Early Childhood Experiences in Language Arts
Early Literacy
Ninth Edition

Early Childhood Experiences in Language Arts
Early Literacy

NINTH EDITION

Jeanne M. Machado
Emerita, San Jose City College

WADSWORTH
CENGAGE Learning™

Australia • Brazil • Japan • Korea • Mexico • Singapore • Spain • United Kingdom • United States

WADSWORTH
CENGAGE Learning

Early Childhood Experiences in Language Arts: Early Literacy, **Ninth Edition**

Jeanne M. Machado

Acquisitions Editor: Christopher Shortt

Development Editor: Tangelique Williams

Assistant Editor: Caitlin Cox

Editorial Assistant: Linda Stewart

Media Editor: Ashley Cronin

Marketing Manager: Kara Parsons

Marketing Assistant: Dimitri Hagnere

Marketing Communications Manager: Martha Pfeiffer

Project Manager, Editorial Production: Christy Krueger

Creative Director: Rob Hugel

Senior Art Director: Maria Epes

Senior Print Buyer: Becky Cross

Permissions Text Acquisitions: Mardell Glinski Schultz

Production Service: Graphic World Inc.

Text Designer: Carolyn Deacy

Copy Editor: Graphic World Inc.

Cover Designer: Bartay Studio

Cover and Interior Images: © Wadsworth Cengage Learning

Compositor: Graphic World Inc.

For product information and technology assistance, contact us at **Cengage Learning Customer & Sales Support, 1-800-354-9706.**

For permission to use material from this text or product, submit all requests online at **cengage.com/permissions.** Further permissions questions can be e-mailed to **permissionrequest@cengage.com.**

Library of Congress Control Number: 2008939029

ISBN-13: 978-1-4354-0012-2

ISBN-10: 1-4354-0012-7

Wadsworth
10 Davis Drive
Belmont, CA 94002-3098
USA

Cengage Learning is a leading provider of customized learning solutions with office locations around the globe, including Singapore, the United Kingdom, Australia, Mexico, Brazil, and Japan. Locate your local office at **www.cengage.com/international.**

Cengage Learning products are represented in Canada by Nelson Education, Ltd.

For your course and learning solutions, visit **www.cengage.com/education.**

Purchase any of our products at your local college store or at our preferred online store **www.ichapters.com.**

Printed in The United States of America
1 2 3 4 5 6 7 13 12 11 10 09

BRIEF CONTENTS

v

CONTENTS

SECTION 5

Speech Growth: Conversation, Expression, and Dramatization

PREFACE

Early Childhood Experiences in Language Arts: Early Literacy is a state-of-the-art teacher-training text designed to help those working in the early childhood education field provide an opportunity-rich program full of interesting, appropriate, and developmental language arts activities. As new terms are encountered, definitions are provided, and a running glossary reinforces comprehension of key concepts. It is both a practical "how-to" manual and a collection of resources that includes a large number of classic, tried-and-true activities. The No Child Left Behind Act legislation and the subsequent development of new standards, guidelines, benchmarks, and assessment requirements have been given comprehensive coverage. All of these have significantly influenced early childhood language arts program planning and instruction.

The first few chapters present a detailed account of language acquisition, young children's early communicative capacities, growth milestones, and age-level milestones (infancy through preschool), along with suggested professional techniques to promote each child's self-esteem and potential. Additional material in Chapter 1 has been provided so that infants' diverse needs can be identified as early as possible. The characteristics of attuned and sensitive caregiver behaviors have been highlighted, and an expanded list of newly published books for infants and toddlers is included.

Because a comprehensive and dynamically planned early childhood language arts curriculum consists of four broad, interrelated areas—speaking (oral), listening, writing, and reading—each is fully explored and described in a separate text section. Visual literacy, a new language arts focus, is given textual coverage due to young children's growing interactions with visual technologies. The text urges early childhood education students to create classroom activities not only based upon children's needs and potential but also based upon beginning teachers' unique talents and skills and their memories of the language-related activities that delighted them in childhood. It is hoped that confidence and skill gained by the reader will help provide young children with an enthusiastic, knowledgeable teacher-companion who enjoys and encourages children in their discovery of the language arts.

Infant and toddler chapters are intended to increase the reader's understanding of infant and toddler communication abilities and the role of adult behavior in promoting language growth. Toddlers' physical development and concurrent mushrooming verbal abilities and language usage is discussed. Infant/toddler special needs may be reognized as quickly as possible when milestones are considered. Because the number of children with special needs who are enrolled in early childhood programs has dramatically increased, teachers' ability to create language-rich environments and interact as enthusiastic, supportive, dynamic, observant companions and collaborators has become critical. The influence of Vygotsky's theories, particularly scaffolding and webbing, are emphasized. Assessment strategies and the development of children's literacy portfolios have also received attention. Recommended literature and classics, appropriate to children's age levels, as well as activity ideas and patterns for storytelling and flannel board sets, provide the student with resource ideas to try out in early childhood classrooms. Young children's progress in the understanding and use of print in daily life has been explained. Children's curiosity and their natural ability to become communicators are described to give the reader increased confidence in children's ability to learn. Parent tips to extend language and provide literacy-enriched home environments and activities are presented, and text suggestions urge educators to honor children's homegrown literacy knowledge and skills. The text helps educators recognize that families may use various and diverse vocabulary and literacy-building strategies.

The ninth edition has noted current public and legislative interest in those prekindergarten experiences that equip young children with the necessary background to master with ease the task of beginning reading. Research and activities promoting phonological and phonemic awareness are discussed in detail, as is the alphabetic principle. Sections concerned with developmentally appropriate instruction in these areas outline the current concern regarding curricula and their relationship to children's activities, interests, and life experiences.

The diversity in preschool classrooms is addressed, in particular the fact that nonnative English-speaking children are abundantly present in many geographical areas of the United States. Cultural differences are increasingly common, and this new edition, like former editions, urges teachers to respect, understand, and dignify each child's uniqueness as they promote the English language arts.

Educators are concerned with neurolinguistic research in the field of young children's brain capacities and development. Discussion of these findings and of their effect on planned language arts curricula has been included. Educators

are urged to share their thinking aloud, when appropriate, and define new vocabulary words to promote children's analysis and problem-solving abilities and vocabulary growth.

The text does not neglect the importance of family and educator attitudes about young children's communicative abilities from birth onward. It alerts adults to act in ways that promote rather than impede growth in children's language arts skills and abilities.

NEW FEATURES

The ninth edition includes a number of new features to promote the student's mastery of each chapter's content, as well as other features carried forward from previous editions. It has updated referenced material, yet where possible, it retains classic findings and recommendations that are still pertinent and valuable.

◆ *Discussion Vignettes*—a continuing reader-friendly feature, these short vignettes introduce chapters, add real-life situations, and pique student interest. The *Questions to Ponder* promote reflection and class discussion.

◆ *Key Terms*—important terms to know are listed in alphabetical order at the beginning of each chapter, in color where they appear within the chapter, in a running glossary at the bottom of the page on which they appear, and again in the glossary at the back of the book. Reinforcement and cross-referencing enhance comprehension for the student.

◆ *Helpful Websites*—Websites of professional organizations, associations, public entities, and colleges or universities are identified at the end of each chapter. A brief description of a chapter-related item accompanies many provided listings, as do suggestions that will narrow the student's search.

◆ *Activities*—this feature appears at the ends of chapters in which ideas for child or adult activities are presented. This allows for uninterrupted reading of theory and later examination of activities suggested by the author.

◆ *Additional Resources*—this section follows each chapter's summary. It presents readings for students wanting further depth, reinforcement of chapter topics, and information to aid in pursuit of special interests. Resources such as commercial educational materials and professional organizations where further information can be obtained are also included.

◆ *Book Companion Website*—The book companion website to accompany the ninth edition of *Early Childhood Experiences in the Language Arts* is the student's link to Internet information and contains numerous features to augment and extend the text and promote teaching skills and text comprehension. The book-specific website at www.cengage.com/education/machado offers students a variety of study tools and useful resources such as chapter overviews and notes, tutorial quizzes, web links, frequently asked questions, discussion questions, glossary/flashcards, student activities, resources, readings, web activities, and more.

ANCILLARIES

Instructor's Manual

The Instructor's Manual includes suggested training session discussion topics and classroom exercises promoting the exchange of ideas and active student participation and application of each chapter's content. Answers to review questions, test items, multimedia resources, and suggested student assignment sheets are part of the manual.

PowerLecture

This one-stop digital library and presentation tool includes preassembled Microsoft® PowerPoint® lecture slides by Jennifer Prior, Northern Arizona University. In addition to a full Instructor's Manual and Test Bank,

PowerLecture also includes ExamView® testing software with all the test items from the printed Test Bank in electronic format, enabling you to create customized tests in print or online.

Book Companion Website

The book companion website offers instructors access to password-protected resources such as an electronic version of the instructor's manual and PowerPoint slides.

PROFESSIONAL ENHANCEMENT BOOK

Another supplement to accompany this text is the *Language Arts and Literacy Professional Enhancement* booklet for students. This book, which is part of Wadsworth Cengage Learning's Early Childhood Education Professional Enhancement series, focuses on key topics of interest to future early childhood teachers and caregivers. Students will keep this informational supplement and use it for years to come in their early childhood practices.

WEBTUTOR TOOLBOX

WebTutor™ Toolbox for WebCT™ or Blackboard® provides access to all the content of this text's rich book companion website from within your course-management system. Robust communication tools—such as a course calendar, asynchronous discussion, real-time chat, a whiteboard, and an integrated e-mail system—make it easy for your students to stay connected to the course.

ABOUT THE AUTHOR

The author's experience in the early childhood education field has included full-time assignment as a community college instructor and a department chairperson. Her duties included supervision of early childhood education students at two on-campus laboratory child development centers at San Jose City College and Evergreen Valley College, as well as child centers in the local community. Her teaching responsibilities encompassed early childhood education, child development, and parenting courses.

She received her MA from San Jose State University and her vocational community college life credential with coursework from the University of California at Berkeley. Her experience includes working as a teacher, a director, and an early childhood education consultant in public early childhood programs, parent cooperative programs, and private early childhood centers. Ms. Machado is an active participant in several professional organizations that relate to the education and well-being of young children and their families. She is a past president of CCCECE (California Community College Early Childhood Educators) and the Peninsula Chapter of the California Association for the Education of Young Children. Her authoring efforts with Dr. Helen Meyer-Botnarescue produced a 2007 text for student teachers titled *Student Teaching: Early Childhood Practicum Guide,* sixth edition. An additional text, *Employment Opportunities in Education,* was co-authored with Romana Reynolds in 2006. Both are published by Wadsworth Cengage Learning.

Currently, Ms. Machado consults with teachers and administrators and interacts with young children in classrooms in Cascade, Idaho, and San Jose, California.

ACKNOWLEDGMENTS

The author wishes to express her appreciation to the following individuals and agencies.

The students at San Jose City College, AA Degree Program in Early Childhood Education

Arbor Hill Day Care Center, Albany, New York

San Jose City College Child Development Center administrators, teachers, and staff

Evergreen Valley College Child Development Center personnel, San Jose, California

James Lick Children's Center, Eastside High School District, San Jose, California

Kiddie Academy, Albany, New York

Piedmont Hills Preschool, San Jose, California

Pineview Preschool, Albany, New York

St. Elizabeth's Day Home, San Jose, California

W.I.C.A.P. Head Start, Donnelly, Idaho

Cascade Elementary School preschool class, Cascade, Idaho

Christopher Shortt and the Staff at Wadsworth Cengage Learning

In addition, special appreciation is due the reviewers involved in the development of this edition:

Karen Roth, National-Louis University

Sandra Crosser, Ohio Northern University

Tim Rasinski, Kent State University

Leanna Manna, Villa Maria College

Kellie Jo Sullivan, Brazosport College

Karen Davis, Southwest Georgia Technical College

Ellen M. Curtin, Texas Wesleyan University

Sharon Radebaugh, Middle Georgia Technical College

Josephine Fritts, Ozarks Technical Community College

Nancy Peterson, Utah Valley State College

Susan Baxter, El Camino Community College

Tom Yawkey, The Pennsylvania State University

Angela Salmon, Florida International University

Linda Aiken, Southwestern Community College

Priscilla Smith, Gwinnett Technical College

TO THE STUDENT

Because you are a unique, caring individual who has chosen an early childhood teaching career or who is currently working with children, this text is intended to help you discover and share your developing language arts gifts and talents. Create your own activities; author, when possible, your own "quality" literary, oral, and writing opportunities for young children. Design your activities and base them on an understanding of current research and theory found in the text. Consider the wisdom you have gained through your past experiences with children. Share your unique perspective and those language arts–related experiences that excite you now and delighted you when you were a child.

In this text, I urge you to become a skilled teacher who interacts, collaborates, and becomes a conversationalist, "a subtle opportunist," getting the most possible out of each child-adult situation while also enjoying these daily exchanges yourself. Your joy in language arts becomes their joy.

A file box or binder collection of ideas, completed sets, patterns, games, and so on, carefully made and stored for present and future use, is suggested. Filling young children's days with developmental, worthwhile experiences will prove a challenge, and your collection of ideas and teaching visual aids will grow and be adapted over the years.

In this text, I attempt to help you become increasingly skilled at what you may already do well, and I also urge you to become the kind of teacher who is described as creating classroom experiences and, at times, miracles in which a light is cast on each child to make him or her shine and be appreciated by others. Suggested activities and review sections at the end of chapters give immediate feedback on your grasp of the chapter's main ideas and techniques. Because I am growing too, I invite your suggestions and comments so that in future revisions I can refine and improve this text's value.

You can make a difference in young children's lives. Ideally, this text will help you become the kind of teacher who does.

SECTION 1

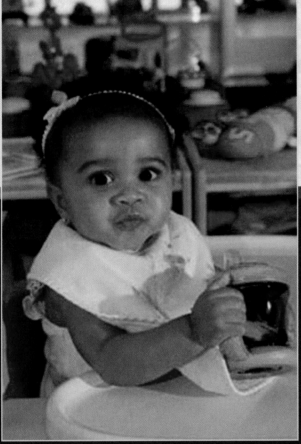

Language Development:
Emerging Literacy
in the Young Child

CHAPTER 1

Beginnings of Communication

OBJECTIVES

After reading this chapter, you should be able to:

◆ Compare two theories of human language emergence.

◆ Identify major factors that influence language development.

◆ Discuss the reciprocal behaviors of infants, parents, and caregivers.

◆ Create or demonstrate three child-adult play activities for infants 1 to 6 months or infants 6 to 12 months.

◆ Explain the significance of infant signaling.

KEY TERMS

affective sphere	echolalia	resonation
articulation	equilibrium	responsive mothers
attachment	gaze coupling	rhythm
auditory acuity	holophrases	sensory-motor
babbling	language	development
cognition	moderation level	signing
communication	neurolinguistics	spatial-temporal
cooing	parentese	reasoning
cues	perception	synapses
dual coding	phonation	

A NEW SIGN

Noah, 10 months, had a new sign for "cracker" that he had used a few times during the day at the infant center. He was very pleased when his "sign" resulted in someone bringing him a cracker. At pick-up time, one of the staff believed it important to talk to Noah's dad. Mr. Soares did not really understand what the teacher, Miss Washington, was talking about when she said "signing." Miss Washington gave Mr. Soares a quick explanation. He smiled proudly and then said, "That's great. I'll talk to his mom and let her know."

QUESTIONS TO PONDER

1. Miss Washington had a new language-related topic for the next staff meeting. What would you suspect it was?

2. Did this episode tell you something about the language-developing quality of the infant center?

3. What do you know about male infants and their signing ability compared with that of female infants? Could you describe infant signing behavior?

(If you are hesitating, this chapter supplies answers.)

In this chapter the reader is acquainted with those elements in an infant's life that facilitate optimal growth in communication and language development. Socioemotional, physical, cognitive, and environmental factors that influence, promote, or deter growth are noted. Recommended interaction techniques and strategies are supported by research and reflect accepted appropriate practices and standards. As foundational aspects of infant communication are presented, *boxed* descriptions of the attuned and engaged behaviors caregivers make with infants are provided. Caregivers establish a relationship with each infant in their care, and the quality of that relationship serves to motivate each infant to engage in learning (McMullen & Dixon, 2006). Higher levels of warmth are connected to positive caregiver sensitivity. Gerber, Whitebook, and Weinstein (2007) note that the quality of caregiver practices has been linked to children's brain development and cognitive functioning.

For you to become the kind of educator children deserve, one who enhances language growth, you should begin by believing that most infants are able and natural communicators from birth onward unless some life circumstance has modified their natural potential. Infant care facilities with well-planned, positive, and growth-producing environments that are staffed with skilled, knowledgeable, and well-trained adults who offer developmentally appropriate activities provide a place where infants can and do thrive.

Each infant is a unique combination of inherited traits and environmental influences. Structural, hormonal, and chemical influences present prenatally may have affected the growth and development of the fetus (Gould, 2002).

Researchers confirm that newborns seem to assimilate information immediately and are interested in their surroundings. Some suggest an infant possesses "the greatest mind" in existence and is the most powerful learning machine in the universe. During the third trimester of pregnancy, most mothers notice that their babies kick and move in response to music or loud noises. The sound of speech may draw a less spirited reaction, but there is little question that fetuses hear and react to a wide variety of sounds.

Technology can now monitor the slightest physical changes in breathing, heartbeat, eye movement, and sucking rhythm and rates. Researchers suggest that babies begin learning how to carry on conversations quickly and sucking patterns produce a **rhythm** that mimics that of give-and-take dialogues. Infants respond to very specific maternal signals, including tone of voice, facial changes, and head movements.

Greenspan (1999) suggests what may happen when interacting with a 1- or 2-month-old baby at a relaxed time after a nap or feeding:

> . . . when you hold him at arm's length and look directly into his eyes with a broad smile on your face, watch his lips part as if he's trying to imitate your smile. (p. 31)

Babies gesture and make sounds and seem to hold up their ends of conversations, but at times, they appear to suppress output and channel their energy into seeing and hearing. Their eye contact with their caregivers, called **gaze coupling**, is believed to be one of their first steps in establishing communication. Infants can shut off background noises and pay attention to slight changes in adult voice sounds.

An attuned adult would:

- ◆ *notice infant actions, including gestures, body positioning, noisemaking, eye gazing, and any shift from listening to watching.*
- ◆ *make face-to-face contact frequently.*
- ◆ *display admiration, affection, and pleasure and smile frequently.*
- ◆ *provide verbal and nonverbal communication.*
- ◆ *seek to maintain and prolong eye contact.*

---

rhythm — uniform or patterned recurrence of a beat, accent, or melody in speech.
gaze coupling — infant-mother extended eye contact.

GENETIC INHERITANCE AND EMERGING BEHAVIORS

The qualities an infant inherits from parents and the events that occur in the child's life help shape the child's language development. Gender, temperament, and a timetable for the emergence of intellectual, emotional, and physical capabilities are all genetic givens. In the short 4 to 5 years after birth, the child's speech becomes purposeful and similar to adult speech. This growing language skill is a useful tool for satisfying needs and exchanging thoughts, hopes, and dreams with others. As ability grows, the child understands and uses more of the resources of oral and recorded human knowledge and is well on the way to becoming a literate being.

The natural capacity to categorize, invent, and remember information aids the child's language acquisition. Although unique among the species because of the ability to speak, human beings are not the only ones who can communicate. Birds and animals imitate sounds and signals and are believed to communicate. For instance, chimpanzees exposed to experimental language techniques (American Sign Language, specially equipped machines, and plastic tokens) have surprised researchers with their language abilities. Some have learned to use symbols and follow linguistic rules with a sophistication that rivals that of some 2-year-olds. Researchers continue to probe the limits of their capabilities. However, a basic difference between human beings and other species exists.

It is the development of the cerebral cortex that sets humans apart from less intelligent animals. Our advanced mental capabilities, such as thought, memory, language, mathematics, and complex problem solving, are unique to human beings.

Humans have the unique species-specific ability to test hypotheses about the structure of language. They can also develop rules for a particular language and remember and use them to generate appropriate language. Within a few days after birth, human babies recognize familiar faces, voices, and even smells and prefer them to unfamiliar ones.

Over the past few decades, infant research has advanced by leaps and bounds to reveal amazing newborn abilities. Long before they can talk, for example, babies remember events and solve problems. They can recognize faces, see colors, hear voices, discriminate speech sounds, and distinguish basic tastes. When you combine the psychological and neurological evidence, it is hard not to conclude that babies are just plain smarter than adults, at least if being smart means being able to learn something new (Gopnik, Meltzoff, & Kuhl, 1999).

INFANT ACTIONS PROMPT CAREGIVER BEHAVIORS

The human face becomes the most significantly important communication factor for the infant, and the facial expressions, which are varied and complex, eventually will influence infant body reactions (interior and exterior). Caregivers strive to understand the infant's state of well-being by interpreting the infant's face and postures, as infants also search faces in the world around them.

Figure 1–1 identifies a number of signals infants use and their probable meanings. Response and intentional behavior become apparent as infants age and gain experience. Infants initially respond with various preprogrammed gestures such as smiling, intent and interested looking, crying, satisfied sucking, and snuggling. Soon these behaviors are followed by active demanding and attention-seeking patterns in which attempts to attract and solicit caregiver attention rapidly become unmistakable and intentional.

Researchers are studying the roles of facial expressions, gestures, and body movements in human social communication (Figure 1–2). Early expressions that look like smiling may occur minutes after birth and are apparent in the faces of sleeping babies, whose facial expressions seem to constantly change. Researchers

INFANT ACTS	PROBABLE MEANING
turning head and opening mouth	feeling hungry
quivering lips	adjusting to stimuli
sucking on hand, fist, thumb	calming self, feeling overstimulated
averting eyes	tuning out for a while
turning away	needing to calm down
yawning	feeling tired/stressed
looking wide-eyed	feeling happy
cooing	feeling happy
appearing dull with unfocused eyes	feeling overloaded, needing rest
waving hands	feeling excited
moving tongue in and out	feeling upset/imitating

FIGURE 1–1 Born communicators.

FIGURE 1–2 "Wow, that is interesting!"

studying infant smiling during an infant's first week of life, such as Dondi et al. (2007), suggest that infants smile in various behavioral states, including during brief alertness, drowsiness, active sleep, and quiet sleep, but they also confirm what many parents have noticed—smiling most often occurs in deep sleep.

Caregivers observe that infants search for the source of the human voice and face. An infant may become wide-eyed and crane his neck and lift his chin toward the source. His body tension increases as he becomes more focused and somewhat inactive. Most caregivers respond to these signals by picking up the infant and cuddling him.

An attuned adult would:

◆ *be aware of opportunities to soothe and touch and engage in some way with an infant.*

◆ *pick up and hold an infant gently while providing firm support.*

◆ *note an infant's well-being and comfort.*

◆ *attempt to interpret an infant's facial and body signals.*

DEFINITIONS

Language, as used in this text, refers to a system of intentional communication and self-expression through sounds, signs (gestures), or symbols that are understandable to others. The language-development process includes both sending and receiving information. Input (receiving) comes before output (sending); input is organized mentally by an individual long before there is decipherable output.

Communication is a broader term, defined as giving and receiving information, signals, or messages. A person can communicate with or receive communications from animals, infants, or foreign speakers in a variety of ways. Even a whistling teakettle sends a message that someone can understand. Infants appear to be "in tune," focused on the human voice, hours after birth.

Speech is much more complex than simple parroting or primitive social functioning. The power of language enables humans to dominate other life forms. The ability to use language secured our survival by giving us a vehicle to both understand and transmit language and to work

---

language — the systematic, conventional use of sounds, signs, or written symbols in a human society for communication and self-expression. It conveys meaning that is mutually understood.

communication — the giving (sending) and receiving of information, signals, or messages.

cooperatively with others. Language facilitates peaceful solutions between people.

INFLUENCES ON DEVELOPMENT

A child's ability to communicate involves an integration of body parts and systems allowing hearing, understanding, organizing thoughts, learning, and using language. Most children accomplish the task quickly and easily, but many factors influence the learning of language.

Research suggests that babies instinctively turn their heads to face the source of sound and can remember sounds heard before birth. This has prompted mothers to talk to, sing to, and read classic literature and poetry to the unborn. Research has yet to document evidence of the benefits of these activities.

Of all sounds, nothing attracts and holds the attention of infants as well as the human voice—especially the higher-pitched female voice. "Motherese," a distinct caregiver speech, is discussed later in this chapter. Dietrich, Swingley, and Werker (2007) note:

> Infants begin to acquire their language by learning phonetic categories. At birth infants seem to distinguish most of the phonetic contrasts used by the world's languages. However, over the first year, this "universal" capacity shifts to a language-specific pattern in which infants retain or improve categorization of native-language sounds but fail to discriminate many non-native sounds. (p. 16030)

Rhythmic sounds and continuous, steady tones soothe some infants. A number of commercial sound-making products that attempt to soothe can be attached to cribs or are imbedded in plush stuffed animals. Most emit a type of static or heartbeat sound or a combination of the two. Too much sound in the infant's environment, especially loud, excessive, or high-volume sounds, may have the opposite effect. Excessive household noise can come from televisions or other sources. Many have described sensory-overload situations when infants try to turn off sensory input by turning away and somehow blocking that which is at the moment overwhelming, whether the stimulus is mechanical or human. This blocking includes falling asleep.

Although hearing ability is not fully developed at birth, newborns can hear moderately loud sounds and can distinguish different pitches. **Auditory acuity** develops swiftly. Infants inhibit motor activity in response to strong auditory stimuli or when listening to the human voice and attempt to turn toward it. Some researchers see this as an indication that infants are geared to orient their entire bodies toward any signal that arouses interest (Figure 1–3). Infants' body responses to human verbalizations are a rudimentary form of speech development (Figure 1–4).

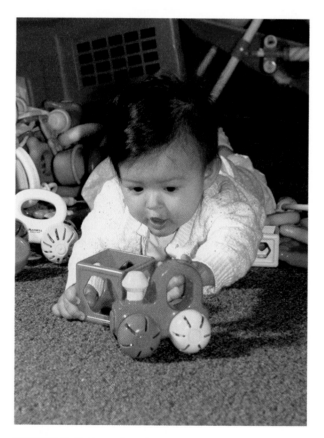

FIGURE 1–3 Sound-making toys attract attention.

---

auditory — relating to or experienced through hearing.
acuity — how well or clearly one uses the senses; the degree of perceptual sharpness.

AGE	APPROPRIATE HEARING BEHAVIORS
birth	awakens to loud sounds
	startles, cries, or reacts to noise
	makes sounds
	looks toward then looks away from environmental sounds
0–3 months	turns head to hear parent's or others' speech
	reacts to speech by smiling
	opens mouth as if to imitate adult's speech
	coos and goos
	seems to recognize a familiar voice
	calms down when adult's voice is soothing
	repeats own vocalizations
	seems to listen to and focus on familiar adults' voices
4–6 months	looks toward environmental noise (e.g., barking, vacuum, doorbell, radio, TV)
	attracted to noise-making toys
	babbles consonant-like sounds
	makes wants known with voice
	seems to understand "no"
	reacts to speaker's change of tone of voice
7–12 months	responds to own name
	may say one or more understandable but not clearly articulated words
	babbles repeated syllables or consonant- and vowel-like sounds
	responds to simple requests
	enjoys playful word games like Peak-a-boo, Pat-a-cake, etc.
	imitates speech sounds frequently
	uses sound making to gain others' attention

FIGURE 1–4 Auditory perception in infancy.

Sensory-motor development, which involves the use of sense organs and the coordination of motor systems (body muscles and parts), is vital to language acquisition. Sense organs gather information through seeing, hearing, smelling, tasting, and touching. These sense-organ impressions of people, objects, and life encounters are sent to the brain, and each **perception** (impression received through the senses) is recorded and stored, serving as a base for future oral and written language.

Newborns and infants are no longer viewed as passive, unresponsive "mini-humans." Instead, infants are seen as dynamic individuals, preprogrammed to learn, with functioning sensory capacities, motor abilities, and a wondrous built-in curiosity. Parents and caregivers can be described as guides who provide opportunity and act *with* newborns rather than *on* them.

Beginning Socialization

A child's social and emotional environments play a leading role in both the quality and the quantity of beginning language. Many researchers describe communicative neonatal behaviors that evoke tender feelings in adults. Human children have the longest infancy among animals. Our social dependency is crucial to our individual survival and growth. Much learning occurs through contact and interaction with others in family and social settings. Basic attitudes toward life, self, and other people form early, as life's pleasures and pains are experienced. The young child depends on parents and other caregivers to provide what is needed for growth and **equilibrium** (a balance achieved when consistent care is given and needs are satisfied). This side of a child's development has been called the **affective sphere**, referring to the affectionate feelings—or lack of them—shaped through experience with others (Figure 1–5). Most experts believe that each

---

sensory-motor development — the control and use of sense organs and the body's muscle structure.
perception — mental awareness of objects and other data gathered through the five senses.
equilibrium — a balance attained with consistent care and satisfaction of needs that leads to a sense of security and lessens anxiety.
affective sphere — the affectionate feelings (or lack of them) shaped through experience with others.

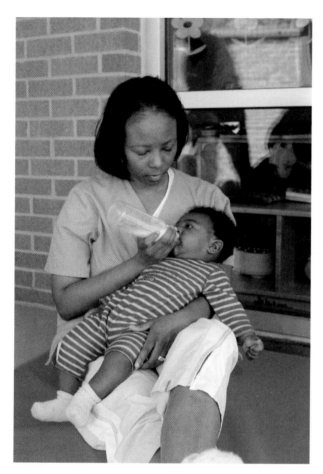

FIGURE 1–5 Care and attention in the early years influence language development.

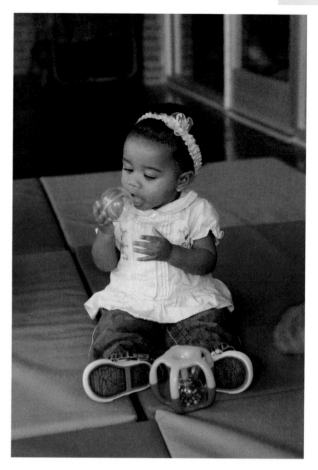

FIGURE 1–6 An infant who feels comfortable and whose needs are satisfied is alert to the world.

time an infant takes in information through the senses, the experience is double-coded as both a physical/cognitive reaction and as an emotional reaction to those sensations.

Textbooks often speak indirectly about the infant's need to feel loved consistently, using words like *nurturance, closeness, caring,* and *commitment.* The primary goal of parents and caregivers should be handling the infant and satisfying the child's physical needs in a way that leads to mutual love and a bond of trust (Figure 1–6). This bond, often called **attachment,** is an event of utmost importance to the infant's progress. A developmental milestone is reached when a baby responds with an emotional reaction of his own by indicating obvious pleasure or joy in the company of a parent or caregiver. Attachment is formed through mutual gratification of needs and reciprocal communication influenced by the infant's growing cognitive ability. The two-way nature of the attachment process is also referred to as bonding.

> Another idea about attachment, or bonding, is that babies and young children develop "internalized working models" that are systematic pictures of how people relate to one another—theories of love. (Gopnik et al., 1999, p. 178)

---

attachment — a two-way process formed through mutual gratification of needs and reciprocal communication influenced by the infant's growing cognitive abilities. It is sometimes referred to as bonding or a "love affair" relationship.

The special feelings an infant develops for a main caregiver later spreads to include a group of beloved family members. If an attachment bond is evident and consistent care continues, the child thrives. Social interaction with an empathic and attuned caregiver plays the major role in the growth and regulation of the child's nervous system, and it helps the infant develop the strength needed to become socially competent (Gould, 2002).

Newborns seem to have an individual preferred level of arousal, a **moderation level**, neither too excited nor too bored. They seek change and stimulation and seem to search out newness. Each human may possess an optimal level of arousal—a state when learning is enhanced and pleasure peaks. Mothers and experienced caregivers try to keep infants at moderate levels of arousal, neither too high nor too low. One can perceive three states during an older infant's waking hours: (1) a state in which everything is all right and life is interesting; (2) a reactive state to something familiar or unfamiliar, when an observer can see an alert "what's that?" or "who's that?" response; and (3) a crying or agitated state. One can observe a switch from feeling safe or happy to feeling unsafe or unhappy in a matter of seconds (Figure 1–7). Loud noises can startle the infant and elicit distressed crying. Infants control input and turn away or turn off by moving their eyes and head or body and by becoming fussy or falling asleep.

Greenspan (1999) urges parents and caregivers of infants to improve their observational skills.

As you sharpen your observational skills and pay attention to the times when your baby seems to have more trouble becoming calm and sharing attention with you, you'll begin to assemble a truly revealing developmental profile of your child. You'll start recognizing whether an unpleasant smell, an unexpected hug or cuddle, or a piercing noise overwhelms your child. Don't forget, though, that

FIGURE 1–7 With tears still wet, this infant has moved on to observing another feature of his environment.

even a crying, finicky baby is capable of a lot of looking and listening. You may receive some very expressive looks from your three-month-old when he's got a gas bubble in his stomach! If you rub his back while murmuring sympathetically, he may be encouraged to keep his looking and listening skills even when he's not feeling so good. He may be able to use your soothing sounds and touches to calm him. Practicing under slightly stressful conditions will make him into a stronger looker and listener later on. (p. 201)

An attuned adult would:

◆ *observe closely.*

◆ *assess infants' needs and work to satisfy them.*

◆ *notice reactions to room sounds—sound intensity or rhythm or other features.*

◆ *calm infants when necessary by trying a variety of strategies.*

◆ *use an attention-getting voice, voice variety, and/or high-pitched tones.*

---

moderation level — an individual preferred state of arousal between bored and excited when learning and pleasure peak.

Parent and Caregiver Attitudes and Expectations

As was mentioned earlier, research indicates that parents' and caregivers' attitudes and expectations about infants' awareness and sensory abilities may be predictive of developmental growth.

> Certainly there are many possible explanations for developmental differences. But the fact remains: The earlier a mother thought her baby would be aware of the world, the more competent her baby grew to be. Why was this so? It is because the mothers treated the babies according to their expectations. In home visits, researchers observed that mothers who knew more about their infants' abilities were more emotionally and verbally responsive to their babies. They talked to them more. They provided them with more appropriate play materials and initiated more stimulating experiences. And they were more likely to allow their babies to actively explore the world around them. (Acredolo & Goodwyn, 2000, p. 102)

Growing Intellect

Other important factors related to the child's mental maturity or ability to think are ages, stages, and sequences of increased mental capacity that are closely related to language development. Language skill and intellect seem to be growing independently, at times, with one or the other developing at a faster rate. The relationship of intelligence and language has been a subject of debate for a long time. Most scholars, however, agree that these two areas are closely associated. Researchers suspect the mind's most important faculties are rooted in emotional experiences from very early in life.

The natural curiosity of humans requires discussion here. Curiosity can be defined as a compulsion (drive) to make sense of life's happenings. Over time, exploring, searching, groping, and probing by infants shift from random to controlled movements. At approximately 8 months of age, infants begin to possess insatiable appetites for new things—touching, manipulating, and trying to become familiar with everything that attracts them. Increasing motor skill allows greater possibilities for exploration. Skilled caregivers of infants are kept busy trying to provide novelty, variety, and companionship while monitoring safety. The curiosity of infants seems to wane only when they are tired, hungry, or ill.

Cultural Ideas Concerning Infant Communication. Cultural and social forces affect language acquisition. They influence young lives through contact with group attitudes, values, and beliefs. Some cultures expect children to look downward when adults speak, showing respect by this action. Other cultures make extensive use of gestures and signaling. Still others seem to have limited vocabularies or believe that engaging in conversations with infants is inappropriate.

THEORIES OF LANGUAGE EMERGENCE

Many scholars, philosophers, linguists, and researchers have tried to pinpoint exactly how language is learned. People in major fields of study—human development, linguistics, sociology, psychology, anthropology, speech-language pathology, and animal study (zoology)—have contributed to current theory. The following are major theoretical positions.

Behaviorist/Environmentalist (or Stimulus-Response) Theory

As parents and main caregivers reward, correct, ignore, or punish the young child's communication, they exert considerable influence over both the quantity and quality of language usage and the child's attitudes toward communicating. Under this theory, the reactions of the people in a child's environment have an important effect on a child's language development. In other words, positive, neutral, and negative

FIGURE 1–8 Enjoyable conversational interactions occur early in life.

reinforcement play a key role in the emergence of communicational behaviors.

The child's sounds and sound combinations are thought to be uttered partly as imitation and partly at random or on impulse, without pattern or meaning. The child's utterances may grow, seem to stand still, or become stifled, depending on feedback from others (Figure 1–8). This theory is attributed to the work of B. F. Skinner, a pioneer researcher in the field of learning theory.

Maturational (Normative) Theory

The writings of Arnold Gesell and his colleagues represent the position that children are primarily a product of genetic inheritance and that environmental influences are secondary. Children are seen as moving from one predictable stage to another, with "readiness" the precursor of actual learning. This position was widely accepted in the 1960s, when linguists studied children in less-than-desirable circumstances and discovered consistent patterns of language development. Using this theory as a basis for planning instruction for young children includes (1) identifying predictable stages of growth in language abilities and (2) offering

appropriate readiness activities to aid children's graduation to the next higher level.

Predetermined/Innatist Theory

Under this theory, language acquisition is considered innate (a predetermined human capacity). Each new being is believed to possess a mental ability that enables that being to master any language to which he has been exposed from infancy. Chomsky (1968), a linguistic researcher, theorizes that each person has an individual language acquisition device (LAD). Chomsky also theorizes that this device (capacity) has several sets of language system rules (grammar) common to all known languages. As the child lives within a favorable family climate, his perceptions spark a natural and unconscious device, and the child learns the "mother tongue." Imitation and reinforcement are not ruled out as additional influences.

Chomsky notes that 2- and 3-year-olds can utter understandable, complicated sentences that they have never heard. More current theory also suggests that young children are equipped with an implicit set of internal rules that allows them to transform the sequences of sounds they hear into sequences of ideas—a remarkable thinking skill. Theorists who support this position note the infant's ability to babble sounds and noises used in languages the child has never heard.

Cognitive-Transactional and Interactionist Theory

Under a fourth theory, language acquisition develops from basic social and emotional drives. Children are naturally active, curious, and adaptive and are shaped by transactions with the people in their environment. Language is learned as a means of relating to people. Others provide social and psychological supports that enable the child to be an effective communicator. L. S. Vygotsky's major work, *Thought and Language* (1986), suggests that children's meaningful social exchanges prepare them for uniting thought and speech into "verbal thought." This inner speech development, he theorizes, promotes oral communication and is the basis for written language. Drives stem from a need for love and care, and the need prompts language acquisition.

Children are described as reactors to the human social contact that is so crucial to their survival and well-being. They are natural explorers and investigators. The adult's role is to prepare, create, and provide environments and events. Children's views of the world consist of their mental impressions, which are built as new life events are fit into existing ones or as categories are created for new events. Language is an integral part of living; consequently, children seek to fit language into some pattern that allows understanding. With enough exposure and with functioning sensory receiving systems, children slowly crack the "code" and eventually become fluent speakers. The works of Jean Piaget, Jerome Bruner, and J. McVicker Hunt have promoted a wide acceptance of this theory by early childhood professionals.

Vygotsky (1980) argues that language learning is, in part, biological but that children need instruction in the zone between their independent language level and the level at which they can operate with adult guidance. Bodrova and Leong (1996) list four basic principles underlying the Vygotskian framework:

1. Children construct knowledge.
2. Development cannot be separated from its social context.
3. Learning can lead development.
4. Language plays a central role in mental development.

The early childhood practitioner adopting Vygotsky's ideas would believe both the teacher's behaviors and the child's active physical manipulation of the environment influence and mediate what and how a young child learns or "constructs" mentally.

In other words, without the teacher's social interaction, a child does not learn which characteristics are most important or what to notice and act upon. The teacher's role is to find out through thoughtful conversation, observation, and collaboration what concept a child holds during a jointly experienced happening and to aid the child to further mental construction(s). Consequently, under Vygotskian theory, teachers can affect young children's cognitive processes—the way they think and use language. Other individual and societal features that affect children's thinking are family, other children and people in their lives, and society at large, including language, numerical systems, and technology. Children learn or acquire a mental process by sharing or using it in circumstances with others, and then move forward in an independent manner.

Constructivist Theory

Proponents of constructivist theory propose that children acquire knowledge by constructing it mentally in interaction with the environment. Children are believed to construct theories (hypothesize) about what they experience and then put happenings into relationships. Later, with more life experiences, revisions occur and more adequate explanations are possible. Constructivists point to young children's speech errors in grammar. Internal rules have been constructed and used for a period of time, but with more exposure to adult speech, these rules change and speech becomes closer to adult forms. The rules young children used previously were their own construct and never modeled by adult speakers. Clay (1991), in *Becoming Literate*, points out:

> We know that children operate on some kind of language rules to form plurals and the past tense of verbs and negatives, and we know that many of the rules they seem to use could not have emerged from anything they have heard adults use. They must have been constructed by children themselves. (p. 66)

Planning for language development and early literacy using a constructivist perspective would entail offering wide and varied activities while emphasizing their interrelatedness. Teachers and parents are viewed as being involved jointly with children in literacy activities from birth onward. The overall objective of a constructivist's approach is to promote children's involvement with interesting ideas, problems, and questions. Teachers would also help children put their findings and discoveries into words, notice relationships, and contemplate similarities and differences. Children's hands-on activity is believed to be paired with mental action. A secure, unstressed environment encourages the development of children's ability to cooperate, respect one another, exercise curiosity, gain confidence in themselves, and figure things out on their own. They become autonomous learners.

Other Theories

There is no all-inclusive theory of language acquisition substantiated by research. Many relationships and mysteries are still under study. Current teaching practices involve many different styles and approaches to language arts activities. Some teachers may prefer using techniques in accord with one particular theory. One goal common among educators is to provide instruction that encourages social and emotional development while also offering activities and opportunities in a warm, language-rich, supportive classroom, center, or home. Educators believe children should be included in talk and treated as competent language partners.

This text promotes many challenging activities that go beyond simple rote memorization or passive participation. It offers an enriched program of literary experience that encourages children to think and use their abilities to relate and share their thoughts.

The text is based on the premise that children's innate curiosity, their desire to understand and give meaning to their world, and their predisposition equip them to learn language. Language growth occurs simultaneously in different yet connected language arts areas and all other curriculum offerings. Children continually form,

modify, rearrange, and revise internal knowledge as experiences, activities, opportunities, and social interactions are encountered. Children's unconscious mental structuring of experience proceeds in growth spurts and seeming regressions, with development in one area influencing development in another.

RESEARCH ON INFANTS' BRAIN GROWTH

Rich early experience and time with caring and loving families or early childhood educators has become even more important as researchers of **neurolinguistics** make new discoveries about infants' and young children's brain growth. Although awed by the brain's exceptional malleability, flexibility, and plasticity during early years and its ability to "explode" with new **synapses** (connections), scientists also warn of the effects of abuse or neglect on the child's future brain function.

It is estimated that at birth, each neuron in the cerebral cortex has approximately 2,500 synapses, and the number of synapses reaches its peak at 2 to 3 years of age, when there are about 15,000 synapses per neuron.

A new discipline called cognitive science has appeared, uniting psychology, philosophy, linguistics, computer science, and neuroscience. New technology gives researchers additional tools to study brain energy, volume, blood flow, oxygenation, and cross-sectional images. Neuroscientists have found that throughout the entire process of development, beginning even before birth, the brain is affected by environmental conditions, including the kind of nourishment, care, surroundings, and stimulation an individual receives. The brain is profoundly flexible, sensitive, and plastic and is deeply influenced by events in the outside world. The new developmental research suggests that humans' unique evolutionary trick,

---

neurolinguistics — a branch of linguistics that studies the structure and function of the brain in relation to language acquisition, learning, and use.
synapses — gap-like structures over which the axon of one neuron beams a signal to the dendrites of another, forming a connection in the human brain. They affect memory and learning.

their central adaptation, their greatest weapon in the struggle for survival, is precisely their dazzling ability to learn while they are babies and to teach when grown-ups (Gopnik et al., 1999).

Early experience has gained additional importance and attention. New scientific research does not direct families to provide special "enriching" experiences to children over and above what they experience in everyday life. It does suggest, however, that a radically deprived environment could cause damage. Gould (2002) reports that various types of unpredictable, traumatic, chaotic, or neglectful environments can physically change the infant's brain by overactivating the brain's neural pathways. According to Gould, these changes may include a change in the child's muscle tone, profound sleep difficulties, an increased startle response, and significant anxiety. Life experiences are now believed to control both how the infant's brain is "architecturally formed" and how intricate brain circuitry is wired. Infant sight and hearing acuity need to be assessed as early as possible given this new information. If a newborn's hearing disability is diagnosed and treated within 6 months, the child usually develops normal speech and language on schedule (Spivak, 2000).

With new technology, hearing tests are far more accurate and can pinpoint the level of hearing loss in babies who are only a few hours old. (See Helpful Websites at the end of this chapter for further information.) The American Academy of Pediatrics recommends that all infants be examined by 6 months of age and have regular checkups after age 3.

Researchers, such as Wingert and Brant (2005), provide a description of what is believed to be happening in infants without limitations:

> Science is now giving us a much different picture of what goes on inside their [babies] hearts and heads. Long before they form their first words or attempt the feat of sitting up, they are already mastering complex emotions—jealousy, empathy, frustration—that were once thought to be learned much later in toddlerhood.

They are also far more sophisticated intellectually than we once believed. Babies, as young as 4 months, have advanced powers of deduction and an ability to decipher intricate patterns. They have a strikingly nuanced visual palette, which enables them to notice small differences, especially in faces, that adults and older children lose the ability to see. Until a baby is 3 months old, he can recognize a scrambled photograph of his mother just as quickly as a photograph in which everything is in the right place. (p. 33)

Older debates about nature (genetic givens) versus nurture (care, experiential stimulations, parental teaching, and so on) are outdated (Figure 1–9). Nature and nurture are inseparably intertwined, and innate endowments enable babies to use their powerful learning mechanisms to take advantage of the information they receive from grown-ups. The interaction and interplay between both are critical in determining brain development and which neural pathways and circuitry will diminish, possibly disappear, or grow stronger and become permanent.

Nash (1997) describes a growth spurt that occurs in the infant's brain shortly after birth.

> After birth, the brain experiences a second growth spurt, as the axons (which send signals) and the dendrites (which receive them) explode with new connections. Electrical activity, triggered by a flood of sensory experiences, fine-tunes the brain's circuitry—determining which connections will be retained and which will be pruned . . . . Each time a baby tries to touch a tantalizing object or gazes intently at a face or listens to a lullaby, tiny bursts of electricity shoot through the brain, knitting neurons into circuits as well defined as those etched onto silicon chips. The results are those behavioral mileposts that never cease to delight and awe parents. (p. 120)

OLD THINKING . . .	NEW THINKING . . .
How a brain develops depends on the genes you are born with.	How a brain develops hinges on a complex interplay between the genes you are born with and the experiences you have.
The experiences you have before age three have a limited architecture impact on later development.	Early experiences have a decisive impact on the architecture of the brain and on the nature and extent of adult capacities.
A secure relationship with a primary caregiver creates a directly favorable context for early development and learning.	Early interactions do not just create a context; they affect the way the brain is "wired."
Brain development is linear: the brain's capacity to learn and change grows steadily as an infant progresses toward adulthood.	Brain development is nonlinear: there are prime times for acquiring different kinds of knowledge and skills.
A toddler's brain is much less active than the brain of a college student.	By the time children reach age three, their brains are twice as active as those of adults. Activity levels drop during adolescence.

FIGURE 1–9 Rethinking the brain. (From Shore, R. [1997]. *Rethinking the brain.* New York: Families and Work Institute. Reprinted with permission.)

Many scientists believe that in the first few years of childhood there are a number of critical or sensitive periods, or "windows," when the brain demands certain types of input. If a child's brain is not stimulated during a specific window of time, consequences occur. For example, researchers posit vision will not be normal if by approximately 6 months an infant is not seeing things in the world around him. In neurobiological literature, these special periods are described as "critical periods" or "plastic periods," and they are believed to be one of nature's provisions for humankind to be able to use environmental exposure to change the anatomy of the brain and make it more efficient.

Kantrowitz (1997) points out:

> **Every lullaby, every giggle and peek-a-boo, triggers a crackling along his neural pathways, laying the groundwork for what could someday be a love of art or a talent for soccer or a gift for making and keeping friends. (p. 152)**

Other scientists are skeptical and observe clear evidence of differential abilities to learn language during certain time periods is not easily forthcoming. They suggest that critical periods may seem to exist only because brain structures have already developed through early experiences, affecting the way in which one perceives and interprets the world. These neuroscientists note that the subject of critical periods is hotly debated. One thing is clear— children who learn a second language between 3 and 7 years of age perform like native speakers on various tests, whereas children who learn a second language after puberty speak it with an accent.

Wardle (2003) believes brain research also supports early second language learning, for it suggests that young children have the brain capacity and neural flexibility to undertake the challenging task. She observes that second language learning creates new neural networks that increase the brain's capacity for all sorts of future learning, not just language learning.

What specific courses of action do brain researchers recommend?

- Providing excellent child care for working parents
- Talking to babies frequently
- Cuddling babies and using hands-on parenting

◆ Using **parentese**, the high-pitched, vowel-rich, singsong speech style most adults readily undertake when interacting with babies that helps babies connect objects with words

◆ Giving babies freedom to explore within safe limits

◆ Providing safe objects to explore and manipulate

◆ Giving babies regular eye examinations and interesting visual opportunities

◆ Providing loving, stress-reduced care for the child's emotional development

Cowley (1997) describes "red flag behaviors" that should alert parents to possible infant learning difficulties.

◆ 0–3 months: Does not turn when you speak or repeat sounds like coos.

◆ 4–6 months: Does not respond to the word *no* or changes in tone of voice. Does not look around for sources of sounds, for example, a ringing doorbell, or make babbling sounds similar to adult speech such as *p*, *b*, and *m*.

◆ 7–12 months: Does not recognize words for common items, turn when you call his name, imitate speech sounds, or use sounds other than crying to get your attention (Figure 1–10).

Educators and families agree that infant care should be provided by knowledgeable adults who realize that early experiences and opportunities may have long-term developmental consequences and that caregivers should provide rich, language-filled experiences and opportunities. Many educators worry that "excessive pressure" for inappropriate skills at early ages may cause later problems. Adults' enthusiasm for creating "super babies" may motivate them to offer meaningless age-inappropriate activities.

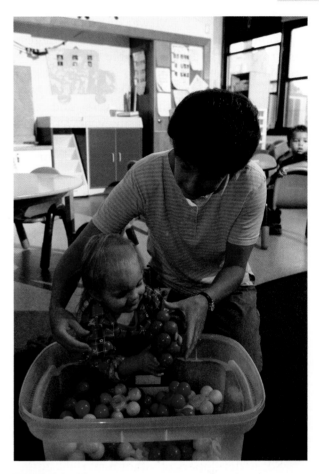

FIGURE 1–10 Emotional health is built from nurturing contact with others.

Greenspan's (1999) observations make it clear that certain kinds of emotional nurturing propel infants and young children to intellectual and emotional health and that affective experience helps them master a variety of cognitive tasks. He states:

As a baby's experience grows, sensory impressions become increasingly tied to feelings. It is the **dual coding** of experience that is the key to understanding how emotions organize intellectual capacities and indeed create the sense of self. (p. 78)

---

parentese — a high-pitched, rhythmic, singsong, crooning style of speech. It is also known as motherese or baby talk.
dual coding — the belief that infants' experiences and emotions influence cognition.

Coles (2004), a reviewer of brain research, also points out that growing evidence suggests that thinking is an inseparable interaction of both **cognition** and emotion (feelings, desires, enthusiasms, antipathies, etc.). Interactive emotional exchanges with caregivers and their reciprocal quality are increasingly viewed as being critical to human infants' growth and development, including language development. Early childhood caregivers realize:

> . . . the adult a baby will someday become is the end result of the thousands of times a parent or caregiver comforted her when she cried, helped her to play well with others in the sandbox and sang just one more lullaby before she finally closed her eyes for the night. Each of these seemingly simple acts gently shapes a child's growing sense of self. (Kantrowitz, 2000, p. 6)

The importance of environmental feedback is considerable. Feedback by caregivers includes giving words of praise and providing caregiver attention, and it promotes the emotional satisfaction an infant feels when he is successful in doing something he set out to do.

Some developers of infant materials, equipment, books, and services suggest they can speed brain development, "lock-in a baby's smarts," and promote emotional well-being. Families may feel considerable pressure to find ways to accelerate early childhood experiences and believe that it is up to them to find products and services. Most educators believe this is unnecessary and suggest spending time with infants and providing natural parenting, such as playing, engaging in reciprocal talk, and simply putting plastic mixing bowls on the floor. Honig (2007) concurs and points out that when an infant shakes a bell or pulls a toy on a string to make it move, he is delightedly learning he can get a specific effect. She notes scientists use these same strategies in their laboratories every day.

ADDITIONAL COMMUNICATIVE ABILITIES IN INFANCY

Newborns quickly make their needs known. They cry, and their parents or caregivers respond. Adults feed, hold, and keep infants warm and dry. The sounds of footsteps or voices or a caring touch often stops infants' crying. Babies learn to anticipate. The sense perceptions they receive begin to be connected to stored impressions of the past.

Infants are very powerful in shaping relationships with significant caregivers. They are a wonderful combination of development, potential development, and cognitive flexibility. An infant can perceive from caregivers' behavior a willingness to learn from the infant and respond to his patterns of behavior and rhythms of hunger. This is accomplished by a caregiver's close observation of the infant's vocal and body clues, which indicate the child's state of being. At some point, the caregiver notices that a pattern of mutual gazing is established. Then a type of proto-conversation begins with caregiver vocalizations followed by infant response and noisemaking. Two important developmental tasks that confront infants are learning to regulate and calm themselves and learning to interact and "play" with caregivers. The first may be difficult for some infants, but the second seems to come naturally.

The infant is a noisemaker from birth. The child's repertoire includes sucking noises, lip smacking, sneezes, coughs, hiccups, and, of course, different types of cries. As an infant grows, he makes vocal noises, such as **cooing** after feeding. During feeding, slurping and guzzling sounds indicate eagerness and pleasure. Cooing seems to be related to a child's comfort and satisfaction. Cooing consists of relaxed, low-pitched vowel sounds that are made in an open-mouthed way; for example, *e* (as in see), *e* (get), *a* (at), *ah*, and *o, oo, ooo*. The infant appears to be in control of this sound making.

---

cognition — the process that creates mental images, concepts, and operations.
cooing — an early stage during the prelinguistic period in which vowel sounds are repeated, particularly the *u-u-u* sound.

Discomfort, by comparison, produces consonant sounds, made in a tense manner with the lips partly closed and the tongue and the ridge of the upper or lower jaw constricting airflow.

Families who attend to infant crying promptly and who believe that crying stems from legitimate needs rather than attempts to control tend to produce contented, trusting infants. Advice for families of colicky babies consists of holding and carrying the infant more frequently in an effort to soothe.

Infants differ in numerous ways from the moment of birth. In speaking to parents about the unique differences in infants, Greenspan (1999) notes the following:

> For most babies, swaddling (gently but firmly bundling the baby's arms and legs in a receiving blanket wrapped around their bodies) is soothing. Other babies enjoy a body massage in which their limbs are gently flexed and extended.
>
> Up until recently, scientists assumed that all human beings experienced sensations in similar ways. We now know that individuals perceive the same stimulus very differently. Your feathery touch could feel tickly and irritating on your newborn's skin, while another baby might take delight in the same caress. (p. 91)

The individual pace of development varies. Whether an infant reaches developmental milestones on the early or late side of normal seems to bear little relation to either cognitive skills or future proficiency (Raymond, 2000). However, in most cases, milestones in language development are reached at about the same age and in a recognizable sequence (Figures 1–11 and 1–12).

Babies learn quickly that communicating is worthwhile because it results in action on the part of another. Greenspan (1999) warns that unless a child masters the level we call two-way intentional communication, normally achieved by an 8-month-old infant, the child's language, cognitive, and social patterns ultimately develop in an idiosyncratic, piecemeal, disorganized manner. There is a high degree of relationship

AGE	RESPONSES
newborn	is startled by a loud noise
	turns head to look in the direction of sound
	is calmed by the sound of a voice
	prefers mother's voice to a stranger's
	discriminates many of the sounds used in speech
1–2 months	smiles when spoken to
3–7 months	responds differently to different intonations (e.g., friendly, angry)
8–12 months	responds to name
	responds to "no"
	recognizes phrases from games (e.g., "Peak-a-boo," "How big is baby?")
	recognizes words from routines (e.g., waves to "bye-bye")
	recognizes some words

FIGURE 1–11 Examples of the typical order of emergence of responses to sounds and speech in the first year, with approximate ages. (From Berko Gleason, J. [1997]. *The development of language* [4th ed.]. Boston: Allyn and Bacon. Copyright © 1997 by Pearson Education. Reprinted by permission of the publisher.)

between a caregiver's responsiveness and a child's language competence. By 9 to 18 months of age, the more responsive mothers promoted greater language facility and growth.

Infants quickly recognize subtle differences in sounds. This helps infants calm down and pay attention—in other words, listen. Infants move their arms and legs in synchrony to the rhythms of human speech. Random noises, tapping sounds, and disconnected vowel sounds do not produce this behavior.

There is a difference between people in an infant's life. Some talk and touch. Others show delight. Some pause after speaking and seem to wait for a response. The child either "locks on" to the conversationalist, focusing totally, or breaks eye contact and looks away. It is almost as though the infant controls what he wants to receive. Of course, hunger, tiredness, and other

AGE	NONWORD VOCALIZATIONS
newborn	cries
1–3 months	makes cooing sounds in response to speech (*oo, goo*)
	laughs
	cries in different ways when hungry, angry, or hurt
	makes more speechlike sounds in response to speech
4–6 months	plays with some sounds, usually single syllables (e.g., *ba, ga*)
6–8 months	babbles with duplicated sounds (e.g., *bababa*)
	attempts to imitate some sounds
8–12 months	babbles with consonant or vowel changes (e.g., *badaga, babu*)
	babbles with sentencelike intonation (expressive jargon/ conversational babble)
	produces protowords

FIGURE 1–12 Examples of the typical order of emergence of types of nonword vocalizations in the first year, with approximate ages. (From Berko Gleason, J. [1997]. *The development of language* [4th ed.]. Boston: Allyn and Bacon. Copyright © 1997 by Pearson Education. Reprinted by permission of the publisher.)

factors also influence this behavior and may stop the child's interest in being social.

The special people in the infant's life adopt observable behaviors when "speaking" to them, just as the infant seems to react in special ways to their attention. Talking to babies differs from other adult speech in that the lyric or musical quality of speech seems more important than words. Infants listening to these long, drawn-out vowels experience an increase in heart rate. At the same time, it speeds up the brain's ability to recognize connections between words and objects. Educators believe "baby-talk" speech modifications can vary among cultures. The attention-holding ability of this type of adult speech may help the infant become aware of the linguistic function of vocalizations (Sachs, 1997). Mothers sometimes raise their voice pitch to a falsetto, shorten sentences, simplify their syntax and vocabulary, use nonsense sounds, use a slower tempo, and use longer pauses than in adult conversations. They maintain prolonged eye contact during playful interchanges. Most infants are attracted to high-pitched voices, but a few infants seem to overreact and prefer lower speech sounds. Infants can pick up higher-pitched sounds better than lower-frequency ones, which may be why they are entranced by the high-pitched coos and singsong nature of parentese. Parents' voices when talking to their infants can be described as playful, animated, warm, and perhaps giddy. Falk (2004) proposes that parentese forms a scaffold for infants' language acquisition, and caregivers often use vocal means to placate and reassure. They attempt to control their infant's state of well-being. Falk notes that vowels are lingered over, phrases are repeated, and questions carry exaggerated inflections.

A mutual readiness to respond to each other appears built-in to warm relationships. The infant learns that eye contact can hold and maintain attention and that looking away usually terminates both verbal and nonverbal episodes. They learn a great deal about language before they ever say a word. Most of what they learn at a very early age involves the sound system of language.

Crying

Crying is one of the infant's primary methods of communication. Cries can be weak or hardy, and they provide clues to the infant's general health. Crying is the only way an infant can affect his situation of need or discomfort. Infants begin early in life to control the emotional content of their cries. Many parents believe they can recognize different types of crying, such as sleepy, frightened, hungry, and so on, especially if infant body actions are observed concurrently. Researchers have discovered that parents do indeed accurately infer the intensity of an infant's emotional state from the sound of the cry itself, even if the baby is not visually observed. Even adults inexperienced with infants seem to possess this ability.

Child development specialists advise adult alertness and responsiveness to minimize crying. Crying will take place in the best of circumstances, and research has indicated that there are some positive aspects of crying, including stress reduction, elimination of toxin in tears, and reestablishment of physical and emotional balance. However, although crying may have its benefits, it is not recommended that infants be left to cry, but rather that adults continue to attempt to soothe and satisfy infant's needs.

A baby's crying may cause strong feelings in some adults, including anger, frustration, irritation, guilt, and rejection. Successful attempts at soothing the infant and stopping the crying give both the infant and the caregiver satisfaction, feelings of competence, and a possible sense of pleasure. When out-of-sorts infants cease crying, alertness, attentiveness, and visual scanning usually happen and/or the infants fall asleep (Figure 1–13). Infant-caregiver interaction has been described as "a rhythmic drama," "a reciprocal ballet," and "a finely tuned symphony." All of these touch on the beauty and coordination of sound-filled moments between the adult and child.

Emotions are expressed frequently in crying as the infant nears his first birthday. Fear, frustration, uneasiness with novelty or newness, separation from loved ones, and other strong emotions can provoke crying through childhood and beyond.

Infant care providers in group programs engage in frank staff discussions concerning infant crying. Normal and natural staff feelings concerning crying need open discussion so that strategies can be devised in the best interests of both the infants and staff members. Many techniques exist to minimize crying and also to monitor the crying levels of individual infants so that health or developmental problems can be spotted quickly.

Smiling and Laughing

True smiling can occur before 6 months of age and is usually associated with a caretaker's facial, auditory, or motor stimuli. Laughter

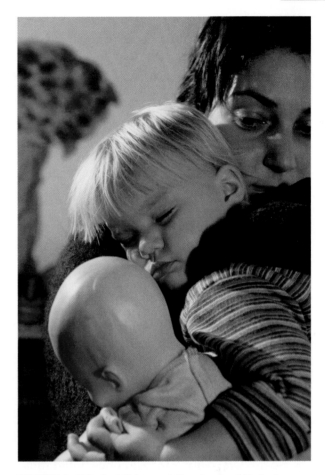

FIGURE 1–13 A child may fall asleep while being soothed.

may occur as early as 4 months of age and is believed to be a good predictor of cognitive growth. Some developmental experts suggest that the earlier the baby laughs, the higher the baby's developmental level is. In the second half of the first year, infants smile at more complex social and visual items. Laughter at this age may be full of squeals, howls, hoots, giggles, and grins. Incongruity may be noticed by the infant, and laughter follows. If an infant laughs when he sees the family dog in the driver's seat with its paws on the wheel, the child may be showing recognition of incongruity—the child has learned something about car drivers.

Responsive caregivers promote infant smiling. Ainsworth and Bell (1972) concluded that

responsive mothers, those who are alert in caring for the infant's needs, had babies who cried less frequently and had a wider range of different modes of communication (Figure 1–14). These responsive mothers created a balance between showing attention and affording the infant autonomy (offering a choice of action within safe bounds) when the infant became mobile. They also provided body contact and involved themselves playfully at times.

Gonzalez-Mena (2007) notes there may be times when infant's needs are met and the infant still cries. She recommends:

> If you've done all you can to meet the needs and the baby's still crying, it is not a reflection on you, your caring, or your skills—it's about allowing emotions to be expressed instead of repressed. When babies understand that what they feel is okay with the people around them, they have a better chance of learning to calm themselves—or in technical terms, learn self-regulation, a problem solving skill. (p. 23)

Gonzalez-Mena (2007) states she does not mean to for the adult to exit completely and let the infant "cry it out"; instead one should make periodic contact and continue to reassure the infant. Naturally, most caregivers will try checking for possible discomfort and use calming strategies that have been successful in the past. *An attuned adult:*

- *notices infant reactions to auditory stimuli.*
- *is aware of infant preferences.*
- *notices if an infant has an attachment to a caregiver and/or expresses pleasure in another's company.*
- *seeks to help the infant maintain a state of balance and a comfort level.*
- *is attentive and consistent in recognizing and satisfying a child's needs.*
- *has sufficient energy and seeks to engage frequently with an infant.*

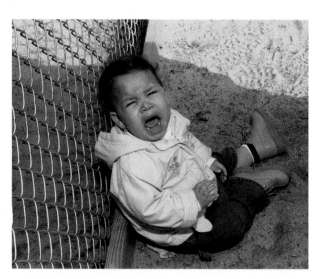

FIGURE 1–14 A quick parental response to crying is appropriate and recommended.

- *monitors an infant's health and safety and observes closely.*
- *provides a variety of experience and sensory materials for exploration.*
- *uses words to accompany child and adult actions.*
- *records milestones in development and uses them to guide caregiver interactions.*
- *is playful, gives attention, and provides feedback to an infant's efforts.*

Infant Imitation

Acredolo and Goodwyn (2000) suggest that infants as young as 1 or 2 days old may imitate parent head movements and facial behaviors; they explain:

> This inborn push to mimic others gets babies into a problem-solving mode from the very beginning. And as we mentioned earlier, babies thrive on problem solving. The payoff is such a pleasant one—Dad sticks around to interact some more, and baby is amused. Imitation is such an important developmental

---

responsive mothers — mothers who are alert and timely in responding to and giving attention to infants' needs and communications.

component that Mother Nature has not left it up to chance. She has made sure that each of us begins life's journey with a necessary tool in hand. (p. 185)

Babbling

Early random sound making is often called **babbling**. Infants the world over babble sounds they have not heard and that they will not use in their native language. This has been taken to mean that each infant has the potential to master any world language. Close inspection shows repetitive sounds and "practice sessions" present. Babbling starts at about the fourth to sixth month and continues in some children through the toddler period. However, a peak in babbling is usually reached between 9 and 12 months. Periods before the first words are spoken are marked by a type of babbling that repeats syllables, as in *dadadadadada*. This is called **echolalia**. Infants seem to echo themselves and others. Babbling behavior overlaps the stages of making one and two or more words, and may end for some children at about 18 months of age.

Infants who are deaf also babble. In play sessions, they will babble for longer periods without hearing either adult sound or their own sounds, as long as they can see the adult responding. However, these children stop babbling at an earlier age than do hearing children. It is not clearly understood why babbling occurs, either in hearing or hearing-impaired children, but it is thought that babbling gives the child the opportunity to use and control the mouth, throat, and lung muscles. Researchers trying to explain babbling suggest that infants are not just exercising or playing with their vocal apparatus. Instead, they may be trying out and attempting to control their lips, tongues, mouths, and jaws to produce certain sounds. A child's babbling amuses and motivates the child, acting as a stimulus that adds variety to the child's existence.

In time, the child increasingly articulates clear, distinct vowel-like, consonant-like, and syllabic sounds. *Ba* and *da* are acquired early because they are easy to produce, whereas *el* and *ar* are acquired late because they require a sophisticated ability to articulate sounds. Although babbling includes a wide range of sounds, as children grow older, they narrow the range and begin to focus on the familiar language of the family. Other sounds are gradually discarded. Almost any feature of environment may promote verbal attempts.

Physical contact continues to be important. Touching, holding, rocking, and engaging in other types of physical contact bring a sense of security and a chance to respond through sound making. The cooing and babbling sounds infants make may also draw caregivers into "conversations." Babies learn to wait for the adult's response after they have vocalized, and both infants and adults are constantly influencing one another in establishing conversation-like vocal interactions (Figure 1–15). The active receiving of perceptions is encouraged by warm, loving parents who share a close relationship. Secure children respond more readily to the world around them. Children who lack social and physical contact or those who live in insecure home environments fall behind in both the number and range of sounds made; differences start showing at about 6 months of age. Sound imitation eventually becomes syllable imitation, and short words are spoken near the end of the child's first year.

Stages of Vocalization

Stoel-Gammon (1997) outlines stages in infants' production of sounds and notes that vocalization types typically overlap from one stage to another.

> **Stage 1 (birth to 2 months): Reflexive vocalization. Characterized by crying, fussing, vegetative sounds like coughing,**

---

babbling — an early language stage in sound production in which an infant engages in vocal play with vowel and consonant sounds, including some sounds not found in his or her language environment.
echolalia — a characteristic of the babbling period. The child repeats (echoes) the same sounds over and over.

FIGURE 1–15 Infants' vocal and playful interactions with caregivers are the precursors of conversations.

burping, sneezing, and some vowel-like sounds.

Stage 2 (2–4 months): Cooing and laughter: Characterized by comfort-state vocalizations and chuckles.

Stage 3 (4–6 months): Vocal play. Characterized by very loud and very soft sounds, yells and whispers, very high and low sounds—squeals and growls, raspberries (bilabial trills), and sustained vowels.

Stage 4 (6 months and older): Canonical babbling. The appearance of sequences of consonant-vowel syllables with 'similar-to–adult' timing, 'near-to-a–word' utterances, reduplicated babbles (bababa), and variegated babbles (bagidabu). The infant's ability to hear his and others' vocalization takes on increased importance. The vocalization of babies with deafness decreases.

Stage 5 (10 months and older): Jargon stage. Babbling overlaps the early period of meaningful speech and is characterized by strings of sounds and syllables uttered with a rich variety of stress and intonation. Sound play, containing recurring favorite sequences, or even words, may occur. (p. 21)*

A Shared Joint Attention Milestone

By the last half of the first year, children begin to take part in a new type of interaction with their caretakers. They share attention given to objects with another person by following that individual's gaze or pointing, responding to the individual's emotional reaction to an event, and imitating that person's object-directed actions (Nelson & Shaw, 2002). This gives adults who notice this behavior a chance to pair words with objects. First words or sounds are usually simple associates of objects or situations. The infant simply voices a shared reference. Nelson and Shaw note that the leap from shared reference associations to meaningful language requires the child to integrate skills with communicative patterns and conceptual knowledge. The child is then standing on a first communicative step.

INFANT SIGNALING/SIGNING

During the latter part of the first year, alert caregivers notice hand and body positions that suggest the child is attempting to communicate (Figure 1–16). Researchers suggest that parents pair words with easy-to-do gestures. At the age of 1 year, children cannot gain enough mastery over their tongues to form many words. Gesturing with their fingers and hands is simpler. For example, infants as young as 7 months may bang on a window to get a family cat's attention or reach out, motion, or crawl toward something or someone they want. The use of signs continues until the child's ability to talk takes off. Some educators believe **signing** may spark other critical thinking skills and lead to

*From Berko Gleason, J. (1997). *The development of language* (4th ed.). Boston: Allyn and Bacon. Copyright © 1997 by Pearson Education. Reprinted by permission of the publisher.

---

signing — a body positioning, sound, action, gesture, or combination of these undertaken by an infant in an effort to communicate a need, desire, or message.

GESTURE	POSSIBLE MEANING
allows food to run out of mouth	satisfied or not hungry
pouts	displeased
pushes nipple from mouth with tongue	satisfied or not hungry
pushes object away	does not want it
reaches out for object	wants to have it handed to him
reaches out to person	wants to be picked up
smacks lips or ejects tongue	hungry
smiles and holds out arms	wants to be picked up
sneezes excessively	wet and cold
squirms and trembles	cold
squirms, wiggles, and cries during dressing or bathing	resents restriction on activities
turns head from nipple	satisfied or not hungry

FIGURE 1–16 Some common gestures of babyhood. (From Hurlock, E. B. [2009]. *Child development* [5th ed.]. New York: McGraw-Hill. Copyright © 2009. Reproduced by permission of The McGraw-Hill Companies, Inc.)

better intelligence quotient (IQ) scores when testing begins.

Toward the end of the child's first year, pointing becomes goal-oriented—the infant will point to a desired object. As time progresses, more and more infant body signaling takes place. Signals are used over and over, and a type of sign language communication emerges. It can be a "signal and sound system" understood by caregivers. When caregivers respond appropriately, the infant easily progresses to word use and verbal aptitude. Signing by infants and young toddlers is believed to stimulate brain development, particularly brain areas involved in language, memory, and concept development.

Some studies of communication gestures note that infants with more advanced gestures have larger vocabularies and that girls seem slightly more advanced in gesturing than do boys. (This paragraph offered an answer to one of the questions in this chapter's beginning vignette. The next paragraph answers another.)

Well-meaning parents or caregivers may choose not to respond to infant gestures and signals, thinking this will accelerate or force the use of words. The opposite is thought to be true. Alert parents who try to read and receive signals give their infant the message that communication leads to fulfillment of wishes. Successful signaling becomes a form of language—a precursor of verbal signals (words). Some experts believe baby signers by age 2 are better at both expressing themselves and understanding others' speech and, on average, have slightly larger vocabularies than their peers who do not sign. Sitting down at the child's level at times when the infant is crawling from one piece of furniture to another may facilitate the adult's ability to pick up on signaling. Watching the infant's eyes and the direction the infant's head turns gives clues. Infants about 8 months old seem fascinated with the adult's sound-making ability. They often turn to look at the adult's lips or want to touch the adult's mouth.

Early childhood educators employed by infant-toddler centers need to know their center's position regarding expected educator behaviors. Most centers expect educators to actively pair words with adult or child signs, encourage child use of signs, and learn and respond to each child's individual sign language.

UNDERSTANDING

Most babies get some idea of the meaning of a few words at about 6 to 9 months. At about 10 months of age, some infants start to respond to spoken word clues. Somewhere between 8 and 13 months, the child's communication, whether vocal or a type of gesture, becomes intentional as the child makes a connection between responses, his behavior, and parent or early childhood educator responses (Figure 1–17). A game such as Pat-a-cake may start the baby clapping, and "bye-bye" or Peek-a-boo brings about other imitations of earlier play activities with the parents. The child's language is called passive at this stage, for he

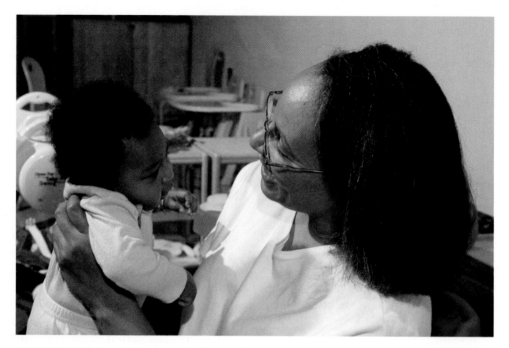

FIGURE 1–17 Caregivers provide face-to-face conversation that promotes infants' own attempts to communicate.

primarily receives (or is receptive). Speaking attempts will soon become active (or expressive). Vocabulary provides a small portal through which adults can gauge a little of what the child knows. There is a point at which children expand nonverbal signals to true language.

Older infants still communicate with their caregivers through many nonverbal actions; one common way is by holding up their arms, which most often means, "I want to be picked up." Other actions include facial expression, voice tone, voice volume, posture, and gestures such as "locking in" by pointing fingers and toes at attention-getting people and events.

Although infants at this stage can respond to words and changes in caregivers' facial expressions, voice tone, and voice volume, actions and gestures also carry feelings and messages important to infants' well-being. Understanding the tone of caregivers' speech comes before understanding the words used.

Gopnik et al. (1999) describe what happens when infants are about 1 year old.

One-year-old babies know that they will see something by looking where other people point; they know what they should do to something by watching what other people do; they know how they should feel about something by seeing how other people feel. (p. 243)

FIRST WORDS

Before an understandable, close approximation of a word is uttered, the child's physical organs need to function in a delicate unison and the child must reach a certain level of mental maturity. Close to 12 months of age, the speech centers of the brain have developed the capacity to enable the infant to produce his first word—a great accomplishment and milestone. The child's respiratory system supplies the necessary energy. As the breath is exhaled, sounds and speech are formed with the upward movement of air. The larynx's vibrating folds produce voice (called

phonation). The larynx, mouth, and nose influence the child's voice quality (termed **resonation**). A last modification of the breath stream is **articulation**—a final formation done through molding, shaping, stopping, and releasing voiced and other-than-voiced sounds that reflect language heard in the child's environment.

Repetition of syllables such as *ma*, *da*, and *ba* in a child's babbling occurs toward the end of the first year. If *mama* or *dada* or a close copy is said, parents and caregivers show attention and joy. Language, especially in the area of speech development, is a two-way process; reaction is an important feedback to action.

The term *protoword* is often used for the invented words a child may use during the transition from prespeech to speech. During this transition, a child has acquired the difficult concept that sounds have meaning and is unclear only about the fact that one is supposed to find out what words exist instead of making them up.

Generally, first words are nouns or proper names of foods, animals, or toys; words may also include *gone*, *there*, *uh-oh*, *more*, and *dat* ("what's that?"). Greetings, farewells, or other social phrases, such as *peek-a-boo*, are also among the first recognizable words.

Monolingual (one-language) children utter their first words at approximately 11 months of age; the range is from about 9 months to about 16 months. At about a year and a half the child learns approximately one new word every 3 days. Most experts believe that talking alone shows no link to mental development at age 2, but a child's comprehension of words is paramount. Experts conclude that there is little scientific evidence to suggest that late talkers will become less fluent than early talkers. Some children acquire large numbers of object names in their first 50 to 100 words. The first spoken words usually contain *p*, *b*, *t*, *d*, *m*, and *n* (front of the mouth consonants), which require the least use of the tongue and air control. They are shortened versions, such as *da* for "daddy," *beh* for "bed," and *up* for "cup." When two-syllable words are attempted, they are often strung together using the same syllable sound, as in *dada* or *beebee*. If the second syllable is voiced, the child's reproduction of the sound may come out as *dodee* for "doggy" or *papee* for "potty."

At this stage, words tend to be segments of wider happenings in the child's life. A child's word *ba* may represent a favorite, often-used toy (such as a ball). As the child grows in experience, any round object seen in the grocery store, for instance, will also be recognized and called *ba*. This phenomenon has been termed *overextension*. The child has embraced "everything round," which is a much broader meaning for ball than the adult definition of the word.

Following is a list of words frequently understood between 8 and 12 months of age: *mommy*, *daddy*, *bye-bye*, *baby*, *shoe*, *ball*, *cookie*, *juice*, *bottle*, *no-no*, and the child's own name and names of family members.

A child finds that words can open many doors. They help the child get things and cause caregivers to act in many ways. Vocabulary quickly grows from the names of objects to words that refer to actions. This slowly decreases the child's dependence on context (a specific location and situation) for communication and gradually increases the child's reliance on words—the tools of abstract thought. Children learn very quickly that words not only name things and elicit action on another's part but also convey comments and express individual attitudes and feelings.

An attuned adult:

◆ *nurtures infant curiosity.*

◆ *uses words and gestures in communication.*

◆ *builds a sign language relationship with infants.*

---

phonation — exhaled air passes the larynx's vibrating folds and produces "voice."
resonation — amplification of laryngeal sounds using cavities of the mouth, nose, sinuses, and pharynx.
articulation — the adjustments and movements of the muscles of the mouth and jaw involved in producing clear oral communication.

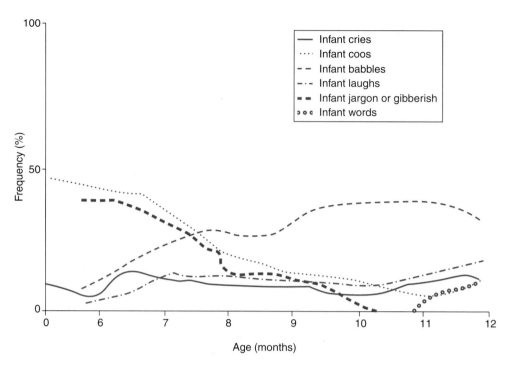

FIGURE 1–18 Approximate frequency of child utterances from 6 to 12 months.

♦ tries to judge the intensity of infants' emotions.

♦ offers a choice of child actions and explorations within safe limits.

♦ responds to and promotes reciprocal communication.

♦ pairs words with actions and objects.

♦ observes the direction of infants' gazes for clues to infants' moment to moment interests.

♦ continues to be at eye level when possible.

♦ expects and recognizes invented words.

♦ encourages first word use by repeating word back to child and connecting the child's word to objects or actions as appropriate.

♦ guesses frequently about a child's meaning in communication.

♦ works toward a child's success at using words to fulfill his desires, needs, and interests.

TODDLER SPEECH

Toddlerhood begins, and the child eagerly names things and seeks names for others. The child echoes and repeats to the best of his ability. At times, the words are not recognizable as the same words the caregiver offered. When interacting with young speakers, an adult must listen closely, watch for nonverbal signs, scan the situation, and use a good deal of guessing to understand the child and respond appropriately. The child's single words accompanied by gestures, motions, and intonations are called **holophrases**. They usually represent a whole idea or sentence.

While the child is learning to walk, speech may briefly take a backseat to developing motor skill. At this time, the child may listen more intently to what others are saying.

The slow-paced learning of new words (Figure 1–18) is followed by a period of rapid

holophrases — the expression of a whole idea in a single word. They are often found in the speech of children at about 12 to 18 months of age.

growth. The child pauses briefly, listening, digesting, and gathering forces to embark on the great adventure of becoming a fluent speaker.

IMPLICATIONS FOR INFANT CENTER STAFF MEMBERS

The importance of understanding the responsive, reciprocal nature of optimal care giving in group infant centers cannot be overestimated. The soothing, calming, swaddling, rocking, sympathizing, and responding behaviors of infant care specialists help infants maintain a sense of security and a relaxed state, calmness, and equilibrium.

Weissbourd (1996) describes the type of adult a child needs.

> **All children should have a continuous relationship with a consistently attentive and caring adult who treats them as special—and not just another inhabitant of this world—who is able to stimulate and engage.**
>
> **Responsive mothers—those who ignore few episodes and respond with little delay—have infants with more variety, subtlety, and clarity in noncrying communications . . . Mothers who vocalize and smile frequently have been found to have infants who vocalize and smile frequently. (p. 61)**

The emotional well-being of infants has been given increased attention as research on infant development uncovers its importance. Physician Chet Johnson (2005) points out:

> **The research shows how powerful emotional well-being is to a child's future health. A baby who fails to meet certain key "emotional milestones" may have trouble learning to speak, read, and later, do well in school. By reading emotional responses, doctors have begun to discover ways to tell if a baby as young as 3 months is showing early signs of possible psychological disorders, including depression, anxiety, learning disabilities and perhaps autism. Instead of just asking if they're crawling or sitting we're asking more questions about how they share their world with their caregivers. (p. 35)**

See Figure 1–19 for infants' emotional milestones.

At about 4 months, babies begin to gaze in the direction in which caregivers are looking. Caregivers are able to follow the line of vision of babies as well. Well-trained caregivers will naturally comment and offer language labels and a running commentary. This process is known as *joint attentional focus*. When adults know that the infant does not yet understand language, most adults behave as if the child's response is a turn in the conversation. Adult caregivers need to read both nonverbal and vocalized cues and react appropriately (Figure 1–20). They need to be attentive and loving. Learning to read each other's signals is basic to the quality of the relationship. Liberal amounts of touching, holding, smiling, and looking promote language and the child's overall sense that the world around him is both safe and fascinating. Recognizing the child's individuality, reading nonverbal behaviors, and reacting with purposeful actions are all expected of professional infant specialists, as is noticing activity level, moods, distress threshold, rhythms of the body, intensity, sense of adventure, distractibility, adaptability, and attention span.

There are many skills that well-trained caregivers possess, beginning with holding the infant firmly yet gently and making soft, gentle sounds while moving smoothly and holding the infant close. Others are identified in the following list.

An attuned adult:

◆ *talks in a pleasant, soothing voice; uses simple language; and makes frequent eye contact.*

◆ *emphasizes and expects two-way "conversation"; hesitates; and pauses for an infant response.*

AGE	EMOTIONAL/SOCIAL CHARACTERISTICS
Birth to around 3–4 months	At birth, the infant is able to feel fear and contentment and is self-absorbed. During first 3–4 months, infant becomes aware of the environment around him and is attentive and interested. Seems able to calm self at times. Develops deliberate responses. Focuses on the faces of people and smiles at them. Eyes may widen in anticipation. May react to strong scents or odors. Has a developing sense of security. Holding and touching may reduce stress, and rhythmic motion may soothe. May enjoy swaddling. Pays attention and reacts to sounds. Some infants are oversensitive to some types of sounds. Reacts to visual cues, especially from care provider's face.
Around 5–6 or more months	Displays emotions such as surprise, joy, and frustration. Falls in love with care provider. Beams with delight at times. Able to see the pattern formed by features on care provider's face. Smiles in recognition. May display sorrow and annoyance. Builds a stronger relationship with primary care provider. Begins to realize he can make things happen. Is comforted by physical closeness. Develops feelings of being loved, valued, and esteemed by others. Easy to tell when infant is happy. Sense of self is a reflection of care provider's emotional interactions with infant. May experience jealousy.
Around 10 or more months	Initiates two-way communication. Notices where care provider looks and often follows by also looking. Tries to catch care provider's eye and gives physical cues to others to obtain a desired action, such as being held. May use signs and signals to make things happen. May respond to rhythm with rhythmic movements. Expects his action will prompt a reaction. May mimic gestures. May express fear, anger, anticipation, caution, and surprise with strangers. Responds to name, words, and sounds, and attempts to imitate them. Is curious and perhaps assertive and negative at times. May experience a sense of loss at something removed. May show fear if care provider looks angry, frowns, or stares (not recommended). Seeks pleasure and enjoys stimulating self (for example, touching toes and participating in adult-infant games that involve moving or touching body parts, such as "This Little Piggy."

Note: This is not intended to be a complete inventory of emotional milestones; research in identifying infant emotional development and capacity is still in its infancy. Notice social skill and emotional response is intertwined and dependent on environmental and human experience. |

FIGURE 1–19 Emotional milestones and social skill characteristics.

◆ makes a game out of the infant's smiles, sounds, and movements when the infant is responsive.

◆ speaks clearly.

◆ explains what is happening and what will happen next.

◆ is consistently attentive.

◆ does not interrupt the infant's vocal play, jargon, or self-communication.

◆ engages in word play, rhyme, chants, and fun-to-say short expressions.

◆ is an animated speaker and a responsive companion.

◆ may, with an older infant, attempt to offer simple finger plays.

◆ plans real and concrete participatory activities with textures, sights, and sounds.

◆ encourages soundmaking and provides noisemaking and musical toys.

◆ labels objects, happenings, actions, and emotions.

◆ uses highly intonated speech that may be high pitched at times with very young infants.

FIGURE 1–20 "You can do it. Just take one small step."

◆ *speaks distinctly with clear enunciation to help children identify phonemes.*

◆ *emphasizes, at times, one word in a sentence.*

◆ *uses repetition but avoids overdoing it.*

◆ *gives feedback by responding with both words and actions.*

◆ *creates and pursues game-like strategies and techniques.*

◆ *serves as a coexplorer.*

Being playful and initiating singing conversations with infants can be enjoyable and may lay the foundation for later music activities. Both recorded and live musical sounds are part of an auditory-rich environment for infants. For identified early childhood goals and additional caregiver activities, see Figure 1–21.

Williams (2008) urges caregivers to explore the world outside the classroom or home with older infants and toddlers.

Teachers can support children's explorations and interactions with the natural world much as they support other learning: with the belief and hope that each child will be encouraged to become a geologist, biologist, zookeeper, veterinarian, or preschool teacher, regardless of how dirty the job may be. (p. 25)

Think about watching or feeling raindrops, experiencing mud, touching a caterpillar, smelling flowers, or hearing birds. The reality and beauty of natural landscapes surrounds us, and there are multiple ways to experience it safely with infants and toddlers.

Remember that infants are alike yet uniquely different. Some sensitive infants may appear overwhelmed and require little stimuli to maintain equilibrium. Others will thrive in an environment that provides a multitude of people, sights, sounds, and new activities. Each infant provides a challenge one must "puzzle out" to decide best courses of action—what works, what does not work, and what is best.

Because infants' first sensory experiences are part of emotional relationships with caregivers,

AGE	ADULT GOALS	ADULT ACTIVITY
birth to 2 months	1. to create a trusting, intimate relationship 2. to take pleasure in the reciprocal infant-adult interactions 3. to help infant calm and regulate himself 4. to verbally communicate and promote a two-way pattern of responses 5. to maintain eye contact and spend time face to face 6. to seek to create an appropriate environmental moderation level	1. anticipate and satisfy infant needs 2. show interest and provide positive reactions and joy in the infant's presence and communicative attempts 3. provide sights, sounds, touches, and playful companionship 4. talk, croon, whisper, sing, and mimic infant gesture 5. repeat infant sounds 6. provide a comfortable environment that satisfies the child's needs
2–6 months	1. to keep alert to infant attempts to communicate distress or needs 2. to strengthen growing bond of enjoyment in adult-infant "together time" and explorations 3. to recognize child individuality, moods, likes and dislikes, uniqueness 4. to encourage "you talk" and "I talk" behaviors 5. to see infant gestures as possibly purposeful 6. to hold child's eye contact when speaking and gain child's attention with animated speech 7. to use clear and simple speech	1. provide adult-infant play time and joint new experiences 2. provide infant exploring of sights, sounds, music, and play materials and indoor and outdoor environments 3. offer "talking" opportunities with others 4. name child's actions, toys, happenings while changing, bathing, and feeding 5. play baby games such as Pat-a-cake 6. use talk and touch as a reward for the child's communication attempts 7. repeat child sounds and gestures
6–12 months	1. to pursue infant interests, tailoring your talk to child focus 2. to promote the idea that language is used for naming and describing 3. to play with rhythm and rhyme in adult-infant communications 4. to speak clearly, emphasizing new words when appropriate 5. to show delight in child's verbal and physical accomplishments 6. to pair your words with actions, happenings, and objects 7. to recognize and respond appropriately to child signaling and words 8. to make sure sound level and noise is appropriate 9. to listen for intent, not perfection 10. to provide safe environment conducive to child exploring and action	1. expand the child's world with neighborhood trips, people, playthings, and experiences 2. name and describe happenings, emotions, actions, and environments as things take place 3. introduce and read board books to the child, letting child explore them himself 4. sing songs, perform finger plays, play word games with visual and touching actions 5. listen and pause for infant response 6. name body parts, colors, and objects 7. tell simple stories 8. delight in the world and its joyful pursuits with the child

FIGURE 1–21 Adult goals and activities for language development during infancy.

caregivers' efforts to provide developmental care go hand in hand with providing positive emotional support in daily reciprocal exchanges between the child and adult. The terms *child-centered* and *child-focused* need to be coupled with reactive, observant, playful, and nurturing adult behaviors. This type of infant care is nearly impossible when adult-infant ratios are inadequate.

Generally, the types of adults who promote language are those who are alert to the child's achievements, notice them, and enjoy interacting, as well as adults who can offer novelty, assistance, and enthusiasm in addition to focusing on the child's interests. Clark (2007) suggests that adults view young children as being actively engaged in search for meaning. Besides being increasingly competent communicators, they are also avid researchers and explorers of their environment.

BABY GAMES AND EXPLORATIONS

Almost daily, infants seem to increase the ways they can explore and enjoy verbal-physical games. Most mothers or infant educators create their own games and activities that are enjoyable to both infants and caregivers. They become aware of their infants' focus and reactions to people, toys, and other environmental features; they then build activities and interactions based on child interest. Games that deal with child anticipation often elicit smiles or giggles. Playing classics such as Peek-a-boo or Johnny Jump Up or hiding an object under a cloth has delighted generations of children. More newly devised activities include tying a soft tinkling bell to the wrist or leg of an infant or connecting a soft ribbon from an infant's ankle to an overhead mobile (under adult supervision).

Experts recommend that, from a baby's earliest days, caregivers begin with simple imitation games during face-to-face interaction, making sure to pause long enough for the infant to take in the information and mount a response. The best distance for these games is 8 to 12 inches away from the child's face.

Imitation of the baby's movement is also suggested, as is rewarding the baby's effort with attention or smiles.

Caregivers spend considerable time supervising active infants; it usually takes little effort to supply brief running remarks. Pausing is as important as talking. A caregiver who has primarily a policing orientation that is full of "no-no's" and little else misses a large amount of language-building opportunities.

It is obvious that infants 6 months and older watch, imitate, and attempt physical and verbal contact with other infants and children. There is a strong attraction to other small people and animals. Most young infants prefer to be in the same room with a favored caregiver. Only as they become mobile and older do they explore other people and adjacent rooms and areas on their own.

The following classic language and body action play has brought delight to generations of infants. The most enjoyed play activities include tickling, bouncing, and lifting with accompanying words and rhymes.

THIS LITTLE PIGGY

(Each line is recited while holding a toe, moving toward the pinkie.)

> *This little pig went to market. This little pig stayed home. This little pig had roast beef. This little pig had none. This little piggy cried, "Wee, wee, wee, wee!" all the way home.*

(First published in 1728.)

PAT-A-CAKE

(Recited while helping the child with hand clapping.)

> *Pat-a-cake, pat-a-cake, baker's man.*
> *Bake me a cake as fast as you can.*
> *Pat it and prick it and mark it with a "B."*
> *And put it in the oven for baby and me.*

SO BIG

> *Say, "Look at you—so big!" Slowly raise both of the infant's arms up, extending them over the child's head while saying, "[child's name] is so-o-oh big" and then slowly bring the arms down.*

Repeat.

> *Say the child's name slowly as you raise the infant close to your face at eye level. Then say, "So-o-oh big." Then gently say, "Wow, wow, wow—what a baby. A so-o-oh big baby!" with a big smile.*

Other play games are found in the Activities section.

MUSICAL PLAY

Music, singing, and musical expression appear to be a central part of the crucial interaction that occurs between caregivers and infants as infants develop over the first year of life. Two types of musical or singing interaction take place: (1) a soothing go-to-sleep lullaby-style interaction and (2) a playful, upbeat adult behavior that might be described as rhythmic and joyful. The first style is seen as caregivers attempt to regulate or promote a particular infant state (such as relaxation, contentment, or sleep), and the second style, the communication of emotional information (such as mutual enjoyment and love of music).

Common sense tells us that certain musical experiences enrich infants' lives and may soothe both infants and caregivers. Experts believe babies as young as 3 months can distinguish between certain melodies. Musical infant babbling has been described as tonal and rhythmic babble (Gordon, 1986). Tonal babble is babbling in a single pitch, the babble sounding like a monotone singer. In rhythmic babble the child's body or voice displays a rhythmic beat or quality.

Much of the music offered to infants may be accompanied by caregiver singing. Nursery, cultural, and folk tunes can be introduced in intimate and pleasant settings. Simple, safe musical instruments are enjoyed, and moving to music is natural to young children. Wolf (2000) suggests that educators start with songs they love, ones sung to them as children. Others suggest using children's music recorded by well-known performers. Names like Raffi, Ella Jenkins, Hap Palmer, Tom Hunter, and others are familiar to most early childhood educators. Some educators recommend Bach preludes and Vivaldi's *Springtime* Symphony along with other classical pieces. Two benefits of musical activities for some older preschoolers and primary children are enhanced abstract reasoning and **spatial-temporal reasoning**.

Scientists are finding that the human brain may be "prewired" for music. They suspect that some forms of intelligence are heightened by music. Although controversial at present, some educators believe learning musical skills in childhood can help children do better at mathematics. Only more studies with more children will prove whether music produces lasting benefits in cognition.

See Additional Resources at the end of this chapter for favorite musical and movement activities and song books.

READING TO INFANTS

Some parents read books during a mother's later stages of pregnancy, believing the practice will produce some positive results. Research findings suggest that infants remember and give greater attention to stories read to them before their birth. Conclusive research evidence is yet to verify this. Zambo and Hansen (2007) suggest that from birth to 3 months, read-alouds are purely an emotional connection between the infant and caregiver.

> **Being held, feeling good, and having a familiar, conforming voice are more important than the kind of book or the content of the story. Lullabies, singsong stories, and other repetitive, rhythmic experiences bring joy and comfort to infants and establish a special time together for child and caregiver. (p. 34)**

Between 6 and 12 months, some infants will sit and look at a picture book with an adult.

---

spatial-temporal reasoning — the mental arrangement of ideas and/or images in a graphic pattern indicating their relationships over time.

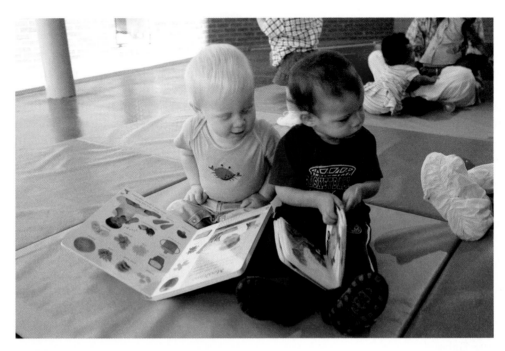

FIGURE 1–22 Ryan is trying to turn a page.

It is the sound of the reader's voice that gets the young child's attention, even before the child's focus shifts to the pictures. The warmth and security of being held and the reader's voice make for a very pleasurable combination.

The child may want to grab pages and test the book in his mouth or try to turn pages. His head may swivel to look at the adult's mouth. If the child has brought a book to the adult, he will usually want to sit on the adult's lap as both go through the book. Children get ever more adept at turning pages as their first birthday nears (Figure 1–22). Familiar objects in colorful illustrations set on white or plain backgrounds and large faces seem to be particularly fascinating. Infants seem to respond well to and enjoy the rhyme they hear.

Adult reading to infants younger than 12 months of age is increasingly recommended, for researchers believe the infant is learning about the sound patterns in words and how words are formed. Book-reading techniques include reading something the adult enjoys with average volume and expression, using gesturing or pointing when called for, promoting child imitation, letting the child turn sturdy pages, and making animal or sound noises. A good rule of thumb is to stop before the child's interest wanes. Adults may find that many infants enjoy repeated reading of the same book during the same sitting. Some parents are very adept at sharing picture books. These parents find **cues** in book features, such as familiar objects, events depicted, sounds, colors, and so on, that give the infant pleasure, as may be evidenced by the adult saying, "It's a dog like our Bowser!" Skilled early childhood educators realize it is the colorful illustrations that attract, so they name and point to features. They also attempt to make illustrations relevant to the child's past experience.

Colorful books with sturdy or plastic-coated pages or cardboard books are plentiful. Books of cotton fabric and ones with flaps to lift and peek under, soft furry patches to feel, rough sandpaper to touch, and holes to look through or stick a finger through are books that include enjoyable sensory exploration. Homemade

cues — prompts or hints that aid recognition, such as a parent pointing to and/or saying "teddy bear" when sharing a picture book illustration. This is done because the infant is familiar with his own teddy bear.

collections of family photographs have delighted many young children. Picture books with simple, large illustrations or photos that are set against a contrasting background and books that are constructed to stand on their own when opened are also popular.

There are a number of literary classics (although not all experts agree to the same titles) that most children in our culture experience. Many of these involve rhyme and rhythm. They have, over time, become polished gems passed onto succeeding generations. Some of these are songs that have been published as books, and include:

Here We Go Round the Mulberry Bush

One, Two, Buckle My Shoe

Hush-a-Bye Baby

Twinkle, Twinkle, Little Star

Rock-a-Bye Baby

Ba Ba Blacksheep

RECORDINGS

Growing numbers of CDs, tapes, and videos are being produced for infants. Infants listen and sometimes move their bodies rhythmically. Research is yet to confirm the educational or language-developing benefits claimed by manufacturers of infant recordings whether audio or visual. In *The Journal of Pediatrics*, Interlandi (2007) reports a new study that included a group of 1,000 families and reviewed the use of infant DVDs; this report suggests that babies who watch recordings fared worst with DVDs than with several other types of programming in terms of educational or language-developing benefits.

> Exposure to educational shows, like "Sesame Street," and non-educational ones, like "SpongeBob SquarePants," had no net effect on language, researchers said—but for every hour that infants 8 to 16 months spent watching the baby DVDs, they understood six to eight fewer words, out of a set of 90, than infants who didn't watch. (p. 14)

EARLY EXPERIENCE WITH WRITING TOOLS

As early as 10 to 12 months, infants will watch intently as someone makes marks on a surface or paper. They will reach and attempt to do the marking themselves. Large chalk, thick crayons, or large crayon "chunks" are recommended for exploring, but caregivers are reminded to supervise closely because of infants' tendency to put small objects in their mouths. Large-sized paper (for example, torn apart grocery brown bags) taped at the edges to surfaces and chalkboards work well. The child may not realize the writing tool is making marks but may imitate and gleefully move the whole arm. Many believe it is simply not worth the effort to supervise very young children during this activity and save this activity until the children are older.

MONITORING INFANT DEVELOPMENT

Stark, Chazen-Cohen, and Jerald (2002) point out that normal paths of development within various domains serve as reference points to assess infant competence. A number of factors in an infant's life influence the child's overall development, communication abilities, and language growth.

Early educators are aware that a mother's improper prenatal health and diet, negative home environment, and other life circumstances may cause biological problems such as premature birth, low birth weight, a disability, or a regulatory disorder. After birth, factors such as maternal depression, poverty, family homelessness, stress, family caregiving behaviors, and lack of family support systems may affect children's emotional, physical, intellectual, and social development and competence. Early childhood programs recognize that family-school communications and interactions can be crucial. They establish working relationships with families and a variety of community network and support agencies.

Infant assessments undertaken by educators try to identify strengths and developmental areas where the infant and/or family may need supportive assistance to promote optimal infant growth. Maternal health histories sometimes provide clues, as do home visits and daily or periodic educator-family interactions. An examination of whether the school's schedules, activities, staff, and curriculum need to change or adapt takes place frequently so that each child's individual needs have every chance of being met.

Infants should be observed daily with an eye toward assessing developmental milestones and mental and physical health, and educators must be knowledgeable of ages and stages. In a busy center, making dated notes is suggested as new, questionable, or important behaviors are observed. A notepad in a handy pocket is recommended, as are frequent staff meetings to discuss individual infant language behaviors and developments. This is followed by planning sessions that create individual learning plans and family consultation when necessary.

Eiserman and associates (2007) note that hearing loss may be an "invisible" condition, especially for infants and toddlers with moderate, mild, or unilateral hearing losses, because these children may not exhibit observable symptoms of loss until they are older. Before the use of modern screening tools, infants with hearing loss typically remained unidentified until 2½ years of age (Harrison, Roush, & Wallace, 2003)—far too late for optimal language development (Eiserman et al., 2007). Dramatic improvements in hearing screening technology and growth in the number of hospitals that do at-birth screenings have occurred in the past 10 years. Educators realize hearing loss can occur at anytime, either swiftly or gradually. The American Speech-Language-Hearing Association (2001, 2004) estimates approximately 35 percent of preschoolers (including infants) will have repeated episodes of ear infection that nearly always cause a temporary loss that can significantly disrupt language acquisition. Screening hearing during infancy and beyond is a recommended practice, as is caregiver vigilance. For a listing of additional milestones in infant development, consult the Book Companion Website.

IMPLICATIONS FOR FAMILIES

Family attitudes about their infant's communicating abilities may influence the infant's progress, in part by affecting how the family responds to the infant.

These attitudes are the early roots of the critical partnership between adult and child and the child's sense of feeling lovable and powerful. Consequently, they influence the child's assessment of self.

Special infant projects to promote later school success have provided information in this area. Positive home factors mentioned include the following:

- A lot of attention by socially responsive caregivers
- Little or no disruption of bonding attachment between the infant and his primary caregiver during the first year
- Availability of space and objects to explore
- Good nutrition
- Active and interactive exchanges and play time
- Parent knowledge of developmental milestones and the child's emerging skills
- Parent confidence in infant handling
- Maintenance of the child's physical robustness
- Positive attention and touching in play exchange

Parent (or family) stress and less-than-desirable quality in child-parent interactions seem to hinder children's language development. Because most families face stress, a family's reaction to stress, rather than stress itself, is the determining factor. In today's busy families, time spent with infants and young children needs to remain a family priority.

Good advice for families includes not worrying about teaching as much as creating a rich and emotionally supportive home atmosphere. A rich atmosphere is one that offers opportunity and companionship rather than expensive toys and surroundings. Current research indicates that families who spontaneously speak about what the child is interested in and who zoom in and out of the child's play as they go about their daily work are responsive and effective families. Also, families should know early and late "talkers" usually show little difference in speaking ability by age 3. The variation between children with respect to the onset and accomplishment of most human characteristics covers a wide range when considering what is normal and expected.

Munir and Rose (2008) describe healthy social behavior in infancy as well as infants who display possible early autistic behaviors.

> Healthy infants as young as 6 or 8 months do communicate and respond nonverbally to social cues. Most look up or turn at the sound of their name. By 12 months, they typically babble and point at objects. By 16 months, they say single words; by 24 months, two-word phrases. In contrast, children with autism seldom make meaningful eye contact or respond to familiar voices. They may never speak. Their play is often repetitive and characterized by limited imagination. Others may simply flap their hands in excitement or disappointment.
>
> On their own, none of these signs means a child has autism or another development disorder. Nevertheless, if a child has any of these signs, he or she merits evaluation. (p. 64)

Regardless of the setting, the experts agree the primary need of infants and toddlers is emotional connection (Lloyd-Jones, 2002). Human relationships are the key, and emotional development is critical for growth. Children of the poor, who are considered to be at-risk, may escape at-risk status if they share the following commonalities. They live in large, extended families that provide supportive language stimulation and encouragement, and they have no other social or biological risks present. Their families manage to safeguard their infants' and older children's health. Intervention and social service programs may also have been accessible. It is the isolated poor families with multiple risk factors, including abusive home environments, whose children are the most negatively affected.

SUMMARY

Each child grows in language ability in a unique way. The process starts before birth with the development of sensory organs. Caregivers play an important role in a child's growth and mastery of language.

Perceptions gained through life experiences serve as the base for future learning of words and speech. Babbling, soundmaking, and imitation occur, and first words appear.

A number of environmental factors, including poverty, may influence a child's language acquisition. Adults' attitudes concerning infants' intellectual and communication abilities are important also. Most children progress through a series of language ability stages and milestones at about the same ages (Figure 1–23) and become adult-like speakers during the preschool period. The way children learn language is not clearly understood, hence the numerous differing theories of language acquisition.

Technology has permitted neuroscientists to research infant abilities in greater depth than ever before. Research has enlightened educators who are awed by discoveries concerning infant's learning capacities and abilities to sort and categorize human speech sounds. Deprivation, abuse, and neglect can affect infants' brain function, as can sight and hearing acuity.

Early in life, infants and parents form a reciprocal relationship, reacting in special ways to each other. The quality and quantity of caregiver attention becomes an important factor in language development.

The child progresses from receiving to sending language, which is accompanied by gestures and nonverbal communication. From infancy, the child is an active participant, moving closer to the two-way process required in language usage and verbal communication.

Staff members in infant care programs can possess interaction skills that offer infants optimal opportunities for speech development. Constant monitoring of each child's progress

INFANT'S AGE	STAGES OF LANGUAGE DEVELOPMENT
before birth	Listens to sounds. Reacts to loud sounds.
at birth	Birth cry is primal, yet individual—vowel-like. Cries to express desires (for food, attention, and so on) or displeasure (pain or discomfort). Makes eating, sucking, and small throaty sounds. Hiccups. Crying becomes more rhythmic and resonant during first days. Shows changes in posture—tense, active, or relaxed.
first days	Half cries become vigorous; whole cries begin to take on depth and range. Coughs and sneezes.
1 month	Three to four vowel sounds apparent. Seems to quiet movements and attend to mother's voice. Eating sounds mirror eagerness. Sighs and gasps. Smiles in sleep.
2–3 months	Coos and makes pleasurable noises (babbling) and blowing and smacking sounds. Most vowel sounds are present. Open vowel-like babbles may begin. Consonant sounds begin, usually the following—*b, d, g, h, l, m, n, p, t*. Markedly less crying. Smiles and squeals and may coo for half a minute. Peers into faces. Adults may recognize distinct variations in cries (i.e., cries that signal fear, tiredness, hunger, pain, and so on). Focuses on mother's face and turns head to her voice. May be frightened by loud or unfamiliar noise. May blow bubbles and move tongue in and out.
4–5 months	Sound play is frequent. Social smiling more pronounced. Can whine to signal boredom. May laugh. Reacts to tone of voice. Seems to listen and enjoy music. Likes adult vocal play and mimicking. Favorite people seem to induce verbalness. Babbles several sounds in one breath. Body gestures signal state of comfort or discomfort. Attracted to sounds. Approaching 6 months of age, may start to show understanding of words often used in household. Turns head and looks at speaking family members. Consonant sounds more pronounced and frequent.
6–8 months	Increased babbling and sound making; repeats syllables; imitates motions and gestures; uses nonverbal signals; vocalizes all vowel sounds; reduplication of utterances; more distinct intonation. Increases understanding of simple words. Enjoys making noise with toys and household objects. Repeats actions to hear sounds again. May blow toy horn. Delights in rhythmic vocal play interchange, especially those that combine touching and speaking. Twists and protrudes tongue, smacks, and watches mother's mouth and lips intently. May look at picture books for short period or watch children's television programs.
9–10 months	May make kiss sounds. Increasing understanding of words like *no-no, mommy, daddy, ball, hat,* and *shoe*. May play Pat-a-cake and wave bye-bye. May hand books to adults for sharing. Uses many body signals and gestures. May start jargonlike strings of sounds, grunts, gurgles, and whines. Listens intently to new sounds. Imitates.
11–14 months	Reacts to an increasing number of words. Speaks first word(s) (usually words with one syllable or repeated syllable). Points to named objects or looks toward named word. Makes sounds and noises with whatever is available. Imitates breathing noises, animal noises (like dog's bark or cat's meow), or environmental noises (like "boom" or train toot). Uses many body signals, especially "pick me up" with arms outstretched and reaching for another's hand, meaning "come with me." May understand as many as 40 to 50 words. At close to 15 months, one word has multiple meanings. Jargonlike strings of verbalness continue. The child's direction of looking gives clues to what the child understands, and the child may have a speaking vocabulary of 10 or more words. Uses first pretend play gestures such as combing hair with a spoon-shaped object, drinking from a pretend cup, pretending to eat an object, and pretending to talk with another on a toy telephone.

FIGURE 1–23 Milestones in developing language behavior.

in reaching milestones is undertaken to ensure that each child's needs are evaluated. Recognized needs can then receive staff attention and program particulars can be adjusted.

ADDITIONAL RESOURCES

Readings

Acredolo, L., & Goodwyn, S. (2000). *Baby minds: Brain-building games your baby will love to play.* New York: Bantam Books

Jahromi, L. B., & Shifter, C. A. (2007). Individual differences in the contribution of maternal soothing to infant stress reduction. *Infancy, 11*(3), 1061–1099.

Karp, H. (2002). *The happiest baby on the block.* New York: Bantam Dell.

Learner, C., & Dumbro, A. (2005). *Bringing up baby: Three steps to making good decisions in your child's first years.* Washington, DC: Zero to Three.

Murray, C. G. (2007). *Simple signing with young children: A guide for infant, toddler, and preschool teachers.* Beltsville, MI: Gryphon House.

Infant Books

Alborough, J. (2000). *Hugs.* Cambridge, MA: Candlewick Press.

Aston, D. H. (2006). *Mamma outside, mama inside.* New York: Henry Holt.

Bauer, M. D. (2003). *Toes, ear, and nose.* New York: Little Simon.

Boyton, S. (2004). *Moo baa, la la la!* New York: Simon & Schuster.

DK Publishing Inc. (1998). *Touch and feel farm* [sensory board book]. New York: Author.

Hindley, J. (2006). *Baby talk: A book of first words and phrases.* New York: Candlewick Press.

Katz, K. (2000). *Where is baby's belly button?* New York: Little Simon.

Miller, M. (1998). *Baby faces.* New York: Little Simon.

Oxenbury, H. (1981). *Dressing.* New York: Little Simon.

Oxenbury, H. (1995). *I hear.* New York: Candlewick Press.

Saltzberg, B. (2004). *Noisy kisses.* San Diego: Red Wagon.

Shott, S. (1996). *Baby's world.* New York: Dutton.

Watanabe, K. (2003). *My first Taggies book: Sweet dreams.* New York: Scholastic.

Infant Play Games

Lansky, V. (2001). *Games babies play: From birth to twelve months.* New York: Book Peddlers.

Rowley, B. (2000). *Baby days: Activities, ideas, and games.* New York: Hyperion.

Wilner, I. (2000). *Baby's game book.* New York: Greenwillow.

Infant Music, Movement Activities, and Song Books

Beall, P. C., & Nipp, S. (1996). *Wee sing for baby.* New York: G.P. Putnam Publishing.

Burton, M. (1989). *Tail, toes, eyes, ears, nose.* New York: Harper and Row.

Long, S. (2002). *Hush little baby.* San Francisco: Chronicle Books.

Manning, J. (1998). *My first songs.* New York: Harper-Collins.

Nursery songs. (1997). New York: McClanahan Book Co.

Raffi. (1996). *Singable songs for the very young: Great with a peanut butter sandwich.* Rounder.

Shore, R. (1998). *Bach and baby bedtime* [cassette or CD]. Huntington Beach, CA: Youngheart Music.

Helpful Websites

KidSource Online
http://www.kidsource.com
Readings and resources for educators and parents are available.

National Federation of Families for Children's Mental Health
http://www.ffcmh.org
Contains information on government policy and research. Spanish publications available.

National Parent Information Network
http://npin.org
Contains readings and parenting resources.

Parents (American Parents, Parents, and Family Circle Magazine)
http://www.parents.com
Tracks infant and toddler development by week or month. Select Babies or Toddlers link.

Sensory Awareness Foundation
http://www.sensoryawareness.org
Lists available infant experiences.

U.S. Department of Education
http://www.ed.gov
Presents reading research concerning children from birth through age 6. Select Publications link.

Zero to Three
http://www.zerotothree.org
Contains information on family-child bonding.

Book Companion Website

Read about "Educator Actions That Matter during Infancy." Additional infant-adult interaction games, readings, web activities, exercises, and web links are included, along with an annotated infant book list. Use an outline that will help you train future staff members who have no knowledge of signing. A review on early recognition of autistic behaviors is presented for those who are interested.

STUDENT ACTIVITIES

1. What parental expectations of infants might interfere with the infant's ability to develop the idea he is an effective communicator? List three or four. Give examples from your own experience if possible. Compare your list with that of a classmate.

2. Observe two infants (birth to 12 months). Note situations in which the infants make sounds and how adults (parents or teachers) react to the sound making.

3. Sit with a young infant facing you. Have a notepad handy. Remain speechless and motionless. Try to determine what moment-to-moment needs the child has, and try to fulfill each need you recognize. Try not to add anything new; just respond to what you think the child needs. Write a description of the needs observed and your feelings.

4. Try sharing a colorful, simple book with an 8- to 12-month-old. What behaviors did you observe?

5. Create a new game, rhyme, or movement word play, and test it on an infant 6 to 12 months of age.

6. Locate three books you think would be appropriate for older infants, and share them with the class.

7. Observe three children younger than 1 year of age each interacting with an adult for one 10- to 30-minute period. Try parks, family homes, or doctors' waiting rooms. Take notes concerning their verbal ability and conversational interactions. What language-developing techniques were present? Which child would you choose to be if you could change places with one of the observed children? List your reasons why.

8. Read and then pair up with a classmate to discuss and react to the following. Keep notes.

   What research actually shows is that infant-directed speech which is high-pitched, sing-song, repetitive and drawn out is the type of speech that infants in their first year of life not only hear better but also the language to which they are most responsive. In the first year speaking to infants in a way that gets a response is far more important than using "proper" adult grammar and words. It's not so much what parents say as that they say anything at all. Using "baby talk" beyond one year is probably not the best idea. (Ciccarelli, 2006, p. 3E)

CHAPTER REVIEW

A. Write your own theory of language acquisition. (A child learns language . . .) Compare and contrast your theory with those in this chapter.

42

B. Finish the following: Early childhood educators working in group infant care programs who wish to give infants opportunities to acquire language should carefully monitor their ability to . . . (list specific techniques).

C. Write definitions for the following: articulation, bonding, echolalia, moderation level, infant signing phonation, critical brain growth periods, larynx, and joint attention milestone.

D. Explain the difference between cooing and babbling.

E. Finish the following passage: Language is a kind of game infants learn—a game played with precise recognizable rules. To learn the game, it is best to have adults in your life who . . .

F. Select the best answer.
1. Environmental factors that can affect future language development start
   a. at birth.
   b. before birth.
   c. during infancy.
   d. during toddlerhood.
2. The tone of a parent's voice is
   a. understood when a child learns to speak in sentences.
   b. less important than the parent's words.
   c. understood before actual words are understood.
   d. less important than the parent's actions.
3. In acquiring language, the child
   a. learns only through imitation.
   b. is one participant in a two-part process.
   c. learns best when parents ignore the child's unclear sounds.
   d. does not learn by imitating.
4. Select the true statement about babbling.
   a. Why babbling occurs is not clearly understood.
   b. Babbling is unimportant.
   c. Babbling predicts how early a child will start talking.
   d. Babbling rarely lasts beyond 1 year of age.
5. How a child acquires language is
   a. clearly understood.
   b. not important.
   c. only partly understood.
   d. rarely a subject for study.

G. With a partner, create a parent billboard drawing or other pictorial artwork and relate it to infant language development. Write a clever caption (slogan). Share with the group. (Example: Picture of an infant and father. Caption: "Hey big daddy, that sweet talk and hug are just what I needed." [Not very clever? You can do better.])

H. What is the significance for early childhood educators of current discoveries concerning young children's brain growth?

INFANT-ADULT PLAY GAMES

What are presented here are classics that have pleased a good number of infants for a good number of years. You are urged to try your hand at creating others. Pleasurable features to add to your creations are sound variety, rhymes, noises, emphasized words, and touching and encouraging infant movements.

WHAT HAVE WE HERE?

Here's two little eyes big and round
And two little ears to hear all sounds,
One little nose smells a flower sweet,
One little mouth likes food to eat.
Here are ten little fingers to grasp and
*   wiggle,*
Tickle ten toes and there's a giggle.
Here's a button on a tiny tummy
Around and around—that feels funny!

ROUND AND ROUND

(This is a frequently used tickling verse of English mothers.)

Round and round the garden (Said
*   slowly while circling the baby's palm)*
One step, two steps (Walking fingers
*   toward a tickling spot at neck,*
*   stomach, or underarms, and said a*
*   little faster)*
Tickle you there! (Said very fast)

TWO LITTLE EYES

Two little eyes that open and close.
Two little ears and one little nose.
Two little cheeks and one little chin.
Two little lips that open and grin.

BABY RIDES

This is the way baby rides, (Bounce in-
*   fant on knees; with each new verse,*
*   bounce a little faster)*
The baby rides, the baby rides.
This is the way baby rides, so early in
*   the morning.*

This is the way the farmer rides . . .
This is the way the jockey rides . . .

LITTLE MOUSE

Hurry, scurry little mouse
There he is down at your toes. (Touch
*   child's toes)*
Hurry, scurry little mouse
Past your knees up he goes. (Touch
*   child's knees)*
Hurry, scurry little mouse
Up to where your tummy is. (Touch
*   child's tummy)*
Hurry, scurry little mouse
He wants to give you a mousy kiss.
*   (Give child a loud kiss)*

HERE WE GO

Here we go up, up, up (Lift child's legs
*   up)*
Here we go down, down, down (Lower
*   child's legs down)*
Here we go backward and forward
*   (Sway child backward and forward)*
And here we go round and round
*   (Move child's legs in air)*

WHAT HAVE WE HERE?

These are baby's fingers, (Touch child's
*   fingers)*
These are baby's toes, (Touch child's
*   toes)*
This is baby's belly button, (Touch
*   child's tummy)*
Round and round it goes! (Tickle
*   child's tummy button)*

WHOA HORSE

Giddy-up, giddy-up, giddy-up horsey
*   (Bounce child on knees—last line,*
*   let child slip over knees while slid-*
*   ing lower on adult's extended legs)*
Giddy-up, giddy-up, go, go, go. Giddy-
*   up, giddy-up, Whoa!*

CHAPTER 2

The Tasks of the Toddler

OBJECTIVES

After reading this chapter, you should be able to:

◆ Discuss phonology, grammar, and semantics.

◆ List three characteristics of toddler language.

◆ Identify adult attitudes and behaviors that aid toddlers' speech development.

KEY TERMS

concept	morpheme	pragmatics
grammar	morphology	prosodic speech
inflections	over-regularization	semantics
inner speech	phoneme	symbols
joint attention	phonetics	syntax
modifiers	phonology	telegraphic speech

THE TODDLER TEACHER

Kelsa (26 months) and her grandfather entered the classroom. He drew me aside after his granddaughter had run off to the housekeeping area. With a smile he shared what Kelsa had done and said to him. "We were watching TV, and I commented on something," he said. "She got up and stood right in front of me. Next, she cupped my cheeks with her hands and said, 'Look at me when you say words.'" He laughed. I explained, "Sometimes with toddlers we can understand their words only if they speak right into our face."

QUESTIONS TO PONDER

1. Is this a teacher strategy that helps toddlers?

2. Was the teacher's explanation to Kelsa's grandfather sufficient, or would a longer explanation have been better?

3. Is Kelsa's language acquisition advanced or about average for her age?

If you were amazed at the infant's and the 1-year-old's ability, wait until you meet the toddler! Toddlerhood marks the beginning of a critical language-growth period. Never again will words enter the vocabulary at the same rate; abilities emerge in giant spurts almost daily. When children stop and focus on things, from specks on the floor to something very large, concentration is total—every sense organ seems to probe for data.

Toddlerhood begins with the onset of toddling (walking), a little before or after the child's first birthday. The toddler is perched at the gateway of a great adventure, eager to proceed, investigating as she goes, and attempting to communicate what she discovers and experiences (Figure 2–1). "The bags are packed" with what has been learned in infancy. The

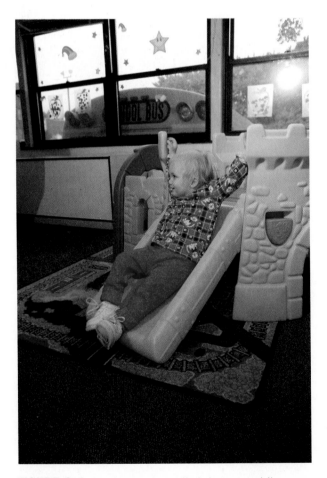

FIGURE 2–1 Exploring a small slide is a toddler adventure.

child will both monologue and dialogue as she ages, always knowing much more than can be verbally expressed. During toddlerhood she uses words whose meanings have been rooted in social acts and may have significance.

Toddlers are action-oriented. McMullen (1998) points out that they simultaneously act on and perceive the world around them. She believes one can see toddlers' thoughts because their thinking is a sensorimotor activity; only at a later age does higher-level thinking happen, allowing toddlers to think first and then act.

By the age of 2, toddlers' brains are as active as those of adults. The metabolic rate keeps rising, and by the age of 3, toddlers' brains are two and a half times more active than the brains of adults—and they stay that way throughout the first decade of life (Shore, 1997). Quindlen (2001) compares the working rate of a toddler's mind to an adult's mind as that of a race car to a lawn tractor.

An important milestone during the toddler period occurs when the toddler uses symbolic (speech) communication rather than communicating primarily through body actions and gestures. This is made possible by the child's growing mental capability and the richness of the child's affective and life experiences. Many experts believe that a warm, close relationship with a caregiver promotes the child's communication ability and provides satisfaction in itself. Experts agree that the primary need of toddlers (and infants) is emotional connection.

From a few spoken words, the toddler will move to purposeful speech that gains what is desired, controls others, allows personal comments, and accompanies play. It becomes evident that the toddler recognizes the give and take of true conversation. She also realizes the difference between being the speaker and being the one who listens and reacts—the one who persuades or is persuaded, the one who questions or is questioned. Toddlers become aware that everything has a name and that playfully trying out new sounds is an enjoyable pursuit. The child's meanings for the few words she uses at the start of the toddler period may or may not be the same as common usage. As children age, they will continually and gradually modify their private meanings of the words in their speaking vocabulary to conform to public meanings.

Cambourne (1988) describes the enormous complexity of learning to talk:

> When one has learned to control the oral version of one's language, one has learned literally countless thousands of conventions. Each language spoken on the Earth today (some three or four thousand) comprises a unique, arbitrary set of signs, and rules for combining those signs to create meaning. These conventions have no inherent "rightness" or "logic" to them, just as driving on the right or left side of the road has no intrinsic rightness or logic to it. Yet each language is an amazingly complex, cultural artifact, comprising incredibly complex sets of sounds, words, and rules for combining them, with equally numerous and complex systems for using them for different social, personal, and cognitive purposes. (p. 252)*

Even though toddlers have an innate predisposition for learning to communicate, they face four major tasks in learning the rule systems of language: (1) understanding phonology (the sound system of a language); (2) learning syntax (a system of rules governing word order and combinations that give sense to short utterances and sentences, often referred to as *grammar*); (3) learning semantics (word meanings); and (4) learning pragmatics (varying speech patterns depending on social circumstances and the context of situations). The understanding of these rule systems takes place concurrently— one area complementing and promoting the other. Rule systems form without direct instruction as toddlers grope to understand the speech of others, to express themselves, and to influence others both verbally and nonverbally. We can think of the toddler as one who tests many hypotheses—the kind of thinker who over time can unconsciously discover and formulate the rules of language.

Language emergence is but one of the toddler's achievements. Intellectually, toddlers' process, test, and remember language input. They develop their own rules, which change as they recognize what are and are not permissible structures in their native language. Other important developmental achievements intersect during late toddlerhood as children increasingly shift to symbolic thinking and language use. Gains in social, emotional, and physical development are apparent, as are issues of power and autonomy.

PHONOLOGY

Toddlers learn the **phonology** of their native language—its phonetic units and its particular and sometimes peculiar sounds. This is no easy job! The young language learner must sort sounds into identifiable groups and categories while she is possibly experiencing the speech of a variety of people in various settings. Because spoken language is characterized by a continuous flow of word sounds, this makes the task even more difficult.

After the child learns sounds, she learns sound combinations. A **phoneme** is the smallest unit of sound that distinguishes one utterance from another—implying a difference in meaning. English has 46 to 50 phonemes, depending on which expert is consulted. Language from a phonetic perspective might be conceived as a continuous sequence of sounds produced when air is pushed through the throat and mouth, and then received and recognized by sensitive ear structures.

Languages are divided into vowels and consonants. When pronouncing vowels, the breath stream flows freely from the vocal cords; when pronouncing consonants, the breath stream is blocked and molded in the mouth and throat area by soft tissue, muscle tissue, and bone, with

*From Brian Cambourne, *The Whole Story*. Copyright ©1988.

---

phonology — the sound system of a language and how it is represented with an alphabetic code.
phoneme — the smallest unit of speech that distinguishes one utterance from another.

the tongue and jaw often working together. The child focuses on those sounds heard most often. The toddler's speech is full of repetitions and rhythmic speech play. Toddler babbling of this type continues and remains pleasurable during early toddlerhood. Sounds that are combinations of vowels and consonants increase. Vowels are acquired early, and most studies suggest that vowel production is reasonably accurate by age 3 (Donegan, 2002). Low, nonrounded vowels (that is, *i, o, u*) are favored during infancy. Consonant sounds that are difficult to form will continue to be spoken without being close approximations of adult sounds until the child reaches 5 or 6 years of age or is even slightly older (Figure 2–2). Early childhood teachers realize that, in many instances, they will have to listen closely and watch for non-verbal clues to understand child speech.

It is a difficult task for the child to make recognizable sounds with mouth, throat, and breath control working in unison. Perfecting the motor control of speech-producing muscles is a sophisticated skill that comes ahead of many other physical skills. It requires precise and swift movements of the tongue and lips. This is all but fully developed when most other mechanical skills are far below levels of their future accomplishment.

Much of early speech has been described as unintelligible or gibberish. The toddler seems to realize that conversations come in long strings of sound. Rising to the occasion, the child imitates the rhythm of the sound but utters only a few understandable words.

Toddlers hear a word as an adult hears it. Sometimes, they know the proper pronunciation but are unable to reproduce it. The child may say "pway" for *play*. If the parent says "pway," the child objects, showing confusion and perhaps frustration. Toddler talk represents the child's best imitation, given present ability. Parents and teachers are urged to look at toddlers' speech mistakes as evidence that children are learning in an intelligent way.

Adult-to-child talk can be defined as "child-directed speech," that is, a set of speech modifications commonly found in the language adults use to address young children. Most speech researchers divide adult-child language into five main categories: pedagogy, control, affection, social exchange, and information.

The pedagogy mode is characterized by slow adult speech that is overenunciated or overemphasizes one or two words. This type of adult speech is "tailor-made" for 1- or 2- year-olds trying to segment the speech stream into comprehensible units.

Many adults tend to label happenings and objects with easy-to-learn, catchy variations, such as *choo-choo*, *bow-wow*, and so forth. Additional parental language techniques include the following:

1. Labeling themselves as "Mommy" or "Daddy," instead of "I" or "me" in speech.
2. Limiting topics in sentences.
3. Using short and simple sentences.
4. Using repetition.

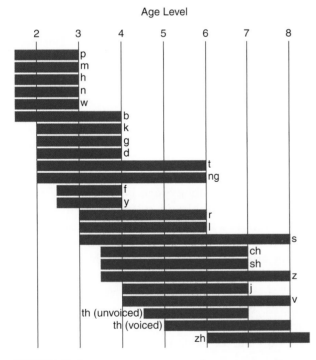

Age Level

FIGURE 2–2 Consonants—age of acquisition. (Reprinted with permission from Sander, E. K. [1972]. When are speech sounds learned? *Journal of Speech and Hearing, 37,* 55–63. Copyright American Speech-Language-Hearing Association. All rights reserved.)

5. Expanding or recasting children's one-word or unfinished utterances. If the toddler says "kitty," the parent offers "Kitty's name is Fluff."

6. Using a wide range of voice frequencies to gain the child's attention and initiate a communication exchange.

7. Carrying both sides of an adult-child conversation. The adult asks questions, and then answers them too. This technique is most often used with infants but is also common during the toddler period. The adult is modeling a social exchange.

8. Echoing a child's invented word. Many toddlers adopt a special word for a certain object. The whole family may use the child's word in conversational exchanges also.

When adults feel infants and toddlers are able communicators, it is reflected in their actions and speech. This can, and usually does, increase children's communicative abilities and opportunities.

Early childhood educators believe caregivers should treat toddlers as communicating children, and avoid childlike or cutesy expressions. They offer simple forms of speech and easy-to-pronounce words whenever possible, especially when they introduce new words.

Views on adult use of baby talk after the infancy period stress the idea that the practice may limit more mature word forms and emphasize dependency. On the other hand, adults may offer simplified, easily pronounced forms, such as *bow-wow* for a barking poodle. They later quickly switch to harder-to-pronounce forms when the child seems ready. In the beginning, though, most adults automatically modify their speech when speaking with toddlers by using short sentences and stressing key words.

Children progress with language at their individual rates and with varying degrees of clarity. Some children speak relatively clearly from their first tries. Other children, who are also progressing normally, take a longer time before their speech is easily understood. All basic sounds (50 including diphthongs) are perfected by most children by age 7 or 8.

Morphology

A **morpheme** is the smallest unit of language standing by itself with recognized meaning. It can be a word or part of a word. Many prefixes (*un-*, *ill-*) and suffixes (*-s*, *-ness*, *-ed*, *-ing*) are morphemes with their own distinct meanings. The study of morphemes is called **morphology**. There are wide individual differences in the rates toddlers utter morphemes (Figure 2–3). It is unfortunate if early childhood teachers or families

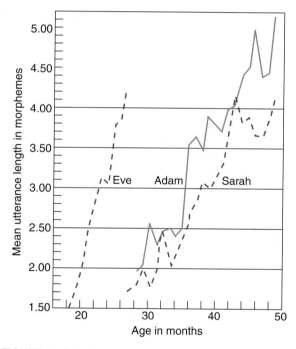

FIGURE 2–3 Individual rates in morpheme usage. (From Brown, R., Cazden, C., & Bellugi-Kilma, U. [1969]. The child's grammar from I to III. In J. P. Hill [Ed.], *Minnesota Symposium on Child Psychology* [vol. 2]. Minneapolis: University of Minnesota Press, p. 29. Copyright © 1969 The University of Minnesota Press. Used with permission.

morpheme — the smallest unit in a language that by itself has a recognizable meaning.
morphology — the study of the units of meaning in a language.

attempt to compare the emerging speech of toddlers or equate greater speech usage with higher ability, thus giving the quiet toddler(s) perhaps less of their time.

Between the ages of 2 and 4 years, children gradually include a variety of different morphemes in their spontaneous utterances. There seems to be a common sequence in their appearance.

SYNTAX

Languages have word orders and rules, and young children speak in word order and follow the rules of their native tongue. Children typically acquire the rules of grammar in their native language, with little difficulty, from normal communicative interactions with adults.

The rules for ordering words in sentences do not operate on specific words, but on classes of words such as nouns, verbs, and adjectives, and a relatively small number of syntactical rules can account for the production of a very large number of sentences. In some languages, the subject of a sentence follows the verb; in other languages, it precedes the verb.

Modifiers (descriptive words) in some languages have gender (male and female forms), but in others they do not. Plurals and possessive forms are unique to each language. Young speakers will make mistakes, but adults marvel at the grammar the child does use correctly, having learned the rules without direct instruction. One can compare children's mastery of **phonetics** to their mastery of **syntax**. The child's mastery of phonology is gradual, but the child's use of correct syntax is almost completely mastered from early beginning attempts.

By age 2, and sometimes as early as 18 months, children begin to string together two or more holophrases and have thereby arrived at the telegraphic stage. All telegraphic speech consists of acceptable grammatical sequences that are the precursors of the sentence.

From all the perceptions she has received and the words spoken to and about her, the child has noted regularities and has unconsciously formed rules, which are continually revised. Chukovsky (1963) describes this task:

> It is frightening to think what an enormous number of grammatical forms are poured over the poor head of the young child. And he, as if it were nothing at all, adjusts to all the chaos, constantly sorting out in rubrics the disorderly elements of words he hears, without noticing as he does this, his gigantic effort. If an adult had to master so many grammatical rules within so short a time, his head would surely burst. (p. 31)

Grammar involves the way sounds are organized to communicate meaning. With grammatical knowledge the young child can produce and understand a wide range of new, novel, grammatically correct, and meaningful sentences. As the child learns to talk during preschool years, she may construct many ungrammatical sentences and use words in unusual ways. The errors of the 2-year-old disappear as the child gains more control over language, but new kinds of errors appear in 3-year-olds, who are trying new forms of expression. An understanding of the general rules of grammar develops before an understanding of the exceptions to the rules. Correct grammar forms may change to incorrect forms as the child learns new rules. Slobin (1971) gives an interesting example of this phenomenon:

> In all of the cases which have been studied . . . the first past tenses used are the correct forms of irregular verbs—came, broke, went, and so on. Apparently

---

modifiers — words that give a special characteristic to a noun (for example, a large ball).
phonetics — pertaining to representing the sounds of speech with a set of distinct symbols, each denoting a single sound.
syntax — the arrangement of words as elements in a sentence to show their relationship.
grammar — the rules of a specific language that include both written and spoken utterances and describe how that specific language works and the forms of speech that conform to the rules that well-schooled speakers and writers observe in any given language.

these irregular verbs in the past tense—which are the most frequent past tense forms in adult speech—are learned as separate vocabulary items at a very early age.

Then, as soon as the child learns only one or two regular past tense forms—like helped and walked—he immediately replaces the correct irregular past tense forms with their incorrect over-generalizations from the regular forms. Thus children say "it came off," "it broke," and "he did it" before they say "it comed off," "it breaked," and "he doed it." Even though the correct forms may have been practiced for several months, they are driven out of the child's speech by the **over-regularization**, and may not return for years. (p. 103)

In later years, during elementary school, the child will formally learn the grammar rules of the English language. What the child has accomplished before that time, however, is monumental. The amount of speech that already conforms to the particular syntactical and grammatical rules of language is amazing. The child has done this through careful listening and by mentally reorganizing the common elements in language that have been perceived.

The toddler's growing use of intonation and **inflections** (changes in loudness of voice) adds clarity, as do nonverbal gestures. The child is often insistent that adults listen.

The toddler's system of nonverbal signals, body postures, and motions that were used in late infancy continues and expands, becoming part of the toddler's communication style (Figure 2–4). Many signals translated by mothers or care providers to strangers leave strangers bewildered as to how the mother or another adult could possibly know what the child wants. It may seem impossible based on what the stranger observed and heard.

English sentences follow a subject-verb-object sequence. The three fundamental

FIGURE 2–4 Teachers try to identify each child's individual communication style.

properties of sentences are verb-object, subject-predicate, and modification, and most all human languages have rules for these basic sentential structures.

Learning grammar rules helps the toddler express ideas, and her understanding of syntax helps the child to be understood.

Our knowledge of the rules of combination determines how we construct and understand an infinite number of sentences from a finite vocabulary. Syntax gives language its power.

A person who listens closely to the older toddler will sometimes hear the child self-correct speech errors. Toddlers talk to themselves and to their toys often. It seems to aid the storage of words and memory. The toddler understands adult sentences because the child has internalized a set of finite rules or combinations of words.

---

over-regularization — the tendency on the part of children to make the language regular, such as using past tenses like -*ed* on verb endings.

inflections — the grammatical "markers" such as plurals. Also, a change in pitch or loudness of the voice.

SEMANTICS

Semantics is the study of meanings and acquisition of vocabulary. It probes how the sounds of language are related to the real world and life experiences. The toddler absorbs meanings from both verbal and nonverbal communication sent and received. The nonverbal refers to expressive associations of words, such as rhythm, stress, pitch, gesture, body position, facial change, and so on. Adults perform important functions in the child's labeling and concept formation by giving words meaning in conversations.

The toddler who comes from a home that places little emphasis on expressing ideas in language may be exposed to a relatively restricted range of words for expressing conceptual distinctions. Every early childhood center should offer opportunities for children to learn a rich and varied vocabulary to refer to various experiences and to express ideas (Figure 2–5).

In toddler classrooms, teachers have many opportunities to name objects and happenings as the day unfolds. Using teacher gesturing along with words (or pointing to illustrations and photographs in simple picture books or classroom signs) helps the toddler form a connection between what is seen and heard. Repeating words with voice stress can be done in a natural way while monitoring whether the child is still interested.

Word meanings are best learned in active, hands-on experiences rather than "repeat-after-me" situations. Meanings of words are acquired through their connotations, not their denotations, that is, in situations that consist of feelings and verbal and nonverbal messages with physical involvement. The word *cold,* for instance, means little until physically experienced. Toddlers assume that labels (words) refer to wholes instead of parts (the creature, not the tail) and to classes instead of items (all horses, not one horse) (Cowley, 2000).

When an older infant is first learning to talk, the same sound often serves for several words; for instance, *bah* can mean "bottle," "book," "bath," and "bye." And sometimes infants use one sound to name an object and also to express a more complicated thought; for example, a child may point to a ball and name it, but later may say the same word and mean, "I want to play with the ball. Roll it to me."

The child's **concept** building is an outgrowth and result of a natural human tendency to try to make sense of the surroundings. Attending to and pondering about the relationships, similarities, and differences in events and happenings, and mentally storing, remembering, and retrieving those ideas and impressions are important aspects of concept development. With young children's innate curiosity, drive, and desire to explore and experience, concepts are continually being formed, reformed, and modified.

Examples of toddler behavior demonstrate that conceptual conclusions happen daily in group and home care settings. When a child blows a whistle-shaped toy, licks and bites a plastic fruit, tightly clings to an adult when a

FIGURE 2–5 Play brings toddlers together in social situations.

---

semantics — the study of meanings associated with words and the acquisition of vocabulary.
concept — a commonly recognized element (or elements) that identifies groups or classes; usually has a given name.

dog barks, or says "hot" when pointing to a water faucet, one can see past experiences are basic to the child's concept development.

To understand how concept development is individual and based on life experiences, ask yourself what makes a cup a cup. How many distinguishing features can you list? Ask another adult to do the same. You will both probably list some of the following characteristics:

- has a handle
- holds liquids and substances
- is often round on top, tapering to a smaller round base or can be cylindrical
- is used as a standard measurement in cooking (8 ounces)
- is made from clay, plastic, glass, metal, or other solid substances
- can be used to drink liquids

Adults speaking about cups understand one another because they usually recognize the same distinguishing characteristic(s). If asked to get the cup on the shelf, they won't get a glass. A toddler using the word cup often means his personal drinking cup.

A toddler may overuse concepts in new situations. Perhaps a bandage on the tip of a brother's finger will be called a thimble. For a short time, all men are daddies, a cow may be called a big dog, and all people in white are feared. As mental maturity and life experiences increase, concepts change; small details and exceptions are noticed. Toddlers may use a word to refer to a smaller category than would adults. An example of this phenomenon is the toddler's use of the word *dog* only in reference to the child's pet rather than all dogs encountered.

Concepts, often paired mentally with words, aid categorizing. Concept words may have full, partial, or little depth of meaning. The toddler's level of thought is reflected in speech. When counting to three, the toddler may or may not know what "three" represents. Words are **symbols**.

Pan and Gleason (1997) explain how young children acquire word meaning and also the symbolic nature of words:

> First, it is important to note that the meaning of a word resides in speakers of a common language, not in the world of objects. The word is a sign that signifies a referent, but the referent is not the meaning of the word.
>
> Let us assume that a child learns that the word *kitty* refers to her cat; in this case, the actual cat is the referent of the word *kitty*.
>
> There is nothing intrinsic to cats that makes one or another name more appropriate or fitting—the relationship between the name and the thing is thus arbitrary, and it is by social convention in a particular language that speakers agree to call the animal by a particular word. This arbitrary relationship between the referent (the cat) and the sign for it (the word *cat*) is symbolic.

In a few words the relationship between a word and a referent is not arbitrary; an example of this is the word *hiss*. In this case the word resembles the sound; other words, such as *tick-tock*, *tinkle*, and *woof*, also fall in this category.

A toddler's firsthand sensory experiences are very important. Stored mental perceptions are attached to words. Words are only as rich as the experiences and depth of understanding behind them.

The activities and experiences found in subsequent chapters will help the early childhood teacher enrich the child's concepts by providing deeper meanings in a wide range of language arts. Every activity for young children—a total school program—gives them a language arts background full of opportunities to explore by handling, tasting, using their bodies, smelling, and touching, as well as by seeing and listening.

---

symbols — things that stand for or suggest (such as pictures, models, word symbols, and so forth).

PRAGMATICS

The subtleties of our language are multifaceted. **Pragmatics** is the study of how language is used effectively in a social context, or the practical aspect of oral communication. It is the study of who can say what, in what way, where and when, by what means, and to whom (Figure 2–6). Language is a tool in questioning, ordering, soothing, ridiculing, and engaging in other social actions. One can request quiet in the form of a question such as, "Can't anyone get a peaceful moment around here?" or talk longingly about the candy in a store for the purpose of obtaining it without making a direct request—as in, "Oh, they have my favorite kind of chocolate bar!".

The language that young children use to express desires, wishes, concerns, and interests becomes a reflection of their social selves. When a toddler communicates effectively, the toddler receives feedback from others. Many times, a sense of well-being elicited by positive events helps the child shape a feeling of competency

---

PRAGMATIC SKILLS

1. taking turns in a conversation with another

2. knowing you are supposed to answer when a question is asked

3. noticing nonverbal body cues, signals, gestures, and signs and then responding

4. introducing a topic in a conversation for the listener to understand

5. having the ability to stay on the subject of a conversation

6. maintaining the right amount of eye contact; not staring or turning away too frequently

7. using different communicative styles that suit different communicative partners

8. learning that in certain situations talking is inappropriate

FIGURE 2–6 Pragmatic skills.

---

and self-esteem. Not yet socially subtle in speech, the toddler has not learned the pragmatically useful or appropriate behaviors of older children. Toddlers seem to have just one goal: to get messages across by gaining adult attention regardless of who is present and in what situation. The world, from the toddler's perspective, revolves around the toddler and her need to communicate.

ATTACHMENT AND DEVELOPMENT OF LANGUAGE SKILLS

Attachment problems can slow communicative development. Observers describe infants and toddlers in less-than-adequate care situations as fearful, apathetic, disorganized, and distraught. If responsive social interaction and adult feedback exchanges are minimal, limited, frightening, or confusing, the infant or toddler may display a marked lack of interest in holding or obtaining adult attention. During toddlerhood these children can fall behind in speech development. Lally (1997) describes the importance of toddler social interaction:

> Infants and toddlers develop their sense of who they are from the adults who care for them. They learn from their caregivers what to fear, what behaviors are appropriate, and how their communications are received and acted upon. They learn how successful they are at getting their needs met by others, what emotions and intensity levels of emotions to safely display, and how interesting others find them. (p. 288)

FIRST WORDS

Any time between 10 and about 22 months is considered within the normal range for first words. A vocabulary growth spurt happens

---

pragmatics — the study of how language is used effectively in a social context; varying speech patterns depending on social circumstances and the context of situations.

around 18 to 22 months (Strickland & Schickedanz, 2004). First words are "building blocks" and "content words" (nouns, verbs) that carry a lot of meaning. They usually consist of names of important people or objects the toddler encounters daily and include functional words such as *up*, *out*, *night-night*, and *bye-bye* used in social contexts (Figure 2–7). Easy-to-pronounce words are more likely to be included in toddlers' early expressive vocabularies.

Single words can frequently go further than naming by representing a meaningful idea (a holophrase). The task of the adult includes both being responsive and guessing the child's complete thought. This may sound simple, but many times it is difficult and frustrating. Many factors influence the degree of adult responsiveness and talkativeness, particularly in child center settings—room arrangements, adult-child ratios, level of staff training, and other emotional and environmental factors. The greatest inhibitor of adults' speaking and responding to children seems to be adults' talking to one another instead of the children. Professionals save chatting for breaks and afterschool meetings. The nature of the work in a group care program can easily be described as emotion packed and demanding, in addition to rewarding and challenging. On the surface, the general public may not see or understand skilled verbal interactions taking place between toddlers and caregivers. What seems to be random, natural playfulness and verbal responsiveness can be really very skilled and professionally intentional behavior. The same, of course, is true regarding family behavior.

Adults sometimes question the practice of responding to toddlers' grunts and "uhs"; instead they respond only to toddlers' spoken words. Many toddlers seem to understand everything said to them and around them but get by and satisfy most of their needs with sounds and gestures. The points for adults to consider are that the child is performing and learning a difficult task and that speech will soon follow. The message that responsive adults relay to children when rewarding their early attempts with attention is that children can be successful communicators and that further attempts at speech will get results.

Sound effects
baa baa, meow, moo, ouch, uh-oh, woof, yum-yum

Food and drink
apple, banana, cookie, cheese, cracker, juice, milk, water

Animals
bear, bird, bunny, dog, cat, cow, duck, fish, kitty, horse, pig, puppy

Body parts and clothing
diaper, ear, eye, foot, hair, hand, hat, mouth, nose, toe, tooth, shoe

House and outdoors
blanket, chair, cup, door, flower, keys, outside, spoon, tree, TV

People
baby, daddy, gramma, grampa, mommy, [child's own name]

Toys and vehicles
ball, balloon, bike, boat, book, bubbles, plane, truck, toy

Actions
down, eat, go, sit, up

Games and routines
bath, bye, hi, night-night, no, peek-a-boo, please, shhh, thank you, yes

Adjectives and descriptives
allgone, cold, dirty, hot

FIGURE 2–7 Children's earliest words: examples from the vocabularies of children younger than 20 months. (From Berko Gleason, J. [1997]. *The development of language* [4th ed.]. Boston: Allyn and Bacon. Copyright © 1997 by Pearson Education. Reprinted by permission of the publisher.)

FROM EGOCENTRIC SPEECH TO INNER SPEECH

During the toddler period, observers notice that words or short phrases spoken by adults are remembered and spoken out loud. The toddler's "hot," "no," "kitty," or similar words accompany the child's actions or a simple viewing of objects at hand. Vygotsky (1986) has called this "egocentric" speech, which is ultimately and usefully tied to the toddler's thinking.

As the child matures, this type of speech slowly becomes **inner speech**, part of the child's thinking process. Egocentric speech is regulatory, that is, useful in helping the child regulate (manage) her own behavior. As adults, we see examples of this regulatory function when we talk ourselves through particular perplexing situations. For example, "First the key goes in the lock, then turn the handle, and the bar moves to the left."

SYMBOLIC GESTURING

It is old-fashioned to believe that real communication does not exist before a child's first words (Figure 2–8). Researchers have helped us understand that gestures and signs (signals) occur in tandem with early vocalizing. Young toddlers can possess a rich repertoire of signals, and female infants tend to rely on or produce them with slightly greater frequency than male infants. Signs have been defined as nonverbal gestures symbolically representing objects, events, desires, and conditions that are used by toddlers to communicate with those around them. They literally can double a young toddler's vocabulary.

Toddlers' interest in learning hand signals (signing) varies greatly. Conducting an infant-toddler program in which signing is a regular part of the curriculum has become popular. Some toddlers may use 20 or more signs for various objects, feelings, and needs; other toddlers mixed only a few gestures with their beginning words. Both would be displaying normal development.

The use of words and symbols to influence other people in predictable ways requires the child to represent mentally the relationship between the symbol (word or gesture), the meaning for which it stands, and the intended effect on the other person. A symbol—a word, a picture, a dance—exists because of human intention to infuse some tangible form—a sound, a mark, a movement—with meaning and thereby to comment on or take action in the social world.

Various researchers have studied a child whose parents felt that their child was capable of learning nonverbal as well as verbal labels. The parents informally concocted signs on the spot for new events without any reference to a formal sign language system. Figure 2–9, from a study by Acredolo and Goodwyn (1985), describes the signs and gives the age the signs appeared in the child's communicative behaviors and the age the child said the word represented by the sign. The list of signs includes the signs the child learned with and without direct parent teaching.

Gestures are integral companions of toddler verbalizations. Adults may have modeled the gestures in their adult-child interactions. A family's signals are "read" by toddlers, and a hand held palm up is usually read as "give it to me." Toddlers show their understanding by

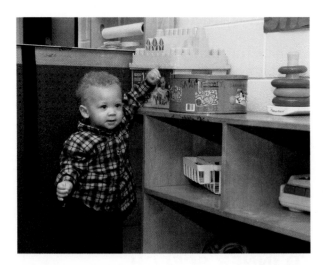

FIGURE 2–8 Gestures often indicate a child's desire or need.

SIGNS	DESCRIPTION	AGE OF SIGN ACQUISITION (MONTHS)	AGE OF WORD ACQUISITION (MONTHS)
flower	sniff, sniff	12.5	20.0
big	arms raised	13.0	17.25
elephant	finger to nose, lifted	13.5	19.75
anteater	tongue in and out	14.0	24.0
bunny	torso up and down	14.0	19.75
Cookie Monster	palm to mouth plus smack	14.0	20.75
monkey	hands in armpits, up-down	14.25	19.75
skunk	wrinkled nose plus sniff	14.5	24.00
fish	blow through mouth	14.5	20.0
slide	hand waved downward	14.5	17.5
swing	torso back and forth	14.5	18.25
ball	both hands waved	14.5	15.75
alligator	palms together, open-shut	14.75	24.0
bee	finger plus thumb waved	14.75	20.00
butterfly	hands crossed, fingers waved	14.75	24.0
I dunno	shrugs shoulders, hands up	15.0	17.25
hot	waves hand at midline	15.0	19.0
hippo	head back, mouth wide	15.0	24.0
spider	index fingers rubbed	15.0	20.0
bird	arms out, hands flapping	15.0	18.5
turtle	hand around wrist, fist in-out	15.0	20.0
fire	waving of hand	15.0	23.0
night-night	head down on shoulder	15.0	20.0
X-mas tree	fists open-closed	16.0	26.0
mistletoe	kisses	16.0	27.0
scissors	two fingers open-closed	16.0	20.0
berry	"raspberry" motion	16.5	20.0
kiss	kiss (at a distance)	16.5	21.0
caterpillar	index finger wiggled	17.5	23.0

FIGURE 2–9 Symbolic signs, in order of acquisition, produced by case study subject. (From Acredolo, L. P. & Goodwyn, S. W. [1985]. Symbolic gesturing in language development. *Human Development, 28,* 53–58. Reproduced with permission from S. Karger A. G.)

behaviors. Toddlers can and do invent new gestures; consequently, signing is not simple, imitative behavior. Pointing is probably the most commonly used gesture of toddlers. Eventually, words are preferred and gesturing remains as an accompaniment of speech. We have all slipped back into a gesturing mode as we search for words in conversation, and hand gestures are used automatically to convey the word(s) that we cannot quite express.

Early childhood educators employed by infant-toddler centers need to know their centers' position regarding expected language-developing behaviors. Most centers expect educators to pair words with adult hand signs, to encourage toddler use of signs, and to learn and respond to each child's individual sign language. To do this, teachers must be alert to children's cues, in particular noticing what in the environment attracts them so that words can be supplied and the children's intentions "read." Teachers' behaviors should reflect their awareness, intentional efforts, and attention to toddlers' efforts to communicate. Their continual goal is to establish a warm, emotionally fulfilling connection to each child in their care.

Toddlers are very interested in exploring. Teachers should "hang back" when toddlers interact with other toddlers and try not to interrupt play. Becoming social with peers is given priority and promoted.

Teachers of toddlers do a lot of "word modeling." They attempt to be both calm and fun companions. Most will tell you that after a full day with toddlers they look forward to conversing with adults.

TWO-WORD SENTENCES	MEANINGS
<u>Dat</u>* car	nomination
Daddy <u>dare</u>	location
<u>See</u> kitty	identification
<u>More</u> cookie	repetition, recurrence
Milk <u>allgone</u>	nonexistence
<u>Sit</u> chair	action—location
<u>No</u> car, <u>no</u> want dat	negation
<u>Todd</u> shoe, <u>mine</u> toy	possession, possessor
<u>Big</u> cup	attribute description
Jin <u>walk</u>, truck <u>go</u>	agent—action
<u>Kiss</u> you, <u>fix</u> car	action—direct object
<u>Where</u> ball?	question

*Underlined words are pivots.

FIGURE 2–10 Pivot words in toddlers' two-word sentences.

FIRST SENTENCES

The shift from one word to a two-word (or more) stage at approximately 18 months is a milestone. At that time, the toddler has a speaking vocabulary of about 50 words; by 36 months, upward of 1,000 words. It is crucial in talking about vocabulary to acknowledge that children not only acquire new words as they get older but also expand their understanding of old words.

If one looks closely at two-word utterances, two classes of words become apparent. The smallest group of words is made up of what are called "pivot words." Examples of toddlers' two-word sentences, with pivot words underlined, are shown in Figure 2–10. Pivot words are used more often than other words, and seem to enter the vocabulary more slowly, perhaps because they are stable and fixed in meaning. In analyzing two-word toddler comments, one finds they are both subject-predicate and topic-comment in nature. Frequently stressed syllables in words and word endings are what toddlers first master, filling in other syllables later. At times, toddlers

use *-um* or *-ah* as placeholders for syllables and words. They replace these with correct syllables and words as they age.

Understanding of grammar rules at this two-word stage is displayed even though many words are missing. Toddlers frequently use a simple form and, almost in the same breath, clarify by expansion (by adding another word). The invention of words by toddlers is common. One 18-month-old had her own private word for "sleep," consistently calling it "ooma." Families trying to understand their toddlers get good at filling in the blanks. They then can confirm the child's statement and can add meaning at a time when the child's interest is focused.

TODDLER-ADULT CONVERSATIONS

Toddlers control attending or turning away when interacting with others, as do infants. At about 1 year, they understand many words and begin to display turn-taking in conversation, with "you talk, I answer" behaviors. **Joint attention** starts around 10 months of age. At this time infants develop intentional communication and willingly share emotions, intentions, and interest in the outside world. To do this, the child has to be sure that both she (the speaker) and her intended receiver are focused on the same thing. She does this by capturing another's attention, establishing the topic of conversation, and maintaining attention on the topic by looking back and forth.

Her communication usually consists of one or more of the following: looking, pointing, gesturing, showing, giving, making sounds, and changing her facial expression.

Toddlers learn that speech deserves attention and that speech is great for getting adults to notice them. They seem to revel in the joint-endeavor aspect of conversations.

Toddlers are skillful communicators. They converse and correct adult interpretations, gaining pleasure and satisfaction from language exchanges. The following incident shows more than toddler persistence:

A first-time visitor to the home of a 20-month-old toddler is approached by the toddler. The visitor eventually rises out of his chair, accompanies the toddler to the kitchen, gets a glass of water, and hands it to the child. The toddler takes a tiny drink, and returns, satisfied, to the living room. Parents were not involved. Thirst, itself, was unimportant. The pleasure gained by the child seemed to motivate her actions.

For the child to accomplish her ends, the following actions occurred. The visitor:

1. focuses attention on child.
2. realizes a "talking" situation is occurring.
3. listens and maintains a receiver attitude.
4. corrects his own behavior, guesses at the child's meaning, and tries new actions.
5. realizes the conversation is over.

While the toddler:

1. stands in front of visitor; searches face to catch eye; makes loud vocalization, dropping volume when eye contact is made; observes visitor behavior.
2. repeats first sound (parents understand, visitor does not) and observes visitor reaction.
3. grabs visitor's hand, vocalizes loudly, and looks in visitor's eyes.
4. tugs at hand, uses insistent voice tone, and gestures toward the kitchen.
5. pulls visitor to sink and uses new word (visitor does not understand); corrects through gestures when visitor reaches for the cookie jar.
6. corrects visitor's guess (milk), gestures toward water, and holds out hand.
7. drinks a small sip and hands back the glass, smiles, and walks away.

This type of behavior has been called *instrumental expression* because vocalization and nonverbal behaviors were used to obtain a certain goal.

The toddler seeks out people willing to listen and learns from each encounter. Adults modify and adapt their speech based on the abilities they observe in the child. This is done intuitively by use of shorter and less complex comments, and it changes when adults notice increased capacity (Figure 2–11).

Many experienced caregivers describe a time when some toddlers in their care remain very close. During this time, the toddler's behavior is characterized by clinging to a primary caregiver, watching adult lips intently, showing decreased interest in toys or playing independently, frequently bringing objects to the caregiver, and attempting to say words. The duration and appearance of these behaviors is unique to each toddler, and some do not display them at all. Families can worry about spoiling the toddler, if these behaviors persist, and educators urge families to satisfy children's needs for increased

joint attention — child's awareness that he or she must gain and hold another's focus during communicational exchanges to get his or her message understood.

FIGURE 2–11 Children seek out people willing to show interest in what they are doing.

attention and language input. Usually the child will emerge with a longer attention span and branch out to explore a wider world.

CHARACTERISTICS OF TODDLER LANGUAGE

The speech of young children speaking in two-word, or longer, sentences is termed **telegraphic** and **prosodic**. It is telegraphic because many words are omitted because of the child's limited ability to express and remember large segments of information; the most important parts of the sentence are usually present. Prosodic refers to the child's use of voice modulation and word stress with a particular word or words to give special emphasis and meaning. Telegraphic speech can be defined as utterances that are devoid of function words and resemble messages sent by telegraph, for instance, "Jimmy truck" could represent "That truck belongs to Jimmy" or "Give me my truck." Meanings often depend upon context and intonation of the utterance.

For additional toddler language characteristics that may appear before the child's third birthday, see Figure 2–12.

Negatives

No discussion of older toddlers' language would be complete without mentioning the use of "no." There seems to be an exasperating time when children say "no" to everything—seemingly testing whether there is a choice. Young children first use "no" to indicate nonexistence. Later it is used to indicate rejection and denial. Even when the child can speak in sentences longer than three words, the "no" often remains the first in a sequence of words. A typical example is "No want go bed." Soon, children insert negatives properly between the subject and the verb into longer utterances, as sentence length increases. Of all speech characteristics adults remember, toddlers' use of negatives and their avid energetic demands to be "listened to" stick in the memories of their caregivers.

AIDS TO TODDLER SPEECH DEVELOPMENT

The swift rate of new words entering toddlers' vocabularies indicates that educators caring for them should begin to become increasingly specific with descriptive terms in their speech. If a truck is blue, a comment like "The blue truck rolled in the mud" is appropriate. If an object is on the bottom shelf, in the top drawer, or under the table, those words can be stressed. A color, number, or special quality, like fast or slow, big or little, or many other adjectives and adverbs, can be inserted in simple comments.

Playing detective to understand toddlers will always be part of adults' conversational style. Teachers may request that toddlers look directly at them when they communicate so that teachers can better hear each word and determine intent.

telegraphic speech — a characteristic of young children's sentences in which everything but the crucial word(s) is omitted, as if for a telegram.
prosodic speech — the child's use of voice modulation and word stress to give special emphasis and meaning.

TODDLER LANGUAGE CHARACTERISTICS

- Uses two- to five-word sentences.
  "Baby down."
  "Baby boom boom."
  "No like."
  "No like kitty."
  "Me dink all gone."
  "See me dink all gone."
- Uses verbs.
  "Dolly cry."
  "Me going."
  "Wanna cookie."
- Uses prepositions.
  "In car."
  "Up me go."
- Adds plurals.
  "Birdies sing."
  "Gotta big doggies."
  "Bears in dat."
- Uses pronouns.
  "Me big boy."
  "He bad."
- Uses articles.
  "The ball gone."
  "Gimme a candy."
- Uses conjunctions.
  "Me and gamma."
- Uses negatives.
  "Don't wanna."
  "He no go."
- Runs words together.
  "Allgone," "gotta," "gimme," "lookee."
- Asks questions.
  "Wa dat?"
  "Why she sleep?"
- Does not use letter sounds or mispronounces spoken words.
  "Iceam," "choo" (for shoe), "member" (for remember), "canny" (for candy).
- Sings songs.
- Tells simple stories.
- Repeats words and phrases.
- Enjoys word and movement activities.

FIGURE 2–12 Toddler language characteristics.

Many experts offer adults advice for providing an optimal toddler environment for language stimulation. The following are some specific tips.

- Expose the child to language with speech neither too simple nor too complex, but just slightly above the child's current level.
- Stay in tune with the child's actual abilities.
- Omit unreasonable speech demands, yet encourage attempts.
- Remember that positive reinforcement is a more effective tool than negative feedback.
- Accept the child's own formulation of a language concept.
- Provide a correct model.
- Make a point of being responsive.
- Follow the child's interest by naming and simple discussion.

Other suggested pointers follow.

- Explain what you are doing as you work.
- Describe what is happening.
- Display excitement for the child's accomplishments (Figure 2–13).
- Talk about what the child is doing, wanting, or needing.
- Pause and listen with ears and eyes after you have spoken.
- Encourage toddler imitation of gestures and sounds.
- Imitate the child's sounds playfully at times.

Language and self-help skills blossom when 2-year-olds have opportunities to participate in "real" activities such as cutting bananas (using a plastic knife), emptying baskets, sponging off the table, and helping sweep the floor.

The following adult behaviors are included in appropriate practices identified by the National Association for the Education of Young Children (NAEYC) (Bredekamp & Copple, 1997):

Adults engage in many one-to-one, faces-to-face conversations with toddlers. Adults let toddlers initiate language, and wait for a response, even from children whose language is limited. Adults label or name objects, describe events, and reflect feelings to help

FIGURE 2–13 Educators are alert to recognizing and commenting on a child's accomplishments.

children learn new words. Adults simplify their language for toddlers who are just beginning to talk (instead of "It's time to wash our hands and have a snack," the adult says, "Let's wash hands for snack time!"). Then, as children acquire their own words, adults expand on the toddler's language.

Toddler-adult activities can include:

◆ setting out two or three familiar objects and asking the child to get one.

◆ calling attention to interesting things you see, hear, smell, taste, or feel.

◆ showing and labeling your facial features and the child's in a mirror.

◆ labeling and pointing to objects around a room.

◆ verbally labeling items of clothing as the child is dressing and undressing.

◆ labeling the people in the toddler's world.

Toddler-adult language and movement play are recommended. One classic play activity follows. Others are located in the Activities section.

TAKE YOUR LITTLE HANDS

Take your little hands and go clap, clap, clap.

Take your little hands and go clap, clap, clap.

Take your little hands and go clap, clap, clap.

Clap, clap, and clap your hands.

Take your little foot and go tap, tap, tap.

Take your little foot and go tap, tap, tap.

Take your little foot and go tap, tap, tap.

Tap, tap, and tap your foot.

Take your little eyes and go blink, blink, blink.

Take your little eyes and go blink, blink, blink.

Take your little eyes and go blink, blink, blink.

Blink, blink, and blink your eyes.

Take your little mouth and go buzz, buzz, buzz.

Take your little mouth and go buzz, buzz, buzz.

Take your little mouth and go buzz, buzz, buzz.

Buzz like a bumblebee.

Take your little hand and wave bye, bye, bye.

Take your little hand and wave bye, bye, bye.

Take your little hand and wave bye, bye, bye.

Wave your hand bye-bye.

Language Through Music

Toddlers are music lovers. If a bouncy melody catches their ear, they move. They obtain plenty of joy in swaying, clapping, or singing along.

Many can sing short, repeated phrases in songs, and some toddlers will create their own repetitive melodies (Figure 2–14). Words in songs are learned when they are sung repeatedly. Adult correction is not necessary or appropriate. Playful singing and chanting by adults is a recommended language-development technique.

Educators can encourage young children's creativity with music. If teachers always focus on everyone singing the same words and/or doing the same actions, they may not be using music to promote creative expression. Fortunately, with the uninhibited and exuberant toddler this is not a problem; teachers are going to see some fantastic "moves" and hear some unique lyrics and takeoffs on songs and dances. The author enjoys remembering the time a 2-year-old composed his own song—"Zipper your do da."

The social component in musical games is also a language facilitator. Joining the fun with others gradually attracts even the youngest children (Figure 2–15). A toddler can be introduced to the joy of moving to a new song with others; mutual musical listening and participation in music experiences at small group times add new avenues for language growth.

One technique educators frequently engage in with music is to verbally describe how a particular child is moving to music. ("Johnny is lifting his knees high up to his tummy.") This encourages children's movement to music and should be used when appropriate. The adult can extend two index fingers for the shy or wobbly child to grip, thereby creating a dance partnership. This allows the child to release at any time. Gently swaying or guiding movements to the music may increase the child's enjoyment.

The following criteria for selecting sing-along songs, recorded music, and songbook selections is recommended.

1. a short selection for toddlers
2. repetitive phrases
3. reasonable range (C to G or A)
4. simple rhythms

Try to find pieces that represent the ethnic and cultural diversity of attending children and include folk music.

Suggested music resources are found in the Appendix.

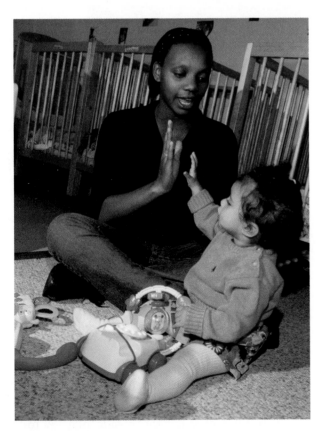

FIGURE 2–14 Toddler teachers sometimes sing nursery songs that include hand motions.

FIGURE 2–15 Making music is a popular preschool activity.

SYMBOLIC PLAY

At approximately 12 to 15 months, toddlers will begin to engage in symbolic (pretend) play. This important developmental leap allows the child to escape the immediate and firsthand happenings in her life and use symbols to represent past experiences and imagine future possibilities. The acts of toddler pretend play observed by adults are widely diverse and depend in part on the child's life experiences. Greenspan (1999) describes a parent observing a young toddler's symbolic play:

> . . . he tenderly puts his teddy bear to be inside an empty shoe box, and the parent recognizes the child is starting to grasp that one thing can stand for, or symbolize, another. Because he can picture what a bed looks and feels like in his mind, he is able to pretend that a hollow, rectangular box is really a symbol for a bed. When the parent comments that his teddy bear "is sleeping in his bed," he will eventually comprehend that the word "sleeping" stands for the bear's activity in the bed. As soon as he can articulate the sounds, the toddler will himself use the word symbol "sleeping" to describe an elaborate pattern of behaviors that he has observed. (p. 200)

One can always find toddlers who will talk into toy phones, spank dolls, grab the wheel of toy vehicles, and accompany motor movements with sounds, speech, and *vrooms*. Some reenact less common past experiences that are puzzling to their teachers. Gowen (1995) suggests the teacher techniques listed in Figure 2–16.

MAKING FRIENDS

Often, toddler play is side-by-side play. A toddler may watch what a neighboring peer is doing and may sometimes imitate the peer's actions.

Comment on what the child is doing.

Examples:

Child pushes truck, saying, "Brummm."
Say, "I hear your truck coming."

Child puts baby bottle to doll's mouth.
Say, "You're feeding your baby. You're such a good mommy!"

Imitate the child's action.

Examples:

Child pushes truck, saying, "Brummm."
Push another vehicle and make motor sound.

Child pretends to drink from toy cup.
Pick up another cup and pretend to drink from it.

Reinforce the child's symbolic play.

Examples:

Child pretends to feed doll.
Say, "You're such a good mommy!"

Child pushes toy across floor.
Say, "Boy, you can really make that car go!"

Child puts toy dishes on table.
Say, "You've got the table all ready!"

Make indirect suggestions.

Examples:

Child is playing with toy beings.
Say, "I think your baby [this horse, this man] is hungry [is sleepy, needs a bath]."

Child fed milk to doll from toy baby bottle.
Say, "Your baby's had her dinner. I bet she's sleepy now."

Child pushes car, then stops it.
Say, "Is your car out of gas?"

Child puts plates on table.
Say, "I'm hungry. May I have a hamburger?"

Make direct suggestions.

Examples:

Pick up round, red paper scrap.
Say, "This can be our pizza, OK?"

Put rectangular block (size of a stick of butter) on the table.
Say, "Let's pretend this is our butter."

Model symbolic-play behaviors.

Examples:

Put undressed doll in box, rub square block on a piece of fabric, and pretend to bathe the doll.

Hop toy person to toy car, put it in, and say in a low voice, "I'm going shopping. See you later."

FIGURE 2–16 Techniques for promoting symbolic play through caregiver-child interaction. (From Gowen, J. [1995]. The early development of symbolic play. *Young Children, 50*[3], 75–84. Reprinted by permission of the author.)

However, two toddlers playing in an organized, shared-goal play situation is infrequent. Toddlers are usually in-their-own-world-of-discovery people, but they do at times pick up play ideas from one another. Social graces may be absent, yet some beginning empathy for others may be apparent when one toddler communicates by patting or hugging a crying peer. Poole (1999) describes the difficulties toddlers face in building peer friendships;

It's hard work for toddlers to learn how to play with one another. At first, some may examine their playmates as if they were inanimate objects, such as a doll or a ball, pinching and poking without understanding that their actions can hurt.

Toddlers also don't always have control over their strong emotions.

It takes time to learn not to hug too hard or to say "Hello" rather than swipe at a friend's face. Even when toddlers begin to sense that such behavior is frowned upon, they may continue testing the limits. (p. 37)

By 15 to 18 months of age, many toddlers participate in joint physical activities and may more fully enjoy others' company. By age 2, they often pair off with a peer and have favorite companions. Young toddlers' emotions may erupt when sharing classroom playthings, causing friendships to change quickly. It is then, at age 2, that words can help children attract companions and repel others. Two-year-olds mimic increasingly and use words a friend uses.

LEARNING FROM MOTHERS— EARLY STUDIES

Burton White's projects have influenced many early childhood educators. His writings highlight the importance of the environment and the adult's nurturing behaviors. He believes toddlerhood is "a critical childhood growth stage" (1987). While observing mothers from all economic levels and watching their children's progress, he identified maternal skills that he suggested accounted for the competence in the observed children. He commended the nurturing ability, ingenuity, and energy of his observed group of mothers. White believed that mothering can be a vastly underrated occupation.

The following describes some of White's identified mother behaviors:

> Mothers talk a great deal to their children, and usually at a level the child can handle. They make them feel as though whatever they are doing is usually interesting. They provide access to many objects and diverse situations. They lead the child to believe that he can expect help and encouragement most, but not all of the time. They demonstrate and explain things to the child, but mostly on the child's instigation rather than their own. They are imaginative, so that they make interesting associations and suggestions to the child when opportunities present themselves. They very skillfully and naturally strengthen the child's intrinsic motivation to learn. (p. 121)

More and more evidence highlights the importance of family and caregiver attitudes and beliefs concerning toddlers' and young children's experiences with books and literacy activities. Families who believe reading is a source of enjoyment and entertainment have children with more positive views about books and the reading experience. Adults taking to heart this evidence will make "toddler book reading times" times of pleasure and enjoyment rather than times to pass on the information in the book. The more families talk with toddlers, croon to and sing with them, read picture books together, and point out and name objects, the more firmly synaptic connections in the brain are reinforced and the less likely they are to disappear.

RECOGNIZING DIFFERENCES IN LANGUAGE GROWTH

Early childhood teachers are better able to identify accelerated, normal (average), and delayed speakers at about 18 months of age. What causes diversity is too complex to mention here, but some factors can be inferred, and others have been previously mentioned. Families' and caregivers' responses to children's nonverbal and verbal attempts to communicate toward the end of the first year and into the second year can be a determining factor.

> Sooner or later families and caregivers become aware of [the] child's emerging capacity of language acquisition. Some choose to feed the growth of language by going out of their way to talk a great deal to their children. Some provide language input effectively by careful selection of suitable words and phrases and by exploiting the child's interest of the moment. Others provide a great deal of input but with considerably less skill and effectiveness. Others show minimal attention to the language interest of children or for other reasons provide negligible amounts of language input (White, 1987, p. 110).

INTRODUCING TODDLERS TO BOOKS

Toddlers show an interest in simple, colorful books and pictures and enjoy adult closeness and attention. Pointing and naming can become an enjoyable game. Sturdy pages that are easily turned help the toddler. A scrapbook of favorite objects mounted on cardboard individualizes the experience. Clear contact paper and lamination will add life and protection.

Board books (usually stiff, coated, heavy cardboard) for toddlers allow exploratory play and may offer colorful, close-up photographs or illustrations of familiar, everyday objects. These books promote the child's naming of pictures and active participation at book-reading times.

Toddler books are plentiful, and school collections include both fiction and nonfiction. Experts and librarians recommend volumes that are colorful, simple, inviting, realistic, and contain opportunities that encourage child involvement. With durable, glossy, wipe-clean page coating and smaller-than-average picture-book size, board books allow small and sometimes sticky hands to explore without tearing sturdy covers or pages.

Because a toddler may move on quickly to investigating other aspects of the environment, adults offering initial experiences with books need to remember that when interest has waned, it is time to respect the search for other adventures (Figure 2–17).

Other hints concerning the introduction of books, from Kupetz and Green (1997), are as follows:

◆ Do not expect to quiet a rambunctious toddler with a book.

◆ Pick a time when the child seems alert, curious, and interested.

◆ Establish a special reading time (although books can be read anytime).

◆ Use your voice as a tool to create interest.

◆ Be responsive.

◆ React positively to all of the child's attempts in naming objects, turning pages, or attempting any form of verbalization (Figure 2–18).

Toddlers with past experiences with picture books may have certain expectations for adult-child book sharing. They may want to cuddle with a blanket, sit in adult laps, turn pages for themselves, point to and question book features, name objects, watch the adult's mouth during reading, and so on. Exhibiting

FIGURE 2–17 The "right" book can hold a toddler's attention.

flexibility and following the child's lead reinforces the child's social enjoyment of the book.

Educators should be cautioned about the practice of requiring a group of toddlers to sit and listen to a story together. The key words are group and require. Toddler group times are of short duration and planned for active child participation. As toddlers age, they maintain focus for longer periods. Educators of toddlers might try sharing a picture book with a few children. When they do so, they endeavor to keep the experience warm, comfortable, and intimate.

What can toddlers begin to understand during the reading of picture books? Besides knowing that photographs and illustrations are

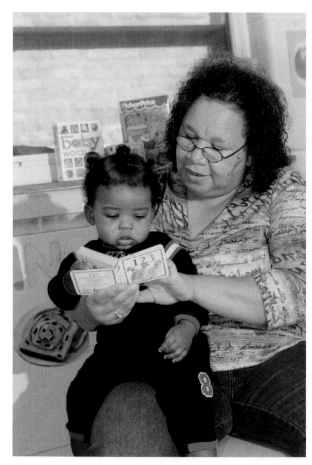

FIGURE 2–18 Toddlers often name what they see in book illustrations.

between the covers of books, the toddler gathers ideas about book pleasure. As the child touches pictured objects, the child may grasp the idea that the objects depicted are representations of familiar objects. The toddler can notice that books are not handled as toys.

Very young children's reading-like behaviors may surprise their teachers especially when they observe the independent activity of older infants and toddlers with their favorite books. Almost as soon as the older toddler becomes familiarized with particular books through repetitive readings, he begins to play with them in reading-like ways. Attracted by the familiar object with which she has such positive associations, the toddler picks up the book, opens it, and begins attempting to retrieve some of the

language and its intonations. Almost unintelligible at first, this reading-like play rapidly becomes picture-stimulated, page-matched, and story related.

Near 2 years of age, the toddler probably still names what is pictured but may understand stories. The toddler may grasp the idea that book characters and events are make-believe. If a particular book is reread to a child, the child can know that the particular stories in books do not change, and what is to be read is predictable. Sometimes the toddler finds that she can participate in the telling by singing, repeating character lines, and making physical motions to represent actions; for example, "knocking on the door" and saying "moo."

Selecting Toddler Books

Books for toddlers should be:

- repetitive and predictable.
- rhythmical.
- illustrated with simple, familiar, easy-to-identify colorful objects, animals, toys, and so on.
- filled with feel, touch, and smell opportunities.
- sturdy, with easy-to-turn pages.
- set with few words on each page.
- relatively short, with simple, concise story lines about common, everyday life and environmental experiences.
- formatted with illustrations matched to the text on each page.

Additional desirable features of toddler-appropriate books often include simple, uncomplicated storylines; colorful, well-spaced illustrations or photographs; opportunities for the toddler to point and name familiar objects; sensory features; predictive books (ones allowing the child to guess or predict successfully); and strong, short rhymes or repetitive rhythms. "Touch and feel" books are particularly enjoyed, as are sturdy, heavy board pages. Novelty books that make noise, pop-up books, and books with easy-to-use moving parts capture a toddler's attention. Now is the time to also share the strong rhyming rhythms of Mother Goose and introduce two classics: *Mary Had a Little Lamb* and *Pop Goes the Weasel*.

Adults sing with toddlers, do finger plays, act out simple stories like *The Three Bears* with older toddlers participating actively, or tell stories using a flannel board or magnetic board, and allow children to manipulate and place figures on the boards.

Electronic Books

Books with electronic features provide another way to engage toddlers with stories and print. Each book differs, but many have colorful illustrations that move, flash, "talk," or make musical sounds and noises. Pressing an area, button, icon, or symbol activates prerecorded features. But the research of Zimmerman and Christakis (2007) alerts early childhood educators to possible ill effects of early media exposure, particularly children's media viewing before the age of 3. Their study conclusions note that viewing of either violent or nonviolent entertainment television before age 3 was significantly associated with subsequent attentional problems 5 years later. The viewing of any content type at ages 4 to 5 was not associated with attentional problems. Another research study by the same researchers (Christakis and Zimmerman, 2007) examined violent television viewing during preschool years and its associated increased risk of children's antisocial behavior during school-age years. Other researchers (Dworak et al., 2007) have concluded that a link exists between television and computer game exposure and children's sleep patterns, diminished verbal cognitive performance, and their learning and memory abilities. Though Dworak and associates' research was conducted with a small group of school-age children and more extensive research is needed to further probe preschooler's noneducational game playing, early educators should note and consider its possible importance.

Most educators and parents agree that electronic books, noneducational games, and television do attract toddlers but that interest wanes quickly unless the media is shared with a responsive adult.

Scribbling

In most home environments, toddlers see others writing and want to try it themselves. Large, chunky crayons and nontoxic markers are easily manipulated by toddlers at about 18 months of age. They usually grasp them in their fist and use a scrubbing motion. They have some difficulty placing marks where they might wish, so it is best to use very large sheets of sturdy paper taped to a tabletop. Brown bags cut flat or untreated shelf paper work well. The act of scribbling can serve several useful purposes, including enhancing small muscle coordination, exercising cognitive abilities, promoting social interaction, and allowing emotional release. It can also be seen as a precursor to an interest in symbols and print. An important point in development is reached when the child moves from linear scribbles to enclosed shapes and at a later age begins realistic, representational drawing. Some Asian families may place a high emphasis on drawing activities for young children, and their children's work at school often reflects more comfort and experience with art materials and writing tools.

BEGINNING LITERACY

During toddlerhood, some children gain general knowledge of books and awareness of print. This is viewed as a natural process, which takes place in a literate home or early learning environment. Toddlers learn through imitation, by reacting and constructing their own ideas, and by internalizing social action as an apprentice to others (loved ones, early childhood educators, and so on). Immersing toddlers in language activities facilitates their literacy development. It is possible to establish a positive early bonding between children and book-sharing times—a first step toward literacy. Some toddlers who show no interest in books will, when exposed to books at a later time, find them as interesting as other children. Parents need to understand that a literary interest can be piqued throughout early childhood. The fact that a toddler may not be particularly enamored with books or book-sharing times at a particular stage is not a matter of concern. It may simply be a matter of the child's natural, individual activity level and her ability to sit and stay focused in an environment that holds an abundance of features to explore.

Musical Activities

Musical play with toddlers can help promote literacy skills. Activities can include:

◆ focused listening experiences.

◆ play that focuses on or highlights discrimination of loud and soft and fast and slow, rhythms, repeated patterns, tones, words, and so on.

◆ the use of repetitive beats, catchy melodies or words, clapping, tapping, rocking, galloping, marching, motions, and body actions.

◆ coordination of movement and music in some way.

◆ creative and imaginative opportunities.

◆ experiences with a variety of simple, safe musical instruments.

◆ the singing of age-appropriate songs.

Music activities often can be used to create an affectionate adult-child bond. Singhal (1999) describes toddlers participating in adult and child music activities:

> Toddlers are beings in motion, and music is the perfect vehicle for directing and freeing their movements. They feel and internalize the steady beat of adult motions. Contrary to popular belief, toddlers can also be excellent listeners. They are fascinated by sound, whether it's a bee buzzing or a clarinet melody. The different shapes, feel and sounds of simple rhythm instruments also mesmerize toddlers. Being able to make a steady sound on his own on an instrument such as the drum is very empowering to a young child who wants to "do it myself!"

Even though at this age children may not be willing to echo back chanted tonal and rhythm patterns, it is still important that they hear them. The patterns are being "recorded" in their minds for future reference.

Singing, listening, and music-making are a completely natural and enjoyable part of a young child's being. (p.22)

Toys

Certain types of toys have a strong connection to toddlers' emerging language development (Figure 2–19). Musical toys, dolls and stuffed animals that make noises or talk, and alphabet toys, including magnetic alphabet letters,

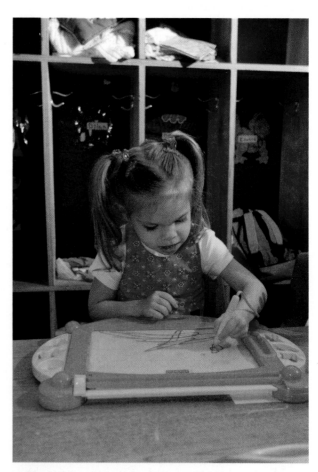

FIGURE 2–19 Certain toys promote early scribbling behavior.

can be described as language-promoting toys. Noisemaking toys or recordings, both audio and visual, capture the toddler's attention. Manipulative toys for toddlers are becoming increasingly available. Songs and music are also enjoyed by toddlers and offer another language-inputting opportunity; however, some educators are concerned about the quantity, quality, and subject matter of audiovisuals that possibly may be replacing adult-child language interaction.

FREEDOM TO EXPLORE

Greenspan (1999) emphasizes how toddler problem solving develops and describes its relationship to "freedom to explore" (within supervised limits).

> An ability to solve problems rests on the even more basic skill of seeing and deciphering patterns. It is the ability to understand patterns that lets a toddler know if she takes two steps here and two steps there that she'll be able to reach her favorite toy. She becomes a successful navigator not only because her muscles are coordinated, but also because her growing brain now enables her to understand patterns. Toddlers learn to recognize how one room leads to another, and where you are in relation to them. They can meaningfully explore the world long before they are able to express their wishes and thoughts in words.

The Comical Toddler—Exploring Humor

Adults may not realize that children begin honing their own comedic skills at impressively early ages. They point out that a child's reaction to physical stimuli, seen in activities such as tickling and bouncing, takes a new form sometime after the first birthday by becoming visual or oral rather than tactile. Toddler silliness or "joking" behavior can be seen as rudimentary attempts at humor and can be appreciated as child-initiated attempts to get

others' reactions to the ridiculous, the unexpected, or their play on words.

ADVICE TO PARENTS OF TODDLERS

Verbally responsive and playful people, and a "toddler-proof" home equipped with objects and toys the toddler can investigate, will help facilitate a toddler's emerging language skills. An adult sitting on the floor or on a low chair near a toddler at play can promote toddler communication and also help the adult see things from the child's vantage point.

Objects and toys need not be expensive and can be designed and created at home. Social contact outside the home is important also. Toddlers enjoy branching out from the home on excursions into nature and community with caring adults. Local libraries may offer toddler story hours, and play groups are increasingly popular and sponsored by a wide number of community groups. Exposing the toddler to supervised toddler play groups gives the child "peer teachers" and promotes social skills. Typically, toddlers play side-by-side rather than cooperatively, but beginning attempts at sharing and short give-and-take interactions take place.

Some toddlers may frequently ask for the names of things and can be insistent and impatient about demands. Words will be learned during real events with concrete (real) objects. Children continue to generate language when their early efforts are accepted and reinforced. Situations that involve positive emotions and those that involve multiple sensory experiences also evoke child language production.

Regularly involving toddlers in educative conversations with educational toys and simple books prompts language growth. Patience and interest—rather than heavy-handed attempts to teach—are best. Getting the most from everyday experiences is a real art that requires an instructive yet relaxed attitude and the ability to talk about what has captured the child's attention. A skilled adult who is with a toddler who is focused on the wrapping paper rather than the birthday present will add comments about the wrapping paper. Or at the zoo, in front of the bear's cage, if the child is staring at a nearby puddle, the adult will discuss the puddle. Providing words and ideas along the child's line of inquiry, and having fun while doing so, becomes second nature after a few attempts.

Skilled adults tend to modify their speech according to the child's ability. They speak clearly, slowly enunciate and slightly exaggerate intonation, and pause between utterances. They may end their sentences with the "focused-upon" new word and emphasize it in pitch and stress. They also add to sentence length and complexity, providing that which is just a little beyond the child's level. Parent talk that sensitively and effectively suggests and instructs primes the child's language growth. If the home language is not English, Gonzalez-Mena (2006) suggests supporting children's development of that language, for it serves as a foundation for the later learning of a second language (in this case, English). This is aided by a strong school-home partnership.

The following two books contain a number of adult-child interactive games. They are good resources for parents and teachers.

> Silberg, J. (2002). *Games to play with two-year-olds.* Bettsville, MD: Gryphon House.
>
> Silberg, J. (2002). *Games to play with toddlers.* Bettsville, MD: Gryphon House.

Parents may need to become aware of the consequences that can result from home or center environments where toddlers experience chaos, unpredictability, violence, and frightening experience as a daily reality. Honig (1999) describes these toddlers as quick to be startled, aroused, angry, defiant, fearful, or withdrawn. She describes the chemical activity in their brains as abnormal. Building intimate, warm, trusting relationships is the best way to teach a child's brain that it need not send the body messages to release high levels of stress hormones. Honig recommends that nurturing providers offer each child interpretable, orderly, soothing, and loving experiences daily to support optimal brain development.

SUMMARY

Language ability grows at its fastest rate of development during the toddler period. Young children accomplish difficult language tasks. They learn their native language sounds (phonetics) and successfully produce an increasing number of sounds. Grammar rules form and reform as the child gets closer to reproducing mature speech patterns. The child listens more carefully, noticing regularities and meanings (semantics) of words and gestures.

Concepts develop, serving as categories that help the child organize life's events. Many concepts are paired with words. Word symbols aid communication and language by allowing the child to speak and to be understood. Parents' conversations and the child's firsthand exploration through sense organs give depth to new words.

Toddlers are active in conversations, speaking and listening, sometimes correcting, trying to get the message across to whomever in the family will listen. Toddlers talk to themselves and their toys in one-word and then two-word (or more) sentences. These sentences are barely recognizable at first but gain more and more clarity as children age.

Differences between children's speech output may be noticed, and responsive, sensitive adults are language-promoting companions. Toddler books are enjoyed and plentiful, but researchers suggest non-educative electronic media viewing may produce undesirable effects for children under age 3.

ADDITIONAL RESOURCES

Readings

Acredolo, L. P., & Goodwin, S. W. (2000). *Baby mind: Brain-building games your baby will love to play.* New York: Bantam Books.

Fischer, B., & Medvic, E. (2003). *For reading out loud: Planning and practice.* Portsmouth, NH: Heinemann.

Nichols, J. (1998). *Storytimes for two-year-olds.* Chicago: American Library Association.

Owens, R. (2001). *Language development.* Boston: Allyn and Bacon.

Toddler Books

Albee, S. (2003). *Blue's checkup.* New York: Simon and Schuster. (A visit to the doctor.)

Barton, B. (1986). *Trucks.* New York: Crowell. (Vivid color and objects that move.)

Blonder, E. (1988). *My very first things.* New York: Gossett. (Board book.)

Cousins, L. (1991). *Farm animals.* New York: Tambourine.

Cowley, J. (1999) *Mrs. Wishy-Washy.* East Rutherford, NJ: Philomel Books. (Board book.)

Darling Kindersley (2003). *Are lemons blue?* New York: Author. (Playful.)

Davenport, Z. (1995). *Mealtime.* New York: Ticknor & Fields. (Colorful illustrations.)

Davenport, Z. (1995). *Toys.* New York: Ticknor & Fields. (Common toys and objects.)

Dyer, J. (1996). *Animal crackers.* New York: Little, Brown. (A delectable collection of pictures, poems, and lullabies for the very young.)

Elya, S. M. (2006). *Beebe goes shopping.* New York: Harcourt.

Fleming, D. (2006). *The cow who clucked.* New York: Henry Holt. (Sounds and silliness that delight.)

Hoban, T. (1985). *What is it?* New York: Greenwillow.

Kunhardt, D. (1942). *Pat the bunny.* New York: Golden Touch and Feel Books.

Lynn, S. (1987). *Farm animals.* New York: Macmillan.

McCue, L. (1987). *Ten little puppy dogs.* New York: Random. (Board book.)

Newcome, Z. (2002). *Head, shoulders, knees, and toes.* Cambridge, MA: Candlewick Press.

Oxenbury, H. (1988). *Tickle, tickle.* New York: Macmillan.

Prelutsky, J. (Ed.) (1988). *Read-aloud rhymes for the very young.* New York: Alfred Knopf Publishers.

Price, M., & Claverie, J. (1987). *Show and tell me.* New York: Tuffy Books Inc.

Tafuri, N. (1987). *Where we sleep.* New York: Greenwillow.

Weeks, S. (2006). *Overboard!* New York: Harcourt (Bright, cheerful and fun.)

Whitford, R. (2005). *Little yoga: A toddler's first book of yoga.* New York: Holt, Henry Books for Young Readers. (Expect to try yoga positions with toddlers.)

Helpful Websites

ECRP—Early Childhood Research & Practice
http://ecrp.uiuc.edu
Includes articles about research on toddler development.

IbcTech
http://www.thebestkidsbooksite.com
Identifies recommended books on many topics.

Kid Source Online
http://www.kidsource.com
Includes a speech development outline. Select NICHCY for information about speech and language disorders.

National Parent Information Network
http://npin.org
Provides related websites for parents and teachers. Select Parent-Teacher Communication and then Quality Infant-Toddler Care for reading that assesses quality.

Book Companion Website

Visit the book companion website to read about behaviors that teachers use to develop toddlers' language and to learn more about syntax. You will also find out how to tell if toddlers are forming unconscious mental rules concerning language. In addition, you will find exercises focusing on toddler computer use and exposure to interactive story books, including an informative question-and-answer section. Also available are the criteria used for selecting toddler books and a recommended toddler book list.

STUDENT ACTIVITIES

1. Make a book for toddlers from magazine illustrations or from photographs of common objects familiar to toddlers. Pages should be sturdy. Cut away any distracting backgrounds. If desired, outline objects with a wide-tip felt pen and protect pages with clear adhesive plastic or slip into page protectors. (An old binder works well to hold the pages.) Test your book on toddlers, and share your results.

2. Using only gesturing, get the person sitting next to you to give you a tissue or handkerchief or to tell you that one is not available.

3. Observe three toddlers (15 to 24 months old). Write down consonant sounds you hear. Record the number of minutes for each observation.

4. Using the following scale, rate each of the statements that follow. Talk about your ratings in a group discussion.

1	2	3	4	5
Strongly Agree	Agree	Can't Decide	Mildly Disagree	Strongly Disagree

   a. Toddlers can be best understood when adults analyze their words instead of their meanings.

   b. Some parents seem to have a knack for talking to young children and probably do not realize they possess this skill.

   c. The labeling stage is a time when children learn concepts rather than words.

   d. Learning language is really simple imitation.

   e. The study of semantics could take a lifetime.

   f. A toddler who does not like books is not progressing properly.

   g. After reading this chapter, I will not react to toddler grunts.

   h. Parents whose toddlers are speaking many words have purposely taught words to their children.

   i. It is a good idea to have a special place in the home where books are enjoyed with a toddler.

   j. It is best to give the toddler specific words for things, such as pickups instead of trucks, or bonnet instead of hat.

5. You notice your sister is ignoring her toddler's sign language attempts. What would you say or do? Be specific.

CHAPTER REVIEW

A. Match each word in Column I with the phrase it relates to in Column II.

COLUMN I	COLUMN II
1. phonology	a. "Allgone cookie." "Shoe allgone."
2. grammar	b. toddler goes through a naming or labeling stage
3. dis? dat?	c. toddler unconsciously recognizes word order
4. pivot	d. the sound system of language
5. alphabet	e. each world language has its own
6. symbol	f. as active as an adult
7. toddler brain	g. a word represents something

B. Write a brief description of experiences that could promote a toddler's learning the word *hat*. (Example: Parent points to a picture of a hat in a book and says, "Hat.")

C. List five identifying characteristics of the following concepts: van, rain, needle, and giraffe.

D. Return to question B. How many of your examples involved the child's sensory exploration of a hat? Why would this aid the child's learning?

E. Why is the toddler period called the prime or critical time for learning language?

F. Select the best answer.

1. Most children clearly articulate all English letter sounds by age

   a. 7 or 8.   c. 5.
   b. 6.   d. 24 months.

2. Most concept words used correctly by toddlers are
   a. labels and imitative echoing.
   b. fully understood.
   c. used because identifying characteristics have been noticed.
   d. rarely overused.

3. From beginning attempts, children
   a. reverse word order.
   b. use full simple sentences.
   c. use stress, intonation, and inflection in speaking.
   d. are always clearly understood.

4. One should _____ insist that the toddler pronounce "tree" correctly if he or she is saying "twee."

   a. always   c. usually
   b. never   d. tactfully

5. A toddler's one-word sentence, "Wawa," may mean
   a. "I want a drink of water."
   b. the child's dog, Waiter, is present.
   c. the child's father's name is Walter.
   d. any one or none of the above.

6. A child's first word is usually spoken between _____, and this is considered within the normal range.
   a. 10 and 22 months
   b. 9 and 20 months
   c. 11 and 25 months
   d. 8 and 18 months

TODDLER FAVORITES

TURTLE

There once was a turtle
that lived in a box.
He swam in the puddle
and climbed on the rock.

He snapped at a mosquito.
He snapped at a flea.
He snapped at a minnow
and he snapped at me.

He caught the mosquito.
He caught the flea.
He caught the minnow.
But he didn't catch me!

Author Unknown

TEDDY BEAR, TEDDY BEAR

Teddy Bear, Teddy Bear, turn all
   around,
Teddy Bear, Teddy Bear, touch the
   ground.

Teddy Bear, Teddy Bear, read the news,
Teddy Bear, Teddy Bear, shine your
   shoes.

Teddy Bear, Teddy Bear, go upstairs,
Teddy Bear, Teddy Bear, say your
   prayers.

Teddy Bear, Teddy Bear, turn out the
   lights,
Teddy Bear, Teddy Bear, say
   GOODNIGHT!

Author Unknown

THE LITTLE WHITE DUCK (SONG)

There's a little white duck sitting in
   the water,
A little white duck doing what he
   oughter;
He took a bite of a lily pad,
Flapped his wings and he said,
"I'm glad I'm a little white duck
   sitting in the water,"
quack, quack, quack.
There's a little green frog swimming in
   the water,
A little green frog doing what he
   oughter;
He jumped right off the lily pad,
that the little duck bit and he said
"I'm glad I'm a little green frog
   swimming in the water,"
glumph, glumph, glumph.
There's a little black bug floating on
   the water,
A little black bug doing what he oughter;
He tickled the frog on the lily pad
That the little duck bit and he said,
"I'm glad I'm a little black bug float-
   ing on the water,"
chirp, chirp, chirp.
There's a little red snake lying in the
   water,
A little red snake doing what he oughter;
He frightened the duck and the frog so
   bad,

He ate the little bug and he said,
"I'm glad I'm a little red snake lying
    in the water,"
sss, sss, sss.
Now there's nobody left sitting in the
    water,
nobody left doing what he oughter;

There's nothing left but the lily pad,
the duck and frog ran away. It's sad. . . .
That there's nobody left sitting in the
    water,
boo, hoo, hoo.

Author Unknown

CHAPTER 3
Preschool Years

OBJECTIVES

After reading this chapter, you should be able to:

◆ Identify characteristics of typical preschool speech.

◆ Describe differences in the language of younger and older preschoolers.

◆ Discuss the development of language skills in preschoolers.

KEY TERMS

consonant

expressive
  (productive)
  vocabulary

metalinguistic
  awareness

overextension

receptive
  (comprehension)
  vocabulary

regularization

vowel

ON AND ON AND ON …

Wilford is 4 and eager to speak in groups. He rambles, goes on and on, and both bores and loses his audience. Renee, his teacher, waits, patiently listening, but occasionally interrupts him to say, "Thank you, Wilford, for sharing with us." Sometimes this stops him, but often it does not.

QUESTIONS TO PONDER

1. Is this "stream of consciousness" talking typical of 4-year-olds? Is this a behavior found in some adults?

2. What teacher strategies might help Renee?

3. Describe three program activities that might help Wilford.

The preschool child's speech reflects sensory, physical, and social experiences, as well as thinking ability. Parents and teachers accept temporary limitations, knowing that almost all children will reach adult language levels.

During the preschool years, children move rapidly through successive phases of language learning. By the time youngsters reach their fifth year, the most challenging hurdles of language learning have been overcome.

Teachers should interact with the children and provide appropriate learning opportunities and activities. An understanding of typical preschool speech characteristics can help the teacher do this.

Background experiences with children and child study give a teacher insight into children's language behavior. The beginnings of language, early steps, and factors affecting the infant's and toddler's self-expression were covered in Chapters 1 and 2. This chapter pinpoints language use during preschool years. Although speech abilities are emphasized, growth and change in other areas, as they relate to speech, are also covered.

In addition to the child's home environment, playing with other children is a major factor influencing language development. Finding friends in his age group is an important benefit of attending an early childhood center. In a place where there are fascinating things to explore and talk about, language abilities blossom (Figure 3–1).

It is almost impossible to find a child who has all of the speech characteristics of a given age group, but most children possess some of the characteristics that are typical. There is a wide range within normal age-level behavior, and each child's individuality is an important consideration.

For simplicity's sake, the preschool period is divided into two age groups: young, or early, preschoolers (2- and 3-year-olds) and older preschoolers (4- and 5-year-olds).

YOUNG PRESCHOOLERS

Preschoolers communicate needs, desires, and feelings through speech and action. Close observation of a child's nonverbal communication can help uncover true meanings. Raising an arm, fiercely clutching playthings, or lying spread-eagle over as many blocks as possible may express more than the child is able to put into words. Stroking a friend's arm, handing a toy to another child who has not asked for it but looks at it longingly, and following the teacher around the room are behaviors that carry other meanings.

One can expect continued fast growth and changing language abilities, and children's understanding of adult statements is surprising. They may acquire 6 to 10 new words a day. Figure 3–2 displays children's stunning vocabulary growth from ages 1 through 7.

Squeals, grunts, and screams are often part of play. Imitating animals, sirens, and environmental noise is common. The child points and pulls to help others understand meanings. Younger preschoolers tend to act as though others can read their thoughts because, in the

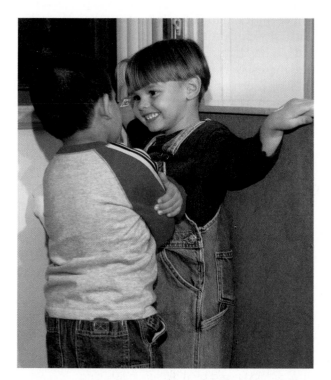

FIGURE 3–1 Children often share their ideas concerning how or what they might play.

VOCABULARY GROWTH

10–14 months	first word	First words are usually nouns instead of verbs.
12–18 months	two words a week; close to 50 by 18 months	Child looks at something (or someone), points, and then says one or two words. Mispronunciations are common.
18–24 months	200 words	Some toddlers constantly ask "What dat?" or just "Dat?" They want objects named.
2–3 years	500 words	Questions, questions, questions! Mispronunciations still happen, and consonants may be substituted for one another in some words.
3–4 years	800 words	Preschoolers start to use contractions ("won't," "can't") as well as prepositions ("in," "on") and time expressions ("morning," "afternoon"). They may also make up words.
4–5 years	1,500 or more words	Children speak with greater clarity, can construct five- and six-word sentences, and make up stories.
5–7 years	11,000 words	Children retell and discuss stories. They have many words at hand and will know more than 50,000 as adults.

FIGURE 3–2 Vocabulary growth.

past, adults anticipated what was needed. A few children may have what seems to be a limited vocabulary at school until they feel at home there.

A difference between the child's **receptive** (or **comprehension**) **vocabulary** and his **expressive** (or **productive**) **vocabulary** is apparent, with the productive vocabulary lagging behind the receptive vocabulary. The receptive vocabulary requires that a child hear a word and anticipate or react appropriately; the production of a word means the child speaks the word at an appropriate time and place.

Children begin to acquire the more complex forms of grammar during this time period, including past tenses, embedded clauses, and passive constructions. Creative mistakes happen, such as "he breakeded my bike," which indicates that the child is noticing consistent patterns and applying them to the language system as he understands it.

The words used most often are nouns and short possessives: *my, mine, Rick's.* Speech focuses on present events, things are observed in newscaster style, and "no" is used liberally. As preschoolers progress in the ability to hold brief conversations, they must keep conversational topics in mind and connect their thoughts with those of others. This is difficult for 2-year-olds, and true conversational exchange with playmates is brief, if it exists at all. Although their speech is filled with pauses and repetitions in which they attempt to correct themselves, early preschoolers are adept at conversational turn taking. Talking over the speech of another speaker at this age occurs only about 5 percent of the time.

Speech may be loud and high pitched when the child is excited (Figure 3–3), or it may be barely audible and muffled when the child is embarrassed, sad, or shy. Speech of 2- and 3-year-olds tends to be uneven in rhythm, with comments issued in spurts rather than in an even flow like the speech of older children.

There seems to be an important step forward in the complexity of content in children's

---

receptive (comprehension) vocabulary — the comprehension vocabulary used by a person in listening (and silent reading).
expressive (productive) vocabulary — the vocabulary a person uses in speaking and writing.

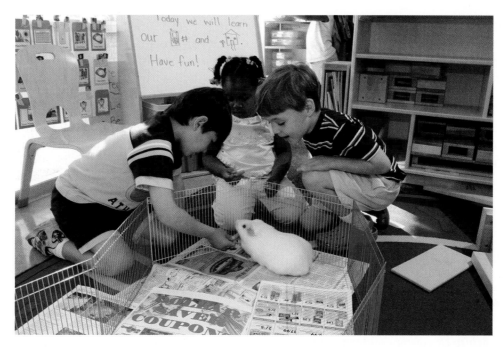

FIGURE 3–3 Speech can be limited when children are very interested.

speech at age 2. They may begin making comments about cause and effect and sometimes use conjunctions, such as *'cause, 'ah,* and *'um,* between statements.

Young preschoolers' talk is self-focused and mostly concerned with their intentions and feelings, why they wanted or did not want to do certain things, or what they wanted other people to do. Statements such as "I'm painting" or "I'm not climbing on the steps!" are commonplace.

Much of the time very young preschoolers' play focuses on recreating the work of the home and family—cooking, eating, sleeping, washing, ironing, infant care, and imitations of family events and pets (Figure 3–4). Play of slightly older preschoolers is more interactive. The child continues self-play but also explores other children, adults, environments, and actions. Eventually, most preschoolers understand that it is usually worth their while to share toys and take turns because when other playmates are around it is more fun. Two-year-olds may believe, as one preschooler remarked to his teacher, that "share means you give it away." When children begin

FIGURE 3–4 Teachers encourage the verbalizations of preschoolers.

exploring these other play options, "what's happening" in play becomes a speech subject, along with brief verbal reactions to what others are saying and doing.

A desire to organize and make sense of their experiences is often apparent in young preschoolers. Colors, counting, and new categories of thought emerge in their speech. There is a tendency for them to live out the action words they speak or hear in the speech of others. An adult who says "We won't run" may motivate a child to run; in contrast, an adult who says "Walk" might be more successful in having the child walk. This is why experienced teachers tell children what they want children to do rather than what they do not want them to do.

The Subdued 2-Year-Old

In any given group of young children, a few may appear subdued and quiet, having a tendency toward what many might call shyness. These children may possess a natural inclination that tends to inhibit spontaneous speech. Strong emotions can cause muscle tension, including tension in the larynx. Some adults asked to speak in front of a group experience this phenomenon. It can also affect speech volume. Most preschool teachers have worked with children whose speech was difficult to hear. Often, these children seem restrained when faced with unfamiliar situations. Older preschoolers may become more outgoing and talkative or may continue to be less talkative and somewhat subdued when compared with their more boisterous counterparts. Teachers respect these children's natural inclinations and tendencies.

Verb Forms

In English, most verbs (regular forms) use *-ed* to indicate past tense. Unfortunately, many frequently used verbs have irregular past-tense forms, such as *came, fell, hit, saw, took,* and *gave.* Because the child begins using often-heard words, early speech contains correct verb forms. With additional exposure to language, children realize that past events are described with *-ed* verb endings. At that point, children tack the *-ed* on regular verbs as well as on irregular verbs, creating words such as *broked, dranked,* and other charming past-tense forms. This beautiful logic often brings inner smiles to the adult listeners. Verbs ending with *-ing* are used more than before. Even auxiliary verbs are scattered through speech— "Me have," "Daddy did it." Words such as *wanna, gonna,* and *hafta* seem to be learned as one word, and stick in children's vocabulary, being used over and over.

A term for children's speech behavior that indicates they have formed a new internal rule about language and are using it is **regularization**. As children filter what they hear, creating their own rule systems, they begin to apply the new rules. An expected sequence in forming rules for past-tense verb usage follows.

- Uses irregular tense endings correctly (e.g., *ran, came, drank*).
- Forms an internal rule when discovering that *-ed* expresses past events (e.g., *danced, called, played*).
- Over-regularizes; for example, adds *-ed* to all regular and irregular verbs that were formerly spoken correctly (e.g., *camed, dided, wented, goed*).
- Learns that both regular and irregular verbs express past tense, and uses both.

In using plural noun forms, the following sequence is common.

- Remembers and uses singular forms of nouns correctly (e.g., *ball, dog, mouse, bird*).
- Uses irregular noun plurals correctly (e.g., *men, feet, mice*).
- Forms an internal rule that plurals have "s" or "z" ending sounds.

---

regularization — a child's speech behavior that indicates the formation and internalization of a language rule (regularity).

◆ Applies rule to all nouns (e.g., *balls, mens, dogs, feets, birds, mices, or ballsez, dogsez, feetsez*).

◆ Achieves flexible internal rules for plurals, memorizes irregular plural forms, and uses plurals correctly.

Key-Word Sentences

The 2-year-old omits many words in sentences, as does the toddler. The remaining words are shortened versions of adult sentences in which only the essentials are present. These words are key words and convey the essence of the message. Teachers attempt to relate questionable child utterances to concurrent child activity to grasp a child's meaning. Sentences at this stage are about four words long. Some pronouns and adjectives, such as *pretty* or *big*, are used. Very few, if any, prepositions (*by, on, with*) or articles (*a, an, the*) are spoken. Some words are run together and are spoken as single units, such as "whadat?" or "eatem," as are the verb forms mentioned earlier. The order of words (syntax) may seem jumbled at times, as in "outside going ball," but basic grammar rules are observed in most cases.

Pronouns are often used incorrectly and are confused, as in "Me all finish milk," and "him Mark's." Concepts of male and female, living things, and objects may be only partly understood, as shown in the example of the 3-year-old who says of a special toy she cannot find, "Maybe it is hiding!". This probably indicates she hasn't yet learned that hiding can be done only by an animate object.

Questions

Wh- questions (where, what, why, who) begin to appear in the speech of the young preschooler. During the toddler period, rising voice inflection and simple declarative utterances such as "Dolly drink?" are typical. At this stage, questions focus on location, objects, and people. Occasionally, their questions display a special interest in causation (why), process (how), and time (when). This reflects more mature thinking that probes purposes and intentions in others. Figure 3–5 shows one child's question development. Questions are frequent, and the child sometimes asks for an object's function or the causes of certain events. It is as if the child sees that things exist for a purpose that in some way relates to him. The answers adults provide stimulate the child's desire to know more. Questions about words and word meanings appear, such as "Why is his name Ang?".

Vocabularies of the young preschooler range from 250 to more than 1,000 words (Figure 3–6). An average of 50 new words enters the child's vocabulary each month. Gartrell (2007) notes that children are like sponges. They absorb

AGE	
age 2	raises voice pitch at sentence ending: "Me go?" "All gone?"
	uses short "what" and "where" questions: "Whas dat?" "Where kitty?"
age 3	asks yes-no questions
	begins to use "why" questions
	begins to use auxiliary verbs in questions: "Can I have gum?" "Will you get it?"
	begins to use "how" questions: "How you do that?"
age 4	adds tag endings: "Those are mine, okay?" "You like it, huh?" "That's good, isn't it?"
	inverts auxiliary verbs in questions: "Why are you sad?" "Why aren't we staying with gramma?"
	begins to use complex and two-part questions and statements: "I will tell him how to do it if you like." "What can I do when he won't come?" "I don't know what to do." "Why does it fall down when the door slams?"

FIGURE 3–5 Question development.

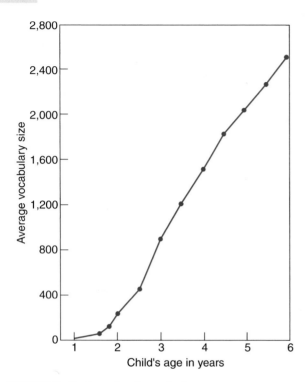

FIGURE 3–6 Growth of vocabulary.

information from the world around them and incorporate it into their growing beings.

CATEGORIES IN CHILDREN'S THINKING

Children organize a tremendous amount of sensory and experiential happenings by forming mental categories. Studies point out that young children can be quite sophisticated in how they group objects and think about their groupings. Young preschoolers' categories differ from those of older children. The young preschooler tends to focus on superficial properties such as the "look" of something and where it is found. A younger child may focus on the teacher's fuzzy sweater by wanting to touch and rub it and saying "soft." An older preschooler may talk about its number of buttons, or patterns, or its similarity to his own sweater or other

sweaters he has seen. Preschoolers often put items together in terms of their visual similarities rather than grouping items according to more fundamental likenesses.

Overlapping Concepts

Younger preschoolers commonly call all four-footed furry animals "dog," and all large animals "horse." This reflects **overextension**, in which the child has overextended and made a logical conclusion because these animals have many of the same features, can be about the same size, and therefore fit the existing word. This phenomenon is seen in the examples given in Figure 3–7.

Concept development, defined in Chapter 2 as the recognition of one or more distinguishing features or characteristics, proceeds by leaps and bounds during preschool years and is essential to meaningful communication. Details, exceptions, and discrepancies are often discussed in 4-year-olds' conversations. The younger preschooler can be described as a "looker and doer" who engages in limited discussion of the features of situations. The excitement of exploration and discovery, particularly of something new and novel, is readily apparent in preschool classrooms. Children typically crowd around to see, touch, experience, and make comments about objects and events. Teachers notice the all-consuming focusing and the long periods of watching or touching, usually followed by verbalizing and questioning an event or experience.

Running Commentaries

As children play, their actions are sometimes accompanied by a running self-commentary or "stream of consciousness" talking concerning what they are doing or what is happening (Figure 3–8). It can be described as a kind of verbal thought process, like mentally talking to oneself. It seems to increase in complex play situations as the child problem solves and talks it through.

---

overextension — in the early acquisition of words and their meanings, the application of a word to include other objects that share common features, such as "water" being used to describe any liquid.

WORD	OBJECT OR EVENT FOR WHICH THE WORD WAS ORIGINALLY USED	OTHER OBJECTS OR EVENTS TO WHICH THE WORD WAS LATER APPLIED
mooi	moon	cakes, round marks on windows, writing on windows and in books, round shapes in books, tooling on leather book covers, round postmarks, letter *O*
buti	ball	toy, radish, stone spheres at park entrance
sch	sound of train	all moving machines
em	worm	flies, ants, all small insects, heads of timothy grass
fafer	sound of trains	steaming coffee pot, anything that hissed or made a noise
va	white plush dog	muffler, cat, father's fur coat

FIGURE 3–7 Some examples of overextensions in the language of 1- and 2-year-old children. (From Clark, E. V. [1975]. Knowledge, context, and strategy in the acquisition of meaning. In D. P. Dato [Ed.], *Georgetown University round table on languages and linguistics, 1975. Developmental psycholinguistics: Theory and applications.* Washington, DC: Georgetown University Press. Used with permission.

Situation:	Four- and five-year-old girls playing with water	
	COMMENTARY	**CHARACTERISTIC**
Debbie:	"Two of those make one of these." (playing with measuring cups)	Talking to self.
Debbie:	"Two cups or three cups ... whoops it went over."	Talks about what happened.
Tifine:	"Stop it or else I'll beat you up." (said to Debbie)	Does not respond to another's speech.
Debbie:	"This is heavy." (holding the 2-cup measuring container full of water)	Describes perception.
Christine:	"Is it hot?" (Christine just dropped in)	
Debbie:	"Feel it and see." "It's not hot." (feeling the water)	Hears another; answers appropriately. Child talking to self.
Debbie:	"I'm finished now. Oh this is awfully heavy—I'm going to pour it into the bottle."	Talking about what she perceives and what she is doing.

FIGURE 3–8 Conversation during play activity.

Researchers suggest multiple reasons for preschoolers' private speech. These include the following: (1) talking to themselves is a way of giving themselves directions for their intended actions, (2) they need a sensorimotor activity as a reinforcer or "crutch" because their cognitive schemes are not yet well developed, and (3) it is more efficient for them to talk their ideas through in words rather than silently.

Self-talk may help children sequence actions, control their own behavior, use more flexible modes of thinking, and manipulate the goals they are trying to achieve in their play.

Talking to self and talking to another can occur alternately. Toys, animals, and treasured items still receive a few words. Statements directed to others do not usually need answers. Private speech rarely considers another's point of view. A conversation between young preschoolers may sound like two children talking together about different subjects. Neither child is really listening or reacting to what the other says. When a very young preschooler does wish to talk directly to another child, it is sometimes done through an adult. A child may say, "I want truck," to an adult, even if the child playing with the truck is standing close by.

Other researchers who have examined self-talk suggest a number of possible developmental benefits. These include:

♦ practicing newly recognized language forms.
♦ obtaining pleasure through play with word sounds.
♦ exploring vocal capacities.
♦ reliving particular significant events.
♦ creating dialogue in which the child voices all participants' parts, perhaps helping the child later fit into social settings.
♦ experimenting with fantasy, thereby accommodating the creative urge.
♦ attending objectively to language.
♦ facilitating motor behavior in a task or project.

Whatever its benefits, self-talk is natural, common behavior. By the age of 5, the child's self-talk is observed infrequently. As children approach the age of 3, both dialogue and monologue are apparent. Observers of play conversations find it difficult to determine just how much of each is present.

Teachers who conduct group times with younger preschoolers are familiar with children who ramble on and on; the teachers deal with this behavior by using a variety of techniques. Some teachers try to encourage "my turn, your turn" behaviors. A kitchen timer, a ping-pong paddle held by each speaker, or a turned-on flashlight to signal a child that his speaking turn is over are strategies other teachers have devised. Teachers also try to draw focus back to the subject at hand by saying, "Amy, yes, dogs do use their tongues when they drink. It is Jeremy's turn to tell us about his dog now."

Repetition

Repetition in speech is common. Sometimes it happens randomly at play, and at other times it is done with a special purpose. A young child may repeat almost everything said to him. Most young preschoolers repeat words or parts of sentences regularly. Children's growing language skills allow them to create repetitions that rhyme, as in "oogie, woogie, poogie bear," which greatly please them. They quickly imitate words that they like; sometimes, excitement is the cause. Rhyming words or rhyming syllables may promote enjoyable mimicking and younger preschoolers are particularly fascinated and attracted to words that rhyme. Repetition of rhyming words seems to help children remember things (just as adults mentally repeat new telephone numbers), such as "Get up at eight and you won't be late."

Free associations (voiced juggling of sounds and words) occur at play and at rest and may sound like babbling. Many times, it seems as though, having learned a word, the child must savor it or practice it, over and over (Figure 3–9).

Lack of Clarity

About one in every four words of the young preschooler is not readily understandable. This lack of clarity is partially caused by an inability

FIGURE 3–9 Elsa Beth calls this "bussing" her teeth.

to control the mouth, tongue, and breathing and an inability to hear subtle differences and distinctions in speech. Typically, articulation of all English speech sounds, especially some **consonant** blends, is not accomplished until age 7 or 8. Young preschoolers are only 40 to 80 percent correct in articulation. This lack of intelligibility in children can be partly attributed to the complexity of the task of mastering the sounds. Although children may be right on target in development, their speech may still be difficult to understand at times.

The young preschooler may have difficulty with the rate of speech, phrasing, inflection, intensity, syntax, and voice stress. Faulty articulation and defective soundmaking can also contribute to the problem. The child who attempts to form the longest utterances is the one who is hardest to understand. The child who omits sounds is less clear than the one who distorts them. As a rule, expect omissions, substitutions, and distortions in the speech of 2- and 3-year olds, for they will be plentiful.

By 3 years of age, children's pronunciation patterns are not yet fully like those of adults, but the basic features of the adult phonological system are present. Most children can produce all of the **vowel** sounds and nearly all of the consonant sounds in at least a few words, but their productions are not 100 percent accurate.

Young children typically omit sounds at the ends of words, saying, for example, *ba* for "ball." Middle consonants in longer words are also passed over lightly—*ikeem* for "ice cream" or *telfone* for "telephone." Even beginning sounds may be omitted, as in *ellow* for "yellow."

Substitutions of letter sounds are also common, for example, *aminal* and *pasghetti*. Until the new sound is mastered, one consonant may even take the place of another; *wabbit, wun,* and *wain* are common examples. Children who cannot yet produce all of the speech sounds accurately can generally hear the differences between *w* and *r*, or *t* and *th*, when they are pronounced by others.

Dramatic Play

Short play sequences that involve acting or imitating the behavior of family begin at home and school. Speech usually accompanies the reenactments. Although young children at this age play side-by-side, most of this dramatic play starts as solitary activity. Common play themes include talking on the phone, caring for a baby, or cooking (Figure 3–10). Dolls, toys, and dress-up clothes are usually part of the action and may serve to initiate this type of play. Observers of 2- and 3-year-olds in classrooms find it hard to determine whether children are engaged in joint planning of play or are simply playing in the same area with the same kinds of playthings. Preschools purposely purchase multiple dolls so that many children can feed and rock "their babies" when they see others doing it.

ADVICE FOR FAMILIES AND EARLY CHILDHOOD EDUCATORS

Parents sometimes worry about a child who stops, stammers, or stutters when speaking. Calling attention to this speech and making demands on the child cause tension, making the situation worse. All children hesitate, repeat, stop, and start in speaking—it is typical behavior. Searching for the right word takes time, and thoughts may come faster than words. Adults need to relax and wait. Speech is a complex process of sending and receiving. Maintaining patience and optimism and assuming a casual "I'm listening" stance is the best course of action for the adult. Many schools routinely send home informational material to alert parents to age-level speech characteristics.

Teachers frequently encounter child statements that are seemingly illogical and they suspect, if they acknowledge them, that the child will soon provide more information. Child

---

consonant — (1) a speech sound made by partial or complete closure of the vocal tract, which obstructs air flow; (2) an alphabet letter used in representing any of these sounds.

vowel — a voiced speech sound made without stoppage or friction of air flow as it passes through the vocal tract.

FIGURE 3–10 Dress-up play may be enhanced if a mirror is provided.

logic is there, but teachers know that they are not privy to inner thought processes or children's past experiences. With more information, what at first appeared illogical turns out to have beautiful logic.

Frequently, a listening teacher will feel on the edge of understanding what a child is trying to say. This happens with both younger and older preschoolers struggling at times to put into words what they are thinking. Acceptance and interest are appropriate (Figure 3–11).

Attentive interaction with positive feedback is recommended for adults who live or work with 2- and 3-year-olds. Reacting to the intent of the child's message is more helpful than concentrating on correctness. In other words,

FIGURE 3–11 "Me eatem!"

focus on what is said rather than the way it is said. A lot of guessing is still necessary to determine what the child is trying to say. The adult's model of speech will override temporary errors as the child hears more and more of it.

By simply naming objects, adults can encourage children to notice how different items are similar and can help children gain new information about the world. Helping children see details and relationships in what they encounter is useful if done in a matter of fact rather than a pressured way or an "I'm trying to teach you something" manner. Connecting past events to present events may aid their understanding.

Children's hearing should be checked regularly because even a moderate hearing loss may affect speech production. Preschoolers are particularly prone to upper respiratory infections and ear problems.

BOOKS FOR YOUNGER PRESCHOOLERS

Many picture books are available for younger preschoolers. Experts suggest books for this age group that have:

- themes, objects, animals, or people that are familiar and within their range of life experience.
- clarity of content and story line.
- clear, simple illustrations or photographs with backgrounds that do not distract from the intended focus.
- themes concerning everyday tasks and basic human needs.

Most 2- and 3-year-olds enjoy actively participating in story reading, but they can be very good listeners as well. Participation can include pointing, making noise, repeating dialogue, or performing imitative body actions. Books that are repetitive and predictable offer the enjoyment of anticipating what will come next. For children who are used to being read to at bedtime, the calming effect of listening to the human voice becomes very apparent during story reading when heads nod or children act sleepy.

Chapter 9 covers the topic of introducing preschool children to literature.

OLDER PRESCHOOLERS

As younger preschoolers get older, adults can expect the following:

- longer sentences with more words per sentence
- more specificity
- more "ing" endings on verbs
- increased correctness in the forms of the verb "to be"
- use of more auxiliary verbs
- more facility with passive-voice verbs, including "did" and "been"
- changes in negative sentences, from "No want" to "I don't want"
- changes in question forms, from "Car go?" to "Where did the car go?"
- changes in mental categories
- additional clarifications in articulation of speech sounds

By the time they are between 4 and 5 years of age, most preschoolers' speech is similar to adult use; their sentences are longer, with almost all words present rather than only key words (Figure 3–12).

Preschoolers' play is active and vocal, and they copy each other's words and manner of speaking. A word such as "monster," or more colorful words, may swiftly become of interest and spread rapidly from child to child. Remember the joy that both younger and older children exhibited with the phrases: "zip-a-dee-doo-dah," "bibbidi-bobbidi-boo," "scoobidoobi-do," "blast off," "fuzzy-wuzzy," and "ooey-gooey"? Every generation of preschoolers seems to have their own favorite sayings, and new ones are constantly appearing.

The older preschooler's social speech and conversations are heard and interpreted to a greater degree by others of the child's age. The child learns and practices the complexities of social conversation, including (1) gaining

FIGURE 3–12 Rene is explaining why she selected a certain puzzle piece.

another's attention by making eye contact, touching, or using words or catch-phrases like "Know what?"; (2) pausing and listening; (3) correcting himself; (4) maintaining attention by not pausing, so as not to let another speaker jump in; (5) taking turns in conversing by developing patience and trying to listen while still holding in mind what he wants to say.

Friendships

The young preschooler may develop a new friend or find another he prefers to play near or with. At ages 2 and 3, friendships are usually temporary, changing from day to day. Friendships of older preschoolers are more stable and lasting. By ages 4 and 5, there seems to be a desire to remain compatible and work out differences, therefore creatively maintaining a type of play acceptable to both. Negotiation, clarification, and open-mindedness flourish during play. A friend's needs and requests are handled

with sensitivity, and flexibility characterizes conversations. Needless to say, spats, "blow-ups," and the crushed feelings accompanying rejection sometimes occur. Verbal interaction between children adds a tremendous amount of verbal input and also promotes output.

Group Play

Joint planning of play activities and active make-believe and role-playing take on new depth in older preschoolers. Most 4- and 5-year-olds' main concern seems to be interacting with age-mates. Twosomes and groups of play companions are typical in older preschoolers' classrooms and play yards (Figure 3–13). As speech blossoms, friendships blossom and disintegrate (Figure 3–14). Speech is used to discourage and disallow entrance to play groups when running from newcomers is impossible. Speech is found to be effective in hurting feelings, as in statements such as "I don't like you" or "No girls." Children find

FIGURE 3–13 Group play encourages social development and social connectiveness.

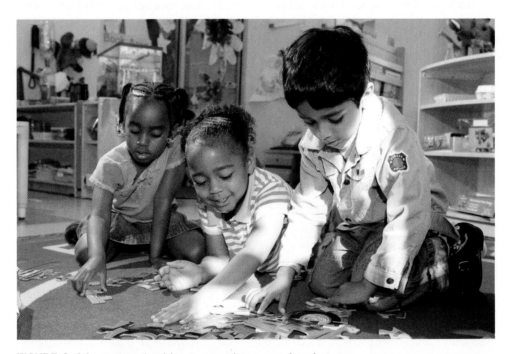

FIGURE 3–14 "Bosom buddies" enjoy the same play choices.

that verbal inventiveness may help them join play or initiate play.

In group play, pretending is paramount. Make-believe play appears to be at its zenith. Many children grow in the ability to (1) verbally suggest new directions and avenues of fantasy, (2) engage in verbal negotiation, (3) compromise, (4) argue, and (5) become a group's leader by using the right words. Popular children seem to be those who use speech creatively and become enjoyable companions to others.

Violent statements such as "I'm going to shoot you" or "cut you up" are sometimes heard, and these tend to reflect television viewing or media drama. The reality-fantasy dividing line may become temporarily blurred in some play situations, causing some children considerable anxiety.

Older preschoolers talk "in character" as they elaborate their dramatic play. If a scenario calls for a mother talking to a baby or teenagers talking, preschoolers adopt appropriate speech. Imitations of pop singers or cartoon characters are common. Role-taking is an important skill in mature communication, indicating that social and dramatic play and improvisation are effective means of facilitating growth in communicative competence.

Four-year-olds seem to boast, brag, and make lots of noise. However, apparently boastful statements such as "Look what I did" may just be the child's attempt to show that he is capable and to share his accomplishments. Although preschoolers enjoy being with their peers, they quickly and easily engage in quarreling and name-calling. Sometimes, they do battle verbally. Typically, 3- to 5-year-olds disagree over possession of objects or territory, and verbal reasons or verbal evidence may help them win arguments. Many conflicts are resolved and lead to continued play. Speech helps children settle their affairs with and without adult help.

As a child develops a sense of humor, giggling becomes part of the noise of play. Silliness often reigns. One preschool boy thought it hilarious to go up to a teacher named Alice and say, "What's your name, Alice?" and then run off laughing—quite mature humor for a 4-year-old! Preschoolers may distort and repeat what a caregiver says, making changes in sounds and gleefully chanting the distorted message. Teachers who want to cultivate children's ability to understand and appreciate humor try to plan activities and present materials that challenge children's ability to interpret humor.

Argument, persuasion, and statements aimed at controlling others are frequently heard during play. Older preschool children are able to state reasons (Figure 3–15),

FIGURE 3–15 Emily is explaining why the rabbit in the book is naughty.

request information, give explanations, utter justifications for their behavior, and verbally defend themselves. At times, establishing authority in disagreements seems paramount to compromising.

Inner Speech

Much of a child's speech during early preschool years is made up of comments about what the child is currently doing or what he has done. A subtle shift takes place during the later preschool years, when inner speech becomes apparent and the child more frequently plans, monitors ideas, and evaluates silently. The child is still talking about his accomplishments and actions in a look-at-me fashion, but a greater portion of his self-commentary is unspoken.

Exploring the Conventions of Conversation

Children learn language by reinventing it for themselves, not by direct instruction. They crack the code through exposure and opportunities to converse. They actively, although unconsciously, ingest and discover the rules of the system. Their speech errors often alert adults to the inner rules of language being formed.

Conversations have unwritten rules and expectations, the "you-talk-I-talk" sequence being the most apparent. Some preschoolers (3- and 4-year-olds) may delight in violating or "playing" with the conventions of conversation. Sometimes preschoolers deliberately mislead (usually to tease playfully) or use "taboo" bathroom talk, nonsense talk, or unexpected tone when they are capable of verbally responding at a more mature level. Most teachers sense the child may be asserting independence by rejecting conversational convention. One teacher termed this "going into the verbal crazies" to reject what another child or adult is saying, therefore attempting to change or control the situation. By violating conversational convention, children may clarify how conversational interaction should take place.

Relational Words

More and more relational words appear as the child begins to compare, contrast, and revise stored concepts with new happenings. The following teacher-recorded anecdote during a story-telling activity shows how the child attempts to relate previously learned ethics to a new situation.

> During story telling Michael repeated with increasing vigor, "He not berry nice!" at the parts of the story when the wolf says, "I'm going to blow your house down." Michael seemed to be checking with me the correctness of his thinking based on his internalized rules of proper moral conduct. (Machado, 2008, p. 16)

Perhaps because adults stress bad and good or because a young child's inner sense of what is and what is not correct is developing, teachers notice that preschoolers often describe feelings and people within narrow limits. One is pretty or ugly, mean or nice. Shades of meaning or extenuating circumstances seem yet to be understood. Beck (1982) observed:

> Three-year-old children are usually able to describe the world around them, and four-year-old children are also creatures of their senses. They are concerned with the smell of a thing, the touch of a thing, the look of a thing, and the sound of a thing. Sometime during their fourth year children's well-developed, sensory awareness begins to take on conceptual dimensions. They begin to notice function or use and they begin to see it comparatively. They come to see relationships between several objects and/or several events, and in comparing one to the other, they are learning the principle of categorization. (p. 153)

Although the words "big" and "little" are commonly used by preschoolers, they are overused. Many other comparison words give children trouble, and one hears "biggerer," "big-big-big," and "bestus one" to describe size. Time words elicit smiles from adults as children wrestle with present, past, and future, as in "zillion days" or "tomorrower." Number words are difficult for some children to handle, and expressions such as "whole bunches" and "eleventeen" are sometimes heard.

Although 4-year-olds are able speakers, many of the "plays on words," double meanings, and connotative language subtleties that are important in adult speech are beyond children's understanding. Their creative uses of words at times seem metaphoric and poetic and are valiant attempts to put thoughts into words. Half-heard words and partially or fully learned words are blended together and are, at times, wonderfully descriptive. The author still laughs about the 4-year-old who called her "Mrs. Eye Shadow."

Speech and Child Behavior

There is tremendous variety in the ways children can modify their voices, and they may speak in a different pitch or rhythm when speaking to different people. They can whine, whisper, change volume, and distort timing and pronunciation.

Some children discover that by increasing volume or changing tone they can affect others' behavior. They find that speech can show anger or sarcasm and can be used aggressively to hurt others.

Preschoolers may mimic the speech of "bad guy" media characters. Acts of aggression, clothed in the imitated speech and actions of a TV character, can become part of this type of play. Purposeful echoing or baby talk can irritate or tease. Excessive talking is sometimes used to get one's way, and "talking back" may occur.

Some children find that silence can get as much attention from adults as loud speech. Tattling on another may simply be a way of checking for correctness, or it can be purposeful.

Through trial and error and feedback, the child finds that words can hurt, gain friends or favor, or satisfy a wide range of needs. Because preschoolers are emotion-packed human beings, their statements range from expressions of

"you're my buddy" to "you're my enemy" within a matter of minutes.

What may appear to be violent statements may be just role-playing or make-believe competition. To some adults, preschooler speech may appear loud and wild. Their speech seems overly nasal and full of moisture that sprays out in some words. A young child may have frequent nasal colds and congestion during this period. Preschoolers tend to stand close to others and their volume increases when they feel strongly about their subjects.

Impact Words

Not all speech used by older preschoolers is appreciated by adults. Name-calling and offensive words and phrases may be used by active preschoolers to gain attention and reaction from both adults and children. Children discover that some phrases, sentences, and words cause unusual behavior in others. They actively explore these and usually learn which of these are inappropriate and when they can be used. Gartrell (2007) notes that children often hear others use expletives spoken when emotions run high. Children learn that most of this type of talk has "impact value." If certain talk makes people laugh or gives the children some kind of positive reward, it is used over and over.

Bathroom words seem to be explored and used as put-downs and attention getters. As every parent and teacher knows, young children experiment with language related to the body, and particularly to the private parts, going to the bathroom, and sexuality. In fact, children's use of sexual words can make it seem as if they know more than they do. Giggles and uproarious laughter can ensue when these words are used, adding to the child's enjoyment, and new teachers may not know how to handle these situations. The school's policy regarding this matter can be a subject for staff discussion. Generally, newly spoken bathroom talk should be ignored unless it is hurtful, or the child should be told that the place to use the word is in the bathroom. This often remedies the behavior because the child's enjoyment of it is spoiled without an audience. Alternatively, it might suffice to firmly say, "That's a word that hurts. His name is Michael," or in a calm but firm voice, "That kind of talk is unacceptable." Preschoolers love using forbidden words, especially when they play together. What parents and teachers can control is what is said in their presence.

Sound Words

In our culture, children are particularly fond of repeating conventionalized sounds reputedly made by animals ("arf-arf," "meow," "baa") as well as action sounds for toy vehicles ("putt-putt," "beep," "varoom"). When a child is playing the baby in home reenactment dramatic play, "wa-wa" will be heard frequently. Rough-and-tumble outside play may be accompanied by cartoon-strip sounds like "pow," "bam," and "zap." In addition, a good number of 4-year-olds can distinguish rhyming words, and they enjoy creating them.

Created Words

Created words such as "turner-overer" for pancake turner, "mudpudders" for rain boots, or "dirt digger" for spade are wonderfully descriptive and crop up occasionally in child speech, perhaps as a means of filling in gaps in their vocabularies. Many cite young children's fascination with the functions of objects in their environment as the reason such words are created. Children love making up words, including nonsense words, and revel in their newly gained abilities to do so.

Word Meanings

During later preschool years children often become focused on what words mean and they begin to think and wonder about words. They begin to understand that words are arbitrary symbols with no intrinsic connection to their meaning but rather are representatives of meaning. The young child who says, "Templeton has a big name; my name is small," is displaying a recognition of word length or number of syllables.

Reality and Nonsense

Some preschool children can enjoy the absurd, nonsensical, and ridiculous in their experiences and find humor in the unexpected. Others, at a different stage in their cognitive development with another orientation, insist on knowing the right way—the real, the accepted, the "whys and wherefores"—and will see no humor in what confuses them or contradicts the "usual order of things."

A number of preschoolers view life and surroundings seriously, literally. Others can "play" in speech with the opposite of what they know to be true. We know this is true in some adults also. Some simply do not seem to enjoy what most of us may find humorous.

There is considerable "language play" in nursery rhymes, fairy tales, and classic stories and children discover wonderful, fun ways to repeat things that story characters say. They may gleefully stomp up a hallways saying, "Fee, fi, fo, fum, here I come!". They may build bridges with blocks and make play figures "trip, trap, trip, trap" across them. Teachers are careful not to suppress a child's delight in absurdity by insisting on exact or literal renditions of things. Teachers encourage nonsense play by appreciating a child's inventions or nonsensical propositions. They may model some silliness or nonsense themselves. For example, the teacher might invert words in a sentence well known to the children to evoke child laughter by saying, "And the dogs go meow and cats say bow-wow." And then the teacher would hope the children would either correct her or join in the game, producing their own inversions.

Myths Concerning Speech and Intelligence

A large and mature vocabulary at this age may tend to lead teachers to think a child has superior intelligence. Making conclusions about children based on language ability at this age has inherent pitfalls considering the many factors that could produce limited or advanced vocabulary, particularly when one considers cultural differences, bilingualism, and the child's access to "language-rich environments." At later ages language usage does seem to be related to school success.

Common Speech Patterns of Older Preschoolers

Four-year-olds often rhyme words in their play and speech, as previously mentioned. Older preschoolers engage in self-chatter, as do younger ones. Older preschoolers continue to make errors in grammar and in the use of the past tense of verbs ("He didn't caught me"), adjectives ("It's biggerer than yours") (Figure 3–16), time words ("The next tomorrow"),

and negatives ("I didn't did it"). But preschoolers' skills are increasing at this age, and their use of forms of the irregular verb "to be" improves such as "I am so," or "Mine are hot, and yours are cold." Sentence structure comes closer to adult usage, including use of relative clauses and complex and compound sentence forms. Articulation of letter sounds is still developing; about 75 percent of English letter sounds are made correctly. Omissions of letter sounds (*'merca* for "America") and substitutions (*udder* for "other") are still present.

Older preschoolers may have a vocabulary of much more than 1,500 words. They are learning new words and new concepts while they also enrich and solidify their knowledge of known words by establishing multiple links among words and concepts. Many 4-year-olds are very concerned about the correct names of things and detect errors in the speech of others. Because the older preschooler is an active explorer, his questions still probe the "purposefulness" of objects or actions (as in "Why is the moon in the sky?"). The 4-year-old becomes an active problem solver and tends to explain things through visually noted attributes; for example, "A cow is called that 'cause of its horns."

Preschoolers may not be able to talk about their solutions to problems. Although they can respond to and solve questions posed verbally, they may not be able to explain their thinking. A child at this age can transform questions; for example, if asked to carry a message asking a person whether she is ready, the child will correctly ask her, "Are you ready?"

Most 4-year-old children enjoy books, stories, and activities with words. More and more of their time is spent on these pursuits.

The 4-year-old may still stutter and clutter and stop speech when there is stress or excitement. The less-mature speech of a best friend might be copied, and nonverbal expression is most often a part of communication. However, most 4- and 5-year-olds are avid speakers. They are interested in exploring the real world and make-believe worlds.

A wide range of individual speech behavior is both normal and possible. Knowing some

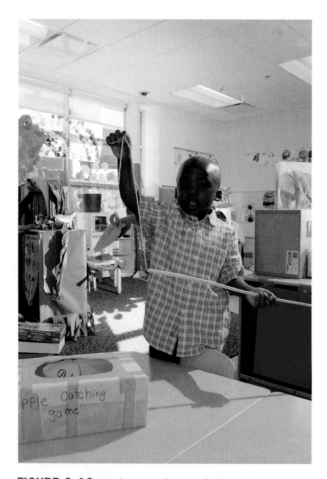

FIGURE 3–16 It's bigger than a shark.

typical behaviors can help the teacher understand young children. Some younger preschoolers may have the speech characteristics of older preschoolers, whereas some older preschoolers have the characteristics of younger preschoolers. Each child is unique in his progress and rate of acquiring language skills.

Metalinguistic Awareness and Brain Growth

Teachers and parents hope that preschool language arts experiences will, when the time comes, help children learn to read and write with ease. Preschoolers may begin to notice words as objects. **Metalinguistic awareness** can be defined as a knowledge of the nature of language as an object. Children begin to notice words as objects and later become able to manipulate them to learn to read and write and to accomplish a host of other ends, such as using metaphors, creating puns, and using irony. Pan and Gleason (1997) observe:

> Before children can engage in flexible uses of words, they must have an implicit understanding that words are separate from their referents. Young children often consider the name of an object another of its intrinsic attributes. They believe, for instance, that if you called a horse a cow, it might begin to moo. Later children learn that words themselves are not inherent attributes of objects, which allows them to move beyond literal word use and adopt a metaphoric stance. (p. 327)

A critical restructuring of the brain begins at about age 4 when a surge in learning is happening. The brain is beginning to eliminate weak connections but is still eagerly seeking information from the senses. Early childhood educators and many researchers are urging that a national emphasis and priority be given to early childhood education, especially in the key areas of language learning, mathematics, music education, and problem-solving skill development.

SUMMARY

Knowing typical and common language development characteristics helps the teacher understand that children are unique individuals. Rapid growth of vocabulary and language skills is part of normal growth. Errors in the speech of young preschoolers (aged 2 to 3) make verbalizations partly understandable. Key words in the correct order give adults clues to what is intended. Self-talk during the child's play usually describes what the child is doing and may alternate with social comments.

Teachers can use their knowledge of early childhood language development in many ways, such as alerting the staff about a child's need for hearing tests or special help and helping parents who are concerned with their child's speech patterns.

The speech of older preschool children (aged 4 to 5) is very similar to adult speech. Children in this age group explore words and begin to understand their power. Make-believe play peaks and is often accompanied by a child's imitation of the speech used by others in their lives. Some newly learned speech may be irritating to school staffs and families, but it can indicate intellectual and social growth. Exploring and enjoying books occupies more of the children's time. Exploring the real and fantasy worlds with words becomes children's active pursuit during the early childhood years.

There is no "average" child when it comes to language development; individual differences exist and are treated with acceptance and optimism (Figure 3–17).

Added interest and emphasis on language fundamentals during preschool years has occurred in light of research on brain growth and function.

---

metalinguistic awareness — a conscious awareness on the part of a language user of language as an object in itself.

CHILD'S AGE

2–2½ years	joins words in sentences of two or more words knows name has vocabulary of more than three words understands long spoken sentences and simple commands begins using plurals and past tense changes pitch and/or loudness for specific meaning begins using forms of verb ''to be'' uses a few prepositions uses ''I,'' ''me,'' and ''you''	uses about 25 phonemes articulates about 10 to 12 vowel types and about 12 to 15 consonants points to and names objects in pictures names five to eight body parts enjoys rhythm in words, nursery rhymes, finger plays, and simple stories understands and responds to almost all of adult speech generalizes by calling round objects ball, and so on
2½–3 years	begins to use negatives, imperatives, and commands shows variety in question types adds as many as two to three words to vocabulary daily names items in signs and books uses three- or four-word sentences enjoys fun with words	follows simple directions points to body parts when asked names many common objects uses an increasing number of nouns, verbs, and pronouns draws lines and circular forms in artwork knows words or lines from books, songs, and stories
3–4 years	asks why, what, where, how, and when questions loves word play makes closed figures in art begins using auxiliary verbs tells sex and age utters compound sentences with connecting ''and . . . er . . . but,'' and so on engages in imaginary play with dialogue and monologue says full name follows two- and three-part requests relates ideas and experiences uses adverbs, adjectives, and prepositions answers who, what, and where questions names some colors and is interested in counting	looks at books while alone and enjoys reading times talks about relationships memorizes a short song, poem, finger play, or story repeats three digits and two to three nonsense syllables if asked uses adjectives and pronouns correctly can copy a recognizable circle or square well if shown a model can imitate a clapping rhythm starts to talk about the function of objects can find an object in group that is different can find missing parts of wholes can classify using clear, simple distinctions knows names of common shapes
4–5 years	has vocabulary of more than 1,500 words uses sentences of five to six (or more) words may use impact, shock, and forbidden words may use words of violence argues, convinces, and questions correctness shares books with friends acts out story themes or recreates life happenings in play has favorite books likes to dictate words notices signs and print in environment uses etiquette words, such as ''please,'' ''thank you,'' and so on enjoys different writing tools knows many nursery rhymes and stories	may add alphabet letters to artwork creates and tells long stories can verbally express the highlights of the day knows many colors can repeat a sentence with six or more words may pretend to read books or may actually read others' name tags holds writing tools in position that allows fine control traces objects with precision classifies according to function asks what words mean is familiar with many literary classics for children knows address and phone number can retell main facts or happenings in stories uses adultlike speech

FIGURE 3–17 Developmental language-related milestones at ages 2 through 5.

ADDITIONAL RESOURCES

Readings

Bowman, B. T., Donovan, M. S., & Burns, M. S. (Eds.). (2001). *Eager to learn: Educating our preschoolers.* Washington, DC: National Academy Press.

Clay, M. M. (2001). *Change over time in children's literacy development.* Portsmouth, NH: Heinemann.

Hart, B., & Risley, T. R. (1999). *The social world of children learning to talk.* Baltimore: Paul H. Brookes.

Jones, E., & Cooper, R. M. (2006). *Playing to get smart.* New York: Teachers College Press.

Ohl, J. (2000, Fall). Linking child care and early literacy. *Child Care Bulletin, 27,* 1–4.

Paley, V. G. (1988). *Bad guys don't have birthdays: Fantasy play at four.* Chicago: University of Chicago Press.

Paley, V. G. (1988). *Mollie is three: Growing up in school.* Chicago: The University of Chicago Press.

Roskos, K. A., Christie, J. F., & Richgels, D. J. (2003). The essentials of early literacy instruction. *Young Children, 58*(2), 52–60.

Helpful Websites

National Child Care Information Center (NCCIC)
http://nccic.org
Staff will research your questions and connect you with information on young children's language and literacy.

National Network for Child Care
http://www.nncc.org
For the ages and stages of 3- and 4-year olds, select Articles & Resources and then select Child Development.

Book Companion Website

Vivian Paley's writings have been treasured and extensively read by early childhood educators. One strategy that aided her understanding of the children in her classroom could easily be replicated. Read about her strategy on the book companion website and discuss her strategy with peers. The findings of a kindergarten readiness study that involved 700 children in an urban California school district will alert you to the communication abilities the study believed important. It points out how instrumental preschool teachers can be in preparing children for kindergarten. Learn some strategies for promoting children's problem solving, vocabulary, and the expression of child discoveries.

STUDENT ACTIVITIES

1. Observe a 2-, 3-, 4-, and 5-year-old for 15-minute periods. (Omit children's names.) Try to write down what is said and a brief description of the setting and actions. Underline typical characteristics described in this chapter. Make comparisons between older and younger preschool children. Add any new language characteristics you notice.

2. Read the following from Justice and Pence (2006) with a peer. Then role-play a situation in which a seasoned early childhood educator is instructing a new classroom assistant by giving examples concerning how she reaches the goal of helping preschoolers learn new words, and promotes vocabulary and word understanding. Then switch roles. Share some of your examples with the total group.

   Justice and Pence (2006) point out children's acquisition of a new word moves from broad, shallow understanding to greater specificity and deeper understanding over time with ongoing exposures to the word in different contexts. Educators support deeper understanding when children hear words many times such as hearing repetitive words in stories, or through hearing the same word or words in varying classroom circumstances, or when adults frequently connect words to real objects, actions, or illustrations. (p. 19)

3. What rules or restrictions concerning the use of inappropriate speech (name-calling, swearing, and screaming) would you expect to find in a preschool center?

4. Write definitions for the following:

consonant	metalinguistic awareness
egocentric speech or private speech	overextension
expressive vocabulary	running commentary
impact words	vowel

CHAPTER REVIEW

A. Associate the following characteristics with the correct age group. Some may seem to fit both categories; choose the most appropriate one. Write the characteristics under the headings "Younger Preschooler" (2- and 3-year-olds) and "Older Preschooler" (4- and 5-year-olds).

"Look, I'm jumping."	repetitions
telegraphic speech	omission of letter sounds
rhyming and nonsense words	adult-like speech
name-calling	bathroom words

nonverbal communication	substitutions
vocabulary of more than 1,500 words	role-playing
talking about what one is doing	planning play with others
stuttering	arguing
talking through an adult	

B. Select the correct answers. Many questions have more than one correct response.

1. The younger preschool child (2 to 3 years old)
   a. may still grunt and scream while communicating.
   b. always replies to what is said to him by another child.
   c. articulates many sounds without clarity.
   d. speaks in complete sentences at 2 years of age.

2. A truly typical or average child
   a. would have all the characteristics of his age.
   b. is almost impossible to find.
   c. is one who speaks better than his peers.
   d. sometimes makes up words to fit new situations.

3. Repetition in the speech of the young child
   a. needs careful watching.
   b. is common for children aged 2 to 5.
   c. can be word play.
   d. happens for a variety of reasons.

4. Name-calling and swearing
   a. may take place during preschool years.
   b. can gain attention.
   c. show that children are testing reactions with words.
   d. happen only with poorly behaved children.

5. A word like "blood" or "ghost"
   a. may spread quickly to many children.
   b. has impact value.
   c. can make people listen.
   d. is rarely used in a preschool group.

6. Most younger preschoolers
   a. cannot correctly pronounce all consonants.
   b. omit some letter sounds.
   c. have similar-to-adult speech.
   d. will, when older, reach adult-level speech.

7. Stuttering during preschool years
   a. happens often.
   b. should not be drawn to the child's attention.
   c. may happen when a child is excited.
   d. means the child will need professional help to overcome it.

8. "Me wented" is an example of
   a. pronoun difficulty.
   b. a telegram sentence.
   c. verb incorrectness.
   d. the speech of some 2- or 3-year-olds.

9. Joint planning in play with two or more children is found more often with
   a. 2- to 3-year-olds.
   b. 4- to 5-year-olds.
   c. slowly developing children.
   d. male children.
10. Knowing typical speech characteristics is important because teachers
   a. may need to alert their director's attention to a child's difficulty.
   b. can help individual children.
   c. interact daily with young children.
   d. should be able to recognize typical age-level behavior.

CHAPTER 4

Growth Systems Affecting Early Language Ability

OBJECTIVES

After reading this chapter, you should be able to:

◆ Describe sequential stages of intellectual development.

◆ List three perceptual-motor skills that preschool activities might include.

◆ Discuss the importance of an early childhood center's ability to meet young children's social and emotional needs.

KEY TERMS

accommodation	impulsive	social
assimilation	mental image	connectedness
classify	metalinguistic skills	
conceptual tempo	reflective	

AN UNEXPECTED REMARK

Leisel entered the classroom on her first day of work as a coteacher for a class of 4-year-olds. The morning went well until Paynter, a boy, said, "You sure are ugly." Leisel thought, "All right, how should I answer this? Should I just ignore it, believing he is just having a bad day, and let it go until I know more about him?" Instead Leisel said with good humor, "I'm very ugly when I wake up in the morning. My eyes are half awake, and my hair sticks up and goes in spikes. Sometimes I look in the mirror and say, 'Oh no.'"

QUESTIONS TO PONDER

1. Which way would you have chosen to answer? Would your response have been similar to Leisel's? If not, why?

2. How do you think Paynter might have responded to Leisel?

3. How many 4-year-olds know words can be powerful? Few, many, most, or is this more characteristic of older elementary schoolchildren?

The child is a total being, and language growth cannot be isolated from physical, mental, and social-emotional well-being. All body systems need a minimum level of movement (exercise) to keep the body in good working order and to stimulate brain growth. A proper intake of nutritious foods and living conditions that provide emotional security and balance can affect the child's acquisition of language and her general health and resistance to disease. A preschool, child center, or learning center intent on developing language skills focuses on satisfying both physical and emotional needs while also providing intellectual opportunity and challenge by offering a variety of age-appropriate activities (Figure 4–1).

PHYSICAL GROWTH

Physical development limits or aids capabilities, thereby affecting children's perceptions of themselves, as well as the way they are treated by others. Early childhood teachers are aware of these fundamental physical changes that take place in young children. For instance, a

slightly taller, physically active, strong, and well-coordinated child who can ride a two-wheel bike and drop-kick a football may be admired by her peers. These two skills are not usually witnessed during preschool years, but occasionally a child possesses such physical skills. A wide range of physical abilities in individual children exists within preschool groups as in all developmental areas. Bergen, Reid, and Torelli (2001) describe children's physical development of the late toddler period:

> Children of this age show great achievements in gross- and fine-motor development. They are now stable walkers and enjoy going for walks of short duration. Running is a new thrill, and they may seem to go everywhere at a run. Most can climb purposefully to get a desired object out of reach, walk up and down stairs, use riding wheel toys by pushing with their feet, and "dance" to music. They can throw a ball using their whole arm but can't yet catch it. (p. 92)

Preschoolers grow at the rate of 2 to 3 inches in height and 4 to 6 pounds in weight

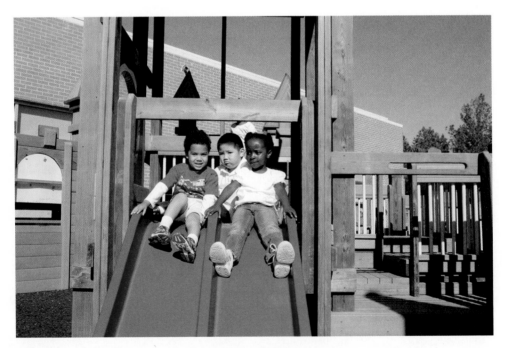

FIGURE 4–1 Outdoor structures can involve different types of physical activity.

a year. At about 18 to 24 months, the child's thumb is used in opposition to just one finger. The ability to use tools and drawing markers with a degree of skill emerges. The nutritional quality of the child's diet exerts an influence on both body and neural development. Monitoring nutrient intake, height, weight gain, and emotional well-being can alert parents to possible deficiencies.

Illness during accelerated growth may produce conditions affecting language development if it damages necessary body systems.

Hearing loss and vision difficulties impair the child's ability to receive communications and learn her native language. A brain impairment may hinder the child's ability to sort perceptions, slowing progress.

Preschools and early learning programs plan a wide range of motor activities; much of the children's time is devoted to playing with interesting equipment in both indoor and outdoor areas (Figure 4–2). The well-known benefits of a healthy mind in a healthy body should be planned for by incorporating daily physical activities that promote well-exercised and well-coordinated muscles into young children's daily programs.

FIGURE 4–2 Outdoor climbing structures can promote development of both large and small muscles.

Planned physical movement opportunities and activities prepare children for academic learning. Movement stimulates learning physiologically, and also helps young children to experience concepts so they can process them cognitively. Teachers often offer children opportunities to solve movement problems by urging them to invent their own solutions. Activities can make abstract concepts (like over and under) concrete when children physically experience them. Teachers can and should ask children to talk aloud about the motor task at hand while they are performing it, according to a study by Winsler, Manfra, and Diaz (2007):

> Findings from a present study showed overall that children from both groups (kindergarten and preschool) do indeed respond to teacher's speech instructions and that performance on motor sequencing and counting tasks improved when children are asked to speak out loud. (p. 28)

PERCEPTION

An infant's physical actions are the vehicle of knowledge. Seeing and trying to touch or act upon the environment are the work of infancy. This early physical stage precedes and develops into the child's **mental image** of her world, and this makes later verbal labeling and speech possible.

As the child matures, perceptual acuity increases; finer detail is seen. Most children achieve 20/20 vision (adult optimum) at age 14. From ages 2 to 5, vision is in the 20/45 to 20/30 range. It is estimated that 20 to 25 percent of preschoolers have some eye problem that, if uncorrected, could delay learning or cause vision loss. Experts advise families and teachers to watch for an eye that slightly turns in or out, squinting, eye closing or head turning when the child is focusing, avoidance of coloring activities or books, and clumsiness or frustration during play. Unfortunately, many eye screening

---

mental image — a "perceptual representation" or mental picture of a perceptual experience, remembered or imagined.

tests performed by school staffs, instead of pediatric eye specialists or professionals, miss an accurate diagnosis.

Hearing acuity increases from birth through ages 4 and 5. At this point, the hearing mechanisms are essentially mature and will not change greatly except through disease or injury. Ohl (2002) points out that in infancy, before babies can speak, they have already figured out many of the components of language and they know which particular sounds their language uses, what sounds can be combined to create words, and the tempo and rhythm of words and phrases. She also states that this information is important because developmental science has taught educators that there is a strong connection between early language development and reading.

> **Both oral language and reading require the same types of sound analysis. The better babies are at distinguishing the building blocks of speech at 6 months of age, the better they will be at other more complex language skills at 2 and 3 years of age, and the easier it will be for them at 4 and 5 years to grasp the idea of how sounds link to letters. (p. 2)**

Kotulak (1996) describes what happens to a child who is born deaf:

> **In a child who is born deaf, the 50,000 nerve pathways that normally would carry sound messages from the ears to the brain are silent. The sound of the human voice, so essential for brain cells to learn language, can't get through and the cells wait in vain. Finally, as the infant grows older, brain cells can wait no longer and begin looking for other signals to process, such as those from visual stimuli. (p. 27)**

Young children are noted for their desire to get their hands on what interests them. If a new child with particularly noticeable hair joins a group, hands and fingers are sure to try to explore its texture. If a teacher wears bright or shiny jewelry, some children will want to touch it. Perceptions are gathered with all sense organs. Experts believe that the main purpose of receiving, organizing, and interpreting what one encounters perceptually is to achieve constancy—a stable, constant world. Development involves changes or shifts in the way a person organizes experience and copes with the world, generally moving from simpler to more complex, from single to multiple and integrated ways of responding.

Researchers exploring infant visual preferences have pinpointed a series of changes in attention-drawing features from infancy to age 5. At approximately 2 months of age a change occurs. The child shifts from having attention captured by movement and edges of people and objects to active search and explore. Later, from age 2 to 5, children change from unsystematic exploring to systematically examining each feature carefully.

Children get better and better at focusing on one aspect of a complex situation: they become selective in focusing their attention, and they ignore the irrelevant and distracting. Life events that cause tension and anxiety can interfere with children's emerging abilities. In complex situations children do best when perceptual distractions are minimized, allowing deep concentration.

Individual differences have been noted in the way children explore their environment and react to problems. Kagan (1971) has described **conceptual tempo** to contrast the **impulsive** child, who answers quickly and may make mistakes, with the **reflective** child, who spends considerable time examining alternatives. A second difference in perception identifies field-independent and field-dependent styles of perceiving. Field-independent children are those good at ignoring irrelevant context, whereas

---

conceptual tempo — a term associated with Jerome Kagan's theory of different individual pacing in perceptual exploration of objects.
impulsive — quick to answer or react to either a simple or complex situation or problem.
reflective — taking time to weigh aspects or alternatives in a given situation.

field-dependent children tend to focus on the total context.

Visual Literacy Skill

Educators interested in visual literacy (viewing skill) describe it as a primary basic human capacity that aids learning and problem solving and that is useful across many educational disciplines—math, science, music, art, language, and so on. Visual literacy, as discussed here, involves young children's understanding and use of symbolic representation. It is not unlike Gardner's spatial-kinesthetic intellectual theory (Gardner, 2000), which focuses on relationships and the ability to notice characteristics and details that lead to ideas and conclusions.

Visual literacy refers to a group of vision competencies a human being can develop by seeing and at the same time having and integrating other sensory experiences. The development of these competencies is fundamental to normal human learning. When developed, they enable a visually literate person to discriminate and interpret the visible actions, objects, symbols, natural or man-made, that she encounters in her environment. Through the creative use of these competencies, she is able to communicate with others. Through the appreciative use of these competencies, she is able to comprehend and enjoy the masterworks of visual communication.

A preschool example of visual literacy skills at work would be the 4-year-old boy who said sadly, "Katrin (a fellow teacher and gifted story-book reader) won't be here for storytime." "Why?" his teacher asked. "She's all dressed up," the boy answered. Katrin had previously left school for a series of dental appointments. On those days the boy noticed she was dressed differently and would then leave school.

The process of visual perception involves several basic parts, including the sensing of information along dual pathways in the brain. An understanding of this process is essential to realizing the power of visual images to move us emotionally and behaviorally and to influence our conscious thought.

The educational philosophy known as the Reggio Emilia approach encourages educators to use visual literacy concepts. Educators who use this approach promote children's expression of ideas through graphic arts, using diverse media and symbol systems to make children's learning visual. The children's work can then be talked about, reflected upon, and refined. This can lead to new perspectives, new avenues of exploration and discovery, and deeper understanding.

Burmark (2002) believes visual literacy is a learned skill and discusses the learning process:

> The process of becoming visually literate is not unlike the process of learning to read. When a child first looks at words on a page, the letters and spaces are meaningless. They appear to be nothing but random shapes—little curves and lines that big people keep pointing at all the time. In time, the child begins to associate those shapes with the sounds coming out of parents' mouths, and is soon able to crack the mysterious code of meaning behind the words on the page. Verbal literacy involves a person's ability to interpret and use spoken and written language to decode the world of words. Likewise, visual literacy relates to a person's ability to interpret and create visual information—to understand images of all kinds and use them to communicate more effectively. (p.79)

The primary literacy of the twenty-first century will be visual—pictures, graphics, images of every kind—and students must learn to process both words and pictures and shift back and forth between them. Teachers can help children become more knowledgeable and more skilled in their use of verbal communications, and can also help them gain skill in using and understanding visual images. Some authors suggest early childhood educators give preference to verbal literacy and written text and de-emphasize visual thinking and learning in their curriculum planning (Karchmer, Mallette, & Leu, 2003). Children will need to know how to make meaning not just from text but also from vast amounts of information conveyed through images.

Perceptual-Motor Skills

Perceptual-motor, or sensory-motor, intelligence has been defined as an action-oriented knowledge, not to be confused with the intelligence that involves thinking and logic. The latter grows during preschool years and beyond, when children can think about and know without acting out in a physical way.

Piaget, the noted Swiss psychologist and researcher, greatly affected early childhood educators' interest in perceptual-motor activities. Piaget and others observed that automatic movements such as crying, sucking, and grasping in infants became controlled, purposeful body movements as the child grew. He speculated that physical movement served as a base for later mental abilities (Figure 4–3).

During the preschool years, the development of motor skills is as important as the development of language skills. Just as there is gradually increasing control over language, movement, and body control in the preschool years, there is also a similar continuing increase in the ability to scan new material, organize one's perception of it, remember it, and perhaps refer to it by some label or assign meaning in some other way. The close ties between motor activities and thought processes indicate that the child needs motor activity involving the five sense organs, as well as large muscle use. Exactly how much of a child's mental activity is dependent on or promoted by physical activity is unknown. Most educators of young children believe that a definite, strong connection exists between development of mental and physical skills.

Motor skill develops in an orderly, predictable, head-to-toe fashion. Head, neck, and upper-body muscles are controlled first (large muscles before small muscles), and center-of-body muscles are coordinated before extremities (fingers and toes). Handedness (left or right) is usually stable by age 5 or 6 (Figure 4–4). Child limitations can occur if motor experience is limited. A child who has had limited experience to run around, to climb, to use her body effectively in activities that demand gross motor skill, may not be ready for the finer adjustments that are required in the motor skills

FIGURE 4–3 Dancing can involve lots of body movement.

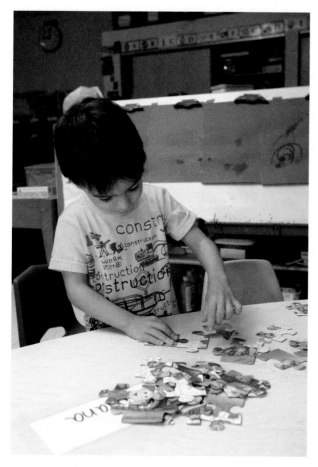

FIGURE 4–4 Manipulating small items such as puzzle pieces requires small muscle control.

of eye movement and hand-eye coordination in her early grades in school.

Montessori's approach (1967a) to educating young children stresses direct manipulation of real objects presented in sequenced form. She designed and constructed many tactile (touching) exploring materials for the young child. She explains her motives:

> The training and sharpening of the senses has the obvious advantage of enlarging the field of perception and of offering an ever more solid foundation for intellectual growth. The intellect builds up its store of practical ideas through contact with, and exploration of, its environment. Without such concepts the intellect would lack precision in its abstract operations. (p. 117)

Preschools are full of appealing equipment and programs that offer a planned approach to the development of sensory-motor skills. They are seen as integral parts of the curricula. School success in later elementary years may also be influenced by the development of perceptual-motor skill.

There seems to be no clearly accepted or defined separate place within the preschool curriculum for sensory-skill development. Some centers identify a series of sequential activities and label them perceptual or sensory-motor activities; their main goal is skill development. In other centers, every activity is seen as developing perceptual-motor skill. Commonly, music activities and physical games deal with physical coordination and endurance. Other programs plan for perceptual-motor activities within their language arts curriculum. What remains important is that this type of emphasis be part of every center's program.

This list of objectives designed to refine perceptual-motor skills is drawn from a number of schools' and centers' goal statements.

- awareness of self in space
- awareness of self in relation to objects
- flexibility
- body coordination
- posture and balance
- awareness of spatial relationships
- rhythmic body movements
- ability to identify objects and surfaces with the eyes closed
- awareness of temperatures by touch
- ability to trace form outlines with fingers
- ability to discriminate color, shapes, similar features, different features, sizes, textures, and sounds
- ability to match a wide variety of patterns and symbols
- ability to identify parts of figures or objects when a small part of a whole is presented
- eye-hand coordination
- familiarity with the following terms: same, different, long, longer, longest, small,

smaller, smallest, big, little, tall, short, wide, narrow, high, low, above, below, on, in, hard, soft, sweet, salty, sour

◆ ability to identify food by tasting
◆ ability to identify smells of various items
◆ ability to identify common sounds

Activities for Perceptual-Motor Development

It is difficult to think of one piece of preschool equipment or one activity that does not address some aspect or component of perceptual-motor development. Figure 4–5 lists perceptual-motor

EXPERIENCES DEALING WITH:	POSSIBLE MATERIALS AND EQUIPMENT
Visual Discrimination	
long, longer, longest	felt or paper strips; sticks; ribbons
small, smaller, smallest	nested boxes; blocks; buttons; measuring cups
big, little	blocks; jars; buttons; balloons; toys
tall, short	felt figures; stuffed toys
wide, narrow	pieces of cloth and paper; scraps of wood; boxes
high, low	jump rope; small ball; see-saw made from small board with tiny block in middle
above, below	felt pieces to place above and below a box with colored stones
Auditory Discrimination	
quiet, noisy	two boxes: one containing something that rattles (such as stones or beads) and one containing cloth or paper
bell sounds	bells of varying shapes and sizes for a variety of tones
falling sounds	feather; leaf; stone; block of wood; cotton
shaking sounds	maracas; baby rattle; pebbles inside coffee can
musical sounds	variety of rhythm instruments
Tactile Discrimination	
textures	sandpaper; tissue; stone; waxed paper; tree bark; velvet; wool; fur; cotton
outline of shapes	thin wooden circle, square, triangle, rectangle; letters cut from sandpaper
recognition of objects	four different-shaped objects, each tied in end of sock—children guess what each is by feeling it (change objects often)
hard, soft	handkerchief; rock; cotton batting; nail; sponge
Taste Discrimination	
identifying food: sweet, salty, sour	small jars: filled with salt, sugar, unsweetened lemonade
trying new foods	variety of vegetables children may not know; samples of fruit juices; honey, molasses, maple syrup
Smell Discrimination	
identifying object by smell	cake of soap; vial of perfume; pine sprig; onion; vials of kitchen spices; orange
Kinesthetic Discrimination	
lifting, racing downhill, swinging, throwing, running, jumping, climbing, bending, stretching, twisting, turning, spinning, balancing	yard and motor play materials

FIGURE 4–5 Perceptual activities.

development activities and equipment, gathered from a broad range of early childhood books and sources. It can serve as a beginning.

COGNITIVE DEVELOPMENT

There are major, opposing views concerning the link between language and thought. One view is that language is the foundation of thought and vital to a person's awareness of the world. Another view suggests that language is dependent on thinking; as intelligence grows, language grows, reflecting thoughts. Vygotsky (1980) has influenced early childhood educators' beliefs by theorizing that language is an actual mechanism for thinking, a mental tool. Language makes thinking more abstract, flexible, and independent from immediate stimuli. It is difficult to determine which of these ideas is closer to the truth, but most educators will agree that language and thought are closely associated.

Many researchers believe very young children, including preschool children, are much more capable of learning than previously thought. The reason that young children's cognitive development and rapid learning curve may have been underestimated is that young children are learning seemingly ordinary things encountered in everyday activities and play. Gopnik (1999) suggests that adults should not assume that children will simply soak up needed knowledge from their environment, but rather, adults can provide "gentle lessons," building language skills and basic numerical understandings (Figure 4–6). Educators who disagree with Gopnik's views may believe that because children are capable learners, it is more important for educators to promote and provide for children's self-discovery.

As the child's brain grows, it is reorganized by experience. Experience changes the brain, but then those very changes alter the way new experience affects the brain. Children who have been passive viewers of life (through electronic media) rather than active listeners (explorers and conversationalists) may lack practice in both auditory analysis and logical and sequential reasoning skills, many experts believe.

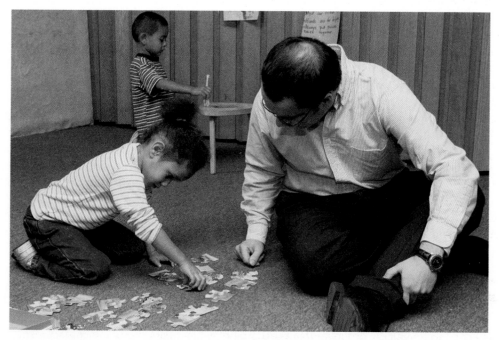

FIGURE 4–6 The adult's words accompany the child's activity choices at times.

Greenspan (1999) suggests that perhaps the most critical role for emotions is to create, organize, and orchestrate many of the mind's most important functions. He states:

> In fact, intellect, academic abilities, sense of self, consciousness, and morality have common origins in our earliest and ongoing emotional experiences. (p. 197)

Greenspan (1999) presents educators with what he perceives to be the fundamental sequential building blocks of mental growth based on human beings' capacity to experience emotions. They include the ability to

- attend.
- engage.
- be intentional.
- form complex, interactive, intentional patterns.
- create images, symbols, and ideas.
- connect images and symbols.*

The idea that the reciprocal emotionally charged interactions between infants and young children and caregivers influence their cognitive development is not new, but increasingly it is given close attention by anyone caring for the very young.

Problem solving has been associated with "literacy behaviors" that come before conventional reading and writing. Once children become higher-level symbolic thinkers, they are able to piece together the mental processes used in everyday problem solving with the symbols needed for reading and writing.

Classifying Information

Intellect is rooted in each particular child's stored perceptual and sensory-motor experiences. Each child interprets happenings and

*From Greenspan, S. I. (1997). Growth of the mind and the endangered origins of intelligence. Copyright © 1997. Reprinted by permission of Da Capo Press, a member of Perseus Books Group.

attempts to connect each to what she already knows. If it fits, the child understands and it all falls together. An example of this might be seen if one watches a 9-month-old learn to make noise come out of a toy plastic horn. At first, the child has no knowledge of how the horn works. When she first blows into it and it makes a toot, the child blows into it repeatedly (and usually happily). After that, the child knows how to toot the horn. Infants, toddlers, and preschoolers can be thought of as having mental groupings (classes and categories). They **classify** what they encounter, including events, people, and objects, before they have words for them. The 9-month-old just described probably has no word associated with what the child knows about the horn. Each mental grouping is distinguished by a set of distinctive features, and objects yet to be classified are examined for the presence of these features. If the horn-blowing infant reacts by trying to blow into a new toy horn of a similar shape, one can be relatively sure the child is forming a class of "horn" mentally. One can expect that this infant will try blowing into any horn shape that comes her way. Later, a word or language symbol can be attached to a class or category, which makes it possible for the child to communicate about what the class or category means to the child or how the child feels about it. Simple words like *doggie, milk,* or *ball* may be among children's earliest categories of the world around them.

Preschool teachers readily see differences between the feelings and meanings expressed by each child. For example, the way that a child reacts when meeting a new large animal may demonstrate what she knows and feels about large animals. Another child's reaction might be entirely opposite.

Putting events and experiences into classes and categories is innate—a natural mental process. The motivation to engage actively with the environment—to make contact, to have an impact, and to make sense of experience—is built into human beings. The mind yearns for

---

classify — the act of systematically grouping things according to identifiable common characteristics, for example, size.

order, and knowledge is built within from what is experienced. Children construct theories or hypotheses about objects and phenomena by putting things into relationships. A child's knowledge is constantly changing, for children are curious and are constantly searching for a variety of experience, fighting to overcome boredom. A new or novel idea or event may greatly affect a child by adding to or changing all a child knows and feels on a particular subject.

As a child's language ability develops, mental classes, categories, and concepts are represented symbolically by words. Words become an efficient shortcut that eliminates the need to act out by gesturing or signaling to make something known to another. Thoughts can be analyzed and evaluated internally as the child grows older. If there exists a common language system between the child and others, it can be used to reveal the child's unique self (Figure 4–7).

Piaget's (1952) terms **assimilation** and **accommodation** describe what happens when infants and children experience something new. Each individual unconsciously structures (internally builds and organizes) what is perceived. If a new experience or event is perceived, it is assimilated into what already mentally existed. If it changes or modifies those existing structures (ideas or thought patterns), the new is accommodated. In other words, children attend to features that make sense to them, and learning involves adding to what is already known or modifying (changing) what is known.

An example of a child trying to make sense of her experience follows:

> . . . after a visit to the hospital to see her dying great-grandmother who was over 90, Amy (age 4) commented, "Ya know, Dad, the Brooklyn Bridge is pretty old. It's going to die soon!" In her struggle to understand life and death, Amy had made a connection between the Brooklyn Bridge and her great-grandmother.

Although children use words that adults know and recognize, the knowledge behind children's words often carries quite a different meaning and understanding.

FIGURE 4–7 Group play exposes children to the ideas of others.

assimilation — the process that allows new experiences to merge with previously stored mental structures.
accommodation — the process by which new experiences or events change existing ideas or thought patterns.

Different Levels of Maturity

The human brain's cortex contains two differently specialized hemispheres. Each hemisphere appears designed for unique functions, different abilities, and styles of thought, including verbal and spatial thinking. Different brain areas are well defined and possess a rich concentration of certain abilities that are not equal among children (Figure 4–8). Naturally, the brain structures of some children may be developing more slowly than those of others, which might affect their ability to learn and may cause teachers to compare them unfairly with children of the same age who have developed more quickly. Consequently, teachers need to pay special attention to how they act when comparing children. Competitive, pressurized lessons can create an unhealthy "I'm not good (smart) enough" attitude that can be self-perpetuating.

Preschool children's statements that seem to be "errors in thinking" on the surface can, on deeper analysis, be seen as quite mature and understandable, not just random guesses. When a child says a camel is a horse with a hump, she should be given credit for seeing the similarity rather than merely corrected.

The child's fantasy world, which appears and is expressed in speech, should be seen as a giant intellectual leap (Figure 4–9). Make-believe is

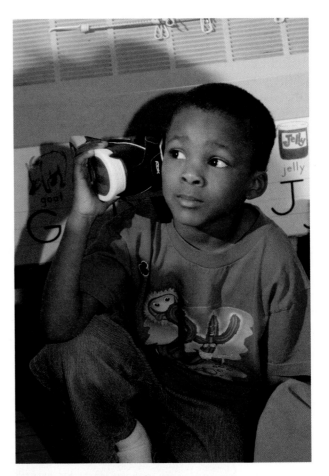

FIGURE 4–9 DelJon's pretend cell phone is his shoe.

1. seeking information (focusing)
2. seeking word labels (concept building)
3. naming, classifying, categorizing, and grouping experiences mentally—objects, ideas, etc. (general to specific; revising concepts)
4. responding and remembering (memorizing and recalling)
5. comparing and contrasting information (abstracting)
6. making inferences and predicting in general ways (predicting)
7. generalizing (inductive thinking)
8. applying known information to new situations (transferring)
9. making hypotheses (educated guesses) and predicting in specific ways (deductive thinking)

FIGURE 4–8 The child's emerging intellectual skills.

internal intellectual creation and/or recreation. A preschooler may say she is someone else—most often this someone else is a hero of sorts or an admired personage, usually from the movies, videos, television, or real life. There may be days when the child wishes to assume the name and identity of a friend or animal. Many children during preschool can readily follow story sequences and identify with book characters. An in-depth discussion of preschoolers and books is found in Chapter 9.

Teachers need to realize that there are differences between adult concepts and child concepts. The child's view of the world is usually based on immediate, present happenings and beginning thought processes. A child's speech is full of many unique misconceptions, conclusions, and errors (as judged by adult standards). These errors arise because of each child's unique way of sorting out experiences—a continuous process of trying to make sense and order out of daily events. Errors based on just a few happenings may be quite logical conclusions. For example, a child may conclude that milk comes from the store, or, when looking at an *n*, that it is a "baby m."

The Teacher's Role

Teachers who work with infants, toddlers, and preschoolers realize that sensory-motor experiences and opportunities with people, toys, and room environments are early intellect-building events. Exploring and experimenting are enhanced by adult provision of materials and equipment. At some point, teachers realize that some actions look as though the child thought first and then acted. At about 10 months, some infants seem to be majoring in dropping and emptying. They drop things from high-chair trays and watch the objects fall, or put things into containers, drawers, or boxes and empty and refill these over and over. One has to smile and think of very young infants as active scientists.

When working with 2-year-olds and young 3-year-olds, teachers notice a good deal of voiced external speech that accompanies play. This speech enables the child to order and organize his or her thoughts, plan and develop solutions, and come to conclusions. A "zone of proximal development" is what Vygotsky (1980) calls the area between what the child can solve alone when faced with problems and experience, and what the child can possibly solve or come to know with the help of adults or more experienced, knowing children. When adults name and explain happenings and talk about relationships, this is seen as a stimulant to both language and mental growth. A teacher trying to put into practice Vygotsky's theories would try to talk with children, becoming a catalyst who names, discusses, and prompts children's exploration and expression of what they have discovered or formulated (Figure 4–10). It is

FIGURE 4–10 Teachers may act as an interested "sounding board" that encourages the child's expression of what he has discovered.

also important that adults know when not to interrupt children's thoughts when they are deeply engaged in play. Dialogue makes much more sense when children seek adult help or when they are companions in activities.

In promoting what children will store (learn and remember), teachers deal with both meaning and feelings. Each intellect-building encounter and interaction with children starts with the adult's supportive acceptance and caring. Purposeful teacher dialogue is often part of child-teacher exchanges. Its goal is to advance further discovery or to help put the discovery or experience into words. A teacher listens and observes closely. This listening may expose aspects of the child's thinking, logic, inner concepts, and feelings.

Working with children daily, teachers strive to understand the logic and correctness behind children's statements. The balance a teacher maintains between gently correcting false impressions and having children discover what they have not understood for themselves is not easy to maintain. Of course, there are many instances in which a child's or another's safety and health could be at risk; at times like these the adult cannot possibly let a child discover the consequences of her actions or lack of action.

As children try to make sense of happenings and experiences, teachers can expect to be asked questions. Four-year-olds can ask hundreds of questions on any given day. Teachers sometimes answer a question with a question. Skillful questioning and sensitive responses from the teacher preserve a child's feelings about expressing worthwhile ideas and make the child more willing to speak and share. These are some examples:

- "I can see you want to have a turn talking too, Emma, and I want to hear you."

- "Would you tell us, Jacob, about the boat you put together this morning?"

- "You thought of a different way to make a hole in your paper; perhaps your friends would like to hear about it."

- "Shayne, you wanted to know how our hamster got out of his cage. Can you see an opening he might have squeezed through?"

- "Did anyone see what happened to Yang's shoe?"

- "I wonder if there's a way for three people to share two pairs of scissors."

Teachers can support children as they converse by encouraging them to step outside their own perceptions to become aware of larger, more generalized patterns in the things they observe. The processes of questioning, predicting, and testing possibilities can be learned firsthand as children solve their own problems. Early childhood educators facilitate children's ability to come to their own conclusions and relate those conclusions to observable evidence, if possible. A teacher may also ask children to compare their ideas with one another in group conversations.

Children may gain **metalinguistic skills** during the preschool years. They are then able to "think about language." Many play with language and words and make comparisons between spoken and written words. Others may be able to analyze words into individual parts and judge what is correct word usage and what is not.

SOCIAL AND EMOTIONAL GROWTH

Interaction with other people is always a major factor in a child's language learning. Children who have positive feelings about themselves—feelings of self-value and security—speak frequently. New contacts with adults outside the home run smoothly as the child branches out from the home.

Feelings and emotions are part of each human conversation. A child's feelings toward adults are generalized to teachers in the early school years. The parent-child bond and its influence on language learning is overwhelming, and unfortunately early educators meet children

---

metalinguistic skills — the ability to think about language as a separate entity.

who don't feel comfortable with adults or groups of other children.

During preschool years, children form ideas of self-identity. It becomes difficult for children to believe in themselves—or their language abilities—if self-esteem is constantly undermined. Figure 4–11 suggests teacher behavior and response in communicating with children to promote social growth.

Erikson (1950) identified a series of social-emotional developments in the young child, which are presented in a shortened form here.

- (Infants) Trust vs. Mistrust. Trust develops from consistent care, which fulfills basic needs (food, warmth, physical contact, and so on), leading to stable and secure feelings rather than anxiousness. A positive view of life forms.

- (Toddlers and two-year-olds) Autonomy vs. Shame and Doubt. Children get to know themselves as separate persons. What they control, decisions they can make, and freedom they may have while still being very dependent become apparent. Awareness of inabilities and helplessness is sensed. Behavior may be testing and full of the word "no."

- (Preschoolers) Initiative vs. Guilt Feelings. Experimentation and active exploration of new skills and directions occur. There are strong emotions at times in resistance to authority figures and rules, yet children are still dependent on adult approval. (p. 145)*

Social development must not be ignored in planning and conducting language activities or in trying to manage groups. Structure and rules are necessary for group living. An individual child's status in the eyes of the group can be enhanced through the sharing and appreciation of the child's ideas and accomplishments and by providing frequent opportunities for the child to lead or help lead the group in activities, which is almost always a confidence and status-building experience.

Teachers should be concerned with a child's **social connectedness**—a term that has been defined as characteristic of people with stable and secure lives, supportive families and friends, and close ties to community and who are accepted as a worthy part of a group and are able to weather life's stresses with a sense of individual identity. A teacher is in control of a school's atmosphere and works with the home and community, thus plays a large role in the development of this aspect of a child's personality.

Preschoolers begin to learn labels for feelings, such as happy, sad, jealous, fearful, and so on. They begin to think of others' feelings. The conscience is forming, and interest in right and wrong is expressed. Teachers who speak of their

In communication, the teacher:
- cares and is ready to give of self.
- listens, intent on understanding.
- adds simple words when the child cannot.
- does not correct speech when this might break down willingness to speak further.
- is available for help in clarifying ideas or suggesting new play and exploring possibilities.
- senses child interests and guides to new real experiences.
- is available when problems and conflicts happen.
- enjoys time spent in child activities.
- establishes friendships with each child.
- talks positively about each child's individual uniqueness.
- is an enthusiastic and expressive communicator.
- offers friendly support while redirecting undesirable social behavior or stating rules.
- notices and respects each child's work.

FIGURE 4–11 Teacher behaviors that are helpful to the child's social growth.

*From Erikson, E. (1950). *Childhood and society*. Copyright © 1950, © 1963 by W. W. Norton & Company, Inc., renewed © 1978, 1991 by Erik H. Erikson. Used by permission of W. W. Norton & Company, Inc.

social connectedness — a term associated with the following human characteristics: is stable and secure, develops close relationships with others, has supportive family and friends, and is deemed a worthy individual by others. Often seen by others as able to transcend stress and possess an individual identity.

own feelings as adults set an example and provide a climate in which children's feelings are also accepted and understood.

Most children explore social actions and reactions. They have a strong desire to spend time with their peers (Figure 4–12). They want to have friends, and in play, they learn to make plans, negotiate, and communicate. Strong emotions accompany much of children's behavior; their total beings speak. When a child feels left out, life becomes an overwhelming tragedy; on the other hand, a party invitation may be a time to jump for joy.

It is through symbolic and pretend play that young children are most likely to develop both socially and intellectually. Opportunities for spontaneous child-initiated social play need to rate high on a center's agenda. The following

list identifies activities that can help children develop a sense of self. These are just a few suggestions; many more are possible.

◆ activities using mirrors
◆ activities using children's photographs and home movies
◆ tracings of the child's outline
◆ activities that involve making name tags and placing names on belongings, drawings, lockers, and projects
◆ activities that identify and discuss feelings
◆ activities concerned with personal opinions
◆ activities that show both similarity to others and individual diversity
◆ activities that build pride or membership in a group
◆ activities that identify favorite pursuits, objects, or individual choices
◆ small group activities involving cooperation

The following is a list of social abilities that serve as a strong foundation for future schooling. Children should be able to

◆ get and hold the attention of adults in a variety of socially accepted ways.
◆ express affection or mild annoyance to adults and peers when appropriate.
◆ use adults as resources after determining that a task is too difficult to handle alone.
◆ show pride in achievement.
◆ lead and follow children of the same age.
◆ compete with age-mates.

Teachers strive to supply a center atmosphere in which a sense of trust and security thrives. Children need to learn to trust people in their world, or else they reject all that these people want to teach them. They need to have faith in those who respect them and accept their feelings, and learn to trust themselves.

Securely attached infants, those who have received responsive and developmentally appropriate care, emerge as confident, energetic toddlers with beginning awareness of self as a

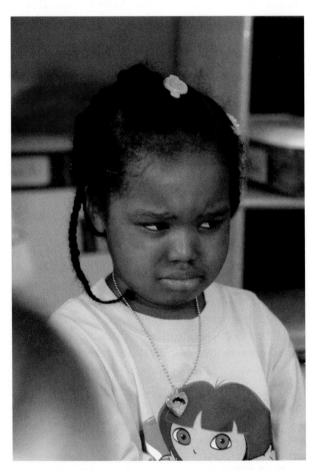

FIGURE 4–12 Being left out feels like the end of the world.

person. Imitative play, self-pretending play, and play that models emotions (hugging or spanking dolls) appear during the child's second year. Empathy for others who are hurt or crying may also be displayed.

As children age, self-acts can be talked about and judged by the child. The author once met a young 3-year-old boy who would sit himself in a chair if he thought he had misbehaved (for example, if he had purposely bumped another with a bike, pushed another, taken another's toy). He would sit only a few moments, and then happily resume play. This type of guidance technique was not used by the staff, but at home, sitting in the "thinking chair" was a common occurrence. The center staff respected the child's behavior and watchfully intervened when behavior warranted urging the child's use of words to solve problems. The child's chair-sitting behavior slowly disappeared as he learned to ask for a turn and gained new social skills.

Whether young children see themselves as "valued identities" depends on their interactions with their care providers and families. The child whose confidence stems from the security of feeling loved, valued, and appreciated as an individual is a child who continues to communicate. Adults contribute greatly to the ever-maturing view the child has of herself.

SUMMARY

Physical, intellectual, and social-emotional growth proceeds concurrently with the child's speech. Understanding these growth systems allows teachers to use appropriate techniques and behaviors. Child characteristics and teacher-provided growth opportunities are included in Figure 4–13.

Perceptual-motor activities are an integral part of many centers' language arts programs. Many educators believe that there is a strong correlation between physical activity during this period and mental growth. Some educators present visual literacy activities to preschoolers,

CHILD CHARACTERISTICS	TEACHER-PROVIDED GROWTH OPPORTUNITIES
• curiosity • ability to learn • interest in what affects the child personally • focus on here and now • intellectual activity • social involvement • physical energy • symbolic thinking • language growth • emotionally "charged" • growth is in spurts with parallel and uneven growth possible in different growth areas	• varied, firsthand experience with abundant sensory materials, objects, and media • teacher enthusiasm for learning • time to explore and make own discoveries • language arts activities • planned program with developmentally appropriate activities and age-suitable classrooms and play yards • supportive assistance when pursuing a line of inquiry • an environment that encourages the development of the child's sense of trust • caring adults and a safe, secure environment • activities and routines to satisfy physical, intellectual, social, and emotional needs • cultural respect and dignity • play with peers • knowledgeable adults who take a personal interest in each individual child's welfare and growth • opportunities for child-initiated project work

*Note: This figure is not intended to be complete but rather to offer highlights of chapter text.

FIGURE 4–13 Growth and opportunity.

believing visual literacy is a learned skill (Figure 4–14).

Adults need to react to and sense the correctness of what seem to be errors in children's thinking. Guiding the child's discovery of concepts is an integral part of early childhood teaching.

A child who trusts can learn. Teachers must accept children's feelings and concentrate on establishing bonds between themselves and the children. This encourages growth of abilities. The feeling tone that lies beneath each human contact and conversation creates a setting for learning.

VISUAL LITERACY ACTIVITIES

- Read Ellen Stoll Walsh's *Mouse paint* (1999, New York: Harcourt/Red Wagon Books [board book]), which discusses how useful color can be.
- Chart color choices. Offer shell pasta that has been colored with yellow, blue, red, and green food coloring. Chart children's choice of the best one to eat. Discuss.
- Display child art with a word in 2- to 3-inch letters that closely connect. Ask children for a word that "talks" for her art. "Does your artwork need a word to go with it?" "If your painting could talk, what would it say?"
- Make graphs. Example: How many came to school in a car or bus, walked, or biked? What kind of pets do we have—dog, cat, bird, turtle?
- Use visual cards as a transition devise. The card selected by the child is the place she chooses to go next. (Book for library area, block for block area, paint can with brush for art area, etc.)
- Find round, square, and triangular objects in illustrations or photos.
- Create a flower garden wall display with a photo of a child's face or child's name in the center of each flower. Children can make flowers using various media.
- Make a "Guess-What-I-Am?" flannel board set using simply shaped objects such as a house, tree, scissors, hat, and so on. Make all shapes with no details and use the same color.
- Line up three photos and have children guess what story they tell.
- Post photographs or images representing honesty, empathy, kindness, helpfulness, beauty, work, responsibility, and so on, that expand children's understanding of human characteristics. Discuss one characteristic daily.
- After a story is read and is familiar, decide how it could be told with pictures, in dance, or with clay instead of using words.
- Collect photos or illustrations of happy, sad, frightened, and so on, multicultural faces. Discuss ones that go together and what emotion is present.

FIGURE 4–14 Visual literacy activities.

ADDITIONAL RESOURCES

Readings

Burmark, L. (2002). *Visual literacy: Learn to see, see to learn.* Alexandria, VA: Association for Supervision and Curriculum Development.

Elias, M., Zins, J., Weisberg, R., Frey, K., Greenberg, M., Haynes, N., Kessler, K., Schwab-Stone, M., & Shriver, T. (1997). *Promoting social and emotional learning: Guidelines for educators.* Alexandria, VA: Association for Supervision and Curriculum Development.

Honig, A. S., & Wittmer, D. S. (1996, January*).* Helping children become more prosocial: Ideas for classrooms, families, schools, and communities. *Young Children, 51*(2), 31–39.

Jensen, E. (2000). *Learning with the body in mind.* San Diego: The Brain Store.

Notari-Syverson, A., O'Connor, R. E., & Vadasy, P. F. (2007). *Ladders to literacy.* Baltimore, MD: Brookes Publishing Co.

Helpful Websites

International Visual Literacy Association (IVLA)
http://www.ivla.org
Contains articles and information on research and conferences.

National Child Care Information Center (NCCIC)
http://www.nccic.org
Lists ages and stages of growth.

National Institute of Mental Health
http://www.nimh.nih.gov
Outlines risk factors affecting social and emotional development and readiness for school. Search the site by using key words Good Start.

Book Companion Website

Use an observational checklist to determine if a classroom promotes both language and cognitive growth or complete an exercise about providing for children's intellectual needs. Conducting an individual research study dealing with stereotypical girl or boy behaviors using an interviewing strategy is suggested. The highlights of *The Boys and Girls Learn Differently* are covered in a book report on the website.

STUDENT ACTIVITIES

1. Observe young children (2- to 4-years-old) in a public place (restaurant, laundromat, grocery store, park, bus, department store). What do the children seem to notice, and how do they investigate what they notice? Write down those environmental objects, people, and so on, and what features capture children's interest (for example, sound, color, texture).

2. Using the chalkboard or a large piece of newsprint (or shelf paper), list, with a small group of other students, the teacher behaviors that might develop a sense of trust and build children's self-esteem.

3. Plan and conduct two activities with preschool children that concentrate on a perceptual-motor skill. Report your successes and failures to the group.

4. With your eyes closed, identify three objects given to you by another person.

5. Pair with another student. Taking turns, have one person take three personal articles and place them on the table or desk in front of the other person. Try to categorize these articles. How many objects can you put in the same category? Can you find a category that includes all of the items?

CHAPTER REVIEW

A. Describe children's development of physical skill, and react to the statement "Physical skills have little effect or influence on young children's language skills."

B. Choose the category that fits best, and code the following words with the headings (1) perceptual-motor development, (2) social-emotional development, or (3) mental development.

1. trust	6. categorizing	11. security
2. concepts	7. predicting	12. generalizing
3. tasting	8. avoiding people	13. balance
4. self-awareness	9. eye-hand skill	14. conscience
5. self-image	10. body image	15. abstracting

C. Read the following teacher behaviors and verbalizations. Write the numbers of those you think would help a child develop healthy social-emotional skills.

1. Recognizing each child by name as the child enters.

2. Pointing out (to others) a child's inability to sit still.

3. Telling a child it is all right to hate you.

4. Keeping a child's special toy safe.

5. Encouraging a child's saying, "I'm not finished," when another child grabs his or her toy.

6. Saying, "Jerome (child) thinks we should ask the janitor, Mr. Smith, to eat lunch with us."

7. Saying, "Hitting makes me angry. It hurts."

8. Planning activities that are either "girls only" or "boys only."

9. Encouraging children who show kindness to others.

10. Allowing a child to make fun of another child and then neglecting to speak to the first "fun maker" about it.

11. Changing the rules and rewards often.

12. Ignoring an irritating behavior that seems to be happening more frequently.

D. Discuss children's vision and hearing acuity and perception during preschool years.

E. Choose the best answer.

1. Most centers agree that perceptual-skill development belongs
   a. somewhere in the program.
   b. in the language arts area.
   c. in the music and physical education area.
   d. to a separate category of activities.

2. The younger the child, the more the child needs
   a. demonstration activities.
   b. to be told about the properties of objects.
   c. sensory experience.
   d. enriching child conversations.

3. Trust usually _____ being able to risk and explore, when considering early child-hood school attendance.
   a. follows
   b. combines
   c. is dependent on
   d. comes before

4. Young children's thinking is focused on
   a. firsthand current happenings.
   b. abstract symbols.
   c. pleasing adults for rewards.
   d. the consequences of their behavior.

5. There is a _____ relationship between language and thought.
   a. well-understood
   b. well-researched
   c. clear
   d. cloudy

VISUAL DISCRIMINA-TION GAMES

1. Children find hidden objects in illustrations or photographs in this activity. Hide cutouts of different shapes made from any adhesive paper in illustrations or photographs. Example: Cut out geometric shapes and simple object shapes (dog, cat, hat, glove, ball, bat, flower, and so on); then stick shapes in a scene cut from a magazine or in a drawing you have created. Ink stamping set shapes or commercial stickers also work. Make a key sheet using duplicate hidden shapes on a blank sheet so that children know what they are looking for. Children can circle or color the object when found.

2. Find objects in the same category, such as food, clothing, shoes, hats, flowers, bugs, cars, and so forth, in a picture book, magazine, or catalog. Example: "Let's see how many different hats we can find."

3. Make a set of index cards onto which you have pasted pictures of food items. Make other categories on other index cards. Mix them up. Paste an item from each category into a medium-sized department-store gift box lid, then sort the index cards into the box lids according to category.

RESOURCES FOR ACTIVITIES AND GAMES

ABB Creations
http://www.itchysalphabet.com
A commercial source for sticker sets, game cards, and alphabet strips.

Treetop Publishing
http://www.barebooks.com
This site has blank, precut puzzles for making photograph puzzles and also supplies stickers, blank books, and game boards. Sticker sheets are available in bugs, cats, dogs, fish, and animals. These can be used to make visual matching games.

Developing Language Arts Programs

CHAPTER 5

Understanding Differences

OBJECTIVES

After reading this chapter, you should be able to:

◆ Discuss Standard and non-Standard English.

◆ Describe the teacher's role with children who speak a dialect.

◆ Discuss early childhood centers' language programs for second-language learners.

◆ Identify common speech problems.

KEY TERMS

accent

auditory processing

bilingual

Black English

cluttering

culture

deafness

deficit perspective

dialect

Ebonics

hearing disabilities

otitis media

scaffolding

selective (elective) mutism

speech and language disabilities

Standard English

subculture

A PROBLEM SOLVED

It was the first song at circle time.

> Good morning, I like the shoes you've got on. / In fact, I like 'em so much, I'm gonna put 'em in a song. / In a song, in a song, / I'm gonna put you and your shoes in a song.

A boy asked if we could put hair in. "Good morning, I like the hair you've got on. . . ." The boy stopped singing. We finished the verse. The boy leaned toward me and said quietly, "But what about Mr. Baker?" "Who's Mr. Baker?" I asked. The boy lifted one hand from his lap and pointed to his left. I saw Mr. Baker, one of the father volunteers who came to tell stories. He was totally bald and trying not to laugh. None of the children found it funny. To leave Mr. Baker out was not funny. A girl whispered loudly to the boy, "Say skin." He leaned toward me and said, "Sing skin this time." The cloud left the boy's face . . . and Mr. Baker gave him a thumbs-up, as if to celebrate another problem solved (Hunter, 2003).

QUESTIONS TO PONDER

1. What is this reading an example of?

2. Could this vignette's song be used in a planned unit of study on diversity? If so, explain how?

3. What do you like about this song activity?

The United States is a multicultural society. It is a vast array of people of different backgrounds and ethnicities. Members of families may be married, remarried, single, gay, straight, birthparents, adoptive parents, and/or unrelated individuals. These families have broken almost all traditional rules for what makes a family but continue to affirm the most basic definition of family: a bond reinforced by love and caring.

Experienced teachers throughout the United States report that the children they teach are more diverse in their backgrounds, experiences, and abilities than were those they taught in the past. Projections suggest that by the year 2025, more than half of the children enrolled in America's school will be members of "minority" groups, not of European-American origin.

The National Assessment of Education Progress, known as the nation's report card, shows an alarming trend. The gap between affluent and poorer students in the United States has widened on important indicators, such as scores on reading, math, and science. In schools in high-poverty areas, 70 percent of children scored below even the most basic level of reading (Alexander, 2004).

Early childhood programs and elementary grade levels are experiencing an influx of Spanish-speaking children in parts of the country with little or no history of ethnic or racial diversity—a trend that is expected to continue at an increasing rate. Barnett, Yarosz, Thomas, Jung, & Blanco (2007) describe expected numbers of English language learners (ELLs):

> The number of children in the United States is growing rapidly, and the vast majority are from homes where Spanish is the primary language (Tabors, Paez, & Lopez, 2003). This trend is even stronger at the preschool level. Hispanic children account for more than 20% of all children under five (Collins & Ribeiro, 2004). Moreover, Hispanic children are more highly represented in public preschool programs because they are more likely to be income eligible for such programs. About 30% of the Head Start population is Hispanic. In the public schools, about 25% of preschool children are Hispanic (Smith, Kleiner, Parsad, & Farris, 2003). Head Start data indicate that Spanish is the dominate language for three-quarters of these children. (p. 277)

Language-minority students are expected to comprise over 40 percent of the school-aged population by 2030.

More children enter school with addictions, diseases, and disorders such as fetal alcohol syndrome, and without having had sufficient sleep, food, or supervision at home. Teachers have found themselves virtually unprepared to deal with the vastly different linguistic and life experiences and abilities of language-diverse children (Figure 5–1).

Early childhood educators recognize that extra efforts made early in some young children's lives can prevent problems with learning to read. Children who are poor, nonwhite, and nonnative speakers are considered much more likely to fail to learn to read adequately.

Early childhood programs and elementary schools are examining older, traditional curriculum and teaching techniques. Quite simply, our school populations have changed. Children deserve teachers and administrators who value diversity and recognize its presence in the classroom. As with other educators, you will be searching for ways to meet young children's varied educational needs.

For many language-limited or language-diverse young children, play opens children to expression; it should be an integral part of any early childhood program. Barrett (2003) has reviewed research concerning preschool enrollment and later reading achievement. A summary of his findings follows.

> Preschool programs can have an important short-term impact on general cognitive development and academic abilities including reading achievement. Effects appear to be larger for intensive, high-quality educational programs targeting children in poverty.

> Long-term findings included the following comments. School success (primarily grade repetition and special education placement) is dependent on verbal abilities; particularly reading plays an important role in accessing new knowledge

FIGURE 5–1 Ethnic and cultural diversity is commonplace in America's classrooms.

from textbook readings and other schoolwork. (p. 57)

Barrett concluded that preschool education in a variety of forms improves general cognitive abilities during early childhood and produces long-term increases in reading achievement. He also notes that additional research on learning and teaching in the early years could provide more guidance for teachers regarding the most productive approaches to the development of abilities and dispositions that facilitate later achievement in reading and other subject-matter areas. The National Early Literacy Panel's research on early literacy education is discussed in Chapter 6.

CHILD-FOCUSED AND CHILD-SENSITIVE APPROACHES

Au (2006) describes what is important to consider when a classroom includes children of diverse backgrounds. Establishing positive relationships with children is key:

It may be helpful for the teacher to have an understanding of the students' cultural backgrounds and the values they bring to school. Once positive relationships and open communication have been established, students will accept the teacher as a role model and as a model of literate behavior. (p. 197)

Program planners are experimenting and refining instructional models. These new approaches are described as child-focused and child-sensitive approaches (Figure 5–2).

A safe classroom environment using these approaches is one that respects differences and uniqueness and energizes young children's ability to communicate desires, fears, and understandings.

The NAEYC (1996) has recommended the following:

For the optimal development and learning of all children, educators must accept the legitimacy of children's home language, respect (hold in high regard) and value (esteem, appreciate) the home culture, and promote and encourage the active involvement and support of all families, including extended and nontraditional family units. (p. 42)

KIDS ARE DIFFERENT

Kids are different
They don't even look the same
Some kids speak different languages
They all have a different name
Kids are different
But if you look *INSIDE* you'll see
The one with brown hair, black hair, red hair
or blond hair,
Is just like you and me.

Author Unknown

FIGURE 5–2 Wall chart.

Young children explore, question, predict, discover, and interact with their early childhood teachers, who are bent on fostering natural curiosity by serving as fellow explorers, feedback agents, providers of opportunity, and facilitators of children's emerging language abilities.

Teachers realize that children whose language skills or patterns are different are just as intelligent and capable as those who speak Standard English. Before discussing language differences, it is important to clarify the intent of this book. The purpose here is to assist teachers (1) to help the children and (2) to help in such a way that it will not actually make matters worse. The teacher's sensitivity to and knowledge of a particular cultural group and its different language patterns can aid a particular child's growth. Preserving the child's feelings of adequacy and acceptance is the teacher's prime goal; moving the child toward the eventual learning of standard forms is a secondary goal.

Early childhood educators strive, through professional associations, individual efforts, and attention to standards, to increase program quality. In doing so, each center needs to examine its program to ensure language learning is not seen as occurring only at language time but from the moment teachers greet each child at the beginning of the day. Every child-adult interaction holds potential for child language learning. The key question is whether each child is receiving optimum opportunity during group care to listen and speak with a savvy adult skilled in natural conversation that reinforces, expands, and extends.

Language acquisition is more than learning to speak; it is a process through which a child becomes a competent member of a community by acquiring both the linguistics and sociocultural knowledge needed to learn how to use language in that particular community. It is particularly important that every individual have equal access to educational and economic opportunity, especially those from groups who have consistently been found on the bottom of the educational, social, and economic heap: African-Americans, Latinos, Mexican-Americans, and Native American people.

STANDARD ENGLISH

Standard English is the language of elementary schools and textbooks. It is the language of the majority of people in the United States. Increasingly, preschool programs are confronted with children whose speech reflects different past experiences and a cultural (or subcultural) outlook that is different from the majority. When attending a preschool or center, these children, by practicing and copying the group's way of speaking, become aware of the group's values, attitudes, food preferences, clothing styles, and so on, and gain acceptance as group members. Some theorize that group membership influences children's manner of thinking about life's experiences.

Standard English usage is advantageous and a unifying force that brings together cultures within cultures, thereby minimizing class differences.

Dialect, as used here, refers to language patterns that differ from Standard American

---

Standard English — substantially uniform formal and informal speech and writing of educated people that is widely recognized as acceptable wherever English is spoken and understood.
dialect — a variety of spoken language unique to a geographical area or social group. Variations in dialect may include phonological or sound variations, syntactical variations, and lexical or vocabulary variations.

English. Dialects exist in all languages and fall into two categories: (1) regional and geographical and (2) social and ethnic. Dialect has been defined as a regional or social variety of language distinguished by pronunciation, grammar, or vocabulary, especially a variety of speech differing from the standard literary language or speech pattern of the culture in which it exists. Two widely recognized dialects in the United States are a New England accent and a Southern drawl. Diverse dialects include African-American English, Puerto Rican English, Appalachian English, and varieties of Native American English, Vietnamese English, and others. Dialects are just as highly structured, logical, expressive, and complex as Standard English.

Boser (2006) notes that experts have been predicting the imminent demise of American dialects for decades because of increased mass media, but the opposite seems true. Boser notes his conclusion is drawn from the work of William Labov, a noted University of Pennsylvania linguist who, with associates, is compiling a new atlas of North American English. This first work to plot all major speech patterns in the continental United States and Canada shows that regional dialects have become more pronounced. Boser points out that although mountains of data have been collected on *how* dialects are changing, understanding of *why* they change remains elusive.

African-American preschoolers who speak **Black English** (African-American English) use advanced and complex syntax, such as linking two clauses, as do their Standard English–speaking peers. Black English is a systematic, rule-governed dialect that can express all levels of thought. African-American English, Black English, and the term **Ebonics** refer to a grammatically consistent speech whose key features include not conjugating the verb "to be" and the dropping of some final consonants from words (Figure 5–3). In the past, many debated whether African-American English is a distinct language or a dialect; the controversy still exists today.

1. extreme reduction of final consonants ("so" for "sold," "fo" for "four," "fin" for "find," "ba" for "bad")
2. phonological contrasts absent, such as -th versus -f at word endings ("baf" for "bath," "wif" for "with")
3. "l" or "r" deleted in words ("pants" for "parents," "doe" for "door," "he'p" for "help")
4. verb "be" used to indicate extended or continuous time ("I be walkin")
5. deletion of some "to be" verb forms ("He sick" or "She talk funny")
6. deletion of s or z sounds when using third person singular verbs ("He work all the time" or "She say don't go")
7. elimination of s in possessives ("Mama car got crashed")
8. use of two-word subjects ("Ben he be gone")
9. use of "it" in place of "there" ("It ain't none pieces left" for "There are no pieces left")

FIGURE 5–3 Some features of African-American vernacular English.

Elevating African-American English to the status of a language has evoked emotional reaction nationwide from both African-Americans and others. Early childhood professionals have mixed opinions. Many educators believe that the professional teacher's primary task is to preserve children's belief that they are already capable speakers and that teachers also should provide the opportunity for children to hear abundant Standard English speech models in classrooms. Linguists and educators do agree on the desperate need to teach some African-American children Standard English, but there is little agreement on how best to do so. Although it has long been suggested that the dialectic features of African-American vernacular English and its phonology create additional challenges for learning to read English, few efforts to test this hypothesis have been undertaken directly. It should also be pointed out that many African-American

Black English — a language usually spoken in some economically depressed African-American homes. A dialect of non-Standard English having its own rules and patterns, it is also called African-American English.
Ebonics — a nonstandard form of English, a dialect often called Black English that is characterized by not conjugating the verb "to be" and by dropping some final consonants from words.

children speak Standard English, not African-American English.

Actually, only relatively minor variations in vocabulary, pronunciation, and grammatical forms are apparent in most dialects.

Speakers of a particular dialect form a speech community that reflects the members' lifestyles or professional, national, family, or ethnic backgrounds. Certain common features mark the speech of the members, and no two members of a particular community ever speak alike because each person's speech is unique. Unfortunately, to some, the term dialect can connote less-than-correct speech. Speech accents differ in a number of ways and are fully formed systems. Children from other than mainstream groups enter school with a set of linguistic and cultural resources that in some respects differ from, and even conflict with, rather than resemble, those of the school culture.

Individuals react to dialects with admiration, acceptance, ambivalence, neutral feelings, or rejection based on value judgments. Most Americans have but a superficial acquaintance with stereotypes of American Southern or New York varieties of English, which have been experienced while listening to advertisements or entertainment media. People make assumptions about an individual's ethnicity, socioeconomic status, and competence based on the way he or she speaks, and unfortunately discrimination is not uncommon.

Just as a child who meets another child from a different part of the country with a different **accent** might say, "You sound funny!" so others may think of dialectic speech as crude or reflecting lack of education. Early childhood teachers are trained to remain nonjudgmental and accepting.

Dialect-speaking teachers, aides, and volunteers (working with children and families of the same dialect) may offer children a special degree of familiarity and understanding (Figure 5–4).

A Standard English–speaking teacher may sound less familiar but affords the child a model for growth in speaking the dominant

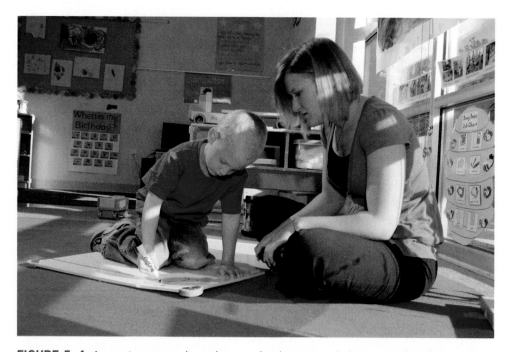

FIGURE 5–4 An assistant teacher who speaks the same dialect can often form a special relationship with a child.

accent — prominence or emphasis given to a word or syllable through one or more of the following factors: loudness, change of pitch, and longer duration (Harris & Hodges, 1995).

language of our society, which is important to his life opportunities.

Although a dialect (or accent) may be an advantage in one's community, it may be a disadvantage outside of that community. When someone begins to learn English, others may feel betrayed because they feel the individual has denied his or her identity and joined forces with those who are rejecting group values.

Accented speech, for this discussion, is defined as distinctive, typical speech habits of an individual or group of individuals associated with a geographical location or region.

WORKING WITH DIALECT-SPEAKING FAMILIES

Many early childhood centers employ staff members who have dialects that the children can easily understand so that children feel at home. Teachers who speak the children's dialect may be eagerly sought and in short supply. Additional insight into the child's culture and the particular meanings of their words is often an advantage for teachers who have the same dialect as the children. They may be able to react to and expand ideas better than a Standard English–speaking teacher.

It is important for teachers to know whether the children are speaking a dialect and to understand dialectic differences. The four most common dialectic differences between Standard English and some common dialects occur in verb forms. These differences occur in the following areas.

◆ Subject-verb agreement
◆ Use of the verb "to be"
◆ Use of present tense for past tense
◆ Use of "got" for "have"

In some areas where a language other than English is spoken, part of the rules of the second language may blend and combine to form a type of English different from the standard. Two examples of this are (1) English spoken by some Native American children and (2) English spoken in communities close to the Mexican-American border.

There are differing opinions about the teaching of preferred Standard English in early childhood centers. In most centers, however, preserving the child's native dialect, while moving slowly toward Standard English usage, is considered more desirable than providing immediate, purposeful instruction in standard forms. Joint family and center discussions can help clarify program goals.

THE TEACHER'S ROLE

Understanding dialectic differences is important to the teacher's understanding of each child. To give young children the best model possible, the early childhood teacher should speak Standard English. The federal government mandates that all children attending American public schools learn English, and instruction in English always begins at some point during the elementary school years.

Many successful teachers have speech accents and also possess other characteristics, abilities, and useful techniques that aid young children's development of language and literacy. It matters very little to children whether the teacher speaks a bit differently from the way they speak. The teacher's attitude, warmth, and acceptance of the dialect and the children themselves are very important considerations (Figure 5–5).

Teachers are in a unique position to build bridges rather than walls between cultures. Teachers' essential task is to create new and shared meanings with the children—new contexts that give meaning to the knowledge and skills being taught. The challenge is to find personally interesting and culturally relevant ways of creating new contexts for children, contexts in which school skills are meaningful and rewarding.

Competence is not tied to a particular language, dialect, or culture. Professional educators realize that language instruction or any other part of the planned curriculum should not reject or be designed to be a replacement of children's language or culture, but rather be viewed as language expansion and enrichment.

FIGURE 5–5 Teacher behavior, actions, and conversations can create children's positive feelings of self-worth.

Early childhood teachers may receive little instruction (teacher training) in the types of language behaviors to expect from diverse speakers; training in how to effect growth in language competencies also may be lacking. Teachers themselves will need to do their own classroom observation and research to identify cultural variations and differences that affect attending children's speech growth and development. Young preschoolers have learned the social speech expectations of their homes and possibly their communities. They know when to speak and when to be silent. At school they infer what is appropriate based on what they hear and observe there. When children begin to use a second language or second dialect, they tend to use words in syntactic constructions found in their native speech or dialect. Because many cultures, including Chinese, Vietnamese, and some Native American communities, expect children to learn from listening, young children from these cultures may be relatively silent

compared with children encouraged to be verbal from birth. Hawaiian children observed by researchers often did not like to be singled out for individual attention and tended to give minimal answers when questioned.

Because impact and swear words are said with emotion and emphasis, it is not uncommon for these words to be learned first and used at the wrong time. In some cultures, children may be encouraged to use "yes" and interrupt adult speech to signify that they are in tune with the speaker.

Some facial expressions or gestures acceptable in one culture may be highly insulting in another. Even the acceptable distance between speakers of different languages varies. Teachers may interpret various child language (or lack of it) as disrespectful without considering cultural diversity. Misunderstandings between children, humorous as they may be to teachers, require sensitive handling.

A child may be a very good speaker of his particular dialect or language, or he may be just a beginner. Staff members working with the young child respect the child's natural speech and do not try to stop the child from using it. The goal is to promote the child's use of natural speech in his native dialect. Standard English can be taught by having many good speaking models available at the center for the child to hear. Interested adults, play activities, other children, and a rich language arts program can provide a setting where children listen and talk freely. Teachers refrain from correcting children's oral language errors and look for meaning and intention. They stress cooperation, collaboration, and frequent conversation.

The teacher should know what parts of the center's program are designed to increase the child's use of words. Teachers can show a genuine interest in words in their daily conversations with the children. Teachers can also use the correct forms of Standard English in a casual way, using natural conversation. Correcting the children in an obvious way could embarrass them and stop openness and enthusiasm.

Delpit (1995) points out that constant teacher correction and focus on correctness impedes the child's "unconscious acquisition" of a language by raising the child's anxiety level and forcing him to cognitively monitor his every word. She provides an example of one 4-year-old's resistance to being taught to answer the teacher's morning greeting with a specific "I'm fine, thank you" response. Delpit's example (1995) follows.

Teacher:	Good morning, Tony. How are you?
Tony:	I be's fine.
Teacher:	Tony, I said, How are you?
Tony:	(with raised voice) I be's fine.
Teacher:	No Tony, I said. How are you?
Tony:	(angrily) I done told you I be's fine. I ain't telling you no more. (p. 94)

Careful listening, skillful response, and appropriate questions during conversations help the child learn to put thoughts into words. The child thinks in terms of his own dialect or language first and, in time, expresses words in Standard English. Delpit (1995) recommends that teachers provide students with exposure to an alternative form and allow children the opportunity to practice that form in contexts that are not threatening, have real purpose, and are intrinsically enjoyable.

Preschool teachers must face the idea that children's language and appearance may unconsciously affect their attitudes about those children and, consequently, teacher behaviors. A teacher may tend to seek out and communicate with children whose speech and appearance is most similar to her or his own. Extra effort may be necessary to converse and instruct. Staff-parent meetings and additional planning are musts to meet the needs of children with diverse language patterns. Pronunciation guides helping teachers say children's names correctly are gathered from families at admitting interviews. This is just a small first step.

Working with culturally diverse children means lots of teacher observation ("kid watching"). This gives clues to each child's preferred or learned style of language interaction.

Sensitive, seasoned teachers will not put some children on the spot with direct questions or requests at group times. They may include additional storytelling or demonstration activities with young children whose native cultures use this type of approach. "Rappin" and words-to-music approaches may appear to a greater extent in some child programs. Drama may be a way to increase language use in other classrooms. To be sure, with the great diversity in today's early childhood classrooms, teachers will be struggling to reach and extend each child's language competence. This is not an easy task. Teachers who work with other than mainstream children learn that their own views of the world, or ways of using language in that world, are not necessarily shared by others.

Suggestions based on the work of Soto (1991), though dated, still present accepted instructional strategies.

1. Accept individual differences with regard to language-learning time frames. Avoid pressures to "rush" and "push" children. Young children need time to acquire, explore, and experience second-language learning.

2. Accept children's attempts to communicate because trial and error are a part of the second-language learning process. Children should be given opportunities to practice both native and newly established language skills. Adults should not dominate the conversations; rather, children should be listened to.

3. Recognize that children need to acquire new language skills instead of replacing existing linguistic skills. Afford young children an opportunity to retain their native language and culture.

4. Provide a stimulating, active, diverse linguistic environment with many opportunities for language use in meaningful social interactions. Avoid rigid grammatical approaches with young children.

5. Valuing each child's home culture and incorporating meaningful active participation will enhance interpersonal skills and contribute to academic and social success.

6. Use informal observations to guide the planning of activities, interactions, and conversations for speakers of other languages.

7. Provide an accepting classroom climate that values culturally and linguistically diverse young children. (p. 102)★

Additional Teacher Tips

A teacher should guard against

◆ correcting children in a way that makes them doubt their own abilities.

◆ giving children the idea that they are not trying hard enough to correct or improve their speech.

◆ discouraging children's speaking.

◆ allowing teasing about individual speech differences.

★From Soto, L. D. (1991, Jan.). Understanding bilingual/bicultural young children. *Young Children* 40(2):30–36.

◆ interrupting children who are trying to express an idea.

◆ hurrying a child who is speaking.

◆ putting children on stage in an anxiety-producing way.

SECOND-LANGUAGE LEARNERS

Many English-language learners live in California, Texas, New York, Florida, and Illinois, but other areas are experiencing sudden growth in this population. Non–English-speaking children, like nonstandard dialect speakers, tend to come from low socioeconomic backgrounds and attend schools with disproportionately high numbers of children in poverty; however, many will not fit this description. A large group of professional, foreign-born technology workers' families reside in some urban areas. In the world today, in many countries it is "natural" to grow up speaking more than one language. More than 70 percent of the world's population does so.

Language-minority children (second-language learners) can be defined as children who speak their native language in social and cultural contexts out of school and have developed the necessary communicative competence. They also are being introduced, in substantive ways, to another language. In this discussion, it is English.

There are two main categories of second-language learners who speak no or very little English. The first category consists of those children who come to this country at a very young age or are born here to immigrants who have lived in areas of the world where language as well as the culture, systems of government, and social structures are quite unlike those of the United States. The second group of learners are native born, such as Native Americans or Alaskan native born children, but speak a different language and are members of a different culture than the mainstream American culture.

The following terms may be used in readings and research publications to describe second-language learners: **bilingual** learner, English as a

bilingual — refers to an individual with a language background other than English who has developed proficiency in the primary language and a degree of proficiency in English.

second-language student, student with limited English proficiency, language-minority learner, English-language learner, and linguistically diverse student.

A bilingual child can be described as a child younger than 3 years of age who learns two (sometimes more) languages at the same time or a child who learns a second language after age 3. Sequential acquisition describes what occurs when a child starts to learn a second language after the first language is only partially established—such as when a young child enrolls in a school where his native language is not spoken.

It is not unusual to find enrolled preschool children who are learning English and also possess different degrees of proficiency in two or more other languages (Figure 5–6). Bilingual children initially might have smaller vocabularies when each language is considered separately. But when one considers that the memory capacity of young children is limited and this restricts their rate of vocabulary acquisition, it is understandable. Bilingual children have two sets of vocabularies to learn. At any particular point during development, one would expect them to know fewer vocabulary items in each language but approximately the same number when both languages are considered.

Many experts suggest that if more than one language is spoken in the home and both languages are spoken well, the infant should be exposed to both from the beginning. However, if, as is so often the case, the first language is spoken exclusively in the home, research indicates the child should be encouraged to develop expertise in a wide range of language functions in the first language, in the expectation that these will easily transfer to the second language (English). Learning his native language allows the child's phonemic sensitivity to develop, which may allow him to gain an alphabetic insight that is needed for learning to read with ease.

The most immediate question the teacher of a bilingual child must face is deciding how well the child is progressing in all the languages the child is learning. A full language assessment with respect to the child's first language and with respect to the child's knowledge of English will probably show that the child's difficulties are limited to the acquisition of English. The testing of young children in multicultural and economically diverse classrooms is a growing practice.

NAEYC has developed screening and assessment recommendations for young English language learners; for downloadable versions go to www.naeyc.org/about/positions.asp.

The phrase "culturally sensitive" refers to whether the test is responsive to social and cultural differences among test takers. Because tests of language always reflect aspects of culture, it is impossible to construct a single test that is absolutely culturally sensitive, and incorporates aspects of all cultures to which children belong.

What is very important, when working with English language learners, is that the learner receives input that is not only comprehensible but just slightly beyond his or her current level of competence.

Knowing common strategies that young children use to learn English as a second language helps teachers. Some follow.

FIGURE 5–6 Arianne speaks Spanish, German, and English.

Children

◆ assume that what people are saying is directly related to the ongoing situation.

◆ learn a few stock expressions or formulaic speech and start to talk.

◆ search for patterns that recur in the language.

◆ make the most of the language they already have.

◆ spend their major effort on getting across meaning and save refinement for later.

Most educators estimate that most second-language–learning children will require 4 to 6 years to become competent users of English, and some will take as long as 5 to 8 years.

An effective early childhood curriculum for second-language should provide for frequent and diverse opportunities for speaking and listening that offer **scaffolding** to help guide the child through the learning process. The curriculum also should encourage children to take risks when speaking, construct meaning, and reinterpret knowledge within comfortable social contexts.

The dilemma that second-language learners may face in early school experiences is likened to a situation in which you can't win. To learn the new language, one needs to be socially accepted by those speaking the language; however, to be socially accepted, one has to be able to speak the new language. Young children often hurdle this bind by using various strategies, including gestures to invite others to play and accept their company. Crying, whimpering, pointing, miming, and making other nonverbal requests may also be tried. Children collect information by watching, listening, and speculating. They may talk to themselves and experiment with sounds or rehearse what they have heard. Telegraphic and formulaic language develops and they may say "Hey!" or "Lookit" over and over to gain attention.

Monolingual and bilingual speakers make inferences about social and linguistic appropriateness based on continued interaction in diverse social situations. Learning a second language includes a number of difficult tasks. The child must

◆ produce sounds that may not be used in the native language.

◆ understand that native speech sounds or words may have different meanings in the new (second) language.

◆ learn and select appropriate responses.

◆ sort and revise word orders.

◆ learn different cultural values and attitudes.

◆ control the flow of air while breathing and speaking.

Tabors (1997) identified four stages when describing the way children pursue learning a second language. These stages follow.

1. There may be a period of time when children continue to use their home language in the second-language situation.

2. When they discover that their home language does not work in this situation, children enter a nonverbal period as they collect information about the new language and perhaps spend some time in sound experimentation.

3. Children begin to go public, using individual words and phrases in the new language.

4. Children begin to develop productive use of the second language.

Researchers have identified many factors that may have an impact on how quickly young children acquire a second language: motivation, exposure, age, personality, aptitude, consistency, attitude, learning style, opportunity and support, and the individual characteristics of the home and family environment.

---

scaffolding — a teaching technique helpful in promoting languages, understanding, and child solutions. It includes teacher-responsive conversation, open-ended questioning, and facilitation of children's initiatives. Also defined as instruction in which a teacher builds upon what the child already knows to help the child accomplish a task and/or suggests breaking a task down into simpler components to promote accomplishment.

An important technique—admitting and recognizing that a child is a classroom resource when it comes to explaining other ways of naming and describing objects or other ways of satisfying human needs—should be utilized by educators. Printed word cards in both languages can be added to the classroom to reinforce this idea.

Research has promoted the idea that bilingual youngsters have not encountered a lifelong setback but instead they may be more imaginative, better with abstract notions, and more flexible in their thinking than monolingual children. They also have been described as more creative and better at solving complex problems. Compared with monolingual children, bilingual children may develop more awareness concerning the nature of language and how it works. Evidence suggests that being bilingual enhances cognitive development. It definitely is a job skill many employers seek.

Some English-only parents, particularly more affluent ones, seek tutors or early childhood programs that offer their monolingual children the opportunity to become second-language learners. Nationally many legislators believe bilingual programs should be available for all children.

Researchers have noticed that bilingualism sometimes improves children's self-esteem and strengthens family ties. Other researchers state that it may cause family distress. Educators have raised concerns about placing bilingual children in English-only preschools and believe that this may result in the children losing the ability to communicate effectively in their native language. This might adversely affect family relationships and conceptual development.

PROGRAM PLANNING FOR SECOND-LANGUAGE LEARNERS

Educators urge program planners who provide second-language learning opportunities to realize that the child's exposure, comfort level, motivation, familiarity, and practice in real communicative contexts are all important considerations. Curriculum developers in early childhood programs that enroll other-than-English-speaking children will have to decide their position on the best way to instruct. A debate rages. One end of the debate espouses native language use, native cultural instruction, and academic learning in the child's native language before instruction in English begins. At the other end, advocates would present English on the child's first day of schooling, with minimal use of the child's native language. Those on this side of the argument believe that the earlier English is introduced and confronted, the greater the child's linguistic advantage. (Policy recommendations put forth by the National Institute for Early Education Research in 2006 say that support for English language learners should be provided in both the home language and English where feasible.)

Educators note the different points of view concerning English language learners, but may choose to create their own programs by using innovative curricula and other instructional techniques. Above all, most educators agree that other-than-English-speaking children need to be perceived as intellectually able, and their teachers should hold high achievement and academic expectations for them as they do for all enrolled children.

Most early childhood centers adopt a variety of plans and methods to help bilingual children. Techniques are often researched and studied by individual staff members and are part of a center's in-service education. Au (2006) recommends that in any curriculum approach educators need to realize that one factor that handicaps the academic advancement of English language learners is some teachers' tendency to be overly concerned about the surface features of language, such as correct pronunciation of English, rather than the content of the ideas students are trying to communicate. She also points out that if students believe that what they have to say is important, they will have the confidence to learn the language needed to express those ideas.

Most programs approach the differences existing between home and school cultures by promoting children's biculturalism. This allows children to have successful experiences both in their families, where one set of values and behaviors prevails, and in school, where another set of values and behaviors may be expected. In a culturally sensitive approach, early childhood professionals would use modeling with culturally diverse children and slowly introduce and increase the practice of teaching via direct inquiry, particularly using verbal questions while they continue to use modeling. This practice would help increase children's verbal skills and their ability to follow directions.

Padron, Waxman, and Rivera (2002) define culturally responsive teaching as teaching that incorporates the everyday concerns of students, such as important family and community issues. The goal of this type of curriculum includes helping children feel more comfortable and confident. Planned activities that relate to the experiences of children's everyday lives are relevant and significant. Cooperative learning activities that involve a small group of young children working together can be planned. This helps develop social skills and positive group relations.

Papadaki-D'Onofrio (2003) lists the following common characteristics of programs that aim to provide students with dual- or multiple-language proficiency and foster academic success.

◆ Development of the mother tongue is encouraged to promote cognitive development and as a basis for learning the second language.

◆ Family and community involvement are essential.

◆ Teachers are able to understand, speak, and use with a high level of proficiency the language of instruction, whether it is their first or second language.

◆ Teachers are well trained, have cultural competence and subject matter knowledge, and continually upgrade their training.

Within the field of early childhood education, there is a need for knowledgeable, trained, competent, and sensitive multilingual/multicultural early childhood educators. Early childhood educators who speak more than one language and are culturally knowledgeable are an invaluable resource in the early childhood setting. In some instances the educator may speak multiple languages or may be able to communicate using various linguistic regionalisms or dialects spoken by the child or family. The educator may have an understanding of sociocultural and economic issues relevant within the local linguistically and culturally diverse community and can help support the family in the use and development of the child's home language and in the acquisition of English. Many experts and researchers advocate recruiting teacher assistants and classroom volunteers who speak children's native tongue.

The value of exposing second-language-learning children to quality books cannot be overlooked (Figure 5–7). Story times and one to-one, adult-child book readings can supply vocabulary and meaning in a way that conversational models alone cannot accomplish. Songs and music can also present language-learning opportunities. Print use in the center environment is another vehicle to promote literacy development. Above all, opportunity for abundant play and interaction with English-speaking children is critical. The most successful methods for teaching a second language include the same techniques mentioned in the monolingual child's learning of his first

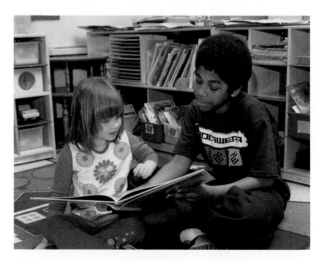

FIGURE 5–7 The introduction of English picture books benefits second-language learners.

language—warm, responsive, articulate adults involved with children's everyday, firsthand exploration of the environment.

Additional suggested teacher strategies and techniques follow.

◆ Provide a safe, accepting classroom environment.

◆ Listen patiently, maintaining eye contact.

◆ Give attention to child attempts.

◆ Respond to meaning rather than speech technicalities or specifics.

◆ Promote sharing and risk taking.

◆ Make classroom activities inviting, interesting, meaningful, and successful.

◆ Emphasize key words in sentences.

◆ Point at objects or touch them while naming them, when possible (Figure 5–8).

◆ Learn how to correctly pronounce the child's name.

◆ Include the child in small groups where there are other child models to follow.

◆ Help the child realize he is unique and special, exactly "as is."

◆ Learn a few useful words in the child's language (for example, *bathroom, eat, stop, listen*).

◆ Gesture and use objects and pictures that give children additional clues, such as a picture-based daily schedule.

◆ Provide activity choices in which the child does not have to interface with others—so-called safe havens.

◆ During activity times, provide enough staff so that teachers can work closely with children and materials.

◆ Use a running commentary technique in interactions. "Serena is painting with red paint." "I'm pinning a name tag on your sweater."

◆ Choose predictable books to share.

◆ Work with a small group at story-reading times.

◆ Use repeated presentations of the same songs at group times.

◆ Link up English-speaking "partners" in noncompetitive games.

A number of researchers have found that when teachers work with second-language learners, they make adjustments similar to those families make when talking to their very young children; these include organizing talk around visual references (real objects, actions, happenings, people, and so on), using simple syntax, producing many repetitions and paraphrases, speaking slowly and clearly, checking often for comprehension, and expanding and extending topics introduced by the child.

During planned teacher-led instruction, it is important for teachers to recognize the second-language learner by using his name; his needs and other children's positive attitudes toward second-language learners should also be recognized. Group seating arrangements, opportunities to sit near a "translating friend," and children's participation as co-members of the group also should be given close attention.

Professional education associations recommend that teachers faced with many different languages in their classrooms consider grouping together, at specific times during the day, children that speak the same or similar languages so

FIGURE 5–8 Objects can be named when the teacher touches them.

that children can construct knowledge with others who speak their home language.

Playmates of second-language learners can be encouraged not only to be aware and accepting of other children but to approach and invite them to play. Through discussion, example, and modeling, children can learn to use gestures, to use simple sentences, to speak slowly, and to repeat themselves or use different words when they think their "friends" do not quite understand. Teachers stress that these new classmates may need help. One classroom regularly scheduled a short picture book reading time when family members shared a book in a language other than English. Children could choose whether to attend. The book would then be repeated in English by their regular teacher, and a discussion period examined how children both attempted to understand and felt during the first reading.

For any child learning English as a second language, making a friend is an important developmental step. Educators often pair children with an English-speaking partner or ease children into play groups for the inherent social and language benefits. Individual differences always exist in any group of young second-language learners, just as they do with first-language learners.

As mentioned earlier, second-language learners can be ignored and left out of peer play. Even when trying to communicate nonverbally, they can be treated as "babies" or as invisible. They may be cast as the infant in dramatic play situations or be the object of a mothering child's attention—perhaps unwanted attention. Other children may speak to them in high-pitched voices and in shortened and linguistically reduced forms as they have observed adults sometimes do with very young children who are learning to speak. Teachers should monitor these peer behaviors and gently discourage them if necessary.

Reaching Families

Home-school instructional support programs have provided books, electronic media, "borrowed" materials and equipment, and "take home" suggestions for homes with limited access to English-language models and storybooks. Encouraging families to continue to maintain their first language and their home language literacy activities, and perhaps increase everyday conversations, is a common practice. Schools usually ask families questions about what types of language exposure a child has had since birth and what types of literacy experiences have been associated with them.

In some cases an interpreter may be necessary. Designing room features and planning curriculum activities that welcome a family's participation in classroom activities and show acceptance are important considerations.

Behaviors Teachers Can Expect

Both teachers and children can be expected to experience some frustration with the second-language-learning process. But preschoolers' language ability is amazing, and teachers will notice more and more understanding of English, then hesitant naming, followed by beginning phrases. If the teacher tries to learn the child's language, the same sequence is apparent. There is usually a period of time when children will try to use their native language with children and teachers. Eventually, they discover that this is not an effective technique unless other children of their native language group are present. Children's beginning communication attempts can consist of trying to get attention, requesting help, protesting, and gesturing, but these may not be effective.

When words are attempted, teachers can expect a Spanish-speaking child to have a problem producing consonant sounds that do not exist in his native language, such as *d, j, r, v, sh, th,* and *s*; beginning-of-word blends, such as *st, sp,* and *sm*; and word endings of *r* blends, such as *-rd, -rt,* and *-rs*. A few other word sounds also will be difficult.

Second-language learners may reach a stage at which they seem to repeat words, and focus intently and rehearse words. This happens not for the purpose of communication but rather so the child can practice through repetition, which is reminiscent of younger preschoolers' private speech or self-talk during play situations. These rehearsing-like behaviors are usually done at a low volume. The first unintelligible utterances that second-language learners issue may be sound experimentation.

CULTURAL DIFFERENCES

Cultural differences in communicating are important for a teacher to understand because cross-cultural communication abounds in many early childhood classrooms. Diversity represents the richness and uniqueness of human life. It is something we value and share with the children. The word multidimensional may best describe today's children.

Multicultural education hopes to prepare children for a diverse society in which differing languages are spoken and customs and values differ. Its goals include communicating despite differences, cooperating for mutual good, fighting bias and discrimination, respecting others' values, and providing for dignity and fair treatment for all.

Early childhood educators realize cultural differences may exist and they listen closely to families to understand family traditions, practices, and hopes for their children and to find common ground so that enrolled children and families will feel comfortable and respected at school. They share their school's philosophy that each child is welcome and precious. They describe state, federal, and professional standards that mandate every enrolled child should learn English when that explanation is necessary. Educators avoid making value judgments and acknowledge they have assumptions concerning what they believe is best and right when educating children in their care. They realize some differences may exist between a family's wishes and a program's philosophy. Areas that are not negotiable—such as a family's request that boys be offered more access to academics or physical development programs than girls—are discussed but school policy does not change.

A study of cultural differences can help teachers receive accurate messages. Gestures and body language of the cultural groups attending a center may differ widely in meaning.

Teachers interested in studying the cultures of enrolled children can start by identifying components of culture. These components include family structure; definitions of stages, periods, or transitions during a person's life; roles of adults and children; their corresponding behavior in terms of power and politeness; discipline; time and space; religion; food; health and hygiene; history; traditions; holidays; and celebrations (Figure 5–9).

The ways in which language is used in different situations vary from one culture to another. People from different cultural groups transact business in different ways; converse with one another in different ways; praise, criticize, and greet one another in different ways; and have different ideas concerning the value of education for their children. Variations in the ways cultures organize the use of language reflect differences in cultural beliefs, values, and goals concerning social roles and relationships in their group.

Some American-born Hispanic children may, like their foreign-born, newly arrived Hispanic contemporaries, have difficulty communicating in English. The temporary status of some Mexican families and their determination

FIGURE 5–9 Teachers studying enrolled children's cultures may find that children's religious observances differ from their own.

to keep alive their non-English mother tongue may account for a lack of enthusiasm to learn English.

In some cultures it is believed that children are not appropriate conversational partners for adults. Children may not be encouraged to initiate conversations about themselves or their interests, and adult talk may not be child-centered. Children may have learned not to look directly at adults when talking. Some children grow up learning that cooperation is more highly valued than competition; others do not.

Cultures are complex and changing, so understanding cultural similarities and differences can be a life's study in itself. **Culture** is defined here as all the activities and achievements of a society that individuals within that society pass from one generation to the next.

Ethnic origin is often a basic ingredient in subcultural groupings. **Subculture** is defined as other than a dominant culture. Class structure also exists in societies consisting of upper, middle, and lower income groups. Often, patterns of child-rearing vary between cultures and classes. Families may express attitudes and values peculiar to their class or culture. Attitudes and feelings of an impoverished group, for instance, often include futility, anger, violence, and loss of trust in anyone or anything.

Teachers try to determine the backgrounds of their attending families, noting the individual nature of children's home communities—housing, income, general numbers, and types of cultural groups—in an attempt to better understand children and provide language-developing experiences. Their ability to respond and relate to what attending children verbalize is enhanced.

What cultural differences can inhibit child speech? Adult models' lengths of sentences or their inability to modify their speech to child levels, neutral or negative environments, family arrangements that require children to be alone for long periods or in which children are expected to be quiet or cannot gain adult attention, and lack of books or early reading experiences are all factors that can affect speech growth. Parents are the primary language teachers in the early years, and language competence grows out of familiar situations such as seeking help or establishing joint attention—situations that provide frameworks in which children learn to make their intentions plain and to interpret the intentions of others.

Okagaki and Diamond (2000) suggest the following teacher strategies.

◆ Have consistent routines.
◆ Learn and sing a family song with the total group.
◆ Encourage children to share their cultural ways.
◆ Encourage children to share something special in their lives with others.
◆ Use photographs of the children's and teacher's families on a bulletin board or class book.
◆ Ask families about the children's favorite music or stories.
◆ Invite families to classroom activities.

PROMOTING ACCEPTANCE

Practitioners may have to field questions from children about another child's speech. Answering in an open, honest fashion with accurate information gives the adult an opportunity to affirm diversity and perhaps correct a child's biased ideas. Negative stereotypes can be diminished or dismissed. Before answering, it is a good idea to clarify what the child is really asking. Examples of teacher statements follow:

"Yes, Paloma speaks some words you don't understand. Her family comes from Guatemala

---

culture — all the activities and achievements of a society that individuals within that society pass from one generation to the next.
subculture — an ethnic, regional, economic, or social group exhibiting characteristic patterns of behavior sufficient to distinguish it from others within an embracing culture or society.

and they speak the Spanish language. Paloma is learning lots of new words at school in the language of her new country—English."

"Quan doesn't talk to you because he doesn't know our words yet. He speaks a different language at his house. He is listening, and one day he will speak. While he is listening and learning words to speak, he wants to play. Show him with your hands and words what you want him to do. He will understand."

Teachers working with culturally diverse children need to watch and listen closely. Children's behavior and movements will give clues to their well-being and feelings of safety in the group. Teachers may need to ease into situations in which unpleasant remarks or actions are directed at a newly enrolled child who speaks a different language and express sadness, such as: "Ricardo has heard some unkind and unfriendly words from you boys in the loft. He is new at school and doesn't know what our school is like. I'm going to try and help Ricardo enjoy his first day in our room."

Working with culturally diverse children also means that educators will guard against alienating children from their own cultural values.

Teachers need to remember that the ability to learn a second language and the syntax of that language is highest between birth and age 6. The same experiences and responsive care that gave rise to language in infancy will work—lots of language activities, labeling activities, listening to picture books, musical activities, play with peers, and the adult's time and confidence in the child's grasp of new-for-him language usage. Just as repetition of experience was needed in infancy, it will again be needed to support the older child's acquisition of a second language.

CULTURAL AWARENESS ACTIVITIES

In planning language activities of all types, every effort must be made to make children aware of cross-cultural similarities and to explore differences. Language arts programming should draw on the linguistic, cultural, and personal experiences of language-diverse children. When

planning instructional activities, it is important to provide opportunities that are familiar to children from their family and community life. Parents and extended family members can be invited to share family stories and artifacts relating to theme units, learning centers, or other program components.

Young children can be exposed to the idea that people eat, sleep, wear clothing, celebrate, dance, sing, live in groups, and speak to one another in common languages, and that they do these things in ways that may be either the same as or different from the ways their families do these things. Planned activities can make comparisons, treating diversity with the dignity it deserves. Skin color, hairstyles, food preferences, clothing, and music are starting points for study. Modeling friendship and cooperation between cultures and planning activities showing dissimilar individuals and groups living in harmony is a good idea. Stories exist in all languages and in most dialects. Some centers ask children and parents to contribute family photos to use to construct a classroom "My Family" book. Each child is asked to dictate a caption for each family photo. The book is permanently placed in the class library collection. When a new child enrolls, new family photos are added. See the Additional Resources at the end of this chapter for related helpful readings.

Identifying quality multicultural and multiethnic picture books is discussed in Chapter 9. Room displays, bulletin boards, and learning centers should also reflect the cultural diversity of attending children.

It is important to plan language arts programs that incorporate different cultural styles of dramatic play, storytelling, and chanting. Librarians can help teachers discover picture books and other materials written in dialects or two-language translations.

Planning for Play

Unfortunately, young children who lack language and social skills may miss out on peer play interactions, which are important in language learning. Educators need to be aware of those children in their classrooms who are alone (Figure 5–10) and perhaps humming, singing, and/or talking to themselves and should expend extra efforts to help them become skilled play companions. This can have a tremendous impact on both language development and social skill growth. Through play and its resultant conversations, peers are teachers. The child who cannot sustain play interactions with peers needs to learn skills associated with maintaining play relationships, which is sometimes tough enough for fluent child speakers. The acts of resolving conflict, sharing, cooperating, collaborating, and negotiating all involve the use of language and are typical parts of preschool peer play.

FIGURE 5–10 Brett watches his parents leave and needs time alone before he turns to play.

Planning play opportunity and experiences is an important teacher task in program planning. This involves observing individual children during play periods and promoting play groups for children experiencing difficulties.

Families as Partners

Translating to families the school's respect for the culture and language of the parent is not an easy job. Knowledgeable educators realize the child's long-range advantage as a future bilingual and bicultural job seeker. Every effort should be made to support family efforts to acquaint their children with the parents' native culture and its language, literature, history, beliefs, values, and heritage.

When working in communities with newly arrived immigrant populations, teachers have to devote considerable time and study to understanding the families and lives of attending children. A strong connection between home and school should exist, with families playing a role in program planning and as assistants or teachers in classrooms. When family literacy rates are less than desirable, teachers have to proceed carefully with suggestions concerning reading to their children. Wordless books and parent storytelling are alternatives. Family literacy programs are discussed in Chapter 19.

Volk and Long (2005) have the following suggestions that help educators honor children's home and school literacy resources.

◆ Guard against a **deficit perspective** that distorts the educator's vision when working with marginalized families.

◆ Gain the perspective that homes, families, cultures, and communities possess "funds of knowledge" literacies and individuals with valuable skills.

◆ Understand that children become literate in many ways.

◆ Recognize that most families value education and believe it is important.

deficit perspective — an attitude or belief that attributes children's school failures to children themselves, or their family or culture.

◆ Recognize that families may use different yet various and effective methods to support literacy.

◆ Believe that children participate in many literacy interactions at home (Figure 5-11).

◆ Realize that children may be surrounded by abundant human and literary resources including networks of support and people of varying ages and abilities.

◆ Recognize that peers help each other and may clarify the teacher's statements.

- doing homework
- reviewing school work, reading teacher letters
- practicing school-related skills
- talking about school work and reading and writing
- using workbooks
- looking at and reading books (their own and others' picture books, school books, library books, coloring books, address books, dictionaries)
- listening to books and letters read aloud by others
- reading/writing greeting cards
- enacting literacy-related cultural roles—playing "school," "church," and "McDonald's"
- watching TV and videos for entertainment and language learning
- playing with a minicomputer, video games, a musical keyboard with letters
- playing children's card games and board games, doing puzzles, collecting baseball cards
- reading/listening to Bible passages and Bible commentaries
- memorizing psalms to recite in church
- writing, reciting, singing, and listening to poems, stories, and songs from families' cultures, from school, and from popular culture, some created by the children
- drawing and writing with crayons, markers, pencils, and pens in notebooks and on pads and loose paper

FIGURE 5–11 Children's home literacy interactions and activities. (From Volk, D., & Long, S. [2005, November]. Challenging myths of the deficit perspective: Honoring children's literacy resources. *Young Children, 60*[6], 12–19.)

PROGRAM TYPES

Controversy exists concerning which type of program is best suited to the child learning English as a second language. A list of common program types follows.

◆ Bilingual program: Two languages are used for instruction.

◆ Transitional bilingual program: Children's first language is used as a medium of instruction until they become fluent enough to receive all of their instruction in English.

◆ Newcomer program: Recent immigrant children with no or limited English proficiency, native literacy skills, or formal education are provided a special academic environment for a limited period. Both elementary-level and secondary-level newcomer programs exist. They provide a welcoming classroom environment. Teachers use instructional strategies to orient children to American life and culture. Bilingual staffs familiar with the children's cultures are secured when possible. The aim of this type of intense program is to prepare children for success in English as a second language, bilingual, or mainstream classes.

◆ Developmental bilingual program: Equal status is given to English and another language, promoting full proficiency in both languages. Academic instruction is given in English and the child's first language. Teachers are proficient in both languages. Mixing and translating language is avoided but acceptable at social times.

◆ Two-way immersion program: This type of program provides integrated language and academic instruction for native English speakers and native speakers of another language. Students are together at least 50 percent of the day and communicate in both languages. This enables English speakers to develop second-language proficiency. Both groups' families must have an interest in bilingualism.

◆ Tutor-assisted program: A special tutor (or teacher) works with a child for a portion of the school day.

A full-immersion program offers an age-appropriate curriculum in a language foreign to the child. Some parents, like Wardle (2003), believe the early years are the optimal time to learn a second language and that every child in America should learn an additional language besides English. Wardle notes that most full-immersion programs in the United States start in preschool, kindergarten, or first grade and students attending these programs are fluent in the foreign language by second or third grade.

Some classrooms combine approaches and program types, and identify elements common to successful English-language learner programs. These include the following, as identified by the Center for Research on Education, Diversity, & Excellence (2001):

- ongoing and guided parental involvement
- professional development for both specialized and mainstream teachers
- the promotion of proficiency in both first and secondary languages
- the use of assessment methods linked to instructional objectives to inform instructional planning and delivery
- developmentally appropriate curriculum
- high standards for language acquisition and academic achievement
- strong staff leadership
- sheltered instruction, an approach that integrates language and content instruction
- academic instruction in English
- special strategies to make content (in activities) meaningful and comprehensive*

Visuals and images (pictorial representations) used while the teacher is talking almost always improve student listening comprehension and reduce recall errors.

Assessment

Assessment is usually undertaken when teachers suspect that a child has difficulty communicating and could profit from specialized

instruction. Schools and programs affected by the federal No Child Left Behind Act or by local, regional, or state standards routinely conduct mandated, periodic testing. The teachers in these programs must document each child's progress. Individual learning plans are developed that include systematic instructional strategies when children are not progressing. The goal is to identify whether a child's language is less advanced than that of other children his age (delayed language) or is deficient when compared with performance on social and/or intellectual tasks (language deficit) or whether the child fits both categories. Screening tests should be conducted by trained professionals.

CHILDREN WITH SPECIAL NEEDS

Special language-development preschool centers with expert personnel are available in most communities for children with easily identifiable communication deficiencies such as hearing loss, visual impairment, and obvious speech impairments. Other children in need of special help may not be identified at the preschool level and may function within the wide range of children considered to be average or typical for preschool ages. In language arts, learning disability is a term that refers to a group of disorders manifested by significant difficulties in the acquisition and use of listening, speaking, reading, or writing. Most programs are reticent to label children as having language learning problems because of their lack of expertise to screen and evaluate children in a truly professional manner. Referral to speech-language pathologists or local or college clinics is suggested to parents when a question exists concerning a particular child's progress. Early childhood teachers are not speech or language pathologists and therefore should not be expected to diagnose language problems or prescribe therapy. Communication disorders are usually divided into two main categories.

Hearing disabilities are characterized by an inability to hear sounds clearly. Such disabilities

---

*From Center for Research on Education, Diversity, & Excellence. (2001). Some program alternatives for English language learning. Practitioner's Brief #3.

hearing disabilities — characterized by an inability to hear sounds clearly. This may range from hearing speech sounds faintly or in a distorted way, to profound deafness.

may range from hearing speech sounds faintly or in a distorted way, to profound deafness. In the United States, approximately 1 out of every 300 children is born with permanent hearing loss (Eiserman, Shisler, Foust, Buhrmann, & White, 2007). It is estimated that by school age nearly 1 out of every 100 students have permanent sensory-neural hearing loss. Undetected hearing loss often results in language delay and language deficits. This not only can affect literacy, but also school achievement, degree of socialization, and readiness for both school and reading instruction. Identification of hearing loss and appropriate intervention before a baby is 6 months old can significantly improve language and cognitive development. See Figure 5–12, a resource published by the American Speech-Language-Hearing Association (ASLHA, 2001).

Speech and language disabilities can affect the way people talk and understand; these range from simple sound substitutions to not being able to use speech and language at all.

SPEECH-LANGUAGE DISABILITIES AND PROBLEMS

More than 13 million people in the United States have some kind of expressive speech disability, the most common problem involving articulation—affecting an estimated 75 percent of people with these types of problems. The rest, approximately 25 percent, have language, voice, and fluency disorders, or a combination of these. Most articulation problems not caused by physical, sensory, or neurological damage respond to treatment. Non-organic causes of problems can include:

- lack of stimulation.
- lack of need to talk.
- poor speech models.
- lack of or low reinforcement.
- insecurity, anxiety, crisis.
- shyness or lack of social confidence.

Language Delay

Language delay may be connected to one or more of the following areas (Taylor, 2002).

- syntax (putting words together to create sentences)
- semantics (using words and understanding their meanings)
- morphology (using word endings, given the language context)
- pragmatics (using social language)
- sequencing (recalling and relating events in the correct order)
- vocabulary (comprehending and using new words)*

Language delay is characterized by a marked slowness in the development of the vocabulary and grammar necessary for expressing and understanding thoughts and ideas. It may involve both comprehension and the child's expressive language output and quality. It is wise for families to consult a speech-language pathologist if the delay is more than 6 months so language therapy if recommended can commence.

A complete study of a child includes first looking for physical causes, particularly hearing loss, and then examining other structural (voice-producing) conditions. Neurological limitations come under scrutiny, as do emotional development factors. Home environments and family communicating styles are also examined.

A language-delayed child may have a small vocabulary, and use short and simple sentences with many grammatical errors. He may have difficulty maintaining a conversation, and often talk about the immediate present rather than future happenings. He can have difficulty understanding others and in making himself understood.

*From Taylor, R. (2002, Mar.). Helping language grow. *Instructor* 111(6): 25–26. Copyright © 2002 Scholastic, Inc. Reprinted by permission.

---

speech and language disabilities — communication disorders that affect the way people talk and understand; range from simple sound substitutions to not being able to use speech and language at all.

HEARING AND UNDERSTANDING	TALKING

HEARING AND UNDERSTANDING

birth–3 months
- startles to loud sounds
- quiets or smiles when spoken to
- seems to recognize your voice and quiets if crying
- increases or decreases sucking behavior in response to sound

4–6 months
- moves eyes in direction of sounds
- responds to changes in tone of your voice
- notices toys that make sounds
- pays attention to music

7 months–1 year
- enjoys games like Peek-a-boo and Pat-a-cake
- turns and looks in direction of sounds
- listens when spoken to
- recognizes words for common items like "cup," "shoe," "juice"
- begins to respond to requests ("Come here," "Want more?")

1–2 years
- points to a few body parts when asked
- follows simple commands and understands simple questions ("Roll the ball," "Kiss the baby," "Where's your shoe?")
- listens to simple stories, songs, and rhymes
- points to pictures in a book when named

2–3 years
- understands differences in meaning ("go-stop," "in-on," "big-little," "up-down")
- follows two requests ("Get the book and put it on the table")

3–4 years
- hears you when you call from another room
- hears television or radio at the same loudness level as other family members
- answers simple "who?" "what?" "where?" "why?" questions

4–5 years
- pays attention to a short story and answers simple questions about it
- hears and understands most of what is said at home and in school

TALKING

birth–3 months
- makes pleasure sounds (cooing, gooing)
- cries differently for different needs
- smiles when sees you

4–6 months
- babbling sounds more speechlike with *many* different sounds, including *p*, *b*, and *m*
- vocalizes excitement and displeasure
- makes gurgling sounds when left alone and when playing with you

7 months–1 year
- babbling has both long and short groups of sounds such as "tata upup bibibibi"
- uses speech or noncrying sounds to get and keep attention
- imitates different speech sounds
- has one or two words (bye-bye, dada, mama), although they may not be clear

1–2 years
- says more words every month
- uses some one- to two-word questions ("Where kitty?" "Go bye-bye?" "What's that?")
- puts two words together ("more cookie," "no juice," "mommy book")
- uses many different consonant sounds at the beginning of words

2–3 years
- has a word for almost everything
- uses two to three words to talk about and ask for things
- speech is understood by familiar listeners most of the time
- often asks for or directs attention to objects by naming them

3–4 years
- talks about activities at school or at friends' homes
- people outside family usually understand child's speech
- uses a lot of sentences that have four or more words
- usually talks easily without repeating syllables or words

4–5 years
- voice sounds clear like other children's
- uses sentences that give lots of details (e.g., "I like to read my books")
- tells stories that stick to topic
- communicates easily with other children and adults
- says most sounds correctly except a few like *l*, *s*, *r*, *v*, *z*, *j*, *ch*, *sh*, *th*
- uses the same grammar as the rest of the family

FIGURE 5–12 Speech and hearing ages. (From "How Does Your Child Hear and Talk?" Reprinted with permission from the American Speech-Language-Hearing Association.)

Besides linguistic problems, a language-delayed child may have problems classifying objects and recognizing similarities and differences. He also may ignore opportunities to play with others.

Additional behaviors a teacher might notice in a language-delayed child include:

◆ less variety in sentence structure.

◆ simple two- and three-word sentences.

◆ less frequent speech.

◆ frequent occurrence of playing alone.

◆ less adept participation in joint planning with classmates.

Early childhood educators concerned about the speech and socialization of "late talkers" should discuss their suspicions with their teaching team and supervisors.

Tabors (1997) points out:

Preschool educators are often called upon to assess whether a child's behavior warrants further investigation for intervention.

Because communicative factors related to language affect children's social behavior, it is often difficult for preschool educators to know where certain behaviors in second-language–learning children are indicative of true developmental delay or are merely due to the pressure of the new social environment to which the children are being exposed. (p. 34)

Teachers might readily agree with the following sample description of a language-delayed child: "Speaks markedly less well than other children of the same age and seems to have normal ability in intellectual, motor, sensory, and emotional control areas, but may be rejected by peers."

Researchers studying differences in the quantity of parent talk with their young children may find a wide disparity between two families—a child from one family could hear 700 utterances each day while a child from another family hears 11,000 utterances. Children in the first category can seem to possess lower-level language skills not caused by any innate problem but rather by an environmental situation.

Teachers working with language-delayed children use the following interactive techniques.

◆ gaining attention with tempting, interest-catching activities

◆ being at eye level, face-to-face, if possible

◆ establishing eye contact

◆ displaying enthusiasm and playfulness

◆ establishing a play activity involving "my turn, your turn" interaction

◆ verbalizing single words, short phrases, or short sentences depending on the child's verbal level

◆ pausing, waiting, and looking expectantly, encouraging the child's turn to talk

◆ repeating teacher statements and pausing expectantly

◆ copying the child's actions or verbalizations

◆ following the child's focus of interest with joint teacher interest

◆ probing the child's interest with logical questions

◆ maintaining close, accepting physical contact and a warm interactive manner

A few children may make a conscious decision not to try to learn Standard English or a new language when they are confronted with a language other than their native language or dialect. A number of reasons for their choice are possible. If others enrolled or teachers speak their native language, they may believe it is not necessary or simply not worth the effort. Families may not give a high priority to learning the new language, or children's enrollment may consist of only a few mornings a week. A child's decision can be temporary or long-term.

The Cloistered Child

Some teachers and educators describe children with inadequate language due to lack of human interactive environments. To be "cloistered" connotes isolation, separation, limited experience, meager human contact, a narrow view of the world, small or sparsely furnished living quarters, and a time-consuming devotion to spiritual contemplation and prayer. In the cloistered child the spiritual contemplation and prayer have been replaced with the passive pursuit of hours and hours of never discussed television and/or other electronic media watching.

The cloistered child is thought to display one or many of the following characteristics.

- limited attention span
- inability to express ideas
- limited language and vocabulary
- inability to draw on past knowledge
- inability to listen
- impulsiveness (says first thing that pops into mind)
- lack of perseverance ("It's work. It's too hard.")
- blunted interest and curiosity
- disorganization
- impatience, inability to wait
- poor conversation skill

To develop what is seen as "missing language and missing experience," experts recommend a curriculum that includes lots of talk, active involvement, time and play with other children, and exposure to literature. Some educators would recommend opportunities to play with peers and plan actions, which facilitate the child's seeing himself in control, along with the promotion of child resourcefulness in seeking help from others.

The Overstressed Child

There are many different reasons why some children have stressful living situations. When young children's stress is connected to new adults, new situations, groups of peers, books and book-reading times, or conversations with an adult, teachers will notice child anxiety and aversion behavior. O'Leary, Newton, Lundz, Hall, O'Connell, Raby, and Czarnecka (2002) describe degrees of stress and possible causative factors teachers should avoid.

Mild stress enhances conscious learning, but too much stress, especially for too long a time, prevents it. Stress speaks primarily to the emotional learning system, and there it works primarily in a negative way.

Extreme stress, caused by too much different information, unrelated information, or information too rapidly introduced or presented within too short a space of time, adds to a negative emotional reaction and clicks in a fear response. This memory is engraved below the level of awareness and becomes conscious as an attitude toward or feeling about the situation or topic. (p. 46)

Fortunately, when no pressure and stress exist, and a safe school environment is experienced, many children who display an initial aversion to certain school activities, including language arts activities, venture forth slowly and their attitudes change. Most early childhood teachers have been acquainted with children who avoid book-sharing times yet listen from another area in the classroom. After a period, they move closer, and eventually they join the read-aloud group. Their former avoidance and what seemed to be apathy becomes anticipation and enjoyment. These children often do not avoid social contact with peers but rather the newness of the group book-reading experience.

Expressive and Receptive Language Difficulties

Educators begin suspecting problems in language development when they observe attending children in a variety of classroom situations, including group times, play times, adult-child exchanges, and social interactions. In lower elementary school grades, including kindergarten, the following characteristics are cause for concern. They are seen as behaviors indicating expressive-language difficulties.

1. limited use of language
2. trouble starting and/or responding to conversation

3. heavy reliance on gesture or nonverbal communication

4. limited or nonspecific vocabulary

5. inappropriate grammar

6. difficulty in sequencing rhymes or stories

Teachers handling preschoolers may think many of these characteristics are typical of younger preschoolers and that they will be corrected as the child approaches kindergarten age. Their program planning and teacher-child interactions aim to erase difficulties, and they would be concerned if growth in a preschooler's language ability and skill was not observable and apparent over time.

Articulation

Articulation disorders involve difficulties with the way sounds are formed and strung together, usually characterized by substituting one sound for another, omitting a sound, or distorting a sound.

If consonant sounds are misarticulated, they may occur in the initial (beginning), medial (middle), or ending positions in words. It is prudent to point out again that normally developing children do not master the articulation of all consonants until age 7 or 8.

Most young children (3 to 5 years old) hesitate, repeat, and re-form words as they speak. Imperfections occur for several reasons: (1) a child does not pay attention as closely as an adult, especially to certain high-frequency consonant sounds; (2) the child may not be able to distinguish some sounds; or (3) a child's coordination and control of his articulation mechanisms may not be perfected. For example, the child may be able to hear the difference between *Sue* and *shoe* but cannot pronounce them differently. About 60 percent of all children with diagnosed articulation problems are boys.

Articulation characteristics of young children include the following.

- ◆ Substitution: One sound is substituted for another, as in "wabbit" for "rabbit" or "thun" for "sun."

- ◆ Omission: The speaker leaves out a sound that should be articulated. He says "at" for "hat," "ca" for "cat," "icky" for "sticky," "probly" for "probably." The left out sound may be at the beginning, middle, or end of a word.

- ◆ Distortion: A sound is said inaccurately but is similar to the intended sound.

- ◆ Addition: The speaker adds a sound, as in "li-it-tle" for "little" and "muv-va-ver" for "mother."

- ◆ Transposition: The position of sounds in words is switched, as in "hangerber" for "hamburger" and "aminal" for "animal."

- ◆ Lisp: The *s*, *z*, *sh*, *th*, *ch*, and *j* sounds are distorted. There are 2 to 10 types of lisps noted by speech experts.

Articulation problems may stem from a physical condition such as a cleft palate or hearing loss, or they can be related to problems in the mouth, such as a dental abnormality. Many times, articulation problems occurring without any obvious physical disability may involve the faulty learning of speech sounds.

Some children will require special help and directed training to eliminate all articulation errors; others seem to mature and correct articulation problems by themselves.

Teacher behavior that helps a child with articulation problems includes not interrupting or constantly correcting the child and making sure that others do not tease or belittle the child. Modeling misarticulated words correctly is a good course of action. Simply continue your conversation and insert the correctly articulated word in your answering comment.

Voice Quality

Teachers sometimes notice differences in children's voice quality, which involves pitch, loudness, resonance, and general quality (breathiness, hoarseness, and so on). The intelligibility of a child's speech is determined by how many of the child's words are understandable. One can expect 80 percent of the child's speech to be understandable at age 3.

Stuttering and Cluttering

Stuttering and cluttering are categorized as fluency disorders. Stuttering involves the rhythm of speech and is a complicated, many-faceted problem. Speech is characterized by abnormal stoppages with no sound, repetitions, or prolonged sounds and syllables. There may also be unusual facial and body movements associated with efforts to speak. This problem involves four times as many males as females and can usually be treated. All young children repeat words and phrases, and this tends to increase with anxiety or stress. It is simply typical for the age and is not true stuttering. A teacher should wait patiently for the child to finish expressing himself and should resist the temptation to say "slow down." An adult talking at a slow, relaxed rate and pausing between sentences can give a child time to reflect and respond with more fluency. Keeping eye contact and not rushing, interrupting, or finishing words is also recommended. Classmates should be prohibited from teasing a peer who stutters.

Trautman (2003) identifies the following causes of stuttering:

> There are four factors most likely to contribute to stuttering, *genetics* (approximately 59% of all people who stutter have family members who stutter); *child development* (children with speech, language, cognitive or development delays are more likely to stutter); *neurophysiology* (research has shown that some people who stutter process speech and language in different areas of the brain than people who do not stutter); and *family dynamics* (fast-paced lifestyles and high expectations can contribute to stuttering). (p. 49)

She notes that most stuttering starts between the ages of 2 and 4 and about 20 percent of children in that age group are affected. Many others in this age group go through a temporary lack of fluency and outgrow it. She points out that if stuttering lasts longer than 3 months and begins after the age of 3; the child will likely need therapy to correct it.

Teachers need to listen patiently and carefully to what the child is saying, not how he is saying it. A speech-language pathologist is the appropriate person to evaluate and plan improvement activities.

Cluttering is more involved with the rate of speaking and includes errors in articulation, stress, and pausing. Speech seems too fast, with syllables and words running together. Listener reaction and good speech modeling are critical aspects of behavior for teachers when a child lacks fluency. Adults who work with a young child refrain from criticizing, correcting, acting negatively, or calling a speech problem to the child's attention. They need to create a warm adult-child relationship if possible, and try to eliminate any factors or conditions that increase problems in fluency. They should work to protect the child's expectation of normal fluency and build the child's self-confidence as a speaker.

Approximately 25 percent of all children go through a stage of development during which they seem to stutter (or clutter) when excited or are searching for a word to express their thoughts. A child who appears to be having a problem may be going through a temporary lack of fluency associated with learning to speak.

Only a minority persists in early childhood stuttering, whereas in the majority of cases, stuttering is temporary and an often short-lived disorder that disappears without formal intervention, apparently on its own. Females evidence a higher recovery rate than do males.

Selective (Elective) Mutism

Occasionally, early childhood teachers encounter silent children. Silence may be temporary or lasting, in which case it will be a matter

---

cluttering — rapid, incomplete speech that is often jerky, slurred, spoken in bursts, and difficult to understand; nervous speech.

for teacher concern. Children with **selective (elective) mutism** are described simply as children who can speak but do not. They display functional speech in selected settings (usually at home) and/or choose to speak only with certain individuals (often siblings or same-language speakers). Researchers believe selective mutism, if it happens, commonly occurs between ages 3 and 5 years. Because child abuse may promote delayed language development or psychological disorders that interfere with communication, such as selective mutism, teachers need to be concerned. School referral to speech professionals leads to assessment and individual treatment programs. School administrators prefer that families make appointments and usually provide families with a description of local resources.

Teachers can help professionals by providing observational data to describe the child's behavior and responses in classroom settings. Many factors can contribute to a particular child's silence or reduced speech. Consequently, teachers are cautioned to avoid a mutism diagnosis. A child's teasing or any other action that causes the embarrassment of a child with a language or speech difference should be handled swiftly and firmly by preschool staff members.

At the beginning of the school year or of a child's enrollment, some children may prefer to watch and observe rather than interact. Speakers of languages other than English may choose to play and speak only to those children and adults who understand their language. These behaviors change as English usage grows and the child feels comfortable and secure at school.

OTHER CONDITIONS TEACHERS MAY CONSIDER PROBLEMS

Frequent Crying

Occasionally, frustrated children will cry or scream to communicate a need. Crying associated with adjustment to a new situation is handled by providing supportive attention and care. Continual crying and screaming to obtain an object or privilege, on the other hand, calls for the following kinds of teacher statements:

"I don't understand what you want when you scream. Use words so I will know what you want."

"Sara does not know what you want when you cry, Ethan. Saying 'Please get off the puzzle piece' with your words tells her."

These statements let the child know what is expected and help him see that words solve problems.

Avid Talkers and Shouters

Occasionally, children may discover that talking incessantly can get them what they want. In order to quiet children, others sometimes give in. This is somewhat different from the common give and take in children's daily conversations or children's growing ability to argue and state their cases.

Language for these children becomes a social weapon instead of a social tool. A child may find that loudness in speech can intimidate others and will out-shout the opposition. If a child behaves this way, it is prudent to have the child's hearing checked. Teachers often change this type of behavior through discussions of "inside" (the classroom) voices and "outside" voices (which may be used on the playground), and also by mentioning how difficult it is to hear a "too loud" voice.

Questioners

At times, children ask many questions, one right after another. This may be a good device to hold or gain adults' attention: "Why isn't it time for lunch?" or "What makes birds sing?" or "Do worms sleep?" The questions may seem endless to adults. Most of the questions are prompted by the child's natural curiosity. Educators' help children find out as much as possible and strive to fulfill the needs of the individual child. Along the way, there will be

---

selective (elective) mutism — a behavior that describes child silence or lack of speech in select surroundings and/or with certain individuals.

many questions that may be difficult or even impossible to answer.

Learning Disabilities

It is estimated that over 5 percent of the nation's students are served in publicly funded learning-disabilities programs. The following signs during preschool years may indicate that a child has a learning disability.

- Starts talking later than other children
- Has pronunciation problems
- Has slow vocabulary growth; is often unable to find the right word
- Has trouble learning numbers, the alphabet, days of the week
- Has difficulty rhyming words
- Is extremely restless and easily distracted
- Has trouble with peers
- Displays a poor ability to follow directions or routines
- Avoids puzzles, drawing, and cutting

Experts point out that the sooner a problem can be identified and treated, the better the outcome is likely to be.

Most programs handling children with learning difficulties strive to pinpoint causative factors, and assess children's present level of functioning. Then programs and/or professional consultants develop individual learning plans (IEPs).

Hearing Problems

A screening of young children's auditory acuity may uncover hearing loss. Rones (2004) estimates that 2 to 3 infants of every 1,000 are born with significant and/or permanent hearing loss and about 70 percent get their ears checked before leaving the hospital. The seriousness of hearing loss is related both to the degree of loss and the range of sound frequencies that are most affected. Because young children develop ear infections frequently, schools alert parents when a child's listening behavior seems newly impaired.

Otitis media is a medical term that refers to any inflammation of the middle ear. There are two types of otitis media: (1) a fluid-filled middle ear without infection and (2) an infected middle ear. Researchers believe that otitis media may affect babbling and interfere with an infant's ability to hold on to a string of utterances in working memory long enough to draw meaning. Many preschoolers have ear infections during preschool years, and many children have clear fluid in the middle ear that goes undetected. Even though the hearing loss caused by otitis media may be small and temporary, it may have a serious effect on speech and language learning for a preschool child. The common cold outranks child ear infection, and a teacher can expect one child in three to be affected on any given day during some seasons of the year.

If undetected hearing distortion or loss lasts for a long period, the child can fall behind. One of three children enrolled in speech and language special treatment therapy is estimated to have a history of middle ear disease (Mody et al., 1999). General inattentiveness, wanting to get close to hear, trouble with directions, irritability, or pulling and rubbing of the ear can be signs a teacher should heed. Other signs to look for include:

- difficulty hearing word endings such as -*ed*, -*ing*, and -*s*.
- problems interpreting intonation patterns, inflections, and stress.
- distractibility.
- inattentiveness.
- asking adults to repeat.
- confusion with adult commands.
- difficulty repeating verbally presented material.
- inappropriate responses to questions.
- watching for cues from other children.
- complaints about ears.
- persistent breathing through the mouth.
- slowness in locating the source of sounds.

---

otitis media — inflammation and/or infection of the middle ear.

- softer or "fuzzier" speech than others.
- aggressiveness.
- loss of temper.★

Hearing loss can be temporary or permanent. Early detection and treatment are important.

Preschool staff members who notice children who confuse words with similar sounds may be the first to suspect **auditory processing** difficulties or mild to moderate hearing loss.

Mild hearing impairment may masquerade as

- stubbornness.
- lack of interest.
- a learning disability.

With intermittent **deafness**, children may have difficulty comprehending oral language.

Severe impairment impedes language development and is easier to detect than the far more subtle signs of mild loss. Most infected ears cause considerable pain, and parents are alerted to the need for medical help. However, if the ear is not infected or if the infection does not cause pain, the problem is harder to recognize.

SEEKING HELP

If a child's speech or language lags behind expected development for the child's mental age (mental maturity), school staff members should observe and listen to the child closely to collect additional data. When speech is unusually difficult to understand—rhythmically conspicuous, full of sound distortion, or consistently difficult to hear—this indicates a serious problem. Professional help is available to parents through a number of resources. Most

cities have speech and hearing centers and public and private practitioners specializing in speech-language pathology and audiology. Other resources include:

- city and county health departments.
- universities and medical schools.
- state departments of education offices.
- the American Speech-Language-Hearing Association.

Experts give the families of hearing-impaired children the following advice.

- Help the child "tune in" to language.
- Talk.
- Provide stimulation.
- Read picture books.
- Enroll the child in an infant-stimulation program during infancy.
- Schedule frequent doctor examinations.
- Join parent organizations with a hearing-impairment focus.
- See the child simply as a child rather than "a hearing-impaired child."

SUGGESTIONS AND STRATEGIES FOR WORKING WITH CHILDREN WITH DISABILITIES AND SPECIAL NEEDS

The following suggestions and strategies are useful with typically developing children but also help children with disabilities and special needs. They apply to educators, administrators and families.

- Investigate whether a child is receiving supportive services at school and/or at an out-of-school location.
- Investigate equipment and media used or developed for specific problems or needs.

★Reprinted with permission from Mody, M., et al. (1999). Speech perception and verbal memory in children with and without histories of otitis media. *Journal of Speech, Language, and Hearing Research, 42*: 1069–1079. Copyright © 1999 by American Speech-Language-Hearing Association. All rights reserved.

auditory processing — the full range of mental activity involved in reacting to auditory stimuli, especially speech sounds, and in considering their meanings in relation to past experience and to their future use.
deafness — hearing is so impaired that the individual is unable to process auditory linguistic information, with or without amplification.

◆ Create and provide visual aids that depict or clarify instructional intent, such as posters and signs with pictures, drawings, or photographs.

◆ Use gestures that clarify words.

◆ Place children next to others who can provide help.

◆ Use cues such as a flashing light or music to gain attention, if necessary.

The Individuals with Disabilities Education Act, through federal and state mandates, ensures that children who have educationally significant hearing loss and certain other disabilities receive free, appropriate, public education. Programs develop a team approach that includes families or others familiar with the child's personality and interests, and professionals who are knowledgeable. This group creates individualized learning plans. Classroom environments are designed to promote learning and child comfort (Katz & Schery, 2006).

ADVANCED LANGUAGE ACHIEVEMENT

Each child is unique. A few children speak clearly and use long and complex sentences at 2, 3, or 4 years of age. They express ideas originally and excitedly, enjoying individual and group discussions. Some may read simple primers (or other books) along with classroom word labels. Activities that are commonly used with kindergarten or first-grade children may interest them. Just as there is no stereotypical average child, language-talented children are also unique individuals. Inferring that these language-precocious children are also intellectually gifted is not at issue here. Young children with advanced language development may exhibit many of the following characteristics. They:

◆ attend to tasks in a persistent manner for long periods.

◆ focus deeply or submerge themselves in what they are doing.

◆ speak maturely and use a larger-than-usual vocabulary.

◆ show a searching, exploring curiosity.

◆ ask questions that go beyond immediate happenings.

◆ demonstrate avid interest in words, alphabet letters, numbers, or writing tools.

◆ remember small details of past experiences and compare them with present happenings.

◆ read books (or words) by memorizing pictures or words.

◆ prefer solitary activities at times.

◆ offer ideas often and easily.

◆ rapidly acquire English skills, if bilingual, when exposed to a language-rich environment.

◆ tell elaborate stories.

◆ show a mature or unusual sense of humor for age.

◆ possess an exceptional memory.

◆ exhibit high concentration.

◆ show attention to detail.

◆ exhibit a wide range of interests.

◆ demonstrate a sense of social responsibility.

◆ show a rich imagination.

◆ possess a sense of wonder.

◆ enjoy composing poems or stories.

◆ use richly descriptive expressions in talking.

◆ are highly attentive listeners who remember exceptionally well.

◆ read print in the classroom environment.

◆ write recognizable words or combinations of words.

◆ have sophisticated computer skills.

◆ express feelings and emotions, as in storytelling, movement, and visual arts.

◆ use rich imagery in informal language.

◆ exhibit originality of ideas and persistence in problem solving.

◆ exhibit a high degree of imagination.

Preschoolers may recognize letters early and show an early focus on printed matter. They may be interested in foreign languages and also exhibit correct pronunciation and sentence structure in their native language. Young children may show an advanced vocabulary and may begin reading before they start preschool.

Unfortunately, young children who may be quiet, noncompetitive, and nonassertive; who are slow to openly express feelings; who rarely make direct eye contact, ask questions, or challenge something they know is incorrect; and who are acting appropriately according to their home culture may not be identified as gifted or talented. For indicators of outstanding verbal and linguistic abilities in Native American and Alaskan native children, see Figure 5–13.

Most experts recommend planning activities within the regular curriculum that promote advanced children's creative thinking. Suggestions include providing the following opportunities.

◆ Fluency opportunities: Promoting many different responses, for example, "What are all the ways you can think of to . . ."

◆ Flexibility opportunities: Having the facility to change a mind-set or see things in a different light, for example, "If you were squirrel how would you feel, . . ."

◆ Originality opportunities: For example, "Make something that no one else will think of."

INDICATORS OF OUTSTANDING VERBAL
AND LINGUISTIC ABILITIES

knows signs and symbols of the traditional culture (at an earlier age and beyond the average child)

recalls legends in greater depth and detail after fewer hearings

is more aware of cultural norms and standards at an earlier age

has great auditory memory

remembers details of "everyday" events

makes up elaborate stories, songs, and/or poems

FIGURE 5–13 Identifying outstanding talent in American Indian/Native American (AI/NA) students. (From U.S. Department of Education, Office of Educational Research and Improvement. [1994]. *Identifying outstanding talent in American Indian and Alaska Native students.* Washington, DC: Author.)

◆ Elaboration opportunities: Embellishing of an idea or adding detail, for example, presenting a doodle or squiggle and asking, "What could it be?"

Some educators believe that teachers can help ward off problems for advanced students by grouping language-advanced children with others of high ability or shared interests. Other educators feel doing so robs peers of the sparkle and insight some peers possess.

Arranging situations in which the child's gifts or talents are seen as a group asset is another tactic, as is promoting individual special assignments and varied projects.

If teachers believe as does Gardner (1993, 2000) in the theory of multiple intelligences (one of which is linguistic intelligence) and in the occurrence of "crystallizing experiences," those teachers will notice the young children who take particular interest in and react overtly to some attractive quality or feature of a language arts activity. These children will tend to immerse themselves and focus deeply. This may be the child who loves to act roles in dramatic play, collects words, is fascinated with books or alphabet letters, creates daily rhymes, or displays similar behaviors. The child may persist and spend both time and effort on his chosen pursuit and displays a definite intellectual gift.

Renzulli (1986) defines the talented child's behavior as

. . . evident when a child displays three basic characteristics . . . above-average ability, creativity, and "task commitment," that special drive and motivation that causes some individuals to persist at something when others would quit. (p. 70)

SUMMARY

Teachers work with children who may differ greatly in language development. One of the teacher's roles is to carefully work toward increasing the child's use of words while providing a model of Standard English through activities and daily interaction. Teachers are careful not to give children the impression that their speech is less worthy than that of others.

Program goals should be clearly understood, as should the needs and interests of children who have developed a language that differs from the language of the school. Cultural differences exist, and teachers need to be aware of them to understand the young child. The teacher can provide activities that start at the child's present level and help the child grow, know more, and speak in both Standard English and his native language. Bilingual programs have become a political issue, and some states have eliminated them.

Speech differences require observation and study by a center's staff. Various language behaviors are considered speech and language disabilities. Families can be alerted to whether their children may need further professional help that a school is unable to provide.

ADDITIONAL RESOURCES

Readings

Beaty, J. J. (1997). *Building bridges with multicultural picture books: For children 3–5.* Upper Saddle River, NJ: Merrill/Prentice Hall.

Cook, R. E., Klein, M. D., & Tessler, A., In collaboration with Daley, S. E. (2004). *Adapting early childhood curricula for children in inclusive settings* (6th ed.). Upper Saddle River, NJ: Pearson/Merrill/Prentice Hall.

Grisham-Brown, J., Hemmeter, M., & Pretti-Frontczak, K. (2005). *Blended practices for teaching young children in inclusive settings.* Baltimore, MD: Paul H. Brookes Publishing.

Hanline, M. F., Nunes, D., & Worthy, M. B. (2007, July). Augmentive and alternate communication in early childhood years. *Young Children, 62*(4), 78–82.

Klein, M., Klein, D., & Chen, D. (2001). *Working with children from culturally diverse backgrounds.* Albany, NY: Delmar.

Meier, D. R. (2003). *The young child's memory for words: Developing first and second language and literacy.* New York: Teachers College Press.

Miller, J. (2000). Teaching and learning about cultural diversity. *The Reading Teacher, 53*(8), 666–667.

Orellana, M. F. (2002). The work kids do: Mexican and Central American immigrant children's contribution to households and schools in California. *Harvard Educational Review, 71*(3), 5.

Swick, K. (2004). *Empowering parents, families, schools and communities during the early childhood years.* Champaign, IL: Stipes Publishing.

Helpful Websites

American Educational Research Association (AERA)
http://www.aera.net
Information on the academic achievement of second-language learners (search Publications).

Aspectos Culturales
http://www.aspectosculturales.com
Review resources for teachers concerning Hispanic culture and language.

Council for Exceptional Children
http://www.cec.sped.org
Contains readings and links to publications.

ERIC Clearinghouse on Disabilities and Gifted Education
http://ericec.org
Includes information about gifted recent immigrant children and warning signs in preschoolers' language development.

Kids Together, Inc.
http://www.kidstogether.org
Contains up-to-date information about disabilities.

National Association for Bilingual Education
http://www.nabe.org
Association for teachers of bilingual children.

National Black Child Development Institute
http://www.nbcdi.org
Addresses issues concerning African-American children.

National Parent Information Center
http://npin.org
Provides information about communication disorders and English-language learners.

Book Companion Website

There are additional readings, web activities, exercises, and websites to explore, or you can participate in a rating activity. Criteria for the selection of Afro-centric books is identified. Check to see if you know what some others may not know concerning children's hearing loss and hearing screening.

STUDENT ACTIVITIES

1. Since vocabulary words can be more easily learned when teachers demonstrate, define, and present words in meaningful contexts, think of how many words might be associated with young English-language learners' body parts and body actions—such as nose, eyes, mouth or scratch, drink, jump, and so on. With a peer create a few activity ideas. Share with the total group. (Example: Building a face drawing with the child group by adding one feature at a time daily and printing its name adjacent to the drawing.)

2. Interview the director of a center that cares for bilingual and/or economically disadvantaged young children. Ask what techniques are used to increase a child's language ability. If there is no early childhood center in your community, give examples of goals or techniques used to increase a disadvantaged child's language ability that you have found from research at a library.

3. Observe a "silent-at-group-time" child at play and lunch period. Try to assess when or under what circumstances this child is more verbal. Take written notes.

4. Knowing that it will be crucial that a newly enrolled 4-year-old English-language learner feels both welcome and special on his first day of school (which with this child happens to be in the second month of school), what will you, the teacher, do to prepare the class? (Example: Ask all enrolled children to practice introducing themselves at opening circle on Hermisio's first day by saying, "Hi Hermisio. Me llamo, Andrew. My name is Andrew.") Devise three other plans of action with a peer. Then share with the total group.

5. Tape your voice in a 5-minute conversation with a friend. Have the recording analyzed for dialect, accent, and Standard English usage.

6. Consider the following children. Which children would you suggest to the center's director as possibly needing further staff observation and expert assessment and help?

   a. Trinh seems roughly 2 years behind his age-mates in vocabulary.
   b. Rashad turns his head toward speakers frequently.
   c. Barbara rubs one ear constantly.
   d. Doan cups his hand behind his ear when spoken to.
   e. Tisha is 3, and one cannot understand her words.
   f. Nelson says, "Why did his folks call him Rocky, when he can't say it? He says his name is Wocky Weed!"
   g. Maria is always stressed and extremely tense when she has to speak.
   h. Benji has a monotone quality to his voice.
   i. Becky reads difficult books without help.

7. React to the following statement concerning Ebonics: Pride and self-respect should be the result of effort and achievement. Providing students who are already at an educational disadvantage with a false sense of pride in the misuse of language is an unwise course of action.

CHAPTER REVIEW

A. Answer the following questions.

1. How can a teacher learn about the cultural background of a child?
2. What should be the teacher's attitude toward children whose speech is different from the teacher's speech?

B. Define the following terms.

1. dialect
2. bilingual
3. stuttering

4. auditory
5. cluttering
6. articulation

7. otitis media
8. subculture
9. Standard English

C. Select the correct answer. Some items have more than one correct answer.

1. Standard English is
   a. the language of textbooks.
   b. often taught slowly to non-Standard English speakers.
   c. often different from English spoken in a dialect.
   d. needed for success in any line of work.

2. Early childhood centers try to
   a. teach children Standard English during the first days of school.
   b. make sure each child feels secure.
   c. plan activities in which language-different children have an interest.
   d. provide for each child's development of word use in his own dialect.

3. Teachers should be careful to guard against
   a. correcting children's speech by drawing attention to errors.
   b. thinking that only Standard English is correct and therefore better than English spoken in a dialect.
   c. giving children the idea that they speak differently or "funny."
   d. feeling that children who come from low-income homes are always disadvantaged when compared with children from middle-income homes.

4. Young children with speech errors
   a. rarely outgrow them.
   b. may need special help.
   c. often do not hear as well as adults.
   d. can hear that what they say is different but do not have the ability to say it correctly.

162

5. Bilingualism in the young child is
   a. always a disadvantage.
   b. sometimes a disadvantage.
   c. a rewarding challenge to the teacher.
   d. a problem when schools make children feel defeated and unaccepted.

D. Explain why designations such as Asian or Hispanic do not accurately describe a child's culture.

E. List teacher techniques appropriate and useful in classrooms enrolling English-language learners.

F. Describe the speech characteristics of children who speak African-American English.

G. Provide two statements that are an example of a deficit perspective attitude.

CHAPTER **6**

Achieving Language and Literacy Goals Through Program Planning

OBJECTIVES

After reading this chapter, you should be able to:

- ◆ Define literacy.
- ◆ Describe emerging literacy in early childhood.
- ◆ Discuss program planning for early childhood language arts activities.
- ◆ Describe assessment's role in program development.
- ◆ Write an activity plan for a language arts activity.

KEY TERMS

activity plans	curriculum models	psychosocial theory
assessment	early literacy	social constructivist
behaviorism	interactionists	theory
child-initiated	literacy	visual literacy
curricula	nativists	webbing
constructivist theory	nurturist	
cultural literacy	phonological	
curriculum	awareness	

QUESTIONABLE LANGUAGE

A group of Asian, English-language-learning boys often played only with each other. I was continually attempting to help them branch out and play with other children. It was slowly happening.

At pick-up time, Mrs. Vu, Tan's mother, asked to speak with me. She had brought her neighbor with her as an interpreter. Moving out of the children's range of overhearing our conversation, her neighbor expressed Mrs. Vu's concern. Some of the Asian boys were using very inappropriate words in their native tongue, laughing and then running away. They had been careful in avoiding this activity when Phan, the bilingual assistant, was near. After assuring Mrs. Vu that we shared her concern and would monitor the children's behavior, I thanked her. Fortunately, we had an impending family meeting.

QUESTIONS TO PONDER

1. Could some kind of planned child activity be used to address this problem?

2. What words would you use if you "caught" the boys in this behavior?

3. Should this behavior be discussed at a family meeting, or is this a private matter?

This text divides language arts into four inter-related areas—listening, speaking, writing, and reading—and also discusses **visual literacy** (viewing) as a primary, basic human capacity closely related to the other language arts areas. Increasing the child's understanding of how language arts combine and overlap in everyday preschool activities helps increase language use and **literacy**. Early childhood teachers realize that when children are taught to read or when a few children begin reading on their own before kindergarten, the learning of reading is dynamically concerned with the *interrelatedness* of the literacy skills of listening, speaking, and print (writing). Learning to read with ease happens more readily when young children listen, converse easily, think with and about words, and have rich vocabularies they have used to express their ideas.

To that end, a unified and balanced approach is recommended, one in which the teacher purposefully shows and stresses connections between areas (Figure 6–1). Past practice and program planning in schools attempted to promote literacy by dividing (segmenting) language arts into separate skills. Educators now believe separate, but integrated, skill activities can be part of a balanced language arts program.

The ages of the children and their past life experiences will decide the literacy activities a teacher plans and presents and the techniques and adult-child interaction the educator deems appropriate. Classes may include children who have been in group settings for 3 or 4 years, children with identified disabilities, children with exceptional abilities, children who are already independent readers, and children just beginning to acquire some basic literacy. Literacy knowledge grows and develops within human relationships with responsive adults and the other children.

Listening (receptive language)
  One hears speech.
  One can listen to another reading orally.
  One can listen and write what one hears.
Speaking (oral expressive language)
  One can speak to a listener.
  One can put speech into written form.
  One can read orally.
Writing
  One can write what is spoken and heard.
  One's writing can be read.
  One's writing can be read and spoken.
Reading
  One can read written words.
  One can listen to another reading.
  One can read speech when it is written.

FIGURE 6–1 Interrelations of early childhood language arts.

VISUAL LITERACY

As discussed in Chapter 4, a number of researchers and experts in the early childhood literacy field believe that, in addition to listening, speaking, writing, and reading, a fifth language

visual literacy — the ability to interpret and communicate with respect to visual symbols in media other than print.
literacy — involves complex cognitive interactions between readers and their texts and between background knowledge and new information. It involves both skill and knowledge and varies by task and setting. Different types of literacy are described—prose, document, quantitative, academic, workplace, and functional.

arts area exists—visual literacy, or viewing. The goals of instruction in the visual literacy area involve promoting young children's visual perception skills. This includes attending behavior, discrimination, identification, analysis, classification, sorting, and categorization of visual images. In other words, a conscious noting of differences in visual characteristics would be undertaken. These characteristics include line, shape, color, number, texture, movement, and dimension, as well as other features. This area of study can be referred to in professional readings as visual thinking, visual intelligence, visual awareness, visual sensitivity, and visual arts. It specifically relates to a child's perception of the world; how she reacts to viewed images; how she sees, feels, and interprets emotions evoked; and how she arrives at insights concerning visual media.

Visual literacy, based on the idea that visual images are a language, is defined as the ability to understand and produce visual messages. It is believed useful in improving children's cognitive, reading, writing, and creative skills.

Visual literacy is currently a field of educator research and study. It has become increasingly important with young children's growing exposure to television, videos, video games, computers, and other mass media. The ability to think critically and visually about images is a crucial skill.

Stieglitz (2008) points out that the sense of sight is the most important and basic source of information concerning one's surroundings. It involves not only the eye but also the brain. Elements of the visual perception process are light, the visual stimulus and its characteristics, eye receptors, the individual's past experiences, previous knowledge and ideas, and the individual's purposes, interests, and feelings at a particular time. All those who work with young children may easily relate to this discussion if they have observed young children's diverse reactions to a person in a white jacket or a large dog. Piaget (1970) noted that individuals do not simply record reality but rather transform it by operation of the intellect.

Morrow and Asbury (2003) believe that the visual literacy area should be integrated with writing, listening, reading, and speaking. They also suggest using instruction that is spontaneous, is authentic, and involves children in problem solving; in addition, they recommend instruction that is direct, explicit, and systematic.

Telling stories using a photograph or drawing, eliciting the children's ideas about story content after viewing a picture book's cover, and discussing children's creative art and the details therein or the emotions they feel give teachers insights into what children are thinking. These activities also reveal children's ability to read visual cues and symbols.

When children and adults are in the process of viewing an image or living an event, they are not involved in the process of critical analysis. Rather, they are absorbing those images and events and actively seeking meaning. This would account for children's barrage of questions if they are interested in a new classroom animal, and also explains a good number of their other questions.

When children are encouraged to express their learning through the medium of graphic arts, they are "documenting" their understandings. They are encouraged to do this in the Reggio Emilia approach. Children trace and revisit their discoveries and actions, making them visible.

The exercise is an instrument for reflection and language development as the children discuss their creations. Reflection can lead to a refinement of ideas and further search and discovery. It can be likened to a scientist writing the results of her inquiry, which then leads to further questions. DeMarie (2001) discusses Reggio Emilia children:

> **It is only through the process of repeated investigations using many different languages to represent their learning that these children begin to see the world differently and to attain higher levels of thinking about the topic. (p. 25)**

The primary literacy of the twenty-first century will be visual. Pictures, graphics, and images of every kind will be processed. Children need experience shifting from word to illustration and illustration to word. Observant teachers have always known that visual images help learners understand and remember complex information and abstract concepts.

LITERACY GOALS—SKILL AND KNOWLEDGE

Any discussion of literacy begins with a working definition. Literacy can be defined as a demonstrated competence in communication skills that enables the individual to function, appropriate to age, independently of society and with a potential for movement in society.

Literacy can be conceptualized as a relatively narrow domain of academic inquiry and educational practice (as in reading), or it can be viewed as an encompassing way of being that involves all forms of communication, including mathematical, scientific, and artistic forms. Literacy definitions change and reflect different historical, cultural, and technological development. New technology is enabling students to access the best information in the shortest time, which allows them to identify and solve problems and communicate this information to others. Reading and writing are but the initial layers of the richer and more complex forms of literacy required in Internet use.

Young children usually progress by developing a knowledge of literacy that includes oral language skill and awareness that written (graphic) marks and words carry meaning. Early superficial understandings about picture books and reading aloud lead to a much deeper understanding of the purpose of reading. Psycholinguistic theory focuses on the unique nature of human language—humans' innate search for order, structure, and meaning. Using this theory as a basis, educators can see how children will initiate their own first steps toward literacy when exposed to language-rich environments in which positive attitudes develop toward language arts activities.

Cambourne's definition of literacy (1988) stresses one's ability to use language in daily life.

> . . . literacy is a word which describes a whole collection of behaviors, skills, knowledge, processes and attitudes. It has something to do with our ability to use language in our negotiations with the world. . . . Reading and writing are two linguistic ways of conducting these negotiations. So are speaking, listening, reflecting, and a host of other behaviors related to cognition and critical thinking. (p. 29)

Cultural literacy can be defined as the possession of the basic information needed to thrive in the current world. Children from poor and illiterate homes tend to remain poor and illiterate unless educational opportunities are available. Another definition states that an individual needs to be socialized to literacy and also develop behaviors such as knowing how and when to ask questions, how to hold a book or listen to a story, and when and how to participate.

WHAT IS EARLY LITERACY?

The term **early literacy** refers to young preschool children's language arts behaviors, concepts, and skills that precede and can develop into a literacy that includes reading, conventional writing, and a larger body of literary knowledge at later ages. It considers change over time in how the child thinks about literacy and the strategies the young child uses in her attempts to comprehend or produce oral or written language.

The act of printing shapes with an underlying logic and children's "pretending to read"

---

cultural literacy — literacy that reflects a culture's knowledge of significant ideas, events, values, and the essence of that culture's identity.

early literacy — speaking, listening, print awareness and writing behaviors, reading of alphabet letters and words, and other skills that evolve and change over time, culminating in conventional literacy.

behaviors are viewed as early forms of reading and writing. Many educators believe that additional research is necessary to understand exactly "what clicks into place" when young children make the transition from early reading and writing to conventional reading and writing. Instructional strategies and behavioral techniques based on that knowledge and the identification of what children understand, and which skills aided that transition, enhance a school's planning ability. Early literacy learning happens best in an atmosphere of social collaboration with peers and others who are more literate.

Figure 6–2 shows a set of particular accomplishments that a successful learner is likely to exhibit during preschool years (Snow, Burns, & Griffin, 1998). These authors state that the list is neither exhaustive nor incontestable, but rather it captures many highlights of the course of literacy acquisition revealed through research.

Early home-life activities start children's literacy development by providing early experiences, including parent models and attitudes. A home environment can be stimulating or drab, rich in literate activities or deficient. Children actively search for meaning, and many have lives in which print surrounds them and picture books are familiar. If children have observed and participated in home reading or writing activities, they often enter group care with interest and a positive attitude

---

Birth to 3-Year-Old Accomplishments

- recognizes specific books by cover
- pretends to read books
- understands that books are handled in particular ways
- enters into a book-sharing routine with primary caregivers
- vocalization play in crib gives way to enjoyment of rhyming language, nonsense word play, etc.
- labels objects in books
- comments on characters in books
- looks at a picture in book and realizes it is a symbol for real object
- listens to stories
- requests/commands adult to read or write
- may begin attending to specific print such as letters in names
- uses increasingly purposive scribbling
- occasionally seems to distinguish between drawing and writing
- produces some letterlike forms and scribbles with some features of English writing

3- and 4-Year-Old Accomplishments

- knows that alphabet letters are a special category of visual graphics that can be individually named
- recognizes local environmental print
- knows that it is the print that is read in stories
- understands that different text forms are used for different functions of print (e.g., list for groceries)
- pays attention to separable and repeating sounds in language (e.g., Peter, Peter, Pumpkin Eater, Peter Eater)
- uses new vocabulary and grammatical constructions in own speech
- understands and follows oral directions
- is sensitive to some sequences of events in stories
- shows an interest in books and reading
- when being read a story, connects information and events to life experiences
- asks questions and makes comments demonstrating an understanding of literal meaning of story being told
- displays reading and writing attempts, calling attention to self: "Look at my story."
- can identify 10 alphabet letters, especially those from own name
- "writes" (scribbles) message as part of playful activity
- may begin to attend to beginning or rhyming sound in salient words

FIGURE 6–2 Developmental accomplishments of literacy acquisition. (Reprinted with permission from *Preventing reading difficulties in young children.* © 1998 by the National Academy of Sciences. Courtesy of the National Academy Press, Washington, DC.)

and an early head start in literacy. They are able to enjoy symbolic dramatic play and eventually attempt symbolic representation in art, block building, and a variety of other preschool pursuits. They communicate ideas, discuss meanings, and probe adults and other children for information. Preschoolers growing awareness and "knowledge of literacy" is evident and can include all language arts areas—reading, writing, speaking, listening, and visual representing.

Becoming literate is an extension and companion of language arts skill. Most children acquire spoken language without sit-down instruction; they all become speakers, although at different rates, unless disease, illness, or trauma interferes. Literacy, on the other hand, is not attained unconsciously or by all in our society. Literacy requires a shared body of understanding, much of which involves a common exposure to oral and written material and a level of proficiency in listening, speaking, reading, and writing. Currently, there is a national effort to help students who are not proficient readers,

and surveys show many children experience literacy problems. Literacy acquisition involves a commitment of time and mental energy plus opportunity. At the preschool level, this commitment is a teacher's commitment to presenting a program that both promotes language arts skills and furnishes a shared body of understandings appropriate to preschoolers.

Elementary school reading textbooks in the early part of the twentieth century were collections of classics. The idea of reading levels was not in vogue, but rather the goal was to have every child learn information and skills that were common to the democratic literate public electorate of the time and necessary to the development of a truly educated man or woman. Literacy today is still seen by some as only referring to reading and writing, but many researchers and early childhood educators are concerned with the taproots of literacy, which may be developed during the preschool period (Figure 6–3).

In the age of electronic information processing, meaningful participation is increasingly

FIGURE 6–3 Teachers are trained to encourage child speech during daily interactions and conversations.

dependent on literacy. Few researchers deny that millions of adult Americans are severely hampered by literacy problems and people who are members of minority groups and poor are disproportionately affected.

To be considered functionally literate, one must have knowledge of shared, common information that is neither set down on paper nor explicitly stated in oral communication and that provides the basis for understanding what is heard or read. This idea is well illustrated by a similar phenomenon that occurs when outsiders listen to an in-group whose members have learned a specialized technical vocabulary. For instance, suppose we are having a difficult time understanding a group of computer buffs. We know they are speaking our language, but we cannot understand the bulk of their conversation. As they chat about bits, blogs, DSL, or TCP/IP, they may not make any sense to us. We then might consider ourselves functionally illiterate in computer terminology.

Real access to concepts of cultural heritage comes from extended, personally meaningful conversations with adults, books read aloud at home, and children reading by choice for pleasure.

In programming, an integrated language/literacy approach that emphasizes child comprehension is suggested by current research. It is one of the goals of this textbook.

LANGUAGE ARTS INSTRUCTION—HISTORICAL ROOTS

In examining the historical roots of language arts instruction one could start with the seventeenth-century theorist René Descartes (1596–1650), a French philosopher who theorized that God was responsible for the innate knowledge in children's minds, and the English philosopher John Locke (1632–1704), whose contrasting position suggested that children's minds at birth were blank and unfilled. Locke (1974) also emphasized the importance of experience in learning.

In the eighteenth century, Johann Pestalozzi (1846–1827) of Switzerland and Friedrich Froebel (1782–1852) of Germany presented yet another theory based on their personal interactions with young children. Both Pestalozzi (Rusk & Scotland, 1979) and Froebel (1974) recommend providing "natural environments" in which sensory experiences produce learning and a natural unfolding. Play, they suggested, was the route to learning and intellectual development, along with social, emotional, and physical development. Froebel introduced the notion of treating children with kindness, caring, and compassion. Many schools of the day offered sparse, sterile classroom environments, with young children seated in rows or at desks. Teachers required rote memorization, repetition, imitation, and strict adherence to rules.

The Twentieth Century

At the turn of the twentieth century in the United States, schools for very young children imitated primary school practices, which included memorization and recitation by children, or they simply offered custodial care. Disciples of Froebel began to influence educators along the eastern seaboard. In the Midwest, John Dewey (1916) began experimenting with young children's educational environments. His beliefs promoted a curriculum of teacher-selected topics, themed units of study, and theme-influenced play areas. His ideas affected language arts instructional practices. Dramatic play and book (library) areas are still with us today, and theme instruction has not disappeared. Formal skill-building activities were avoided, but on-the-spot recognized learning moments (teachable moments) were capitalized upon.

Gesell (1940) was also influential. He suggested that developmental "norms" existed, and he believed that child growth and development were based on maturation. For teachers to be effective, they needed to determine children's readiness for learning on a child-by-child basis.

Maria Montessori (1967a), a physician-educator who in 1907 started her experiment by bringing education to children in a deprived area of Rome, captured the attention of some American early educators. Ideas concerning children's learning through sequenced manipulative materials and special teacher-child interactions were recognized. Some group lessons were believed necessary, but primarily, children self-selected from offered activities and decided their own pace, followed their own interests, and worked independently. Montessori instruction stressed order and self-contained tasks. Activities (tasks) had definite beginnings and endings, which included returning materials to shelves. Many of Montessori's activities approached learning in a sensory way; some were color-coded.

In the 1930s and 1940s, it was widely believed that early exposure to formal reading instruction should wait until the necessary skills had been achieved, which was believed to be somewhere around the age of 6½ (Morphett & Washburne, 1931). These prerequisite skills included auditory and visual discrimination, visual motor skills, and large motor skills.

A change occurred in early educational practice during the 1960s and the 1970s. Children were beginning to be seen as constructing their own knowledge of language from their experiences. Rather than moving children to higher levels of development, teachers were to match experiences to children's current levels. Piaget, a Swiss psychologist noted for his observations of his own children, studied children's cognitive growth. Piaget (1952) theorized that a child passed through several sequential stages and was unable to move to a higher stage unless she had mastered the stage before it. Learning took place as the child made sense of her environment through exploration and manipulation.

Chomsky (1968), who was concerned with language development, believed that acquiring language was a matter of the child's gaining facility with the rules that govern language. These rules were not learned but rather ingested as the child matured and interfaced with more mature speakers. Chomsky theorized that the human brain was uniquely equipped with a

language facilitator that he called the "language acquisition device" (LAD).

Vygotsky (1978), considered a sociocultural theorist, suggested that learning took place through social contact and the development of what he termed "private speech." He emphasized the development of socially shared cognition with adults and peers. Adults (or others) assist the child to move ahead in development by noticing what the next logical step might be.

Morrow and Asbury (2003) have listed how different early constructivist approach theorists and philosophers influenced language arts program planning.

- Use of prepared and natural environments for learning
- Equal emphasis on social, emotional, physical, and intellectual development
- Supportive adults who encourage social interaction to aid learning
- A focus on learning rather than teaching
- Awareness that children must be actively involved to learn

Research in the twentieth century provided educators with additional data focusing on oral language, early writing attempts, development of early reading skills, and alphabet learning and/or alphabet sound learning. It emphasized early reading behaviors. This supported the idea that literacy began at birth. Educators tended to believe that a rich literary environment with activities that aided the development of literacy skills did more to promote children's natural interests than direct reading-readiness instruction did. The whole-language movement promoted young children's access to quality literature together with listening, discussion, and active participation in dramatizing, storytelling, poetry, and picture-book times. Early writing and print-related language arts activities gained wide acceptance.

The focus shifted to developmentally appropriate practice in the 1990s, and educators became aware of instructional strategies to prevent reading difficulties through the development of early skills during the preschool years.

Much of early childhood language arts instruction changed. Many programs are working toward a balanced approach to programming, combining a developmental environment and appropriate literacy experiences with research-based, skill-building activities that equip children to make smooth transitions from nonreader to beginning reader to reader.

In the Present

At no time in our history has the public eye been more intently focused on children's reading and writing achievement and classroom instruction in reading and writing. The National Reading Panel Report in 2000 urged an organized and systematic instructional approach with highly qualified teachers. Morrow and Asbury (2003) describe a comprehensive approach to early childhood literacy

> . . . grounded in a rich model of literacy learning that encompasses both elegance and the complexity of reading and language arts processes. Such a model acknowledges the importance of both form (phonemic awareness, phonics, mechanics, etc.) and function (comprehension, purpose, and meaning) of the literacy processes, and recognizes that learning occurs most effectively in a whole-part-whole context. This type of instruction is characterized by meaningful literacy activities that provide children with both the skills and the desire to achieve proficiency and lifelong literacy learning.
>
> Teaching literacy skills and providing opportunities for learning literacy skills are appropriate for young children as long as the teaching methods are appropriate to the child being taught. In such a program, teachers provide numerous literacy experiences that include the integration of reading, writing, listening, speaking, and viewing. (p. 233)

Early childhood instruction may now include the task of assessing developing skills and making instructional plans based on **assessment** data.

In the many early childhood programs that are affected by the Elementary and Secondary Education Act that includes the No Child Left Behind Act (U.S. Department of Education, 2002), periodic assessment is the rule—not the exception—in kindergartens. Early childhood programs are being asked to be accountable by providing data that show young children's progress in the language arts. They are also asked to work more effectively with children's parents.

The quest to identify the most appropriate and effective means to promote children's literacy development has remained elusive for the last half century (New, 2002). New believes the term *emergent literacy* has been replaced by *early literacy*. From this perspective, literacy begins at birth, is ongoing, and is influenced and interpreted by the surrounding sociocultural context. New suggests that as a nation, we are far from achieving common ground on considering the meanings, means, or purposes of early literacy. What we do know is that preschool educators will encounter children who arrive with research-identified risk factors including living in poverty, residing in single-parent homes, having a parent with low educational attainment, and having a home language other than English (Rimm-Kaufman, Pianta, & Cox, 2000). Early childhood educators will face the challenge of providing preschool experiences and activities that prepare children for kindergarten success in the crucial area of language arts. Children will especially need a background that ensures learning to read with ease when formal reading instruction begins. Goldenberg (2002) notes that productive and effective early childhood experiences and instruction must address the *interrelated* aspects of literacy. These follow.

◆ Understanding and use of print functionally (reading and writing for communication, expression, etc.)

---

assessment — a broad repertoire of behaviors involved in noticing, documenting, recording, and interpreting children's behaviors and performances. Testing is a subset of assessment behaviors in which performances are controlled and elicited in standardized conditions.

◆ Understanding and use of the "alphabetic principle" **phonological awareness**, letter names and sounds, efficient and automatic decoding, i.e., writing)

◆ Motivation and interest in using print for a variety of purposes

◆ Language, cognitive skills, and knowledge necessary for comprehension and communication*

Although there is no consensus about how much of each aspect should be stressed, a successful literacy program addresses each of these in sufficient depth and breadth to promote literacy growth in the earliest and later years.

Goldenberg (2002) points out that although there is wide agreement that phonological awareness is an important aspect of being ready to learn to read, there is less agreement about whether children should receive direct instruction and training or whether phonological awareness should be accomplished in "natural language" activities such as poems, chants, songs, and so on. Proponents of strong phonics and phonological awareness training recommend a different set of practices than do those who emphasize the more contextual uses of literacy. Most early childhood educators search for meaningful and functional literacy activities, but many are introducing phonological skill-developing opportunities that encourage children to generate rhymes and segment phonemes within meaningful activities.

The joint position statement of the International Reading Association (IRA) and the NAEYC, *Learning to Read and Write* (1999), serves as a guide for early childhood language arts program development. It describes developmentally appropriate language arts activities in infancy through the early primary grades. Recommended teaching practices and activities are categorized according to children's age levels. It promotes nurturing adult-child relationships;

print-rich environments; daily reading and discussion of high-quality books; oral opportunities that focus on sounds and meaning; phonemic awareness activities; play that includes play with literacy tools; exposure to print, icons, and words in computer games; and firsthand activities that expand knowledge and vocabulary. No one teaching method or approach is likely to be the most effective for all children, according to the position paper. A variety of teaching strategies suited to child diversity and individuality is recommended.

The National Early Literacy Panel. The National Early Literacy Panel has studied literacy research findings extensively. This group recognizes that building young children's literacy skill works and recognizes that demands on early educators are greater than ever before. The panel hopes to identify appropriate early childhood language arts curricula and discover what additional research may be necessary.

The panel is pursuing answers to many questions, including the following:

◆ What literacy skills and abilities in young children (birth to age 5) predict later reading, writing, and spelling outcomes?

◆ What environments and settings contribute to or inhibit gains in skills and abilities and are linked to later outcomes in reading, writing, and spelling?

◆ What child characteristics contribute to or inhibit gains in children's skills and abilities and are linked to later outcomes in reading, writing, and spelling?

◆ What programs and interventions contribute to or inhibit gains in children's skills and abilities and are linked to later outcomes in reading, writing, and spelling?

The panel has already identified a number of variables that have strong and consistent relationships with later literacy outcomes. After their review of a relatively large number of research studies with a relatively large number of children, the following variables were found (Strickland, Shanahan, & Escamalia, 2004).

*From Goldenberg, C. (2002). Making schools work for low-income families in the 21st century. In S. Neuman & D. Dickinson (Eds.), *Handbook of Early Literacy Research.* Copyright © 2002 Guilford Press.

phonological awareness — the whole spectrum from primitive awareness of speech sounds and rhythms to rhyme awareness and sound similarities; at the highest level, awareness of syllables or phonemes.

Strong Predictors of Positive Literacy Outcomes

- alphabet knowledge
- concepts about print
- phonological awareness
- invented spelling
- oral language (expressive, receptive, vocabulary)
- writing of name
- RAN (rapid automatic naming/lexical access)

In using the predictors, the panel cautions that they reviewed only existing research studies. Other predictors may yet be discovered when additional research becomes available.

Putting Theories in Categories

Binding similar theories loosely together may help language arts program planners realize the theoretical basis for their language program decisions.

The **nativists**, those who believe in the natural unfolding of children without direct teaching from adults, include Rousseau, Pestalozzi, and Froebel. These educators can be conceived as thinkers who led later scholars and researchers to propose maturational theories with ages, stages, and normative behaviors.

Psychosocial theory, which stresses stages of human development, is associated with Freud. It can also be seen as a variant of the nativist tradition. Erikson's psychosocial theory stressed specific tasks to be resolved during stages of human development. The major tasks of toddlers and preschoolers were autonomy and initiative. Theory, along this line of thinking, may have evolved into a philosophy of child-directed learning such as traditional Montessori.

Locke's **nurturist** philosophy can be seen as a precursor of highly didactic preschool practices, although he also advocated offering children experiences to promote learning. Program models promote teachers as dispensers of knowledge, but activities might also be presented. These programs are based on the theory of **behaviorism**.

Interactionists view child development and learning as taking place between children and their environment. Program planners promoting this view subscribe to the **constructivist theory**, believing in children's creation of their own internal knowledge as they interact in both social and environmental pursuits. Piaget would describe this interaction as assimilation, accommodation, and equilibration. Vygotsky would emphasize the importance of language and socially shared cognition **social contructivist theory**). He would recommend promoting assisted and scaffolded learning and encouraging children to use private speech to aid them in solving problems.

Although these theories differ in important ways, they share an emphasis on considering

---

nativists — those who adhere to the theory that children are born with biological dispositions for learning that unfold or mature in a natural way.

psychosocial theory — the branch of psychology founded by Erik Erikson; development is described in terms of eight stages that span childhood and adulthood.

nurturist — one who adheres to the theory that the minds of children are blank or unformed and need educational input or direct instruction to develop and "output" knowledge and appropriate behavior.

behaviorism — the theoretical viewpoint, espoused by theorists such as B. F. Skinner, that behavior is shaped by environmental forces, specifically in response to reward and punishment.

interactionists — those who adhere to the theory that language develops through a combination of inborn factors and environmental influences.

constructivist theory — a theory such as that of Jean Piaget, based on the belief that children construct knowledge for themselves rather than having it conveyed to them by some external source.

social constructivist theory — such as Vygotsky's emphasis on the importance of language and socially shared cognition in exchanges between adult and child when scaffolding was used, and encouraging children's use of private speech to aid problem solving.

children as active learners who are able to set goals, plan, and revise. They recognize that children's cognitive development, which is so closely tied to language development, evolves gradually as children acquire strategies for remembering, understanding, and problem solving (Machado & Botnarescue, 2008).

PHILOSOPHIES OF LITERACY INSTRUCTION

A variety of approaches to literacy instruction, representing different philosophical positions, have emerged, resulting in practices using widely diverse teaching techniques, materials, and assessment methods. Contrasting points of view will probably continue as they have in the past. Currently, educators debate the efficacy of academically oriented versus **child-initiated curricula**. Whole-language versus teacher-directed phonics instruction has also received considerable ongoing attention. Out of these debates the "balanced," "eclectic," "natural," and "centrist" philosophical positions have evolved and become often recommended positions.

In a child-initiated model of instruction, children's self-directed actions are facilitated by a teacher. A teacher facilitates learning by (a) providing children with a wide variety of experiences, (b) encouraging children to choose and plan their own learning activities, (c) engaging children in active learning by posing problems and asking questions that stimulate and extend learning, (d) guiding children through skill acquisition activities as needed, and (e) encouraging children to reflect on their learning experiences.

The staff of each early childhood center drafts a program based on the unique mesh of the staff's personal theories about what they believe is appropriate and effective. If a language arts program focuses on the correct form(s) of language, such as the planned and sequential learning of letter names, sounds,

and so forth, the program could be described as traditional, or conventional. This text urges an approach to teaching language arts that is meaning-based and functional for children, literature-rich, and taught in a balanced and interrelated fashion. This type of program approach believes child knowledge and skill in language arts are reinforced and made meaningful when the reading, writing, listening, and speaking aspects of daily activities are encountered concurrently. A developmentally appropriate program first considers the unique group of children enrolled, their needs, their abilities, their interests, and their families' wishes concerning desirable educational outcomes.

Preschools and child centers have given special attention to developmentally appropriate practice guidelines published by the NAEYC. In designing programs for young children, developmentally appropriate practice has three recognized components: age appropriateness, individual appropriateness, and knowledge and honor of children's social and cultural contexts. Many centers depend on developmentally appropriate practice to form a framework for curriculum and adult interactions with children. Deeply embedded in developmentally appropriate practice is the idea that children have a natural disposition toward learning and actively construct their own knowledge through exploration and interaction with materials, peers, and adults. Educators also realize that low-achieving students often need planned and systematic instruction to acquire skills that will enable them to progress and eventually learn to read with ease.

Developmentally appropriate program planning may aim to strengthen what a child already knows and can do and/or may promote what a child can potentially discover or knows or can newly accomplish. See the Appendix for NAEYC's widely held expectations for 3- to 5-year-olds.

Researchers trying to identify the effect of developmentally appropriate practice on children's cognitive development conclude that

---

child-initiated curricula — a basic tenet underlying this type of curriculum is the belief that true growth occurs when children are free to develop intrinsic interests naturally.

children's receptive language was better in pro-grams with higher-quality literacy environ-ments and when developmentally appropriate activities were more abundant. Many educators believe that outdated views, including extensive whole-group instruction and intensive drill and practice of isolated language arts skills, are not suitable or effective with preschoolers. In terms of cognitive development, the use of develop-mentally appropriate instructional strategies appears to facilitate children's creativity, is as-sociated with better verbal skills and receptive language, and contributes to higher levels of cognitive functioning.

Figure 6–4 offers a possible sequence of children's language learning in both planned and spur-of-the-moment classroom activities.

FEDERAL LEGISLATION AFFECTS LANGUAGE ARTS CURRICULA

In July 2001, the White House Summit on Early Childhood Cognitive Development met and focused on the chain of negative educa-tional events that can result when children are unable to master reading in the lower grades of elementary school. An increased federal emphasis exists on not only reading instruc-tion but also what prepares young children and precedes their kindergarten enrollment (Love, 2003).

The federal No Child Left Behind Act (U.S. Department of Education, 2002) sections dealing with guidelines for reading are designed to improve children's reading in publicly funded schools from kindergarten through third grade. Early Reading First, the portion of the law aimed at improving pre-kindergartener's read-ing achievement, specifies that preschool teach-ers at publicly funded schools must deliver systematic and explicit instruction to increase children's oral language development, print awareness, alphabet knowledge, and phonologi-cal awareness (McGee, 2003). Pushing formal reading instruction into preschool classrooms was not recommended and was not the legisla-tion's intent. The idea that literacy experiences

Child has experiential background observing and participating in a rich language arts school environment.

↓

Child gives attention to classroom activities, demonstrations, behaviors modeled by others, new happenings, teacher presentations, or other classroom events. Child perceives activity to be useful, interesting, or worthwhile.

↓

Child feels comfortable and safe in this situation and feels capable and likely successful. Child understands that teacher expects appropriate classroom behavior.

↓

Child continues focus and concentration on activity that is unfolding and progressing.

↓

Child gathers and selects information and data; develops beginning ideas; may ask questions; and looks, listens, touches as if investigating or trying to find out.

↓

Child may see or state relationships and form hypotheses or conclusions and may discuss points of view.

↓

Child may test ideas or check ideas with teacher or others present.

↓

Child may receive feedback from teacher and/or other children. Child may be uncertain or puzzled.

↓

Child may develop a definite idea and "fit" the newness experienced in the activity into what she already knows. Learning occurs.

FIGURE 6–4 Possible sequence in language learning.

during preschool years are critical for successful learning during elementary school years was a central concern.

The assessment of preschool children and programs for them is a "hot button" topic for many early childhood educators. As of November 2006, 14 states have developed quality rating systems (QRS), 9 are piloting a system either statewide or in one or more communities, and 31 are exploring designing one (*Child Care Bulletin*, 2007).

Educators worry that testing will label very young children, and they are concerned about assessment validity and unfair judgments of programs working with disadvantaged children or second-language learners. A draft position statement created by the NAEYC and the National Association of Early Childhood Specialists in State Departments of Education (NAECS/SDE) lists both (1) a general description of responsibilities of educators concerning assessment and (2) the indicators of assessment effectiveness (NAEYC & NAECS/SDE, 2003):

◆ Make ethical, appropriate, valid, and reliable assessment a central part of all early childhood programs. To assess young children's strengths, progress, and needs, use methods that are developmentally appropriate, culturally and linguistically responsive, tied to children's daily activities, supported by professional development, inclusive of families, and connected to specific, beneficial purposes: (a) making sound decisions about teaching and learning, (b) identifying significant concerns that may require focused intervention for individual children, and (c) helping programs improve their educational and developmental interventions.

◆ Ethical principles guide assessment practices.

◆ Assessment instruments are used for their intended purpose.

◆ Assessments are appropriate for ages and other characteristics of children being assessed.

◆ Assessment instruments are in compliance with professional criteria for quality.

◆ What is assessed is developmentally and educationally significant.

◆ Assessment evidence is used to understand and improve learning.

◆ Assessment evidence is gathered from realistic settings and situations that reflect children's actual performance.

◆ Assessments use multiple sources of evidence gathered over time.

◆ Screening is always linked to follow-up.

◆ Use of individually administered, norm-referenced tests is limited.

◆ Staff and families are knowledgeable about assessment.

Standardized testing tends to lead to standardized teaching—one approach fits all—the opposite of the kind of individualized diagnosis and teaching that is needed to help young children continue to progress in reading and writing (IRA & NAEYC, 1999).

More about the No Child Left Behind Act (NCLB)

The No Child Left Behind Act's provision that federal grants be contingent on the fact that all enrolled children at primary schools make "adequate yearly progress" in reading created shock waves throughout public educational systems. As a result, regional areas, states, cities, local communities, school districts, and professional organizations and groups have made attempts to identify age-level literacy characteristics. They have also developed standards and goal statements, pinpointing the literacy skills gained in the early years that may ease children's learning to read. Written standards statements and prescribed curricula can include mandating the time children are to spend in daily classroom literacy-promoting activities. Groups working to address the requirements of the No Child Left Behind Act have also developed, refined, or examined testing alternatives; initiated teacher training and retraining; and pursued various additional efforts. After examining the results of these efforts researchers believe test scores for elementary-aged children have risen only modestly or not at all, and the reading gap remains large.

Early childhood centers attempt to design curricula that are culturally relevant, introduce content and promote varied vocabulary development, instill an enthusiasm for learning, and introduce activities with phonological and phonemic awareness elements. Child observation and documentation activities are now part of the teacher's responsibility in many preschools as well as elementary schools. Child journals, child portfolios, teacher checklists, testing sessions, recording, and observations are commonplace as teachers struggle to identify the literacy growth of each child.

Many educators are involved in debates concerning the wisdom of some or all of the practices that are a result of this federal legislation. Most commonly, they express fears and frustrations involving "pushed down" curriculum formerly introduced in higher grades, literacy or academic activities "crowding out" playtime or other curricular activities, bilingual instructional techniques, and "fairness" in testing. Farstrup (2007) reports that teacher organizations such as the National Education Association and the American Federation of Teachers have made their positions very clear that adequate funding for NCLB has not been made available to support the significant costs of materials, professional development, and required testing programs. The International Reading Association, though expressing strong concerns about the NCLB legislation's possibly overly narrow interpretations and applications of research, still supports the goals of NCLB. Farstrup believes that 5 years of NCLB have resulted in important changes in reading instruction.

Schickendanz (2003) points out that the beliefs of some early childhood educators concerning the code-related aspect of literacy development may create a barrier to their offering literacy instruction (either formal or informal). Code-related components of early literacy consist of phonological awareness, letter name knowledge, knowledge of sound-letter associations, and the insight that letters function to represent sounds in words (that is, the alphabetic principle). Some factors that may influence teachers' behaviors include:

◆ sticking to older, well-known language arts programming activities that ignore new research-based instructional models.

◆ giving a higher priority to other favored daily language arts activities, such as picture book reading, and so on.

◆ receiving teacher training that does not address code-related language development issues.

◆ feeling negative about any "skill' development lessons, whether informal or formal.

Schickendanz goes on to point out that among the revisions and clarifications of the original developmentally appropriate practice guidelines, there is a caution against taking to the extreme such things as the importance of children's play and self-selection of activities and relying on developmental categories as the basis for curriculum and assessment, causing the exclusion of subject-matter content considerations (Schickendanz, 2003). Early childhood educators are as worried as some families are about skill-and-drill sessions, work sheets, and lessons that have no connection to children's backgrounds or interests. Many early childhood educators realize that they may be failing the children who need them the most. Multiple studies show many children from low-income families enter kindergarten a year to a year and a half, on average, behind middle-class children in their language development, as well as other cognitive skills. This is a gigantic lag that dramatically affects children's success in the first grades of primary school and perhaps their entire educational future.

The field is searching for palatable techniques and strategies to incorporate code-related components of literacy mentioned in the No Child Left Behind Act into language arts program planning, particularly for children most in need. The easy part may be intentionally incorporating skill building into daily conversations and daily activities. The hard part may be overcoming teachers' reticence concerning systematic planned skill-based instruction and effectively identifying at-risk children. Educators believe teachers do not need to make children ready for learning; most are quite eager learners.

Criticism and Positive Comments Concerning the No Child Left Behind Act

Some superintendents of urban elementary school districts with large minority and disadvantaged child populations are calling the No Child Left Behind Act the No Teacher Left Standing Act. Because these districts include public schools that have been labeled "in need of improvement," their teachers are struggling and under pressure to show accountable improvement.

Other teachers are angry with the "high standards" and believe the standard equates perfection and is consequently unattainable. Yet others criticize the federal government's amount of funding, saying it is inadequate. After reviewing research undertaken after 2002, some educators question what they feel to be the "meager" research data underpinning the legislation.

Parents, on the other hand, seem to be quite supportive of the No Child Left Behind Act. They are now being told more clearly how much their children are learning at school and how the school is rated, but some families are discouraged by what they feel is excessive homework to attain standards and the amount of required child testing.

One elementary school principal views the No Child Left Behind Act as providing a "tough love" approach that works. His formula for doubling children's reading and math scores in his school was to use a curriculum proven by research and also embrace unpopular testing that prods all students to learn.

State Standards, Head Start Performance Standards, the Head Start Child Outcomes Framework, and Other Frameworks

There are at least three principal reasons for the development and use of standards, according to Kendall and Marzano (2004). These are (1) to establish clarity of curriculum content; (2) to raise expectations for achievement: and (3) to ensure accountability for public education. Most states have state initiatives and standards aimed at preparing preschoolers for kindergarten. Head Start is funded by federal and state funds. Under President George W. Bush's 2003 proposal for improving preschool programs in general and Head Start in particular, states are offered the opportunity to coordinate all preschool programs, including Head Start, in exchange for meeting certain accountability requirements.

States must develop an accountability program that will indicate how well children in individual programs are performing relative to the skills and behaviors identified by the state as prerequisites for effective kindergarten performance. The skills and behaviors should include: pre-reading skills including phonological awareness, letter knowledge, and vocabulary; numeracy; and social-emotional competence.

Curriculum planners and developers in early childhood schools and centers keep standards in mind while preparing a school's program of activities if they receive public funds. Standards adopted at a particular school represent what that school and its teachers expect children to recall, replicate, manipulate, understand, or demonstrate at some point in time—in this case, prior to kindergarten entry.

Early childhood programs nationwide, depending on their state's decision to mandate or recommend their standards, may not be able to design their program of activities, for they may be spelled out in law. Some written standard statements provide examples of child behaviors teachers can observe that indicate child accomplishment or progress toward mastering a particular standard statement. Many state standard statements are in draft or final written form and are available on the Internet or available by contacting a state's Department of Education. The National Institute for Early Childhood Research (NIEER) has a directory of states that have downloadable early childhood (preschool) language and literacy standards (http://www.nieer.org). Another source is http://www.educationworld.com.

Head Start, reauthorized by Congress in 1998, augmented its Head Start Performance Standards, a document that guided language arts program planning along with other curricular areas. In 2000, the Administration for Children and Families (ACF) issued guidelines for devising and implementing outcome-based education plans. Consequently, the Head Start Child Outcomes Framework (U.S. Department of Health and Human Services, 2003) was released. The framework involves eight basic learning and development "domains." Two domains are identified as language development and literacy. Each domain is composed of 27 domain elements and 100 examples of specific indicators of ability. Head Start has shifted from its original focus on social competence and play to literacy and discrete academic outcomes.

The framework gives definition to learning objectives for Head Start and Head Start teachers and could be used to guide curriculum planning and assessment. The objectives include five federally mandated indicators of learning achievement that were set as requirements for Head Start children graduating their programs and entering kindergarten.

The framework also emphasizes the importance of parents' understanding of their vital out-of-school function in promoting language and literacy development. It promotes parents' understanding that children's cumulative life experiences and adult-child interactions from birth on affect language and literacy growth.

All early childhood educators who wish to can use the Head Start framework as a research-based guide and design program activities that work toward the identified outcomes. Individual states may choose to adopt or recognize the Head Start Performance Standards and the Head Start Child Outcomes Framework, in whole or in part, as they endeavor to better coordinate their early childhood programs and also create preschool programs of excellence. To obtain a copy of the Head Start Performance Standards or the Head Start Child Outcomes Framework, go to http://www.hsnrc.org.

The National Association for the Education of Young Children's *Standards and Accreditation Performance Criteria for Early Childhood Programs* (2005b) has been developed through a national effort to identify language and literacy standards. These standards provide guidelines for the content that children are learning, the planned activities linked to these goals, the daily schedule and routines, and the availability and use of materials for children (Strickland & Riley-Ayers, 2006). To review language and literacy standards, guidelines, and performance criteria, search online at http://www.naeyc.org. Proceed to *Academy* for additional NAEYC accreditation information.

To obtain a copy of the Mid-continent Research for Education's Framework for Early Literacy Instruction, search online at http://www.mcrel.org. The framework outlines standards, benchmarks, developmental accomplishments, and child behaviors for pre-K through kindergarten.

Stott (2003) has noted the uncertain feelings and fears about accepting standards, whether state, federal, association, or center created. She has attempted to list both advantages and "downsides" of standards.

Advantages

◆ Standards may help all entering kindergartners start school with similar knowledge and skills.

◆ Preschool standards align with K–12 education standards.

◆ The same learning expectations are set for all students.

◆ Early childhood teachers are provided with guidelines concerning what children need to learn before beginning kindergarten.

◆ The same high standards are used for all children, regardless of geographical area, consequently smoothing child transfer adjustment from school to school.

◆ Standards help preschool teachers put meaningful content into their curricula.

◆ As universal standards, they could guide early childhood educators in curriculum development, including complex grammatical structure and vocabulary.

◆ Standards could specify the necessary knowledge, skills, and competencies.

◆ Greater professionalism may be brought to the early childhood career field.

Disadvantages

◆ The specificity of standards may be too broad or too inflexible.

◆ Assessment and accountability could lead to the identification of narrowly defined skills or facts.

◆ Standards could lead to high-stakes testing.

◆ Curriculum may be constructed to match test items.

◆ Children's social-psychological development or cognitive and creative thought may be ignored.

◆ Less mature children may be labeled failures.

◆ Standards may affect children's self-confidence and motivation.

◆ Teachers may know what to teach but may not know how to teach it.

◆ Families or caregivers may be affected by academic pressures exerted through their children's teachers*

Stott believes that standards in the field of early education are an essential first step for designing a more effective preschool curriculum.

LANGUAGE USE IN ALL CURRICULUM AREAS

Every planned preschool activity uses language in some way. Past experience is basic to all language arts because a child's success often depends on her understanding of what is happening. Language helps children learn, retain, recall, and transmit information. Messages are received through words and nonverbal means. The teacher's speech, behavior, and use of words in planned activities are discussed in the following chapters.

In addition to the early childhood center's planned program, daily sequence of activities, play with peers, and unplanned happenings also stimulate language. Teachers use every oppor-

tunity to add meanings in a natural, conversational way during the preschool day. This generally begins with the teacher's personal greeting or affectionate physical contact as the child enters the center. The "hello" and comments are part of the rituals in preschools that aim to recognize each child's presence each arrival time.

Daily routines are the regular features of a school's program that occur about the same time every day—snacks, toileting, and group activities—in which language is an associate function. Language-related activities are included in both small and large group times; these activities can range from short announcements to literacy-oriented activities the teacher presents or prepares (Figure 6–5).

Planned activities should have a purpose children can understand and in some way connect to what they already know (Figure 6–6). Most, if not all, learning can be made applicable to the child's life. Early childhood practitioners provide real, hands-on experiences in their classrooms when possible. Secondhand activities are second best.

In an activity planting spring seeds, signs or labels adjacent to planted seeds have a practical purpose. The teacher could read the seed packet instructions to the children to find out about planting particulars. If individual planting pots are used, the children and/or teacher could print their names to label them.

Educators are encouraged to use number and measurement terms in preschool activities

FIGURE 6–5 A teacher becomes part of the child group while a student teacher leads an activity.

*From Stott, F. (2003, Nov.). Making standards meaningful. *Early Childhood Today, 18*(3):19–20. Copyright © 2003 Scholastic, Inc. Used with permission.

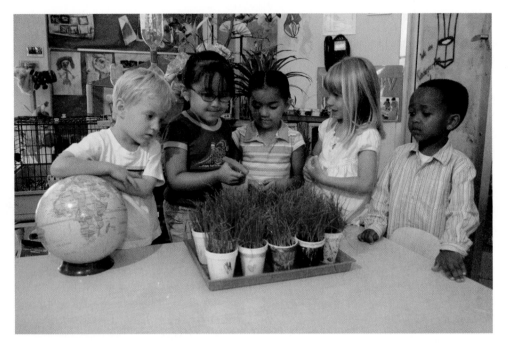

FIGURE 6–6 Many new words can be connected to an activity with growing plants.

in which counting, comparing, adding, or taking away is encountered in planned or unplanned daily happenings. Participation in preschool activities that touch on math knowledge and terminology dramatically reduces the disparities between children from low-income and middle-income families.

LANGUAGE ARTS PROGRAMMING

Preplanned language arts programs develop from identified goals: the knowledge, skills, and attitudes that the school intends to teach (Figure 6–7). Early childhood teachers also

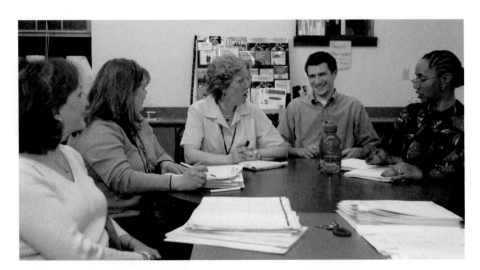

FIGURE 6–7 Staff members, consultants, parents, and community representatives may all be involved in language arts program development.

base teaching techniques on what they believe is best, right, appropriate, and prudent. This, in turn, is connected to views they hold about how, what, when, and where children learn to communicate and use language. The following views about language learning are commonly expressed or implied by staff members involved in planning language arts programs.

◆ Language permeates all planned and unplanned activities.

◆ A dynamic, rich-in-opportunity classroom stimulates communication and exchanges of ideas.

◆ Real experiences are preferred to vicarious ones when practical and possible.

◆ The reciprocal nature of exploring and discovering together should be promoted by teachers.

◆ Play provides many opportunities to learn language.

◆ Teachers' instructional techniques should be skilled and alert to child readiness.

◆ Stressing relationships between objects, events, and experiences is a useful teaching technique.

◆ Individual planning, as well as group planning, is desirable.

◆ Program activities should center on the children's interests.

◆ Literary classics (preschool level) are an important planned-program component.

◆ The entire teaching staff should be committed to and enthusiastic about their planned program and should understand the stated objectives.

◆ An integrated approach to language arts instruction helps children experience the "connectedness" of language arts areas.

◆ Reading and writing is better conceptualized as a developmental continuum.

The best type of planned literacy-promoting program is one that is captivating enough to hold the imagination, engaging enough to sustain active involvement for a period of time, and stimulating enough to motivate further literacy exploration.

Early childhood teachers realize that teachers' goals for attending children may be much different than families' goals. Rather than telling parents what they ought to be doing, it is the school's job to support and complement families' efforts; there is sometimes a need to find community translators to help bridge the gap between home and school.

One can envision an ideal language arts curriculum starting at birth and continuing throughout the child's lifetime. The author sees it as a program of home and life experiences supporting learning and self-discovery in which colorful, interconnected strands of language arts knowledge and skill thread through early childhood and come together in an "'aha' rainbow" when the child successfully decodes her first word, first sentence, or first book. The child then passes through a door equipped to move on into a vast amount of stored human knowledge, discovery, inspiration, creativity, and fantasy. These milestones in development are hopefully accompanied by understanding, rich personal life experiences, natural inquisitiveness, and a belief in the child's own ability and self-worth.

The ideal early childhood curriculum in language arts offers quality child-relevant speaking, listening, early writing, and reading activities in addition to literature opportunities. These activities encourage, sustain, and provide growth, ensuring the necessary foundational knowledge and skill for an easy transition to school and a successful kindergarten year and beyond.

Teacher Training

Your classes in early childhood education, self-study, and your life experiences will influence the early childhood literacy program you will attempt to offer young children. Many times, your ideas will be incorporated into a teaching team's effort to design a planned curriculum.

Your training should have encouraged you to continually improve instructional practice and to analyze what is working and what is not. Questioning and researching are parts of the joy of teaching and can lead to new techniques and insights. When looking for program ideas, be open-minded and look inside to remember what inspired your own literacy development. Do not discount your ability to really focus on children and discover their agenda or your ability as an "innovator" of a language arts program that addresses the needs and interests of each child. The Appendix holds a section of language and literacy specifics that well-prepared candidates (early childhood education majors) should possess. It also cites research-based knowledge and skills. Research has identified the following "critical" teacher behaviors.

- Using new words with children
- Extending children's comments through questioning
- Focusing children's attention on an analysis of books read to them
- Engaging in intellectually challenging conversations
- Placing an importance on child attentiveness during group time
- Obtaining and maintaining children's attention
- Believing academic and social goals are both important
- Providing literacy-learning opportunities and being intentional in instructional efforts to stretch children's thinking
- Supporting children's writing attempts
- Providing knowledge, promoting phonological sensitivity, and instilling child familiarity with the basic purposes and mechanisms of reading, especially to preschoolers with less prior knowledge and skill (at-risk children)
- Giving individual children adequate time to speak
- Planning and implementing small group activities
- Engaging in extensive conversations
- Joining individual children or small groups in the library or writing areas
- Creating a literacy-rich classroom environment with accessible materials
- Ensuring careful organization and management of materials

- Providing opportunities for children to practice skills taught
- Giving guidance in structured lessons for acquisition of skills
- Providing opportunities for children to work independently or in collaborative groups

Programs for At-Risk Preschoolers

The U.S. Department of Education defines a linguistically and culturally diverse child (an educational term) as a child who is either non-English proficient (NEP) or limited-English proficient (LEP). Educators recognize the difficulties many young children may face when entering child care centers or preschools and attempting to learn an unfamiliar language.

High-quality educational programs recognize and promote all aspects of children's development and learning (Figure 6–8). Their goal is to enable all children to become competent, successful, and socially responsible adults.

Preschools and early childhood centers enrolling lower-income families need to consider the following recommendations:

> **Failure to develop an adequate vocabulary, understanding of print concepts, or phonological awareness during the preschool years constitutes some risk for reading difficulties. Hence, we recommend interventions designed to promote growth. At the same time, however, we caution that the focus of intervention should not be limited to overcoming these risk factors in isolation but should be more broadly designed to provide a rich language and literacy environment that methodically includes the promotion of vocabulary, the understanding of print concepts, and phonological awareness. (Snow, Burns, & Griffin, 1998, p. 133)**

Culturally Diverse Musical Experience

The songs and music of childhood are a part of our cultural heritage. The folk songs and ballads that have survived to the present day and the regional tunes parents and teachers offer

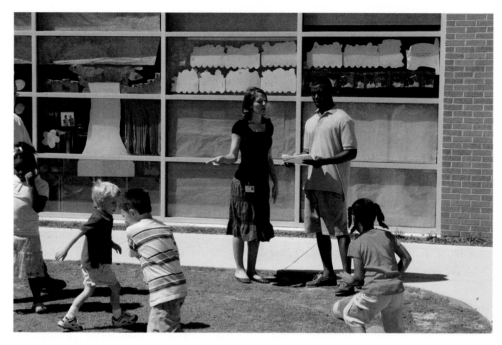

FIGURE 6-8 Completing an observational checklist may happen before activity planning begins.

are part of each child's cultural literacy. Early childhood programs attempt to provide the music of various ethnic groups. Most of these musical experiences give young children the opportunity to form beginning ideas concerning the music and language of diverse peoples.

Musical activities have gained new status and are viewed as language-developing activities. Studies suggest that in cultures in which musical play is actively encouraged, children acquire heightened competencies in motor and communication skills at early ages.

Classroom Environment

Classrooms should be designed to reflect the rich literate environments in which children are immersed outside of school. The use of teacher-made signs that label children's materials, furnishings, or equipment or label areas where children store their belongings and books are helpful. Available paper in various sizes, shapes, and colors that children can write on in their theme play or their independent-time activities encourage child use. All learning experiences should be organized so that

they invite children to participate in literacy events.

Authentic literacy events need to become the focus of the school day as children:

- are signed in daily so that the teacher knows who has arrived in school.
- put away their materials in an appropriate setting, using the signs in the room or their names on their cubbies.
- read recipes and menus as they cook, eat, and learn about healthy nutritional activities; write prescriptions at the play hospital or take phone messages in the house corner.
- read storybooks, write letters, and record observations.

Creating a warm, cozy, friendly environment where children are in a state of relaxed alertness is the goal of educators.

Determining Program Effectiveness

Goals pinpointed through staff meetings and solicited parent input can be finalized in written form to serve as a basis for planning. For one child or many, goals are achieved when teachers and staff plan interesting and appropriate activities for daily, weekly, monthly, or longer periods. In addition to the actual program, materials, and classroom equipment and arrangement, teacher techniques and interactions and other resources aid in goal realization.

Teacher observation and assessment instruments—both commercial instruments and those designed by teachers—add extra data that help in planning programs (Figure 6–9).

Assessment may be defined as an ongoing process of gathering evidence of learning in order to make informed judgments about instructional practice. A listing of commercial preschool language assessments is found in the Appendix.

Carefully planned, recorded, and well-conducted teacher observation is an assessment tool that is hard to beat. Standardized tests all too often do not tell observant teachers anything they do not already know about children. Some assessments attempt to determine ability and accomplishment in a number of language and communication areas; others may be limited to one language skill.

Literacy Portfolios

A number of centers and programs create individual literacy portfolios in an effort to track individual children's literacy development and to complement the school's standardized assessment and reporting methods. A first step is identifying educational goals and purposes that a portfolio might satisfy. Usually this deals with both school and home language arts activities and opportunities. What types of items might be collected is next considered, and then home-school collaboration particulars. Often literacy portfolio development is a joint project undertaken by both teachers and families. Items are collected over time and dated. These can include child work samples, child-dictated text, artwork with recorded comments, photographs of child work or dramatic play, a favorite book list, adult-child interviews, child-created stories or dictation, early writing attempts, alphabet-related examples, word

lists; in short, records of child activities related to speaking, listening, prereading, reading skill development, print awareness, or any activities concerned with child literacy growth.

The portfolio usually travels from school to home and back. This activity informs families about what is happening at school and affords families a review and then insertion of home-collected items. Often children's portfolios become a special book from which children and their families derive pride and pleasure in a child's accomplishments and progress.

Large, album-sized binders are used to accommodate children's artwork in some programs, and many schools use page protectors or clear plastic kitchen storage bags to protect inserts. Items are filed in chronological order when dated. Reviewing a child's portfolio with the child generates considerable interactive conversation and promotes feelings of accomplishment.

Teacher Observation

Many child care centers encourage teachers to continually observe the language skills of attending children. Each child and group may have different needs, and the center attempts to fulfill needs and offer a language arts program that will be growth producing and enriching. Many different observation methods and instruments can be used. Some may be school-designed; others may be commercially produced.

A teacher who is a keen observer and listener gathers information, which guides teacher actions and planning. In their efforts to make an activity relevant, teachers observe attending children's needs, desires, and interests and make individual judgments regarding children's already acquired knowledge, attitudes, and language skills. Educators believe that assessing beyond children's level of performance by looking at ways children learn and interact provides a much richer portrait of children than just identifying levels of skill. As teachers observe, some try to answer the following questions.

◆ What individual language characteristics are present?

SAMPLE OF STAFF-DESIGNED LANGUAGE AND LITERACY CHECKLIST

Child _____ Age _____ (Check if present) Date _____

1. can distinguish illustrations, photographs, and so on from print
2. identifies front/back of books   F_____ B_____
3. notices print in the environment
4. is interested in a book's content and illustrations
5. realizes illustrations can tell a story
6. realizes adults are reading printed text in a storybook
7. realizes print contains names and ideas (storylines)
8. realizes books are authored by people
9. realizes a story she creates can be put into print
10. recognizes her name in print
11. can find her printed name in a group of names
12. chooses books regularly in book areas
13. pretend reads
14. makes up stories
15. can act out stories
16. asks or answers questions about books being read
17. listens to a book attentively
18. handles books with care
19. pretend writes
20. uses alphabet letters in art or constructions
21. knows first letter of her name
22. tries to print name or other words
23. can name a few or many alphabet letters
                few _____ many _____ all _____
24. demonstrates she can hear rhyming words
25. creates a rhyme
26. tells a story with a beginning, middle, and end
       beginning _____ middle _____ end _____
27. has a favorite book
28. can identify words with the same beginning sound
29. knows reading starts at the top left on a page
30. knows there are spaces between words
31. wants her name printed on her work
32. can visually discriminate between alphabet letter shapes
                      few _____ many _____
33. can discriminate between two different speech sounds
34. can perform two- or three-part commands
            Two part _____ Three part _____

35. can predict what might happen in a story based on the cover and illustrations
36. can identify and clap how many syllables are in a three-syllable word
37. recognizes that a letter can be written in uppercase and lowercase form
38. recognizes silly orally spoken mistakes are illogical. (The mouse ate an elephant. The cup fell off the table and hit the ceiling.)
39. can predict what would come next in a simple pattern (AooAo?)
40. controls a writing tool with small motor movement
41. has the ability to attend to and understand conversations, stories, poems, and other oral presentations
42. has a vocabulary (three years, more than 2,000 words; four years, more than 4,000 words; five years, more than 5,000 words)
            average_____ complex _____ varied_____
43. asks questions
44. tells feelings, opinions, ideas, needs, desires, and so forth
                often_____ infrequently _____
45. is a good conversationalist
            initiates _____ listens _____ responds _____
46. pronounces words clearly as expected for age
                clearly _____ average for age _____
47. has increased length of oral sentences
48. uses complex sentences at times
49. discriminates between sounds in words
50. can identify whether a sound in a word is the same or different from another word
51. knows the beginning sound of her name
52. makes an attempt to copy familiar words
53. prints name
54. recognizes common environmental or human symbols
55. is beginning to realize her name is a series of sounds blended together
56. sees visual differences in printed alphabet letters
57. knows the alphabet is a special category of visual graphics
58. can maintain focus of attention in small group instruction (appropriate to age and attention span)

FIGURE 6–9 Sample of a staff-designed language and literacy checklist.

SAMPLE OF STAFF-DESIGNED LANGUAGE AND LITERACY CHECKLIST—cont'd

59. has group social skills such as raising hand, taking turns, asking questions, staying on topic, waiting for answers to her questions, and so on

60. can understand group time rules and participates in formulating them

61. uses language to initiate play with peers

62. makes choices and decisions and verbalizes them

63. can articulate sounds according to developmentally appropriate expectations

64. has developed divergent thinking skills

65. has an adequate grasp of meaningful concepts that are appropriate to age

66. has been exposed to capital alphabet letters used correctly in her name

67. is aware of and/or understands up, down, across, top, bottom, right, and left

68. uses visual cues; for example, follows directions on picture cards

69. is aware computer icons have meanings and knows meanings of a few

70. can find commonalities and differences in oral stories and visual representations

71. can create verbal labels for common objects

72. is aware of some punctuation marks in text

73. has been exposed to the use of computers

74. participates in singing

75. knows about a culture other than her own

76. attempts to write words

77. is familiar with graphs and charts and understands their use in visualizing data

78. understands that symbols are used for objects and events

79. can identify sounds in the environment

*Note: This was gathered from a wide collection of individual state standards and goal statements. It is not intended to be a complete or comprehensive list, but rather a sample of one school's efforts to assess its children's readiness for kindergarten. Some duplication of questions is present.

FIGURE 6–9 *(continued)*

- ◆ How can activities be planned that capture and hold children's interest and enthusiasm?
- ◆ How do my actions and behaviors affect the children's language arts behaviors?
- ◆ Which children are interested in which indoor and outdoor areas?
- ◆ What patterns of language behavior have I noticed?
- ◆ What do children seem eager to talk about or explore?
- ◆ What can I do to provide experience or exploration just beyond what they already know?
- ◆ Which children readily express their ideas?
- ◆ Which children are socially adept and learn language in play with others?

Assessment is a continual, ongoing process. Observation information is confidential and often useful in program planning. Running accounts of child conversations are difficult to obtain because an adult's presence may affect a child's spontaneity. Also, the child's attention span and mobility make it almost impossible to capture more than a few minutes of speech with preschoolers. Many teachers note a few phrases or speech characteristics on a writing pad they carry with them throughout the day. For many teachers, having time just to observe children is considered a luxury. However, observation is important and can be considered an ongoing teacher responsibility in all areas of instruction.

To ensure a language program's quality, plans are changed, updated, and revised based on both the children's progress and staff members' evaluations and observations. Keeping a planned language arts program vital, dynamic, appealing, and appropriate requires continual revision and overhaul.

GOAL STATEMENTS

A particular center may have many or few goal statements, which can be both general and specific.

If standards exist and affect an early childhood program, goals are often identified and listed. Privately funded early childhood programs in most states may choose to look at standards statements but some schools may decide to not incorporate them into their planned program goals and instead develop their own.

A good number of program planners use the NAEYC's (2005a) expectations listing for 3- to 5-year-olds when identifying goals; this listing is found in the Appendix.

Writing Goals

In the process of literacy development, young children can profit from an understanding of the role of the printed word (Figure 6–10). The uses of writing, including recording and transmitting information, recording self-authored creations, and providing entertainment, are important to the quality of human life. Knowing and understanding how writing is used may lead to a realization of the value of learning to read. Writing and reading open each individual to the thoughts, creations, and discoveries of multitudes of people, living and deceased. This discussion is not intended to promote formal early printing instruction but rather to point out that there are basic ideas about writing that must be considered when planning a language arts curriculum that promotes literacy.

There is a strong connection between the child's familiarity with books (and her book-reading experiences) and literacy. Illustrations of the reasons for writing and how writing can satisfy everyday needs can be incorporated into any center's goals for promoting literacy growth.

Most schools concentrate on exposing children to printed words rather than starting actual writing practice in alphabet letter formation.

Reading Goals

Reading skills are multiple and complex and they often involve the coordination of other skills and abilities. Some reading goals that will facilitate later reading skills follow.

- Reads pictures
- Shows an interest in and enjoyment of stories and books

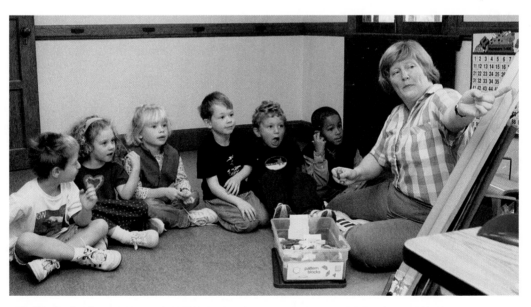

FIGURE 6–10 This group is discussing printed signs that they have found in their school environment.

- Is able to arrange pictures in a sequence that tells a story
- Finds hidden objects in pictures
- Guesses at meanings based on contextual cues
- Reads own and others' names
- Predicts events
- Recognizes letters of own name in other words
- Senses left-right direction
- Guesses words to complete sentences
- Chooses favorite book characters
- Treats books with care
- Authors own books through dictation
- Sees finely detailed differences
- Recognizes and names alphabet letters at times
- Shows interest in libraries
- Shows interest in the sounds of letters
- Watches or uses puppets to enact simple stories
- Has background in traditional literature appropriate for age and ability
- Develops phonemic awareness

FIGURE 6–11 Printed words may accompany new objects in early childhood classrooms.

Goals That Promote Early Literacy

Preschool teachers planning and conducting programs that promote language development in young children try to provide a "classic" literary experience, featuring appropriate age-level materials collected from many cultures and eras. Such a curriculum would serve as a basis of human cultural understanding and would include a wide range of oral and listening materials and activities: books, poetry, language games, puppetry, and storytelling (Figure 6–11). Most teachers believe that early exposure to and familiarity with literary classics can help the child understand what might be encountered later in literature, media, or schooling.

At present, a widely circulated list of classics for preschool children has not been available, but a list of these works has existed in the minds

and hearts of individual teachers. Mother Goose stories are undisputed classics. Two other agreed-upon classic stories are *Goldilocks and the Three Bears* and *Peter Rabbit*. Chapters 9 and 17 present in-depth discussions in this planning area. Whether a story, play, rhyme, or song is considered a "classic," however, is usually a matter of judgment by individual teachers.

Sociocultural Language Goals

Are there important goals teachers need to consider in a democratic society? Many sources suggest the following:

Goal #1: All students are able to communicate effectively with all persons within a multicultural, diverse society.

Goal #2: All students learn to value linguistic diversity and celebrate the cultural expressions of those who are different from themselves.

Goal #3: All students see the value of language and literacy for their own lives.

Early childhood educators can lay the groundwork and monitor attitudes and feelings that in any way degrade other-than-mainstream-language speakers.

A language arts curriculum should include language activities that celebrate cultural diversity. Family and community literacy activities are important considerations. Family stories and literacy-promoting activities and events can be included in center planning. Collaboration with parents reinforces the unique contributions families and neighborhoods make to child literacy growth.

LANGUAGE ARTS CURRICULA

Many early childhood **curriculum models** exist. Some are well known; others are little known. Models usually provide well-defined frameworks to guide program implementation. Child development theories are their underlying foundation. Whether a particular model, a combination of models, or an eclectic model is used, early childhood educators are constantly challenged to examine, reflect, and improve children's daily language arts experiences.

Schools and centers differ widely in **curriculum** development; however, two basic approaches can be identified. In the first, a unit or thematic approach emerges from identified child interest and teacher-selected areas, such as families, seasons, animals, and so on. Using this approach, some centers use children's books or classic nursery rhymes as their thematic starting topic. Others introduce a proposed theme (unit) topic to small discussion groups of children. This offers input from attending children and lets teachers explore children's past experience, knowledge, and interests. Questions children ask and vocabulary used may aid teachers' thematic unit development. Staff and parent group discussion can also uncover attitudes and resources. Goals are considered, and activities are then outlined and scheduled into time slots. Many teachers believe this type of program approach individualizes instruction by providing many interrelated and, consequently, reinforced understandings while also allowing the child to select activities.

The second common instructional approach is to pinpoint traditional preschool subject areas, such as language arts, science, mathematics, art, cooking, and so forth, and then plan how many and what kind of planned activities will take place. This can be done with or without considering a unifying theme. Some teachers believe that this is a more systematic approach to instruction.

In both approaches, the identification of goals has come before curriculum development.

Ages of children, staffing ratios, facility resources, and other particulars all affect planning. After planned curriculum activities take place, teachers evaluate whether goals were reached and modifications and suggestions are noted. Additional or follow-up activities may be planned and scheduled for groups or individual children.

Thematic Inquiry Approach to Language Instruction

Imagine a classroom turned into a pizza parlor or a flower garden. There would be a number of activities occurring simultaneously—some for small groups, others for large groups, and some for individuals. Teachers would be involved in activities, and classroom areas might be set up for continuous, or almost continuous, child exploration. Art, singing, number, movement, science-related, health-related, safety-related, and other types of activities would (or could) be preplanned, focusing on the two themes mentioned previously. The sensory activities could be included so that children could experience the smells, sounds, sights, tastes, and so on, associated with each theme. Planning language arts instruction using this approach allows teachers to use creativity and imagination. It also requires planning time to gather and set up material that might not

---

curriculum models — refers to a conceptual framework and organizational structure for decision making about educational priorities, administrative policies, instructional methods, and evaluation criteria.
curriculum — an overall plan for the content of instruction to be offered in a program.

be found in the school storeroom or supply area. It is easy to see that there could be many opportunities for children's use of speech, listening, reading, and writing, and the natural connection among these activities might be more apparent to the children. Most teachers believe that using a thematic approach is an exciting challenge that is well worth teacher time and effort. They see this approach as one that encourages child-teacher conversations and consequently expands children's language usage and knowledge.

Teachers should not limit their program to traditional themes but should explore and discover beyond the familiar. Teachers can follow children's curiosity and their own childhood interests. Many centers believe that real teaching is found when each staff member gives children what she individually has to offer from the heart as well as the mind.

Considerable staff brainstorming and discussion takes place when deciding which theme topics are suitable, feasible, appropriate, and educationally advantageous for their particular child group and facility.

In constructing a theme, the following steps are usually undertaken.

1. Observe and record a child's interest and/ or teacher drawing from past experience.
2. Identify a topic. (It could be a book, poem, drama, or another category.)
3. Try to discover what children know and want to know.
4. Imagine possible activities (in and out of school).
5. Decide on attempted goals of instruction.
6. Pinpoint range, scope, vocabulary, main ideas, and activities.
7. Discuss room environment, staffing, visitors, and helpers. (What will take place in the classroom or yard or in learning centers?)
8. Make specific plans for individual and group activities.
9. List the necessary materials and supplies.
10. Decide on a culminating activity (usually a recap or "grand finale").
11. Set a timetable if necessary. (Daily schedules may be prepared.)
12. Pinpoint evaluation criteria.

Williams (1997) uses a four-step child-teacher interactive process to jointly plan unit (theme) activities for a group of 4-year-olds. A description of these steps follows.

1. The teacher asks, "What do you wonder?" or "What do you want to know about— (a particular topic, example: the ocean)?" Then the teacher records each child's answer or question in a different color on a wall chart that is posted at the children's eye level. Then the teacher adds her own questions.
2. The teacher asks, "What can we do to find out?" Then the teacher records the children's ideas on a second piece of chart paper. If no one responded, that is acceptable. The teacher instead develops a list of children's questions or ideas that might come up while the unit is in progress, and these are added to the chart.
3. The teacher asks, "What materials do we need?" on a prepared third chart. Materials suggested by the children that do not seem directly related are gently probed by teacher. A child may have a connection to the topic of study not readily seen by the teacher.
4. The teacher asks, "What will you bring (do)?" and "What would you like me to bring (to do)?" The teacher checks with parents about objects and materials suggested by their child. A parent newsletter invites parents to share or bring in additional topic-related items to the classroom.

To promote literacy, teachers think about how each theme activity involves listening, speaking, reading, and writing and how to logically connect these areas during ongoing activities.

Thematic/Literature-Based Instruction

Literature-based instruction, now mandated or recommended in elementary schools in many states, is very similar to what early childhood educators call thematic instruction. Both levels realize the value of literature and its relationship to literacy. A theme in early childhood could be any topic of interest to children. A literacy-based approach uses a classic book or informational book as its central core. A preschool educator would have no problem using a book as a starting place and could plan discussions, drama, art, music, puppetry, and other language arts activities to strengthen various concepts encountered.

Curriculum Webs and Webbing

The use of curriculum webs (or **webbing**) in program planning is popular with some preschool teachers (Figure 6–12). A web can be thought of as a graphic overall picture of what might be included in a theme or unit approach to instruction. Figure 6–13 shows a skeleton web designed for the study of dogs. Under the box "care & needs" one can think of a number of items that could be listed. In fact, the web could become highly detailed as the teacher using it listed concepts associated with the subject—dogs. The object of creating a web is for the teacher to define and refine the web based on the interests and needs of the particular enrolled group. The plan (web) is then translated into planned daily happenings with children's active exploring and participation (Figure 6–14). The goal is to offer activities to engage the students' interest and imagination and to spark their desire to seek out answers, ponder questions, or create responses (Figure 6–15). One of the rewards of teaching is to present or set up an activity that children eagerly select, and perhaps ask a million questions about; in other words, one that has "captured" them and engaged their minds (Figure 6–16).

Webbing is described by one staff member as follows: "To create a plan we choose an idea, brainstorm hands-on activities, and put them on a web." This gives us a sort of road map. It's a process rather than a product.

Reggio Emilia

Early childhood educators studying the Reggio Emilia approach to program planning are re-examining their curriculum. Gandini (1997) describes the teacher's role in the Reggio Emilia approach.

> To know how to plan or proceed with their work, teachers observe and listen to the children closely. Teachers use the understanding they gain in this way to act as a resource for them. They ask questions and discover the children's ideas, hypotheses, and theories. Then the adults discuss together what they have recorded through their own notes, or audio or visual recordings, and make flexible plans and preparations. Then they are ready to enter again into dialogues with the children and offer them occasions for discovering and also revisiting experiences since they consider learning not as a linear process but as spiral progression. (p. 216)

Gardner (1999) identifies how a Reggio Emilia curriculum develops.

> The educators of Reggio Emilia have developed and continuously improved a set of techniques for taking the ideas and actions of young children seriously. Much thought is devoted to the opening exposure to experiences that might constitute themes to be developed in the coming weeks. But it is not possible to plan such a curriculum in advance. Rather, the particular reactions of particular children to particular experiences become the bedrock, the driving force of the "curriculum." The activities of next week (sometimes even the next day) grow out of the results, problems, and puzzles of this week; the cycle is repeated so long as it proves fruitful. Children and teachers are continually reflecting on the meaning of an activity, which issues it raises, how its depths and range can be productively probed. (p. 202)

---

webbing — a visual or graphic method of mapping a possible course of study.

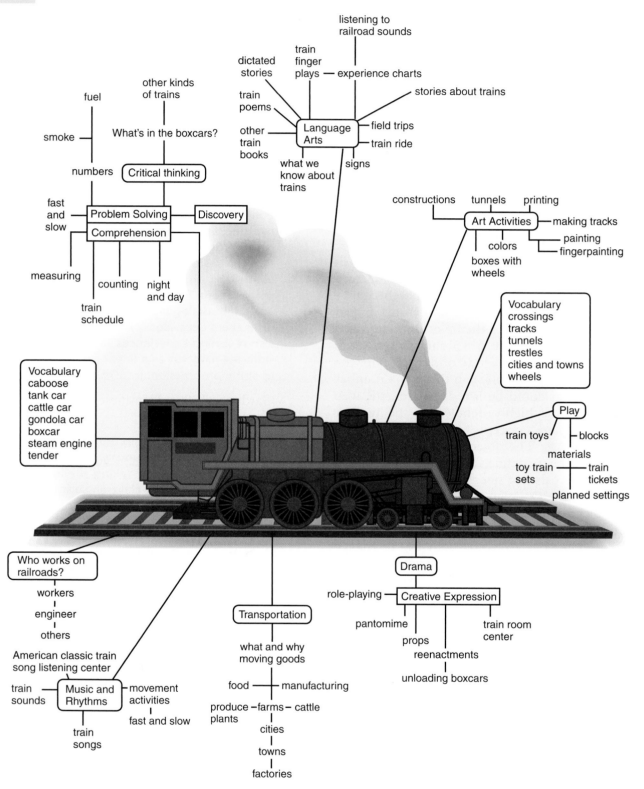

FIGURE 6–12 This webbing example suits a theme based on a picture book about trains, such as Donald Crew's book, *Freight Train*.

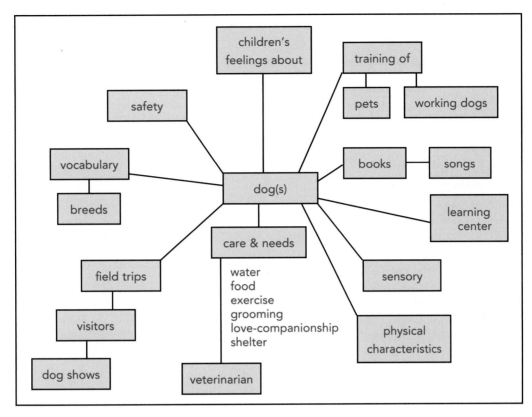

FIGURE 6–13 Topic web—dog(s).

For Hendrick's comparisons of American and Reggian schools, see Figure 6–17.

The Project Approach

The project approach involves integrated teaching and learning. It encourages meaningful, firsthand, relevant study of child-teacher–developed and child-teacher–chosen activities. This program approach is valued by teachers for its flexible and creative aspects, which fit diverse child groups and geographical communities. Children are involved in decision making, program planning, implementation, and evaluation through active teacher-child shared discussion, brainstorming, and project outlining. Teachers also plan activities and experiences. Children are urged to explore and investigate and become testers of ideas as individuals and in study groups. Teachers using thematic unit instruction may feel the

project approach best suits kindergarten and elementary-aged children. Others have incorporated projects into preschool curriculum.

COMMITMENT TO GOALS AND OBJECTIVES

A number of factors determine whether program goals are met.

◆ Enthusiasm and commitment of staff
◆ Staffing ratios
◆ Staff ingenuity and resourcefulness
◆ Methods and techniques used
◆ Resources available
◆ General feeling or tone of center
◆ Examination of sequence (easy to complex)
◆ Parental and community support

OPENING: CHOOSE ONE DOG STICKER FOR YOUR NAME TAG OR TAKE-HOME FILE (STICKERS OF DOG BREEDS)

Large-group Instruction

a. Discussion

Update and review of theme findings and discoveries so far

b. Chart introduction

Different dog breeds have names

Checking opening stickers

Finding similarities and differences

c. Composing

Writing an invitation to a guest speaker—the dog groomer

Requesting a description and, when possible, a demonstration of the dog-care techniques and tools.

d. Song: "Bingo"

Chant: "The Diners in the Kitchen" by James Whitcomb Riley

Poem: "My Puppy" by Aileen Fisher

Small-group Instruction

a. Story time: "Harry the Dirty Dog" by G. Zion or "Dogs" by Dorling Kindersley (2005)

Discussion

Care of dogs

Can dogs do small jobs or work?

Working dog photos

Discovery Time Choices

a. Art

Construct a dog and label using clay or body-part cutouts to paste and label them with the teacher's help

b. Sorting

Assorted dog bones by color, size, and shape

c. Science

How do dogs differ from one another? Examining hair from a variety of dogs and giving each a descriptive label—curly, black, spotted, long, etc.

d. Construction

Making and decorating a large-box doghouse with the teacher's help

e. Cooking and measurement

Making homemade dog bones by reading a recipe chart

f. Writing center

Dictation of a story about a dog, or choosing to do a naming-seven-puppies activity

g. Listening Center

Firehouse dog story on tape

"Bert the Bird Dog" recording

h. Library Center

A selection of books about dogs

i. Yard activities

Exploring walking on all fours

Making dog prints on long paper rolls using sponges or potato prints (teacher directed and supervised)

Hiding-rubber-bones game

Trying to lap water from a bowl (teacher supervised)

Playing with a doghouse construction

FIGURE 6–14 One-day plan during a weekly theme study of dogs (4-year-olds' classroom).

Effort and staff creativity translate goals into daily activities.

Daily Activity Plans

Recognizing children's interests stimulates activity-planning ideas based on what captures and holds the children's attention. Part of the challenge and excitement of teaching is finding ways to be creative in daily activity planning.

Although two staff members work toward the same goal, they may approach the task in different ways. Lesson plans are more frequently used in schools using approaches other than the thematic (unit) approach described earlier but can also be used for individual teacher-conducted activities within theme planning.

WHY DO WEBBING?

Why do webbing? It gives a staff of adults the chance to explore the possibilities of any material or idea in order to make decisions about use: Is it worth doing? Is it likely to generate developmentally appropriate activities? What are the ways we might want to enrich the activity by being prepared with other materials or questions? How long might children's interest continue?

A web is a *tentative* plan. It does not tell you exactly what will happen or in what order. That depends in large part on the children's response. So, first you plan and then you start trying your ideas, *paying attention to what happens,* evaluating, and moving on with further activities.

FIGURE 6–15 Why do webbing? (From Jones, E., & Nimmo, J. [1994]. "Why do webbing?" *Emergent curriculum.* Washington, DC: NAEYC, p. 111. Reprinted with permission from the National Association for the Education of Young Children.)

Lesson plans (or **activity plans**) enable teachers to foresee needs—settings, materials, and staffing. The time that children spend waiting can be minimized. Some teachers pinpoint exactly what words and concepts will be emphasized or what questions asked; other teachers prefer a more spontaneous approach.

Some activities in language arts may require teacher practice beforehand. Others may require visual aids or materials that must be gathered in advance. Planning time is time well spent. Preparation reduces teacher tension and results in child activities that run smoothly.

Teachers must strive to be always aware of child safety and comfort. They must also try to maintain a reasonable level of stimulation somewhere between not very interesting and overly exciting activities so that children are encouraged to process information in a manner that is both pleasurable and efficient. Experienced teachers know when children are interested and

FIGURE 6–16 Creating a sense of wonder and discovery is among the goals of a quality program.

activity plans — written, detailed, step-by-step teaching plans, often including an evaluation section.

AMERICAN	REGGIAN
"Projects" or themes are short lived, extending a day or a week.	"Projects" may be brief but often continue for weeks or months.
"Topics" are used to provide information and (possibly) practice in midlevel thinking skills.	"Topics" are used to pose problems and provoke thought.
Children acquire a shallow smattering of information on many subjects.	Children acquire in-depth knowledge about fewer subjects (i.e., "know more about less").
Inquiry learning focuses on science tables; some problem solving encouraged.	Pronounced emphasis on "provoking" children to propose reasons why things happen and possible ways to solve problems.
Children may show what they know by talking to the teacher about it.	Children show what they know by talking about it but also by using many different media: models, graphics, bent wire, dance, and so forth, to explain their ideas: "You don't know it until you can explain it to someone else."
The individual is emphasized; autonomy, self-responsibility, independence are valued.	Existence within the group is emphasized; sense of community and interdependence are valued.
Children select whatever they wish to participate in each day.	Children select what they want to do but are also encouraged to work in consistent small groups based on their continuing interests.
Time is highly regulated and scheduled.	Time flows easily in an unhurried way.
Record keeping is typically limited to results rather than work in progress—shows what children have learned (checklists, portfolios, observations) or do not know.	Record keeping—Documentation boards record what children "know" at beginning of and during, as well as end of, project; boards used for everyone to *revisit* and recognize their work as it progresses.
Teacher changes at least once a year.	Teachers remain with children for 3 years.
Staffing is teacher, or teacher plus aide.	Staffing is two teachers of equal rank plus services of a *pedagogista* and *aterlierista*.
There is a hierarchy of staff positions (i.e., director, teacher, aide).	There are no directors; everyone accepts various responsibilities.
Confrontation is avoided.	Debate and "confrontation" with different points of view between adults and with children are favored methods of learning for everyone.
Teachers tend to be isolated; policy about and regularity of staff meetings varies.	Close collaboration between *all* teachers occurs regularly and frequently.

FIGURE 6–17 A sampling of some additional comparisons of American and Reggian schools. (From Hendrick, J. [Ed.]. [1997]. *First steps toward teaching the Reggio way.* Upper Saddle River, NJ: Prentice Hall, Inc. © 1998. Reprinted by permission of Prentice Hall, Inc.)

are actively participating. Many teachers say this is one of the greatest joys of teaching.

Group size is an important factor in planning. It is easier for teachers to plan for an entire class group, and sometimes staffing demands it. However, many teachers have explored ways to keep children occupied and supervised while working with small groups. Small groups allow greater intimacy, conversational depth, and opportunity for feedback. Research substantiates

the idea that both children and adults feel more comfortable sharing their thoughts when in small groups. "Instant replays" with small groups can be planned and coordinated. Beginning preschool teachers may not have seen many small group activities modeled by other teachers, but this text recommends them.

Teachers strive to maintain children's attention during activities. Teachers realize that attention is mediated by specific parts of the brain and that neural systems fatigue quickly. After 3 to 5 minutes of sustained activity, children need to rest, but they can recover within minutes too. In a familiar and safe classroom, if a child hears factual information for only 4 to 8 minutes and a teacher is not providing novelty, the brain seeks other stimuli. Perry recommends adding "emotional seasoning" like humor and empathy to teacher presentations and linking facts to related child concepts during activities, in addition to taking advantage of the novelty-seeking property of the human brain. He believes this is a challenging task for teachers of all-aged students.

Figure 6–18 describes how a teacher works toward a variety of goals in a planned two-part activity. Note the preplanned materials the teacher has secured or prepared beforehand.

Detailed written lesson plans help early childhood students feel prepared and relaxed (Figure 6–19). After a period of time, most beginning teachers internalize lesson-planning components and discontinue detailed written plans, although they continue to use lists and outlines.

Watching the class carefully, keeping a notebook in a handy pocket, and writing down small observations can help a teacher remember the interests of a young group. A good guide to unearthing new subjects of interest for a particular class is to notice what has already captured the children's attention. What do the children talk about most often? What do they crowd around? Does the activity promote children's interested questions? What has the longest waiting list? Are children eager to explore a particular object with their hands? Who wants to share something discovered or created? For example, if butterflies interest a group, planned butterfly experiences can add depth to the curriculum.

Activities based on teacher enthusiasm for life and growth, skills, talents, hobbies, and pursuits can fit beautifully into language arts goals. Parent and community resources, including borrowed items and field trips, increase the vitality of programs.

Evaluation

Thinking back over planned activities helps teachers analyze the benefits and possibly leads to additional planning along the same line or with the same theme. Oversights in planning frequently occur, and activities may develop in unexpected ways. Hindsight is a useful and valuable tool in evaluating activities (Figure 6–20).

Often, centers evaluate their planned programs by asking themselves questions such as the following:

- Do children share personal interests and learning discoveries with teachers and/or other children?
- Can teachers enter conversations without diminishing children's verbal initiative?
- Do children become involved in planned activities and room centers?
- Are there times when children listen with interest?
- Are language arts areas (speaking, writing, reading, and listening) connected in a natural way during daily activities?
- Is child talk abundant?

SUMMARY

Traditionally, language arts instruction and planning have been based on the educational theories educators believed to be the best and effective. Historically, theories have, over time, changed, evolved, and emerged. Theorists' and researchers' ideas have been accepted and then come into vogue. Currently, research-based information has influenced federal legislation and publicly funded schools.

Language is part of every preschool activity. This text recommends an integrated approach to early childhood language arts, that is, a program that involves listening, speaking, writing, reading, and viewing.

Public centers identify language arts goals through a group process and consider standards. Activities are then planned. Approaches to activity planning are reviewed. Daily plans carry out what is intended. Assessment instruments are evaluated, and decisions are made concerning whether these instruments are to be used or not used. Staff observation provides data on children's abilities, interests, and skill levels, as well as additional insights that are useful in activity

NOTE: This is a portion of a longer description. The words in italics show how the teacher works toward a variety of goals.

This episode is an account of a sequence of planned activities culminating in a cooking experience for four four-year-old children. Part 1 of the episode details the preparation in the classroom for the purchase of the food and the group's trip to a local store. Part 2 describes the cooking.

The fresh pears at lunch evoked the excited comment "Apples!" from Spanish-speaking Fernando.

"Well, this is a fruit," said Miss Gordon, encouragingly, "but it has another name. Do you remember the apples we had last week?"

"They were hard to bite," said Joey.

"And we made applesauce," said Rosina.

"This fruit is called a pear, Fernando; let's taste this pear now. We'll have apples again."

The teacher responds to what is correct in the child's response, valuing his category association. First, she wants to support communication and willingness to experiment with language; later she gives the correct name. The children strengthen the experience by relating it to previous experience in which they were active.

"Mine's soft," said Joey.

"Can we make applesauce again?" begged Rosina.

The teacher replied, "Perhaps we could do what Janice wanted to do. Remember? To take some home to her family?"

"To my mommy, and my grandma, and Danny."

"Not to my baby," said Rosina. "He's too little. Him only drink milk."

"Tomorrow we'll buy lots of apples," said Miss Gordon.

The teacher is building a sense of continuity by recalling earlier intentions that had been expressed by the children.

She rarely corrects use of pronouns for four-year-olds. She knows the child will learn through greater social maturity and hearing language.

After rest, Miss Gordon asked the children how they could take home their applesauce. "What can we put it in?"

Rosina ran to the house corner and returned with two baby food jars. "I bringed lots," she said. Miss Gordon remembered that Rosina had come to school lugging a bag full of baby food jars, many of which she had put away. "A good idea! And your mommy said she would keep more for us. Let's write a note to tell her we need them tomorrow."

Rosina dictated a note: "I got to bring bunches of jars to school. We are going to make applesauce. I love you, Mommy." Rosina painted her name with a red marker.

The teacher helps children to think ahead to steps in a process.

The use of a tense form, although incorrect, represents learning for the child. The teacher does not correct at this moment, when she is responding to the child's pleasure in solving the practical problem that had been posed. She is strengthening the connection between home and school.

The teacher helps the children learn that writing is a recording of meaning and a way of communicating.

The next day was jar washing and arranging time. Each of the four children put his or her jars on a tray on which there was a large card with the child's name.

Janice put on one jar for her mother, one for her grandmother, one for her brother, and after a pause, one for herself.

Rosina changed her mind. "My baby can have a little tiny bit," she said. So she needed a jar for her father, her mother, her baby, and herself.

Joey and the teacher figured out that he needed six, and that Fernando needed nine!

The children are actively involved in the steps preparatory to the planned activity—an experience in organization that has personal meaning.

The teacher's plan calls for recognition of one's own name and one-to-one counting of family members.

The teacher turned their attention to a chart near the cooking corner. She had made a recipe chart, pasting colored (magazine) pictures next to the names of the items they would need to make the applesauce and had taped a stick of cinnamon to the chart.

Miss Gordon said, "Let's look at the recipe chart. I have a list so we can remember to buy everything."

The children said, "Apples."

Miss Gordon checked her list.

Then, "Sugar."

The children were silent as they looked at the stick of cinnamon taped to the chart.

Miss Gordon suggested, "Smell it. Have we had it before?"

Joey remembered: "Toast! What we put on toast!"

"Yes," said Miss Gordon, and then gave the word, "cinnamon."

The children are having a dual experience—pictorial representation and formal symbol usage.

The teacher supplies the word after the children have revived their direct experience with the phenomenon.

(Biber, Shapiro, & Wickens, 1977).

FIGURE 6–18 Multiple-goal approach.

LANGUAGE ACTIVITY PLAN GUIDE

1. Language activity title _____

2. Materials needed _____

3. Location of activity (to be used when plan is developed for a particular classroom or area) _____

4. Number of children _____

5. Language goal or objective _____

6. Preparation (necessary teacher preparation, including getting materials or objects, visual aids, etc., ready) _____

7. Getting started (introductory and/or motivational statement) _____

8. Show and explore (include possible teacher questions or statements that promote language ability) _____

9. Discussion of key points, discoveries, conclusions, subjects for further study (what vocabulary and/or concepts might be included?) _____

10. Apply (include child practice or application of newly learned knowledge or skill when appropriate) _____

11. Transition statement (needed if activity plan is to terminate or if a second activity immediately follows) _____

12. Evaluation: (1) activity; (2) teacher; (3) child participation; (4) other aspects such as setting, materials, outcomes, etc. _____

FIGURE 6–19 Sample activity plan form.

THINKING BACK

What I planned and how I went about it:

_____
_____
_____

What effect my actions had:

_____
_____
_____

What I could have done:

_____
_____

What effect this action would have had:

_____
_____
_____

What I will do differently next time:

_____
_____
_____
_____

FIGURE 6–20 Thinking back.

planning. Developing literacy portfolios is but one way to display and assess children's growth. Every center has a unique set of goals and objectives. Designing child experiences is done in a variety of ways. Program plans consider attending children's needs and interests.

Evaluating a planned activity after it is presented can pinpoint strengths and weaknesses. This also serves as the basis for further activity planning.

ADDITIONAL RESOURCES

Readings

Labo, L. D., Love, M. S., Prior, M. P., Hubbard, B. P., & Ryan, T. (2006). *Literature links: Thematic units linking read-alouds and computer activities.* Newark, DE: International Reading Association.

Massachusetts Department of Education (2003). *Early Childhood Program Standards for three- and four-year-olds.* Malden, MA: Author.

Neuman, S. B. (2002). *What research reveals: Foundation for reading instruction in preschool and primary education.* Washington, DC: U.S. Department of Education.

Neuman, S., & Roskos, K. (2005). The state of state prekindergarten standards. *Early Research Quarterly, 20,* 125–145.

Venn, E. C., & Jahn, M. D. (2004). *Teaching and learning in preschool: Using individually appropriate practices in early childhood literacy instruction.* Newark, DE: International Reading Association.

Vukelich, C., & Christie, J. (2004). *Building a foundation for preschool literacy: Effective instruction for children's reading and writing development.* Newark, DE: International Reading Association.

Helpful Websites

ERIC—Early Childhood Research & Practice
http://ecrp.uiuc.edu
Provides research articles, theme instruction, project approach information, ERIC standards and assessments, and information about how to develop program goals.

National Association for the Education of Young Children
http://www.naeyc.org
Includes extensive information about program planning.

National Reading Panel
http://www.nationalreadingpanel.org
Reports research-based instructional practices for young children.

Book Companion Website

Standards attempt to identify instructional goals for programs working with young children. You can review the ones the author has put together on the book companion website. It is a combined list of often-mentioned outcomes (goals) in language arts obtained by consulting a number of well-regarded sources. You can test your grasp of chapter content with quiz questions.

STUDENT ACTIVITIES

1. Define literacy in your own words or discuss changes in what skills and knowledge are now required to function in the present "computer age." Share with the class.

2. List 10 reasons for illiteracy in the United States. Then, list 10 ways preschool centers can help a preschooler's early literacy. Ask for a volunteer to make a chart on a large surface that everyone in the classroom can see, listing the reasons for illiteracy that are given by students. Put tallies after ideas to identify what was the most commonly mentioned reason. Make a second large listing of the group's ideas concerning how preschools can promote early literacy.

3. Form two groups of five students. Each group takes 10 to 15 minutes preparing their reaction to the reading that follows.

   Kindergarten teachers have been feeling the pressure of a rising tide of academic expectations and hard-to-accomplish standards. Their colleagues voice the same concerns because kindergartners are now expected to display what had once been the goals of a first-grade curriculum.

   Students in the audience are to identify key statements made by either group.

4. Using any activity plan form, make a written plan for a language development activity. Share your plan with others at the next class meeting. Rate the quality of your participation in the discussion using the following scale (or write a beginning outline for a theme of your own choosing or one that you believe would be of interest to a group of 4-year-old children). Then share your theme ideas at the next class meeting.

   No Input

   Very Little

   Contributed about as Much as Classmates

   A Fair Amount

   Offered Lots of Ideas

5. Look back into your childhood before age 6. What classics, songs, rhymes, and language arts activities did you experience? If you do not remember, answer this alternative question: Which literacy-promoting language activities should not be missed by any child? Be specific, and name poems, books, rhymes, stories, or other literary experiences.

CHAPTER REVIEW

A. Name the four interrelated language arts areas, arranging them in what you believe is their order of appearance in young children. Include the visual literacy area in your discussion.

B. Write three language arts goal statements (what you would want children to have the opportunity to experience and learn). These should be statements that would be included in a program where you are (or will be) employed.

C. Select the correct answer. Each item may have more than one correct answer.

1. Assessment instruments can be
   a. a checklist.
   b. a child interest inventory.
   c. counted on to be valid.
   d. teacher made.

2. Compiling and identifying a center's goal statements ideally involves
   a. children's input.
   b. staff.
   c. parents.
   d. interested community members.

3. Early childhood language arts should be offered to children using
   a. an approach that helps children see relationships between areas.
   b. techniques that promote the child's realization that spoken words can be written.
   c. separate times of day to explore reading and writing without combining these skills.
   d. identified goal statements as a basis for activity planning.

4. When goals are identified, a school (or center) could
   a. retain its flexibility in activity planning.
   b. lose its ability to fulfill children's individual needs if the same activity plans are used from year to year.
   c. keep its program "personal" by continually evaluating and updating.
   d. periodically take a close look at goals to see whether staff commitment is strong or weak.

5. Using commercial assessment instruments
   a. is questionable because reliability varies.
   b. serves as the basis of professional programming.
   c. can mean using teacher-designed assessments is out of the question.
   d. is a group decision.

6. "There is only one correct way to plan and present activities to children." This statement is
   a. true.
   b. false.
   c. partly true because each individual strives to find the one plan that helps planned activities run smoothly and successfully.
   d. incorrect because the plan itself does not ensure success or goal realization.

7. Although language arts goals may be identified, language
   a. is part of every activity.
   b. can be taught through music activities.
   c. skills may grow whether planned activities are offered or not offered.
   d. activities offered daily cannot ensure that goals attempted will be attained.

D. List what positive advantages might be accomplished if a child's literacy portfolio is developed during the child's preschool years.

INDIVIDUAL ACTIVITY

UNDERSTANDING LOCATIONAL WORDS

Note: This is a self-selected child activity set up during a study of transportation for a class of 3- and 4-year-olds. A waiting list is available, so children are ensured a turn.

Purpose: The child will be able to place vehicle "under," "over," "behind," and "in front of" when given verbal directions after becoming familiar with the words in the play situation.

Materials: streets and a highway drawn on a large sheet of paper taped to a table; toy vehicles (car, truck, school bus, van, etc.); blocks, a box, or cardboard to make a highway overpass

Procedure:

1. Place a box with toy vehicles inside in front of the child. "Tell me about what you find in the box." Verbally label each vehicle if the child does not.

2. Pause and let the child talk about the toy vehicles. Introduce overpass and discuss "under" and "over" the bridge.

3. "We're going to take turns. First, I'm going to ask you to put the vehicles in different places. Then, you tell me where you want me to place one of the vehicles."

4. "Can you drive the car under the bridge?" Encourage the child if necessary. Pause. "Which vehicle do you want me to drive under the bridge? Is it the bus or another one?"

5. "My turn. Drive the truck over the bridge." Pause. "Which one do you want me to drive over the bridge?"

6. "Put the bus in front of the car." "Which one do you want me to move in front of the bus?"

7. Proceed until all four location words are introduced and demonstrated. Then, "Tell me where you choose to drive or park the toys. I'll watch you."

8. Allow the child time to play as she wishes. As the child continues with the activity, add comments when appropriate, such as, "You drove the van under the bridge."

GROUP ACTIVITY
VISUAL PERCEPTION

Purpose: matching identical stockings game

Materials: enough matching pairs of stockings for each child in the group (more pairs if possible); socks of any size but different in color or pattern; two bags (separate, putting one sock of each pair in bags); plastic zip lunch bags

Procedure:

Additional activity ideas include:

1. Discussing stockings by examining the differences in socks children are wearing. Talking about how socks are kept together at home, whether a stocking has been lost, and if one visited their home, where stockings are found.

2. Introducing intact pairs in a basket. "To play our game, we need to select one pair from the basket, and then put one sock in one of the provided bags and the second in the other bag. We'll take turns. Mary, choose a pair of socks and tell us something about the pair you choose." Give each child a turn.

3. Putting socks in pairs. "Now we can start our game. I'm going to mix them all together and make a big pile of stockings, and then we'll try to find two stockings that are the same and put them in a plastic lunch bag so that we can keep each pair together. When you find two that match raise your hand. Here is the plastic lunch bag. Keep the socks you've found and put each pair in a plastic sack in front of you." Continue taking turns until all socks are paired. Count or discuss sock pairs, color, size, pattern, and so on.

Reinforcement Activities:

1. Turn this group activity into an individual activity in which one child can pair all the socks. A standing clothes rack or a clothesline can be used.

2. Mittens or shoes can also be matched in a similar group activity. The closer the distinctions are, the more difficult the task will be.

CHAPTER 7
Promoting Language and Literacy

OBJECTIVES

After reading this chapter, you should be able to:

◆ List three roles of a teacher in early childhood language education.

◆ Discuss the balances needed in teacher behavior.

◆ Describe ways a teacher can promote language growth.

KEY TERMS

closure

expansion

explanatory talk

extension

CHILDREN'S LITERACY PORTFOLIOS

Miss Powell, a kindergarten teacher, planned a home visit to each entering child in her fall kindergarten class. At one home, a mother proudly shared the child's preschool literacy portfolio. Miss Powell was able to sit with both her soon-to-be student and the child's mother as they both commented on items in the binder. She found the child was reading a few words and had a huge interest in cats. Although she knew her district would test each child after school started, she was delighted with this home visit.

QUESTIONS TO PONDER

1. How can Miss Powell put to good use the information she now has about this child?

2. Would you suggest that a child literacy portfolio be part of this child's kindergarten experience also?

A good description of a skilled early childhood educator is a "responsive opportunist" who is enthusiastic, who enjoys discovery, and who is able to establish and maintain a warm, supportive environment. When a reciprocal relationship between a child and an adult or between children is based on equality, respect, trust, and authentic dialogue (real communication), child language learning is promoted. Speech is at the foundation of a child's learning life. Teachers need to create a classroom atmosphere where children can expect success, see the teacher as a significant person, are allowed choice, and are able to make mistakes. Ideally, children should join in planned activities eagerly. These activities should end before the child's capacity to focus is exhausted. The child should be able to expect the teacher to listen and respond to the child's communication in a way that respects the child's sense of the importance of the communication.

Studies examining the quality of language environments in American preschools found that many preschools serving poor children scored in the inadequate range. High-quality group book experiences, cognitively challenging conversation, and teacher use of a wide vocabulary were associated with quality environments and young children's subsequent language and literacy development. It is impossible to underemphasize the importance of adult-child interaction. In schools and centers of questionable quality, some children may rarely interact with a preschool teacher and receive little or no individualized attention. These schools fail the children who most need a quality literacy environment to prepare them for later schooling.

Preschool programs can affect intellectual growth during early childhood years, but some of those effects may decline over time. This is not always the case. Children enrolled in the Abecedarian Project, an experimental preschool program that emphasizes language and cognitive development, attained significantly higher reading achievement that lasted through grade eight in elementary school (Campbell & Ramey, 1994). The project took place in rural North Carolina with a study sample of poor African-American children. The intervention program included a pre-literacy and pre-phonics curricula emphasizing phoneme identification. A school-age follow-up component provided families with activities to reinforce basic reading concepts being taught at school. Researchers found that the project affected children's reading and literacy scores in a positive way into early adulthood.

TEACHING STRATEGIES AND BEHAVIORS

Three specific teaching functions that encourage the development of language arts and literacy are discussed in this chapter.

1. The teacher serves as a *model* of everyday language use. What is communicated and how it is communicated are important.
2. The teacher is a *provider* of experiences. Many of these events are planned; others happen in the normal course of activities.
3. The teacher is an *interactor*, sharing experiences with the children and encouraging conversation (Figure 7–1).

These three functions should be balanced, relative to each child's level and individual

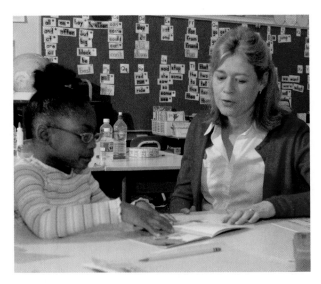

FIGURE 7–1 Sharing books with individual children encourages children to talk about personal interests.

needs. The teaching role requires constant decision making: knowing when to supply or withhold information to help self-discovery and when to talk or listen (Figure 7–2). Basically, sensitivity can make the teacher the child's best ally in the growth of language skills. The importance of teachers' attitudes toward children's talk and teachers' recognition of children's thinking is critical. Researchers studying teacher-child interactions have found that teachers with more education are more responsive and sensitive. Newer, stricter licensing regulations and standards regarding the training of early childhood educators in most states aim to improve the quality of teacher-child interactions. Research consistently shows that training is an important predictor of involved, sensitive teacher-child conversations.

Observing all elements of a program, as well as children's behavior and progress, involves watching, listening, and recording. This can be the most difficult part of teaching because of time constraints and supervisory requirements. In-depth observation is best accomplished when a teacher is relieved of other responsibilities and can focus without distractions. Many teachers who do not have duty-free observation time must observe while on duty. Observation often unearths questions regarding children's difficulties, talents, and a wide range of special needs that can then be incorporated into plans and daily exchanges.

The teacher's role as an observer is an ongoing responsibility that influences all daily teacher-child exchanges and allows the teacher to decide on courses of action with individual children. Knowing children's interests, present behaviors, and emerging skills helps the teacher perform the three aforementioned functions, based on group and individual needs. Teachers must be part detective and part researcher, sifting through the clues children leave, collecting data, testing hypotheses, and examining the way children really are to make a credible record of their growth and development.

Nondirective			Mediating			Directive	
Acknowledge	Model	Facilitate	Support	Scaffold	Co-construct	Demonstrate	Direct
Give attention and positive encouragement to keep a child engaged in an activity.	Display for children a skill or desirable way of behaving in the classroom, through actions only or with cues, prompts, or other forms of coaching.	Offer short-term assistance to help a child achieve the next level of functioning (as an adult does in holding the back of a bicycle while a child pedals).	Provide a fixed form of assistance, such as a bicycle's training wheels, to help a child achieve the next level of functioning.	Set up challenges or assist children to work "on the edge" of their current competence.	Learn or work collaboratively with children on a problem or task, such as building a model or block structure.	Actively display a behavior or engage in an activity while children observe the outcome.	Provide specific directions for children's behavior within narrowly defined dimensions of error.

FIGURE 7–2 *Continuum of teaching behaviors.* (From Bredekamp, S., & Rosegrant, T. [Eds.]. "Reaching potentials through transforming curriculum, assessment, and teaching." In *Reaching potentials: Transforming early childhood curriculum and assessment,* [Vol. 2, p. 21]. Washington, DC: National Association for the Education of Young Children. Reprinted with permission.)

Listening intimately is highly advisable. Providing an environment that is conducive to growth depends partially on being on a child's or group's wavelength. Conversations are more valuable when teachers try to converse and question based on the child's line of thought. Activities provided should increase children's ability to think and rethink and therefore make sense from what they encounter.

Unplanned teacher talk can be viewed as less important than talk in teacher-guided activities. If a teacher thinks this way, it can limit his ability to support problem solving, child discovery, and child expression of events important to the child. The listening and observing behavior of teachers increases the quality and pertinence of teachers' communicative interactions.

THE TEACHER AS A MODEL

Teachers model not only speech but also attitudes and behaviors in listening, writing, and reading. Children watch and listen to adults' use of grammar, intonation, and sentence patterns and imitate and use adults as examples. Consider the different and similar ways teachers verbally interact with young children by examining Figure 7–3.

An early and classic study by Bernstein, who studied British families in 1962, concluded that a recognizable style of verbal interaction based on social class exists. Working-class speakers, Bernstein believed, used a restricted code type of speech, whereas middle-class speakers used both elaborated code and restricted code speech in some verbal exchanges. Restricted code speech characteristics include the following:

◆ specific to a current physical context
◆ limited
◆ stereotyped
◆ condensed
◆ inexact
◆ nonspecific
◆ short in sentence length
◆ vague and indefinite

Example A
Child: "It's chickun soup."
Teacher: "That's right."

Example B
Child: "It's chickun soup."
Teacher: "Yes. I see chicken pieces and something else."
Child: "It's noodles."
Teacher: "Yes, those are long, skinny noodles. It's different from yesterday's red tomato soup."
Child: "Tastes good. It's 'ellow."
Teacher: "Yellow like the daffodils in the vase." (Pointing.)

Example C
Child: "Baby cry."
Adult: "Yes, the baby is crying."

Example D
Child: "Baby cry."
Adult: "You hear the baby crying?"
Child: "Uh-huh."
Adult: "Maybe she's hungry and wants some milk."
Child: "Wants bottle."
Adult: "Let's see. I'll put the bottle in her mouth."
Child: "Her hungry."
Adult: "Yes, she's sucking. The milk is going into her mouth. Look, it's almost gone."

FIGURE 7–3 Adult verbal styles.

Elaborate code speech, in Bernstein's view, is

◆ more differentiated.
◆ more precise.
◆ not specific to a particular situation or context and affords opportunities for more complex thought.

Speakers' styles of communication were seen by Bernstein as powerful determining factors in the young child's development of cognitive structures and modes of communication. He believed that young children exposed exclusively to restricted code speakers are at an educational disadvantage in school settings where elaborated code speech predominates. The major assumption behind this view is that middle-class ways of talking with children support literacy development, whereas working-class ways of talking with children inhibit literacy development.

Many other researchers have investigated verbal exchanges between parents and children to pinpoint connections between adult talk and its relationship to child speech, thinking ability, and literacy. More current studies describe parents' high-level and low-level distancing strategies in verbal exchanges. High-level distancing strategies include:

◆ drawing conclusions.
◆ inferring cause-and-effect relationships.
◆ planning.
◆ evaluating consequences.
◆ evaluating effect.

Low-level distancing strategies include labeling, producing information, and observing. Researchers hypothesized that social class alone does not predict children's cognitive and linguistic outcomes. Early childhood educators observing young children would agree.

It is suggested that early childhood teachers focus on studying their ability to use **explanatory talk** in child-teacher verbal exchanges. Explanatory talk consists of conversation concerning some connection between objects, events, concepts, and/or conclusions that one speaker is pointing out to another (Figure 7–4). Teachers commonly and typically explain their intent and actions to children and provide explanations in response to child comments and questions. This is a preferred behavior in early childhood teachers' verbal interactive exchanges. Some examples follow.

> "The blocks go on the shelf. We will know where to find them when we want to use them, and no one will trip on them."

> "The window was open, and the wind blew into our classroom. It knocked over

FIGURE 7–4 Explanatory talk also occurs when a child explains her connection to a book's illustration.

the small cups where our seeds were planted."

> "I'm putting my snack dish in the tub on the table when I'm finished. Mrs. Gregorio will come and get the tub after snack time."

This explanatory style sometimes carries over into teachers' personal lives. Teachers report family members often say to them, "Yes, I know why you're doing that!"

Adults should use clear, descriptive speech at a speed and pitch easily understood. Articulation should be as precise as possible. Appropriate adult models during infancy and the toddler period would have the following characteristics, which are also desirable in teachers of preschoolers.

> . . . being a good model involves more than merely speaking clearly, slowly, and appropriately. A good model uses a variety of facial expressions and other forms of nonverbal communication; associates talking with understanding and affection;

---

explanatory talk — a type of conversation characterized by a speaker's attempt to create connections between objects, events, concepts, or conclusions to promote understanding in the listener.

provides happy, pleasant experiences associated with talking; and takes advantage of various timely situations. . . .

Teachers also need to be sure that reward in the form of attention is present in their teaching behavior as they deal with young children's attitudes, skills, and behaviors in language arts activities (Figure 7–5). Educators should use language patterns with which they feel comfortable and natural and should analyze their speech, working toward providing the best English model possible. Familiar language patterns reflect each teacher's personality and ethnic culture. Knowing what kind of model one presents is important, because knowing that there is room for improvement can help a teacher become more professional.

Modeling the correct word or sentence is done by simply supplying it in a relaxed, natural way rather than in a corrective tone. The teacher's example is a strong influence; when a teacher adds courtesy words ("please" and "thank you," for instance), these words appear in children's speech. Finishing an incomplete word by adding an ending or beginning may be appropriate with very young speakers. (The child may say

"na na"; the teacher would provide "banana.") Completing a phrase or offering complete sentences in Standard English suits older speakers. Although adult modeling has its limits in facilitating spontaneous language, it is an essential first step in learning language.

After hearing corrections modeled, the child will probably not shift to correct grammar or usage immediately. It may take many repetitions by teachers and adults over time. What is important is the teacher's acceptance and recognition of the child's idea within the verbalization and the addition of pertinent comments along the same line.

When adults focus on the way something was said (grammar) rather than the meaning, they miss opportunities to increase awareness and extend child interest. Overt correction often ends teacher-child conversation. Affirmation is appropriate; the teacher should emphasize the child's intended message.

Adults can sometimes develop the habit of talking and listening to themselves rather than to the children; it is hypnotic and can be a deterrent to really hearing the child. If one's mind wanders or if one listens only for the purpose of refuting, agreeing, or jumping to

FIGURE 7–5 Giving attention can be a form of reward for some children.

value judgments, it interferes with receiving communication from others. Teachers need not be afraid of silences and pauses before answering. The following listening suggestions are recommended.

◆ Work as hard to listen as you do to talk.
◆ Try to hear the message behind the words.
◆ Consciously practice good listening.

One teaching technique that promotes language skill is simple modeling of grammar or filling in missing words and completing simple sentences. This is called **expansion**. It almost becomes second nature and automatic after a short period of intentional practice. When using an expansion, the adult responds to the child by expanding the syntactic composition of the child's utterance. For example, the child's "It is cold" might be followed by "The window pane felt cold when you pressed your nose against it." The teacher's expansion is contingent and responsive, focusing on what the child was experiencing. Although using the strategy of expansion is a widely accepted and practiced teacher behavior, Crawford (2005) notes there is little research evidence that it has any positive effect. Evidence showing a negative effect is also yet to be found. Even without research validating the technique, many educators believe that the practice is still valuable, and when additional research takes place it will confirm their actions. While using expansion, the teacher can also promote wider depth of meaning or spark interest by contributing or suggesting an idea for further exploration. Additional conversation usually occurs.

The teacher is a model for listening as well as speaking. Words, expressions, pronunciations, and gestures are copied, as is listening behavior. A quiet teacher may have a quiet classroom; an enthusiastic, talkative teacher (who also listens) may have a classroom where children talk, listen, and share experiences. The way children feel about themselves is reflected in their behavior. When teachers listen closely,

children come to feel that what they say is worthwhile.

Modeling good printscript form (classroom or center manuscript print) is important (Chapter 16 deals with this topic). Children seem to absorb everything in their environment, so it is necessary to provide correctly formed alphabet letters and numerals on children's work, charts, bulletin boards, and any displayed classroom print.

Teachers' use and care of books are modeled, as are their attitudes toward story and nonfiction book experiences. Through their observations of teachers' actions, children begin to develop ideas about how books should be handled and stored.

One teacher who wanted to model storytelling of personal stories divided a large paper into eight sections; in each section she drew a picture of different stages in her life. She showed this to her class and asked them to pick a picture, which she then related in storytelling. Teachers also model poetry reading and its use, dramatization, puppet play, and many other language arts activities.

What we are communicates far more eloquently than anything we say or do. This is an old saying that was not written expressly for teachers of young children; nonetheless it is a good addition to this discussion. According to Au (2006), teachers must demonstrate the kind of literacy they want students to show. They must see themselves as readers and writers and convince students of the value of reading and writing. In doing so, they help young children gain an appreciation for literacy in their own lives. With picture books, some of the ways this is accomplished is by selecting and sharing books with an obvious enjoyment factor, by building on children's interests, and by discussing enjoyed book sections as these relate to individual children. An educator on any teaching day can model his or her thinking by talking aloud to promote children's thinking along the same lines. This is often done when

---

expansion — a teaching technique that includes the adult's (teacher's) modeling of words or grammar, filling in missing words in children's utterances, or suggesting ideas for child exploration.

sharing a book, but there are many additional opportunities.

> "Today we have three boys sitting together in our circle whose names start with the letter 'J' ... Jacob, Joseph and Joshua."

> "You made a new color when your yellow paint touched the blue paint."

> "I wonder what would happen if I put this sign that says 'Keep Out' on the door of the playhouse. Let's find out."

> "This book says Bill and Will slid downhill. Those words rhyme—Bill, Will, downhill."

> "I hear the same sound at the end of Emma, Olivia, and Isabella's names— Emma, Olivia, Isabella. And in Isabella's name I hear the sound two times."

> "What a sad face Corduroy has. His mouth turns down at its corners."

> "If I pour too much juice into this cup, it will spill. I don't want to do that so I'll stop a little way below the top."

THE TEACHER AS PROVIDER

As providers, preschool teachers strive to provide experiences that promote literacy. Fortunately, the number of interesting language arts activities one can offer children is almost limitless. Teachers rely on both their own creativity and the many resources available to plan experiences based on identified goals. Early childhood resource books, other teachers, teacher magazines, workshops, and conferences all contribute ideas.

Gathering activity ideas and storing them in a personal resource file is suggested, because it is almost impossible to remember all the activity ideas one comes upon. An activity file can include new or tried-and-true activity ideas. Developing a usable file starts with identifying initial categories (file headings) and then adding more heads as the file grows. Some teachers use oversized file cards; others use binders or file folders. Whatever the file size, teachers find that files are very worthwhile when it comes to daily, weekly, and monthly planning. Often, files are helpful when ideas on a certain subject or theme are needed or when a child exhibits a special interest. A file collection is not used as the basis for activity planning but rather as a collection of good ideas or ideas you might like to try at a later time.

A large number of activity ideas are presented in following chapters. Your creativity can produce many others. Here are some suggestions for separate file headings (categories):

◆ Audiovisual Activities
◆ Bulletin Board Ideas
◆ Child Drama Ideas
◆ Children's Books
◆ Circle Time Ideas
◆ Classroom Environment Ideas
◆ Listening Centers
◆ Reading Centers
◆ Writing Centers
◆ Dramatic Play Stimulators
◆ Dramatic Play Theme Ideas
◆ Experience Stories
◆ Field Trip Ideas
◆ Finger Plays
◆ Flannel Board Ideas
◆ Free and Inexpensive Material Resources
◆ Language Game Ideas
◆ Listening Activities
◆ Listening Center Ideas
◆ Magazine (Child's) Activities
◆ Patterns
◆ Perceptual-Motor Activities
◆ Poetry
◆ Printscript Ideas
◆ Puppets
◆ Reading Readiness Ideas
◆ Rebus Stories
◆ Seasonal Ideas
◆ Conversation Starters
◆ Stories for Storytelling
◆ Visitor Resources

Greenberg (1998) paints a colorful picture of what early childhood educators might provide as they strive to offer age-appropriate language activities. Her activity ideas include the following:

> . . . sing lively jingles and soothing lullabies; enjoy laughing lap games and forever intriguing Mother Goose rhymes; recite delightful poems and golden oldie childhood chants; join in choral chanting (or choral reading) of rhymes and fun poems; listen to audio and video cassettes containing songs (including the alphabet song) and rhythmic activities done by real pros—and sing, swing, clap, tap and dance along with them; play traditional preschool and kindergarten games such as London Bridge, Los Pollitos Dicer, and Who Stole the Cookies from the Cookie Jar?; read high-quality books—which have lovely language with pleasing, interesting rhythms, rich vocabulary, and predictable repetitions picking up on a particularly catchy word or phrase and playing with it; act silly with four-, five-, six-, seven- and eight-year-old children, latching onto a word a child says and fooling around with it; or engage in entertaining word games with a few children or the group. (p. 39)

As a provider of materials, a teacher must realize that every classroom object can become a useful program tool to stimulate language. From the clock on the wall to the doorknob, every safe item can be discussed, compared, and explored in some way (Figure 7–6). Because most school budgets are limited, early childhood teachers find ways to use available equipment and materials to their fullest.

Each teacher is a unique resource who can plan activities based on personal interests and abilities. Most teachers are pleasantly surprised to see how avidly their classes respond to their personal interests. When the teacher shares enthusiasm for out-of-school interests, hobbies, projects, trips, and individual talents, he can help introduce children to important knowledge. Almost anything appropriate can be presented at the child's level. Whether the teacher is an opera buff, scuba diver, gourmet cook, stamp collector, or violin player, the activity should be shared in any safe form that communicates special interest and love of the

FIGURE 7–6 Madison has an interest in insects so her teacher supplies both opportunity and equipment.

activity, and the specific vocabulary and materials relating to the activity should be presented. Enthusiasm is the key to inspired teaching.

Providing for Abundant Play

Abundant opportunities for play are important to the child's language acquisition. Considerable research shows that child's play is in fact more complex than it is commonly believed to be. It provides a rich variety of experiences: communication with other children, verbal rituals, topic development and maintenance, turn taking, intimate speech in friendships, follower-leader conversations, and many other kinds of language exchanges. Peer play helps develop a wide range of communicative skills. Except when the children's safety is in question, children's natural ability to pretend should be encouraged, and the flow of this kind of play should proceed without the teacher's interference. Children will want to talk to teachers about their play, and the teacher's proper involvement is to show interest and be playful themselves at times.

If a child has chosen to engage a teacher in conversation instead of play, or during play, the teacher should be both a willing listener and a competent, skillful conversationalist. Opportunities for play and opportunities to engage both children and adults in extended, warm, and personal conversations should be readily and equally available to the child.

Young children explore constantly. They want to do what they see others doing. Play opportunities usually involve manipulating something. When deeply involved in play, children may seem to be momentarily awestruck in their search for meanings, but soon they will approach adults with questions or comments.

When one observes preschoolers at play, it is obvious that they learn a great deal of language from each other. They gain skills in approaching other children and asking if they can play, or just nonverbally joining a play group in progress. They begin to understand what attracts others to them, how to imitate another child's actions or words, how to express affection or hostility, how to assume a leadership role, how to negotiate, and how to follow or refuse playmates' requests. These and other play skills help them stay engaged in a play group for a longer period of time.

Preschoolers at play may even argue over correct language use. Some observers believe that the majority of language teaching that takes place in the 4-year-olds' classroom is child-to-child teaching.

A resourceful teacher will strive to provide a variety of play by regarding all of a center's area (and furnishings) as a possible place (or object) for safe and appropriate play. Creative use can be made of each foot of floor space. Children need large blocks of uninterrupted time to construct knowledge and actively explore their problem-solving options in an environment thoughtfully and carefully prepared by the teacher.

Providing Accurate and Specific Speech in All Content Areas

Although this text concentrates on teacher-child interactions in the subject field, language arts, other content areas, such as mathematics (numbers), social studies, health and safety, art, music, movement, and so on, will be subjects of teacher-child conversations and discussions. The same teacher techniques that are useful in building children's language competence and vocabulary in language arts are equally useful for other content areas. Every subject area has its own vocabulary and common terms that can overlap other fields of study. For example, the teacher may discuss "applying" paints during an art activity and "applying" an antibacterial on a wound or scratch. If children are focused on the number of muffins on a tray, or whether there are enough scissors to go around, then teacher comments include number words.

Teacher comments should be as accurate and specific as possible in light of what the teacher believes the children might already know or have experienced (Figure 7–7). Purposeful teacher conversation adds a little more information than the children already know, and reinforces and adds depth to words already in the children's vocabulary. When working

FIGURE 7–7 Teachers' comments are based on their knowledge of individual children.

with numerals or other subjects, the teacher should use terminology that is appropriate to the subject area but at a level the children will understand. For example, the teacher might say "Let's count the muffins" or "The tool in your hand is a wire whip" or "The metal cylinder attached to the wall is a fire extinguisher. Fire extinguishers have something inside that can be sprayed out to put out fires." In movement or music activities, many descriptive terms can be added to teacher directions, and conversations such as hop, jump, stretch or soft, loud, high, and low. These are easily understood while the child is in the process of experiencing them. The quality of the words children hear is crucial for their later school and language performance (Kalmar, 2008). Children build meaning as adults and teachers make comments, provide information, comfort them, guide them, praise and encourage their efforts, and display excitement and enthusiasm for the world around them. Sometimes, teachers are reluctant to use big, new words such as the word *hibernate* (Neuman & Roskos, 2007). Neuman and Roskos urge educators to remember that teacher words and phrases are one of the main sources for giving children new

knowledge. They stress giving explanations and examples and suggest saying,

> "When an animal goes to sleep for the winter, we say it is hibernating."
>
> Then, provide opportunities for children to practice their new language by saying "Do you remember what we call it when animals go to sleep for the winter? We call it hibernating." (p. 10).

The teacher prompts children's use of the words that the teacher provides. Most times a teacher is careful to define new words immediately after using the new terms. In number activities, number words are used in the presence of a corresponding number of objects. In movement activities, types of movement are discussed with quick demonstrations.

It is important to introduce new terms in a natural conversational tone rather than within the framework of an obvious lesson. Leading a child or groups of children to new discoveries offers the teacher an opportunity to use specific and accurate terms and also makes children feel like partners in the discoveries.

In the theme (unit) approach to instruction, there is often identifiable terminology attached to the theme. Teachers sometimes outline the terms that might be encountered in a particular unit and try to include these specific terms in conversations. A unit on birds could include many terms and specific names that a teacher might need to research.

THE TEACHER—AN EDUCATOR WHO INTERACTS

An educator can be defined as a person who is always interested in what a child is saying or doing. This person encourages conversation on any subject the child selects, is never too busy to talk and share interests and concerns, and listens with the intent to understand. Understanding the child's message makes the educator's response more educationally valuable. Time is purposely planned for daily conversations with each child. When teachers talk about what they are doing, explain why particular results occur, and let children ask questions about procedures and results, children will have more exposure to and experience with extended forms of discourse. These private, personal, one-on-one encounters build the child's feelings of self-worth and open communications. Conversations can be initiated with morning greetings such as the following:

> "Alphonse, I've been waiting to talk to you.
>
> "Tell me about your visit to Chicago."
>
> "How is your puppy feeling today, Andrea?"
>
> "Those new blue tennis shoes will be good for running in the yard and for tiptoeing, too."

Educators are aware of the "reciprocal opportunity" that is always present in work with young children. Teachers try to really hear verbal communications and sense nonverbal messages. They give undivided attention (if possible), which lends importance to and shows interest in children's ideas and also rewards children's efforts to use language and initiate social contact. A teacher can respond skillfully, first clarifying what the teacher thought she heard and then adding to the conversation and attempting to stimulate more verbal output, child discovery, some new feature or detail, or a different way of viewing what has captured the child's interest. The correctness of children's verbal expression of their thoughts, feelings, requests, or other intent is accepted and corrected only when it is socially unacceptable speech.

Studies of teacher-child interaction have discovered that some teachers were warm and accepting but offered children little invitation to talk. These teachers found it quicker and easier to anticipate students' needs and thus failed to seize opportunities that would make children want and need to talk.

Teachers can emphasize the mental or symbolic component of an activity and help children identify problems or dilemmas by suggesting that children put their ideas into words. Teachers may need to raise their own awareness of their interactions with children, in other words, rate themselves on their ability to expand children's verbal output and accuracy (Figure 7–8). Many educators advise

FIGURE 7–8 Notice this teacher's effort to make eye contact with the child as she speaks.

preschool educators to realize the importance of adult-child language interactions, and point out that in a child's first 5 years the child's language growth is entirely dependent on what people say to him—on how much they speak to him, about what things, in what dialect or language, and in what manner, whether gentle and explaining or peremptory and imperative. When a preschool teacher attends to certain events in the classroom, she reveals to children what she values, which hopefully includes preschoolers' literacy efforts.

It is wise to be aware and up to date on topics of special interest to preschoolers. Current popular toys, cartoon figures, community happenings, sports, recording artists, movies, and individual family events may often be the focus of young children's conversations. When a teacher has background knowledge, such as what current Disney characters are popular or familiar to her students or which children have a new infant sibling at home, her responses when children discuss these items can be more pertinent and connected to the reality of enrolled children's lives.

Early childhood educators use a technique called **extension**. Building on a child's statement, the teacher adds information, factual data, or additional meaning. This can both add vocabulary and clarify some aspect or concept encountered in the conversational interchange. The child's "It spilled" might be answered with "Yes, Quan's hand knocked the cup over."

Many teachers have used a conversational interaction technique called **closure**. It involves pausing, specifically, hesitating in the middle of a sentence or at sentence endings. It is a technique that prompts guessing by the child, and the teacher is willing to accept any guess. Most often, children's guesses are logical but may not be what the teacher expected. Those children with a sense of the ridiculous may offer off-the-wall guesses equally acceptable to the teacher. It often promotes further dialogue. The teacher's saying "The sun disappeared behind a . . ." might elicit "hill," "mountain," "building," "tree," "cloud," or other possibilities from the child. The teacher's saying "Coats are hung in the . . . by the front door" is an example of middle-of-the-sentence closure or a fill-in statement.

In looking at individual children, Covey (1989) reminds us of what we know in our hearts to be true, fair, and compassionate. Each child is to be valued for his identity as a person and for his unique individuality, separateness, and worth. Comparisons between children cloud our view. Traits teachers may see as negative can be fostered by the environment we offer and our own perceptions of correct student behavior. An educator's job, according to Covey, is to recognize potential, then coddle and inspire that potential to emerge at its own pace. Weitzman (1992) urges teacher waiting behavior. When you wait, you give the child time to initiate or to get involved in an activity. You are, in effect, giving her this message: "You're in control—I know you can communicate, so you decide what you want to do or say. I'll give you all the time you need." Studies of adult-child interactions have shown that adults give children approximately one second in which to respond to a question. After one second, the adult repeats and rephrases the question or provides the answer. One second! Most children need much longer than one second to process the question and figure out their response.

Adult speech containing a relatively high proportion of statements or declaratives has been associated with accelerated language development in young children. Adult-child conversations tend to last longer if adults add new relevant information. If adults verbally accept and react to children's statements with "oh, really?" or "I see," when they are trying to grasp

---

extension — a teaching strategy in which an adult expands the child's information by adding new, additional, related information or meaning.

closure — a conversation technique that prompts children to verbally guess and complete or fill in a teacher's sentence. The teacher pauses or hesitates, which prompts the child to finish a teacher verbalization.

a child's meaning, additional conversation seems to be promoted.

When a teacher answers a child by showing interest, this rewards the child for speaking. Positive feelings are read internally as an automatic signal to continue to do what we are doing. Many experts suggest that teachers should guide and collaborate to promote children's independent problem solving in any given situation. Most often, teachers show their attention by listening to, looking at, smiling at, patting, or answering a child, or by acting favorably to what a child has said or done.

In Figure 6–18 in the previous chapter, the teacher and children were planning and participating in an activity. Children displayed interest and enthusiasm. This figure illustrates the teacher's thinking. She is guiding, providing, and interacting in a way that promotes children's verbal expression and use of writing. It is easy to see that children exposed to this type of interaction with an adult are learning far more than language. In the example, language and thought are paired. There are obvious growth opportunities in both. How many similar situations in joint planning and joint problem solving are possible in the average classroom? The opportunities are limitless!

Note also that in Figure 6–18 not once did the teacher interact in a test question manner by asking, "What color are apples?" or "What is this called on the recipe chart?" Rather, her verbal comments provoked children's discovery. When she prompted and it was obvious children were unfamiliar with a word (for example, cinnamon), the teacher offered it.

For those who want to ask thought-provoking questions, the work of Kucan (2007) provides another guide. As discussed earlier, teachers can get into the habit of primarily asking questions that call for a "right" answer, a memory question. This type of question does not call for interpretation, application, analysis, synthesis, explanation, evaluation, inference, prediction, comparison, contrasting or connecting ideas. Critical thinking, judgment, and problem solving are required to answer these questions. Try to identify what is asked for in the following.

1. What might happen if Emma grabs Maria's paint without asking?

2. In our story, Josh carried all the eggs in a basket. Could we use something to carry our small blocks outside? We don't have a basket.

3. Saucedo said he was sorry when he knocked down Kai's block tower. What else might he have done to show Kai he was sorry?

4. What happened to make Ahmad so angry in our story? Would you do what Ahmad did?

5. Our pet, Missy, gets so frightened when people gather around her cage. What rules should we make?

6. Noah said, "The ant ate an elephant," and you all laughed. Why?

7. When Latanya said, "It won't work if you do that," what did she mean? Why wouldn't the scissors work?

Although some may seem to fit in more than one category, you should agree that all of these examples required much more thinking than a memory-checking question. Teachers trying to determine their questioning skills can test themselves using Figure 7–9.

Teachers often act as interpreters, especially with younger preschoolers. The child who says "Gimme dat" is answered with "You want the red paint." Do not worry about faulty teacher interpretations! Most children will let teachers know when they have interpreted incorrectly by trying again. Then the teacher has the opportunity to say, "You wanted the blue paint, Taylor."

Consider the dialog of the language-developing teacher below. Did the teacher's speech interactions accomplish the goal?

Goal #1: Use language slightly more complex than the child's.

Child: "Those are cookies."

Teacher: "Yes, they're called gumdrop mountains because they come to a point on the top."

TEST YOUR QUESTIONING AND RESPONDING ABILITIES

Answer the following using A = always, S = sometimes, N = need to work on this, or U = unable to determine.

1. Do I respond to child-initiated comments 100 percent of the time? _____
2. Do I keep to the child's topic and include it in my response? _____
3. Do I ask questions that prompt children to see or discover an aspect that they might not have perceived or discovered? _____
4. Am I aware of the favorite subjects and interests of individual children and ask questions along these lines? _____

   Are my questions appropriate in light of the children's development levels? _____
5. Do I often answer a child's comments using teacher echolalia?

   Child: "I went to the zoo."

   Teacher: "Oh, you went to the zoo."

   Or would my answer more likely be, "What animals did you see?" _____
6. Are my questions usually open ended? _____
7. Are my questions thought-inducing, or are they merely seeking correct answers? _____
8. Do I provide a specific response to children's questions? _____
9. Do my questions take place in the context of mutual trust and respect, based on my genuine friendliness, unconditional acceptance, warmth, empathy, and interest? _____
10. Do many of my questions seem to put a child "on-the-spot" or fluster a child? _____

FIGURE 7–9 Assess your questioning and responding abilities.

Goal #2: Speak with young or limited-language children by referring to an action, object, person, and/or event that is currently happening.

Teacher: "You're climbing up the stairs."

Goal #3: Base your reactive conversation on the meaning the child intended. There are two ways to do this: (1) repetition ("Pet the dog" to child's "Pet dog"); (2) expansion (the child says, "play bath," and the teacher expands with, "You want to play with your toys in the bath tub").

Goal #4: Use recasting. (The child says, "You can't get in," and the teacher responds, "No, I can't get in, can I?")

Goal #5: Use "I see," "Yes," or a similar expression to indicate I am listening.

Encouraging children to tell about happenings and how they feel is possible throughout the preschool day (Figure 7–10). A teacher may find it harder to interact verbally with quiet children than with those children who frequently start conversations with the teacher. The teacher should be aware of this tendency and make a daily effort to converse with all attending children. A teacher's role includes associating language with pleasure and enjoyment.

Teachers shift to more mature or less mature speech as they converse with children of differing ages and abilities. They try to speak to each according to his understanding. They use shorter, less complex utterances and use more gestures and nonverbal signals with infants, toddlers, and speakers trying to learn English. Generally, the ability to understand longer and more complex sentences increases with the child's age.

At times, it will be prudent for the teacher to pause or refrain from speaking. Young children who are talking to themselves, directing their actions with self-talk, will appear to be in their own little world. Intrusion by an adult is not expected by the child, nor is it necessary. Children usually think out loud while they are

FIGURE 7–10 Bending or kneeling puts adults at an appropriate level to engage in intimate conversation.

deeply absorbed in self-pursued activities. Adult talk at these times can be interruptive.

The teacher who interacts in daily experiences can help improve the child's ability to see relationships. Although there is current disagreement as to the teacher's ability to promote cognitive growth (the act or process of knowing), attention can be focused and help provided by answering and asking questions. Often, a teacher can help children see clear links between material already learned and new material. Words teachers provide are paired with the child's mental images that have come through the senses. Language aids memory because words attached to mental images help the child retrieve stored information.

Intellectually valuable experiences involve the teacher and adult as active participants in tasks with the child. Adults can label, describe, compare, classify, and question, supporting children's intellectual development. As the teacher interacts by supplying words to fit situations, it should be remembered that a new word often needs to be repeated in a subtle way. It has been said that at least three repetitions of a new word are needed for adults to master the word; young children need more. In some cases, when a new word is very salient and the child is highly motivated, a child may acquire the word after a single, brief exposure. This is called *fast mapping*, and children also more readily learn new words that are conceptually similar to words they already know (Wasik, 2006). Repeated exposure to a new word in the same and other meaningful contexts is still recommended in most situations. Walley, Metsala, and Garlock (2003) researched the ease with which children learn new words. They note that new words that are phonologically similar to a known word are also easier to acquire. If the child's vocabulary contains *hat*, *mat*, and *cat*, which contain similar morphemes, similar words may be learned readily.

Teachers often hear the child repeating a new word, trying to become familiar with it. To help children remember a new word, Bennett-Armistead, Duke, and Moses (2005) suggest making sure the words you say around the new word give clues to the word's meaning. For example, instead of saying "That is a fox," say "It is an animal called a fox. It looks like a small dog and has a big, fluffy tail." The best way to make a new word *real* to young children is to relate the new word to the child's own experiences and ideas.

There are times when a teacher chooses to supply information in answer to direct child questions. There is no easy way for the child to discover answers to questions such as "What's the name of today?" or "Why is that man using that funny stick with a cup on the end?" A precise, age-level answer is necessary, such as "Today is Monday, May 9" and (while demonstrating) "It's a stick, called a plunger. It pushes air and water down the drain and helps open the pipes so that the water in the sink will run out." As a provider of information, the teacher acts as a reference and resource person, providing the information a child desires. If the teacher does not wish to answer a question directly, she may encourage the child to ask the same question of someone else or help the child find out where the answer is available.

Child: "What's lunch?"

Adult: "Come on, we'll go ask the cook." *or* "Let's look at the menu. It lists all the food being served today. I'll read it to you."

A teacher can help the child focus on something of interest. The child's desire to know can be encouraged. Repetition of words and many firsthand activities on the same theme will help the child form an idea or concept. The child may even touch and try something new with the teacher's encouragement. Can teachers promote children's curiosity about words? By being aware that children sometimes ask about words they do not understand, educators can reward the child's interest with attention. Statements might include the following:

"You now have another word for car. It is the word *automobile*."

"A good question, Erin."

"I'm happy you asked what 'slick' means Josie."

"A new word in this book will be fun to say. The word is *skedaddle* and it means to move very quickly."

"When you hear a word that puzzles you, raise your hand. Ask about it, please."

"What a wonderful word that is!"

The teacher's reaction supplies children with feedback to their actions. The teacher is responsible for reinforcing the use of a new word and gently ensuring that the children have good attitudes about themselves as speakers.

Every day, the teacher can take advantage of unplanned things that happen to promote language and speech. The following provides an illustration.

While children were sitting in a story group, John noticed that a mobile, hung from the ceiling above, was spinning. "Look," said John pointing, "it's moving!" "How come?" said another child. "Someone must have touched it," said Mary. "Stand up, Mary, and see if you can touch it," added the teacher, standing up and reaching, herself, "I can't reach it either." "Maybe it spins itself," contributed Bill. "No, it can't spin itself," said another child. "Let's see," said the teacher. She got a piece of yarn with a bead tied to the end and held it out in front of the children. It was still. Then she held it near the mobile, which was in a draft of a window. The string swayed gently. "The window, the window is open," suggested the children. "Yes, the wind is coming through the window," said John. "And making it move," said all the children, pleased with their discovery. The teacher held the string so the children could blow at it. "Look, I'm the wind," said one of them. That afternoon, outside, the children were given crepe paper streamers to explore wind direction. They were also read *Gilberto and the Wind*, which tells what can happen when wind blows the sail of a boat, the arm of a windmill, the smoke from a chimney, and a child's hat and hair.

Being able to make the most of an unexpected event is a valuable skill. Moving into a situation with skill and helping the child discover something and tell about it is part of promoting word growth (Figure 7–11).

COMMON TEACHER STATEMENT	POSSIBLE CONSEQUENCES
"Tell me more."	expands
"Did you mean . . . ?"	clarifies
"Where did you see . . . ?"	specifying
"Who said . . . ?"	
"When did the bike . . . ?"	
"Whose name shall I write on . . . ?"	specifying possession
"This belongs to . . . ?"	
"Please tell Juan . . ."	conversing with others
"Choose one person to help you."	
"Can you show . . . ?"	provides information
"Tell me again . . ."	rephrase or repeat
"What would happen if . . . ?"	guessing or problem solving
"Thang thinks . . ."	valuing others' ideas
"Taylor says . . ."	
"What could we try . . . ?"	problem solving
"Where should we put . . . ?"	creative thinking
"What's a good name for . . . ?"	
"Who had the last turn to talk . . . ?"	turn taking
"Show me with your hands."	clarifies
"What will you need to . . . ?"	specifies
"What will you do first . . . ?"	
"Do you have a question for me?"	clarifies
"Did something happen that I didn't see?"	
"Did anyone hear a sound?"	listening skill
"Show me your hand when you want to tell us something."	turn taking

*This is not meant to be a complete or comprehensive listing. Each language exchange with children is a challenge and opportunity.

FIGURE 7–11 Sample teacher interaction verbalization.

Teachable Moments

You have probably run across the phrase "teachable moments" in your training and perhaps have become adept at using this strategy. It involves a four- to five-step process.

1. Observe a child or a child group's self-chosen actions and efforts.

2. Make a hypothesis about exactly what the children are pursuing, exploring, discovering, playing with, and so on.

3. Make a teacher decision to intervene, act, provide, extend, or in some way offer an educational opportunity to further growth or knowledge related to the child-chosen agenda. This can be done a number of ways, so this step often involves teacher contemplation.

4. Determine exactly what you will do or provide. Take action. Often, this can be as simple as asking a question such as, "You are putting small pieces of torn paper in Andy's cage. What do you think Andy is going to do with them?" or by silently providing wedge-shaped blocks to a group of children racing small cars down a ramp.

Or perhaps you decide to let a child who has been watching the kitchen helper hand-whip eggs try the hand-whip himself.

5. As a final step, consider having the children tell, act out, communicate, dictate, or in some way represent what has been experienced, if this is appropriate.

A watchful teacher, who is working to promote early literacy skills, may easily connect teachable moments to relevant opportunities involving literacy skills.

Time Constraints

Comments such as, "You finished," "That's yellow," "How colorful," "It's heavy," "I like that too," or "A new shirt," may give attention, show acceptance, provide encouragement, and reinforce behavior. They feel like suitable and natural comments or responses, and they slip out almost unconsciously. In a busy classroom, they often are said in haste when the teacher may have no time for an extended conversation because she is supervising a group of children. In other words, the best a teacher can do, time permitting.

Consciously trying to be specific and expanding takes focus, effort, and quick thinking, but with practice, it can become second nature with teacher statements such as, "You pushed your chair in under the table," "In your drawing I see red and blue," "You helped your friend Alejandra by finding her book," "Those are shoes with lights," "Tell me more about your kitten," and "Returning your crayons to the box helps others find them." Teachers' specific and/or descriptive comments promote literacy.

SCAFFOLDING

Scaffolding is a teaching technique that combines support with challenge. This includes responsive conversation, open-ended questions, and facilitation of the child's initiatives. Adults estimate the amount of necessary verbal support and provide challenging questions for child growth in any given situation. The idea is to promote the child's understanding and

solutions. The adult attempts to build upon what a child already knows to help the child accomplish a task or may suggest breaking down the task into simpler components. As the child ages, his autonomous pursuit of knowledge will need less adult support. The author is reminded of the 4-year-old who described the workings of a steam locomotive. His knowledge of trains and related terminology was way above that of other children his age and even his teacher. Someone in this child's life had supplied the type of "scaffolding" (support with challenge) that allowed the child to follow an interest in trains.

It is believed that children need experiences and educational opportunities with adults who carefully evaluate, think, and talk daily occurrences through. What specific teacher verbalizations and behaviors are suggested in scaffolding? Ones that

- offer responsive and authentic conversation.
- offer a facilitation of the child's initiatives.
- use open-ended questions.
- prompt.
- promote language by using modeling of slightly more mature language forms and some language structures that are new to children.
- offer invitations for children to express thoughts and feelings in words.
- promote longer, more precise child comments.
- invite divergent responses.
- offer specific word cues in statements and questions that help children grasp further information, for example, *what, who, why, because, so, and, next, but, except, if, when, before, after*, etc.
- provoke lively discussions and quests for knowing more about subjects that interest them.
- increase collaborative communication with adults and other children.

Scaffolding is not as easy as it first may appear to teachers. What is opportunity and challenge for one child may not be for the next. In scaffolding, teacher decision making is constant and complex. An educator using scaffolding believes understanding, discovery, and problem solving can be guided. Rather than always being dependent on adults for help, the child actually is moved toward becoming an independent thinker. Adults who accompany children at home or at school can use a scaffolding approach to talk through and plan activities as simple as setting the table, cleaning the sink, getting an art area ready for finger painting, or taking care of the needs of the school pet.

What is right or wrong becomes less important than the child's expression of his own conclusions. The child is encouraged to verbalize the "whys" of his thinking. For example, "Royal thinks the rabbit eats paper because he saw Floppy tearing paper into small pieces inside the cage."

Valuable teacher collaboration with children sustains the momentum of the search, actions, or exploration. Small group projects are often a natural part of children's block area play and can also be promoted in other aspects of daily play and activities. For example, a lemonade stand can be managed by a small group, or a present or card can be designed for a sick classmate at home and then completed and mailed by a small group of children.

TEACHER INTERACTIVE STYLES

A central task for the educator is to find a balance between helping a child consolidate new understanding and offering challenges that will promote growth. Some educators believe that there are two teaching styles—transmission and interpretation. Transmission teaching is the traditional style, in which children's knowledge is thought to be acquired through the teacher talking, sharing books, and explaining classroom events and experiences. Interpretation teaching, on the other hand, is based on the understanding that children reinterpret information for themselves, and consequently, the teacher's role involves dialogues that support the children's efforts to verbalize their ideas and actual experiences.

One can easily see how easy it is to become a transmission teacher. It is overwhelmingly modeled in a teacher's own schooling. An interpretation teacher really listens and does not monopolize conversations by a display of what the teacher knows. Achieving balance between these two styles is the key. Educators both transmit and interpret.

In promoting developing language arts and literacy in early childhood, an interpretation style would not only help children talk about what they know but also help them put ideas and impressions in print by offering to take dictation or by using some other form of expression. The teacher's role is to provide the occasions, resources, and enabling climate for the pursuit of individual meaning.

Teachers can be fun-filled and playful companions at times, exhibiting their love and enthusiasm for life and the child's company. This side of teachers comes naturally to some adults and less easily to others. Perhaps some of us remember adults from our own childhood years who were able to engage themselves in adult-child interactions that could be described as joyful playing. Early childhood practitioners bent on language development are careful not to dominate conversations at these times but rather to be responsive companions.

Interaction in Symbolic Play Situations

Pretend play (symbolic play) teacher interactions take both understanding and finesse. The teacher may wish to preserve the child's chosen play direction and not encroach upon self-directed imaginative activity but, at the same time, may wish to promote the child activity by giving attention, and therefore status, to the child's pursuit. There will definitely be many times when teacher interaction may be deemed intrusive because of the child's deep involvement. At those times teachers simply monitor at a distance. In other instances, particularly with younger preschoolers, teacher interaction may enrich the child's experience.

Smilansky (1968) pioneered attempts to train children who were less able to engage in appropriate pretend play. Through adult modeling and assuming a play role in reenacted real-life experiences and through outside-of-play intervention by making suggestions, giving directions, asking questions, and clarifying behavior, she successfully taught some study children to engage in and sustain sociodramatic play.

Stressing Language Connections

The teacher interested in stressing connections between classroom language arts events and activities, as is done in an integrated approach or a whole-language approach, may often purposefully make the following comments.

> "I am writing down your ideas."
>
> "This printing I am reading says 'Please knock.'"
>
> "Do you want me to read what is printed on the wall?"
>
> "I can print that word."
>
> "What does the sign for your parking garage need to say?"
>
> "You seemed to be listening to the story I was reading."
>
> "Yes, *s* is the first alphabet letter in your name."
>
> "You want me to print your name on your work, right?"
>
> "I can read what this small printing on the box says."

Accepting Approximations

Just as parents accept and celebrate inaccurate and incorrect language and writing attempts because they are seen as signs of growth, teachers also give attention to beginning attempts and provide encouragement. Lively, interesting environments and experiences where children offer their ideas and comments, feeling safe from criticism and insensitive grammar correction, help children risk and push ahead.

Handling Interruptions

Children often interrupt adults during planned activities. When an idea hits, they want to share it. Their interruptions can indicate genuine involvement and interest, or they can reflect a variety of unrelated thoughts and feelings. Teachers usually acknowledge the interruption, accept it, and may calmly remind the one who interrupts that when one wants to speak during group activities, one should raise one's hand first. Other teachers believe preschoolers' enthusiasm to speak is natural and characteristic. These teachers believe asking children to raise their hands during group discussions is best reserved for a later age. Interruptions give the teacher an opportunity to make a key decision that affects the flow of the activity. Will the interruption break the flow of what is going on, will it add to the discussion, or is it best discussed at a later time? The teacher may decide to defer a comment, or accept being sidetracked and briefly digress from the main subject, or develop the interruption into a full-blown teacher-group discussion. Examples follow:

Situation:	The teacher is telling a flannel-board story about a squirrel preparing for winter by hiding nuts in a tree.
Child:	"My cat climbs trees."
Teacher:	"Michael, I've seen cats climb trees."
	(a short acknowledgment)
Teacher:	"Michael's cat climbs trees, and the squirrel is climbing the tree to hide the nuts he is storing away for winter."
	(The teacher acknowledges, but refers listener back to the story line.
Teacher:	"Michael, you can tell me about your cat that climbs trees as soon as we finish our story."
	(The teacher defers discussion until later.)

Because preschoolers are action-packed, they enjoy activities that include an opportunity to perform the action words they encounter in books, discussions, or daily happenings (Figure 7–12). Teachers can promote "acting out" words with their own behaviors. Some descriptive words are easily enacted. *Pounce, stamp, sneak, slither, creep, slide,* and many other appealing action words exist. *Enormous, droopy, sleepy, tired,* and other descriptive words can be connected to visual reproductions.

Incorporating the children's ideas and suggestions into group conversations and giving children credit for their ideas make children aware of the importance of their expressed ideas.

"Kimberly's idea was to . . ."

"Angelo thinks we should . . ."

"Christal suggests that we . . ."

"Here's the way Trevor would . . ."

Using Sequential Approaches to Instruction

Teachers need a clear understanding of how children learn words and concepts. Figure 7–13 includes guidelines for the teacher's words and

FIGURE 7–12 "I'm this big, teacher."

actions to accompany the child's progress toward new learning.

One approach to teacher interaction during structured, planned, or incidental activities, described by Maria Montessori (1967b), is called three-stage interaction. It shows movement from the child's sensory exploration to showing understanding, and then to verbalizing the understanding. An example follows.

Step 1: *Associating Sense Perception with Words.* A cut lemon is introduced, and the child is encouraged to taste it. As the child tastes, the adult says, "The lemon tastes sour," pairing the word sour with the sensory experience. Repetition of the verbal pairing strengthens the impression.

Step 2: *Probing Understanding.* A number of yellow fruits are cut and presented. "Find the one that tastes sour," the teacher suggests. The child shows by his actions his understanding or lack of it.

Step 3: *Expressing Understanding.* A child is presented with a cut lemon and grapefruit and asked, "How do they taste?" If the child is able to describe the fruit as sour, he has incorporated the word into his vocabulary and has some understanding of the concept.

When using the three-step approach, Montessori (1967b) suggests that if a child is uninterested, the adult should stop at that point. If a mistake is made, the adult remains silent. The mistake indicates only that the child is not ready to learn—not that he is unable to learn. This verbal approach may seem mechanical and ritualistic to some, yet it clearly illustrates the sequence in a child's progress from not knowing to knowing.

The following example of a variation of the Montessori three-step approach includes additional steps. In this teaching sequence, the child asks the teacher how to open the tailgate of a dump truck in the sandbox.

CHILD ACTIVITY	TEACHER ACTIONS
• focuses on an object or activity	• Name the object, or offer a statement describing the actions or situation. (supplies words)
• manipulates and explores the object or situation using touch, taste, smell, sight, and sound organs	• Try to help the child connect this object or action to his past experience through simple conversation. (builds bridge between old and new)
• fits this into what he already knows; develops some understanding	• Help the child see details through simple statements or questions. (focus on identifying characteristics)
	• Use "Show me … " or "Give me … " prodding statements that call for a nonverbal response. (prompting)
	• Put child's action into words. (Example: "John touched the red ball.") (modeling)
	• Ask the child for a verbal response. "What is this called?" "What happened when … ?" (prompting)
• uses a new word or sentence that names, describes, classifies, or generalizes a feature or whole part of the object or action	• Give a response in words indicating the truth factor of the response. "Yes, that's a red ball" or "It has four legs like a horse, but it's called a cow." (corrective or reinforcing response)
	• Extend one-word answers to full simple sentence if needed. (modeling)
	• Suggest an exploration of another feature of the object or situation. (extend interest)
	• Ask a memory or review question. "What did we discover when … " (reinforcing and assessing)

FIGURE 7–13 Language learning and teacher interaction.

TEACHER INTENT:	TEACHER STATEMENTS:
1. Focus attention.	"Look at this little handle."
2. Create motivation, defined as creating a desire to want to do or want to know (note that in this situation this is not necessary because the child is interested).	"You want the tailgate to open." (Pointing)
3. Provide information.	"This handle turns and opens the tailgate." (Demonstrating)
4. Promote child's attempts or practice.	"Try to turn the handle."
5. Give corrective information, feedback, or positive reinforcement.	"The handle needs to turn." "Try to push down as you turn it." (Showing how) Or, "You did it; the tailgate is open."

Steps 1 through 5 are used in the following situation in which the teacher wants the child to know what is expected in the use of bathroom paper towels.

1. "Here's the towel dispenser. Do you see it?"

2. "You can do this by yourself. You may want to dry your hands after you wash them."

3. Demonstration: "First take one paper towel. Dry your hands. Then the towel goes into this wastebasket."

4. "You try it."

5. "That's it. Pull out one towel. Dry your hands. Put the towel in the wastebasket."

"Now you know where the dirty paper towels go. No one will have to pick up your used towel from the floor. You can do it without help now like some of your classmates."

Statements of this kind help the child learn both the task and the vocabulary. The ability to provide information that the child needs, without talking too much, is one of the skills required of a really excellent teacher. Most theorists believe that the successful completion of a task is a reward in itself. Others believe that an encouraging verbal pat on the back is in order.

The same dump truck scene detailed earlier could be handled using a discovery approach, instead of a teacher-directed sequence, with the following types of questions. "Did you see anyone else playing with this dump truck? Is there a button to push or a handle to turn that opens the tailgate? What happens if you try to open the tailgate with your hand?"

The goal of prompting in a child-adult conversation is to encourage the child to express ideas perhaps more precisely and/or specifically. It is used slightly differently with younger preschoolers, as shown in the following examples.

Young preschooler: "Cookie."

Adult: "You want a cookie?"

Child: "Dis cookie."

Adult: "You want this brown cookie?"

Older preschooler: "I want that cookie."

Adult: "You want one of these cookies. Which cookie do you want, the chocolate cookie or the sugar cookie?"

Child: "The chocolate one."

Can teachers really make a difference in the level and quality of children's language development? Very significant correlations have been found between both the frequency of informative staff talk, the frequency with which the staff answered the children, and the language comprehension scores of the children. Interaction does require teachers to "wonder out loud." They express their own curiosity while at the same time noticing each child's quest to find out what makes others tick and what the world is all about. How can teachers interact skillfully?

◆ Expand topics in which the child shows interest.

◆ Add depth to information on topics of interest.

◆ Answer and clarify children's questions.

◆ Help children sort out features of events, problems, and experiences, reducing confusion.

◆ Urge children to put what is newly learned or discovered into words.

◆ Cue children into routinely attending to times when the adult and child are learning and discovering together through discussion of daily events.

Dealing with Children's Past Experiences

A teacher encounters a wide range of children's perceptions concerning the way children think they should communicate with adults. A child's family or past child care arrangements may have taught the child to behave in a certain way. With this in mind, the teacher can almost envision what it means to be a conversationalist in a particular family or societal group. Some families expect children to interrupt; others expect respectful manners. Wild, excited gesturing and weaving body movements are characteristic of some children, whereas motionless, barely audible whispering is typical of others. Teachers working with newly arrived children from other cultures may see sharp contrasts in communication styles. Some children verbally seek help, whereas others find this extremely difficult. Some speak their feelings openly; others rarely express them. To promote child learning, a teacher needs to consider how she, their teacher, will interface to help each child understand that school may be very different than home.

Past child care experiences may have left their mark. A 4-year-old child named Perry seemed to give one teacher insight into how speech can be dramatically affected by past undesirable child care arrangements. The following is that teacher's observations and conclusions.

> Perry sat quietly near the preschool's front door, ignoring all play opportunities, and holding his blanket until his mom's return on his first day at school. He only spoke or looked up when teachers tried repeatedly to engage him in conversation and activities. He sat on adults' laps silently when they tried to comfort him, and ate food quickly and then returned to his waiting place near the door. The real Perry emerged a few weeks later as a talkative, socially vigorous child.

> Our verbal statements and actions concentrated on rebuilding trust with adults and other children; only later was language-developing interaction possible.

It can be difficult for a child to engage an adult in conversation, as was the case with Perry. Seeking the availability of a teacher or caregiver and ensuring one's right to her attention and reply often calls for persistence and ingenuity in a poor-quality child care situation. Perry may have long before given up trying, and decided it was best to "just stay out of the way."

Children's Inquisitive Honesty

Young children rarely limit their questions or modify their responses to the teacher for the purpose of hiding their ignorance, as older children sometimes do. During conversations, most young children intent on answers will probe enthusiastically for what they want to know. Teachers actively promote guesses and appreciate error making in an atmosphere of trust. They interact in conversations by focusing child attention, posing questions, discussing problems, suggesting alternatives, and providing information at the teachable moment.

Outdoor Play and Literacy

Interacting to promote literacy during outdoor play challenges educators, but it is possible to offer some materials and activities that include a literacy feature. Probably the most common way is to try to read books on a blanket, in the shade, in the playhouse, or under a tree. Sidewalk chalk activities and games can be fun and might include printing names to jump on or over, or printing simple directions that read "Stamp your feet" or "Follow this line." Snapping instant photos and writing captions with the photographed child is a favorite activity. Occasionally labeling bikes A, B, C, etc. with hang-on cards might improve letter recognition, but caution is needed here. Overzealous teachers whose aim is to "teach on all occasions" should skip this discussion because children need lots of undirected time and freedom to pursue their own agendas, particularly when out of doors and using their own creative play ideas.

THE TEACHER AS A BALANCER

In all roles, the teacher needs to maintain a balance. This means

- giving, but withholding when self-discovery is practical and possible.
- interacting, but not interfering with or dominating the child's train of thought or actions.
- giving support, but not hovering.
- talking, but not overtalking.
- listening, but remaining responsive.
- providing many opportunities for the child to speak.
- being patient and understanding.

As is most often the case, when adults know the answer, many may find it difficult to be patient so children can figure out the answer for themselves.

To maintain a balance, the educator is a model, a provider, and one who interacts, while matching his behavior and speech to the ability of each child. As a model, the teacher's example offers the child a step above—but not too far above. In doing this, the teacher watches and listens while working with individual children, learning as much from the child's misunderstandings or speech mistakes as from correct or appropriate responses and behavior. This does not mean a teacher can't just enjoy talking with children. It means the teacher is ready to make the most of situations, while both child and adult find pleasure in each other's company and learning together. The teacher orally reflects and guards against being overly invasive.

There is an old story about two preschool boys who discover a worm in the play yard.

First child:	"Boy it tickles! Look at him!" (He holds the worm up to be seen.)
Second child:	"Let's show it to teacher."
First child:	"No way—she'll want us to draw a picture of it and make us print 'worm'!"

A teacher's attitude toward child growth in language should be one of optimism; provide the best learning environment and realize the child will grow and learn new language skills when he is ready and sometimes with the educator's help. Early childhood centers plan for as much growth as possible in language abilities.

Teachers thoughtfully screen their comments and conversation to ensure they are free of sexist or biased attitudes, or stereotypes. If a teacher is talking about a stuffed teddy bear or the school's pet guinea pig (whose sex is yet to be discovered), use of the pronoun "it," rather than "he" or "she," is recommended.

Give children the opportunity to re-express what they have discovered, felt, or learned with classroom art materials, building blocks, dramatic play props, and so on. This is another way to promote their language growth and further expression of ideas.

SUMMARY

Teachers function as models, providers of opportunities for language growth, collaborators, and interacting adults. Children copy behaviors and attitudes of both adults and peers. Teacher skills include extending and expanding child conversations. Conversations are a key factor in the child's growing language competence. Extending means adding new information, and expanding means completing a child's statement so that it is grammatically complete.

Words are symbols for objects, ideas, actions, and situations. The teacher can increase the learning of new words and ideas by helping children recognize links between the past and present.

Teachers observe and listen closely so that teacher comments are pertinent and timely. An atmosphere of adult-child trust and acceptance of child ideas, whether valid or incorrect, is recommended.

The three teacher roles discussed in this chapter are model, provider, and interacting adult. A delicate balance exists in teaching functions. Every day decisions are made that affect children's language learning opportunities.

ADDITIONAL RESOURCES

Readings

Denton, P. (2007). *The Power of our words: Teacher language that helps children.* Turner's Falls, MA: Northeast Foundation for Children.

Epstein, A. S. (2007). *The intentional teacher: Choosing the best strategies for young children's learning.* Washington, DC: National Association for the Education of Young Children.

Fassler, R. (2003) *Room for talk: Teaching and learning in a multilingual kindergarten.* New York: Teachers College Press.

Grainger, T. (1999). Conversations in the classroom: Poetic voices at play. *Language Arts, 76*(4), 292–297.

Isenberg, J., & Jalongo, M. (2001). *Creative expression and play in early childhood.* Upper Saddle River, NJ: Merrill/Prentice Hall.

Jones, N. P. (2005). Big jobs: Planning for competence. *Young Children, 60*(2): 86–93.

Routman, R. (2000). *Conversations.* Portsmouth, NH: Heinemann.

Schultz, K. (2003). *Listening: A framework for teaching across differences.* New York: Teachers College Press.

West, K. (1998). Noticing and responding to learners. *The Reading Teacher, 51*(7), 550–559.

Helpful Websites

Child & Family—Canada
http://www.cfc-efc.ca
Search for readings and resources.

Iowa State University Extension
http://www.exnet.iastate.edu
Search Publications for information about nurturing language skills.

National Association for the Education of Young Children
http://www.naeyc.org
Provides articles, publications, and other information.

National Parent Information Network
http://npin.org
Go to Virtual Library. Use "preschool language" as a search term. Sign up for free "Parent's Guide to Preschool" and find an article concerning talking to children about personal safety skills.

Book Companion Website

Do a study of one classroom's child conversation boosters. Your rating of teacher verbalizations and actions can be compared with peer ratings in another exercise. Suggestions for additional readings are also included in the book companion website. Some children are more difficult to engage in conversation, and as a teacher, you will need to develop new strategies to reach them. In a suggested exercise, you will first identify these types of children by select descriptors and then devise a possible strategy. Example: the very active child who is always in motion and rarely sits.

STUDENT ACTIVITIES

1. Pair up with a classmate. Switch between being the child and teacher in the following situations, and attempt to use scaffolding strategies to help the child successfully solve his/her task or problem. Share your results with the total group.

   A. Rahjon (age 4) is trying unsuccessfully to have the large dump truck in the sandbox lift its bed and dump a load of sand.

   B. Margot (age 3½) is attempting to dress a large doll but seems to be unable to do so because the doll clothes have zippers and large buttons.

   C. Charlie's (age 4) job entails setting a small snack table with a plate, cup, napkin, and spoon for four children. It is his first time doing so and he is hesitating, somewhat bewildered, and looks to the teacher for help.

2. Pretend you are having a conversation about a teacher's car that the children observed being towed away for repair. You are attempting to extend the topic of conversation, wringing as much out of the experience as possible while monitoring child interest and knowledge. Create possible teacher conversational comments in b to g after reading the example in a.

   a. Recap what you noticed and promote children's remembrance.

      Example: "I saw a tow truck driver climb out of the tow truck cab."

   b. Explain some aspect of the situation by giving reasons.

   c. Describe a cause-and-effect feature of the situation.

   d. Compare this situation with another.

   e. Talk about what might happen to the teacher's car.

   f. Comment about what the teacher could do in this situation besides calling a tow truck.

   g. Ask how the children would feel if it were their parents' car.

   h. List six other aspects of the situation that could be discussed.

   Compare your answers with those of a group of classmates. Now discuss further teacher-planned activities that could increase and expand children's comments, questions, or understanding. Share with the entire group.

3. Listen intently to three adults. (Take notes.) How would you evaluate them as speech models (good, average, poor)? State the reasons for your decisions.

4. Tape-record or videotape your interaction with a group of young children for a period of 15 minutes. Analyze your listening, questioning, sentence structure, extending ability, and pronunciation.

5. In groups of four or five peers, develop a listing (on a wall chart or chalkboard) of language-stimulating classroom visitors. Prepare a one-page visitor information sheet to help the visitor understand how to structure the visit to offer a literacy-rich classroom experience. Choose two members of the group to role-play a situation in which the head teacher or director and a guest visitor discuss the visitor information sheet.

6. Consider the following slogans. Explain and elaborate their meanings or create five other slogans that would mirror some of this chapter's ideas or suggestions, and then share them with the total group.

   Intent not correctness.

   Your topic, not mine.

   The wrong answer is right.

   Logic not mechanics.

   Give them eyes and ears.

   Responsive opportunist here!

   Shh! Here comes the teacher.

7. Read the following quote. Discuss its relationship to child language growth.

   The small Zulu also didn't have just one daddy. He had the dadoos, his father's brothers and other male adults who talked to him about hunting, showed him how to make a little bow and arrow and all of this kind of stuff. They spent time with him and they "joyed in his presence," as someone once defined love. So on into adult life there was for both the boys and the girls this abundance of love and affection and attention and tenderness. (Lair, 1985)

8. Fill out the checklist in Figure 7–14, and compare your ratings with those of your classmates.

CHAPTER REVIEW

A. Name three functions of the early childhood teacher mentioned in this chapter. Omit balancer; if you remembered this function, there will still be another three.

B. List five examples of each of the functions you listed for question A.

C. Following is an observation of a teacher and children. After reading it, indicate what you believe was appropriate behavior and inappropriate behavior on the part of the teacher in regard to language development.

Situation: Teacher is conducting a sharing time with Joey, Anna, Maria, and Chris.
Teacher: "It's time for sharing. Please sit down, children."
Joey: "I want to share first!"
Teacher: "You'll have your turn. You must learn to wait."
Anna: "I can't see."

1. Every center happening should encourage speech.
2. It takes considerable time and effort to have personal conversations with each child daily.
3. Each child is entitled to a personal greeting and goodbye.
4. "How are you?" is a good opening remark.
5. A child who bursts out with something to say that has nothing to do with what is presently happening must have something important on his mind.
6. Pausing silently for a few moments after speaking to a shy child is a good idea.
7. Most new vocabulary words are learned at group times.
8. Saying, "John stepped over the green block," is unnecessary, for the child knows what he has done.
9. All children have home interests that teachers can discuss with them.
10. At mealtimes, it is best to remain quiet while children enjoy their food.
11. If the child talks about a bathroom function, ignore it.
12. When Adam says, "Girls can't drive trucks," tell him he is wrong.
13. Teachers really need to talk more than they listen.
14. Saying, "Tell him you don't like it when he grabs your toy," is poor technique.
15. I don't think it's possible to use a lot of language-building techniques and still speak naturally and comfortably with a child.
16. Teachers should model a playful attitude at times.

FIGURE 7–14 Opinion poll.

Teacher:	"Yes you can. Maria, you're sitting quietly and not talking. You may go first."
Maria:	"This is a book about Mickey. Mickey clips."
Joey:	"What's clips, teacher?"
Teacher:	"You're next, Joey."
Joey:	"Mickey on TV, teacher. Tomorrow I went to the fire station. The firefighter let me wear his badge, like this."
Chris:	"Firefighter's truck red. Goes whee-whee."
Teacher:	"It's Joey's turn, Chris. Would you wait to talk?"
Anna:	"I want to go, now!"
Teacher:	"Anna, you must have your turn to share before you can go."
Anna:	"I see a butterfly on the window."
Teacher:	"Later, Anna. You can go outside later."

D. Select the correct answers. All have more than one correct reply.
1. The teacher is a model for
   a. speech.
   b. attitudes.
   c. speech more often than parents may be.
   d. speech only during planned activities.

2. It is more important for young children to
   a. like to speak than to speak correctly.
   b. participate than to sit quietly.
   c. speak than to listen.
   d. have the teacher tell them about something than to explore it themselves.
   e. feel comfortable with a teacher than to speak clearly.

3. Teachers reinforce learning by
   a. using speech to solve problems.
   b. giving attention to the child's use of a new word.
   c. motivating the child's "wanting to know."
   d. linking the old with the new ideas.

4. When speaking, the teacher should
   a. attempt to use natural language patterns.
   b. speak in full sentences.
   c. make sure each child responds by speaking.
   d. refrain from "overtalking."

5. Preschool children
   a. are also speech models.
   b. rarely teach others new words.
   c. play and use words in play.
   d. have growing vocabularies only when teachers act appropriately.

E. Different adults have different styles of communicating with young children. The following is a comparison of two mothers trying to teach the same task to their child.

First Mother: "All right, Susan, this board is the place where we put the little toys; first of all, you're supposed to learn how to place them according to color. Can you do that? The things that are all the same color you put in one section; in the other section you put another group of colors, and in the third section you put the last group of colors. Can you do that? Or would you like to see me try it first?"

Child: "I want to do it."

Second Mother (introducing the same task): "Now I'll take them all off the board; now you put them all back on the board. What are these?"

Child: "A truck."

Second Mother: "All right, just put them right here; put the other one right here; all right, put the other one there."

Write a brief comparison of the two mothers, but pretend they are two teachers.

F. Choose the one best answer.

1. Briana is staring at the wall clock. The teacher might say
   a. "You're wondering what time it is."
   b. "You are looking at our classroom clock. It tells us what time it is."
   c. "Tell me about the clock."
   d. "You've noticed our clock. Do you have one at your house?"

2. Scaffolding in teacher-child conversations is
   a. encouragement and laddering.
   b. supportive assistance to help the child express and try out language.
   c. supplying data and information.
   d. telling the child his right and wrong conclusions.
   e. letting the child work things out independently.

SECTION 3

Listening:

Literate Beginnings

CHAPTER 8

Developing Listening Skills

OBJECTIVES

After reading this chapter, you should be able to:

◆ List five types of listening.

◆ Discuss teaching techniques that promote good listening habits.

◆ Demonstrate how to plan an activity that promotes a listening skill.

◆ Present a listening activity to a group of preschoolers.

◆ Tell a story that involves purposeful child listening.

KEY TERMS

alliteration	listening	phonemic
continuant	comprehension	awareness
grapheme	level	rimes
hearing	onsets	
listening	orthography	

UNEXPECTED ANSWER

Claire, an early childhood teacher, circled her classroom of 4-year-olds during the first week of school, trying to make conversation and listen intently to each child at free choice time. When she noticed Anna painting at the easel, Claire stood by and admired her work before saying "I can see many different colors in your painting. There is blue paint and an alphabet letter, too. It looks like an 'a.'" Anna, a tiny child, barely able to reach the top of the paper with her paint brush, responded, "Actually, it is a lower case 'a' that makes a long vowel sound, and this color is aquamarine."

QUESTIONS TO PONDER

1. When children know more than you expect them to know, what is a prudent course of action?

2. How should Claire respond to being corrected by Anna?

3. Anna has told the teacher a lot about herself, including . . . ?

Listening skill is the first language arts skill learned, and it develops before a child speaks. Many children develop the ability to listen carefully to the speech of others during infancy and early childhood; others do not. Because language growth has been described as a receiving process followed by a sending process, a child's listening ability is important to speaking and future reading and writing success.

Hearing and listening are quite different. **Hearing** is a process involving nerves and muscles that reach adult efficiency by age 4 to 5. Listening is a learned behavior, a mental process that is concerned with hearing, attending, discriminating, understanding, and remembering. It can be improved with practice. Listening affects social interactions, one's level of functioning, and perhaps one's overall success in life. Researchers estimate that we listen to 50 percent of what we hear and comprehend only 25 percent of that.

Listening skill can be described as passive and receptive, but it involves active thinking and interpretation. Lively conversations between adults and young children who feel free to verbalize reactions to life's happenings promote listening and speaking. Children offer more verbal comments in school settings in small, relaxed groups in which comments are accepted and appreciated. Young children sometimes learn that it is best to keep quiet in some classrooms. In other classrooms, every child's opinion counts and classroom discussions are frequent and animated.

There are usually many opportunities to listen in early childhood centers. Teacher-planned or child-created play is a source of many sounds (Figure 8–1). A quality program sharpens a child's listening and offers a variety of experiences. Listening is not left to chance; planned programs develop skills.

FIGURE 8–1 Toddlers are often fascinated by musical sounds.

RESEARCH ON LISTENING

Although current research is limited concerning both listening and whether direct instruction in listening skill is effective, studies conducted in the 1950s and 1960s showed that listening instruction led to measurable gains in listening comprehension. Active involvement following listening activities may help more than passive activities.

listening — a mental process that includes attending, hearing, discriminating, understanding, and remembering.
hearing — the facility or sense by which sound is perceived.

Listening is not a discrete skill or generalized ability, but a cluster of specific abilities closely related to those needed in the reading task. Early childhood professionals should be aware of the early development of a child's **listening comprehension level**.

TYPES OF LISTENING

Listening occurs in many ways. A person does not always listen for knowledge but may listen to a sound because it is pleasing. The first time children discover the sounds made by pots and pans, they are fascinated. Preschoolers often make their own pleasurable or rhythmic sounds with whatever is available.

The human voice can be interesting, threatening, or monotonous to a child, depending on past experience. Silence also has meaning. Sometimes teachers suspect that a child has a hearing problem, only to find that the child was inattentive for other reasons.

Children may listen but not understand. They may miss sound differences or listen without evaluating what they hear. Listening involves a variety of skills and levels. To provide growth opportunities, teachers should be aware of various listening skills, as shown in Figure 8–2. A child may rely on a combination of the skills described.

The goal of a good program in early childhood language arts is to guide the young child toward development of these listening levels. The listening process contains three stages the child moves through in efficient listening (Figure 8–3). When a sound occurs, it is remembered by thinking about its features: location, pitches, intensity, newness, and so on.

TODDLER LISTENING EXPERIENCES

Parents and center staff members can engage toddlers in a number of activities to stimulate listening. Body-action play of the old "coochee-coo" variety, "This Little Piggy," and simple rhymes and repetitions are recommended. Connecting noises and sounds with toys and objects and encouraging the child to imitate show the child that joy and soundmaking go hand in hand. Rhythmic clapping, tapping, and pan beating in sequence or patterns can be enjoyable (Figure 8–4). Musical toys and recordings add variety and listening pleasure. Encouraging

Appreciative listening. The child finds pleasure and entertainment in hearing music, poems, and stories. It is best to begin with this type of listening because it is passive, but personal, for each child.

Purposeful listening. The child follows directions and gives responses.

Discriminative listening. The child becomes aware of changes in pitch and loudness. Sounds become differentiated in the environment. Eventually, the child is able to discriminate the speech sounds.

Creative listening. The child's imagination and emotions are stimulated by her listening experiences. Thoughts are expressed spontaneously and freely through words or actions, or both.

Critical listening. The child understands, evaluates, makes decisions, and formulates opinions. To encourage this critical listening, the teacher may pose such questions as "What happens when we all talk at once?" or "What if everyone wanted to play in the playhouse at the same time?" The child must think through the responses, decide the most logical solution to the problem, and present a point of view.

FIGURE 8–2 Some of the ways a child listens.

listening comprehension level — the highest grade level of material that can be comprehended well when it is read aloud to a child.

RESPONDING TO STIMULI	ORGANIZING THE STIMULI	UNDERSTANDING THE MEANING
awareness	sequencing and	(classification;
focus	synthesizing	integration;
figure-ground	scanning	monitoring)
discrimination		

←————————————————————— Memory —————————————————————→

Stage 1—Responding to stimuli. Was there sound? Where was it? Which sound was it? Was there more than one sound? Were the sounds the same?

Stage 2—Organizing the stimuli. What was the sequence of the sounds? What was the length of time between sounds? Have I heard that sound before? Where have I heard it?

Stage 3—Understanding the meaning. What do the sounds and words mean?

FIGURE 8–3 Stages of the listening process.

FIGURE 8–4 Drums capture interest quickly and provide listening pleasure.

children to watch facial expressions as different human sounds are produced and locating environmental sounds together are additional techniques in developing children's listening skills.

Adults exercise care in sound volume and quality; at all age levels, extra loud, shrill, vibrating, or emergency alert sounds can be frightening.

Purposeful Listening Activities

The intent of purposeful listening practice is to increase the child's ability to follow directions and instructions, perform tasks, and respond appropriately in some fashion. Teachers can use a three-step method to help very young preschoolers gain skill in this type of listening.

1. Tell the children what you are going to tell them.

2. Tell the children.

3. Tell the children what you told them.

Example:

1. "I'm going to give you an envelope, and tell you where to take it."

2. "Take the envelope to the cook, Mrs. Corelli, and then come back to our classroom."

3. "You took the envelope to Mrs. Corelli and returned. Thank you."

Purposeful, attentive listening takes concentration. Teachers can perfect a "what I'm saying next is important" tone and consequently create a desire in children to listen. Statements such as "You might want to know how" or "You can listen closely to find out" or "If you'd like a turn, watch and listen" may also provide the motivation to listen closely.

Planned, purposeful listening activities can include activities that encourage children to listen in order to

◆ do something for themselves.

◆ tell another how to do something.

◆ operate some type of toy or equipment.

◆ carry a message.

◆ recall details.

◆ put objects in a special order or sequence.

◆ see how many names or facts they can remember.

◆ learn new skills, such as singing new songs or chanting or doing finger plays.

Appreciative Listening Activities

Appreciative listening deals with light listening when enjoyment or pleasure is paramount. A wide variety of recorded and live appreciative listening experiences is possible. Background music can accompany favorite preschool pursuits. Chanting a remembered selection of words gives the children a double treat of hearing voices in unison and feeling part of a group. Some appreciative listening builds moods, touches emotions, and adds another dimension to experience. The world is full of beautiful and not-so-beautiful sounds. Programs attempt to offer listening experiences that are aesthetically pleasing environmental sounds such as familiar home and community sounds plus pleasant sounds in found in nature.

Possible appreciative listening activities include:

◆ moving to music.

◆ discussing music, rhythms, and sounds.

◆ talking about favorite sounds.

◆ talking about happy, sad, or funny feelings that sounds produce.

◆ tapping, clapping, or moving to music or rhythmic speech.

The benefits of introducing a music curriculum to young children are multiple. Music offers another means of expression for children. It can build vocabulary, establish a sense of internal rhythm, develop an awareness of pitch and intonation in voice, and create an understanding of language concepts such as loud, soft, fast, and slow. Singing promotes the development of syntax and memorization skills.

There is a predictable pattern in children's learning of any song. Words are learned first, then rhythms and other elements. Traditional nursery songs are plentiful, are appropriately pitched, and contain repetition of melodic and rhythmic patterns. Music is a "language builder."

Favorite Traditional Songs

"Old MacDonald Had a Farm"

"Dinah"

"Teddy Bear"

"Eensy, Weensy Spider"

"I'm a Little Teapot"

"Hot Cross Buns"

"The Bus"

"Twinkle, Twinkle, Little Star"

"Yankee Doodle"

"Did You Ever See a Lassie?"

"If You're Happy"

"Ring Around a Rosy"
"Oh, Dear, What Can the Matter Be?"
"Skip to My Lou"
"Down by the Station"
"Looby Loo"
"Bingo"
"The Bear Went over the Mountain"

Partial List of Language Features Found in Songs

- vocabulary
- predictability
- story line and sequence
- rhyming
- repetition
- cultural literacy significance
- rhythmic beat
- concept development
- appreciative listening
- purposeful listening
- discriminative listening
- creative listening
- coordination of words and physical movement

CRITICAL LISTENING ACTIVITIES

Critical listening requires the children's evaluation of what is heard and comprehended. It requires contemplation and reflection, and some preschoolers develop considerable skill in this area and use it frequently. These children seem able to weigh the new against what they already know and feel and are eager to discuss differences. Other children seem rarely to hold any opinion or particular viewpoint and are reticent to share thoughts. Activities that involve critical thinking can be ones in which

- a problem is discussed and solutions are offered and evaluated.
- a probable outcome or guess is prompted.

- a real or make-believe feature is pinpointed using some criteria.
- personal preferences or dislikes are discussed.
- group votes are reviewed and outcomes are anticipated.
- errors of some type are discovered or detected.
- feelings of others are predicted.
- inconsistencies are discovered.

DISCRIMINATIVE LISTENING ACTIVITIES

Discriminative listening has gained increased attention as a result of current research and because of national legislative efforts to improve American children's reading ability. To discern whether a sound or sound pattern is the same or different, one uses discriminative listening skill. This skill is necessary when a child attempts to decode words in early reading.

The preschool teacher who plans a "Listening Detective" activity in which preschoolers catch the teacher in a mistake—such as "he huffed and he puffed and he blew the tree down" after the group is well acquainted with *The Three Little Pigs*—is presenting a discriminative listening exercise. Imitating a clapping pattern is another, as is finding rhyming sounds or matching xylophone notes.

CREATIVE LISTENING ACTIVITIES

Many classroom literacy activities create an emotional response or reaction. Audiovisual media can do so also. Discussion after read-alouds and other literacy events may reveal child feelings and imaginative ideas. Children may then be encouraged to create their feelings and ideas in subsequent art, drama, or other form of expression.

Creative listening has been used as a strategy to unleash creative potential. Who among us hasn't had an "aha" experience when listening or had a mental picture form while experiencing a piece of music?

TEACHER SKILLS

Good listening habits are especially important in school situations. Teachers need to assess their own listening habits and abilities in their daily work with children. If they expect undivided attention from children, they must also give undivided attention to them. Most of us have been told in teacher training to bend or lower ourselves to child eye level when we speak to children, but how often do we do this when we listen to them?

Two factors may decrease teachers' ability to listen and model listening behavior: (1) they may not have had experienced teachers in their own schooling (including college professors) who listened with care and valued child inquiry, and (2) teachers are so busy imparting information that they miss the profound questions and comments of young children. This type of interactive style teaches children to sit passively and withdraw. It teaches most vividly what the teachers least suspect they have transmitted.

Instructions from teachers should be clear and simple, with a sequence of what comes first, next, and last. Usually, instructions need not be repeated when given clearly and simply. Often, when the attention of the group is required, a signal is used. Any distinctive, easy-to-hear, pleasant sound or visual signal can alert children that it is time to listen. The silent pause before beginning an activity can be used effectively to focus attention on listening. Katz and Schery's (2006) suggestions for educators who handle young children with hearing loss also apply to teachers of younger preschoolers and English language learners. Suggestions include:

- Speaking using an ordinary tone/volume.
- Making sure the child's attention is focused on the speaker.
- Talking naturally and clearly and using simple phrases or simple but complete sentences depending on the child's language level.

- Clarifying idioms. Do so in context. For example, explain "It's raining cats and dogs" when you have used the expression after dashing inside during a cloudburst.
- Checking with the child to ensure comprehension. Sometimes asking "Tell me what I just said" provides information to the teacher about how much a child understands.
- Showing real-life pictures when reading or talking about a topic and using simple signs.
- Pointing, or having on hand an example of the object you're explaining.
- Being aware of background noise which can mask essential auditory information.
- Reducing classroom noise with acoustically treated low ceilings, carpet, and well-fitted doors.
- Putting rubber tips or old tennis balls on the bottoms of chair legs to reduce noise. (p. 95)*

Additionally Katz and Schery suggest positioning children to provide a hearing advantage and being sure that lighting is appropriate.

Teachers sometimes use a short song, finger play, or body-movement activity to stimulate interest and draw the group together (Figure 8–5). This helps children focus on what is to follow.

Encouragement and smiles at any time of the day can reward individual listening. Positive, specific statements, such as, "Ramon, you listened to what Jan had to say before you started talking" or "It's quiet, and now we can all hear the beginning of the story," give children feedback on expected listening behavior. The following are sample teacher statements that can promote a group's ability to listen.

At the Beginning

◆ "When I see everyone's eyes, I'll know you're ready to hear about . . ."

◆ "We'll begin when we can all hear the clock ticking."

*From Katz, L., & Schery, T. K. (2006). Including children with hearing loss in early childhood programs. *Young Children*, 61(1): 86–95. Copyright © 2006 NAEYC. Used with permission from the National Association for the Education of Young Children.

FIGURE 8–5 A body-movement activity helps capture attention.

- "I'm waiting until everyone can hear before I start. We need to be quiet so that everyone can hear about . . ."
- "It seems everyone is listening; it's time to begin."
- "We take turns speaking. Skye is first, then . . ."

During the Activity

- "Wyatt had his hand up. Would you like to tell us about your idea?"
- "It's Maria's turn to tell us . . ."
- "We can hear better when just one person is talking. Louis, you go first, then Cristalee."
- "Ethan, it's hard to wait when you want to talk. Khesia is talking now; you can be next." (Later add, "Ethan, thank you for waiting for Khesia to finish. Now we will hear what you wanted to tell us.")
- "Everyone wants to tell us about their own pets. Raise your hand—I'll make a waiting list so that we can hear everyone." (Make the list quickly and hold it up.) "Isaac, your name is first."

At Activity's End

- "We listened so quietly. We all heard every word of that story."
- "Everyone listened to what their friends said."
- "We listened and found out a lot about . . ."

Additional examples of teacher talk that promotes listening are as follows:

- "We are going to do two things right now."
- "Listen. Pick up your rug square; that's the first thing to do. Then put your square right here on this pile on the table. You were listening, Polly, thank you."
- "Listen and then you'll know who will hold the door open. Today it's Rudy's job. Whose job is it? Right, it is Rudy's job today."
- "Eyes open. Lips closed. It's listening time."
- "I can't hear when everyone is talking. Mario, it is your turn."
- "It's Adrian's time to talk now. That means no one else is talking."
- "Let's wait until it is quiet, then we are all ready to listen to the story."
- "When I see everyone's eyes looking in my eyes, I'll know you are ready to listen."
- "That was attentive listening. Everyone was quiet while Joni told us about her painting."

◆ "Josh has something important to say. Let's listen so that we all hear what he is going to tell us."

◆ "I know it's hard to wait, Cleota, but Rick is talking now. Wait. It will be your turn next."

◆ "What are we going to do after we pour the milk in the bowl? Yes, Brenda, we said we had to stir with the spoon. Good listening, Brenda."

◆ "Now let's think of another sound we might hear if we go to the window and listen."

◆ "It is my turn to speak, and your turn to listen."

Rewarded behavior is usually repeated and becomes a habit. Teachers should consistently notice correct listening behavior and comment favorably about it to the children.

How can one recognize good listening habits? Characteristics of children with listening skills follow. Good listeners

◆ look toward a speaker's face.

◆ filter out distractions.

◆ can concentrate on the speaker's message.

◆ can repeat back what the speaker said.

◆ interrupt infrequently (Figure 8–6).

◆ ask clarifying questions that make sense.

◆ seem to think about what has been said.

Examine Figure 8–7; it is an example of a teacher attempting to promote listening skill and other language development strategies.

AUDITORY PERCEPTION

Ears respond to sound waves. These sounds go to the brain and become organized in relation to past experience. The same process is used in early childhood and later when the child learns to read. Language development depends on the auditory process.

Educational activities that give practice and help perfect auditory skills usually deal with the following objectives.

◆ sustaining attention span

◆ following directions or commands

FIGURE 8–6 These two girls are listening closely to the story and probably will not interrupt the reader.

A GROUP ACTIVITY

At group time, Rachel, a preschool teacher, gathered the children, and silently waited while they settled in before beginning. "Let's see who is with us today. If you hear your name, give me one clap. Gage." Gage claps one time. "Gage heard his name, and I heard one clap. I'll whisper the next name. If you hear your name give me two claps." Two claps are heard. "Good listening, Mara." Rachel continues until all in the group have been recognized by name.

Rachel then reaches for a story book. "In this book there is something Nathan and Nicholas Alexander want, but they can't see it. Let's look at the book's cover and I will read its title. Then I think you can guess." She places her hand under each word and reads *Nathan's Fishing Trip*. Children's hands shoot up, and Skylar guesses fish. Others agree. "Lulu Delacre wrote this story," Rachel continues. She turns to the title page and comments, "Look carefully at the pictures (illustrations), do you see Nicholas Alexander? He has a big two word name, but Nicholas Alexander is a very small mouse." She fans the book closer so that all can see. Rachel starts the story, but interrupts briefly to show a large drawing of a hook and a few colored fishing lures. When the word hook and lure are mentioned on the third page, she traces the hook shape as she talks about its sharpness. The book reading proceeds to its conclusion.

A discussion includes confirming that fish was a good guess. Rachel mentions it was a particular fish, a trout. She asks why Nathan and Nicholas Alexander may have decided to free the trout. Children's ideas are offered and discussed. Rachel then says, "Nathan and Nicholas Alexander have names beginning with the letter 'N' just like Nicole." She makes a quick "N" on a sheet of paper and holds it up.

A fishing game with fish shapes follows. This was prepared by Rachel beforehand. She explains some of the fish in the plastic washtub have the letter "N" printed on them, while other do not. "If you want a turn with the fishing game raise your hand." Rachel says. A waiting list is printed by Rachel, who selects one child and asks, "Do you want to choose a friend to play with you?" The child indicates a friend. Rachel lines out their names on the waiting list, and points to and reads the next child's name who is to have the next turn.

FIGURE 8–7 Rachel's group activity.

- imitating sounds
- identifying and associating sounds
- using auditory memory
- discriminating between sounds (intensity, pitch, tempo)

The intensity of a sound is its degree of force, strength, or energy. Pitch is the highness or lowness of sound. Tempo is the rate of speed of a sound, in other words, the rhythm of the sound that engages the attention.

Auditory Activities

A wide range of auditory activities can be planned. The following goals often serve as the basis for planning. Simple skills come before more difficult ones.

- recognizing own name when spoken
- repeating two nonsense words, short sayings, chants, poems, finger plays, or any series of words
- reporting sounds heard at home
- imitating sounds of toys, animals, classrooms, rain, sirens, or bells
- telling whether a sound is near or far, loud or soft, fast or slow, high or low, same or different
- identifying people's voices
- identifying and repeating rhythms heard
- retelling a story, poem, or part of either
- trying to perform first one-part and then two-part directions
- recalling sounds in sequence
- coordinating listening skills with body movements in a requested way
- enjoying music, stories, poems, and many other language arts, both individually and in groups

SETTINGS FOR LISTENING

When preparing listening activities, the teacher can plan for success by having activities take place in room areas with a minimum of distracting sounds or objects. Screens, dividers, and bookcases are helpful (Figure 8–8). Heating and lighting are checked, and comfortable seating is provided. Decisions concerning the size of a group are important. In general, the younger the children, the smaller the group the teacher will attempt to instruct, and the shorter the length of the activity.

Listening cannot be forced, but experiences can be provided that create a desire to listen. Some schools offer children the choice of joining a group listening activity or playing quietly nearby. Teachers find that an interesting experience will attract children who are playing nearby. When activities are enjoyable and successful, the child who was hesitant may look forward to new experiences. A teacher can turn on or turn off attention by ending, changing, or modifying activities when necessary. The teacher should watch carefully for feedback; this will help the child develop active listening. A skillful teacher will complete the learning activity before the group becomes restless. When an activity is planned for which listening is required, it is important to consider that an active preschooler may have to struggle to remain seated for any extended period of time.

Evaluating Teacher Behaviors

Teachers planning activities need to consider the following questions. Why will a child listen to this activity? What factors or features could be included? What teacher behaviors, speech, or actions encourage child listening? How do I, as a teacher, develop "a listening habit" in children and promote specific listening skills? Can I judge when I have captured child attention? Can I assess which children listen well and which children listen poorly? These are quite a few questions to be answered, and you may have thought of others. A good place to start is to analyze your own classroom experiences. Hopefully, you experienced a memorable class or teacher whose class you loved to attend. List the factors that made that teacher or class special. Usually mentioned are the teacher's personality, her style of teaching, and techniques that the teacher used to make students feel special, competent, smart, accepted, and so on. Also often mentioned are the teacher's use of the classroom's physical space, enjoyed activities, and perhaps other adults or children in the classroom. The author remembers vividly the grammar school teacher who always skillfully read an interesting and exciting book

FIGURE 8–8 Bookcases have been added to make this classroom area a quiet spot.

after recess. She read with great enthusiasm, animation, and pleasure. Going back to the questions under discussion, we will take a closer look at each.

Why do children listen to an activity? A number of reasons are possible.

- The activity relates in some way to past experience.
- The children are curious about something new (Figure 8–9).
- There is a motivation to listen because of something the children want to know that personally affects them.
- The children enjoy the company of the people present.
- Something has happened to capture their attention.
- They can hear clearly without distractions and/or can easily see what is going on.
- They are physically comfortable.
- They have no physical, emotional, social, or personal distracting life situation upon which they are focused, such as hunger, lack of sleep, emotional pain, and so on.

What teacher behaviors, speech, or actions might influence child listening?

- enthusiasm
- animation (but not overly so)
- acceptance
- recognition of children by name
- establishment of a you-talk turn, I-talk turn interaction
- eye contact
- listening skill
- patience
- clear and appropriately paced and pitched speech
- panning of a group with the eyes to gauge children's avid or waning attention and adjusting accordingly
- voice variety
- appropriate voice volume
- eye-level contact
- planning for enough time so that there is not a rushed feeling
- elimination of distractions such as two children sitting together who might "act up" or

FIGURE 8–9 Breaking your own egg is a new experience for many children.

other noises in the classroom that interfere with listening

◆ lowered voice volume to gain attention

◆ stating of rules about turn-taking behavior, hand raising, and interrupting

◆ use of an attention-getting gathering activity at the beginning of the activity

Can I judge when I have captured attention or the activity has captured child attention? If you watch, you will know when they are with you, "all ears" so to speak. It is one of the joys of teaching. The feeling of communion never grows old. Ask any practicing teacher.

Can I assess which children listen well and which need help developing listening skill? If you are watchful, yes. However, there are days when even the best listeners will be distracted.

Speak-Listen Group Times

Kindergarten and some early childhood programs are offering older preschoolers "talking-listening" social skill groups. The goal of this activity is to give children who desire to speak the chance to discuss child- and teacher-selected topics in a social setting. This structured activity promotes active listening. In elementary school, this group experience is usually termed "active listening" time or "community circle."

Children are seated in a circle so that they can look at the person speaking and easily hear everyone's comments. In preschools, the circle times are kept short and intimate, with small groups of children.

Teachers structure this type of talking-listening time as follows:

1. The teacher announces a talk-listen circle as a choice of activity.

2. The teacher names the topic or elicits one from the group. It might be cats because a picture book has been shared, or worms because one has been found, or it might be an open-ended statement like, "After school I like to go home and . . ."

3. A chart depicting expected talk-listen circle behavior is introduced or reviewed. "We'll be looking at the person speaking. We'll listen with our ears." The teacher

may choose to introduce only looking at others during children's first circle, and listening another time.

4. The teacher states, "Each of us will have a turn to speak. If you don't want a turn to speak, you can say 'Pass'."

5. The teacher speaks first, modeling a short sentence—"My cat is gray and likes to sleep in a sunny window." Then she proceeds around the circle.

6. A very short group evaluation can take place when all have had a turn. Was it easy to wait for your turn? Did you see others' eyes while you were talking? (Children's answers are given in turn.)

Teachers may continue if discussion is still of interest with statements such as, "We've all had a turn. Raise your hand if you've something more to tell. Anyone can choose to leave our talking-listening time."

A number of common behaviors occur at preschool discussion times. An egg timer might have to be used with the child who drones on and on. The same children may pass day after day, or the same children may choose to participate in circle discussions. A child may not stick to the announced topic, but all comments are accepted and appreciated by the teacher.

Because listening closely and group discussion may be new to preschoolers and because individual developmental levels vary, children may either quickly or slowly grasp the social and listening skills offered. To encourage listening and speaking in turn, some programs use cardboard cutouts of lips and ears attached to tongue depressors. The speaker holds the stick with the lips while listeners hold ear sticks.

Of course, many unplanned discussions take place in most preschool classrooms. This type of structured group time encourages young children's social discussion—a skill useful in future classrooms.

Listening Centers

Special listening areas, sometimes called listening posts, can become a part of early childhood classrooms. Enjoying a quiet time by oneself or listening to recorded materials fascinates many children. Headsets plugged in to a jack or terminal help block out room noise. Partitions cut distractions. Clever listening places where children can settle into become favorite spots, such as

◆ large packing boxes lined with soft fabrics and pillows.

◆ old, soft armchairs.

◆ a bunk or loft.

Videos, audio cassettes, DVDs, CDs and CD players, photographs, picture sets, and books offer added dimensions to listening centers. Recordings of the teacher reading a new or favorite story can be available at all times for children's use (Figure 8–10). These recordings are sometimes called read-alongs and are also

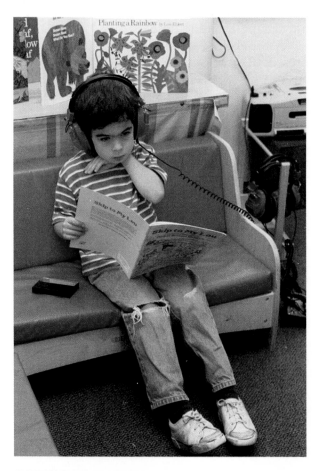

FIGURE 8–10 Listening with earphones puts this child into deep thought.

available from commercial sources. Their quality varies widely, so it is recommended that they be reviewed before they are purchased.

When teachers realize how much future educational experience depends on how well language is processed through children's listening, listening activities and listening centers gain importance. Many of today's children have passively listened to considerable electronic media but may be particularly lacking in the practice of auditory analysis and logical sequential reasoning.

Children can record, with adult help, their own descriptions of special block constructions together with accompanying drawings or photos. "Why I like this book" talks can be made about a special book. Children can record comments about their own pieces of art. A field-trip scrapbook may have a child's commentary with it. Recorded puppet scripts and flannel board stories can be enjoyed while the child moves the characters and listens. The child can explore small plastic animals while listening to a recorded story. Possibilities for recorded activities are limited only by preparation time and staff interest.

Children's ages are always a factor in the use of audiovisual equipment. Listening centers need teacher introduction, explanation, and supervision.

Recorded Media

Some companies specialize in recordings for children that are designed to improve listening skills. These recordings involve children in listening for a signal, listening to directions, or listening to sounds. Some recordings include body-movement activities along with listening skills.

Not all recordings contain appropriate subject matter for young children. Before purchasing one for children, the teacher should listen to it and judge its quality. Tape recorders can fascinate children. They can be valuable tools for listening activities. Under the teacher's supervision or after being given instructions for use, children can explore and enjoy listening.

Books with themes concerned with listening are good springboards to discussions about listening skills. See books listed in the Additional Resources section at the end of this chapter.

MUSIC AS A LISTENING ACTIVITY

A type of activity called "focused listening" occurs in many music activities. Children may be attending to specific sounds and words that give directions. Singing games often call for child response or child silence (or pause). To remember and sing a song (or parts of songs), staying in tune and rhythm, entails not only focused listening but also auditory discrimination and intellectual processing. Suggestions for music activities in early childhood centers follow.

- songs and recordings that give directions
- songs and recordings that contain certain sounds that serve as a cue for response in speech, movement, or both
- music that highlights particular rhythm instruments, drums, bells, sticks, and so forth
- music with environmental sounds
- music with songs that promote creative child response
- background music accompanying play and exploration

See the Appendix for suggested recordings.

ARE THERE DIFFERENCES IN CHILDREN'S LISTENING ABILITIES?

There are wide differences in children's listening abilities. As teachers become familiar with the children enrolled in their classes, they may notice that some children display abilities that allow them to note fine differences in sounds. Other children, who are progressing normally, will not acquire these skills until they are older.

PHONOLOGICAL AWARENESS

Phonological awareness skills are believed to be predictive of a child's ease in learning to read. Researchers have begun to investigate how to enhance these skills before children enter kindergarten. Rhyming; segmenting morphemes and syllables in words; using discriminative and critical listening, phonemic contrasting, and phonemic games emphasizing beginning letter sounds in words; commenting on alphabet letter sounds; and engaging in other such sounds-of-language activities could all be categorized as phonological skill-building opportunities. These types of activities might aid all 4- and 5-year-olds and be particularly valuable for at-risk children. Making these activities relevant and interesting can be a teaching challenge. Activities can become an outgrowth of many daily planned happenings. See the Listening Activities section at the end of this chapter for suggestions.

Phonological awareness is developmental—it develops in stages, the first and easiest being the awareness that our language is composed of words (Figure 8–11). Language learners progress and become aware that words are made up of word parts (that is, syllables), and in the last and most difficult stage, they become aware

1. Realizes language is composed of words
2. Can hear syllables in words
3. Can separate syllables or clap syllables
4. Identifies rhyming words
5. Can create rhyming words
6. Can recognize words beginning with the same alphabet sound
7. Can recognize ending sounds in words and match words that end with the same sound
8. Is able to blend sounds into words
9. Can create words by substituting or moving sounds

Note: Children's developing skills tend to follow a common progression, but some children can display a unique, individual progression.

FIGURE 8–11 Phonological awareness and children's developing skills.

that syllables are made up of individual sounds (that is, phonemes).

What did a large national reading panel conclude after reviewing research concerning phonetic awareness?

◆ Phonetic awareness instruction is effective in teaching children to attend to and manipulate speech sounds in words.

◆ Phonetic instruction is effective under a variety of teaching conditions and with a variety of learners.

◆ Teaching sounds in language helps children learn to read.

◆ Phonetic awareness helps children decode new words as well as remember how to read familiar words.

◆ Phonetic awareness boosts reading comprehension.

◆ Phonetic awareness helps all types of children, including normally developing readers, readers at risk for future reading problems, disabled readers, preschoolers, kindergartners, and first- through sixth-grade children learning to read English as well as other languages.

◆ Phonetic awareness helps some children learn to spell in English as well as other languages.

◆ Phonetic awareness instruction is most effective when children are taught to manipulate phonemes with alphabet letters, when instruction is explicitly focused on one or two types of phoneme manipulations rather than multiple types, and when children are in small groups.

◆ Phonetic awareness instruction should be suited to the child's level of development, with easier tasks being used for younger children.

◆ Teaching alphabet letters is important.

◆ Teaching children to blend phonemes helps them decode.

◆ It is important to teach letter shapes, names, and sounds so that children can use letters to acquire phonetic awareness.

◆ Phonetic awareness instruction is more effective when it makes explicit how children are to apply phonetic awareness skills in reading and writing tasks.

◆ Phonetic awareness instruction does not need to consume long periods of time to be effective.

◆ Computers can be used to teach phonetic awareness effectively.

◆ Phonetic awareness helps learners understand and use the alphabetic system to read and write.

◆ Phonetic instruction is a critical foundation piece.

◆ Phonetic instruction should be offered in short periods and be as relevant as possible.

◆ Early phonetic instruction cannot guarantee later literacy success.

Phonological awareness typically begins at approximately age 3 and improves gradually over many years. Phonological awareness refers to the general ability to attend to (listen to) the sounds of language as distinct from its meaning. A subskill, **phonemic awareness**, can be defined as understanding that spoken language can be analyzed into strings of separate words and that words can be analyzed in sequences of syllables and phonemes within syllables. English consists of approximately 41 to 44 phonemes, depending on the dialect (Ehri & Nunes, 2006). Few words have but one phoneme. Most words contain a blend of phonemes.

Young children begin to notice sound similarities in the words they hear. They enjoy rhymes, language play with words, repeated syllables, and **alliteration**. Because children's

---

phonemic awareness — the insight that every spoken word can be conceived as a sequence of phonemes, and/or the awareness that spoken words are made up of sounds, and the ability to segment a word into its constituent sounds.

alliteration — the repetition of the initial sounds in neighboring words or stressed syllables, for example, "The foam flowed free and fizzy."

books contain these features, close listening at story time is certainly one way to develop phonemic awareness.

Eventually, but usually not until kindergarten or early first grade, children can hear all the sounds in a word and can segment a word into each of its sounds, or phonemes. Is there a sequence in the development of phonemic awareness? Most educators agree that simultaneous learning is more characteristic. Activities associated with phonemic awareness are listed and described at the end of this chapter.

Learning about phonemes is not new. What is new is the importance assigned to phonemes. There is great pressure on teachers to make sure that young children know how to use them to decode words. Barone (2003) discusses successful implementation of phoneme instruction in kindergarten:

> . . . teachers built their instruction of phonemes around children's own language and experiences. They moved from what was known by the students to less familiar territory. They expected all of their students to participate and use whole-group sessions for assessment as well. From these activities, they moved to small groups in which individual student needs can be met. (p. 347)

Educators without a strong English language background need to be aware that phonemes are different from alphabet letters used in spelling words. Ehri and Nunes (2006) point out:

> Phonemes are different from the letters that are used as written units symbolizing phonemes in the spelling of words (Venezky, 1970, 1999). Letters that perform this function are called **graphemes**. Graphemes may consist of one letter for example, P, T, K, A, N, or multiple letters, such as CH, SH, TH, CK, EA, IGH, each symbolizing one phoneme.
>
> Graphemes and phonemes combine to form words. (p. 111).

And:

> If you find it difficult to distinguish the separate phonemes in words, this is because there are no boundaries in speech marking where one phoneme ends and the next begins. Rather, phonemes are folded into each other and co-articulated to produce seamless speech. (p. 111).

Can an early childhood program include the goal of developing phonemic awareness? Is phonological awareness training helpful for 4- to 5-year-old preschoolers who are at risk for reading difficulties? Research evidence points to a "yes" answer to both questions. A study by Brady, Fowler, Stone, and Winbury (1994) reports:

> Brady and associates (1994) studied 43 inner-city children aged 4 to 5 years. At the outset, fewer than half could generate rhymes, and none could segment simple words into phonemes or read any words.
>
> The 21 children who received training were closely matched to 21 who did not on receptive vocabulary, age, and initial phonological abilities.
>
> In the post-tests, 12 of the 21 controls were still unable to generate any rhyme, and only one could segment any words into phonemes. In contrast, all but one of the trained groups could generate rhymes, and six succeeded in full phonemic segmentation. (Snow, Burns, & Griffin, 1998, p. 188)

What exercises were included in this phonemic awareness training?

- directing children's attention to rhyme
- segmenting morphemes and syllables (e.g., "Say a little bit of *butterfly*" and "Can you say 'butterfly' without the 'but'?")
- categorizing sounds (e.g., "Which word doesn't belong: *mop, top, pop, can*?")
- identifying syllables ("Do you hear 'doe' in *window*?"

---

grapheme — the sum of all written letters and letter combinations that represent one phoneme.

- illustrating phonemic contrasts (e.g., /p/ vs. /b/)
- allowing children to experience relevant articulation gestures
- using segmentation and identification games at the phonemic level (e.g., "Say a bit of *boat*.")
- segmenting phonemes in two- and three-phoneme words using a "say it and move it" procedure

Educators planning to incorporate phonemic awareness training for at-risk 4-year-olds are urged to investigate projects like the Abecedarian Project (Campbell & Ramey, 1994).

PHONEMIC AWARENESS SKILL

A child with phonemic awareness may have phoneme segmentation skill, a skill that allows her to hear phoneme segments in a word. A phoneme is the smallest unit of speech distinguishing one utterance from another. The International Reading Association (1998) concludes that research findings support the idea that phonemic awareness predicts reading success. They can only speculate on why the strong relationship exists:

> One likely explanation is that phonemic awareness supports understanding the alphabetic principle—an insight that is crucial in reading an alphabetic **orthography**. The logic of alphabetic print is apparent to learners if they know that speech is made up of a sequence of sounds (that is, if they are phonemically aware). (p. 6)

Research in this area is motivated by the accepted conclusion that a good number of children having difficulty learning to read cannot hear sound sequences in words.

One clever research team introduced a guessing game in which children listened to phonemic hints by a troll character concerning presents they would receive by guessing the word correctly. Hints were stretched-out phonemes in familiar words. In English, this might be done with *d-o-ll?*, *c-a-r?* or other short words. No alphabet letters need to be mentioned in this kind of activity.

Hearing individual phonemes is not an easy task. Hearing the "separate" words in a sentence is also difficult. When researchers and educators talk about developing children's phonemic awareness, they are talking about developing children's ability to hear such sounds, and particularly to analyze words into their separate sounds. Children hear and isolate letters with **continuant**, or sustainable, sounds first. The sounds articulated in the letters *a, e, i, o, u, f, l, m, n, r, s, u,* and *z* are easier to sustain than the stop sounds articulated in the letters *b, c, d, g, h, j, k, p, q, t,* and *x*. Therefore, it is easier for children to hear the continuant sounds in the word *mom* than the stop sounds in the word *bat*.

Five or more different levels of phonemic awareness have been identified (Adams, 1990).

1. The most primitive level—that measured by knowledge of nursery rhymes—involves nothing more than an ear for the sounds of words.

2. At the next level, the oddity tasks require the child to methodically compare and contrast the sounds of words for rhyme or alliteration; this requires not just sensitivity to similarities and differences in the overall sounds of words, but also the ability to focus attention on the components of sounds that make them similar or different.

3. The tasks at the third level, blending and syllable splitting, seem to require (a) that the child have a comfortable familiarity with the notion that words can be subdivided into these small, meaningless sounds corresponding to phonemes and (b) that

---

orthography — the representation of the sounds of a language by written or printed symbols.
continuant — a consonant or vowel that may be continued or prolonged without alteration during one emission of breath.

she be comfortably familiar with the way phonemes sound when produced "in isolation" and, better yet, with the act of producing them that way by oneself.

4. The phonemic segmentation tasks require not only that the child have a thorough understanding that words can be completely analyzed into a series of phonemes but, further, that she be able to so analyze them, completely and on demand.

5. The phoneme manipulation tasks require still further that the child have sufficient proficiency with the phonemic structure of words that she is able to add, delete, or move any designated phoneme and regenerate a word (or a non-word) from the result.*

Phonemic awareness is required to make connections between single alphabet letters and sounds. It is therefore one of the first steps, or first skills, on the road to learning to read. Some preschool children can and do read the printed names of classmates and may have a large number of words memorized by sight, but tackling other words they see and sounding them out is impossible without phonemic awareness skill.

In-depth teaching in this area would focus on a number of language features including **rimes** and **onsets**, before single phonemes (other than onsets). In spoken syllables, onsets are any consonants before a vowel in a syllable; rimes are the vowel and any consonants after it in a syllable (Figure 8–12).

Several researchers have shown that young children are competent at analyzing spoken words into onsets and rimes but not into phonemes when onsets or rimes consist of more than one phoneme. There is usually more than one phoneme in the onset, the rime, or both. An example of this is the fact that children can mentally analyze the word *smiles* into /sm/ and /ilz/, but not into /s/, /m/, /i/, /l/, and /z/. Educators

FIGURE 8–12 Onsets and rimes.

ONSET	RIME
b-	-ack
st-	-ale
p-	-ick
s-	-ame
pl-	-ay
cl-	-ick

have identified 500 primary-grade words that can be derived from a set of only 37 rimes. The fact that young children can split spoken words into onsets and rimes more easily than into phonemes (when phonemes are parts of onsets and rimes) raises the possibility that children use onsets and rimes rather than phonemes to pronounce new print words. Research findings suggest that (1) reading instruction predicated on the assumption that young children learn to pronounce unfamiliar print using phonemes is developmentally inappropriate and (2) young children use their knowledge of onsets and rimes rather than a knowledge of phonemes to pronounce unfamiliar print.

What questions will early childhood staff members discuss before providing phonemic awareness activities? (1) Most certainly, Is it developmentally appropriate? (2) Do children typically develop phonemic knowledge and phonic knowledge without direct teaching? Direct teaching does not have to be intensive and systematic to be effective for a majority of children. At least three fourths of children typically develop phonemic knowledge and phonic knowledge without much direct teaching. (3) Will some children need and benefit from additional help in developing phonemic awareness? Various sources suggest that somewhere between 15 and 20 percent of children show a need for such additional instruction, whether it be provided in the classroom or not. (4) What are recommended instructional techniques to help

*From Adams, M. J. (1990). Beginning to read: Thinking and learning about print. Copyright © 1990 Massachusetts Institute of Technology. Used with permission from The MIT Press.

rimes — the vowel and any consonants after it in a syllable.
onsets — any consonants before a vowel in a syllable.

children gain phonics knowledge and phonemic awareness in the context of meaningful activities and language play? Many educators and phonics advocates recommend the following:

1. Read and reread favorite nursery rhymes, and enjoy tongue twisters and other forms of language play together.

2. Reread favorite poems, songs, and stories; discuss alliteration and rhyme within them; and play with sound elements (e.g., starting with *cake*, remove the *c* and consider what different sounds could be added to make other words, like *take, make, lake*).

3. Read alphabet books to and with children, and make alphabet books together.

4. Discuss words and make lists, word banks, or books of such words that share interesting spelling-sound patterns.

5. Discuss similar sounds and letter-sound patterns in children's names.

6. Emphasize selected letter-sound relationships while writing with, for, or in front of children.

7. Encourage children to play with magnetic letters and to explore letter-sound relationships.

8. Help children write the sounds they hear in words.

9. When reading together, help children use prior knowledge and context plus initial consonants to predict what a word will be, then look at the rest of the word to confirm or correct. This is especially important for helping children orchestrate prior knowledge with context and letter/sound cues in order to not merely identify words but to construct meaning from texts, which, after all, is the primary purpose of reading.

Phonological awareness activities should be embedded within a rich literacy context that also integrates reading, writing, and literature with the use of oral language across the curriculum. It requires children to be thoughtful, which does not happen when they passively complete worksheets or engage in drill sessions. It focuses on patterns, not rules.

Phonemic Awareness Activities

Teachers of young children should recognize the important role they can play in contributing to young children's phonemic awareness and realize it can become a natural outgrowth of a wide variety of language-related activities and not become relegated to a "one-time-a-day" status.

These activities can take place in the daily context of a developmentally appropriate program. The goal of any phonemic awareness activity is to facilitate children's perception that speech is made up of a series of sounds. Activities that easily fall into the category of phoneme awareness activities are wordplay and word-game activities.

It is suggested that the reader study the references found in the Additional Resources section at the end of this chapter and search for other resources to uncover how educators have developed awareness programs for young at-risk children.

Using Book Discussions to Develop Phonemic Awareness

A teacher's comments about a book the teacher is reading aloud can explicitly point out and analyze phonemic features, for example, "Those words start with the same sound: listen—*cap, cape,* and *coat.*" See this chapter's Additional Resources section for a list of children's books that are helpful in developing phonemic awareness.

OTHER LISTENING ACTIVITIES

Listening activities are used to increase enjoyment, vocabulary, and skill. In this chapter, the activities focus on the development of auditory skills through listening and response interactions. Activities that further develop these skills through the use of books and stories are found in later chapters.

Chapter 14 gives a great deal of encouragement and helps you conduct circle or group activities. If you will be trying out activities in this chapter, it is best to skip ahead and read Chapter 14 first.

Every classroom has some signal that alerts children to a change in activities or a new opportunity. This can range from a few notes on a classroom musical instrument to more creative signals. Usually, a short invitational and attention-getting statement will be used to pique children's curiosity, such as:

◆ "Gail has a new game for you in the rug area today."

◆ "Time to finish what you are doing and join us."

◆ "Madelyn is in the story-time center with a book about Clifford, the big, red dog."

◆ "Our clapping song begins in two minutes."

In some centers, children are simply asked to finish up what they are doing and join their friends in a particular room area. The enjoyment of already-started finger plays, chants, songs, or movement captures their attention and they are drawn in. This is a great time to recognize all children by name, as in the following (to the tune of "She'll Be Coming Round the Mountain").

"Susie is here with us, yes, yes, yes." (Clap on yes, yes, yes.)
"Larry's here with us, yes, yes, yes." (Continue until all children are recognized, and end with the following.)
"We are sitting here together,
We are sitting here together,
We are sitting here together, yes, yes, yes."

Early childhood programs that promote poetry, child dictation, storytelling, and authorship can institute a listening and discussion activity centered around what is called "an author's chair." Usually, the child-sized chair is specially decorated and used at one time of the day, or a sign is affixed—Author's and/or Reader's Chair. Children are invited to share their own efforts or share a favorite or brought-to-school picture book. Teachers may find a need to establish time limits for ramblers or may allow audience members to choose to leave quietly when they wish.

Riddles are another way to develop children's listening skills.

LISTENING RIDDLES FOR GUESSING

Rhyming Animal Riddles

A tail that's skinny and long,
At night he nibbles and gnaws
With teeth sharp and strong.
Beady eyes and tiny paws,
One called Mickey is very nice.
And when there's more than one
We call them _____. (Mice)

He has a head to pat.
But he's not a cat.
Sometimes he has a shiny coat.
It's not a hog, it's not a goat.
It's bigger than a frog.
I guess that it's a _____. (Dog)

No arms, no hands, no paws, but it can fly in the sky.
It sings a song
That you have heard.
So now you know
That it's a _____. (Bird)

Sharp claws and soft paws,
Big night eyes, and whiskers, too.
Likes to curl up in your lap,
Or catch a mouse or a rat.
Raise your hand if you know.
Now all together, let's whisper its name very slow _____. (Cat)

Riddle Game

(Children take turns calling on others with raised hands.)

I'll ask you some riddles.
Answer if you can.
If you think you know,

Please raise your hand.
Don't say it out loud
Till ___?___ calls your name.
That's how we'll play this riddling game.

Guessing Game

A beautiful flower we smell with our nose.
Its special name is not pansy but a _____.
   (Rose)

I shine when you're playing and having fun.
I'm up in the sky and I'm called the _____.
   (Sun)

If you listen closely you can tell, I ring and
   chime because I'm a _____. (Bell)

You've got 10 of me, I suppose, I'm on your
   feet and I'm your _____. (Toes)

I'm down on your feet, both one and two
Brown, black, blue, or red, I'm a _____.
   (Shoe)

I sit on the stove and cook what I can.
They pour stuff in me, I'm a frying _____.
   (Pan)

It is helpful to have magazine pictures of a rose, the sun, toes, shoes, and a pan, plus a real bell to ring behind you as you speak. Riddles appropriate for young children who have little experience with rhyming follow.

Body Parts Riddle

If a bird you want to hear,
You have to listen with your _____. (Ear)

If you want to dig in sand,
Hold the shovel in your _____. (Hand)

To see an airplane as it flies, look up and
   open up your _____. (Eyes)

To smell a pansy or a rose,
You sniff its smell with your _____. (Nose)

When you walk across the street you use two
   things you call your _____. (Feet)

If a beautiful song you've sung, you used your
   mouth and your _____. (Tongue)

All these parts you can feel and see are parts
   of your _____. (Body)

Tracing hands or drawing any body part they choose (on a picture with missing hands, feet, and so forth) is a fun follow-up activity for 4½-year-olds.

The following stories and games also can be used to enhance listening skills. These activities help specifically with the skill of listening and following directions.

Sit-Down/Stand-Up Story

Say to the children, "Let's see if you can stand *up* and sit *down* when I say the words 'Listen: Stand *up!*' You all are standing. Sit *down!* Good listening; we're ready to start." Then, tell the children the following story.

When I woke up this morning, I reached down to the floor for my slippers. Then I stood up and slipped them on. Next, I went downstairs to the kitchen. I opened the refrigerator, picked up the milk and sat down to drink. When I finished drinking, I tried to stand up, but I was stuck in the chair. I pulled and pulled, but I was still sitting.

"Don't sit on the chairs," my dad called from upstairs. "I painted them."

"It's too late! I'm sitting down," I answered.

"Hurry down here and help me."

Dad pulled and pulled, but I didn't come up.

"I'll go get our neighbor, Mr. Green. Maybe he can pull you up," Dad said. Dad and Mr. Green pulled and pulled.

"What'll I do?" I said. "The children will be waiting at school for me." Then I got an idea. "Go get the shovel," I said. Well, that worked. They pushed the shovel handle down and I came up.

You know, I think I'm stuck in this chair, too. Look, I am. _____ (child's name) and _____ (child's name), please help me.

Everyone else please sit.

After my story, let's see if just _____ (child's name) and _____ (child's name) can show us with their hands which way is *up*, and which way is *down*.

A good follow-up is to talk about what can be seen in the room that is up above the children's heads and down below their heads, or say this poem together:

When you're up—you're up,
And when you're down—you're down.
But when you're halfway in between,
You're neither up nor down.

SUMMARY

Listening skill is learned behavior. The ability to listen improves with experience and exposure, although young children vary in their ability to listen. Listening ability can be classified by type—appreciative, purposeful, discriminative, creative, and critical.

Planned activities, teacher interaction, and equipment can provide opportunities for children to develop phonetic and phonemic awareness.

Listening cannot be forced, but experiences can be provided so that a desire to listen is increased. Signals and attentive teacher encouragement can help form habits. Settings that limit stimuli and control the size of groups are desirable. When teachers are watchful and act when children seem restless or uninterested during planned activities, listening remains active. One of the responsibilities of the teacher is to plan carefully so that young children consistently want to hear what is being offered.

ADDITIONAL RESOURCES

Children's Books with Listening Themes

Borten, H. (1960). *Do you hear what I hear?* New York: Abelard-Schuman. (Describes the pleasures to be found in really listening.)

Brown, M. W. (1951). *The summer noisy book.* New York: Harper and Row. (It can be easily made into a "guess what" sound game.)

Fisher, A. (1988). *The house of a mouse.* New York: Harper and Row. (Mouse poems can be read in a tiny teacher voice. It is full of rhyming text.)

Glazer, T. (1982). *On top of spaghetti.* New York: Doubleday. (Teacher sings a silly story.)

Guilfoile, E. (1957). *Nobody listens to Andrew.* Chicago: Follett. (The no-one-ever-listens-to-me idea is humorously handled.)

Johnson, L. (1967). *Night noises.* New York: Parents Magazine Press. (Discusses listening to noises in bed at night.)

Lloyd, D. (1986). *The sneeze.* New York: Lippincott. (The child listens to questions.)

Novak, M. (1986). *Rolling.* Riverside, NJ: Bradbury Press. (The sounds of a storm dominate this story.)

Showers, P. (1961). *The listening walk.* New York: Thomas Y. Crowell. (Good book to share before adventuring on a sound walk.)

Spier, P. (1971). *Gobble, growl, grunt.* New York: Doubleday. (Lots of variety in animal sounds, with brilliant illustrations included.)

Zolotow, C. (1980). *If you listen.* New York: Harper and Row. (This is a touching tale of a child who, missing her father, turns to listening.)

Children's Books Promoting Phonemic Awareness

Bayer, J. (1992). *A, my name is Alice.* New York: Dutton. (Alliteration.)

Brown, M. W. (1991). *Good night moon.* New York: Harper. (Rhyming.)

Carle, E. (1994). *The very hungry caterpillar.* New York: Scholastic. (Blending and segmenting.)

Christelow, E. (2000). *Five little monkeys jumping on the bed.* New York: Clarion. (Rhyming.)

Guarino, D. (1997). *Is your mama a llama?* New York: Scholastic. (Rhyming.)

Hutchins, P. (1986). *The doorbell rang.* New York: William Morrow. (Blending and segmenting.)

Martin, B., Jr. (1997). *Polar bear, polar bear, what do you hear?* New York: Henry Holt. (Blending and segmenting.)

Peek, M. (1985). *Mary wore her red dress and Henry wore his green sneakers.* New York: Clarion. (Rhyming.)

Trapani, I. (1997). *I'm a little teapot.* Watertown, MA: Charlesbridge. (Rhyming.)

Readings

Adams, M. B., Foorman, B., Lundberg, I., & Beeler, T. (1996). *Phonemic awareness in young children.* Baltimore: Brookes.

Bennett-Armistead, V. S., Duke, N. K., & Moses, A. M. (2005). *Literacy and the youngest learner: Best practices for educators of children from birth to 5.* New York: Scholastic Inc.

Elster, C. A. (1994). I guess they do listen: Young children's emergent readings after adult read-alouds. *Young Children, 49*(3), 26–31.

Hennings, D. G. (1990). *Communication in action.* Boston: Houghton Mifflin.

Wolvin, A., & Coakley, C. G. (1996). *Listening.* Madison, WI: Brown & Benchmark.

Readings on Phonological Awareness

Adams, M., Foorman, B., Lundberg, I., & Beeler, T. (1997). *Phonemic awareness in young children: A classroom curriculum.* Baltimore: Paul H. Brookes.

Byrne, B., & Fielding-Barnsley, R. (1993). Evaluation of a program to teach phonemic awareness to young children: A one year follow-up. *Journal of Educational Psychology, 55,* 104–111.

Floyd, S., & Yates, W. (2001). *Curriculum-aligned thematic phonological awareness treatment.* Lake City, SC: Susan Floyd.

Opitz, M. F. (2000). *Rhymes and reasons: Literature & language play for phonological awareness.* Portsmouth, NH: Heinemann.

Paulson, L., Noble, I., Jepson, S., & van den Pol, R. (2001). *Building early literacy and language skills.* Longmont, CO: Sopris West.

Yopp, H. K. (1992). Developing phonemic awareness in young children. *Reading Teacher, 45,* 696–703.

Yopp, H. K., & Yopp, R. H. (2000). *Oo-pples and bonoo-noos: Songs and activities for phonemic awareness.* Orlando: Harcourt School.

Game Making and Construction

Silberg, J., & Jones, R. (1995). *500 five-minute games: Quick and easy activities for 3-6 year olds.* Beltsville, MD: Gryphon House.

Silberg, J., & Noll, C. K. (1997). *300 three-minute games: Quick and easy activities for 2-5 year olds.* Beltsville, MD: Gryphon House.

Helpful Websites

KidSource Online
http://www.kidsource.com
Presents phonemic awareness and reading information.

Learning Disabilities Association of America
http://www.ldanatl.org
Provides information on central auditory processing problems in children.

National Child Care Information Center
http://npin.org
Features child literacy and early phonetic awareness information.

Book Companion Website

Many additional listening activities that develop specific listening skills are included. Read about six listening comprehension areas that are identified on the book companion website. Participate in web investigations or try quizzes that reveal your mastery of this chapter. A few exercises urge you to get acquainted with ideas concerning children's listening abilities.

STUDENT ACTIVITIES

1. Choose one of the listening activities found in this chapter, one from another source, or one you create. Present the activity to a group of preschoolers, modifying the activity to suit the child group if necessary. Then answer the following questions.
   a. Was the activity interesting to the children?
   b. Were they able to perform the auditory perception tasks?
   c. Would you change the activity in any way if you presented it again?

2. Find or create five additional listening activities. Provide information regarding the source, name of activity, materials needed, description of activity, and objective. Cite the source or state the title of the book where you found the activity idea. If the idea is original, indicate this by using the word *self*.

3. Practice the listening story in this chapter entitled "Sit-Down/Stand-Up Story," or find another listening story. At the next class meeting, tell the story to a classmate. Share constructive criticism.

4. Create a recorded activity in which children will in some way analyze what they hear and share responses with the teacher. An activity that requires logical or sequential listening could also be attempted. Share your recording and accompanying objects and/or visuals at the next class session.

5. Watch a listening activity in a preschool center, and then answer the following questions.
   a. How did the teacher prepare the children for listening?
   b. What elements of the activity captured interest?
   c. How was the children's interest held?
   d. Did the teacher have an opportunity to recognize the children's listening skill?
   e. Did the children's listening behavior during the activity seem important to the teacher?
   f. Was this the kind of activity that should be repeated? If so, why?

6. Write a one-page paper concerning your feelings about phonological or phonemic awareness instruction for preschoolers. Consider that many other countries, including the United Kingdom, expect preschoolers to know both alphabet letter names and letter sounds before entering kindergarten. Bring your paper to class and pair up with three others to discuss each person's feelings and ideas. Share main points in your discussion with the entire class. Hand in your paper and your four-member discussion-group notes to the instructor.

7. With the new emphasis on phonemic awareness development during preschool years, the commercial development and publication of phonemic awareness activities is bound to happen. What could be the inherent problems preschool teachers might face if they relied heavily on these commercially produced materials? List your main points.

8. Do talk-listen circle times seem overly structured to you, or do you believe that they may be appropriate for today's generation of "media-saturated" children? Elaborate.

9. Discuss with two classmates the teacher techniques used in Figure 8–7. List your ideas and share them with your training class.

CHAPTER REVIEW

A. Five types of listening have been discussed. After each of the following statements, identify the listening type that best fits the situation.

1. After hearing an Indian drum on a recording, Brett slaps out a rhythm of his own on his thighs while dancing around the room.

2. During a story reading of *The Three Little Pigs*, Mickey blurts out, "Go get 'em Wolfie!" in reference to the wolf's behavior in the story.

3. Kimmie is following Chris around. Chris is repeating, "Swishy, fishy co-co-pop," over and over again; both giggle periodically.

4. Debbie tells you about the little voice of small Billy Goat Gruff and the big voice of Big Billy Goat Gruff in the story of *Three Billy Goats Gruff*.

5. Peter has asked whether he can leave his block tower standing during snack time instead of putting the blocks away as you requested. He wishes to return and build the tower higher. He then listens for your answer.

B. Select the correct answers. All have more than one correct reply.

1. Most parents unconsciously teach preschoolers
   a. to develop auditory perception.
   b. attitudes toward listening.
   c. to listen to their teachers.
   d. many words.

2. A teacher can promote listening by
   a. demanding a listening attitude.
   b. using a signal that alerts children and focuses attention.
   c. encouraging a child.
   d. telling a child she is not listening.

3. Critical listening happens when the
   a. child relates what is new to past experience.
   b. child disagrees with another's statement.
   c. child makes a comment about a word being good or bad.
   d. teacher plans thought-provoking questions and the child has the maturity needed to answer them.

4. Children come to early childhood centers with
   a. individual variation in abilities to listen.
   b. habits of listening.
   c. all the abilities and experiences needed to be successful in planned activities.
   d. a desire to listen.

5. Children's ability to follow a series of commands depends on
   a. their auditory memory.
   b. how clearly the commands are stated.
   c. how well their ears transmit the sounds to their brains and how well their brains sort the information.
   d. how well they can imitate the words of the commands.

C. Assume the children are involved in an activity when they are suddenly distracted by a dog barking outside the window. List four things you could say to the children to draw their attention back to the activity. If you wished to use their focus on the barking for a spontaneous listening activity, how would you proceed?

D. What elements of music might promote listening skills?

E. Describe three listening activities, stating the objective of each activity and giving a description of the activity.

F. Define phonemic awareness, onset, and rime.

G. What factors have contributed to a new interest in phonological awareness?

LISTENING ACTIVITIES

Note: The following activities will have to be evaluated for age-level appropriateness and use with a particular group of children. They are provided here as examples of listening activities but may or may not be appropriate for your teaching situation.

ACTIVITIES ASSOCIATED WITH PHONOLOGICAL AWARENESS

- read-alouds, especially ones with repetition in words, phrases, and alliteration
- singing songs, especially those with repetitions or word play
- reading nursery rhymes and poetry
- engaging in language play—using silly words
- seeing words as separate entities

- noticing spaces between words
- labeling objects in the classroom; using word lists and charts
- counting words in a sentence or on a picture-book page
- raising one's hand on hearing a designated word
- clapping syllables
- counting syllables
- hearing different sounds in words and identifying them
- recognizing rhyming words
- using name tags; playing name activities and name games
- hearing sounds in their name by "stretching it out"
- playing with fun-to-say words— *rattata-ta*, *bibbity bobbity boo*, *licky sticky*, and so on
- rhyming a word with teacher's word

- allowing children to create their own rhyme
- thinking of words that start the same as teacher's word
- identifying beginning sounds in words
- associating sounds with written words
- matching sounds
- rhyming with children's names
- playing games with children's names
- making an "'A' stands for . . ." list and so on
- generating new rhyming words
- moving sounds to make new words

Note: These suggested activities are not presented in an age-level or skill-level order.

PHONEMIC AWARENESS ACTIVITIES

- using alphabet books, songs, rhymes, charts, toys, and games
- providing rhyming experiences—recognizing, identifying, and creating
- matching rhyming pictures
- clapping on rhyming words
- recognizing words beginning with the same letter—alliteration
- recognizing words beginning with the same sound
- hearing initial, middle, and ending sounds
- knowing the sounds alphabet letters make
- putting sounds together
- manipulating sounds
- naming words that start with the same letter
- counting sounds in words
- taking away sounds in words
- substituting sounds in words

- writing alphabet letters
- knowing the shapes of alphabet letters
- naming letter shapes
- trying to write words
- trying to read words
- making words with magnetic letters
- typing words or using alphabet stamp sets to form words
- grouping picture cards according to beginning, middle, and ending sounds
- making a list of same-sound beginnings
- matching sounds with alphabet letters
- comparing the number of syllables in words
- finding words with the same beginning and ending sounds
- playing with alphabet letter puzzles
- hunting for alphabet letters in the room
- making personal alphabet books

Note: These are not listed in sequential order, nor is the listing meant to be comprehensive.

RECOGNIZING VOICES GUESSING GAME

Purpose: To practice discriminative listening and auditory memory skills

Materials: Individual snapshots of school personnel; a recording of different school staff members' voices reading sequential paragraphs in a story or describing the work they perform

Procedure: Line up snapshots in view of the children after each is identified. "Here are some snapshots of people we know. Now we're going to listen and try to guess who is talking. Raise your hand if you think you know."

At the conclusion of the activity, show the photos one by one and name each.

A great follow-up is guessing children's voices using the same game format. This can be set up as an individually chosen activity after being introduced at a group time or can be used with a group.

BUILD A BURGER

Purpose: To practice purposeful listening

Materials: Cutouts of foods that are added to hamburger buns—onion slices, lettuce, tomato slices, cheese slices, pickles, salsa, meat patties, bacon, mayonnaise, mustard, and catsup; cutout paper buns or clay bun halves; paper plates; chart paper (optional)

Procedure: Ask the children what kinds of food they like on their hamburgers. After the group discusses the things they like, say, "I'm going to show you pictures of some of the things you've said you liked on your hamburger and some things I like. Here are onion slices; Marion said she liked them." Go on to show and name all the cutouts. "You can build a hamburger for a friend in this game. You'll have to listen closely to find out what she chooses to have you put between the buns." Teacher can print each child's selection on chart paper. (Of course, the real thing would be more fun—provide plastic gloves or use plastic sandwich bags for real food handling.)

SOUND CANS

Purpose: To match similar sounds by using discriminative listening skills

Materials: Cans with press-on or screw-off lids; cards large enough to hold two cans; outline of circles of can bottoms (made with dark pen); two circles for each card (large different color index cards work well); best to use cans that are impossible for children to open or to securely tape cans shut; pairs of cans filled with same materials, such as sand, paper clips, rocks, rice, beans, nuts, and bolts

Procedure: This is a solitary activity or one that children can choose to play with others. It can be used in a learning center. An introduction like the following is necessary. "Here are some cans and cards. The way you play this game is to shake one can and then shake all the rest to find the one that sounds the same as the first can. Let's listen to this can." Shake it. "Now I'm going to try to find the can that sounds just like this one when I shake it." Pick up another and ask, "Does this sound the same?" Shake the first and second cans. "No, this sounds different, so I'm going to shake another can." Go on until the mate is found and placed beside the first can on the card.

This activity is a classic one, and many sound sets are found in preschool programs. (Sets are also commercially manufactured.)

"CAN YOU SAY IT AS I DO?" ACTIVITY

Purpose: To imitate sounds

Materials: None

Procedure: The teacher says, "Can you change your voice the way I can?"

"My name is (teacher softly whispers her name)." With changes of voice, speed, and pitch, the teacher illustrates with a loud, low, or high voice, speaking fast or slow, with mouth nearly closed or wide open, when holding nose, and so on.

The teacher then asks for a volunteer who would like to speak in a new or funny way. "Now, let's see if we can change our voices the way Billy does. Do it any way you want, Billy. We'll try to copy you."

The teacher then gives others a turn. This activity may be followed up with a finger play with voice changes, like the "Five Little Astronauts" activity in Chapter 14.

"LISTEN, OOPS A MISTAKE!—INTERRUPT ME PLEASE."

Purpose: To associate and discriminate among word sounds and objects; to listen for inconsistencies

Materials: Four or five common school objects (such as a pencil, crayon, block, toy, cup, and doll) and a low table, or photographs or drawings of objects

Procedure: Talk about calling things by the wrong name, being sure to discuss how everyone makes mistakes at times. Begin with something like, "Have you ever called your friend by the wrong name?"

Teacher: When you call your friend by the wrong name, you've made a mistake. Look at the things on the table. I am going to name each of them. (Teacher names them correctly.) All right, now see if you can hear my mistakes. This time I'm going to point to them, too. If you hear a mistake, raise your hand and say, "Oops, a mistake!" Let's say that together once: "Oops, a mistake!" Are you ready? Listen: *crayon, ball, doll, cup.*

Change objects, and give the children a chance to make mistakes while others listen. This activity can later be followed with the story *Moptop* (by Don Freeman, Children's Press), about a long-haired red-headed boy who is mistaken for a mop.

ERRAND GAME

Purpose: To follow verbal commands

Materials: None

Procedure: Start a discussion about doing things for parents. Include getting objects from other rooms, from neighbors, and so on. Tell the children you are going to play a game in which each person looks for something another has asked for.

Teacher: "Get a book for me, please. Can you find a leaf?"

Items to ask for include a rock, a blade of grass, a piece of paper, a block, a doll, a crayon, a toy car, a sweater, a hat, clothes, a hanger, a blanket, and so forth. Send children off one at a time. As they return, talk to each about where the item was found. While the group waits for all members to return, the group can name the returned items. Put them in a row, ask children to cover their eyes while one is hidden, and then ask the children to guess which item was removed.

If interest is still high, the teacher can make a request that the items be returned and repeat the game by sending the children for new items.

BLIND WALK

Purpose: To depend on listening to another child's verbal directions

Materials: Scarves, bandanas, or cloth strips

Procedure: Discuss blindness and guide dogs. Pair children and blindfold one child. Ask the guide to hold the blindfolded child's hand and take a classroom walk. Ask the guide to talk about where children are going, and urge the blindfolded child to use her hands to feel objects, and so forth. Change blindfolds, giving the guide a chance to also go on a guided walk. (Some children may object to blindfolds or act fearful. Respect their wishes.) Conduct a brief follow-up discussion. (Activity courtesy of WICAP Head Start, Donnelly, Idaho)

JACK-IN-THE-BOX

Purpose: To discriminate sounds by listening for a signal and responding to it

Materials: None

Procedure: Recite the following rhyme in a whispered voice until the word pop is reached. Using hand motions, hide your thumb in your fist and let it pop up each time the word pop is said.

> *Jack-in-the-box, jack-in-the-box, where can you be?*
>
> *Hiding inside where I can't see? If you jump up, you won't scare me. Pop! Pop! Pop!*

Suggest that children squat and pretend to be jack-in-the-boxes. Ask them to listen and jump up only when they hear the word pop. Try a second verse if the group seems willing.

> *Jack-in-the-box, jack-in-the-box, you like to play.*
>
> *Down in the box you won't stay. There's only one word I have to say. Pop! Pop! Pop!*

PIN-ON SOUND CARDS (ANIMALS AND BIRDS)

Purpose: To associate and imitate sounds and use auditory memory

Materials: Safety pins or masking tape; file cards (3-by-5) or self-stick memo paper with pictures of birds and animals (gummed stickers of animals and birds are available in stationery stores and from supply houses); suggestions: duck, rooster, chick, owl, goose, woodpecker, horse, cow, cat, dog, sheep, lion, mouse, turkey, bee, frog, donkey, seal

Procedure: Have a card pinned on your blouse or shirt before the children enter the room. This will start questions. Talk about the sound that the animal pictured on your card makes. Practice it with the children. Ask who would like a card. Talk about the animal and the sound it makes. Imitate each sound with the group. Have children imitate animal noises, and ask the child with the right card to raise her hand or stand up. Then prompt the child to finish "That's me; I'm a . . . ?" Children

usually like to wear the cards the rest of the day and take them home, if possible.

SOUND STORY

This story contains three sound words. Every time one of the words is mentioned, the children should make the appropriate sound.

Say, "When you hear the word *spinach*, say 'yum, yum, yum.' When you hear the word *dog*, bark like a dog. When you hear the word *cat*, meow like a cat." Then, recite the following story.

> Once upon a time, there was a little boy who would not taste SPINACH. Everyone would say, "Marvin, why won't you taste SPINACH?" Marvin would say, "I think SPINACH is yuk!!!" Marvin's DOG Malcolm loved SPINACH. Marvin's CAT Malvina loved SPINACH. If Marvin didn't eat his SPINACH, Malcolm the DOG and Malvina the CAT would fight over who would get the SPINACH. The DOG and CAT would make so much noise fighting over the SPINACH that everyone in the neighborhood would say, "If you don't stop that noise, you will have to move away." Marvin loved his house and he didn't want to move away from the neighborhood. Malcolm the DOG loved his house and he didn't want to move away from the neighborhood. Malvina the CAT loved her house and she didn't want to move away from the neighborhood. What could they do?

Let the children tell you the answer. This game is a great deal of fun, and the children never tire of hearing the story. You can make up your own sound stories. You can also add rhythm instruments to make the sounds instead of voices. Spinach can be changed to any food—enchilada, wonton, bratwurst, grits, sweet potato pie, and so on.

FUNNY OLD HAT GAME

Gather a bag of old hats (such as new or discarded paper party hats). Pass the hats out to the children, or let the children choose them.

Say, "We're ready when our hats are on our heads. We're going to put our hats in some funny places and do some funny things. Listen."

"Put your hat between your knees."
"Put your hat under your arm."
"Put your hat over your shoes."
"Put your hat under your chin."
"Touch the top of your hat."
"Sit on your hat."
"Stand on your hat."

Encourage the children to choose a place to put the hat, and then say, "Where's the hat? Where's the hat, [child's name]. Can you see the hat, hat, hat?" (This can be chanted.) "Under the chair, under the chair—I can see the hat, hat, hat."

SEE IF YOU CAN GAME

Collect objects from around the classroom (for example, scissors, ruler, eraser, cup, chalk). Put them on the floor on a large piece of paper. Say, "I'm not going to say its name. See if you can tell me what object I am talking about. Raise your hand if you know." (Keep giving hints until the children guess.)

"What has two circles for two fingers?" (Scissors)

"It's long and thin with numbers printed on one side." (Ruler)

"What makes pencil marks disappear?" (Eraser)

"You can fill it with milk." (Cup)

"What's white and small and writes on the chalkboard?" (Chalk)

CAN YOU DO THIS?

Children imitate hand and body movements of teacher or other children. "Can you put your hands on your chin, knees, elbows, and so on?"

WHAT HAS CHANGED? GAME OR CAN YOU KEEP A SECRET? GAME

Purpose: To listen for the purpose of correctly identifying a missing object.

Materials: A bag with hats, scarves, belts, pins, socks, gloves, shoes, and so on

Procedure: The teacher can ask a group to examine her closely because something is going to change or look different. The teacher asks the children to close their eyes or look down, or the teacher can turn her back to the children and quickly slip on one item from the bag. "If you know, keep it a secret. We will help your friends by giving them some clues that will help them discover what changed. Is it above my neck? Say yes or no. Is it above my belt?" and so on. Child volunteers can be used to change themselves after the game is learned.

272

SECTION 4

Introducing Literature

CHAPTER 9

Children and Books

OBJECTIVES

After reading this chapter, you should be able to:

◆ Name three goals for reading books to young children.

◆ Describe criteria for book selection.

◆ Demonstrate suggested techniques for reading a book to a group of children.

◆ Design a classroom library center.

◆ Explain quality book features.

◆ Discuss multicultural and multiethnic book use.

KEY TERMS

characterization	genre	realism
fairy tales	narrative	visualization
fiction	nonfiction	

A VOLUNTEER READER

Mr. Mead, LaVon's grandfather, arrives in the 4-year-old's classroom shortly after nap time and goes to the rocking chair. There is a small commotion in the book center as a few children dash for the reading shelf. A line of children clutching one book forms. The first in line peeks at Mr. Mead, who is reading a book and already has a child curled up on his lap, the child's face registering the intent of enjoying every minute. There is an air of magic and hopeful anticipation on the waiting children's faces. Mrs. Rex, the teacher, moves a few chairs in a row for the "waiters."

QUESTIONS TO PONDER

1. One can hear Mr. Mead's laughter and a child's giggle. What would you like to know about Mr. Mead's reading technique?

2. What children's attitudes are being formed, and how might these affect their future academic success?

Picture books are an important beginning step on a child's path to literacy, as well as an excellent source of listening activities for the young child. Seeing, touching, and interacting with books is part of a good-quality program in early childhood education. Books play an important role in language development.

A child's first being-read-to experience can be thought of as his first curriculum. It is a curriculum rich in pleasant associations: a soft lap, a warm bath, and a snugly bed. This initial literature curriculum uses common words in uncommon ways, titillates the senses, nurtures curiosities, adds to the memory, and stretches the imagination. When handled with care, reading experiences at home and at school can create positive attitudes toward literature and help motivate the child to learn to read. Attitudes toward literacy are most easily established early in life.

Many families read to their children; others do not (Figure 9–1). Children from many low-income families are more dependent on school experiences for their literacy development than middle-class children. In fact, a teacher may offer some children their first contact with stories and books. Teacher and child can share the joy of this very pleasant experience. Many believe next to giving a child a hug, reading aloud is probably the longest-lasting experience that families can put into a child's life. Reading aloud is important for all the reasons that talking to children is important—to inspire them, to guide them, to educate them, to bond with them, and to communicate feelings, hopes, and fears. In the beginning, the child is usually more interested in the reader than the book or story.

Teachers know that book-sharing time is an opportune time for teachers to help children build vocabulary, extend phonological awareness, and develop familiarity with literate forms. Reading books aloud to children exposes them to grammatical forms of written language and displays literate discourse rules in ways that conversation cannot. Discussions can encourage children to analyze the text, and these discussions can have a powerful effect on the development of complex oral language, vocabulary,

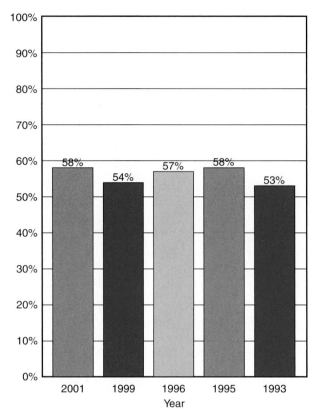

*Based on children who have yet to enter kindergarten.

FIGURE 9–1 Percentage of children ages 3 to 5* who were read to every day by a family member. (From U.S. Department of Education, National Center for Education Statistics, *National Household Education Survey,*1993, 1999, and 2003.)

and story understanding—all critical abilities that young children will need when faced with later literacy tasks.

Early childhood teachers agree that book-sharing sessions are among their favorite times with children. Teachers introduce each new group of children to favorite books that never seem to lose their magic. There will be times when young children are rapt with enjoyment during picture-book readings, and at such times, the lucky reader will understand the power of literature and realize his responsibility as the sharer of a vast treasure. The value of offering thoughtfully selected books in a skilled way will be readily apparent.

What, exactly, do picture books offer young children? They open the door to literacy and create the opportunity to influence attitudes, broaden understanding, savor diversity, vicariously experience drama, expand the imagination, gain vocabulary and information, hear the rhythm of language and words, and enjoy the visual and aesthetic variety in illustrations. Another advantage is that young children learn to respond to the messages in children's stories that are told or read to them and in doing this they use the kind of language and thought processes that they will use in learning to read.

As you read through this chapter, other benefits of reading aloud to children will occur to you, and you will clarify your thoughts about the benefits you consider of primary and secondary importance. You will become acquainted with the cultural universals of story structure and form, which help us remember by providing meaningful frameworks. Stories make events memorable.

A special kind of language is found in books. Oral language differs from written language in important ways. Although many young children communicate well and have adequate vocabularies, they do not construct sentences in the same manner found in their picture books. Knowing the way books "talk" makes children better predictors of words they will discover in their early reading attempts.

Each child gets his own meaning from picture-book experiences. Books cannot be used as substitutes for the child's real-life experiences, interactions, and discoveries, because these are what help make books understandable. Books add another dimension and source of information and enjoyment to children's lives.

Although most teachers believe reading books in a preschool classroom is an important classroom literacy activity, Dickinson's research (2001) found that children in about one-third of the preschool classrooms studied listened to books read in a large group for 25 minutes or

less each week. In only about 25 percent of the classrooms did children listen to stories weekly in large groups for more than 50 minutes. Reading to children individually and in small groups was also rare. Were this study's conclusions an anomaly? Let's hope so.

AGE AND BOOK EXPERIENCES

Careful consideration should be given to selecting books that are appropriate to the child's age. Children younger than 3 (and many older than this age) enjoy physical closeness, the visual changes of illustrations, and the sound of the human voice reading text. The rhythms and poetry of picture books intrigue them. Experts point out that very young children's "syntactic dependence" is displayed by their obvious delight in recognized word order. The sounds of language in picture books may be far more important than the meanings conveyed to the very young child. Teachers of 2- and 3-year-olds may notice this by observing which books children select most often. Four-year-olds are more concerned with content and **characterization**, in addition to what they previously enjoyed in picture books. Fantasy, **realism**, human emotions, **nonfiction**, and books with a variety of other features attract and hold them.

BRIEF HISTORY OF CHILDREN'S LITERATURE

The idea that children need or deserve entertainment and amusement is a relatively new development. Until the mid-eighteenth century, books for children instructed and aimed to improve young children, particularly their moral and spiritual natures.

---

characterization — the way an author presents a character by describing character verbalizations, actions, or thinking, or by what other characters say, think, or do about the character.

realism — presents experience without embellishment to convey life as it appears in a natural world limited by the senses and reason.

nonfiction — prose that explains, argues, or describes; usually factual.

Folk tales were sung and told in primitive times, and stories of human experience were shared. Storytellers often attempted to reduce anxieties, satisfy human needs, fire the imagination, and increase human survival, among other aims. Orally passed down, tales appeared in most of the world's geographical locations and cultures. Much of today's **fiction** reflects elements of these old tales and traditional stories.

Early American children's literature was heavily influenced by English and Puritan beliefs and practices. Books that existed before William Caxton's development of printing in fifteenth-century England were hand-copied adult books that children happened to encounter in private wealthy households. Caxton translated *Aesop's Fables* (1484) from a French version and printed other adult books that literate English children found interesting. *Aesop's Fables* is considered the first printing of talking animal stories. Themes of other books in Victorian England included romances of chivalry and adventure, knights in shining armor, battles with giants, and rescue of lovely princesses and other victims of oppression.

Victorian families read to their children, and minstrels and troubadours were paid to sing narrative verses to the families of rich patrons. The English Puritans were dedicated to a revolution founded on the deep conviction that religious beliefs form the basis for the whole of human life. Writers such as Bunyan, author of *A Book for Boys and Girls* (1686), were intent on saving children's souls.

Chapbooks (paper booklets) appeared in England after 1641. Initially, they were intended for adults, but eventually, they fell into children's hands. They included tiny woodcuts as decoration, and later woodcuts were used to illustrate the text. Salesmen (chapmen) traveled England selling these small, 4-by-2½-inch editions to the less affluent. Chapbooks written to entertain and instruct children followed, as sales and popularity increased. Titles included *The Tragical Death of an Apple Pie* and *The History of Jack and the Giants*.

John Newbery and Thomas Boreman are recognized as the first publishers of children's books in England. Chapbooks, although predated, are considered booklets. Most of these newly printed books were instructional, but titles like *A Little Pretty Pocket-Book* (Newbery, 1744) were advertised as children's amusement books (Figure 9–2). In 1765, Newbery published *The Renowned History of Little Goody Two Shoes, Otherwise Called Mrs. Margery Two Shoes.* The book chronicles Goody's rise from poverty to wealth. Newbery prospered. Other publishers followed with their own juvenile editions, many with themes designed to help children reason and use moral judgment to select socially correct courses of action.

During the earliest years of our nation, many children had no schooling and could not read. Those few who could read often read works intended for adults, such as Jonathan Swift's *Gulliver's Travels* (1726). Reading was considered unimportant for children in agricultural society. Only the need for a literate workforce in the new industrialized society of the 1800s caused time to be set aside for children's education and more attention to be paid to books intended for children.

Books used as school readers in early America contained subject matter of both a religious and a moral nature.

By the mid-1800s, adventure stories for older boys gained popularity with Mark Twain's *Adventures of Tom Sawyer*, published in 1876. Louisa May Alcott had created *Little Women* in 1868 as a girl's volume.

Picture Books

Toward the end of the nineteenth century, some picture books became artistic. English and French publishers produced colorful illustrations of charm, quality, and detail. The books of Randolph Caldecott, Maurice Boutet

---

fiction — imaginative narrative in any form of presentation that is designed to entertain, as distinguished from that which is designed primarily to explain, argue, or merely describe.

FIGURE 9–2 Excerpts from *A Little Pretty Pocket-Book*, published by John Newbery, 1744.

de Monvel, and Kate Greenway had captivating drawings that overshadowed the drab and homely illustrations that were typically found in American picture books.

Although not intended or recommended for children, comic picture sequences, like those of A. B. Frost, appeared in American magazines from 1880 to 1890. Their humor was shared by families. Two American picture books resembling Frost's slapstick humor gained acceptance from American librarians: Gelett Burgess's *New Goops and How to Know Them* (Lippincott, 1928) and Palmer Cox's *Brownies* (1927).

E. Boyd Smith, an American, created illustrations for *The Story of Noah's Ark* (Houghton Mifflin, 1905), which are described as both artistic and humorous. The books Smith created delighted children and adults with colorful panoramic illustrations. Librarians speaking of Smith's illustrative work described it as honest, true, "better than any done by an American artist." The cost of full-color printing escalated,

and illustrative color in picture books was not to reappear in the United States and become widely affordable until the later 1920s and 1930s. Little Golden Books became popular, and European books with colorful illustrative art were imported to the United States for those who could afford them.

Lynch-Brown and Tomlinson (1998) believe the establishment of book awards improved American picture books.

By the 1920s a class of professional writers devoted solely or almost solely to writing literature for children—as opposed to moral reformers, teachers, and clerics as authors—produced a larger quantity and better variety and quality of children's books than had been seen to that point. This development was hastened by the establishment in 1922, under the auspices of the American Library Association, of the first of the great American children's book awards, the Newbery Medal.

In 1938, with the establishment by ALA of the Caldecott Medal for illustration, more and better artists were encouraged to enter the field of children's books as well. For the remainder of the 20th century, book award programs were effectively used to create interest in children's books generally and to promote awareness of specific types of books. Competition for the most prestigious awards resulted in better, more original works. (p. 124)

Extraordinary black-and-white illustrations drawn by Wanda Gág in *Farm Sale* (Coward-McCann, 1926) and *Millions of Cats* (Coward-McCann, 1928) and a lithographic technique used in her other books captured both children's fancy and book reviewers' praise. Her drawings complemented and reinforced her text. Together, the effect was polished and eminently suitable for her folk tales. The combination of Wanda Gág's text, drawings, and format constitute its lasting distinction.

American picture books for children began to reflect a worldview of children's literature. Colorful illustrations appeared in school readers. Stories for young children set in foreign countries were widely acclaimed during the 1930s. *Madeline* (Simon & Schuster, 1939), by Ludwig Bemelmans, is still found on most suggested early childhood reading lists.

The child-study movement and research at numerous universities and institutions during the late 1920s and 1930s led some well-known researchers to believe that young children's interests focused on "the-here-and-now." This was translated as home objects and environments, community settings, airplanes, trains, local workers and professionals, and "everyday matters." Approved and recommended book lists guided parents' selection of preschool books as early as 1913.

It is thought that Russian information and "how-to" books of the 1940s and 1950s increased nonfiction picture-book production in the United States. Books concerning machines and how they worked, insects, and science concepts became abundant. Illustrations included photographs.

Some of the changes in picture-book publishing during the 1960s occurred because several individuals spotlighted the lack of African-Americans in story lines and illustrations. The civil rights movement affected the social consciousness of many teachers and families.

Only a few research surveys conducted in the 1970s and 1980s attempted to pinpoint the numbers of picture-book representations for Mexican-Americans, Asian-Americans, or Native Americans. It is reasonable to say they were minimal in number.

Although published multicultural literature for young children increased and became an important part of language arts education, cultural accuracy that helps young children gain a "true" sense of the culture depicted (a so-called insider's view) is a relatively recent development. This type of picture book is eagerly sought by most early childhood educators.

The current trend toward publishing more multicultural literature to compensate for the almost total absence of it as recently as 35 years ago will continue as schools become more diverse and society becomes more accepting of different voices and viewpoints.

Picture books dealing with the reality of young children's daily lives, their families, and living problems (such as stress, fear, moving, and appearance) began appearing in larger numbers in the 1970s and 1980s, broadening subject matter believed appropriate and of interest to children. These books, many classified as "therapeutic," often attempted to build self-esteem or help young children cope in difficult situations. Characters in picture books always had problems to be solved by creative thinking and self-insight, but these new stories dealt more frequently with life situations children could not change themselves.

Literacy concerns and the whole-language movement (1980s to 1990s) have dramatically increased educators' ideas of the importance of quality literature in early childhood curriculum. More and more activities are based on children's reactions to books and language arts activities offered by their teachers.

Creative technology has entered the children's book field with glitz, bang, and flashing color. The computerized picture book has voice, sound effects, and interactive features not previously thought possible. There are an amazing number of book-technology products that capture attention, hold attention, and attempt to teach and entertain preschoolers. Fortunately, many young children treat them as novelties after a short period and seek traditional read-alouds with the special people in their lives. How smart they are! Nothing can replace someone who answers your every question, relates the book to you and your unique life experiences, and treats you special by choosing to spend time with you in an activity they, too, enjoy.

Today's picture books have historical roots. Some have outlived the generation of children for whom they were produced and are classics of quality. It is those that you, as a teacher of young children, will endeavor to find and share along with the "classics of the future."

WHERE TO START

This chapter contains a list of picture books to be considered merely as a starting point. Because the quality of a book is a subjective judgment, your favorites may not appear on this list. There are many other books of quality; each teacher should develop a personal collection. Librarians and bookstore salespeople can offer valuable suggestions and advice.

QUALITY

Judging quality means reading and viewing a picture book to find out whether it contains something memorable or valuable. For every good book you discover, you may wade through a stack that makes you wonder whether the authors have any experience at all with young children. Remember, appropriate material for a 4-year-old may not suit a younger child.

Each book you select may have one or more of the following desirable and valuable features.

- character development (such as *Madeline* by Ludwig Bemelmans, the wolf in *Goldilocks and the Three Bears*, or *Beady Bear* by Don Freeman)
- color (*Little Blue and Yellow* by Leo Lionni)
- an example of human courage, cleverness, or grit (such as *Peter Rabbit*, created by Beatrix Potter)
- aesthetic appeal (*Rain Rain Rivers* by Uri Shulevitz)
- wordplay (*Tikki Tikki Tembo* by Arlene Mosel)
- listening pleasure (*Make Way for Ducklings* by Robert McCloskey)
- nonsense (*What Do You Do with a Kangaroo?* by Mercer Mayer)
- onomatopoeia (the naming of a thing or action by a vocal imitation of the sound associated with it, as in *buzz* and *hiss*)
- suspense (*Deep in the Forest* by Brinton Turkle)
- humor or wit (*Nothing Ever Happens on My Block* by Ellen Raskin)
- fantasy (*Where the Wild Things Are* by Maurice Sendak)
- surprise (*Harry the Dirty Dog* by Eugene Zion)
- repetition (*The Little Engine That Could* by Mabel Bragg)
- hope (*The Carrot Seed* by Ruth Krauss)
- charm (*George and Martha* by James Marshall)
- sensitivity (*The Tenth Good Thing about Barney* by Judith Viorst)
- realistic dialogue (*Can I Keep Him?* By Steven Kellogg)
- cultural insight (*On a Hot, Hot Day* by Nicki Weiss)
- action (*Caps for Sale* by Esphyr Slobodkina)
- predictability (*Brown Bear, Brown Bear, What Do You See?* by William Martin)

The preceding is only a partial listing. A book can excel in many different ways. An outstanding feature of many good stories is that they can cause the reader or listener to smile with recognition and think, "life is like that" or

"I've been there myself." This promotes a positive feeling of connectedness.

The theme of respect for individual differences in Bill Peet's *Huge Harold*, the gentleness of Uri Shulevitz's *Dawn*, or the tenderness of Charlotte Zolotow's *My Grandson Lew* may fit your criteria of quality. The runaway fantasy of Frank Asch's *Popcorn* and Tomie de Paola's *Strega Nona* might tickle your fancy.

The panoramic scenes of Mitsumasa Anno's *Anno's Counting Book*, the patterns and contrasts in Ezra Jack Keats' *The Snowy Day*, or the fun of discovery in Janet and Allan Ahlberg's *Each Peach Pear Plum* might help a book become one of your favorites because of visual appeal.

For humor and wit, you might choose Steven Kellogg's *There Was an Old Woman*, Leah Komaiko's *Annie Bananie*, Robert Kraus's *Leo the Late Bloomer*, James Marshall's *Yummers*, Mercer Mayer's *Frog, Where Are You?*, or a selection of others that may make you laugh. You might never forget the way you trip over your tongue while reading about Jack, Kack, Lack, Mack, Nack, Ouack, Pack, and Quack in Robert McCloskey's *Make Way for Ducklings* or Arlene Mosel's *Tikki Tikki Tembo*. If you enjoy surprise or an ending with a twist, you might be delighted by Brinton Turkle's *Deep in the Forest* or Jimmy Kennedy's *The Teddy Bears' Picnic*. The sound pleasure in Wanda Gág's *Millions of Cats* or the onomatopoeia in Mabel Bragg's *The Little Engine That Could* might make these books memorable.

You might relive your experience of city living in *Tell Me a Mitzi* by Lore Segal. Perhaps discovering the facts through the colorful, precise artwork in Ruth Heller's *Chickens Aren't the Only Ones* will attract you to the world of nonfiction. You may look for books to promote children's phonological awareness, like Bill Martin Jr. and John Archambault's *Chicka Chicka Boom Boom* or Cheryl Hudson's *Afro-Bets ABC Book*. Unforgettable characters like Leo Lionni's *Frederick*, Don Freeman's *Corduroy* and *Dandelion*, Eugene Zion's *Harry by the Sea*, or Ludwig Bemelmans's demure individualist *Madeline* may be counted among your friends

as you search for quality. Jewels will stand out, and you will be anxious to share them with children.

You will be looking for fascinating, captivating books. Some captivate by presenting believable characters.

Character-drawing is like a tremendous, complicated conjuring-trick. Appealing to imagination and goodwill, diverting attention by sheer power of technique, the writer persuades us (for the period of reading and sometimes for long afterward) to accept the identity of certain people who exist between the covers of his book. The timeless appeal of *The Cat in the Hat* by Dr. Seuss (Theodore Geisel) needs to be mentioned here. Virtually everyone in the English-speaking world who learned to read in the last 50 years is familiar with the book (Freeman, 2007). Freeman believes that it may be another 50 years or more before a similarly two-sided genius (artist and educator) comes along to fashion a story so very easy to read and so very hard to put down. Some picture books fascinate to the extent that worries are forgotten, and the child lives in the fantasy world of the story during its reading and beyond.

Speaking about a true literature-based curriculum, teachers need to watch for stories that "catch on," stories that fulfill some deep understanding of human intentions, or express a developmental concern, or arouse our curiosity: these are the stories that should lead a curriculum of hearing stories, knowing them, and—if they appeal— reliving them through writing, drama, or retelling.

You will want to choose classics so that from the very beginning, the child has a chance to appreciate literature. Not everyone will agree as to what is a modern-day classic. *Where the Wild Things Are*, by Maurice Sendak, continues to cause arguments among adults about whether it is truly a classic. Teachers observe that some adults don't like it very much, but nearly all children really respond to it. Many people think that Sendak is very much attuned to kids' wavelength.

Knowing about family lifestyles, home language, and community individuality aids book selection and planning. Some schools order 50 percent of their books in the children's home language. The relevance of a farm book is bound to be different for farm children, yet the human universality depicted may make it an attractive choice for urban children.

Many early childhood classrooms and child care settings across all geographical boundaries and income levels do not have the resources to build libraries with sufficient numbers of quality books for young children. Far too much reliance can be placed on the generosity of parents and community members to supply additional quality literature for classroom libraries. Many centers do fundraising to supplement their budgets. Families may need guidance or suggested book lists because some don't realize grocery store books and some mass-produced paperback books lack quality.

Award-Winning Books

Each year, the Association for Library Services to Children (American Library Association) recognizes the artist it believes has produced "the most distinguished American picture book for children" with the Caldecott Medal and Honor awards. Early childhood educators look for these and other award-winning books. Other awards given to books include the following:

- Newbery Medals
- International Reading Association Children's Book Awards
- The Parent Choice Awards
- Coretta Scott King Awards
- National Jewish Book Awards
- Catholic Book Awards
- The Children's Africana Book Awards
- newspaper awards
- magazine reviews and recognitions found in *Book Links* (American Library Association) and *Language Arts* (National Council of Teachers of English)
- local public library awards or recognitions

Illustrations

In many quality picture books, the story stands well by itself. The illustrations simply visualize what is written. In others, illustrations play a dominant role and are an integral part of the entire action. Picture books can be defined by as books that rely on a combination of illustrations and **narrative**, with both being integral to the complete work. Fortunately, many picture-book illustrations are created by highly talented individuals. Justice and Lankford (2002) point out that about 95 percent of children's visual attention during storybook sharing is focused on the book's illustrations.

Young children may or may not have grasped the idea that book illustrations are drawn, created, or photographed by real people. The following happened to a student teacher at Evergreen Valley College Child Development Center.

> During a book reading activity the student teacher displayed the cover of the book *The Wide-Mouthed Frog*, and then read the title, the author's name and said "This book's pictures were drawn for us by Jonathan Lambert." One four-year-old girl queried "Was it the frog or a people?" The book's cover has a large colorful green frog illustration.

A wide range of artistic styles exists in picture-book illustration, including line drawings, woodcuts, water colors, collage, crayon, pastels, oil paint, and photography. The style of art can be representational, impressionistic, expressionistic, cartoon, abstract, stylized, surrealistic, or a style that defies categorization. The true artist is one who is able to enter the realm that his work evokes and move as

---

narrative — in general, a story, actual or fictional, expressed orally or in writing.

freely there as if it were the kingdom of his birth. As a consequence, the artist can show us things that we would not have seen as mere visitors.

Illustrations help give words reality. For young children, illustrations promote visual literacy. Additional benefits follow.

◆ provision of pleasure

◆ nourishment of the imagination

◆ promotion of creative expression

◆ development of imagery

◆ presentation and exploration of various styles and forms for the communication of ideas

◆ awareness of the functions of languages

◆ acquisition of metalinguistic awareness (defined as a sense of what printed language is all about)

Picture-book illustrations are often familiar objects in lifelike settings, and publishers are careful to emphasize figures rather than backgrounds. In addition to the simple, true-to-life depictions preferred by young preschoolers, illustrations of pure fantasy and illustrations that contain more detail appeal to older preschoolers.

Many teacher interactive behaviors may occur in read-aloud activities. Among the interactive behaviors research has identified in read-aloud activities are questioning, scaffolding dialogue and responses, offering praise or positive reinforcement, giving or extending information, clarifying information, restating information, directing discussion, sharing personal reactions, and relating concepts to life experiences. A teacher reading this list can never again believe that read-aloud book times are the simplest, easiest time of the day, although they will probably remain one of the teacher's favorite times (Figure 9–3). Children will have spontaneous and unconscious responses to books, including thoughts that agree or disagree, and other feelings and attitudes. At times children's responses to read-alouds are unexpected,

FIGURE 9–3 Schools provide as many one-on-one readings as staff and time allow.

immediately voiced, and can make the act of reading to young children a delightful experience because the teacher shares the excitement, concentration, joy, and laughter.

Format

A book's format is defined as its overall and general character, that is, the way the book is put together. Decisions concerning format by book publishers and author/illustrators include the size and shape of the cover and interior pages, paper quality, printing colors, typesetting, content of each page, and binding. A book's format can enhance its narrative, appeal, and subsequent enjoyment, or it can confuse, frustrate, and alienate the reader. A book can reflect a thoughtful attempt to create a classic volume of enduring worth and value or represent a sacrifice of quality for the sake of quick profit.

Genre, another way of categorizing books, concentrates on a book's content. Narrative is either poetry or prose. Prose can be further

genre — a category used to classify literary works, usually by form, technique, or content.

classified as fiction or nonfiction. The category of fiction includes excursions into sheer fantasy as well as more plausible stories about people or situations that could be, could have been, or might be. The latter group is classified as realistic fiction.

IF ONLY THEY WOULD CHOOSE BOOKS AND BOOK-RELATED ACTIVITIES

Many early childhood teachers are worried that busy money-tight families do not have the time or resources to make books part of children's lives. Consequently, they are expending extra effort and attention to books and book-related activities. Emergent literacy research has alerted educators to the idea that preschoolers who are read to and who are interested in stories and books are more successful students in the beginning years of elementary school and in accomplishing reading. Educators monitor how many children select classroom book-related activities and library areas and also monitor the amount of time each child is so engaged (Figure 9–4).

Teacher planning and thoughtful analysis can increase child interest. Thinking of classroom schedules and book-reading times more critically can initiate change and creative and imaginative presentation of activities. Time spent reading to children can be viewed as only one part of a book's introduction. What precedes and what follows are equally important. Practitioners need to ask themselves the following: How is this book relevant to children's lives? What can I do to increase child involvement and interest? What will make children eager to be part of story times? How can I discover child thoughts about what has been read and then build in further experiences? What can follow this story time, and will children give me clues? In other words, how can this book become part of their lives and at the same time be highly enjoyed? After attempting to answer these and other teacher questions, one can see that simply reading to children may not be enough to reach a teacher's true goals. Teachers spend considerable time in the classroom library (book center) themselves. One teacher technique is to introduce a new book or other printed material every day. Teachers think seriously about book variety, availability, child comfort and adequate lighting. They determine a plan to "sell" the books they introduce.

FIGURE 9–4 This classroom has been able to promote child self-selection of books.

READING BOOKS TO YOUNG CHILDREN

Because children can gain so much from books, the teacher's way of presenting them is very important. The primary goal of a read-aloud event is the construction of meaning that develops in the interactive process between adult and child and the development of children's positive attitudes toward the activity.

Becoming this type of teacher requires the teacher to view children as active, individual learners. In previewing Tomie de Paola's picture book *Strega Nona* (1975) for a group reading, a teacher might think as follows:

What past experiences has this group had with pasta?

What follow-up, extending activities could be planned?

What teacher questions would guide a discussion that probes children's feelings and ideas?

How can I make the "overflowing," "too much" concept a real experience?

The teacher's goal should be to lead each child to understand that books can be fun and interesting, can hold new experiences, and can be enjoyed alone or in the company of others (Figure 9–5).

Children who enjoy read-alouds usually seek out other books. Preschool teachers think of the preschool years as a critical period for children to become addicted to books, when urges are felt as irresistible and objects that gratify the urge are also experienced as irresistible. The educator who wishes to capture a young child needs to ensure that early and repeated gratification from book-reading times exists.

Books that you reject after reviewing them will have been recognized as being inappropriate or missing their appeal with young children. You may judge them as having no redeeming social value; to be dull and uninteresting; or to contain violence, unfortunate representations, unclear messages, or poor models of behavior. A book's construction and format may be undesirable. Of the over 90,000 children's books currently in print, many will not meet the quality standards you set.

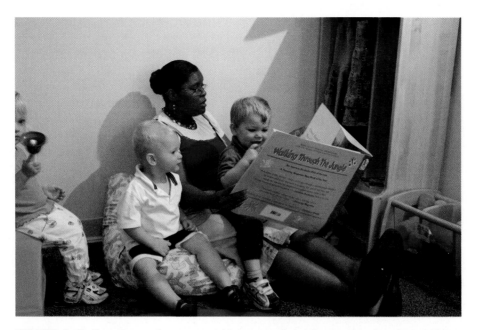

FIGURE 9–5 Creating enjoyment and interest when sharing big books involves promoting the children's positive interest toward books.

Most educators are eager to learn more about new children's books and are already quite knowledgeable. Picking books for a specific child's interest and then selecting books to suit some unique classroom situation or event are ongoing teacher tasks.

In a diverse society, offering multicultural and ethnically representative literature is a must for young children. Although age-recommended lists are available, most teachers actively pursue additional publications. Librarians, publishers, and children's bookstores are excellent resources. Anti-bias themes and sex-equity themes are also eagerly sought to ensure book models give young children every chance to value themselves as individuals.

Sales of children's books to affluent parents, who want to give (perhaps literally) their child every educational advantage, are growing. Hopefully, they are actually taking the time to share them with their children.

It is the teacher's responsibility to encourage the children's interest because not every child in preschool is interested in books or sees them as something to enjoy. Although children cannot be forced to like books, they can acquire positive feelings for them. Some of the positive feelings depend on whether children feel successful and competent during reading time. This, in turn, depends on how skillfully the teacher acts and reacts and how well the book sessions are planned. The key is to draw reluctant children into the story by making story times so attractive and vital that children simply cannot bear to stay away.

An important additional goal in reading books to children is the presentation of knowledge. Books can acquaint the child with new words, ideas, facts, feelings, and happenings. These are experienced in a different form than spoken conversation. In books, sentences are complete; in conversation, they may not be. Stories and illustrations follow a logical sequence in books.

Teachers ought to be concerned with whether the child comprehends what is read. To ensure comprehension, the books must offer significant content, something that relates to the child's everyday experience. Humor and fantasy, for example, are common in favorite picture books. Usually, these books are not merely frivolous. A closer reading will often reveal that they deal with universal human emotions or imaginations. Comprehension is aided by open discussion. Children should be free to ask questions that will help them connect the book's happenings to their own past experiences. The more outgoing and talkative children often clear up misunderstandings of the whole group when books are discussed. Those who work with young children often notice children's innate tendency to try to make sense and derive meaning from the happenings in their lives.

Teachers can show that books may also be used as resources. When a child wants to find out about certain things, teachers can refer to dictionaries, encyclopedias, computers, or books on specialized subjects. The teacher can model the use of books to find facts. When a child asks the teacher a question about some subject of special interest and the teacher says, "I don't know, but I know where we can find out," the teacher can demonstrate how books and other resources can be used for finding answers. The teacher tells where to look and follows through by showing the child how the information is found. The joy of discovery is shared, and this opens the door to seeking more answers.

In contrast, "pressure-cooker" programs, which promise to have 4-year-olds reading before kindergarten, often feature drill sessions designed to develop technical reading skills (such as decoding words). When these drill sessions, which are usually meaningless and boring to young children, are connected to picture-book readings, they could endanger the young child's budding love affair with books.

Many children pick up reading knowledge and reading skills as they become more familiar with book features. They will see regularities and differences in the book's illustrations and text that will aid them in their eventual desire to break the code of reading. An early type of reading has been witnessed by all experienced early childhood teachers. It is called imitative reading, and is defined as the child's reading the story from pictures, and sometimes speaking remembered text. Certain techniques can be used to encourage imitative reading.

- ◆ reading picture books to children daily
- ◆ planning repeated reading of new and old favorites
- ◆ reliving enjoyed parts in discussions
- ◆ being attentive to children's needs to be heard "reading"
- ◆ issuing positive encouragement about your enjoyment of what the children have shared
- ◆ expecting some creative child deviation from the actual story
- ◆ suggesting or providing additional ways children could "read" a book (for example, into a tape recorder)
- ◆ viewing the children's activity as emerging literacy and behavior to value as a milestone

Some preschoolers may begin to understand that the teacher is not telling a story or just reading illustrations but instead the teacher is reading the print (marks) in the book from left to right. The print may first look like strange rows of marks. As knowledge of the marks expands, the child may learn that the marks are single or grouped alphabet letters forming words, and that those words have spaces between them. Eventually the idea that alphabet letters represent sounds may become clear and then children may realize that the reader (teacher/adult) knows these sounds and can therefore "read" and speak words aloud. Many preschoolers recognize single words in books, particularly those that have been read and reread to them often. Some preschoolers develop a small sight word vocabulary and a few become actual readers of simple text. Eventually children come to know that readers use different parts of the text—such as words, photographs and illustrations, graphs, visual images, and the context of reading—to discern meaning.

Educators encourage children to learn how to care for books and where and how they can be used. Attitudes about books as valuable personal possessions should be instilled during early childhood. A number of emerging behaviors and skills will be noticed as children become fond of books. Learning to read is a complex skill that depends on smaller skills, some of which children develop during story times and by browsing through books on their own.

Using Literature to Aid Conflict-Resolution Skills

Concerned with rising levels of violence in our society, early childhood teachers are attempting to use picture books and stories to help children identify and define problems, a first step in conflict resolution. Books can be a valuable tool. Illustrations and book text may help children learn the conflict-resolution skills of **visualization** and empathy by providing nonviolent resolution to story-line disputes, portraying different types of conflicts, and giving examples of peacemaking at work.

BOOK SELECTION

Teachers are responsible for selecting quality books that meet the school's stated goals; often, teachers are asked to select new books for the school's collection. Book selection is not an easy task for teachers. When choosing books, educators must give much thought to each book's content and its relevance to particular children. They must be sensitive to how children might personalize a story. Teachers keep in mind family situations, cultures, religions, and social biases when they select. Some books

---

visualization — the process, or result, of mentally picturing objects or events that are normally experienced directly.

may fill the needs completely; others may only partially meet the goals of instruction. The local library offers the opportunity to borrow books that help keep storytelling time fresh and interesting, and children's librarians can be valuable resources.

Even when careful thought has been put into selecting a book, one child may like a book that another child does not. Some stories appeal more to one group than to another. Stories that are enjoyed most often become old favorites. Children who know the story often look forward to a familiar part or character. Selected books should match the children's needs, and their changing interests. They need books that range from simple to more difficult. They need books that are relevant and reflect the social and cultural reality of their daily lives.

Professional books and journals abound with ideas concerning the types of books that children like best. Some writers believe that simple fairy-tale picture books with animal characters that possess lifelike characteristics are preferred. Others mention that certain children want "true" stories. Most writers agree the success of any book for young children depends on its presentation of basic human tasks, needs, and concerns based on children's perceptions, and at a level at which they can respond. Condescending books that trivialize their concerns and efforts and present easy answers to complex problems are discarded for meaningful ones.

Many writers provide a list of selection criteria that is sensitive to *intergenerational representation* in picture books. Recommendations follow.

◆ Characters should be portrayed realistically and have experiences and emotions with which children can immediately identify.

◆ The story should unfold sequentially. There may be tension or conflict to be reduced or resolved. The simple plot necessitated by the length of a picture book allows young children to become involved immediately in the action, discover the problem, and understand the resolution.

◆ The theme should relate to children's needs, understandings, and interests. A simple story can develop a significant theme.

◆ The story should establish a time and place. Older people are present in all cultures.

◆ The story involves rhythm, repetition, and a careful choice of words.*

Many parents and educators have concerns about the violent nature of some folk and **fairy tales**. Others believe that children already know the world can be a dangerous and sometimes cruel place. Many old stories involve justice—good things happening to people with good behavior and bad things happening to people with bad behavior. Individual teachers and staff groups may decide that some folk tales are too violent, gory, or inappropriate for the age or living circumstances of attending children. Each book needs examination. It is likely that, at times, staff opinions will differ.

Some beginning teachers worry about book characters such as talking bears and rabbits. Make-believe during preschool years is an ever-increasing play pursuit. Most educators are not concerned if bears talk if the message of their speech is something with which children can identify. But, they reject other stories that may seem more realistic if the problems the characters face have little to do with children's emotional lives.

The clear-cut story lines in many folk and fairy tales have stood the test of time and are recommended for a teacher's first attempts at reading to preschoolers. Good literature has something of meaning to offer any reader of any age, although on different levels of comprehension and appreciation. Each child will interpret and react to each book from an individual point of view, based on his unique experience.

Early childhood educators should include books depicting people with disabilities so that

*From James, J. Y., & Kormanski, L. M. (1999, May). Positive intergenerational books for young children. *Young Children, 54*(3): 37–43. Copyright © 1991.

---

fairy tales — folk stories about real-life problems, usually with imaginary characters and magical events.

children can understand and accept people with varying abilities. This group of individuals has been overlooked and inadequately presented in children's books. It is prudent to be on the lookout for this type of picture book.

You will want to introduce books with excellent language usage, ones that enchant and create beautiful images using the best grammatical structure, vocabulary, and imaginative style—in other words, memorable quality books.

Kinds of Books

Children's book publishing is a booming business. Many types of books are available, as illustrated in Figure 9–6, which lists various categories in the left column. The figure identifies the major genre classifications and formats of children's books used in preschool classrooms, but it excludes poetry, which is discussed in another chapter. Many books do not fit neatly into a single category; some books may fit into two or more categories.

TYPES	FEATURES TEACHERS LIKE	FEATURES CHILDREN LIKE
Storybooks (picture books) • family and home • folktales and fables • fanciful stories • fairy tales • animal stories • others	sharing moments seeing children enthusiastic and attentive making characters' voices introducing human truths and imaginative adventures sharing favorites easy for child to identify with small creatures	imagination and fantasy identification with characters' humanness wish and need fulfillment adventure excitement action self-realization visual variety word pleasure
Nonfiction books (informational) also referred to as *content books*	expand individual and group interests develop "reading-to-know" attitudes encourage finding out together provide accurate facts contain scientific content	provide facts; allow for discovery of information and ideas discuss reality and how things work and function answer "why" and "how" supply new words and new meanings
Wordless books	promote child speech, creativity, and imagination	provide opportunity to supply their own words to tell the story promote discovery of meanings include color, action, and visual variety
Interaction books (books with active child participation built in)	keep children involved and attentive build listening for directions skills	provide for movement and group feeling promote individual creativity and expression appeal to senses have manipulatable features
Concept books (books with central concepts or themes that include specific and reinforcing examples)	promote categorization present opportunities to know about and develop concepts many examples	add to knowledge visually present abstractions
Predictable books (books with repetitions and reinforcement)	permit successful guessing build child's confidence promote ideas that books make sense	provide opportunity to read along are repetitive build feelings of competence

FIGURE 9–6 Categories of children's books. *(continued)*

TYPES	FEATURES TEACHERS LIKE	FEATURES CHILDREN LIKE
Reference books (picture dictionaries, encyclopedias, special subject books)	provide opportunity to look up questions with the child promote individualized learning	provide answers are used with teacher (shared time) are resources that answer their questions
Alphabet and word books (word books have name of object printed near or on top of object)	supply letters and word models pair words and objects are useful for child with avid interest in alphabet letters and words can include letter and word play	discover meanings and alphabet letters and words see names of what is illustrated
Novelty books (pop-ups, fold-outs, electronic books, stamp and pasting books, activity books, puzzle books, scratch-and-sniff books, hidden objects in illustrations, talking books)	add sense-exploring variety stimulate creativity come in many different sizes and shapes motor involvement for child many include humor	encourage exploring, touching, moving, feeling, smelling, painting, drawing, coloring, cutting, gluing, acting upon, listening to a mechanical voice, and getting instant feedback
Paperback books and magazines (Golden Books, *Humpty Dumpty Magazine*)	are inexpensive come in a wide variety many classics available	include activity pages
Teacher- and child-made books	reinforce class learnings build understanding of authorship allow creative expression record individual, group projects, field trips, parties promote child expression of concerns and ideas build child's self-esteem	allow child to see own name in print provide opportunity to share ideas with others are self-rewarding
Therapeutic books (books helping children cope with and understand things such as divorce, death, jealousy)	present life realistically offer positive solutions and insights present diverse family groups deal with life's hard-to-deal-with subjects	help children discuss real feelings
Seasonal and holiday books	accompany child interest may help child understand underlying reasons for celebration	build pleasant expectations add details
Books and audiovisual combinations (read-alongs)	add variety offer group and individual experiencing opportunities stimulate interest in books	project large illustrations can be enjoyed individually
Toddler books and board books (durable pages)	resist wear and tear	are easy to use (ease in page-turning
Multicultural and cross-cultural books (culturally conscious books)	increase positive attitudes concerning diversity and similarity	introduce a variety of people
Oversized books (big books)	emphasize the realities in our society have extra large text and illustrations	are easy-to-see in groups have giant book characters

FIGURE 9–6 *(continued)*

A vast and surprising variety of novelty books are also in print: floating books for bath time; soft, huggable books for bedtime; pocket-sized books; jumbo board and easel books (Scholastic); lift-the-flap books; flipbooks (Little, Brown & Co.); books that glow in the dark; sing-a-story books (Bantam); potty-training books (Barron's); and even books within books.

Oversized Books (Big Books)

Big, giant, and jumbo (24-by-36 inches) are descriptors used to identify oversized books. Publishers are mass producing this size book because of their increased popularity with both early childhood educators and whole-language curriculum advocates.

Because they are easily viewed by groups of children, oversized books have been added to teacher curriculum collections. New and classic titles abound. Because the text is large, it is not overlooked by young children. Found in soft and hard cover versions with brilliant-colored illustrations, some have accompanying audio tapes and small book editions. Teachers use chalkboard gutters or art easels as book holders.

Enlarged texts (Big Books) allow groups of children to see and react to the printed page. Active participation and unison participation can be encouraged. Using a hand to underline words while reading, the teacher can focus attention on print and its directionality. Recommended Big Books are listed in the Additional Resources section at the end of this chapter.

Alphabet Books

Singing and learning the "Alphabet Song" is often a child's first introduction to the alphabet, one that precedes and promotes an interest in alphabet books. For a further discussion of alphabet books and print awareness, see Chapter 16.

Nonfiction Books

Teachers may encounter and share nonfiction books that answer children's questions, are related to a curriculum theme, or serve another teaching purpose, such as providing pictorial information. Nonfiction books can teach concepts and terms associated with various topics, people, places, and things children may never encounter in real life. A book with a simplified explanation of how water comes out of a faucet serves as an example. Nonfiction (books) may be perceived as more appropriate for older grades, and a real revolution has occurred in recent years in the writing and production of nonfiction books for young children. Much of the knowledge of our society, and many other societies, is accumulated in our nonfiction text (Duke, 2007). Duke notes:

- **Using nonfiction reference materials in the classroom allows children to see one important and common reason that people read.**
- **For some children, reading nonfiction reference materials may be an especially compelling reason to read.**
- **Reading nonfiction reference materials may help deepen concepts of print and genre knowledge.**
- **Reading nonfiction reference materials provides a forum for building computer literacy.**
- **Reading nonfiction for reference provides another tool for developing comprehension and world knowledge. (p. 13)**

Teachers may ignore informational picture books, believing they will not hold children's attention. They may not know that many are related in cumulative story form, some are wordless, and others have rhythmic features or include poetry. Most cover interesting topics, pique curiosity, and offer scientific or precise vocabulary. Figure 9–7 offers tips on selecting quality nonfiction titles.

Teachers realize that photographs, realistic drawings, paintings, collages, and other images should be accurate because young readers attend most directly to illustrations. If informational books sacrifice this, reject them.

Teachers doing computer searches and selecting books or other reading material for the classroom consider the necessity that they may have to emphasize to children that just because

LANGUAGE

Does the material:

- use simple, straightforward vocabulary?
- include some specific scientific or technical terms?
- present special or technical terms or context?
- use short, direct sentences?

IDEAS AND ORGANIZATION

Does the material:

- present one idea at a time?
- provide specific and concrete information?
- show relationships among ideas that are explicit and simple (for example, sequence, cause-effect, descriptions)?
- use short paragraphs that begin with a clear topic sentence followed by details?
- use bold titles and headings?

GRAPHICS AND FORMAT

Does the material use:

* illustrations and graphics to support and provide content?
* clear relationship between text and illustrations?
* illustrations that elaborate and clarify the written text?
* type size that is 14 point or larger?

FIGURE 9–7 Tips on selecting informational texts.

written material is found in print it may not necessarily be true and factual. A nonfiction book may be one or more people's opinion rather than widely accepted fact. Elementary school teachers purposely offer conflicting readings to promote discussion and critical thinking. At the preschool level, critical analysis is more commonly promoted during oral discussions.

Given a choice of reading materials, young children are as likely to state a preference for informational picture books as for fictional ones. The effects of immersing young children in nonfiction picture books are not fully documented in research. Most practicing teachers know children readily use and consult them. Examples of classroom nonfiction books follow.

Amos, J., & Solway, A. (2000). *Scholastic first encyclopedia*: *Animals and nature*. New York: Scholastic.

Barton, B. (2001). *My car*. New York: Greenwillow Books.

Hirschi, R. (1987). *What is a bird?* New York: Walker.

Stein, S. (1985). *Mouse*. New York: Harcourt, Brace, Jovanovich.

Yabuuchi, M. (1985). *Whose footprints?* New York: Philomel Books.

Story Songs

A growing number of favorite books put to music, and favorite songs published as books, are available. An adult sings as pages are turned. Teachers can introduce this literary experience and encourage children to join in. The added advantage of visual representations helps induce the child to sing. The novelty of a teacher singing a book also offers a possible incentive for the child to select this type of book because of his familiarity with an already memorized and perhaps enjoyed song. Word recognition is sometimes readily accomplished. Popular books of this type include the following:

de Paola, T. (1984). *Mary had a little lamb*. New York: Holiday House.

Kovalski, M. (1987). *The wheels on the bus*. Boston: Little, Brown & Co.

McNalley, D. (1991). *In a cabin in a wood*. New York: Cobblehill/Dutton.

Interactive Technology

Technology and young children's books have been combined by companies like LeapFrog, Fisher-Price (PowerTouch Learning System), and Publications International (ActivePAD). With a touch of the finger or a stylus, a young child can flip pages, hear any particular word pronounced, hear a book read by a clear voice, select the reader's pace, play games, hear word definitions, and take quizzes. Some models have light attachments and a microphone. Some teach phonics; encourage children to pronounce phonemes, words, and sentences; and prompt children to record their names, which are then put into stories. Some models focus on writing skills and enable children to trace alphabet letters, work mazes, or engage in dot-to-dot activities or handwriting exercises. Individual companies have developed over 70 children's book titles.

Families are lured by educative features, and some preschools are adding electronic books to their book collections. Prices vary, but they usually are not prohibitive for the average center.

Criteria for Read-Aloud Book Selection

Consider the attention span, maturity, interests, personality, and age of children you are targeting when selecting books. Developing broad literary and artistic tastes is another important idea.

The following is a series of questions a teacher could use when choosing a child's book to read aloud.

1. Could I read this book enthusiastically, really enjoying the story?

2. Are the contents of the book appropriate for the children with whom I work?

   a. Can the children relate some parts to their lives and past experience?

   b. Can the children identify with one or more of the characters?

   Look at some children's classics, such as *Mother Goose*. Almost all of the stories have a well-defined character with which children share some common feature. Teachers find that different children identify with different characters—the wolf instead of one of the pigs in *The Three Little Pigs*, for example.

3. Does the book have directly quoted conversation?

   a. If it does, this can add interest; for example, "Are you my mother?" he said to the cow.

4. Will the child benefit from attitudes and models found in the book? Many books model behaviors that are unsuitable for the young child. Also, consider the following questions when analyzing a book for unfavorable racial stereotypes or sexism.

5. Who are the "doers" and "inactive observers"?

6. Are characters' achievements based on their own initiative, insights, or intelligence?

7. Who performs the brave and important deeds?

8. Are value and worth connected to skin color and economic resources?

9. Does language or setting ridicule or demean a specific group of individuals?

   a. Are individuals treated as such rather than as one of a group?

   b. Are ethnic groups or individuals treated as though everyone in that group has the same human talent, ability, food preference, and hairstyle, taste in clothing, or human weakness or characteristic?

   c. Do illustrations capture natural-looking ethnic variations?

10. Does this book broaden the cross-cultural element in the multicultural selection of books offered at my school?

    a. Is the book accurate and authentic in its portrayal of individuals and groups?

11. Was the book written with an understanding of preschool age-level characteristics?

    a. Is the text too long to sit through? Are there too many words?

    b. Are there enough colorful or action-packed pictures or illustrations to hold attention?

    c. Is the size of the book suitable for easy handling in groups or for individual viewing?

    d. Can the child participate in the story by speaking or making actions?

    e. Is the fairy tale or folktale too complex, symbolic, and confusing to have meaning?

12. Is the author's style enjoyable?

    a. Is the book written clearly with a vocabulary and sequence the children can understand?

    b. Are memorable words or phrases found in the book?

    c. Are repetitions of words, actions, rhymes, or story parts used? (Anticipated repetition is part of the young child's enjoyment of stories. Molly Bang's *Ten, Nine, Eight* contains this feature.)

13. Does the story develop and end with a satisfying climax of events?

14. Are there humorous parts and silly names? The young child's humor is often slapstick in nature (pie-in-the-face, all-fall-down type rather than play on words). The ridiculous and far-fetched often tickle them. See Tomie de Paola's *Pancakes for Breakfast* (Harcourt, Brace, Jovanovich), a wordless book.

15. Does it have educational value? (See Figure 9–8.)

    a. Could you use it to expand knowledge in any special way? See Maureen Roffey's *Home, Sweet Home* (Coward), which depicts animal living quarters in a delightful way.

    b. Does it offer new vocabulary? Does it increase or broaden understanding? See Masayuki Yabuuchi's *Animals Sleeping* (Philomel) for an example.

16. Do pictures (illustrations) explain and coordinate well with the text? Examine Jane Miller's *Farm Counting Book* (Prentice Hall) and look for this feature.

Some books meet most criteria of the established standards; others meet only a few. The age of attending children makes some criteria more important than others. Schools often select copies of accepted old classics. These titles are considered part of our cultural heritage, ones that most American preschoolers know and have experienced (Figure 9–9). Many classics have been handed down through the oral tradition of storytelling and can contain archaic words, such as *stile* and *sixpence*. *Green Eggs and Ham* and *The Cat in the Hat* by Dr. Seuss (Random House) are newly recognized classics that were included in a National Education Association online survey of children's top 10 favorite books. Most teachers try to offer the best in children's literature and a wide variety of book types.

CULTURALLY CONSCIOUS AND CULTURALLY DIVERSE BOOKS

Multicultural literature can be defined as children's literature that represents any distinct cultural group through accurate portrayal and rich detail. Educators urge teachers to evaluate multicultural children's literature by examining both literary quality and cultural consciousness. A different definition of multicultural literature states that multicultural literature is about some identifiable "other," a person or group, that differs in some way (for example, racially, linguistically, ethnically, culturally) from the Caucasian-American cultural group. Publishers are beginning to create books depicting gay and lesbian families in loving relationships, such as *Molly's Family* (2004). When a center is selecting books, staff members will need to

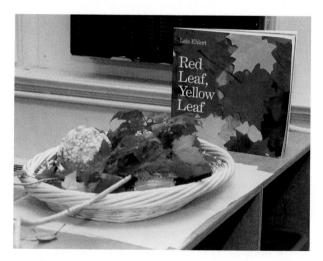

FIGURE 9–8 Color words are easily learned with this book and adjacent real leaves.

A PARTIAL LISTING

"Ba, Ba, Black Sheep"	"Little Girl with a Curl"	"Row, Row, Row Your Boat"
Chicken Little	"Little Jack Horner"	"Silent Night"
"There Was a Crooked Man"	"Little Miss Muffet"	"Simple Simon"
Goldilocks and the Three Bears	*The Little Red Hen*	"Sing a Song of Sixpence"
"Here We Go Round the Mulberry Bush"	"Little Robin Redbreast"	"Take Me Out to the Ball Game"
"Hey Diddle, Diddle (the Cat and the Fiddle)"	"London Bridge Is Falling Down"	*The Three Bears*
"Hickory, Dickory, Dock"	"Mary Had a Little Lamb"	*The Three Billy Goats Gruff*
"Humpty Dumpty"	"Mary, Mary, Quite Contrary"	"The Three Blind Mice"
"Jack and Jill"	"Old King Cole"	*The Three Little Pigs*
Jack and the Beanstalk	"Old Mother Hubbard"	"To Market, to Market"
"Jack Be Nimble"	"The Old Woman Who Lived in a Shoe"	"Twinkle, Twinkle, Little Star"
"Jack Sprat"	"Peter Piper"	*Ugly Duckling*
"Little Bo Peep"	"Pop Goes the Weasel"	"You Are My Sunshine"
"Little Boy Blue"	"Ride a Cock Horse (Banbury Cross)"	
	"Rock-a-Bye Baby"	

FIGURE 9–9 Stories, songs, rhymes, and poems considered classics for preschoolers. Many can be found in picture-book form.

discuss whether books depicting gay and lesbian families fit into their book collection.

The question of authenticity or, more correctly, what constitutes an accurate portrayal of a culture, has plagued educators for years Teachers try hard to present an authentic portrayal of cultural reality in the books they select. Multicultural books offer opportunities for children to learn to recognize similarities, values differences, and also respect common humanity. Children need literature that serves as a window into lives and experiences that are different from their own, and literature that serves as a mirror reflecting themselves and their cultural values, attitudes, and behaviors.

The books listed in the Additional Resources section at the end of this chapter include not only African-Americans, Asian-Americans, Hispanic Americans/Latinos, and Native Americans but also subgroups of different and distinct groups under each heading. Other world groups are also included.

When offering multicultural and multiethnic books to young children, no attempt to give these books special status is suggested. Children's questions and comments that arise are discussed

as all interesting books are discussed. These books are not shared only at certain times of year or for recognized celebrations but are included as regular, standard classroom fare.

Harris (1993) believes the following characteristics are part of authentic multiethnic and multicultural literature.

- Books include the range of character types or people found within the culture, although not necessarily in one book. The characters should not be idealized, but neither should stereotypes predominate. There should be doctors, teachers, truck drivers, cooks, and individuals with other occupations.
- Illustrations should not consist of caricatures of a group's physical features. Rather, the illustrations should reflect the variety found among members of any group.
- Speech adopted by characters should have linguistic authenticity.
- Names of characters should reflect cultural traditions of a group.
- Food should not be used as a short-hand signifier of a group; for example,

rice is not a code word for Asian or Asian-American.

- **The beliefs and values of characters as well as their worldviews should reflect the diversity found in the group's communities.**
- **Writers should understand pivotal family roles and family configurations.**
- **Members of groups should portray members as intelligent problem solvers.**
- **Authenticity derives from insider knowledge about a culture acquired as a member or through extensive study, observation, and interaction.***

"Hispanic" children's literature does not refer to one culture but rather a conglomerate of Central and South American cultures. Hispanics have been poorly represented in children's literature until recently. Books that existed were often folktales or remembrances of an author's childhood.

In picture books classified as depicting the Asian culture, one may find Chinese, Japanese, Korean, Taiwanese, Laotian, Vietnamese, Cambodian, and Filipino cultural experiences depicted. Increasingly, published books about Asians deal with Asian assimilation into the American mainstream. One can find numerous books dealing with Asian folktales. Yet to be written are plentiful picture books from the Vietnamese, Cambodian, and Laotian cultures, but they are slowly appearing.

Books concerning Native Americans can be easier to locate. Most are folktales, but some deal with rituals, ceremony, everyday life, family joys, and problems. Books depicting Middle Eastern cultures are scarce. Again, the teacher needs to screen for stereotypical characteristics. The National Black Child Development Institute (2006) convened a group of national scholars to analyze the reading gap between African American and Caucasian children. Findings and recommendations include the following:

Books read to children are most effective when they mirror children's culture.

*From Harris, V. J. (1993). From the margin to the center of curricula: Multicultural children's literature. In Spodek, B., & Saracho, O. (Eds.). *Language and literacy in early childhood education*, Vol. 4, pp. 123–140. New York: Teachers College Press. Copyright © 1993 by Teachers College Press, Columbia University. All rights reserved.

High-quality reading instruction and a cultural approach is a key to building strong literacy skills.

Learning the alphabet, phonics, spelling and writing are essential to literacy, but it is also important to help children make meaning of what they are reading (or what they are listening to). (p. 1)

A listing of children's multicultural books is included in the Additional Resources section at the end of this chapter.

Moral and Nonviolent Education

A good number of educators are offering picture books whose story lines include moral dilemmas and conflict resolution. These lead to classroom group discussion. Because many stories involve a moral problem or conflict to overcome, it is not difficult to find positive models of character's actions, words, and behaviors. The author recommends selecting books

- with well-defined dilemmas.
- with characters who model levels of reasoning readily understood or slightly above those of the child group audience.
- that suggest a variety of appropriate follow-up activities.
- of high quality with powerful plots, lively characters, and a satisfying conclusion.
- that portray clear and logical consequences.
- that promote critical thinking skills.
- that have characters who embody a wide variety and mixture of physical, social, and emotional features and show a balanced representation of morals considered good and evil.

BIBLIOTHERAPY

Bibliotherapy, literally translated, means book therapy. Teachers, at times, may seek to help children with life problems, questions, fears, and pain. Some professionals believe that books can help children cope with emotional concerns. At some point during childhood, children may deal with rejection by friends, ambivalence toward a new baby, divorce, grief, or death, along with other strong emotions.

Fairy tales can reveal the existence of strife and calamity in a form that permits children to deal with these situations without trauma. These tales can be shared in a reassuring, supportive setting that provides a therapeutic experience. A small sampling of books considered to be therapeutic in nature follows.

Alexander, M. (1971). *Nobody ever asked me if I wanted a baby sister.* New York: Dial. (Jealousy.)

Blegvad, L. (1985). *Banana and me.* New York: Margaret K. McElderry Books. (Fear.)

Gershator, P. (2004). *The babysitter sings.* New York: Henry Holt. (Separation.)

Greenfield, E. (1994). *Sweet baby coming.* New York: HarperCollins. (Birth of a sibling.)

Hazen, B. S. (1987). *Fang.* New York: Atheneum. (Bravery.)

Le Tord, B. (1987). *My Grandma Leonie.* New York: Bradbury Press. (Death.)

Mayer, M. (1968). *There's a nightmare in my closet.* New York: Dial. (Fear.)

Parr, T. (2001). *It's okay to be different.* Boston: Little Brown. (Rejection.)

Viorst, J. (1973). *The tenth good thing about Barney.* New York: Atheneum. (Death of a pet.)

READING BOOKS TO YOUNG CHILDREN

Teachers read books in both indoor and outdoor settings, to one child or to many. Koralek (2007) suggests that teachers look beyond the library corner as the only place to display, share, and read books with young children. Books can be linked to all areas of the curriculum, she feels. Her recommendations include carrying books outdoors, placing them near discovery tables, and displaying them alongside dress-up clothes. Other suggested areas are block areas, housekeeping areas, window seats where natural outdoor settings can be viewed, theme and display areas, and room settings where counting or number concepts are explored. Other room areas with comfortable seating should not be overlooked.

Teachers need to assess their ability to make books and book-reading times exciting and personally relevant and rewarding to each young child. In successful classrooms, observable child behaviors include eager attendance at book-reading times, joyous participation, active dialogue, and self-selected investigation and time spent in the classroom library.

How the teacher achieves this is critical. Most of us have seen well-meaning adults use reading techniques that are questionable and defeat the adult's purpose in reading. Your goals should include making reading aloud times an activity of intrinsic interest to the children, adding to children's comprehension of the world, and stimulating children's imagination. Some educators encourage the storybook reader to make comments and ask questions during the reading experience to increase child comprehension. Others believe maintaining the flow and tempo of the story to be paramount so that the story's literary quality remains intact. The first story readers might query factual details, child opinions, or during the reading ask children to infer, label, evaluate, summarize, elaborate, and predict. They might also make comments that point out, explain, or build bridges to children's experiences during story reading. While others, following the second method, would instead save teacher comments and questions for an after-story discussion. A beginning teacher can attempt to ascertain if either approach is at work at their center. Or perhaps both approaches are used or the center has its own unique approach to reading aloud.

The burden of making reading interesting falls on the teacher. A teacher must also strive to make the book's content relevant to each child. This means relating and connecting story elements to children's lives and their past experiences whenever possible. This can be likened to building a bridge to the world of books—a bridge that children will be eager to cross because books are pleasurable and emotionally satisfying. Building these positive attitudes takes skill. A step-by-step outline is helpful in conducting group story times.

Step 1. *Think about the age, interests, and special interests of the child group and consider the selection criteria mentioned in this chapter.* If you are required to write a lesson plan for sharing a particular book, identify possible unfamiliar vocabulary and what child comprehension goals you are planning to achieve. Read the book to yourself enough times to develop a feeling for characters and the story line. Practice dialogue so that it will roll smoothly. For example, you might not be able to read *The House That Jack Built* unless you have practiced the incremental refrain. In other words, analyze, select, practice, and prepare.

Step 2. *Arrange a setting with the children's and teacher's comfort in mind.* The illustrations should be at children's eye level, and the teacher should face the audience as she speaks. A setting should provide comfortable seating while the book is being read. Some teachers prefer small chairs for both children and teachers; others prefer rug areas. Avoid traffic paths and noise interruptions by finding a quiet spot in the classroom. Cutting down visual distractions may mean using room dividers, curtains, or furniture arrangements.

Preschoolers who are read to in small groups make greater language gains than when they are read to in larger groups. Some classrooms use "instant replays" of storybook readings when adult supervision affects group size.

Step 3. *Make a motivational introductory statement.* The statement should create a desire to listen or encourage listening: "There's a boy in this book who wants to give his mother a birthday present"; "Monkeys can be funny, and they are funny in this book"; "Have you ever wondered where animals go at night to sleep?"; "On the last page of this book is a picture of a friendly monster." Then briefly introduce the author and illustrator.

Step 4. *Hold the book to either your left or right side.* With your hand in place, make both sides of the page visible. Keep the book at the children's eye level.

Step 5. *Begin reading.* Try to glance at the sentences and turn to meet the children's eyes as often as possible so that your voice goes to the children. Also watch for children's body reactions including facial expressions, and try to ascertain whether children are engaged and understanding or have quizzical looks. Speak clearly with adequate volume, using a rate of speed that enables the children to both look at illustrations and hear what you are reading. Enjoy the story with the children by being enthusiastic. Dramatize and emphasize key parts of the story but not to the degree that the children are watching you and not the book. Change your voice to suit the characters, if you feel comfortable doing so. A good story will hold attention and often stimulate comments or questions. Savor it and deliver each word. Try not to rush unless it adds to the drama in places.

Step 6. *Answer and discuss questions approvingly, and if necessary or prudent increase child interaction by guessing about or labeling character actions.* If you feel that interruptions are decreasing the enjoyment for other children, ask a child to wait until the end when you will be glad to discuss it. Then do it. If, on the other hand, most of the group is interested, take the time to discuss an idea, but be careful to resist the temptation of making a lengthy comment that will disrupt the story. Sometimes, children suck their thumbs or act sleepy during reading times. They seem to connect books with bedtime; many parents read to their children at this time. By watching closely while reading, you will be able to tell whether you still have the children's attention. You can sometimes draw a child back to the book with a direct question like, "Debbie, can you see the cat's tail?" or by increasing your animation or varying voice volume. Wondering out loud about what might happen next may help.

Step 7. *You may want to ask a few open-ended discussion questions at the end of the book.* Keep them spontaneous and natural—avoid testing questions. Questions can clear up ideas, encourage use of vocabulary words, and pinpoint parts that were especially enjoyed. "Does anyone have a question about the fire truck?" You will have to decide whether to read more than one book at one time. It helps to remember how long the group of children can sit before getting restless. Story times should end on an enthusiastic note, with the children looking forward to another story. Some books may end on such a satisfying or thoughtful note that discussion clearly is not appropriate; a short pause of silence seems more in order. Other times, there may be a barrage of child comments and lively discussion.

Many children's comments incorporate the story into their own personal vision of things and indicate that the text has meaning for them. Personal meanings are confirmed, extended, and refined as children share their interpretations with others. The focus in after-book discussions is on meaning, and the goal is to "make sense of the text."

Judging oneself on the ability to capture and hold children's attention during group reading times is critical. Many factors can account for children's attention wandering, so analyze what can or did interfere with classroom focus. Factors to consider include group size, seating comfort, temperature, the way the light shines on the book, the child who cannot sit next to a friend without talking or touching, and so on, and, of course, the teacher's presentation skills. One teacher who hated distractions created a sign that read, "Story time; please wait to enter our room." The book itself may also need closer scrutiny.

Independent Reading

Teachers should examine daily programs to ensure that children have time to pursue favorite books and new selections (Figure 9–10). It is ridiculous to motivate then not allow self-selection or time for children to spend looking at and examining introduced books page by page at their own pace.

Additional Book-Reading Tips

◆ Check to make sure all of the children have a clear view of the book before beginning.

◆ Watch for combinations of children sitting side-by-side that may cause either child

FIGURE 9–10 There should be plenty of time to enjoy books with a friend.

to be distracted. Rearrange seating before starting.

◆ Pause a short while to allow children to focus at the start.

◆ If one child seems to be unable to concentrate, a teacher can quietly suggest an alternative activity to the child. Clear understanding of alternatives or lack of them needs to be established with the entire staff.

◆ If one points to or makes references to print on a page occasionally, children will take notice, make more comments about print, and ask questions about it more frequently (Ezell & Justice, 2000).

◆ Moving a distracted child closer to the book, or onto a teacher's lap, sometimes works to improve attention.

◆ When an outside distraction occurs, recapture attention and make a transitional statement leading back to the story: "We all heard that loud noise. There's a different noise made by the steam shovel in our story. Listen and you'll hear the steam shovel's noise."

◆ Personalize books when appropriate: "Have you lost something and not been able to find it?"

◆ Skip ahead in books, when the book can obviously not maintain interest, by quickly reading pictures and concluding the experience. It is a good idea to have a backup selection close by.

◆ Children often want to handle a book just read. Make a quick waiting list for all who wish to go over the book by themselves.

◆ Plan reading sessions at relaxed rather than rushed or hectic times of day.

◆ Handle books gently and carefully.

◆ At times when a new word with multiple syllables appears, repeat it, emphasizing syllables. Clap word syllables such as *festival* (fes-ti-val) and *interpreter* (in-ter-preter). This technique is primarily used with children nearing kindergarten age.

◆ Remember it is not so much what you are reading but how you read it.

◆ Choose material to suit yourself as well as the group. Select a story type that you like.

◆ Lower or raise your voice and quicken or slow your pace as appropriate to the text. Lengthen your dramatic pauses, and let your listeners savor the words and ideas.

◆ Introduce vocabulary words associated with the book sharing experience—*cover, title, author, illustrator, front, first page, beginning, print, middle, ending, turn, words, pictures, last page, ending, back cover.*

◆ Read a book a child has brought to school before you read it aloud to children. Share suitable "parts" only if necessary.

◆ Handle a child comment such as, "I've heard it before," with a recognizing comment such as, "Don't tell how it ends" or "See if you see something different this time."

Clarifying the Act of Reading

Teachout and Bright (2007) have developed a way to promote children's ideas about the act of reading a book based on the work of Kibby (2005). The approach is a "think out loud" technique (reading the illustrations) involving nine steps. It can be used with children who have little or no acquaintance with picture books or those with wider experience. The nine steps attempt to "walk" children through a teacher-led book-reading session with a familiar book. The nine steps follow.

1. Explain that children can read the story even if they are not sure what the print says.

2. Choose a story the class is familiar with and reread it.

3. Begin by "reading" the pictures, describing in simple words what you see. Use your knowledge of the storyline and the visual clues in the illustrations to explain slowly what is happening. Read one page at a time, stopping to allow the children to absorb your comments.

4. Be extremely transparent in your thoughts. Explain your thought process as you study each page.

5. Call on a child who can read independently to read a page after you have (picture) read three or four pages.

6. Continue allowing successful and non-successful readers to participate.

7. Ask questions to help children who get stuck, directing them to the visual clues on the page.

8. Build on responses. Often, our children answer questions with short phrases.

9. Follow up with more lessons on reading the pictures. Continue the lessons reading the illustrations until children are comfortable with the routine of reading.*

*From Teachout, C., & Bright, A. (2007). Teachers on teaching: Reading the pictures. A missing piece of the literacy puzzle. *Young Children, 62*(4):106–107. Copyright © 2007 NAEYC. Used with permission from the National Association for the Education of Young Children.

Teachout and Bright work with pre-kindergartners in a class where 59 percent of the children are English language learners. For the fifth item in the previous list, you may not have a preschooler who reads independently in your group but reading the pictures can still be instructionally developmentally appropriate. Figure 9–11 lists other book features a teacher can introduce and discuss.

Teachers who want to enhance children's understanding of a book's story line can elicit children's ideas about what might happen in a new book. Focusing on the book's cover and showing a few select interior illustrations aid children's predictions.

The teacher prints these child suggestions on chart paper, labeling each comment with the child's name. An after-book discussion can return to children's predictions. Each suggestion is given merit as another possible story

POSSIBLE FEATURES	TEACHER TALK
cover	"The front of this book is called the cover. It tells us something about who will be in our story."
print	"These marks say the names of the two authors who wrote the story—Justin Richardson and Peter Parnell."
illustrator	"Here is the name of the man who drew the pictures—Henry Cole." (underline name with hand) "Pictures in a book are called illustrations."
title	"*And Tango Makes Three* is the book's title." (pointing)
page	"We turn one page at a time. On the first and second pages we see an illustration of where the story takes place."
first word and its location	"The first word on this page begins the story. It is the word *In* and starts with a capital I". (In this particular book the "I" is larger and darker than the other print on the page.)
last word and punctuation	"The last word in our story is *sleep*, and it has a small dot after it. This is called a *period*."
back cover	"This book's back cover has an illustration with lots of penguins. Some storybooks in our classroom library might have an illustration on their back covers, but others may not."

Author's note: This figure gives examples of teacher talk that provide children with basic book features. It doesn't recommend that all book features be mentioned whenever a book is shared. But it does describe what is possible. As children age, other features can also be talked about, such as alphabet letters, syllables, spaces between words, similar sounds, rhyming sounds, spellings, and so on.

The example above uses Richardson, J., & Parnell, P. (2005). *And Tango Makes Three.* New York: Simon & Schuster Books for Young Readers (Illustrated by Henry Cole). The example is not an endorsement for the use of this particular book. It is used here as an example.

FIGURE 9–11 Introducing book features.

happening. How close the child's prediction comes to the storybook's plot is not the point.

Many teachers are more interested in building a love of books during preschool years than talking about book characteristics. But others believe that they are able to add to children's knowledge of books without diminishing children's enjoyment. What may preschoolers know about books?

- They contain stories and information.
- They can be read by adults and older children.
- A book has an author, and maybe an illustrator.
- The name of an author is usually printed on the book cover.
- Books have a front and back cover and first page.
- Adults read a page starting at the top left and read horizontally across the line of words.
- The last word on a page is usually printed on the right bottom corner.
- There are spaces between words.
- Words are made of alphabet letters.
- Letters are printed in capitals and small letters.

This is not a complete listing. Some children may know much more, including letter sounds, punctuation marks, and other print features.

Paraphrasing Stories

Paraphrasing means putting an author's text into one's own words, and this is done when some teachers realize the book or some other factor is interfering with children's ability to maintain attention. It brings the book to a speedy conclusion. By tampering with the text, the teacher may interfere with a book's intent, message, and style. Many professionals find this objectionable and urge teachers to read stories exactly as they are written, taking no liberties, respecting the author's original text. Other educators feel that when a book does not hold the interest of

its audience, it should be saved for another time and place, perhaps another group. Some teachers believe that maintaining children's interest and preserving children's positive attitudes about books supersedes objections to occasional paraphrasing.

Targeting Words for Vocabulary Development

A recommended technique used to promote vocabulary development during book-sharing is referred to as targeting. The teacher attempts to ask open-ended questions during a book's rereading, which allows the teacher to determine unfamiliar vocabulary words and then explain them. Explicit explanations are deemed best. Later, purposeful teacher use of the unfamiliar (target) words during daily or weekly activities takes place, therefore providing additional child exposure and deeper word understanding. To do this the teacher needs to guess which words her class may not know beforehand by scanning the book(s) to be shared.

Building Participation

Children love to be part of the telling of a story. Good teachers plan for child participation when choosing stories to read. Often, books are read for the first time, and then immediately reread, with the teacher promoting as much participation as possible. Some books hold children spellbound and usually take many readings before the teacher feels that it is the right time for active involvement other than listening. Listening skills are encouraged when children contribute to read-aloud sessions and become active, participating listeners. Three-year-olds take a while to settle into appropriate and expected story-time behaviors. A young group may hardly enjoy the physical participation opportunities that a teacher plans ahead of time. This is possible if she has recognized portions of the about-to-be-read picture book where children can chime in, make movements or sounds, or in other ways mirror or duplicate something in the story.

Nonfiction books may not provide opportunities for child involvement. Examining them closely may give the teacher ideas for children's active participation. Many of the benefits young children derive from adult-child readings come through adult reading strategies such as prompting responses, modeling responses for them to copy, asking children to relate responses to real experiences, asking questions, and offering positive reinforcement for children's participation.

Following is a list of additional ways to promote child participation and active listening.

◆ Invite children to speak a familiar character's dialogue or book sounds. This is easily done in repeated sequences: "I don't care," said Pierre.

◆ Pantomime actions: "Let's knock on the door."

◆ Use closure: "The cup fell on the . . ." (floor). When using closure, if children end the statement differently, try saying "It could have fallen on the rug, but the cup in the story fell on the floor."

◆ Predict outcomes: "Do you think Hector will open the box?"

◆ Ask opinions: "What's your favorite pie?"

◆ Recall previous story parts: "What did Mr. Bear say to Petra?"

◆ Probe related experiences: "Emil, isn't your dog's name Clifford?"

◆ Dramatize enjoyed parts or wholes.

Younger preschoolers, as a rule, find sitting without active motor and/or verbal involvement more demanding than older children.

Sharing Your Thoughts

A strategy suggested by Dori (2007) for use with preschoolers and kindergartners involves thinking aloud during read-alouds and during other teaching moments.

> When teachers think aloud, they stop whatever is going on and signal in some way (for example, I point to my head) that their next words will describe

> thoughts that normally are not spoken aloud. Then they talk through their thought processes. (p.101)

And Dori describes the results:

> It's easy to see the effectiveness of think-alouds, because the children's voices begin to chime in as they add their own ideas to the adult's thinking. (p. 103)

Two teaching goals promoted by using this strategy are (1) encouraging children's self-initiated active thinking and (2) encouraging metacognition, the act of thinking about one's own thinking. At kindergarten level, it also helps to create thoughtful readers.

Reading to Individual Children

Teachers without aides and/or volunteers in their classroom may never have undivided time to share books with individual children. One-on-one readings can be the most beneficial and literacy-developing times of all. The dialogue and the personalized attention exceeds what is possible in group readings. In large groups, some children are reluctant to speak and consequently receive less appreciation and feedback. (Small groups are recommended.)

Busy families tend to rely on schools to offer books. Many centers have been clever in promoting home reading. Bulletin boards, lending arrangements, and mandating family classroom volunteering are among the most common tactics.

It is not the simple "I-read-you-listen" type of adult-child interaction with books that really counts. It is the wide-ranging verbal dialogue the adult permits and encourages that gives children their best opportunity to construct a full knowledge of how people use books. Schools consequently include and share reading techniques in their communications with parents.

Teachers plan times to be in the classroom's book center, book corner, library, or book-reading area (whatever it is called). A teacher's presence models interest and allows for individual child readings, questions, and interactions other than at planned group book times.

Rereading Stories

It never ceases to amaze teachers and families when preschoolers beg to hear a book read over and over. Beginning teachers take this statement to mean that they have done a good job, and even veteran teachers confess it still feels good. A teacher who can read the same book over and over again with believable enthusiasm, as if it were his first delighted reading, has admirable technique and dedication. Children often ask to have stories reread because, by knowing what comes next, they feel competent, or they simply want to stretch out what is enjoyable. The decisions that teachers make about fulfilling the request depend on many factors, including class schedules and children's lack of capacity to sit through a second reading (despite their expressed desire to hear it). It is suggested that books be reread often and that teacher statements such as, "I'd like to read it again, but . . ." are followed by statements such as, "After lunch, I'll be under the tree in the yard, if you want to hear the story again."

Requests to "read it again" arise as a natural developmental demand of high significance and an integral part of book exposure. The child's behavior alerts adults to which books hold and preoccupy them. Teachers can think of the behavior as children selecting their own course of study. Multiple copies of favorite books and fresh, new books that extend individual children's "course of study" are provided by alert teachers.

A curious response occurred when the same storybooks were read and reread to 4-year-olds. The researchers attempted to identify the consequences of rereading familiar and enjoyed stories. Children in the study made more detailed comments centering on characters, events, titles, story themes, settings, and the book's language with rereadings. Other results suggest that as children understand particular aspects of stories (gained through numerous rereadings), they shift focus and attend to additional story dimensions overlooked in initial readings.

Early childhood educators with any experience have met children who want to "read" to teachers or peers. Teachers often smile, hypothesizing that the child is using rote memory, but often find that the child is telling his own version of the story. Researchers suggest this indicates a child has displayed a deep understanding and response to the story's meaning.

Teachers decide to introduce books with objects or other visuals for a number of reasons. A chef's hat worn by a teacher certainly gets attention and may motivate a group to hear more about the chef in the picture book. A head of lettuce or horseshoe may clarify some feature of a story. The possibilities are almost limitless. Currently, with the popularity of theme or unit approaches to instruction, a picture book may expand or elaborate a field of study or topic that has already been introduced. If so, some new feature mentioned in a book may be emphasized by using a visual.

When the teacher wears an article of clothing, such as the hat mentioned previously, it may help him get into character. Because children like to act out story lines or scenes, items that help promote this activity can be introduced at the end of the story. Previewing a picture book may make it easier to find an object or person who could add to the storytelling experience.

A teacher at one center wanted to enlarge illustrations in a book that was a classroom favorite. She first used an overhead projector and outlined the enlarged figures on chart paper. She displayed these as she read the book. The experience was enjoyed, and she found posting the enlarged characters around the room drew child interest. Another favorite book was photographed and made into slides. The teacher darkened the lights and read by flashlight while projecting the book's pages. This held the children spellbound, and one child asked if they could "go to the movies" again.

AFTER-READING DISCUSSIONS

How soon after a story is read should discussion, which promotes comprehension of stories, take place? It is obvious that a discussion might ruin the afterglow that occurs after certain books are shared. Teachers are sometimes understandably reluctant to mar the magic of the moment.

The teacher's role during storybook readings is to act as a "mediator" who assists children in two ways: (1) by helping them learn to take knowledge they had gained outside of book-reading experience and use this knowledge to understand the text and (2) by helping them apply the meanings and messages gained from books to their own lives.

Teachers often wonder what type of questions to ask to stimulate book discussions. Open-ended questions work well: "What do you think Asam should do?" "How would you try to find the lost shoe?" "In what ways are your toys different from Ling's toys?" Questions concerning how children feel about book features are helpful. Inviting children's responses and reacting with close accepting listening is suggested. The teacher who conjectures, connects, appreciates, muses, challenges, and questions shows the child how the mature responder interacts with text.

Looking closely at picture books, teachers will find they have a

◆ beginning, which introduces a setting, characters, and a place.

◆ desired goal or outcome or problem.

◆ series of happenings working toward an accomplishment or satisfactory solution often discovered by the main character.

◆ resolution or attainment of a goal.

Understanding this sequence gives hints to pertinent features teachers can probe in after-book discussions that have much more educational value than "What was the dog's name?" or "Did you like the story?" Teachers build on what children say rather than trying to impart or transmit information. What can early childhood teachers expect when children make comments or have questions after book reading?

◆ Ezell and Justice (2000) suggest that book illustrations or book concepts account for approximately 95 percent of children's comments during shared readings. Children's questions about meaning can be less common, and their questions about alphabet letters, words, or letter sounds are infrequent, as are questions concerning the author, illustrator, title, or book's format.

The teacher's focus in asking questions in an after-book discussion is not to check children's knowledge but rather to learn from the child. A preschool teacher's story-reading discussions can be described as negotiated, unfocused interactions in which teachers become aware of the "sense making" children express. The process depends on what children say about their confusions and interpretations and what they understand, together with the teacher's response to the meaning the group seemed to make of the story. Teachers do revisit newly introduced vocabulary words or areas of the book to see if comprehension goals were achieved.

Early childhood teachers could at times consider asking questions that draw attention to major elements of characterization and plot and the moral or deeper implications of a story, if appropriate. The solution that many teachers favor is to wait until children seem eager to comment, discuss, and perhaps disagree, and only then act as a guide to further comprehension. Teachers hope children will think out loud, sharing their ideas with the discussion group. All present are given the opportunity to respond or add comments and cite personal experiences. Teachers using after-book discussions believe book content, word meanings, and ideas are best remembered if talked about.

Some centers designate a time after a story is read as "story time talk." It is described as a time when children's ideas are recorded by the teacher on a "language chart" made of chart paper or butcher paper. This activity gives importance to children's ideas. Writing the children's names by their contributions affords additional status. Children's art related to the book can be appended. Other schools make basket collections of inexpensive small plastic (or other material) figures of story characters, animals, houses, story objects, and so on, to go along with a book. These are so popular one teacher made home-sewn story dolls for the school basket collection.

Discussions can promote print knowledge and include the idea that books are held in a certain way, and pages are turned from front to back. They learn about beginnings and endings of stories, about title pages, authors, and illustrators. They discover that teachers and other adults read print rather than pictures. Children also acquire concepts about print directionality—in English, print is read from left to right and top to bottom—as well as concepts about letters and words—words are made up of letters and are marked by spaces on either side.

STORY OR BOOK DRAMATIZATION

Some early childhood educators encourage child dramatization of favorite picture books and stories. Young children's recollection of literal story details and their comprehension of story features are enhanced if enactment takes place.

Planning for book enactment means teachers start with simple short stories and display various props, objects, costumes, and so forth, to serve as motivator and "get-into-character" aids. In previewing picture books or oral stories for story times, teachers become accustomed to looking for material with repeated words, sentences, or actions (Figure 9–12). These are

FIGURE 9–12 Reenacting "and Grandma caught Annabella before she could run away" was experienced by this story-time group.

the books or story parts that are easy to learn. In the telling of *The Three Little Pigs*, most children will join in with "then I'll huff, and I'll puff, and I'll blow your house down!" after just a few readings.

PICTURE BOOKS AS THE BASIS FOR THEME INSTRUCTION

Early childhood centers are experimenting with using picture books as the basis for theme program planning. Under this approach to program planning, instruction branches out from the concepts and vocabulary present in the book. Usually, the meaning of the story is emphasized, and a number of different directions of study and activities that are in some way connected to the book are conducted. Eric Carle's *The Very Hungry Caterpillar* is a favorite theme opener.

The classroom setting can be transformed into the cabbage patch that Peter Rabbit was so fond of exploring. Activities such as counting buttons on jackets, singing songs about rabbits or gardens, taking field trips to vegetable gardens, and engaging in science experiences in vegetable growing are a few examples of associated activities. A "Stuffed Toy Animal Day" when children bring their own favorite to class might follow the reading of Frank Asch's picture book *Popcorn*. The book *Fast Food* by Freymann and Effers could initiate a study of restaurants.

Memorable experiences connected to classic books can aid literacy development, and an increasing number of early childhood centers are using this approach.

LITERATURE-BASED CURRICULUM

Literature-based reading instruction swept the nation in the 1980s. Many states at the time either recommended or mandated this elementary school approach. Advocates have described a comprehensive literature program as permeating the curriculum. It includes reading aloud to children, making use of informational books, and encouraging children's response to books using drama, art, and child-dictated writing. Walpole and McKenna (2004) describe a high-quality early childhood program that could easily be called a literacy-based model:

> Teachers read and reread books aloud, interactively. They engage children in shared and guided retellings, and help children to act out their favorite books themselves, including chances for pretend readings of books previously read aloud. They model writing about what is read and about what is important to the life of the class.
>
> These activities together (dramatic play, extended language interaction, and reading and writing) provide an authentic window into authentic introduction of letter names, letter sounds, and early phonemic awareness activities appropriate for very young children. (p. 167)

Can an early childhood teacher implement a "literature-based" language arts program? Most early childhood teachers would answer, "Yes, if activities are developmentally appropriate, literature can permeate program planning, but many educators are also choosing to add new research-based instructional techniques."

FROM BOOKS TO FLANNEL (FELT) BOARDS AND BEYOND

Teachers find that a number of books can be made into flannel board stories relatively easily; Chapter 12 is devoted to these activities. Five books that are particular favorites have been adapted for flannel-board presentation. These follow.

◆ *The Very Hungry Caterpillar* by Eric Carle
◆ *The Carrot Seed* by Ruth Krauss
◆ *Johnny and His Drum* by Maggie Duff

◆ *My Five Senses* by Aliki
◆ *Brown Bear, Brown Bear, What Do You See?* by William Martin

Books often open the door to additional instruction with activities or games on the same subject or theme. Whole units of instruction on bears, airplanes, families, and many other topics are possible.

Teachers have attempted to advertise particular books in creative ways. Enlarged book characters might be displayed, or displays of the book of the week or book of the day may be placed in a special spot in a classroom. An attending child's family member may be a special story-time book reader. During a morning greeting to children, a teacher might say, "I have a new book in my lap. See the cover," so she can create excitement for story time.

LIBRARY SKILLS AND RESOURCES

A visit to the local library is often planned for preschoolers. Librarian-presented story hours often result in the children's awareness of the library as a resource. Selecting and checking out one's choice can be an exciting and important milestone. Most early childhood centers also do their best to encourage this family-child activity.

Many libraries have well-developed collections and enthusiastic and creative children's librarians who plan a number of activities to promote literacy. Along with books, you may find computers, language-development computer programs, audio and video CDs, records, book and electronic media combinations, slides, films, children's encyclopedias, foreign language editions, pamphlet collections, puzzles, and other language-related materials and machines.

Finding out more about the authors of children's books can help provide teachers with added insights and background data. One goal of language arts instruction should be to alert children to the idea that books are created by real people. Most children find a photograph of an author or illustrator interesting, as well as stories concerning an author's childhood or reasons for writing a particular picture book.

Becoming more familiar with authors such as Margaret Wise Brown, often called the "Laureate of the Nursery," helps a reader appreciate the simplicity, directness, humor, and the sense of the importance of life that are found in her writings.

Websites that give information about children's book authors and illustrators are helpful, and librarians can guide you to books with autobiographical and biographical information.

Some early childhood centers set up author displays, celebrate author/illustrator birthdays, and encourage visiting authors and illustrators. Letters to authors might be written with child input.

A teacher who has done some reading and wants to mention or quote the children's favorite authors might use items such as the following, which were found in library sources.

◆ Steven Kellogg, author/illustrator of *Can I Keep Him?* "I particularly loved [as a child] drawing animals and birds." (*Fourth Book of Junior Authors and Illustrators*)

◆ Mitsumasa Anno, author/illustrator of *Anno's Alphabet,* "The imaginative eye is the source of all the books I have made for children." (*Fourth Book of Junior Authors and Illustrators*)

◆ Eric Carle, author/illustrator of *The Very Hungry Caterpillar,* "I remember large sheets of paper, colorful paints and big brushes" (speaking of childhood). (*Authors and Illustrators of Children's Books*)

◆ Leo Lionni, author/illustrator of *Little Blue and Little Yellow,* "I like to write about birds because I have birds at home: parrots, pigeons, chickens and finches." (*Authors and Illustrators of Children's Books*)

CHILD- AND TEACHER-AUTHORED BOOKS

Books authored by children or their teachers have many values. They

◆ promote interest in the classroom book collection.

◆ help children see connections between spoken and written words.

◆ contain material based on child and teacher interests.

◆ personalize book reading.

◆ prompt self-expression.

◆ stimulate creativity.

◆ build feelings of competence and self-worth.

Hostetler (2000) describes child-authored books in her classroom.

> The children in my class who are four and five years old love to dictate text and illustrate the pictures for our handmade books. These books become treasures.
>
> The first book the children usually write is about our field trip to the farm. Upon our return from this outing, we encourage the children to each describe something they saw at the farm. Then we add photographs to their transcribed words. (p. 30)

She suggests creating a group-produced classroom book in which each child has a page. The teacher suggests a focal point subject such as something the children would like to have in their pocket or mom's or dad's work. Another idea is to ask older 4-year-olds who will be going to kindergarten soon to help make a book for children coming into their 4-year-olds' classroom. The book will give the new children advice about the good things that might happen at preschool, how to play with others, and so on. Many teachers make an alphabet book as an ongoing class project. When too many "A" pages are collected, a separate "A" book is developed.

If a child-authored book is one of the school's books, the book corner becomes a place where the child's accomplishment is exhibited. Teachers can alert the entire group to new book titles as the books arrive and make a point to describe them before they are put on the shelves.

Child-made books require teacher preparation and help. A variety of shapes and sizes (Figure 9–13) add interest and motivation. Covers made of wallpaper or contact paper over cardboard are durable. The pages of the

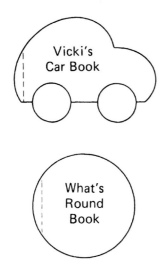

FIGURE 9–13 Book shapes.

BOOKBINDING

One stitch on outside fold.

Two stitches on inside fold.

Masking tape with adhesive facing cover boards.

FIGURE 9–14 One way to bind pages.

books combine child art and child-dictated words, usually on lined printscript paper, or print is enlarged with computer help. Staples, rings, yarn (string), or brads can bind pages together (Figure 9–14). Child dictation is taken word for word with no teacher editing.

The following book, dictated by a 4-year-old, illustrates one child's authorship.

THE WINDOW

Page 1: Once upon a time the little girl was looking out the window.

Page 2: Child's art

Page 3: And the flowers were showing.

Page 4: Child's art

Page 5: And the water was flushing down and she did not know it.

Page 6: Child's art

Teacher-authored books can share a teacher's creativity and individuality. Favorite themes and enjoyed experiences can be repeatedly relived. Books containing the children's, teachers', staff's, parents', or school pets' names are popular. Photographs of familiar school, neighborhood, or family settings are great conversation stimulators. Field trips and special occasions can be captured in book form.

Resources for motivating early childhood teachers to write children's books follow. Some provide insights written by commercially successful children's picture-book authors.

Dahl, K. L. (Ed.). (1990). *Teacher as writer.* Urbana, IL: National Council of Teachers of English.

Holm, K. C. (Ed.). (2008). *Writer's market.* Cincinnati: Writer's Digest Books.

Kovacs, D., & Preller, J. (1993). *Meet the authors and illustrators: 60 creators of favorite children's books talk about their work.* New York: Scholastic Professional Books.

Some educators suggest using what they call caption books with young children. Their caption books carefully place the print at the top left of the page; include photographs that give clues to the print message on the same page; and use short, meaningful sentences that repeat on succeeding pages. These writers also suggest teacher-made books that record nature walks, seasonal events, and holiday celebrations. Urging children to illustrate their favorite stories with their own art is recommended.

Group authorship is another idea. Books in which every child has contributed one or more pages are enjoyable projects and discoveries.

BOOK AREAS AND CENTERS

Classrooms with inviting book storage areas beckon curious browsers. Teachers have become exceptionally clever at devising eye-catching, comfortable, well-lighted, inviting, visually stimulating book-browsing classroom areas.

If an educator is trying to attract children to the book collection or book display area, thought and effort may be necessary to sell the "look-at-books" activity. Use your creativity and use what is at hand, whether it be a sunny interior wall, a tabletop, an old bookcase, or an unused corner.

Thematic and seasonal displays, potted plants, spotlights, and lamps have been used to lure children. Displays in or near the book center can broadcast, lure, shout, reach out, and grab the eyes and ears of passersby, forcing them to stop and pay attention.

Books should be at the child's eye level with book front covers in sight. Book-jacket wall displays and life-size book characters (drawings made by using overhead projectors to increase size then tracing on large sheets of paper) have their own appeal. Comfort and color attract. Softly textured rugs and pillows, comfortable seating, and sprawling spaces prolong time spent in book areas. Low round tables and plump pillows used as seating can also be inviting. Quiet, private spaces that are shielded from outside distractions and sounds and that have good lighting increase the child's ability to stay focused. Hideaways where friends can escape together and experience a book that has captured their attention are ideal.

Guidelines that outline the rules and responsibilities of book handling should be developed by the school. Rules should be designed to encourage children to return books to shelves, turn pages carefully, and respect the quietness of the area. Well-defined boundaries of library centers help books stay put. Teachers should promote the idea that using the area is a privilege and should monitor book centers frequently when younger preschoolers, who may have had little past experience with book collections and libraries, enter the area.

What kind of collection should a well-stocked classroom library center have? Collections often reflect a school's budget and priorities. The purchase of classroom favorites and classics should be the first priority; after that, a well-rounded collection that includes a lot of different topics and categories is recommended. Some centers prize nonfiction books, and consequently, these comprise a large percentage of their class library collection. Their goal is to offer more reality and informational resources as well as fiction that expands and extends children's interests.

Rotating books by removing and storing some books from time to time and providing a different, previously stored set of books will make the area more interesting. Some centers categorize and store related books together and label them with a sign, identified picture, or drawing (such as animals, trains, things that are blue, and so on). Library books supplement the school's collection and may have special classroom-handling rules. Seasonal and holiday books are provided when possible. Paperbacks round out some collections, and multiple copies are considered for younger preschoolers' classrooms. Constant book repair is necessary in most classrooms because of heavy use. A classroom "Book Hospital" box reflects teachers' concern and esteem for books.

Teachers should browse in book centers, modeling both interest and enthusiasm when time and supervision duties permit. It is sad to think of curious children wandering into the book area, selecting a book, trying to grasp meaning from illustrations, wondering how teachers find a story within, and giving up after studying the book closely. Many teachers set up a system so that the story (or nonfiction) can be heard by using an "I-want-to-know-about-this-book" box. Children's name cards are adjacent. The child can select his book, slip his card inside, and place the card in the box. Younger children can find a name card with their picture and do the same. This system works well only if the staff finds the time to share the child-chosen book.

Group Settings

Most classrooms have areas suitable for picture-book reading in groups, besides areas for individual, self-selected browsing and places where children can be in the company of a few others. If these areas are not available, staff members can create them. The reading area should be comfortable and well lit and as far removed from interruptions and distractions as possible. Generally, lighting that comes from behind the children is preferred. Intense, bright light coming from behind the book can make it hard to see. During group readings, one center put a floor lamp in the reading area and dimmed the overhead lights. This setup worked well to cut distractions and focus the group on the reading. Another teacher brought a large packing case into the classroom with a light inside, added comfortable pillows, made a door, and called it the "Reading Box." A large, horseshoe-shaped floor pillow can increase child comfort. Many centers use small carpet sample squares for comfort and to outline individual space.

The number of children in groups is an important consideration; as the size of the group increases, intimacy, the child's ease of viewing, and the teacher's ability to be physically close and respond to each child decrease (Figure 9–15). The ideal group size for story time ranges from 5 to 10 children. Unfortunately, staffing ratios may mandate a much larger group size. Some early childhood centers do "instant replays"—they have many small reading groups in succession, rather than large group reading sessions.

Most centers have developed rules about what behavior is expected from the child, whether the child chooses either to come or not come to a book-reading time, and whether a child can leave before the book's end. If the staff decides to give children a choice, usually the rule is stated thusly, "You need to find a quiet activity inside our classroom until story time is over."

Care and Storage of Books

By setting an example and making clear statements about handling books, the teacher can help children form good book-care habits. However, with time and use, even the sturdiest books will show wear.

Teachers are quick to show their sadness when a favorite book is torn, crayoned, or used as a building block. Some classrooms have signs reading "Books Are Friends—Handle with Care" or "Books are for looking, talking about, and sharing." Teachers are careful to verbally reward children who turn pages gently and return books to shelves or storage areas.

RESOURCES FOR FINDING READING MATERIALS

Public Libraries

Many libraries have book lists of suggested early childhood editions. Often, seasonal books are together in special displays. Ask the librarian about new books, special services, or resources that include films or slides.

FIGURE 9–15 Group size is an important consideration.

Children's Book Stores and Toy Stores

Many stores carry popular new and older titles. Some stock over 15,000 titles.

Teacher Supply Houses and School Supply Stores

Often, a wide selection is stocked, sometimes at school discount prices.

Children's Book Publishers

Catalogs listing new titles, with summaries of contents, are available for the asking.

Book Clubs

Book clubs offer monthly selections of a wide variety of titles. These clubs usually reward schools with free books and teacher gifts that include posters and teaching visuals. Enough order forms for each child's parents are sent on a monthly basis. This offers parents an easy way to order books for their children by having school personnel send and receive orders.

Children's Periodicals

A helpful reference book that describes and evaluates nearly 90 children's magazines is *Magazines for Children: A Guide for Parents, Teachers and Librarians* by Selma Richardson, published by the American Library Association.

Book Week

The Children's Book Council has sponsored National Children's Book Week since 1945 to promote reading and encourage children's enjoyment of books. Mobiles, materials, posters, bookmarks, and book-week kits can be ordered from The Children's Book Council Inc., 12 West 37th Street, 2nd Floor, New York, NY 10018.

Book Services to Families—School Lending Libraries

Preschools that have overnight and weekend book-borrowing privileges promote book use and home enjoyment of books. Manila folders or envelopes, preprinted with the center's name, protect books in transit. Book pockets and cards are available at stationery or school-supply stores. This service can operate with minimal teacher supervision. Parents can help their children pull cards on selected titles if they thoroughly understand the school's system and rules for book borrowing.

FAVORITE CHILDREN'S BOOKS

Generally, children's favorites become your favorites. There is really only one way to develop your own list. Preview books and then try them with children. The Additional Resources section at the chapter's end provides a list of books that are young children's favorites. You can help children learn the value of reading first by falling in love with picture books yourself and then by developing your repertoire for sharing that enjoyment with children.

FAMILY INFLUENCES ON CHILDREN'S READING-LIKE BEHAVIORS

Family influences on the attitudes young children hold about books and book-reading times must be considered. When a first book-reading time is announced, a newly enrolled child's behavior can reflect past experience.

Book reading by families usually starts in infancy, with parents setting up a social reading routine. Physical closeness, comfortable seating, and lighting set the stage; the parent acts as if the child and parent are taking part in a two-part dialogue. The family acknowledges the child's earliest responses, such as looking, pointing, producing vocal imitations of adult speech, turning pages, and so on. The adult may speak for the child, "What's this? A ball, right, that's a ball." As the child responds, the adult subtly asks for more and accepts all attempts. More and more interaction and responsibility for the child's role as a partner in the "reading to" routine is experienced as the child develops. Some adults encourage verbalization and adjust their speech to their child's increasing evolvement and ability. The child experiencing many adult-to-child readings learns what is expected, when to talk, when to

listen, when to turn pages, how to answer adult questions, whether to join in with actions or words, whether to ask questions, and so on.

Many young children have developed a liking for books through being read to regularly from very early in their lives. If so, children soon begin to demonstrate their growing enjoyment of the experience. Their attention span increases, their repertoire of favorite stories expands, and they begin asking that favorites be read over and over. Their avid listening to stories in the secure and close proximity of a loved adult becomes a deeply rewarding human experience.

When a powerful inner drive to want to learn and a natural aptitude for learning are coupled with families who not only select highly predicable stories to read to their children, but who also read in a way that invites children to participate, then learning to reproduce stories through reading-like behavior becomes a relatively simple process. This learning becomes even easier when it is permitted to operate in a non-corrective no-fail environment where children are encouraged to experiment and approximate in their attempts to "read." When these home conditions prevail, children have the opportunity to take the initiative and direct their own learning.

These family techniques are also used effectively by teachers, especially when reading with very small groups or in one-to-one classroom reading situations. Especially useful techniques include the following:

◆ a non-corrective, no-fail environment
◆ invited child participation
◆ encouragement of the child to experiment and approximate in his attempts to "read"
◆ selected books are predictive ones

Reading-like child behavior can include "reading" the book to self or others; mumbling words while paging through a book; joining in with the parent on select pages, passages, and/or book character's verbalizations; offering rhyming and repetitive guesses during an adult reading; and echoing by "reading" slightly behind the adult. Children may also embellish or deviate from a known familiar story, and then return to the original text.

Reading-like behavior called *completion reading* occurs when a reader pauses and the child completes the sentence or story. Families seem to know intuitively where to pause in order to invite their children to complete a sentence or phrase.

Reading-like behavior may include early child knowledge of print. Adults may have pointed to print in picture books, explaining that "it says that here" or "this word is." A family member may move a hand under each word while reading, consequently drawing attention to print. This also gives clues to the direction words are read. An adult may point and ask, "What does this say?" Children also may point to words in books, asking readers the same question. Many young children come to realize that the print in books is significant and connected to what the reader is saying. Some young children actually accomplish the unbelievable feat of the real reading of many words. Others can read simple books and primers before kindergarten.

SUMMARY

The teacher has certain goals when reading books to young children.

◆ promoting child enjoyment and attitude development
◆ acquainting children with quality literature
◆ presenting knowledge
◆ developing children's listening skills
◆ encouraging early literacy (Figure 9–16)

YOUNGER PRESCHOOLER (AGES TWO TO THREE)

- is able to sit and maintain interest while a quality picture book is skillfully read
- is able to browse through a book from cover to cover
- has a favorite book
- points to and talks about objects, people, or features of illustrations when in individual reading sessions
- can name one book character
- brings a book to adults to read
- wants to be present at most book-reading times

- brings a book to school to share
- discusses or acts out story parts at times
- handles book gently
- enjoys library trips
- may point to words or letters
- wants name on his work

OLDER PRESCHOOLER (AGES FOUR TO FIVE)

- obviously enjoys story times
- asks about words
- picks out own name tag
- knows beginning letters of a few words
- wants his ideas and comments written down
- has favorite books and book characters
- can put book events in sequence
- realizes books have beginnings, middles, and endings
- understands authoring
- explains a number of functions of printed words and signs
- asks about the names of letters of his own name
- can tell a book story from memory
- handles and cares for books properly

- discusses and shares books with others
- finds similar letters in different words
- knows spaces exist between words
- recognizes a few words
- tries to decipher words in books
- knows stories in books do not change with rereadings
- is interested in alphabet games, toys, and activities
- tries to copy words or letters from books
- knows alphabet letters represent sounds
- is interested in machines or toys that print words or letters
- wants to make his own book
- knows books have titles and authors
- creates own stories

FIGURE 9–16 Early literacy indicators.

A careful selection of books makes it easier to reach these goals and gives reading activities a greater chance for success. Books vary widely in content and format. Teachers who are prepared can interact with enthusiasm by showing their own enjoyment of language; this helps promote the children's language growth.

Good book-reading technique requires study and practice. Professional interaction is crucial to achieving goals and instilling a love of books.

Settings for group times need to be free of distraction, with optimal comfort and lighting. Book care is expected and modeled by teachers.

ADDITIONAL RESOURCES

Children's Big Books

Crowley, J. (1986). *Mrs. Wishy Washy*. Bothell, WA: Wright Group. (Humorous.)

Hoberman, M. A. (1986*). A house is a house for me*. Ontario: Scholastic-TAB (Rhythm and rhyme.)

O'Donnell, E. L. (1995). *I can't get my turtle to move*. New York: Harcourt Brace School Publishers. (Predictive, colorful, and a drama enactment opportunity.)

Trumbauer, L. (1998). *Sink or float?* Delran, NJ: Newbridge Educational Publishing. (Nonfiction, color photo illustrations.)

Multiethnic and Multicultural Children's Books

Ashley, B. (1991). *Cleversticks*. New York: Crown. (Multiracial class with Chinese-American child who questions his capabilities.)

Bruchac, J., & Ross, G. (1995). *The story of the Milky Way*. New York: Dial Books. (Presents a Cherokee legend with colorful illustrations.)

Buchanan, K. (1994). *This house is made of mud/Esta casa está hecha de lodo*. Flagstaff, AZ: Northland. (In both Spanish and English, poetic language about a home made of mud.)

Caines, J. (1998). *I need a lunch box*. New York: Harper and Row. (Young child in African-American family wishes for a lunch box like his older sister has.)

Carlstrom, N. (1992). *Northern lullaby*. New York: Philomel. (A poetic lullaby set in Alaska featuring native people. For older preschoolers.)

Cave, K. (2003). *One child, one seed: A South African counting book*. New York: Henry Holt.

Chen, C. (2007). *On my way to buy eggs*. New York: Kane/Miller. (Asian tale with an everyday problem that a child solves.)

Child, L. (2000). *I am not sleepy and I will not go to bed*. London: Orchard Books. (A full-of-excuses child and her patient brother.)

Cummings, P. (1991). *Clean your room, Harvey Moon*. New York: Bradbury Press. (African-American family life.)

Dale, P. (1987). *Bet you can't*. Philadelphia: Lippincott. (African-American brother and sister clean room at bedtime.)

Garden, N. (2004). *Molly's family*. New York: Farrar, Straus, and Giroux. (Nontraditional family.)

Garza, C. L. (2005). *Family pictures*. San Francisco: Children's Book Press. (Multicultural families.)

Giovanni, N. (1996). *The genie in the jar*. New York: Holt. (Rhythmic read-aloud with a message of self-esteem and self-discovery.)

Gomi, T. (2001). *I lost my dad*. Brooklyn, NY: Kane/Miller Book Publishers. (A detective story with ethnic characters.)

Greenfield, E. (1991). *I make music*. Inglewood, CA: Black Butterfly Children's Books. (Rhythmic and rhyming, this book encourages young children to join in.)

Greenspun, A. A. (1991). *Daddies*. New York: Philomel. (Photographs of dads and children of diverse cultures.)

Hale, I. (1992). *How I found a friend*. New York: Viking. (Interracial friendship.)

Hamanka, S. (1994). *All the colors of the earth*. New York: Morrow Junior Books. (An exuberant, lovingly illustrated book celebrating the beauty of diverse people.)

Herrera, F. (2000). *The upside down boy*. San Francisco: Children's Book Press. (Adventure and humor.)

Hoffman, M. (1987). *Nancy no-size*. New York: Oxford University Press. (A middle child's self-concept in an urban African-American family is examined.)

Hutchins, P. (1993). *My best friend*. New York: Greenwillow. (Friendship between African-American children.)

Keats, E. J. (1964). *Whistle for Willie*. New York: Viking Press. (A well-known classic featuring an African-American child.)

Keller, H. (1995). *Horace*. New York: Mulberry. (About a spotted leopard who feels out of place in his adopted family of striped tigers.)

Kleven, E. (1996). *Hooray, a pinata*. New York: Dutton. (A diverse way to celebrate birthdays and other special days.)

Lee, C. (2001). *The very kind rich lady and her one hundred dogs*. Cambridge, MA: Candlewick Press. (Especially for dog fanciers.)

Machado, A. M. (1996). *Nina Bonita*. New York: Kane/Miller. (A fanciful story about a rabbit and a dark-skinned Brazilian girl.)

Marcellino, F. (1996). *The story of little Baboji*. New York: Harper Collins/Michael di Capua. (An authentic tale set in India.)

Mora, P. (2005). *Dona Flor: A tale about a giant woman with a great big heart*. New York: Knopf/Random House. (An imagination stimulator.)

Morris, A. (1992). *Tools*. New York: Lothrop, Lee and Shepard Books. (Around the world encountering tool use.)

Perez, A. I. (2000). *My very own room*. San Francisco: Children's Book Press. (A dream for private space.)

Pinkwater, D. M. (1997). *The big orange splot*. New York: Hastings House. (Showcases diversity and pressures to conform.)

Roe, E. (1991). *Con mi hermano/With my brother*. New York: Bradbury Press. (A loving relationship between Mexican-American brothers.)

Rosen, M. (1996). *This is our house*. Cambridge, MA: Candlewick Press. (Opens discussion concerning exclusion.)

Russo, M. (1992). *Alex is my friend*. New York: Greenwillow. (Child's disability handled with feeling.)

Samton, S. W. (1991). *Jenny's journey*. New York: Viking Penguin. (Interracial friendship.)

Schaefer, C. L. (1996). *The squiggle*. New York: Crown. (Asian child delights in imaginative play.)

Spinelli, E., & Iwai, M. (2000). *Night shift daddy*. New York: Hyperion Books. (Ethnic family relationships.)

Waters, K., & Slovenz-Low, M. (1990). *Lion dancer: Ernie Wan's Chinese New Year*. New York: Scholastic. (Color photographs capture a Chinese New Year celebration in New York.)

Williams, V. B. (1990) *"More more more," said the baby*. New York: Greenwillow. (Love and life with multiethnic families with babies. Caldecott Honor winner.)

Zalben, J. (1988). *Beni's first Chanukah*. New York: Henry Holt. (Family traditions are experienced by a small child.)

Volumes Listing Multiethnic and Multicultural Children's Books

Gilliland, H. (1980). *Indian children's books*. Billings, MT: Montana Council for Indian Education.

Jenkins, E. C., & Austin, M. C. (1987). *Literature for children about Asians and Asian Americans*. New York: Greenwood Press.

Marantz, K., & Marantz, S. (1993). *Multicultural picture books: Art for understanding others*. Worthington, OH: Linworth Publishing.

Miller-Lachmann, L. (Ed.). (1992). *Our family, our friends, our world: An annotated guide to significant multicultural books for children and teenagers*. New Providence, NJ: R. R. Bowker.

National Black Child Development Institute. (1995). *Young children and African American literature*. Washington, DC: National Association for the Education of Young Children.

Rand, D., Parker, T., & Foster, S. (1998). *Black books galore! Guide to great African American children's books*. New York: John Wiley and Sons.

Schon, I. (1978). *Books in Spanish for children and adults: An annotated guide*. Metuchen, NJ: Scarecrow Press.

Slapin, B., & Seale, D. (1988). *Books without bias: Through Indian eyes*. Berkeley, CA: Oyate Press.

Favorite Children's Books

Aylesworth, J. (2003). *Goldilocks and the three bears*. New York: Scholastic. (An inquisitive child encounters problems; repetitive dialogue; a classic tale.)

Brown, M.W. (1938, 1965). *The dead bird*. New York: Young Scott Books. (Deals tenderly with the death of a bird.)

Carle, E. (1984). *The very hungry caterpillar*. New York: Penguin-Putnam. (The hungry caterpillar eats through the pictures and emerges as a butterfly on the last page.)

Chorao, K. (1977). *Lester's overnight*. New York: E. P. Dutton. (Family humor about a child's overnight plans and his teddy bear.)

Ets, M. H. (1955). *Play with me*. New York: Viking Press. (A lesson to learn on the nature of animals.)

Flack, M. (1932). *Ask Mr. Bear*. New York: Macmillan. (The search for just the right birthday present for a loved one.)

Freeman, D. (1954). *Beady bear*. New York: Viking Press. (Meet Beady and his courage, independence, and frailty.)

Freeman, D. (1968). *Corduroy*. New York: Viking Press. (The department store teddy who longs for love.)

Freymann, S., & Elffers, J. (2006). *Fast food*. New York: Arthur A. Levine. (Contemporary life.)

Gag, W. (1928). *Millions of cats*. New York: Coward-McCann. (Word pleasure and magic—a favorite with both teachers and children.)

Greene, R. G. (2003). *At grandma's*. New York: Henry Holt. (Grandma's house can be a special place.)

Guilfoile, E. (1957). *Nobody listens to Andrew*. New York: Scholastic Book Services. (An "adults often-ignore-what-children-say" theme.)

Hazen, B. S. (1974). *The gorilla did it*. New York: Atheneum Press. (A mother's patience with a fantasizing child. Humorous.)

Henkes, K. (2005). *Chrysanthemum*. New York: Scholastic (A new classic.)

Hoban, R. (1964). *A baby sister for Frances*. New York: Harper and Row. (Frances, "so human," deals with the new arrival.)

Hutchins, P. (1968). *Rosie's walk*. New York: Macmillan. (A fox is outsmarted.)

Hutchins, P. (1971). *Changes, changes*. New York: Macmillan. (Illustrations of block constructions tell a wordless story of the infinite changes in forms.)

Hutchins, P. (1976). *Goodnight owl!* New York: Macmillan. (Riddled with repetitive dialogue; a delightful tale of bedtime.)

Jenkins, S., & Page, R. (2003). *What do you do with a tail like this?* Boston: Houghton Mifflin. (Humor.)

Keats, E. J. (1967). *Peter's chair*. New York: Harper and Row. (A delightful tale of family life.)

Kennedy, J. (1987). *The teddy bears' picnic*. New York: Peter Bedrick Books. (A delight for the child who has his own teddy bear.)

Kraus, R. (1973). *Leo the late bloomer*. New York: Dutton. (Wonderful color illustrations and a theme that emphasizes individual development.)

Krauss, R. (1945). *The carrot seed*. New York: Harper and Row. (The stick-to-it-tiveness of a child's faith makes this story charming.)

Leonni, L. (1949). *Little blue and little yellow*. New York: Astor-Honor. (A classic. Collages of torn paper introduce children to surprising color transformations, blended with a story of friendship.)

McCloskey, R. (1948). *Blueberries for Sal*. New York: Viking Press. (The young of the two species meet.)

Mosel, A. (1968). *Tiki tiki tembo*. New York: Holt, Rinehart and Winston. (A folktale that tickles the tongue in its telling. Repetitive.)

Potter, B. (1987). *Peter Rabbit's ABC*. Bergenfield, NJ: Frederick Warne. (Clever alphabet letter presentation.)

Provensen, A. (2003). *A day in the life of Murphy*. New York: Holiday House. (A memorable animal story for children who own pets.)

Raskin, E. (1975). *Nothing ever happens on my block*. New York: Atheneum Press. (The child discovers a multitude of happenings in illustrations.)

Scott, A. H. (1972). *On mother's lap*. New York: McGraw-Hill. (There's no place like mother's lap!)

Segal, L. (1970). *Tell me a Mitzi*. New York: Farrar. (New York City life.)

Shulevitz, U. (1969). *Rain rain rivers*. New York: Farrar, Straus and Giroux. (Illustrative fine art.)

Slobodkina, E. (1947). *Caps for sale*. New York: William R. Scott. (A tale of a peddler, some monkeys, and their monkey business. Word play and gentle humor.)

Stevens, J. (1987). *The town mouse and the country mouse*. New York: Holiday House. (One's own house is best.)

Stone, J. (1971). *The monster at the end of this book*. Racine, WI: Western Publishing Co. (Suspense and surprise.)

Viorst, J. (1971). *The tenth good thing about Barney*. New York: Atheneum. (Loss of family pet and positive remembrances.)

Viorst, J. (1976). *Alexander and the terrible, horrible, no good, very bad day*. New York: Atheneum Press. (Everyone relates to the "everything-can-go-wrong" theme.)

Zion, G. (1956). *Harry the dirty dog*. New York: Harper and Row. (Poor lost Harry gets so dirty his family does not recognize him.)

Finding Recommended and Award-Winning Books

American Library Association. (2003). *The Newbery and Caldecott awards: A guide to medal and honor books*. Chicago: Author.

Deeds, S. (2001). *The new books kids like*. Chicago: American Library Association.

Gillespie, J. T. (2002). *Best books for children: Preschool through grade 6*. New Providence, NJ: R. R. Bowker.

Horning, K. T., Lindgren, M. V., Rudiger, H., & Schliesman, M. (2007) *Cooperative Children's Book Center choices, 2007*. Madison, WI: Friends of the CCBC Inc. (University of Wisconsin-Madison).

Temple, C., Martinez, M., Yokata, J., & Naylor, A. (1998). *Children's books in children's hands: An introduction to their literature*. Boston: Allyn and Bacon.

Children's Books Cited in This Chapter

Ahlberg, J., & Ahlberg, A. (1979). *Each peach pear plum: An "I spy" story*. New York: Viking Press.

Aliki. (1962). *My five senses*. New York: Crowell.

Anno, M. (1975). *Anno's counting book*. New York: Crowell.

Asch, F. (1979). *Popcorn: A Frank Asch bear story*. New York: Parents Magazine Press.

Bragg, M. C. (1930). *The little engine that could.* New York: Platt & Munk.

de Paola, T. (1978). *Pancakes for breakfast.* New York: Harcourt Brace Jovanovich.

Duff, M. K. (1972). *Johnny and his drum.* New York: H. Z. Walck.

Gág, W. (1928). *Millions of cats.* New York: Coward-McCann.

Garden, N. (2004). *Molly's family.* New York: Farrar, Straus and Giroux.

Heller, R. (1981). *Chickens aren't the only ones.* New York: Grosset & Dunlap.

Hudson, C. W. (1987). *Afro-Bets ABC book.* Orange, NJ: Just Us Books.

Keats, E. J. (1962). *The snowy day.* New York: Viking Press.

Kellogg, S. (1971). *Can I keep him?* New York: Dial Press.

Kennedy, J. (1987*). The teddy bears' picnic.* New York: Bedrick Books.

Komaiko, L. (1987). *Annie Bananie.* New York: Harper and Row.

Marshall, J. (1972). *George and Martha.* Boston: Houghton Mifflin.

Martin, B., & Carle, E. (1970*). Brown bear, brown bear, what do you see?* New York: Holt, Rinehart and Winston.

Martin, B., Jr., & Archambault, J. (1989). *Chicka chicka boom boom.* New York: Simon & Schuster.

Mayer, M. (1974). *What do you do with a kangaroo?* New York: Four Winds Press.

McCloskey, R. (1941*). Make way for ducklings.* New York: Viking Press.

Miller, J. (1983). *Farm counting book.* Englewood Cliffs, NJ: Prentice Hall.

Peet, B. (1961). *Huge Harold.* Boston: Houghton Mifflin.

Roffey, M. (1983). *Home sweet home.* New York: Coward-McCann.

Sendak, M. (1963). *Where the wild things are.* New York: Harper and Row.

Turkle, B. (1976). *Deep in the forest.* New York: Dutton.

Yabuuchi, M. (1983). *Animals sleeping.* New York: Philomel Books.

Zolotow, C. (1974). *My Grandson Lew.* New York: Harper and Row.

Readings

Bowman, B. (Ed.). (2004). *Love to read: Essays in developing and enhancing early literacy skills in African American children.* Washington, DC: National Black Child Development Institute.

Chambers, A. (1996). *The reading environment: How adults help children enjoy books.* York, ME: Stenhouse.

Gemma, M. (2001, January). Picture books and preschooler's perceptions of school. *Young Children, 56*(1), 71–75.

Hancock, M. (2000). *A celebration of literature and response: Children, books, and teachers.* Upper Saddle River, NJ: Merrill-Prentice Hall.

Jalongo, M. R, (2004). *Young children and picture books.* Washington, DC: National Association for the Education of Young Children.

McCleaf Nespecca, S. & Reeve, J. B. (2002). *Picture books plus: 100 extension activities in art, drama, music, math, and science.* Chicago: American Library Association.

Schon, I. (2001, March). Los ninos y los libros: Noteworthy books in Spanish for the very young. *Young Children, 56*(2), 94–95.

Trelease, J. (1995). *The read-aloud handbook.* New York: Viking-Penguin.

Vestergaard, H. (2005). *Weaving the literacy web: Creating a curriculum based on books children love.* St. Paul, MN: Redleaf.

Helpful Websites

American Library Association
http://www.ala.org
Publications and awards of interest to teachers.

Black Books Galore
http://www.blackbooksgalore.com
Describes themes in books depicting children and families.

Cal State University
http://www.csusm.edu
Search for "Barahona" to find books centered around Latino peoples and culture.

National Institute for Literacy
www.nifl.gov/nifl/pfr.html
Select Partnership for Reading. Free publications including *Big Dreams,* a family book about reading.

The Official Eric Carle Web Site
http://www.eric-carle.com
Presents information about the children's book author.

PBS Teachers
www.pbs.org/teachers
Select "PBS Teachers—Resources for the classroom." Choose "Early Childhood Educators" as a search term to find children's books and links.

Book Companion Website

Web resources include links to picture-book databases, articles, educational games, and curriculum planning ideas. Suggested readings will broaden your investigation of children's literature. A rating activity rates a new teacher's picture-book reading skills. If you've wanted to know more about your favorite picture-book author, a website is suggested. Critical thinking questions probe your views about the value of some book-related preschool activities.

STUDENT ACTIVITIES

1. Select, prepare, and present three books to children. Evaluate your strong points and needed areas of growth. While sharing your three books, try out the technique of thinking aloud. Report your results. (Recommended books to use: Brown, L. (2006). *How to be*; McCarty, P. (2006). *Moon plane*; and Martin, D. (2006). *All for pie, Pie for all.*)

2. Read a children's book to two classmates or to a video camera; take turns evaluating the presentations.

3. Visit a preschool classroom new to you. After observing, develop a book list (10 books) for the class, indicating why each was selected.

4. Interview a local librarian concerning the children's book collection and library services.

5. Pretend you are to make a presentation about the desirable elements and formats of picture books to sixth-, seventh-, or eighth-grade classes interested in creating and then sharing their picture book creations with a small group of preschoolers. What would be your key points? What guidelines or tips concerning reading to preschoolers would you present? List your answers.

6. Create a self-authored picture book. Share it with a small group of young children. Share results, outcomes, and your feelings with fellow students.

7. Visit the local library. Using the form for analyzing a children's book (Figure 9–17), review five books.

8. Do you believe as does Harris (1993) that to author authentic multicultural or multiethnic literature the author either has to have "lived" the experience or studied it deeply? Participate in a class discussion after first listing your main points.

9. Make a list of five nonfiction books that could be used with preschoolers.

10. Read the following.

    My subject today, however, is stereotypes less noticeable and less noticed that have surfaced over my many years of reading and writing about children's books. Or, perhaps they are noticed after all. In my March editorial, "Intergenerational Relationships," I mentioned that children today most likely have grandparents who are younger and more active than those depicted in most stories, who seem to be closer in age and physical condition to the grandparents of those writing and illustrating the books. The resulting chorus of agreement has made me realize that I am not alone in being bothered by these skewed portrayals of the elderly.

FIGURE 9–17 Form for analyzing children's book.

This, in turn, triggered thoughts about another stereotype of the elderly that is perpetrated without much comment. An older character who is scruffily dressed, eccentric, and has a sink full of unwashed dishes, dust an inch high, and a menagerie of dogs or cats in tow is almost always depicted as warm, caring, thoughtful, and sympathetic. But let a character be neatly dressed and coifed, keep a tidy house and yard, and be meticulous in lifestyle, and the resulting image is nearly always that of, at the least, a disagreeable person.

For some reason, the orderliness-equals-nastiness equation is often associated in children's books with affluence. In addition to being very meticulous, the wealthy are nearly always depicted as mercenary, arrogant, and unscrupulous schemers. And as for offspring of affluent parents, they are too-often portrayed as conceited, haughty, and vain. What books do you know that find the wealthy kid on the block the nice one?

Books containing these or any stereotypes shouldn't necessarily be dismissed because of their failings; instead, portrayals should be talked about with children. They should know that one can be neat and still be nice, that affluence isn't always corrupt, that someone from a moneyed family isn't necessarily a snob. Stereotypes won't disappear by sweeping them under the rug; they are best met head-on through discussion and sharing. It's another reason to read with and to children. (Elleman, B. [1995]. Handling stereotypes. *Book Links*, 4[5]:4. Copyright © 1995 American Library Association. Used with permission.)

Discuss with a group of peers. Report the group's comments.

11. Obtain two copies of an inexpensive paperback picture book. Make stick puppets out of characters, objects, and buildings by cutting them out of one copy. Read the book to a small group of preschoolers, and introduce the stick puppets. Put the book and puppets together in a box or basket. Ask which children would like a turn. Have paper and pencil available for a waiting list. Report your experiences to the class.

12. Janine, a student teacher, made the following observation of her cooperating teacher's story time.

Every child was seated on a carpet square cross legged with hands in laps. Mrs. Cordell asked all to "zip their lips and open their ears." Mrs. Cordell started reading the first page with enthusiasm and expression. She used theatrical talent, changing her voice to fit character dialogue. Josh asked a question and Mrs. Cordell simply put her finger to her lips shushing him and then went ahead with her dramatic presentation that included a loud voice which mesmerized the children. She stopped once to ask Ryan to sit still on his carpet square and a few times to praise individual children for their attention. Children focused on Mrs. Cordell, spellbound, but seemed later to start wiggling toward the book's end. They bolted from the reading circle after Mrs. Cordell excused them. I was surprised none of them wanted to talk about the book. I felt I'd seen a teacher performance I couldn't match and dreaded the future when I'd read a picture book and she'd watch me.

React with written notes to be used for a class discussion. Write questions about the student teacher's observation that you would like answered in the class discussion.

13. Design a preschool classroom library center. Include materials and furnishings and show room features such as windows and doors and adjacent activity areas.

14. Observe a classmate reading to a small group of preschool children. Then complete Figure 9–18.

15. Critique one children's magazine using the following terms: literary quality, values found, developmental appropriateness, strengths, and weaknesses. Would you recommend this publication to parents? Why or why not? Identify the publication date, issue, name of publication, and publisher.

		Yes	Can't Determine	No

1. Reader's name: _____
2. Brief description of group (age, number, etc.): _____
3. Location: _____
   Setting: _____
4. How was group gathered? _____
   _____

5. Seating comfort considered? _____
   All saw and heard? If not, explain. _____
   _____

6. Interesting introduction? _____
7. Title and author mentioned? _____
8. Reader's voice appropriate? _____
   If not, describe problem. _____
   _____
   _____

9. Read with expression? _____
   Appropriate? If not, explain. _____
   _____
   _____

10. Book suitable for group? _____
    If not, explain. _____
    _____

11. Book familiar enough for reader to read with ease? _____
12. Did reader give attention and expression to "special"
    or "unique" words, phrases, sentences, or dialogue? ____
    _____

13. How did reader initiate group discussion of story? _____
    _____

14. Were child comments respected and accepted? _____
    If not, explain. _____

15. Any unusual child reactions to book?
    If yes, explain. _____
    _____

FIGURE 9–18 Picture-book reading rate sheet. *(continued)*

16. What reader skills impressed you? _____

_____

17. What reader skills need attention? _____

_____

_____

18. How would you rate this book's holding power on a scale
of 1 (low) to 10 (high)? _____

FIGURE 9–18 *(continued)*

CHAPTER REVIEW

A. Read the following comments by a teacher who is reading to children. Select those comments that you believe would help the child accomplish a goal mentioned in this chapter.

1. "Sit down now and stop talking. It's story time."
2. "Kathy, can you remember how the mouse got out of the trap?"
3. "What part of this story made you laugh?"
4. "John, I can't read any more because you've made Lonnie cry by stepping on her hand. Children, story time is over."
5. "Children, don't look out the window. Look at the book. Children, the book is more interesting than that storm."
6. "Donald, big boys don't tear book pages."
7. "Was the dog striped or spotted? If you can't answer, then you weren't listening."
8. "Mary, of course you liked the story. Everyone did."
9. "Tell me, Mario, what was the boy's name in our story? I'm going to sit here until you tell me."
10. "No, the truck wasn't green, Luci. Children, tell Luci what color the truck was."
11. "Take your thumb out of your mouth, Debbie; it's story time."
12. "You all looked at the book and told me what was in each picture."
13. "One book is enough. We can't sit here all day, you know."
14. "Children, we have to finish this book before we can go outside. Sit down."
15. "That book had lots of colorful pictures."
16. "Well, now we found out who can help us if we ever lose mama in a store."

B. Answer the following questions:

1. Why is it important for the teacher to read a child's book before reading it to the children?

2. How can a teacher help children learn how books are used to find answers?

3. Why should a teacher watch for the young child's reactions to the story while reading it?

C. Select the phrases in Column II that are best connected to items in Column I.

COLUMN I	COLUMN II
1. fairy tales	a. before teacher starts reading to the group
2. first step in planned reading	b. when children show interest in a subject
3. arrange setting with comfort in mind	c. a book with violence
4. stop storytelling to discuss it	d. book may not be appropriate for this age level
5. not appropriate for early childhood level	e. may be too frightening
6. children become restless	f. "Tick-tock," said the clock
7. directly quoted conversation	g. teacher reads the book beforehand
8. "And I'll huff and I'll puff and I'll blow your house down."	h. repetition in *The Three Little Pigs*
9. "So they all had a party with cookies and milk." The end.	i. identification
10. "The rabbit is just like me, I can run real fast."	j. a satisfying climax to a story
11. a book should be read and held	k. in an upright position with the front cover showing
12. books are more inviting when stored this way	l. at children's eye level

D. Describe in step-by-step fashion how you would plan and conduct a group story time.

E. Choose the true statements. Each question may have none or more than one true statement.

1. A book's format
   a. is defined by its content.
   b. includes paper weight.
   c. includes size and shape.
   d. can frustrate children.

2. A teacher's goals when sharing books with children can include to
   a. give information.
   b. promote literacy.
   c. build attitudes.
   d. make them aware of print.
   e. teach listening behavior.

3. Bibliotherapy refers to books that are
   a. nonfiction.
   b. focused on life's happy moments.
   c. helpful in promoting reading skills.
   d. colorful and well illustrated.
   e. written by people with problems.

4. When it comes to different types of books for young children,
   a. most are suitable.
   b. many contain exceptional art.
   c. the fewer words, the greater the enjoyment.
   d. a wide variety exists.
   e. there are more factual than fantasy books published.

5. When preparing to read a picture book to a group of young children, the following was recommended.
   a. Be prepared to dramatize so that children watch you closely.
   b. Skip over old-fashioned words.
   c. Practice until it easily rolls over your tongue.
   d. The larger the audience, the more vivid the experience.
   e. Speak in character dialogue, if it is comfortable for you.

6. Multicultural picture books are
   a. offered to children only at special times and during celebrations.
   b. treated the same as other classroom books.
   c. difficult to find if one is looking for a wide variety of ethnic representation.
   d. widely available and account for about 30 percent of children's picture books published after 1990.

CHAPTER 10
Storytelling

OBJECTIVES

After reading this chapter, you should be able to:

◆ Describe how storytelling can help language growth.

◆ List teacher techniques in storytelling.

◆ Demonstrate the ability to create a story that meets suggested criteria.

◆ Describe promotion of child-created stories.

KEY TERMS

dialogue	participation stories	story
fable	plot	story map
monologue	semiotics	

HEY! GODZILLA!

A tree in our yard was perfect for climbing, with a smooth trunk and a thick layer of tan bark underneath. I watched as Fenton climbed up and out on a limb. He was hanging on the limb with both hands, feet dangling a foot or so above the ground. He seemed unable to let go and unable to swing his legs back up on the limb. As I walked closer to help him, he yelled, "Godzilla help me." Other boys, closer than I, grabbed his legs. He let go, knocking them down with him. They rolled on the ground unhurt. Then Pierre jumped up and said, "My turn," and he headed up the tree.

QUESTIONS TO PONDER

1. Could you create a short story with a beginning, middle, and end about a boy stuck in a tree? Write this story.

2. How would you describe this tree to give listeners a vivid mental image?

Storytelling is a medium that an early childhood teacher can develop and use to increase a child's enjoyment of language. When good stories are told by a skilled storyteller, the child listens intently; mental images may be formed.

Storytelling enables teachers to share their life experiences and create and tell stories in their own way. It is a teacher's gift of time and imagination. Your style of storytelling will be individual and unique, and you will be free to improvise. Beginning teachers do not worry that their version of a favorite story differs from others.

Storytelling can be defined as the seemingly easy, spontaneous, intimate sharing of a narrative with one or many persons. The storyteller relates, pictures, imagines, builds what happens, and crafts characters, all of which is manifested through the storyteller's voice and body.

Storytelling is the act that essentially makes humans human. It defines us as a species. We are shaped by the stories we hear. In storytelling, children leave the "here and now" and go beyond what is seen and at hand. They experience the symbolic potential of language with words themselves, the main source of meaning independent of the time and place they are spoken. Children create imaginative scenarios quickly and easily in everyday play situations.

Early childhood teachers recognize the importance of storytelling in a full language arts curriculum. Good stories that are well told have fascinated young listeners since ancient times. Storytelling is a form of expressive artistry, and storytelling remains one of the oldest and most effective art forms. The oral story, be it aesthetic or pedagogical, has great value. It seems to be a part of the human personality to use it and want it. The art of the storyteller is an important, valuable ingredient in the lives of children.

Storytelling is enjoying a renaissance. The National Storytelling Festival's 3-day celebration held in Jonesborough, Tennessee, draws over 8,000 people each year. Storytelling festivals are held in 40 states. America is rediscovering the magic of storytelling. Regional, intergenerational, multicultural, and multiethnic story themes delight audiences.

In many cultures, oral stories have passed on the customs, accumulated wisdom, traditions, songs, and legends. Storytelling is as old as language itself.

The teacher's face, gestures, words, and voice tell the story when books or pictures are not used. Eye contact is held throughout the storytelling period. The child pictures the story in her mind as the plot unfolds.

How could one describe skilled storytellers? They are gloriously alive, live close to the heart of things, have known solitude and silence, and have felt deeply. They have come to know the power of the spoken word. They can remember incredible details about a good story that interests them. Preschool teachers may know silence only at nap times, but they indeed live close to the heart of young children's forming character and personality and growing intellect.

STORYTELLING AND LITERACY

The promotion of oral literacy is an important consideration for preschool program planners. Oral literacy involves a shared background and knowledge of orally told stories plus a level of competence. Being able to tell a story well depends on a number of factors, including observation of techniques. Natural storytellers, if they exist, are overshadowed by storytellers who have practiced the art. Some adult job hunters find telling a story is a requested part of their job interview and is used to assess intelligence, communication ability, and literacy.

Preschools are sure to offer picture-book readings, but storytelling may be neglected. Some teachers shy away from the activity for a variety of reasons, including not being able to hold their child audience's attention. Young children may be so used to illustration and pictures (books and television) that initial storytelling experiences are foreign to them.

Teachers can increase their skills by observing practiced storytellers, taking classes, or engaging in self-study (Figure 10–1). The best suggestion for a teacher wishing to develop her storytelling skills is to start by relating short,

FIGURE 10–1 Watching a skilled storyteller may increase teacher skill.

significant happenings from daily life—keep it lively. Four-year-olds make a better audience for the beginner storyteller, rather than younger children.

As children observe and listen to the teacher's storytelling, they notice common elements, including beginnings, middles, and story endings. They discover some stories vary little between tellers. They imitate techniques using hand and body gesturing, facial expression, and vocal variation; they speak in character **dialogue**, and they may even copy dramatic pause. They also may attempt to make their audience laugh or add suspense to their stories.

Acredolo and Goodwyn (2000) suggest how young children begin to get "the idea of story":

. . . They hear important people in their lives talking about the past: "Remember what we did today? We went to the zoo! And do you remember what animals we saw?" What's more it's clear that these people are especially pleased when the children themselves also remember. The implication is clear.

Adults literally teach their children about beginnings, middles, and endings by structuring their own narratives in an organized way: "Remember we saw the flamingos when we first went though the gate? And then we went into the snake house and we got scared." (p. 16)

Sharing oral stories and verbally putting daily happenings into words can be cherished for what they are—the building blocks of thinking and imagining, describing, creating, expressing ideas, and later achieving writing and reading skill. Gallas (2003) suggests that not only is the storyteller absorbed in thought during the storytelling experience but the audience is as well.

Over the years as I have watched successive classes create stories for sharing time, I have seen that the storytelling child does one kind of imaginative,

---

dialogue — a conversation between two or more persons or between a person and something else.

synthesizing work that takes skill and thought. The listening children, however, do another kind of imaginative, synthesizing work in order to become part of the story. That work is personal, social, and intellectual. (p. 176)

Educators try daily to really engage children in talk and to celebrate its occurrence. Forget quiet classrooms; strive for talk-filled rooms balanced with quiet times!

Children attempt to make sense of the stories they hear and try to fit them into their lives. Stories can give meaning to events by making connections between them and the real world. The content of stories can have a lasting effect on children.

One benefit that is fostered by teacher storytelling is child story making. Other possible child competencies and understandings promoted by storytelling experiences include developing a sense of

- personal story.
- curiosity about others stories.
- drama.
- a story's power.
- phonemic awareness.
- cultural similarities and differences.
- social and group enjoyment during storytelling.
- gestures and acting actions effective in communicating ideas, feelings, and moods.

Much current research is encouraging teachers to promote child dictation of child-created stories and subsequent dramatization. The teacher then reads the child's work to child groups. Besides the obvious benefits of the speaking and writing involvement in this activity, it is based on child-relevant material. Experts believe that this kind of activity primes children's inner feelings and thinking processes for change and growth, and increases self-awareness and awareness of self in relation to others. All in all, it is a powerful language arts approach.

Gainsley (2003) describes a teacher dictation activity that took place before a firehouse field trip. Children were asked what they might see. The teacher made a list that was checked off during the trip. It was discussed later, along with other things children observed and recalled. Other teacher dictation ideas cited by Gainsley were creating grocery lists, creating new verses for songs, and writing letters and cards.

TELLING STORIES WITHOUT BOOKS

Chapter 9 described the merits and uses of picture books with young children. Storytelling without books has its own unique set of enjoyed language pleasures. Storytelling is direct, intimate conversation. The well-told story's power to hold children spellbound is widely recognized. It is the intimate, personal quality of storytelling as well as the power of the story itself that accomplishes these minor miracles. Yet in order to work this spell, a story must be learned, remembered, and so delightfully told that it catches and holds the attention of the most inveterate wrigglers.

Teachers observe children's reactions as they tell a story. A quizzical look on a child's face can help the teacher know when to clarify or rephrase for understanding. A teacher's voice can increase the story's drama in parts when children are deeply absorbed.

Many educators have noted how quickly and easily ideas and new words are grasped through storytelling (Figure 10–2). This is an additional benefit. Stories are told to acquaint young children with this enjoyable oral language art. Obvious moralizing or attempts to teach facts by using stories usually turn children away.

Storytelling may occur at almost any time during the course of the day, inside or outside. No books or props are necessary, but use of them may focus attention and add to the child's enjoyment. Teachers are free to relate stories in their own words and manner. Children show by their actions what parts of the story are of high interest. The storyteller can increase children's enjoyment by emphasizing these features.

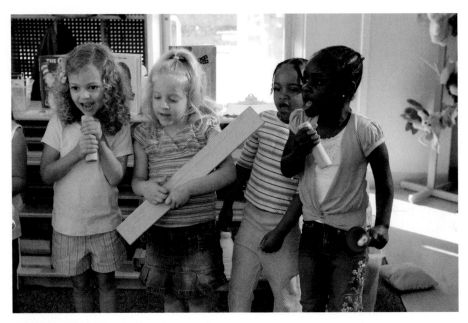

FIGURE 10–2 A story about a singer prompts children to use cylinder blocks.

STORYTELLING GOALS

A teacher seeks to become a skilled storyteller so that she can model storytelling skill while providing another avenue to the development of oral competence. Another goal is to acquire a repertoire of stories that offer children a variety of experiences.

As they relate to storytelling, the teacher's goals also include:

◆ increasing children's enjoyment of oral language.

◆ making young children familiar with oral storytelling.

◆ encouraging children's storytelling and authorship.

◆ increasing children's vocabulary.

◆ increasing children's confidence as speakers.

◆ increasing children's awareness of story sequence and structure.

Storytelling is a wonderful way to promote understanding of audience behaviors and performer behaviors. Teachers experience rewarding feelings when their technique and story combine to produce audience enjoyment and pleasure. Child storytellers gain tremendous insights into the performing arts, their own abilities, and the power of orally related stories. Most reading experts agree that oral competence enhances ease in learning to read and promotes understanding of what is read.

Thoughtful writers have questioned the wisdom of always exposing children to illustrations at story time. By not allowing children to develop mental images, they believe we have possibly distracted children from attaining personal meaning. On the other hand, discussing what children see in a photograph or drawing and conjecturing with them about what is happening, the details they notice, the feelings that they or the person pictured might be having, and what might happen next can be both a visual literacy experience and a motivational strategy to encourage child storytelling. There are benefits children can accrue from both "with visuals" and "without visuals" literacy experiences.

USING PICTURE BOOKS FOR STORYTELLING

At times, a picture book is the source for storytelling. The teacher later introduces the book and makes it available in the classroom's book center for individual follow-up. Used this way, storytelling motivates interest in books.

Many picture books, however, do not lend themselves to storytelling form because illustrations are such an integral part of the experience (Figure 10–3). Books that have been successfully used as the basis for storytelling can be handled in unique ways. An experienced teacher using professional presentation skills in a storytelling experience using *Caps for Sale* (by Esphyr Slobodkina) would make it an audience participation story and would shake a fist at the monkeys. The audience, with only the slightest encouragement, might shake its fists at the peddler.

The following books are recommended for teacher storytelling:

Asbjornsen, P. C. (1972). *The three billy goats gruff.* New York: Harcourt, Brace, Jovanovich.

Galdone, P. (1961). *The old woman and her pig.* New York: McGraw-Hill.

Kent, J. (1971). *The fat cat.* New York: Parents Magazine Press.

After-Storytelling Discussion

Storybook discussions can aid children's narrative abilities. Justice and Pence (2006) urge teachers to help children master narrative skills and to use literate language. Literate language, as they define it, is a specific type of language that is highly precise and is necessary when little context is available—such as telling about an incident or happening in the past without a visual. Justice and Pence suggest that the following discussion activities are aligned to the objectives that characterize important early achievement in narrative knowledge.

1. to discuss the sequence of events in a story
2. to discuss what happens to characters in a story
3. to discuss the location or setting of a story

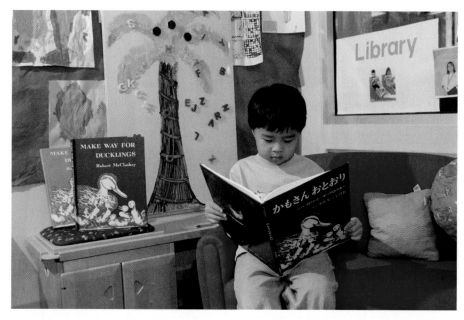

FIGURE 10–3 Some picture books are not good sources for oral storytelling.

4. to discuss reported speech used by characters in a story

5. to identify the high point of a story (pp. 72–73)

An increasing number of multicultural picture books are in print as publishers strive to react to America's changing and diverse school populations. The following are suggested as storytelling sources.

Escardo, M. (2006). *The three little pigs/Los tres cerditos*. San Francisco: Chronicle Books.

Hudson, C. (1999). *Glo goes shopping*. East Orange, NJ: Just Us Books.

Rylant, C. (2007). *Alligator boy*. New York: Harcourt.

Rocco, J. (2007) *Wolf! Wolf!* New York: Hyperion.

Tsubakiyama, M. (1999). *Mei-Mei loves the morning*. Morton Grove, IL: Albert Whitman & Co.

An increasing number of classrooms promote acting out stories after they are read. Immediately following this acting experience, children are urged to create their own stories. These can be taped and later written by adults. These child stories can also be enacted with the story's author or teacher selecting her actors or with actor volunteers.

SOURCES FOR STORIES

Story ideas can be found in collections, anthologies, resource books, children's magazines, films, or story recordings, or they may come from another storyteller. A story idea can also be self-created.

A teacher-created story can fill a void. In any group of young children there are special interests and problems. Stories can expand interest and give children more information on a subject. Problems can possibly be solved by the stories and conversations that take place.

New teachers may not yet have confidence in their storytelling abilities, so learning some basic techniques for selecting, creating, and telling stories can help build confidence. This, together with the experience gained by presenting the stories to children, should convince the teacher that storytelling is enjoyable for preschoolers and rewarding to the teacher.

Teachers telling children personal stories about their lives actually "model" storytelling. They also let children know that their actions and words are the stuff of stories too. Gestures, facial expressions, body language, and variety in tone of voice are observed. This type of storytelling is a natural part of social interaction. With young children, short anecdotes and humorous life incidents work well. "News of the Day Time" is often included in daily schedules.

STORY SONGS

Many stories can be introduced through song. Some of us remember the delightful folk story song that begins "A fox went out on a chilly night" and tells of the animal's adventures. These types of songs may include opportunities for children's oral, physical, and creative expression or for child involvement in the storytelling. A creative teacher can use story songs to complement, extend, and reinforce a multitude of classroom activities. Vocabulary meanings are often more apparent to children when learned in the context of a story song.

Simple, quick definitions by teachers are offered in a conversational tone. Imagine the fun involved in a story song about the saga of a lump of dough becoming a loaf of bread: ". . . and they pushed and pulled me. Oh, how they pushed and pulled" or "It's warm in here. I'm getting hot. Look at me. I'm growing and turning golden brown."

STORY SELECTION

The selection of a story is as important as the selection of a book, because stories seem to have individual personalities. Searching for a story that appeals to the teller and that can be eagerly shared is well worth the time. A few well-chosen and well-prepared stories suiting the individual teacher almost always ensure a successful experience for all. The following selection criteria are commonly used.

Age-Level Appropriateness

Is the story told in simple, easily understood words? Is it familiar in light of the child's life experiences? Is it frightening? Can the child profit from traits of the characters?

Plot

Does the setting create a stage for what is to come? Is there action? Is there something of interest to resolve? Does the story begin with some action or event? Does it build to a climax with some suspense? Does it have a timely, satisfying conclusion? Are characters introduced as they appear?

The stories you will be searching for will have one central **plot**; a secondary plot may confuse children. Action-packed stories where one event successfully builds to another hold audience attention.

Style

Does the story use repetition, rhyme, or silly words? Does it have a surprise ending? Does it include directly quoted conversations or child involvement with speaking or movements? Does the mood help the plot develop?

Values

Are the values and models presented appropriate for today's children? Screen for ethnic, cultural, and gender stereotypes that would lead you to exclude the story or discuss the issue with children.

Memorable Characters

Look for a small number of colorful characters who are distinct entities in contrast to the main character and each other. One should be able to identify and recognize character traits.

Sensory and Visual Images

The visual and sensory images evoked by stories add interest. For example, phrases like "gingerbread cookies, warm and golden" rather than "cookie" and the "velvet soft fur" rather than "fur" create different mental images. Taste, smell, sight, sound, and tactile descriptions create richness and depth.

Additional Selection Criteria

Elements that make stories strong candidates include the following:

◆ an economy of words—a polished quality
◆ a universal truth
◆ suspense and surprise

Themes and Story Structure

Many well-known and loved stories concern a problem that is insightfully solved by the main character. They begin by introducing a setting and characters and have a body of events that moves the story forward to a quick, satisfying conclusion. The story line is strong, clear, and logical. One category of stories described as cautionary seems to have been designed to keep children safe by teaching a truth or moral, consequently helping children make wise decisions.

Storyteller Enthusiasm

Is the story well liked by the teller? Does the teller feel comfortable with it? Is it a story the teller will be eager to share?

Finding a story you love may make it easier for the child to enjoy the story you tell. The easiest door to open for a child is one that leads to something you love yourself. All good teachers know this. And all good teachers know the ultimate reward: the marvelous moment when the spark you are breathing bursts into a flame that henceforth will burn brightly on its own (Figure 10–4).

---

plot — the structure of the action of a story.

FIGURE 10–4 Dressing up may help a teacher tell her story.

MacDonald (1996) advises:

Just jump in. Storytelling is like swimming. You can't do it by sitting on the bank. You have to jump in and start dog paddling. You take a story that you love and think would be fun to tell, and you just start telling it. You keep on doing it until you get good at it. It's that simple, but you've got to start. You'll never do it sitting on the bank. (p. 13)

TYPES OF STORIES

Some stories, particularly folktales and fairy tales, have been polished to near perfection through generations of use. Classic tales and folktales may contain dated words and phrases, but these might be important story parts that add to the story's charm. In retelling the story to young children, a brief explanation of these types of terms may be necessary.

A **fable** is a simple story in which animals frequently point out lessons (morals), which are contained in the fable's last line.

Many great stories, called **participation stories,** have opportunities for active child involvement and the use of props. Props, such as pictures, costumes, and other objects, may spark and hold interest. A cowboy hat worn by the teacher during the telling of a Western tale may add to the mood and can later be worn by children in play or during a child's attempt at storytelling.

Repetitive phrases or word rhythms are used in all types of stories, and chanting or singing may be necessary in the telling. Most stories have problems to be solved through the ingenuity of the main character. This sequence can be explored in teacher's self-created stories.

Some tales, such as the adventures of Anansi, a spider of African origin, have a rhythm and cadence found in no other stories. Anansi stories, researchers believe, exist

fable — a short tale in prose or verse that teaches a moral, usually with talking animals or inanimate objects as main characters.
participation stories — stories with some feature children can enact through physical movements, verbal expression, or both.

today because of an African oral storytelling tradition.

Stories of children of color should be a planned part of the curriculum. Teachers should try to avoid the tendency to just look for stories in their own cultural and ethnic background. The right story, regardless of the characters' ethnicity, will fit emotionally, intellectually, and physically.

Story Ideas

Teachers often begin by telling stories from classic printed sources. Almost any life adventure or happening and any classroom-inspired story works well when it has a touch of drama. Don't be afraid to tell stories other teachers find unsuccessful, and borrow their good ones, too!

Classic Tales

Goldilocks and the Three Bears
Little Red Riding Hood
The Three Little Pigs
The Billy Goats Gruff
The Little Red Hen
The Gingerbread Boy

From Aesop's Fables

The Lion and the Mouse
The Hare and the Tortoise
The Ant and the Grasshopper

Traditional Stories

Hans Christian Andersen, *Ugly Duckling*
Arlene Mosel, *Tikki Tikki Tembo*
Florence Heide, *Sebastian*
Beatrix Potter, *Tale of Peter Rabbit*

It is wise for beginning teachers to not waste their time on material that does not inspire them to feel, "I can't wait to tell this!" You are sure to find such stories if you look.

PRACTICE AND PREPARATION

When a teacher has selected a story, a few careful readings are in order. Try to determine the story's main message and meaning. Next, look closely at the introduction that describes the setting and characters. Study Figure 10–5 and analyze how the selected story fits this pattern. The initial setting often sets up a problem or dilemma. The story can be outlined on a 4-by-6-inch (or larger) cue card to jog your memory during practice sessions (Figure 10–6). Memorizing beginning and ending lines and interior chants or songs is suggested.

Once the story rolls out effortlessly, the storyteller fine-tunes it by practicing dialogue, and identifying pauses, gesturing, and facial expressions. Particular attention should be given to the rising action in the story's body so that one event builds on another until a quick, satisfying conclusion is reached.

In many cultural rituals, an air of magic, soft flickering embers, were part of the storytelling experience. African storytellers would begin, "A story, a story, let it come, let it go." Ritual can mean entering a particular "distraction-free" classroom area, lighting a candle, wearing a special teacher hat, dimming the lights, saying a chant, or engaging in a special finger play that settles and brings anticipation. One clever teacher created a story sack and reached inside and slowly raised her hand to her mouth before beginning. Another teacher found only short,

FIGURE 10–5 Common and classic story pattern form.

Intro. "Once upon a time, there were four little rabbits, Flopsy, Mopsy, Cottontail, and Peter. They lived with their mother in a sand-bank, underneath the root of a very big fir tree."

Theme. Mind your mother.

Problem. Peter disobeys and goes into McGregor's garden.

Rising action.

Peter squeezes under garden gate and eats a lot.

McGregor sees him.

McGregor chases him, and he loses a shoe.

Peter gets caught in a gooseberry net and loses his jacket.

Peter hides in the tool shed in a can full of water.

Peter sneezes, almost gets caught, but jumps out a window.

Peter cries and sees cat (another danger).

Peter makes a dash for the gate and gets free.

Peter gets home without clothes and shoes, goes to sleep, and misses dinner. Mother serves him tea.

Ending lines.

"But Flopsy, Mopsy, and Cottontail had bread and milk and blackberries for supper. And that's the end of the Tale of Peter Rabbit!"

FIGURE 10–6 Cue and file card example. (From Potter, B., *Peter Rabbit*. First published in 1902.)

action-packed stories containing many move-the-body features appealed to his group of 3-year-olds.

Use the following steps in preparing a story: The first step is to divide the story into units of action. As you read the story, you will notice that most divide into an easily definable series of actions or episodes; these can be summarized in brief form, and then the sequence can be learned. The second task is to identify those sections that do need to be memorized verbatim. This may include some words, some repeated phrases, or perhaps some larger sections. A discerning storyteller learns verbatim these repeated sections, because the repetition encourages children to join in as the teller recites the lines.

Participation tales hold child attention. As you tell a story you might be constantly roaming the group, touching every face and drawing each listener back into the story over and over

again. See *Just Like Metoo!*, *To Grandmother's House*, *What Was Behind the Door?*, and *Little Duck Lost* in the Activities section of this chapter. These stories can come to life and grab attention.

Select a setting with few distractions where all can hear, and make child seating comfortable. Do not begin until listeners are ready. Be at a level to maintain eye contact and prepare an introduction that piques children's interest. Use a prop, or tell something about the story's source or author, or discuss a related event, or ask a question to focus attention (Figure 10–7). Your opening phrase is your bridge between the world of ordinary conversation and the world of the story and this crossing is best when both magical and deliberate.

Additional Techniques

The following storytelling techniques and tips should be kept in mind.

◆ Guard against sounding mechanical. Tell the story in your own personal way.

◆ Become familiar with the key ideas. Know the key happenings and their order of appearance in the story.

◆ Develop story sequence pictures.

◆ Practice before a mirror or with another staff member.

◆ Enjoy and live the story as you tell it in your own words. Use gestures.

◆ Maintain eye contact by scanning the group during the telling; watch for children's interest or restlessness.

◆ The teacher should pace the storytelling by going faster during exciting or fast-action parts and slower in serious parts. Adventure stories may feature the unknown or unexpected and include elements of excitement and surprise.

◆ Use a clear, firm voice. Try changing voice volume and tone to fit the story; in some parts of the story a whisper may be most effective. Change your voice to fit the characters when they speak, if you feel comfortable doing so.

FIGURE 10–7 Using pictures or photographs to introduce the setting in your story is sometimes successful.

◆ Make gestures natural complements of the story (large and descriptive for younger children).

◆ Involve the children often, especially with repetitions, rhymes or actions, silly words, or appropriate questions, if the story lends itself to this.

◆ Sit close to the group; make sure all are comfortable before beginning.

◆ Include teachers and children's names and familiar places in the community to clarify meanings or add interest in teacher-created stories.

◆ Start by telling little personal stories about your family, pets, and daily happenings, if you are a novice; move on to simple stories with lots of repetition.

◆ Investigate the cultural backgrounds of children in your care and see if you can find stories that reflect these backgrounds.

◆ Seek out talented storytellers in your community to observe your storytelling or to appear as guest storytellers in your classroom.

◆ Become very familiar with any pronunciations, including proper names and foreign or unfamiliar terms in stories.

◆ Use dramatic pauses to build suspense, after an exclamation, or to facilitate transitions between story events.

◆ Try to communicate characters' attitudes and motivations.

◆ Consider the flavor and language of the particular tradition from which the story comes.

◆ Storytelling comes from the imagination.

◆ Let the story unfold as you picture scenes in your mind.

◆ Slow down. Tales are best shared when spoken at half of normal conversation speed.

◆ No two tellers present their tales in exactly the same way, for each person brings another perspective.

◆ Move your body with your story.

◆ End with confidence.

A storyteller who sees that children are losing interest in a story is free to make changes in it, based on intuition and knowledge of the group. Others would disagree with changing well-known, classic tales, but they do advise changing one's style, pace, or voice volume to draw listeners back to the story.

It is important to remember that even the best storytellers have an occasional flop. If the storyteller is not able to draw the children back to the story, the story may be ended very quickly and tried at a later time, using a revised version.

Teacher-Created Stories

Many teachers find that they have a talent for creating stories and find that a popular character in one story can have further adventures in the next. Remember that "bad guys" in stories are enjoyed as much as "good guys." A character with a problem that needs to be resolved is the basis for many well-known classics.

Whenever a teacher cannot find a story that seems tailor-made for a particular group of children, she can create a story. As teachers use their own stories, they tend to cut and add to them based on the reactions of the children. Take care that themes do not always revolve around "mother knows best" episodes, and watch for sexism and stereotypes when creating a story.

Telling Stories for an Educational Purpose

There are five key elements of a good teacher story: audience, content, motivation, timing, and **semiotics**. Teachers can consider these elements if storytelling for an educative purpose.

Considering *audience*, a story without one is not a storytelling experience! Whether the story includes preschool exploring behavior or some other preschool-important concept, *content* needs to be creatively conceived and made interesting. It can be made interesting by relating it to children's lives. *Motivation* is enhanced when children identify with some story element. Interactive storytelling, where children have some part in the telling, engages unmotivated learners, boosts enjoyment, and holds an audience.

Timing involves telling a story in a progression from beginning, to middle, to end. Pacing, at the right speed, holds attention. *Semiotics* considers cultural and cognitive differences. A story set in an imaginary preschool classroom similar to the children's own classroom and the inclusion of familiar words like block area or bicycle path will help children connect.

The writings of Vivian Paley (1990, 1994) are full of examples of purposeful educative storytelling, and show how one dedicated teacher used storytelling to change and enhance children's lives in and out of school.

Child-Created Stories

Storytelling is probably the first situation in which the child must sustain a **monologue** without the support of a conversational partner. It is a complex cognitive endeavor that involves a kind of "story sense" and "story grammar." To be coherent, a child's story needs to be more than an unrelated series of events, as is often the case with beginning child storytellers. Teachers should realize that for some preschoolers, including those from low-income homes and minority backgrounds, personal storytelling may be their area of strength and giftedness.

As children are exposed to stories told and stories read, they construct their own ideas about the linguistic features of narrative storytelling. They use their stories as a way of expressing certain emotionally important themes that preoccupy them and of symbolically managing or resolving these underlying themes.

Many educators believe that despite our best efforts, we just do not reach young children on the inside, where they hide their stories. They think that teachers fail, at times, to consider children's individual and developmental histories—in other words, who they are and how they think.

Watching children's dramatic play, teachers will see stories "acted out" rather than told.

---

semiotics — observant of signs or symbols. The study of how groups come to share meaning.
monologue — literally "speaking alone."

They will be spontaneous, creative, natural, and seemingly much easier and enjoyable than the act of child storytelling. Teachers can appreciate child actors in dramatic play situations, for they create their own script, improvise, and develop characters in the roles they have chosen or been assigned. At times, dramatic play may seem a series of unrelated events, but surprisingly, the teacher will witness many logically flowing scenarios, such as stories in action or preschool "soaps."

Encouraging child authorship and child storytelling goes hand-in-hand with teacher storytelling. It is an excellent way to develop fluency and elaborated language usage. The importance of the children's sense of "I am an author" is often incorporated into the child's self-concept. This will help children form the habits and knowledge an author needs. One suggestion is to offer activities in which pictures or props are used as motivators. Children's attempts are not edited or criticized but simply accepted. Logic should not be questioned, nor should the sequence of events be corrected. Each story is special. Teachers can think of child-dictated stories as print-awareness activities. Young children may have had limited experiences with adults printing their ideas (Figure 10–8). Child story dictation presents another use of print—a personal important use. Beginning writers do not write because they have something they want to say; they write in order to discover what they have to say, just as they played with blocks and discovered what they could create. This is why dictation is so valuable to the young storyteller. Subtly and over time, dictation helps teach the child-author that a written story is merely an oral story put into print.

If recorded or dictated, the story should be taken verbatim. Some teachers initiate discussions that allow the children to tell what they liked best about a story to alert children to desirable story features. Egg timers may be useful if rambling, long-winded children leave little time for others. Asking for child volunteers to retell stories to other children works in some programs; an announcement may be made that Mark or Susie will be sitting in the storyteller's chair after snack. Teachers tactfully remind children before the volunteer starts her story that questions or comments will be saved until the story is over. An adjacent box of storytelling props may help a child get into character. If the

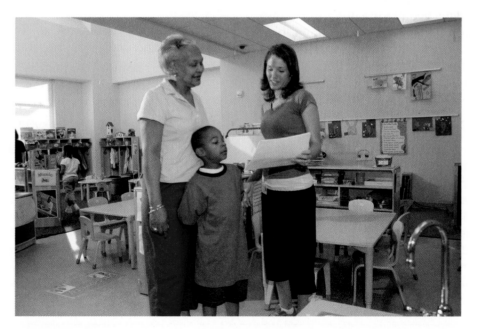

FIGURE 10–8 The teacher explains that Reynolds has dictated a short story to accompany his artwork.

teacher has told *Goldilocks and the Three Bears* using three stuffed bears, a yellow-haired doll, three doll beds, and three dollhouse chairs, chances are children will want to use the same props for their own telling of the story.

Clipboards can be used to list the stories that are created throughout the day. The creation of stories is given status, and sharing these stories is a daily occurrence. Sharing takes place with the child's permission, and the child chooses whether she or the teacher will present the story to the group.

Children's first storytelling attempts often lack sequence, have unclear plots, ramble, and involve long, disconnected events; as children mature and are exposed to stories and books, authorship improves. The goal is not to produce child storytellers but to encourage a love for and positive attitudes toward oral storytelling. The development of child storytelling seems to follow a sequence beginning with children's use of language to create a special or private world. This is believed to be a forerunner to the child's use of language to create a world of make-believe. It leads to the gradual acquisition of the specific conventions that constitute a sense of story. As children mature, their stories increase in length and complexity. Children gradually acquire greater control over the events in their stories, moving from a loose collection of related and unrelated events to a tightly structured narrative that links a set of events to each other and to a common theme.

Working on Comprehension

One important goal in formal reading instruction is promoting children's comprehension of reading material. Early experiences in **story** comprehension take place in preschools when discussions follow oral stories and picture book stories. The goal is to help children organize and understand the ideas, events, and feelings the story produced. Children get their first practice in using logic when they think about story sequence, cause and effect, emotions felt, fantasy versus reality, incongruities, and other story elements. An after-story discussion led by the teacher might focus on

- making a visual graph of some story element (whether the monkeys ate grapes, bananas, melons, etc.).
- asking if anyone has a question about the story.
- listing on a chart what information about alligators was present.
- asking if someone heard a new word or name.
- asking about story noises or actions.
- discussing how children might change something a character did.
- having the children make up a different way to end the story.
- discussing how the children might have solved a problem in the story.
- asking the children if they could show the story in pictures and what would come first and last.
- making a **story map** showing the travels of a story character.
- asking the children's opinion of a story character's behavior as being good or bad—and why,
- asking about a character's possible emotions during story events.

Using Picture Files in Storytelling

Encouraging young children to tell stories while using pictures, photographs, or other visuals stimulates creative thinking and visual literacy skills. What is so interesting to teachers is the diverseness of stories a group of children may relate from the same visual images. Picture files are useful in many language arts activities and are well worth the time spent collecting, mounting, and protecting them with clear contact paper.

---

story — an imaginative tale with a plot, characters, and setting.
story map — a timeline showing an ordered sequence of events.

Story Sequence Cards

Story sequence cards are popular teaching aids. They have a number of purposes. They can be used as a teacher's cue cards when storytelling. They are also a visual aid for children, who are learning that stories progress from a beginning to an end, with events, actions, and happenings occurring in a sequence between. If sequence cards are made available for child use, children will use them for storytelling and retelling. They often line or prop them up and "picture read."

Cards can be made from two picture books torn apart and pasted on cardboard, with or without adjoining print. They can also be made from teacher drawings, photographs, or other pictorial representations. Examine Figure 10–9, which displays picture sequence cards for a story found at the chapter's end called *It Was My Idea*.

SUCCESSFUL DICTATION

Teachers act in the dual role of scribe and facilitator when taking dictation of a child's story. Asking questions to clarify and help the child express ideas is deemed appropriate. Younger children seem to run out of steam after 10 minutes or more of storytelling, and some are done in less than 2 minutes.

Statements that help children start dictating stories follow.

- "Tell me the words you want me to write down on the paper. I'll write them down."
- "Do you have a story to tell?"
- "I'll write down your words."
- "Let's write down what you said about your new puppy."
- "What is the story you would like to tell me?"
- "What are the words to your story?"

During dictation a teacher may guide a child toward developing the sequence of a story or help the child find the story's beginning and end. When working with a child who is more advanced, the teacher might encourage the child's use of dialogue or the child's development of descriptive language.

Two snow geese flying

Geese by lake

Turtle

Geese with turtle flying together

Farmer

Turtle falling into haystack

FIGURE 10–9 Story sequence cards.

The decisions children make mentally during dictation are complex. The child may pause, start, and stop, all of which reflect the child's attention to the task at hand.

Preschool classrooms that announce that the teacher or volunteers are available and start a waiting list for a child-dictated storytelling time find that children accept and look forward to the opportunity. The success of the dictation activity may rely on the promise of dramatization. Linking dictation to children's opportunity to jointly act out before peers what the children have written is believed to be the key (Figure 10–10). Young children's interest in a concrete representation of their stories (the drama or action) coincides with young children's emotional need to establish their individual identity within the group.

Nicolopoulou, Scales, and Weintraub (1994) studying the content of 4-year-olds' dictated stories found differences in boys' and girls' tales. Boys' stories were far less likely than girls' to have either a stable cast of characters or a well-articulated plot. Boys did not develop their themes in a steady and methodical manner as did many girls. Girls' stories focused on creating, maintaining, and elaborating structure, the boys' stories focused on generating action and excitement. Boys' main characters were often big, powerful, and frightening, whereas girls depicted realistic stable family life. Girls' stories created animals that were soft, cute creatures, whereas boys' animals typically were violent, wild, and scary.

Bathroom-type stories or gory stories appear at times in child dictation and should be censored if inappropriate.

Early Writing Skill and Teacher Dictation

Should early childhood educators who are taking dictation from young children simply record what the children say word for word or attempt to become someone who is both sharing the children's ideas and increasing children's ability to relate a story logically? Many educators perform a dual role. Teachers of kindergarten and older children who have acquired the ability to form letters and select words for

Teacher:	Alexandra's story goes like this: (Paraphrasing) "The lady knocked on the door. Her dog was big and fluffly. The lady said, "Do you want to buy my cookies?" The girl in the house told the lady "yes" if the lady could sing a song that would make her dog bark. She did. They had cookies and lemonade under the tree in the yard."
Teacher:	(to Alexandra) Who do you choose to be the lady with the dog and the cookies? (Alexandra chooses Dana.)
Teacher:	Dana will you be the lady? (Dana nods "yes.")
Teacher:	Alexandra choose your dog. (Alexandra chooses Patrick.)
Teacher:	Patrick can you be a dog that barks? (Patrick says, "Okay.")
Teacher:	Now we need a girl in the house. Who do you choose Alexandra? ("Maria," she answers.)
Teacher:	Maria would you play the girl in Alexandra's story? (Maria nods "yes.")
Teacher:	Dana, Patrick, and Maria, please come up here in front. Everyone else can move to where they can see and sit down. Alexandra's play is going to start. (Children move and sit.)
Teacher:	Dana and Patrick, let's start with you moving to the door of Maria's house. "The lady knocked on the door." "Do you want to buy my cookies?"
Teacher:	"I will if you sing a song and your dog barks."
Teacher:	Dana if you don't know a song to sing you can just sing *la, la, la.* "The dog barks." The teacher and the children finish the play sequence. Maria improvises giving Dana coins.
Teacher:	Good acting. Dana really sang a song. Patrick, what a good job of pretending to be a dog. You walked like a dog. Maria that was a good idea—giving money for cookies. A class discussion follows. Children decide to ask Alexandra if the story can be "acted" again.

FIGURE 10–10 Example of a child's story dramatization. (Courtesy of Busy Bee Preschool, Santa Clara, California.)

their writings make every effort to use teaching techniques and strategies that promote a children's desire to write and increase their handwriting skills.

Should early childhood educators help children with *relating skills*? Relating skills would include the ability to speak and later write ideas clearly. To do so when dictating a story the child needs some beginning idea of story structure, what comes first, next, etc. If they are giving a report of something experienced, they need some idea of a sequence of happenings. If they are providing directions that help someone accomplish a task, they will need to have some sequence of actions in mind. If they are dictating a note or message, children will need to identify what facts or information they want the receiver to know.

Early childhood teachers use picture-book readings, storytelling, flannel board stories, story songs, poetry, and other literary activities to provide young children with opportunities to acquire a knowledge of story structure. They point out story sequence in picture-book discussions. Many other preschool activities deal with a sequence of time, actions, and steps needed to complete a task. Teachers gently promote children's clarification of ideas by accepting statements and children's ideas and their opinions. When a teacher makes comments such as "Jacob thinks we should have snack after recess" or "Ethan wants to know if the hamster has been fed," the teacher is restating what she thinks a child has said and this let's the child know she has been either understood or misunderstood. It gives the child the opportunity to correct and try again to express herself more clearly.

What early childhood teacher actions, strategies, and techniques encourage children's dictation of stories and other types of written communication? Some suggestions follow.

◆ Create no pressure to dictate. This is a child-choice activity.

◆ Encourage children to dictate their ideas concerning a real and present happening such as how they made a drawing or block structure, or how a problem was solved, or how a project was completed. They can also be encouraged to relate an important experience or happening, or a message they want to send, or dictate a sign for a dramatic play area, and so on.

◆ Listen raptly at the child's eye level.

◆ Probe for intent.

◆ Help the child articulate what she is trying to communicate.

◆ Help the child begin if necessary.

◆ Talk about what the child has already contributed after dictation starts.

◆ Give a short teacher example, when prudent.

◆ Talk about what you are doing as you take dictation.

◆ Date the child's work, and encourage creation of a title, if the child wishes.

◆ Compliment what features you can when the child dictates something for you to write.

◆ Comment on descriptive word use that adds clarity and interest.

◆ Suggest that the child may want a visual to accompany her words—such as a drawing, etc.

◆ Post the child's work and/or have the child share the writing with others. (Teachers can read and talk about the child's dictation, after asking the child if she wishes the teacher to do so.)

◆ Develop a classroom writing file where children's dictation is kept and explain that all will go home at the end of the week unless the child wants it to go home sooner.

Figure 10–11 gives examples of teacher statements that relate to the dictation suggestions in the above list.

Reaching Reluctant Storytellers

Educators may be faced with some young children who seem unable to initiate stories or who are reluctant interactive audience members. Reaching these children can be a challenge. Telling one's own story involves an element of

Examples of teacher statements probing for intent
"Those are scary words—monster, ghost, and devil. You are trying to tell a scary story, is that right?"
"Your kitten's fur is soft and you are saying you like to feel the soft fur."
"In your story something is going to happen to this very small mouse and you have used the words *little* and *tiny* to describe the mouse."

Examples of teacher statements that commend children's efforts
"You've decided on an interesting title for your story. It tells me your story will be about a cat."
"Your message begins with telling your mom something you want her to know. Is there something else you want to tell her?"
"That's a good start. Now I know you are in a park when your story begins."
"You've said three words—see, here they are."

Examples of helping to get the ball rolling with students
"Lots of stories start with 'Once upon a time.' "
"Is your story about a zoo, and airplane, a clown, or something else?"
"Your first word is . . ."
"Your story is about . . ."

Examples of giving a short teacher story or other writing example
"I wrote a story about how I locked myself out of my car yesterday."
"I wrote a story about my horse, Captain, and how he jumped over a high fence."
"When I write a note, I think about the important things I want the person to know."
"Sometimes just one word in a sign says what I want others to know, like 'danger' or 'hot.' "

Talk about what you are doing as you are doing it, but be careful not to interrupt.
"I'm listening to hear your words."
"I'm starting in the left-hand corner."
"I'm printing the word _____."
"It starts with a 'B.' "
"That word has two syllables: 'door' and 'way.' "
"Joseph is his name, so I printed a capital (big) 'J.' "

Compliment Examples
"You told me three things about your dog. That's neat, because now I know more about him." (content)
"Your story had a beginning, a middle part, and an end. All good stories have those, too." (appropriate story sequence)
"You talked until you were finished and didn't stop to play—good going." (staying focused)
"I liked that word you used. The word was *gigantic*. It's a big word that describes large objects like elephants, skyscrapers, and monster trucks." (vocabulary)

Comment on the child's use of descriptive words.
"You used the word *spotted* to tell me how your dog looks. That tells me he looks different from my dog."
"When you said your favorite cookie was chocolate chip, I knew exactly what kind of cookie it was."
"Your description of the snow floating to the ground told me it was a certain kind of snow."
"When you said you ran very fast, I knew you were in a hurry."

FIGURE 10-11 Teacher dictation statements.

risk. Becoming comfortable speaking before a group may be difficult for some children in light of their innate nature, home culture, or past experience. A classroom alive with "story," dramatization, and performance may slowly reach these children, as the fun, excitement, and "social connectedness" of storytelling become part of their classroom lives. Most child groups have a number of enthusiastic story presenters, who are learning which of their presenter skills or created story parts are enjoyed by their audience. These are willing and eager models.

Some children feel comfortable using active body movements and dance, and it has become integral to their storytelling style. The early childhood educator who introduces storytelling discovers that wild fantasy and vivid imagination are alive and well in most young children.

Storytelling with Young Limited-English Children

Pantomimes of eating dinner, going to bed, dressing, washing one's face and brushing teeth, opening a door with a key, rocking a baby to sleep, and other activities intrigue limited-English speakers. Pantomimes can include words in English and other languages enacted by children and adults. Props are sometimes useful. Guessing is half the fun. Using pantomimes can introduce and enhance the world of storytelling.

A Cut-and-Tell Story

Clever teachers have created cut-and-tell stories that readily capture children's attention. While telling these stories, the teacher cuts a paper shape relating to the story line. *The Boy in the Boat*, an example, follows.

Preparation

Step 1: Fold a piece of 9-by-12-inch (or larger) paper in half.

Step 2: Fold top corners down toward the middle.

Step 3: Fold single sheet up over triangles.

Step 4: Turn over and fold single sheet up.

Those who know how to fold a sailor's hat will recognize the pattern. Tell the story with scissors handy.

> Once there was a boy (or girl) who wanted to be a sailor. He had a sailor's hat. (Show hat shape.) And he had a boat. (Turn the hat so it becomes a boat.) One day he climbed in his boat and floated to the middle of a big lake. It was very hot, for the sun was bright. He took off his shirt and pants and threw them into the water. He had a swimming suit on under his clothes, and he felt much cooler. His boat hit a large rock and the front of his boat fell off. (Cut off front of boat.)

> Then a giant fish took a bite out of the bottom of the boat. (Cut off the bottom.)

> The back of the boat came off when a big bird flew down and sat on it. (Cut off the back of the boat.)

> The boy didn't have but a little boat left and water was reaching his toes, so he jumped overboard and swam to the shore. He watched his boat sink. Then he saw something white floating toward him. What do you think it could be? (Unfold what's left of the boat.)

> His shirt!

Finding Additional Help

Many metropolitan areas have storytelling clubs and associations. Increasingly apparent are individuals and groups bent on preserving cultural and ethnic stories and techniques. One well-known resource for storytelling is the National Association for the Preservation and Perpetuation of Storytelling, P.O. Box 309, Jonesborough, TN 37659.

PARENTS, VOLUNTEERS, AND COMMUNITY STORYTELLERS

It is surprising how many parents, volunteers, and community elementary school-aged children, high school students, and adults will rise to the occasion when asked to tell fictional stories or stories concerning significant life experiences.

Grandparents and other seniors might relate stories from their own unique backgrounds. Stories about contemporary happenings are also valuable. Many of these stories might involve a rich array of multicultural and multigenerational themes and offer wisdom accumulated through many years of living. Stories might also be told in the authentic language of the storyteller.

Intergeneration storytelling benefits both the storyteller and the listener. However, guidelines of suitability will need to be discussed.

Older storytellers and other volunteers should be briefed on appropriate time length, settings, story features, and so forth.

SUMMARY

Teachers offer orally told stories to promote literacy and encourage children's language enjoyment and development of oral abilities.

One goal of storytelling is achieving a feeling of togetherness and enjoyment through the words of a story. Building listening skills, developing vocabulary, and expanding interest are other important goals.

Stories for storytelling can be found in printed sources or borrowed from other teachers. A story can also be created by the teacher. By following suggested techniques and criteria, a successful activity for both children and teachers is possible.

Stories are told in the teacher's own words, with key events clearly in mind. Watching the children's interest and reactions keeps the teacher aware of how well the experience is accepted. Any skill takes practice; storytelling skills improve with use.

Teachers promote child storytelling by encouraging children and recognizing their efforts.

ADDITIONAL RESOURCES

Readings

Brett, D. (1998). *Annie stories: A special kind of storytelling.* New York: Workman.

Fujita, H. (1998). *Stories to play with: Kids' tales told with puppets, paper, toys and imagination.* Little Rock, AR: August House Publishers, Inc.

Gillard, M. (1996). *Storyteller storyteacher.* New York: Stenhouse Publishers.

Hamilton, M., & Weiss, M. (1996). *Stories in my pocket: Tales kids can tell.* Golden, CO: Fulcrum Publishing.

McCord, S. (1995). *The storybook journey: Pathways to literacy through story and play.* Englewood Cliffs, NJ: Prentice Hall.

Mooney, B., & Holt, D. (1996). *The storyteller's guide.* Little Rock, AR: August House Publishers.

Paley, V. (1990). *The boy who would be a helicopter.* Cambridge, MA: Harvard University Press.

Helpful Websites

Brown Bag Bedtime Books
http://www.brownbagbooks.com
Sells read-along stories that include CD recordings.

The Internet Public Library
http://www.ipl.org
Includes some story text. Select KidSpace link, then Story Hour.

Reading Is Fundamental
http://www.rifnet.org
Reviews storytelling history and benefits.

Book Companion Website

Read, analyze, and react to elements in classic stories that create drama. Describe why memorable main characters in your favorite stories are well remembered and may guide your actions. What makes Beatrix Potter's *Peter Rabbit* as real today as he was when you were a child? Answer these in the Internet exercises provided on the book companion website.

STUDENT ACTIVITIES

1. Create a story. In outline form, write the beginning, middle, and ending. Practice telling it to a fellow student. Use your own title or select one of the following:

   The Giant Ice Cream Cone *The Big Birthday Present*

   Magic Shoes *The Police Officer and Mike*

   The Dog Who Wouldn't Bark *The Fastest Bike*

   The Mouse Who Chased Cats *I Have a Bug in My Pocket*

   Billy Found a Dollar

2. Tell a story to a group of children. Write an evaluation of both the story and your skill.

   a. What parts interested the children the most?

   b. What would you change if you told it again?

   c. What techniques were used to hold interest?

3. Create a story song. Share it with your classmates.

4. Find an ethnic or cultural story that could be told to young children. Cite your source and be ready to share the story with fellow classmates.

5. Design an evaluation (rating form) to assess a storyteller's skill.

6. Interview and invite a librarian or experienced adult who tells stories during story hours to share favorite stories with the class.

7. Tell a story to a video camera. Play it back. Look for strong points and areas for growth in skill.

8. Read the following kindergarten teacher's description of an oral storytelling situation.

   Once they were drawn in, they became intensely focused during the story. I couldn't help but notice the deep interest in their faces, and they begged for more. They especially liked stories with jokes about themselves, and with issues that weren't too close to home. For example, they wouldn't have enjoyed a vivid description of an angry mother, but they adored the story in which the janitor had mistakenly replaced their table chairs with those from the toddler room. (Cooper, 1993)

   Knowing preschoolers enjoy a slapstick type of humor, create a story for teacher storytelling. What vivid descriptions would you avoid including in tales to preschoolers—ones you feel are "too close to home"?

9. Have a child under the age of 5 dictate a story to you. Try an "I'll tell you my story, and you tell me your story" technique. Share the results with the class.

349

10. Listen to a commercial storytelling recording. List the techniques used to hold children's interest.

11. List important reasons for teacher storytelling.

12. Using the cue card example (Figure 10–6), tell a fellow student the *Tale of Peter Rabbit*.

13. Read the following storytelling promotion idea.

Create a home-visiting stuffed animal who reports back to school his adventures during his home visit. The class stuffed animal comes in a convenient carrying case with written instructions to parents to help their child record what the stuffed animal experienced. This written and pictorial record (if parents take photos) is presented to the class and becomes part of a book entitled *Geraldo's Adventures*. Often, this book is the most cherished book in the classroom collection.

What would you include in the instructions to families? Put your instructions in written form.

14. Create a story that can be told while each child in the audience moves props that have been distributed beforehand, such as (1) felt pieces on a square of felt, (2) plastic animals, (3) blocks, (4) paper figures, or (5) other props you create. Test the story and props with a small group of children. Report results to classmates, and write a brief summary for your instructor.

CHAPTER REVIEW

A. Column I lists common preschool characteristics. Select the appropriate storytelling technique or criterion from Column II that matches each item in Column I.

COLUMN I

1. likes to move frequently
2. has had experiences at home, at school, and in community
3. has fear of large animals and bodily harm
4. likes to play with words
5. likes to be part of the group
6. likes to talk

COLUMN II

a. selects stories without cruel monsters or vivid descriptions of accidents
b. "Ducky-Ducky and Be-Bop-Boo went to the park to meet Moo-moo the cow."
c. stories contain familiar objects and animals
d. "What did big bird say to baby bird?"
e. "Help Tipper blow out the candle." "Pretend my finger is a candle and try to blow it out!"
f. "Stand up and reach for the moon like Johnny did in our story. Now close your eyes; is it dark like night? You couldn't reach the moon, but can you find your nose with your eyes closed?"

B. Briefly answer the following questions.

1. Why should storytelling take place often in early childhood centers?

2. What are three resources for stories?

3. What are stereotypes?

C. Select the correct answers. Each item has more than one correct answer.

1. In storytelling, the storyteller not only uses words but also uses
   a. the hands.
   b. the face.
   c. the eyes.
   d. gestures.

2. Recommended techniques used by storytellers are
   a. changing the voice to fit the character.
   b. changing the personality of a character during the story.
   c. stopping without ending a story so that children will listen quietly the next time.
   d. watching children closely and emphasizing the parts they enjoy.

3. Criteria for story selection include
   a. believable characters.
   b. a plot with lots of action.
   c. a possible problem to be resolved.
   d. making sure the story is one that can be memorized.

4. Teachers should not
   a. let children be inattentive during their story.
   b. feel defeated if a storytelling attempt occasionally flops.
   c. put bad guys in stories.
   d. tell the story memorized word for word.

5. During storytelling time, the
   a. child can form her own mental pictures.
   b. teacher can share interesting personal life experiences.
   c. teacher models correct speech.
   d. teacher models creative use of words.

D. Write a paragraph or two describing appropriate teacher strategies and techniques promoting clarity and sequencing when children are dictating their ideas or stories.

E. Give two examples of words, phrases, or sentences that must be memorized when a teacher is telling a particular story. Include story title. (For instance, in *The Three Little Pigs,* the phrase "I'll huff, and I'll puff, and I'll blow your house down" must be memorized.)

SUGGESTED STORIES

THE LITTLE ELF WHO LISTENS

Author Unknown

Do you know what an elf is? No one ever saw an elf, but we can pretend it is a little boy about the size of a squirrel. This elf I'm going to tell you about lived at the edge of a large forest.

He played with chattering chipmunks, with bushy-tailed squirrels, and with hopping rabbits. They were his best friends.

Now, this little elf had something very special. His fairy godmother had given him three pairs of listening ears! That would be six ears, wouldn't it?

There was a big pair of ears, a middle-sized pair of ears, and a tiny pair of ears.

When the little elf wore his big ears, he could hear the faintest (smallest) sounds in the woods—leaves falling from the trees, the wind whispering to the flowers, the water rippling over stones in the little stream. He could hear the dogs barking far, far away. The little elf always told his friends, the squirrels, the chipmunks, and the rabbits, about the dogs, so they could run and hide. They were very thankful.

The little elf wore his tiny ears when the storms came and the wind blew loud and fierce, and when the thunder roared and crashed. The little animals that had only one pair of ears were frightened by the loud noises, but their friend, the elf, told them that the wind and the thunder were important. After them would come the rain, and the rain was needed to help the food to grow.

On most days the little elf wore his middle-sized ears. He liked them best of all. He listened to all the middle-sized sounds with them, not the very loud and not the very soft sounds.

One morning some children came to the woods to pick flowers. "What shall we do with our pretty flowers?" a little girl asked.

A boy called Adam said, "Let's take them to school." "Let's!" the little girl agreed. "We can show them to the other children." The little elf listened, and he wished that he could go to school. He wanted to see and hear what the children did at school.

He told his friends, the squirrels, the chipmunks, and the rabbits, about it, but they said, "No, an elf cannot go to school. School is just for children."

The little elf decided he would go to school anyway. So the next morning he crept out of his warm bed of leaves under the toadstool, and he skipped down the road toward the school.

Soon he came to a big building. Girls and boys were playing out on the playground. There was a red, white, and blue flag flying high on a pole, so the little elf knew this was really the school.

Just then a bell rang, and the children all went inside. The little elf quietly slipped inside too.

You were the girls and boys playing outside. You are the children that the little elf followed.

Which pair of ears do you think he will have to use at school?

—His big ears because you talk too low, as if you were afraid of your own voice?

—His tiny ears because you talk so loud that you sound like a thunderstorm?

—Or his middle-sized ears because you are talking just right—loud enough so everyone in the room can hear, but not so loud that you seem to be shouting? Remember, the little elf likes his middle-sized ears best!

(Suggestions: It is a good idea to show tiny, middle-sized, and big ears drawn on the chalkboard or on paper or on the flannel board. A follow-up to this story could be sorting objects into three groups by size.)

LITTLE DUCK

(This is a good group-participation story. Children imitate the actions with the teacher.)

To introduce the story:

"In this story you will need to listen closely when you hear the words *run, walk, big steps, swim,* and *bang.* When we hear the word *run* we are going to make a running sound. Watch and listen."

The teacher demonstrates and practices with the children, demonstrating each of the action words before starting the storytelling.

Run–Slapping thighs quickly

Walk–Slapping thighs slowly

Big steps–Thumping fists on chest

Swim–Rubbing palms of hands
    together rapidly

Bang—Clapping hands once

Little Duck was scolded for eating too many bugs, so he said to his mother, "I am going to run (action) away. Then I can eat anything I like."

So Little Duck left the barnyard and his own dear mother who loved him. He walked (action) down the road on his little flat feet. (Action)

Little Duck met a cow who was munching hay.

"Have some," offered the cow.

Hay was much too rough for Little Duck to eat because he had no teeth to chew it. He thanked the cow for her thoughtfulness and walked on. (Action) Suddenly, he heard a big BANG. (action) Little Duck trembled with fright.

"Oh, oh, that must be a hunter with a gun," he cried.

Little Duck ran (action) away from there fast. Then Little Duck heard some BIG LOUD steps coming toward him. (Action) He hid in some bushes until the big steps went by.

"Why, that was only a HORSE," said Little Duck happily.

Little Duck met a dog with a bone.

"Have some," said the dog.

"No, thank you," said Little Duck as he walked on. (action)

Little Duck came to a pond. He jumped into the water and swam across the pond. (action) He climbed out of the water and walked on. (action)

Suddenly Little Duck heard a fierce sound, "Grrrrrrowl, Rrrrrrruff."

Right in front of Little Duck sat a fox!

"Yum, yum," said the fox, smacking his lips. "Duck for dinner!"

"Oh, oh!" cried Little Duck as he began to run. (action)

He ran and ran faster and faster. (action) He came to the pond and swam across. (action) The fox was right behind him.

Suddenly there was a loud BANG. (action) When the fox heard the big noise, he turned and ran away. (action)

Little Duck felt safer now, but he kept right on running. (action)

He passed the horse—and the cow—and the dog with a bone. Soon he was back in the barnyard with his own dear mother who loved him.

He said:

"I'm a little duck as you can see,

And this barnyard is the best place for me."

Little Duck knew that being scolded was for his own good, and he never ate too many bugs again. He never ran away again, either. (action)

I'M GOING TO CATCH A LION FOR THE ZOO

Author Unknown, Traditional

I'll get up in the morning (yawn and stretch)

I'll put on my clothes (go through motions)

I'll take a long piece of rope down from the wall (reach up)

I'll carry it over my shoulder (push up arm to shoulder)

Open the door (pretend to turn door handle)

And close the door (clasp hands) I'm going on a lion hunt, and I'm not afraid (slap hands on knees)

Whoops—coming to a hill (climbing with hands)

Now I'm crossing a bridge (pound closed fists on chest)

And I'm crossing a river (motion as though swimming)

Now I'm going through tall grass (rub hands together)

Whoops—I'm walking in mud (poke air-filled cheeks)

I'm going on a lion hunt, and I'm not afraid (slap hands on knees)

Coming to a lion territory—want to catch a lion.

Have to go tippy-toe (fingertips on knees) I'm climbing up a tree (climb up and look all around)

No lion!

Going in a dark cave (cup hands around eyes and look around)

Oh, a lion! I'm scared.

(The trip back home is exactly the same, only in reverse and faster. The cave is first and slam the door is last.) Home at last. I'm not going on any more lion hunts. I've found a lion, and I'm afraid.

(This story is full of child participation and action. It takes teacher practice but is well worth the effort. Note: This is a variation of *Bear Hunt*.)

THE LITTLE RED HEN

See the Appendix for story text. Trousdale (1990) relates her experiences with this story as follows:

> To encourage interactive telling . . .
> I have taken with me stuffed animals for each character. After the story has become thoroughly familiar to the children, the stuffed hen, dog, cat, and rat are given to individual children. I continue to "tell" or narrate the story, but when each character speaks, the child who is holding the hen, or dog, or cat, or rat, speaks that character's words. Holding the animals seems to give the children a sense of security and authority.
>
> In early childhood, many repetitions of the story may be necessary before children remember individual character's lines. (p. 170)

THE LITTLE HOUSE WITH NO DOORS AND NO WINDOWS AND A STAR INSIDE

Author Unknown

(Plan to have an apple, cutting board, and a knife ready for the ending. A plate full of apple slices is sometimes enjoyed after this story.)

Once there was a little boy who had played almost all day. He had played with all his toys and all the games he knew, and he could not think of anything else to do. So he went to his mother and asked, "Mother, what shall I do now?"

His mother said, "I know about a little red house with no doors and no windows and a star inside it. You can find it, if you go look for it."

So the little boy went outside and there he met a little girl. He said, "Do you know where there is a little red house with no doors and no windows and a star inside?"

The little girl said, "No, I don't know where there is a little red house with no doors and no windows and a star inside, but you can ask my daddy. He is a farmer and he knows lots of things. He's down by the barn and maybe he can help you."

So the little boy went to the farmer down by the barn and said, "Do you know where there is a little red house with no doors and no windows and a star inside?"

"No," said the farmer, "I don't know, but why don't you ask Grandmother. She is in her house up on the hill. She is very wise and knows many things. Maybe she can help you."

So the little boy went up the hill to Grandmother's and asked, "Do you know where there is a little red house with no doors and no windows and a star inside?" "No," said Grandmother, "I don't know, but you can ask the wind, for the wind goes everywhere, and I am sure he can help you."

So the little boy went outside and asked the wind, "Do you know where I can find a little red house with no doors and no windows and a star inside?" And the wind said, "OHHHH! OOOOOOOOOOOO!" And it sounded to the little boy as if the wind said, "Come with me." So the little boy ran after the wind. He ran through the grass and into the orchard and there on the ground he found the little house—the little red house with no doors and no windows and a star inside! He picked it up, and it filled both his hands. He ran home to his mother and said, "Look, Mother! I found the little red house with no doors and no windows, but I cannot see the star!"

So this is what his mother did (teacher cuts apple using a horizontal slice making two halves). "Now I see the star!" said the little boy. (Teacher says to children) "Do you?"

THE PANCAKE WHO RAN AWAY

(a folktale)

Once upon a time there was a mother who had seven hungry children. She made a delicious light and fluffy golden pancake.

"I'm hungry," said one child. "I want some pancake."

Then all the other children said the same thing, and the mother had to cover her ears because they were so loud.

"Hush, shush!" said the mother. "You can all have some as soon as the pancake is golden brown on both sides."

Now the pancake was listening and did not want to be eaten, so it hopped from the pan and rolled out the door and down the hill.

"Stop, pancake!" called the mother. She and all her children ran after the pancake as fast as they could. The pancake rolled on and on.

When it rolled a long way, it met a man.

"Good morning, pancake," said the man.

"Good morning Mandy-Pandy-Man!" said the pancake.

"Don't roll so fast. Stop and let me eat you," said the man.

"I've run away from the mother and seven hungry children and I'll run away from you Mandy-Pandy-Man." It rolled and rolled down the road until it met a hen clucking and hurrying along.

"Good morning, pancake," said the hen.

"The same to you, Henny-Fenny-Hen."

"Pancake don't roll so fast, stop and let me eat you," said the hen.

"No, no," said the pancake. "I've run away from the mother and the seven hungry children, Mandy-Pandy-Man, and I'll run away from you." And it rolled on and on.

It met a rooster.

"Good morning, pancake," said the rooster.

"The same to you, Rooster-Zooster," said the pancake.

"Stop so I can eat you," said the rooster.

"I've run away from the mother and the seven hungry children, Mandy-Pandy-Man,

Henny-Fenny-Hen, and I'll run away from you," said the pancake. And it rolled on and on until it met a duck.

"Good morning, pancake," said the duck.

"The same to you, Quacky Duck," said the pancake.

"Stop so I can eat you," said the duck.

"I've run away from the mother and the seven hungry children, Mandy-Pandy-Man, Henny-Fenny-Hen, Rooster-Zooster, and I'll run away from you," said the pancake. On and on the pancake rolled until it met a goose.

"Good morning, pancake," said the goose.

"The same to you, Goosey-Loosey," said the pancake.

"Stop so I can eat you," said the goose.

"I've run away from the mother and the seven hungry children, Mandy-Pandy-Man, Henny-Fenny-Hen, Rooster-Zooster, Quacky Duck, and I'll run away from you." The pancake rolled on and on. Then, the pancake met a pig at the edge of a dark wood.

"Good morning, pancake," said the pig.

"The same to you Piggy-Wiggy," said the pancake.

"That wood is dark; don't be in such a hurry! We can go through the wood together. It's not safe in there," said the pig.

The pancake thought that was a good idea, so they went along together until they came to a river. The pig was so fat he could float across, but the pancake had no way of crossing.

"Jump on my snout," said the pig, "and I'll carry you across." So the pancake climbed on the pig's snout. "Oink!" said the pig as he opened his mouth wide and swallowed the pancake in one gulp. And that's how it was . . . pancakes are for eating, and the pig had his breakfast.

It Was My Idea

One winter two snow geese were on their way south flying high in the sky. They looked down and saw a beautiful lake. They were tired and hungry, so they landed together, splashing across the sparkling water. There were seeds and bugs everywhere, and they ate their fill. A talkative turtle poked his head up from the water, and talked, and talked, and talked. "We'll get no rest here," said one goose to the other. The turtle overheard, and said, "I want to see the world. Take me with you. Will you? Will you? Will you?" The geese laughed. "Now, how can we take you with us?" they said. "I'll get a stick. If you both hold it in your beaks, I can clamp down in the middle with my strong snapping mouth," explained the turtle. "It won't work turtle, you couldn't stop talking that long," laughed a goose. The turtle talked, and talked, and talked. Finally, the geese said, "Yes," just to shut him up. The three took off together with turtle biting the stick and hanging between them. Soon they flew over a farm. A farmer in the field looked up. He had never seen such a sight. He called to his wife, "Look at those clever birds, aren't they smart?" Turtle called back as he fell from the sky, "It was my idea." Turtle was very lucky to fall into a giant haystack. He was happy and ready to start a new adventure on the farm.

(This is a "bare bones" version of this tale. The author suggests you embellish it by adding descriptive words and developing further characterization. Invoke color and use sounds. Add details suiting your own personal style.)

MORE PARTICIPATION STORIES

JUST LIKE METOO!

(Children imitate what Metoo does. Metoo does things a little faster each day. Metoo was always late for school. Speedee was always on time.)

Once upon a time, Metoo came to live at Speedee's house. He thought, "I'd like to do what Speedee does, but I can't learn everything at one time. Each day I'll do one new thing."

On Monday, when the alarm went off, Metoo jumped out of bed just like Speedee and washed his hands and face at 7:30 in the morning. (Jump up, wash hands and face, sit down.)

On Tuesday, when the alarm went off, Metoo jumped out of bed and washed his hands and face and brushed his teeth at 7:30 in the morning. (Jump up, wash hands and face, brush teeth, sit down.)

On Wednesday, when the alarm went off, Metoo jumped out of bed just like Speedee and washed his hands and face, brushed his teeth, and dressed by himself at 7:30 in the morning. (Jump up, wash hands and face, brush teeth, dress self, sit down.)

On Thursday, when the alarm went off, Metoo jumped out of bed just like Speedee, washed his hands and face, brushed his teeth, dressed by himself, and ate his breakfast at 7:30 in the morning. (Jump up, wash hands and face, brush teeth, dress myself, eat breakfast, sit down.)

On Friday, when the alarm went off, Metoo jumped out of bed, just like Speedee, washed his hands and face, brushed his teeth, dressed himself, ate his breakfast, and waved goodbye to Speedee's mother who was on her way to work at 7:30 in the morning. (Very rapidly, jump up, wash hands and face, brush teeth, dress self, eat breakfast, wave goodbye, sit down.) Speedee and Metoo walked to school together. Metoo wasn't late for school!

On Saturday, when the alarm went off, Metoo turned over and shut it off. (Move right arm across body slowly, as if shutting off alarm.) He had heard Speedee say, "This is Saturday. Nobody goes to school on Saturday."

TO GRANDMOTHER'S HOUSE

(Before beginning this story, draw the picture in Figure 10–12 on the chalkboard or on a large sheet of paper. You can draw homes from different cultures, such as grass huts, flat top South American types, teepees, igloos, and so on. During the telling let your fingers, hands, and arms show Clementine's actions during her travels.)

One day Clementine's mother said, "I'm making cookies. I need some sugar. Please go to Grandma's house and borrow a cup of sugar." "Yes, Mother, I'll go right away," said Clementine.

FIGURE 10–12 Clementine's travels.

Clementine climbed up the first mountain. Climb, climb, climb. (Make climbing motions with arms.) Climb, climb, climb.

When she got to the top of the mountain she slid down. (Make sliding motion with hands.)

At the bottom of the mountain was a wide, wide lake. Clementine jumped in and swam across. Swim, swim, swim. (Make swimming arm motions.)

Clementine climbed the next mountain. Climb, climb, climb. (Make climbing hand motions.) Then she slid down the other side. (Make sliding motions.)

Next, Clementine crossed the bridge. Tromp, tromp, tromp. (Make feet move up and down.) Tromp, tromp, tromp.

Clementine climbed the third mountain. Climb, climb, climb (motions). Then she slid down the other side (motions).

Clementine's grandmother was standing next to her house. "Hello, Grandmother, may I have a cup of sugar? My mother's making cookies." "Yes, dear," said Grandmother, and she came out of the house with a little bag.

"Goodbye, Grandmother," Clementine said. Climb, climb, climb. She slid down the other side and crossed the bridge. Tromp, tromp, tromp. She climbed the middle mountain. Climb, climb, climb (motions). Then she slid down the other side (motions). She swam the lake with the bag in her teeth and her head held high. Swim, swim, swim (motions). Next, she climbed the mountain. Climb, climb, climb (motions). Then she slid down the mountain (motions) to her house.

When she went into the house, she gave her mother the sugar. Her mother said, "This is brown sugar. I wanted white sugar." "I'll go to Grandmother's," said Clementine.

Clementine climbed the first mountain. Climb, climb, climb (motions). She slid down the other side (motions). Then she swam the lake. Swim, swim, swim (motions).

She climbed the second mountain. Climb, climb, climb (motions). She slid down the other side (motions) and crossed the bridge. Tromp, tromp, tromp (motions).

She climbed the third mountain. Climb, climb, climb (motions). Then she slid down the other side (motions).

Grandmother was working in her garden. "Hello, Grandmother," said Clementine. "Two visits in one day. How nice," said Grandmother.

"But I can't stay this time either. Mother needs white sugar instead of brown," said Clementine.

Grandmother went into her house and came out with a little bag.

"You look so tired, Clementine!" said Grandmother.

"I am," said Clementine.

"Take the shortcut home," said Grandmother.

So Clementine did. She walked straight home on the path at the foot of the mountains.

(This story can be lengthened by having the mother request additional ingredients and by Clementine taking cookies to Grandmother after they are baked. White or wheat flour is another possibility, as is raisins or nuts.)

WHAT WAS BEHIND THE DOOR?

(Teacher says the following to children: "I need you to help me tell this story! Do you suppose that you can remember all of the sounds that we have talked about? In this story, you can make the animal noises that Granny hears. When the story says, Granny heard a dog, say, 'Bow Wow!' [and so on—see list at end of story]. Listen carefully.")

Granny sat in a big armchair knitting Tommy a sweater. All of a sudden she heard a dog say ". . ." (Bow Wow).

"Gracious!" said Granny. "I do believe there's a dog behind the door. Should I have a dog in the house?"

"Oh yes," answered the dog behind the door. "I'm a good dog. I don't jump on people."

"Very well," said Granny, and she went on knitting the sweater for Tommy. All of a sudden Granny heard a cat say ". . ." (Meow).

"Gracious!" said Granny. "I do believe that there is a cat behind the door. Should I have a cat in the house?"

"Oh yes," answered the cat. "I am a good cat. I do not scratch the furniture."

"Very well," said Granny, and she went on knitting Tommy's sweater. All of a sudden Granny heard a bird say ". . ." (Peep Peep).

"Gracious!" said Granny. "I do believe that I heard a bird behind the door. Should I have a bird in the house?"

"Oh yes," answered the bird. "I am a good bird. I sing very sweetly."

"Very well," said Granny, and she went right on knitting a sweater for Tommy.

All of a sudden, Granny heard a lion say ". . ." (Grrrr).

"Gracious!" said Granny. "I do believe that there is a lion behind the door. This is too much!" Carefully, Granny opened the door; because she wasn't sure she liked having a lion in the house.

And what do you think she found hiding behind her door? There was Tommy. He had been making those noises after all!

Suggest: "Can you all make the noises Tommy made?"

Dog—Bow Wow
Cat—Meow
Bird—Peep Peep
Lion—Grrrr

"What other animal sounds do you know?"

LITTLE DUCK LOST

(full of sounds and action)

Cow—"Moo Moo"
Cat—"Meow Meow"
Duck—"Quack Quack"
Horse—"Neigh Neigh"
Pig—"Oink Oink"
Mouse—"Squeak Squeak"
Dog—"Bow Wow"
Rooster—"Cock-a-doodle-do"

The animals on the farm were noisy one morning. The rooster (Cock-a-doodledo) was crowing. The cow (Moo Moo) was mooing. The dog (Bow Wow) was barking, and the cat (Meow Meow) was meowing. Everybody was looking for Little Duck (Quack Quack). Little Duck (Quack Quack) was gone. The cow (Moo Moo) looked all through the sweet clover in the pasture but no Little Duck (Quack Quack). The horse (Neigh Neigh) galloped into the next field, but no Little Duck (Quack Quack). The fat, fat pig (Oink Oink) pushed all the mud out of his puddle. He could not find Little Duck (Quack Quack).

Then the animals hurried down to the pond once more to look for Little Duck (Quack Quack). They all called him. (Everybody calls "Little Duck.") There was no Little Duck (Quack Quack). The animals were quiet as they walked back to the barn. They had looked everywhere, but could not find Little Duck (Quack Quack).

Suddenly, a little mouse (Squeak Squeak) came scurrying out of the barn. How he squeaked! He led the animals back into the barn and over to his nest in a quiet corner and there was Little Duck (Quack Quack) asleep on the mouse's (Squeak Squeak) nest. What a shout the animals gave! (Everybody calls "Wake up!") They had found Little Duck (Quack Quack). They woke him with their shouting. Little Duck (Quack Quack) was rushed back to the duck pond, where, after all, little ducks (Quack Quack) belong.

An additional story is found in the Appendix.

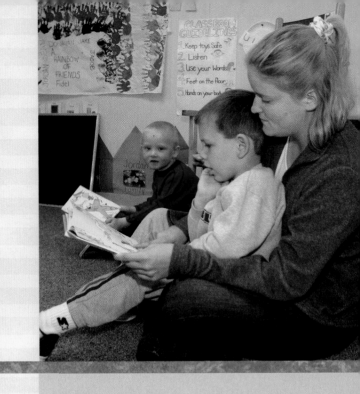

CHAPTER 11

Poetry

OBJECTIVES

After reading this chapter, you should be able to:

◆ Discuss poetry elements.

◆ Demonstrate the ability to present a poem.

◆ Create a poem that appeals to young children.

KEY TERMS

alliteration	figurative language	poems
assonance	metaphors	similes
couplets	nursery rhymes	verses
diction	personification	

FRECKLES

I notice Yolanda staring at my arm one day. She was new and had moved here from Arizona. She asked, "What are those?" It was summer, and my freckles really stood out. "They are called freckles," I said. She answered, "Have you tried to get them off?" I replied, "I tried buttermilk one time because someone told me buttermilk would make them go away. But it didn't work." She thought about that for a moment and said, "Have you tried soap and water?" I laughed, and told her that soap and water did not work either. Later that day, Yolanda walked by saying, "Sprinkles, speckles, freckles," while smiling up at me. "That's a rhyme, Yolanda," I answered.

QUESTIONS TO PONDER

1. What do you think about Yolanda's logic?

2. Would freckles or Yolanda's created rhyme be something to talk about with children at a sharing time?

3. Were the teacher's verbal responses appropriate?

Children's poetry is an enjoyable vehicle for developing listening skills. Activities that involve poetry hold many opportunities to promote language and literacy by associating pleasure with words. Poetry has a condensed quality that makes every word important. It prompts imagery through its sensory descriptions and can introduce enchanting tales. Nonsense verse appeals to the preschoolers' appreciation for slapstick.

The repetitive format of rhymes makes them "memorable." Repetition is a strategy for learning with pleasure. Expectancies are set up and gloriously materialize. Children's desire to hear more is intensified. The language of rhyme becomes easily fixed in memory; it can become part of a child's linguistic and intellectual resources for life.

Poetry is a perfect test for what language can do; it is full of wordplay. Poets have always used language in special ways, and in poetry, we have a vehicle for looking at the use of words, that is, the choosing of the one special word that fits perfectly. We need to share with children words "that taste good"—that tickle the tongue, tease the ear, create images in the mind's eye, delight us with their trickery, and amuse us with their puzzles and complexities.

Appropriate children's poetry is plentiful and varied. In addition to fast action and mood building, there is the joy of the rhythm of the words in many **poems**. Some rhythms in classic rhymes are so strong that they can motivate children to move their bodies or clap. The nursery rhymes "Jack and Jill," "Twinkle, Twinkle, Little Star," and "The Little Turtle" are good examples. Rhythm encourages children to join in orally, experiment with language, and move to the rhythmic sounds. Some poems appeal to the emotions; others, to the intellect (Figure 11–1).

A preschool child with beginning literacy might be described as a child familiar with Mother Goose rhymes and other contemporary and classic poems, and one who knows

FIGURE 11–1 Poetry can hold a child's attention.

that rhyming words sound alike. Three-year-olds delight in silly and playful poetry.

LEARNING OPPORTUNITIES

Poetry provides an opportunity for a child to learn new words, ideas, and attitudes and to experience life through the eyes of the poet. To remember how many days there are in a month, many people still recite a simple poem learned as a child. If you are asked to say the alphabet, the classic ABC song of childhood may come to mind.

Poetry has form and order. It is dependable and also easy to learn. Simple rhymes are picked up quickly, as most parents have seen from their children's ability to remember television commercials. Children in early childhood centers enjoy the accomplishment of memorizing short **verses**. They may ask to share the poems they have learned with the

---

poems — metrical forms of composition in which word images are selected and expressed to create powerful, often beautiful impressions in the listener and/or enjoyable rhythmic responses in young children.
verses — lines of a poem or poetry without imaginative or conceptual power.

teacher, just as they ask to sing songs they know (which are often poems set to music).

The teacher should provide encouragement, attention, and positive comments to the child who responds to poetry. As with picture-book reading, storytelling, and other language activities, the goal of the teacher in regard to poetry is to offer children pleasure and enjoyment of the language arts while expanding their knowledge and interest.

Poetry, then, is used for a variety of reasons, including the following.

◆ familiarizing and exposing children to classic and contemporary poetry that is considered part of our literary heritage
◆ training children to experience the pleasure of hearing sounds
◆ providing enjoyment through the use of poems with silly words and humor
◆ stimulating children's imaginations
◆ increasing vocabulary and knowledge
◆ building self-worth and self-confidence
◆ encouraging an understanding of rhyming

POETRY AND EARLY READING ABILITY

Poems, rhymes, and chants acquaint young children with language in repeated pleasant patterns and with catchy rhythms, such as "The Grand Old Duke of York." Drop the words in this rhyming chant (found in Chapter 14). Use da-Da, da-Da, da-Da, etc., and see how easy it is to isolate and sense the accented words and syllables. Pointing out rhyming words helps teach a child that different words can share some of the same sounds.

Experts believe children's ability to discriminate, create rhyming words, and sense the rhythm of words is closely related to early reading ability.

Educators agree that a great deal of general evidence indicates that both early awareness of rhyme and nursery rhyme knowledge facilitate literacy acquisition. It is a significant predictor of later progress in reading and spelling. A relationship exists between early rhyme awareness and later phonological skills. Nursery rhyme knowledge is a strong predictor of word attack and word identification skills when children begin early reading. The connection between rhyme awareness and the child's subsequent acquisition of literacy-related skill demonstrates that a developmental pathway to reading involves rhyme. Repetition of consonant sounds in the lyrics of **nursery rhymes** like "cock-a-doodle-doo, dee-doodledee doodle-dee doodle-dee-doo" certainly demonstrates rhyme and **alliteration**.

Children develop skill in identifying rhyme at an early age. The relationship between rime units and words that rhyme is obvious: words that rhyme share the same rime unit. Refer back to the discussion of phonemic awareness and rimes in Chapter 8. Children's knowledge of nursery rhymes is believed to be predictive of their success in spelling 2 to 3 years later.

SELECTION

Poetry introduces children to characters with fun-to-say names such as

◆ "Jonathan Bing" by Beatrice Curtis Brown.
◆ "Mrs. Peck Pigeon" by Eleanor Farjeon.
◆ "Godfrey Gordon Gustavos Gore" by William Rands.

The characters can live in familiar and far-fetched settings, such as.

◆ under the toadstool, from "The Elf and the Dormouse" by Oliver Herford.
◆ the animal store, from "The Animal Store" by Rachel Field.

---

nursery rhymes — folk sayings with rhyming words for very young children.
alliteration — repetition of beginning consonant sounds.

◆ in a little crooked house, from *Mother Goose.*

And they have various adventures and difficulties.

◆ "The kids are ten feet tall," from "Grown-Up-Down Town" by Bobbi Katz
◆ "Christopher Robin had wheezles and sneezles," from "Sneezles" by A. A. Milne
◆ "Listen, my children, this must be stopped," from "The Grasshoppers" by Dorothy Aldis

Teachers select poetry that they can present eagerly and that they believe children will like. Delight in words is a natural outcome when the poem suits the audience. Teachers look for poems of quality and merit. Three elements exist in good poetry: (1) distinguished **diction**, (2) carefully chosen words and phrases with rich sensory and associated meanings, and (3) significant content. Much of classic poetry has a song quality and a melody of its own. Poetry can say something to children, titillate them, recall happy occasions or events, or encourage them to explore.

Teachers have found traditional eighteenth-century nursery rhymes are still popular with today's children. Favorite rhymes with strong four-beat **couplets** ("Humpty Dumpty" and others) were repeated with the teacher exaggerating the beat (as children do). This technique held group interest.

Categories of verse popular with most preschoolers have one or more of the following characteristics.

◆ simple story line ("Jack Be Nimble")
◆ simple story line with finger play ("This Little Piggy")
◆ story in song with repeated chorus ("London Bridge")
◆ verse/story with nonsense words ("Hey, Diddle, Diddle")

◆ descriptions of daily actions ("Little Jack Horner")
◆ choral reading in which youngsters could join in with rhymed words ("To Market, to Market")

No child should miss the fun, wit, and wisdom of Mother Goose. Literacy, in part, depends on a child's exposure to cultural tradition. Mother Goose is an American tradition. Make a list of Mother Goose characters. You will be surprised at how many you remember.

Practicing teachers recommend the following poetry selection criteria.

◆ Begin with poems that are sure to please.
◆ Select poems that have strong rhythm and rhyme.
◆ Find poems that play with sound or are humorous.
◆ Look for content that deals with things that are familiar to children's lives.

Once children have been bitten by the poetry bug, focus on rhythm and rhyme, and explore how various poets use sound devices such as alliteration or onomatopoeia.

Types of Poetry

There are several types of poetry, described as follows:

◆ lyric melodic: descriptive poetry that often has a song quality
◆ narrative poetry: tells a story or describes an event or happening
◆ limerick: a poem with five lines of verse set in a specific rhyming pattern that is usually humorous
◆ free verse poetry: does not rhyme
◆ nonsense poetry: often ridiculous and whimsical (Figure 11–2)

---

diction — clarity of speech; enunciation.
couplets — stanzas of two rhyming lines.

"What's did you do?"   said the shoe.

"I sat on the hog,"   answered the dog.

"Is he dead?"   asked the bread.

"That is not funny!"   said the bunny.

"Is that a hat?"   said the cat.

"No, it is not,"   replied the clock.

"Well, what is it then?"   asked the hen.

"Stop. This poem is too silly!"   said Uncle Willy.

FIGURE 11–2 A whimsical poem.

POETRY ELEMENTS

A particular poem's rhythm is influenced by sounds, stress, pitch, and accented and unaccented syllables. Manipulation of one or all of these features creates a particular idea, feeling, or message. Some rhythms are regular; others are not. The enjoyable quality of the Mother Goose rhymes stems from their strong rhythm and cadence. In poetry, authors use rhythm to emphasize words or phrases, consequently capturing children's immediate attention. Exciting, dramatic rhythms and relaxed, soothing rhythms can be included in the same poem. Poetry's rhythm is capable of making children feel that they are actively participating rather than merely listening.

Children's literature is full of rhyming words and rhyming names. Poetic rhyme can occur within sentences or at line endings. Children often rhyme spontaneously, during play (Figure 11–3). Nonsense rhymes have given joy to generations of children; sayings like stomper-chomper, icky-sticky, and Dan, Dan, elephant man, can spread immediately among children.

Alliteration (defined as the occurrence of two or more words having the same initial sounds, **assonance**, or vowel sounds) is often used in poetry. All types of repetition are characteristic of children's poetry.

Visual images are stimulated by the poet's use of sensory words and **figurative language** (nonliteral meanings). A poet may provide a new way of looking at things by comparing

FIGURE 11–3 Darren created the rhyme "High in the sky" during this activity.

---

assonance — the repetition of words of identical or similar vowel sounds followed by different consonant sounds.
figurative language — language enriched by word images and figures of speech.

previously unconnected objects or events. **Similes** (direct comparisons between two things that have something in common but are essentially different) or **metaphors** (implied comparisons between two things that have something in common but are essentially different) are often found in poetry. Giving human characteristics and emotions to inanimate objects and animals (**personification**) is also commonplace, and talking dishes, trains, birds, bears, and pancakes are plentiful in children's poems.

The format of printed poetry (type size and style, page layout, punctuation, and capitalization) has been used to heighten enjoyment and highlight the subject matter. One can find poems printed in the shape of a tree or in a long, narrow column of single words.

TEACHER TECHNIQUES

If a poem is read or recited in a conversational manner, rather than in a singsong fashion, the rhyme is subtle and enjoyable. Singsong reading and recitation may become tiresome and difficult to understand.

Most teachers know that reciting from memory requires practice, so the poems they memorize are a few favorites. However, memorization can create a mechanical quality, as the teacher focuses on remembering rather than enjoyment.

Often, poetry is shared through teacher readings from lap cards. A poem should be read smoothly without uncalled-for hesitation. This means the teacher has to prepare by reading the poem enough times for it to roll off the tongue with ease, savoring the words in the telling.

The enjoyment of poetry, like other types of literature, can be increased by an enthusiastic adult. Careful reading of poetry is necessary because of poetry's compactness, and tendency to make every word count.

When encouraging children to join in and speak favorite poetry lines, sensitive handling is in order. A teacher can suggest, "Let's say it together" or "Join me in saying this poem if you like." A child should not be singled out or asked to recite without volunteering. Some gregarious children will want to share poems they have learned. A number of repetitions of a favorite verse may be needed before it is totally remembered. Children usually start with a few words or phrases.

Giving careful attention to both pitch and stress is important. Another important element when reading poetry aloud is juncture, where one makes the breaks in the poem. Your awareness of juncture will make or break your presentation. The natural tendency is to break at the end of the printed line, which may lead to artificial segmenting, not intended by the poet. Look at Figure 11–4. Read the first two lines as one sentence without pausing at the word *tree*. Now, read the poem stopping at each line's end and you'll see what artificial segmenting means.

A technique that works well for "a change of pace" is to use music without lyrics but with a strong repeated beat as a backdrop for poems or teacher-created rhymed lines. The result is chant-like or rap-like and promotes children's joining in and at times also clapping.

Poetry charts displayed on a stand next to the teacher are a helpful device for capturing attention and freeing a teacher's eyes to meet those of the children. When reading from a chart, quickly glance at a line and then turn so that the words are transmitted to the children. The elementary school poetry chart in Figure 11–5 was posted near the storage of classroom books. Children were encouraged to think of other things a book might say about book care and handling. The teacher wrote these child-dictated poems and posted them at the chart's bottom and identified them with the child's name.

---

similes — comparisons of two things that are unlike, usually using the words *like* or *as*. Example: "Love is like a red, red rose."

metaphors — figures of speech in which a comparison is implied by analogy but is not stated.

personification — a metaphorical figure of speech in which animals, ideas, things, etc., are represented as having human qualities.

I am a pine tree
growing on a hill.
I can stand so very,
very still. All at
once the wind
begins to blow.
I bend to and fro,
to and fro, to and fro.

FIGURE 11–4 A rhyming chart.

A POETRY CHART

Be gentle
Turn pages slow
I don't want to
Rip you know!
　　　　　by Ashad

I fall apart
In the rain
Pages crinkle
It's a pain!
　　　　　by Ling

If after you hold me
You put me back
Others will find me
On the book rack.
　　　　　by Rena

Inside my cover
A story hides
Pick me up
And look inside.
　　　　　by Juan

If you've never
Been to the zoo
Animals inside
Might frighten you.
　　　　　by Sierra

Sticky hands
Make a mess
When I'm clean
I look my best.
　　　　　by Carla

My printed words
Will make you laugh
This book's about
A funny giraffe.
　　　　　by Hensie

Don't walk away
I'm lonely today
Look at me
Before you play.
　　　　　by Lori

When you hold me
In your hands
And turn my pages
I feel grand.
　　　　　by Omar

I'm not safe
On the floor
Where feet kick
And make me sore.
　　　　　by Bradford

FIGURE 11–5 If books could talk, what would they say?

Young children sometimes create their own rhymes. The teacher can jot them down for display or to be taken home by the children. "Amber, pamber, big fat bamber," created by a child, may interest other children, and the teacher who has recorded it might share it at group time as a rhyme created by a playmate.

Poems dictated by children should be recorded verbatim, with no editing or teacher suggestions. Each creation is regarded as special. Lionni's *Frederick*, a wonderful picture book, helps children understand rhyming. This book's last two lines read

> "But Frederick," they said, "you are a poet!"
>
> Frederick blushed, took a bow, and said shyly, "I know it."

Ways to Introduce Children to Poetry

Posting poems in conspicuous places may help create interest, particularly if pictures or illustrations are placed adjacent to the poems. A poetry tree, made by placing a smooth tree limb in plaster of paris, can have paper leaves with poems on the back that can be selected at group times. A poem of the day (or week) bulletin board has worked well in some classrooms.

Pictures and flannel boards can be used in poetry presentation to interest and help children focus on words. Other props or costumes that relate to the poem (such as a teddy bear or police officer's hat) will gain attention. Some of the best collections of poems have no pictures; others have an illustration for each poem.

OLD CLASSICS

"Here We Go 'Round The Mulberry Bush"
"London Bridge Is Falling Down"
"Rock-a-Bye Baby"
"Row, Row, Row Your Boat"
"Sing a Song of Sixpence"
"Three Blind Mice"
"Twinkle, Twinkle Little Star"
"I'm a Little Teapot"
"Pop Goes the Weasel"

NEW CLASSICS

"You Are My Sunshine"
"Take Me out to the Ball Game"
"Blue-Tailed Fly"

FIGURE 11–6 Nursery songs—old and new classics.

A poem can be enjoyed indoors or outdoors, or between activities as a "fill-in" when the teacher or children are waiting.

Mounting cut magazine pictures and trying to think up words that rhyme with what is pictured is a rhyming activity many teachers favor. For example, "Here's a cake, let's give it to . . ."

Nursery songs emphasize rhyme, rhythm, alliteration, and playful enjoyment. Their predictability delights, and children acquire an immediate sense of accomplishment when they join in with words or movement. Classic rhyming nursery songs are listed in Figure 11–6.

SOURCES

A fine line divides finger plays, body and movement games, chants, songs, and poems. All can involve rhyme and rhythm. Poems presented later in this chapter are primarily the type that children would merely listen to as they were being recited, although some do contain opportunities for child participation.

Many fine picture books contain rhymed verse and can enhance a center's poetry program (Figure 11–7). Collections, anthologies, and books of children's poetry are available at the public library, bookstores, and school supply stores, as well as in children's and teachers' magazines.

Teachers also can create poetry from their own experiences. The following suggestions for creating poems for young children help the teacher-poet by pointing out the special features found in older classics and quality contemporary poetry.

- ◆ Include mental images in every line.
- ◆ Use strong rhythms that bring out an urge to chant, move, or sing.
- ◆ Use frequent rhyming.

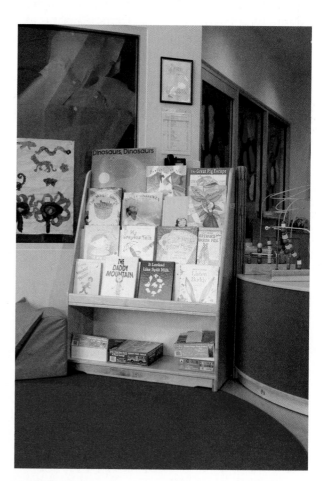

FIGURE 11–7 Books in rhyme are plentiful and selected for classroom libraries.

◆ Use action verbs often.

◆ Make each line an independent thought.

◆ Change the rhythm.

◆ Use words that are within the children's level of understanding.

◆ Use themes and subjects that are familiar to the young child.

Teacher-created poems promote child-created poems.

Many teachers search for ethnic poems that allow them to offer multicultural variety. No one cultural group has a corner on imagination, creativity, poetic quality, or philosophic outlook. Each has made important contributions to the total culture of the country and the world.

Recalling the poems and verses of one's own childhood may lead a teacher to research poems by a particular poet. Remembering appealing poetry elements may also help a teacher find poetry that may delight today's young child. Poetry collections are cited in the Additional Resources section at the end of this chapter.

SUGGESTED POEMS

The poems that follow are examples of the type that appeal to young children.

IF I WERE AN APPLE

If I were an apple
And grew on a tree,
I think I'd drop down
On a nice boy like me.

I wouldn't stay there
Giving nobody joy;
I'd fall down at once
And say, "Eat me, my boy!"

Old Rhyme

BUTTONS

Buttons on a sweater,
Buttons on a skirt,
Buttons on a dress,

Buttons on a shirt,
Buttons on pajamas,
Buttons on a gown,
Buttons that I button up,
Or I button down,
Buttons that are hidden,
Buttons right in sight,
Buttons that are red and blue,
Yellow, green, or white,
Buttons made of leather,
Buttons made of glass,
Buttons made of bits of wood,
Buttons made of brass,
Buttons, lots of buttons,
Buttons big and small,
Buttons with two eyes or more,
Or no eyes at all.
"You're cuter than a button,"
My Aunt Sue said to me.
Just what button does she mean?
Which one could it be?

Anita E. Posey (from *Rings and things and other poems.* Copyright ©1967)

ANIMAL CRACKERS

Animal crackers, and cocoa to drink,
That is the finest of suppers, I think;
When I'm grown up and can have what
    I please
I think I shall always insist upon these.
What do you choose when you're offered a
    treat?
When Mother says, "What would you like
    best to eat?"

Is it waffles and syrup, or cinnamon toast?
It's cocoa and animals that I love the most!

The kitchen's the coziest place that I know:
The kettle is singing, the stove is aglow,
And there in the twilight, how jolly to see
The cocoa and animals waiting for me.

Daddy and Mother dine later in state,
With Mary to cook for them, Susan
    to wait;
But they don't have nearly as much fun as I

Who eat in the kitchen with Nurse
   standing by:
Having cocoa and animals once more
   for tea!

"Animal Crackers," © 1917, 1945 by Christopher Morley.
From *Chimneysmoke* by Christopher Morley. Reprinted by
permission of Harper and Row Publishers, Inc.

ONE STORMY NIGHT

Two little kittens,
One stormy night
Began to quarrel,
And then to fight.

One had a mouse,
The other had none;
And that's the way
The quarrel begun.

"I'll have that mouse,"
Said the bigger cat.
"You'll have that mouse?
We'll see about that!"

"I will have that mouse,"
Said the eldest son.
"You shan't have the mouse,"
Said the little one.

The old woman seized
Her sweeping broom,
And swept both kittens
Right out of the room.

The ground was covered
With frost and snow,
And the two little kittens
Had nowhere to go.

They lay and shivered
On a mat at the door,
While the old woman
Was sweeping the floor.

And then they crept in
As quiet as mice,
All wet with the snow,
And as cold as ice.

And found it much better
That stormy night,

To lie by the fire,
Than to quarrel and fight.

Traditional

WHISKY FRISKY

Whisky frisky,
Hipperty hop,
Up he goes
To the tree top!

Whirly, twirly,
Round and round,
Down he scampers
To the ground.

Furly, curly,
What a tail,
Tall as a feather,
Broad as a sail.

Where's his supper?
In the shell.
Snappy, cracky,
Out it fell.

Anonymous

TO MARKET

To market, to market,
To buy a fat pig,
Home again, home again,
Jiggety jig.
To market, to market,
To buy a fat hog,
Home again, home again,
Jiggety jog.
To market, to market,
To buy a plum bun,
Home again, home again,
Market is done.

Mother Goose

SECRETS

Can you keep a secret?
I don't suppose you can,
You mustn't laugh or giggle
While I tickle your hand.

Anonymous

OLIVER TWIST

Oliver-Oliver-Oliver Twist
Bet you a penny you can't do this:
Number one—touch your tongue
Number two—touch your shoe
Number three—touch your knee
Number four—touch the floor
Number five—take a dive
Number six—wiggle your hips
Number seven—say number eleven
Number eight—bang the gate
Number nine—walk the line
Number ten—start again.

Traditional

RAINDROPS

"Splash," said a raindrop
As it fell upon my hat;

"Splash," said another
As it trickled down my back.

"You are very rude," I said
As I looked up to the sky;

Then another raindrop splashed
Right into my eye!

Anonymous

PRETENDING

I'd like to be a jumping jack
And jump out from a box!
I'd like to be a rocking horse
And rock and rock and rock.
I'd like to be a spinning top
And twirl around and round.
I'd like to be a rubber ball
And bounce way up and down.
I'd like to be a big fast train
Whose wheels fly round and round.
I'd like to be a pony small
And trot along the ground.
I'd like to be so many things
A growly, scowly bear.
But really I'm a little child
Who sits upon a chair.

Anonymous

SLOW TURTLE, FAST RABBIT

Turtle and Rabbit went walking each day.
They moved along in the funniest way.
Turtle talked s-l-o-w-l-y but he listened
*   well.*
Rabbit hopped fast and had much to tell.
He hopped in circles around turtle slow.
He talked and talked about all he did
*   know.*
Rabbit, of course, knew of every disaster
And he spoke out in spurts like a TV fore-
*   caster.*
"Molefellinahole." "Roosterflewintoapole."
Words shot out of his mouth like an arrow
*   in flight.*
Turtle, a good listener, understood them all
*   right.*
Turtle answered,"T-o-o b-a-d t-h-a-t i-s s-o
*   s-a-d."*
Rabbit went on to relate,
"Snakeateawholecakegottastomachache."
"Bearlosthercub."
"Antwasswallowedbyabigyellowbug."
Turtle said, "N-o h-a-p-p-y n-e-w-s t-o-d-a-y?"
"Ohsureiknowsomething," he did say.
"Skunkfellinthewellandhelosthissmell!"

J.M.M.

THE ISLAND OF A MILLION TREES

I took my ship and put out to sea
Sailing to the Island of a Million Trees.
Lucky Duck flew on the deck
There was Happy Me, and Lucky Duck
*   sailing free.*

To Million Tree Island we sailed our ship.
Neal the Seal asked to join our trip.
The ship was big so we said, "yes."
Happy Me, Lucky Duck, Neal the Seal, our
*   new guest.*

The wind did blow and along we flew
Sailing, playing, eating lunch, too.
We heard a meow from a floating raft
And rescued a kitty named Sweet Little Taff.
There was Happy Me, Lucky Duck, Neal
*   the Seal, and Sweet Little Taff.*

Sailing free to the Island of a Million Trees.

We drifted east and drifted west.
A storm stirred the waves, we could not rest.
A voice cried out from the gray fog
And over the side climbed Sailor Bob.

There was Happy Me, Lucky Duck, Neal
    the Seal,
Sweet Little Taff and Sailor Bob.
Off to the Island of a Million Trees.
Off in the distance we spotted land
With a million trees and mile of sand.
Closer and closer our boat did go.
Hands on the oars we started to row.
There was Happy Me, Lucky Duck, Neal
    the Seal,
Sweet Little Taff, and Sailor Bob.
Stepping onto the Island of a Million Trees.

                              Danielle Tracy

Permission granted by Danielle Tracy, 2008.

MAYTIME MAGIC

A little seed
For me to sow . . .
A little earth
To make it grow . . .

A little hole,
A little pat . . .
A little wish,
And that is that

A little sun,
A little shower . . .
A little while,
And then—a flower!

                              Mabel Watts

Permission granted by Mabel Watts, 1988.

HARRY T. BEAR LEARNS TO RHYME

Harry T. Bear says he can rhyme.
"Harry," I say. "Rhyme the word game."
He says, "Game rhymes with door."
I say, "Game rhymes with name."
"Give me a better word," says he.
"Well then try to rhyme the word bug."

Harry T. says, "Bug rhymes with bear."
"They start with the 'B' sound that's true
But Harry T. no rhyme is there."
He smiles and says, "Rhymes I can do!
Bug rhymes with rug, jug and mug, too."
"Harry T. you've got it hurray!"
That was the start of a very bad day
He could only talk in rhyme you see
His awful rhymes were bothering me.
When I said, "It's time to eat."
He said, "Meat, feet, sweet, tweet and seat."
I said, "I am going to bed."
He said, "Dead, lead and read."
"Stop please." I said "This is hurting my head!"
"But I can say rhymes anytime"
"Enough already," I then cried.
"Please take your rhymes and go outside."
Away he went out the door
My head ached I wanted no more.
As Harry T. Bear walked out of sight
I heard him say light, kite and bite.
Then his voice disappeared into the night.
He'll be back on my bed when I awake
I hope he has no other rhymes to make.

                              Danielle Tracy

Permission granted by Danielle Tracy, 2008

HARRY T. BEAR SAYS HE CAN READ

At night Harry says "Is it time?"
He puts on pajamas when I put on mine
Harry T. Bear hides books in my bed
Under the pillow where I lay my head.

"See," Harry T. says "Black marks
In a straight row
Are alphabet letters
Making words that I know!"

Harry says, "I CAN read books
But you read them best"
He sits and looks
While I read his requests.

Harry picks books 'bout caves and honey,
Or silver fish swimming in streams.
I like books that are funny,

Or have birthday parties with chocolate ice cream.

Together we sit all snuggled tight.
I read the pictures by the lamp's golden light.
Harry T. Bear says, "Please read it again."
But I fall asleep before the book's end.
That's when Harry T. Bear says he reads to me.

Danielle Tracy

Permission granted by Danielle Tracy, 2008.

I Bought Me a Rooster

I bought me a rooster and the rooster pleased me.
I fed my rooster on the bayberry tree,
My little rooster goes cock-a-doodle-doo, dee-doodle-dee doodle dee doodle dee doo!

I bought me a cat and the cat pleased me.
I fed my cat on the bayberry tree,
My little cat goes meow, meow, meow.
My little rooster goes cock-a-doodle-doo, dee-doodle-dee doodle dee doodle dee doo!

I bought me a dog and the dog pleased me.
I fed my dog on the bayberry tree,
My little dog goes bark, bark, bark.
My little cat goes meow, meow, meow.
My little rooster goes cock-a-doodle-doo, dee-doodle-dee doodle dee doodle dee doo!

Traditional

Note: This is a cumulative poem that takes teacher practice; additional verses include as many animals as you wish.

The Chickens

Said the first little chicken,
With a queer little squirm,
"I wish I could find
A fat little worm!"

Said the next little chicken,
With an odd little shrug:
"I wish I could find
A fat little bug!"

Said the third little chicken
With a small sign of grief:
"I wish I could find
A green little leaf!"

Said the fourth little chicken,
With a faint little moan:
"I wish I could find
A wee gravel stone!"

"Now see here!" said the mother,
From the green garden patch,
"If you want any breakfast,
Just come here and scratch!"

Anonymous

Talking Animals

"Meow," says cat.
"Bow-wow," says dog.
"Oink," says pig.
"Croak," says frog.

Hen says, "Cluck."
Lamb says, "Ba."
Cow says, "Moo."
and babies "Wah."

Lion says, "Roar."
Mouse says, "Squeak."
Snake says, "Ssssis."
Chick says, "Peep."

Crow says, "Ca."
Bears growl.
Sheep bleat.
Wolves howl.

Pig says, "Squeal."
Owl says, "Hoot who."
Toad says, "Ree deep."
Cuckoo says, "Cuckoo."

Donkey says, "Hee Haw."
Horse says, "Neigh Neigh."
Turkey says, "Gobble."
And we all say, "HOORAY!"

Note: Last line can also read, "And we say 'Happy Birthday!'"

HERE COMES THE BUS

*Lights flashing, gravel crunching, the big
    yellow door swings open swooshing the
    air.*

*Big kids make faces in the windows and
    the driver smiles down the stairs.*

When I climb in that bus I'm a big kid too

*With my snack in my backpack and my
    new shiny shoes.*

*I'll wave to mom and kiss the glass. Today
    I'll be a kindergartner—at last.*

*I'll make new friends and run and play.
    There are things to do like blocks and
    clay.*

*I'm going to learn to draw and write, and
    spell and make my numbers right.*

*Mom says to share, be kind and good for
    the teacher has rules to tell.*

*I'll sit or stand like teacher says and listen
    for the bell.*

*Since I'm five, I know a lot like alphabet
    letters, left, right, and stop.*

*I can print my name and say colors, too.
    I'm a big kindergartner and that is new.*

J. M. M.

OVER IN THE MEADOW

Over in the meadow, in the sand in the sun,
*Lived an old mother frog and her little
    froggie one.*
*"Croak!" said the mother; "I croak," said
    the one,*
*So they croaked and were glad in the sand
    in the sun.*

Over in the meadow in a pond so blue
*Lived an old mother duck and her little
    ducks two.*
*"Quack!" said the mother; "We quack," said
    the two,*
*So they quacked and were glad in the pond
    so blue.*

Over in the meadow, in a hole in a tree,
*Lived an old mother robin and her little
    birds three.*
*"Chirp!" said the mother; "We chirp," said
    the three,*

*So they chirped and were glad in the hole
    in a tree.*
Over in the meadow, on a rock by the shore,
*Lived an old mother snake and her little
    snakes four.*
*"Hiss!" said the mother; "We hiss," said
    the four,*
*So they hissed and were glad on a rock by
    the shore.*

Over in the meadow, in a big beehive,
*Lived an old mother bee and her little
    bees five.*
*"Buzz!" said the mother; "We buzz," said
    the five,*
*So they buzzed and were glad in the big
    beehive.*

LITTLE BOY BLUE

Little Boy Blue,
Come, blow your horn!
The sheep's in the meadow,
The cow's in the corn.
Where's the little boy
*That looks after the sheep? Under the hay-
    stack, fast asleep!*

Traditional

THE CAT AND THE FIDDLE

Hey, diddle, diddle!
The cat and the fiddle,
The cow jumped over the moon;
The little dog laughed
To see such sport,
And the dish ran away
With the spoon.

Mother Goose

THE LITTLE GIRL WITH THE CURL

There was a little girl
Who had a little curl
Right in the middle of her forehead;
When she was good
She was very, very good,
And when she was bad she was horrid.

Mother Goose

SUMMARY

Poems and verses provide an important literary experience, and exposure to classics is something no child should miss. Poems and verses can be a source of enjoyment and learning for young children. Rhythm, word images, fast action, and rhyme are used to promote listening skill.

Short verses, easily remembered, give children self-confidence with words. Encouragement and attention are offered by the teacher when the child shows interest.

Poems are selected and practiced for enthusiastic, smooth presentations. They can be selected from various sources or can be created by the teacher. Props help children focus on words. Poems are created or selected keeping in mind the features that attract and interest young children.

ADDITIONAL RESOURCES

Readings

Cole, B. (1990). *The silly book*. New York: Doubleday.

Crews, N. (2004). *The Neighborhood Mother Goose*. New York: Harper Collins.

Gable, S. (1999, September). Promoting children's literacy with poetry. *Young Children, 54*(4), 12–15.

Rovetch, L. (2001). *Ook the book and other silly rhymes*. San Francisco: Chronicle Books.

Steptoe, J. (1997). *In daddy's arms I am tall*. New York: Lee & Low Books.

Yolen, J., & Peters, A. F. (2007). *Here's a little poem: A very first book of poetry*. Cambridge, MA: Candlewick.

To find multicultural poetry for young children using an Internet search, use the key words *multicultural poetry, African-American children's poetry, Hispanic children's poetry*, and so on.

Read-Aloud Rhyming Picture Books

Christelow, E. (1998). *Five little monkeys jumping on the bed*. Boston: Houghton Mifflin.

Collins, H. (2003). *Little Miss Muffet*. Toronto: Kids Can Press.

Guarino, D. (1997). *Is your mama a llama?* New York: Scholastic.

Kalan, R. (1989). *Jump, frog, jump*. New York: Mulberry.

Lansky, B. (2004). *Mary had a little jam*. New York: Meadowbrook Press.

Miranda, A. (1997). *To market, to market*. San Diego: Harcourt.

Mosel, A. (1988). *Tikki tikki tembo*. New York: Henry Holt.

Raffi (1990). *The wheels on the bus*. New York: Crown.

Seuss, Dr. (1960). *One fish, two fish, red fish, blue fish*. New York: Random House.

Poetry Collections

Brown, M. (1985). *Hand rhymes*. New York: E. P. Dutton.

Brown, M. (1998). *Party rhymes*. New York: Dutton.

Carle, E. (1989*)*. *Animals, animals*. New York: Philomel.

Carlstron, N.W. (1989). *Graham cracker animals 1–2–3*. New York: Macmillan.

Cousins, L. (1989). *The little dog laughed and other nursery rhymes*. New York: E. P. Dutton.

Delacre, L. (1989). *Arroz con leche: Popular rhymes from Latin America*. New York: Scholastic.

Gander, F. (1985). *Nursery rhymes*. Santa Barbara: Advocacy Press.

Ghigna, C. (1995). *Riddle rhymes*. New York: Hyperion.

Jones, C. (1992). *Hickory dickory dock and other nursery rhymes*. Boston: Houghton Mifflin.

Lobel, A. (1985). *Whiskers & rhymes*. New York: Greenwillow.

Lobel, A. (1986). *The Random House book of Mother Goose*. New York: Random House.

McClosky, P. (1991). *Find the real Mother Goose*. New York: Checkerboard Press.

Moore, H. H. (1997). *A poem a day*. New York: Scholastic.

Prelusky, J. (1986). *Read-aloud rhymes for the very young*. New York: Knopf.

Roemer, H. (2004). *Come to my party and other shape poems*. New York: Henry Holt.

Schlein, M. (1997). *Sleep safe, little whale*. New York: Greenwillow.

Trapani, I. (1997). *I'm a little teapot*. Watertown, MA: Charlesbridge Publishing.

Helpful Websites

The Academy of American Poets
http://www.poets.org
Select "For Educators" link.

Famous Poetry Online
http://www.poetry-online.org
Select Poetry for Children, then Funny Poetry.

Meadowbrook Press
http://www.gigglepoetry.com
The Poetry Class link provides tips on writing humorous poems.

Poets House
http://poetshouse.org
Click on Collection and then Children's Room for information about admission-free poetry activities in New York; or click Collection and then Libraries to find out how the Poets House model can be replicated. Visit News to see how poetry has been introduced in community environments.

Story-It
http://www.storyit.com
Select Rhymes to Print to print nursery rhymes; then investigate Top Sites for Teachers.

Book Companion Website

The book companion website contains poetry activity examples, additional flannel board poems and Mother Goose rhymes. Rhyming picture books are given attention. Web activities are suggested, and a short quiz tests your knowledge of children's poetry.

STUDENT ACTIVITIES

1. Share with the class a poem you learned as a child.
2. Select five poems from any source. Be ready to state the reasons you selected them when you bring them to the next class meeting.
3. Make a list of 10 picture books that include children's poetry. Cite author, title, publisher, and copyright date for each.
4. Create a poem for young children. Go back and review the features most often found in classic rhymes.
5. Use the poem "Here Comes the Bus" from this chapter to initiate a group discussion with older 4-year-olds concerning what they know about kindergarten. One kindergarten teacher and her class developed a book titled *What We Know About Kindergarten.* Might this type of book change 4-year-olds' perceptions and attitudes about attending kindergarten? Discuss your answers with your peer group.
6. Present a poem to a group of preschoolers. Evaluate its success in a few sentences.
7. Find poetry written in free verse that you think might be successful with preschool children.
8. Form groups of three to six students. Using a large sheet of newsprint tacked (or taped) to the wall and a felt pen, list clever ways to introduce poetry to young children; for example, Poem of the Day. Discuss each group's similar and diverse suggestions.
9. Find a source of ethnic children's poetry and share it with class members.
10. Earlier in this chapter it was suggested that you list remembered Mother Goose characters. In a group of four or five classmates, compare your list with others, then with other groups. The group with the longest list then asks other groups with shorter lists to recite a Mother Goose rhyme in unison.

CHAPTER REVIEW

A. List a few reasons why poetry is used with young children.

B. Match each term in Column I to one item in Column II.

COLUMN I	COLUMN II
1. poetry	a. an action verb
2. rhyme	b. self-confidence
3. beat	c. a rhythmic measure
4. order and form	d. mental pictures
5. images	e. words with like sounds

6. remembered
7. interest
8. goal
9. presentation
10. reciting
11. classics
12. song
13. props
14. run
15. source

f. consistent and dependable
g. teacher attention
h. after practice
i. enjoyment
j. promotes listening skill
k. never forced
l. library
m. Mother Goose rhymes
n. musical poem
o. focus attention

C. List the numbers of the statements that you believe agree with the suggestions mentioned in this chapter.

1. Young children must learn to recite.
2. Emphasizing the beat of poetry as you read it always increases the enjoyment.
3. Repeat the poem over and over until a child learns it.
4. Describe to children the mental pictures created by the poem before reading the poem to the children.
5. It really is not too important for young children to memorize the poems they hear.
6. Memorizing a poem can help a child feel competent.
7. Most poems are not shared because teachers want children to gain the factual information the poem contains.
8. Poetry's rhythm comes from its form and order.
9. Memorizing a poem always causes awkward teacher presentation.
10. Teachers may try to author some of their own children's poetry.

D. List elements of poetry that can be manipulated to evoke emotion in listeners.

E. Write an example using a line of poetry or free verse for the following: alliteration, personification, simile, and figurative language.

F. Comment on a poetry reader's tendency to pause at the end of each line when reading poetry aloud.

CHAPTER 12

Flannel (Felt) Boards and Activity Sets

OBJECTIVES

After reading this chapter, you should be able to:

◆ Describe flannel boards and types of flannel board activities.

◆ Make and present three flannel board activities.

◆ Describe teacher techniques in flannel board story presentation.

THE KNOWLEDGEABLE CHILD

Atienza (2004) describes one mother's attempt to prepare her child for kindergarten as follows. Besides reading to her son daily to build his vocabulary . . . she tries to get him socially and emotionally prepared for kindergarten.

> He and his mother are currently reading a stack of books about wiggly critters. Other questions that her child (age four) has asked about have sent mother and son to the library for books on trains, airplanes, space ships, bugs and tornadoes. (p. L2)

QUESTIONS TO PONDER

1. Imagine you are this child's kindergarten teacher. How would you go about creating a flannel board activity on "wiggly critters"?

2. Why do you think nonfiction flannel board activities are so hard to find?

A flannel (or felt) board activity is a rewarding experience for both the child and the teacher. Because the attention of young children is easily captured with these activities, the teacher finds the use of flannel board activities very popular and effective. Children are highly attentive during this type of activity—straining to see and hear—looking forward to the next piece to be put on the flannel board.

Stories to be used with flannel board activities are selected by the same criteria used for storytelling (see Chapter 10). In addition to stories, poetry, and songs, other listening and learning activities can be presented with flannel boards.

FLANNEL BOARD CONSTRUCTION

Boards of different sizes, shapes, and designs are used, depending on the needs of the center. They may be freestanding or propped up in the chalkboard tray, on a chair, or on an easel. Boards can be covered on both sides in different colors. Many are made by covering a sheet of heavy cardboard, display board, prestretched artist's canvas (Figure 12–1), Styrofoam, or wood with a piece of solid-colored flannel or felt (Figure 12–2). The material is pulled smooth and held by tacks, tape, glue, or wood staples, depending on the board material. Sometimes an underpadding is added. Putting wire mesh or a sheet of metal between the underpadding and the covering material makes pieces with magnets adhere. Because all metal does not attract magnets, the mesh or metal needs testing before purchase.

Decisions on which materials to use in flannel board construction are often based on the intended use of the flannel board, material cost, and tools or skills needed in construction. Styrofoam is a good choice if having a lightweight board is important; however, wood-based boards are more durable.

Making a board that tilts backward at a slight angle is an important consideration for a freestanding flannel board because pieces applied to a slanted board stick more securely.

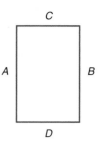

A prestretched *artist canvas* can be obtained at an art and craft store or through artist's supply catalogs. Flannel or felt is available in navy blue or black in 45" widths.

Purchase ¾ yard of 45" yardage to cover a 24" × 36" canvas. Place the flannel or felt on a flat surface, and place the artist canvas face down on the material. Fold over and staple material onto the wood frame in this manner: First, staple side A. Pull the material snugly, and staple side B, then sides C and D making four hospital corners. Trim.

FIGURE 12–1 Directions for artist's canvas flannel board.

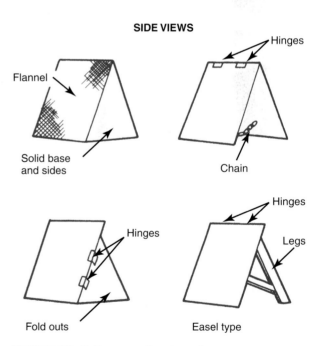

FIGURE 12–2 Freestanding boards.

Stores and companies that sell school supplies have premade boards in various price ranges. See the Additional Resources section at the end of this chapter for a listing of commercial board and set manufacturers.

Although flannel and felt are popular coverings for boards, other materials also work well. Almost all fuzzy textured material is usable. The nap can be raised on flannel or felt by brushing it with a stiff brush. It is a good idea to press a small piece of felt or pellon (fabric interfacing) to a fabric to see how well it sticks before buying the fabric.

Some boards have pockets in the back so that flannel pieces can be lined up and ready for use (Figure 12–3). Some early childhood centers have parts of walls, dividers, and backs of pieces of furniture covered with flannel or felt. A simple homemade freestanding board holder is shown in Figure 12–4.

A tabletop flannel board can be made from a cardboard box (see instructions and necessary materials in Figure 12–5). One clever idea is to use a secondhand attaché case. Using a case that opens to a 90-degree angle, glue a large piece of flannel to the inside of the top lid. When the lid is open, the flannel will be in view.

The case is used for storing sets, and the handle makes it easy to carry.

Display fabrics to which three-dimensional objects will adhere are also available. Special adhesives and tapes are needed for this type of flannel board.

The size of the flannel board's front surface is important. Consider making or purchasing a board no smaller than 24-by-30 inches. The attaché case could be used for individual child's play or for small groups, but it may be too small for larger groups. Most centers obtain or construct both a child's flannel board and a staff flannel board.

FLANNEL BOARD ACTIVITY SETS

Many schools make or purchase flannel board activity sets for teacher use and to accompany children's favorite books and other flannel

Construction:

Obtain a piece of cardboard, of the size you desire for the back of your flannel board, and a large sheet of flannel or heavy wrapping paper. The flannel (or paper) should be several inches wider than the cardboard and about twice as long as the finished chart size. One-inch deep with a back 3 inches high is a good pocket size.

Measure and mark both sides of flannel (paper) at intervals of 3 inches and 1 inch, alternating. Using accordion folds, the first 1-inch section is creased and folded forward over the second 3-inch section, and so on. Pull tight and secure ends.

A pocket chart conveniently holds set pieces in sequence for flannel-board stories and can be useful in other child activities with flannel set pieces.

FIGURE 12–3 Pocket chart.

FIGURE 12–4 Two metal coat hooks screwed to a piece of heavy plywood make a good flannel board holder.

Materials:
cardboard box
art knife or cardboard cutter
adhesive paper
cloth, plastic, or bookbinder's tape
tacky glue (or white school glue)
felt yardage (large enough to cover box)

Directions:

1. Using the cardboard cutter, remove top of box so that only the four sides and bottom remain.
2. As indicated in A, cut box in half lengthwise.
3. Preserve half of box for flannel-board base (B). Tape bottom of box for support. Cut sides diagonally, as shown in C.
4. From the remaining piece of the original box, cut off sides to obtain a rectangular piece of cardboard, measuring approximately 16" × 12".
5. Fit rectangle into diagonally cut box half.
6. Use adhesive shelf paper to decorate flannel board. Use glue to attach felt to the front of the box.

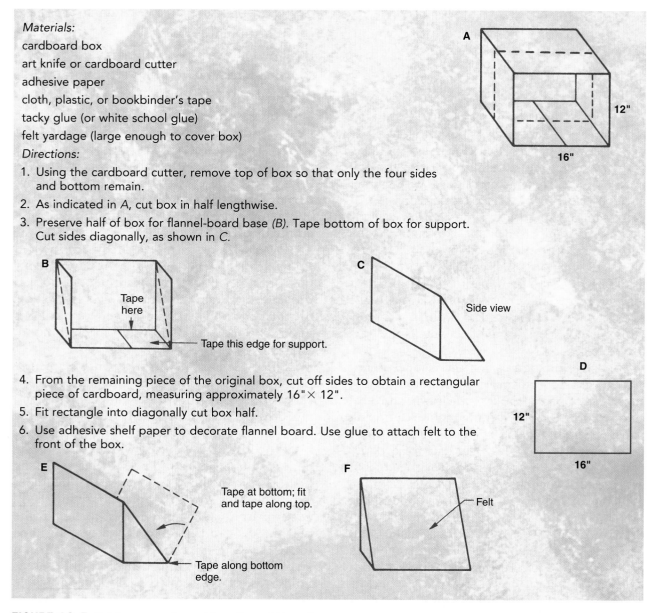

FIGURE 12–5 Tabletop cardboard box flannel board.

board activities. Before making or purchasing set pieces, teachers consider what pieces are central to the story or activity. In telling a story with a flannel board, teachers and children will decide how set pieces are to be placed on the board. Teachers attempt to increase audience understanding and also select what visual pieces are essential in each scene. They choose words that coordinate with the visuals. In stories involving "running away" set pieces, teachers often move a piece in a running movement across the board. As a child relates a tale, his or her version may resemble or creatively deviate from the teacher's presentation. Considerable visual literacy thinking is taking place.

Activity Set Construction

Pieces for flannel board activity sets can be made in a number of ways and from a number of fabrics and papers. Pellon and felt, because of their low cost and durability, are probably the most popular. Heavy-paper figures with flannel backing or felt tape also stick well. Commercial tape, sandpaper, fuzzy velour-flocked wallpaper, Velcro, and used foam-like laundry softener sheets are other possibilities for backing pieces. Premade flannel or felt board sets are available at school supply stores and at most teacher conferences. Most communities have at least one teacher who is a small business entrepreneur specializing in making flannel sets for other teachers.

Shapes and figures for the flannel board activity sets can be traced from books, magazines, or coloring books; self-drawn and created; or borrowed from other sources. Tracing paper is helpful for this purpose. Tracing can be done simply by covering the back of a paper pattern with a heavy layer of pencil lead. Soft art pencils work best. The pattern is then turned over and traced. Another method is cutting the object out, tracing its outline, and then drawing details freehand. Tracing pencils and pens are commercially available and come with directions for use; they can be found at craft stores.

Color can be added to set pieces with felt markers, oil pastels, acrylic or poster paint, embroidery pens, crayons, paints, and colored pencils. Sets take time to make but are well worth the effort. Favorites will be presented over and over again. Pieces can be covered with clear contact paper or can be laminated (fronts only) for durability.

Teachers can be creative with flannel board activity sets by decorating pieces with

- layered felt.
- wiggly eyes (commercially available at variety stores).
- hand-stitched character clothing.
- imitation fur fabric.
- liquid glitter.
- commercial fluorescent paint or crayons.

Most copy machines have the ability to enlarge figures or shrink them. Activity set pieces that are too small are difficult to handle and see. Narrow parts on set pieces should be avoided because they tend to tear with use. Also, try to preserve the size relationship between characters (such as between a mouse and a human figure) as well as the cultural and ethnic diversity of characters.

Pattern transfer books are plentiful and available from craft and sewing stores. Patterns can be ironed on cloth quickly, and it is possible to obtain multiple copies. Publishers of transfer books include Dover Publications in New York and Craftways in Richmond, Calif.

Some schools buy inexpensive picture books and use the illustrations as flannel board set pieces. After the pieces are cut, they are glued to oak tag and backed with some of the materials mentioned earlier.

Proper storage and care will preserve pieces and prolong their usefulness. A flat stocking box or large mailing envelope or manila folder is practical for storage. If pieces become bent, a warm iron can often be used to flatten the pieces. Sets can be stored in plastic page protectors used in three-ring binders (available in stationery stores). Large sealed plastic household bags, as well as plastic envelopes available at teacher-supply stores, can also be used to protect pieces.

Nonfiction Sets

You will find that young children are just as interested in nonfiction topics as they are in narrative stories. Educators, in attempting to build on recognized child interest, construct their own nonfiction flannel board set pieces or find ones commercially manufactured. A true representation of detailed subjects is best. Library or computer research can secure accurate images. Textbooks for elementary schools are another good resource. A robin activity set piece should look like a robin, not just a bird in general. The same goes for other set figures. Distinguishing features should be depicted.

Nonfiction set pieces can also be easily woven into other designed activities, such as categorizing animals by color or number of legs. Referring back to the discussion in Chapter 9 on nonfiction book selection will be helpful.

PRESENTATION

As is the case with most listening activities, a semi-secluded, comfortable setting should be chosen for presentation of flannel board activities. The activity begins with the teacher starting to place pieces on the board in proper sequence as the story or activity unfolds, always focusing on the children's reactions. In this activity, as in many others described in this text, the teacher may be presenting but also watching for reaction. Because pieces are usually added to the board one at a time, they should be kept in an open flat box or manila folder in the teacher's lap, or, better yet, behind the board, stacked in the order they will appear. This is hard to do if the story or activity is not well in mind.

The teacher should periodically check to see whether the set has all its pieces, particularly in large centers where many staff members use the same sets. If pieces are missing or damaged, the teacher or volunteers can make new pieces. New sets are always appreciated by the entire staff and can be developed to meet the needs and interests of a particular group of children.

To present activities with ease, the beginner should

◆ read the story (or activity sequence) and check the pieces to be used.

◆ practice until there is a smooth coordination of words and placement of pieces on the board.

◆ set up the flannel board.

◆ check and prepare pieces in order of their appearance.

◆ place pieces out of view, behind the board within easy reach, or in a lap folder.

◆ gather children.

◆ make seating adjustments if necessary.

◆ respond to children's needs.

◆ Consider group size carefully; the smaller the group, the more intimate and conversational the experience. (As with other language arts presentations, consider planning two presentations to reduce group size.)

◆ introduce the activity with a statement that builds a desire to listen.

◆ tell the story (or present the activity), while watching for reactions from the children.

◆ create drama and suspense with pauses, speaking in characters' voices and moving pieces across the board's surface, if the story calls for this. Let your personality guide you (Figure 12–6).

◆ discuss language development or comprehension (optional). Teachers ask questions or discuss story particulars to elicit children's ideas and comments.

◆ keep pieces flat and store them properly, returning sets to where other staff members expect them to be.

◆ allow children to do their retelling with a flannel board and their own activity sets. Most centers construct one set for teachers and another set for child exploration and activity.

In addition to storytelling activities, sets may be used for songs, poetry, activities with numbers, language development, and other curriculum area activities.

FIGURE 12–6 During this flannel board presentation, children are imitating the teacher's gestures.

SUGGESTED STORIES AND ACTIVITIES

There are many resources for story ideas. Stories created by teachers can be enjoyed as much as commercial sets and classic stories. Sets can improve listening skills and enhance vocabulary and concept development, often within one activity. The visual shapes or pieces are linked to words and ideas. Occasionally, a child's picture book can be presented as a flannel board activity before the book becomes part of the school's book collection.

An available flannel board placed at children's eye level with an adjacent open box of figures or shapes quickly encourages use and creativity. Remembered words, lines, and whole stories are relived in children's play. They often go beyond the familiar, devising their own events. Even sturdy felt pieces will need to be ironed flat occasionally and replaced because of frequent and vigorous use by children. As suggested previously, children's play with the flannel board often follows a teacher presentation but can also be a free choice activity at other times of the day.

Many centers include flannel boards and sets in their language centers along with alphabet letter cutouts. Teachers can use alphabet letter cutouts in daily activities, and many centers routinely have set pieces, such as a particular flower labeled with its name using cutout alphabet letters underneath it. The flannel board is then displayed for children's viewing. A flannel board with the word *Closed* on it may be used to block entrance to a play area or other section of the room.

Suggested picture books that lend themselves to flannel board presentations include the following:

Brett, J. (1989). *The mitten*. New York: Putnam.

Flack, M. (1971). *Ask Mr. Bear*. New York: Macmillan.

French, V. (1995). *Red hen and sly fox*. New York: Simon & Schuster.

Hobson, S. (1994). *Chicken Little*. New York: Simon & Schuster.

Martin, B. (1972). *Brown bear, brown bear, what do you see?* New York: Holt, Rinehart, and Winston.

Neitzel, S. (1989). *The jacket I wear in the snow.* New York: Greenwillow.

Slobodkina, E. (1947). *Caps for sale.* Glenview, IL: Addison Wesley Publishing Company.

Stevens, J. (1995). *Tops and bottoms.* New York: Harcourt.

Young, E. (1992). *Seven blind mice.* New York: Philomel Books.

Zemach, M. (1977). *It could always be worse.* New York: Farrar.

Zuromskis, D. (1978). *The farmer in the dell.* Boston: Little, Brown & Co.

Commercially made sets and activity ideas can be obtained from sources listed in the Additional Resources section.

Many urban school districts allow private preschool teachers in their community to use their central office curriculum centers, which may also hold flannel board resources. Flannel board stories and patterns are found in the Activities section at the end of this chapter.

SUMMARY

A flannel board presentation is one of the most popular and successful listening activities for the young child. Stories are told while figures and shapes are placed and sometimes moved on the board. The children can learn new ideas and words by seeing the visual model while listening to stories and other flannel board activities.

Beginning teachers practice presentations with words and pieces until the activity flows smoothly. The children's feedback is noted. Flannel board activities in many other learning areas besides language development take place in early childhood centers.

A wide variety of fabrics is available for both boards and pieces; felt and flannel are the most commonly used materials for boards.

ADDITIONAL RESOURCES

Commercial Flannel Board and Flannel Board Set Manufacturers

ChildWood, 8040 NE Day Road West, Bainbridge Island, WA 98110; 800-362-9825; http://www.childwoodmagnets.com. (Magnet boards and brightly painted cut-wood pieces; teaching suggestions also available.)

GW School Supply Inc.; 800-234-1065; http://www.gwschool.com. (Boards and sets in a variety of price ranges.)

Learning Wonders; 866-933-PLAY; http://www.learningwonders.com. (Felt sets and boards, multicultural figures, nursery rhymes, community helpers, fairy tales.)

Little Folk Visuals; 800-537-7227; http://www.littlefolkvisuals.com. (Flannel sets and scenes.)

Resource Books with Flannel Board Stories and Set Patterns

Anderson, P. (1972). *Storytelling with the flannel board (Books 1 & 2).* Minneapolis: T. S. Denison & Co.

Briggs, D. (1992). *Flannel board fun: A collection of stories.* New York: Scarecrow Press.

Kreplin, E., & Smith, B. M. (1995). *Ready-to-use flannel board stories, figures and activities for ESL children.* Denver: Center for Applied Research.

Peralta, C. (1981). *Flannel board activities for the bilingual classroom.* Culver City, CA: La Arana Publishers.

Scott, L. B., & Thompson, J. J. (1984). *Rhymes for fingers and flannel boards.* Minneapolis: T. S. Denison & Co.

Taylor, F., & Vaugh, G. (1980). *The flannel board storybook.* Atlanta: Humanics Learning.

Wilmes, L., & Wilmes, D. (1987). *Felt board fun.* Elgin, IL: Building Books.

Readings

Roe, B., Alred, S., & Smith, S. (1998). *Teaching through stories: Yours, mine and theirs.* Norwood, MA: Christopher-Gordon.

Helpful Websites

Fabulous Flannel Fun
http://www.lessontutor.com
Search the site for "flannel boards." An author provides flannel board ideas for making boards and creating cutouts.

Lakeshore Learning Materials
   http://www.lakeshorelearning.com
   A commercial source for boards and sets.

Make Me a Story
   http://www.makemeastory.com
   Select Flannel Board link.

Preschool Printables
   http://www.preschoolprintables.com
   Select Felt Board Stories; then click on 5 Red Apples.

Book Companion Website

A simple method of assessing young children's story comprehension is provided in the book companion website. Think of this exercise as a mini–research study that may tell you if young children can remember more about a story told with the flannel board than a story read aloud from a picture book. Do a computer search using the key words "flannel board stories" to find new stories. A suggested reading list is also included.

STUDENT ACTIVITIES

1. Visit a center to watch a flannel board presentation, or invite a teacher to present an activity to the class.

2. Give a presentation to a small group of classmates. The classmates should make helpful suggestions in written form while watching the presentation, trying to look at the presentations through the eyes of a child.

3. Write an original story for the flannel board. Include patterns for your pieces. Share with your total training group.

4. If video camera equipment is available in your classroom, give a flannel board presentation and evaluate yourself.

5. Make three flannel board sets, using any materials desired.

6. Visit a school supply store and price commercial flannel boards. Compare costs for constructing a flannel board, and report at the next class meeting.

7. Make a personal flannel board.

8. Research stories and sets with multicultural variety.

9. With a group of classmates discuss turning *Roll Over* into a flannel board set. How many set pieces would be needed? How could this set fit into a theme unit? Would you use numeral set pieces? Why? Could set pieces be multicultural? What materials would you need to construct this set? List.

ROLL OVER

Ten in the bed, and the little one said,
"Roll over! Roll over!"
So they rolled over and one fell out.

Nine in the bed, and the little one said:
"Roll over! Roll over!"
They all rolled over and one fell out.

Eight in the bed, and the little one said:
"Roll over! Roll over!"
They all rolled over and one fell out.

Seven in the bed, and the little one said:
"Roll over! Roll over!"
They all rolled over and one fell out.

Six in the bed, and the little one said:
"Roll over! Roll over!"
They all rolled over and one fell out.

Five in the bed, and the little one said:
"Roll over! Roll over!"

They all rolled over and one fell out.

Four in the bed, and the little one said:
"Roll over! Roll over!"
They all rolled over and one fell out.

Three in the bed, and the little one said:
"Roll over! Roll over!"
They all rolled over and one fell out.

Two in the bed, and the little one said:
"Roll over! Roll over!"
They all rolled over and one fell out.

One in the bed, and the little one said,
"Alone at last!"

CHAPTER REVIEW

A. List the types of materials used in board construction.

B. Name the kinds of materials used to make flannel board pieces.

C. In your opinion, what is the best way to color pieces for flannel boards?

D. Why is the use of visual aids valuable?

E. Place the following in correct order.
1. Give a flannel board presentation.
2. Set up area with board.
3. Check pieces.
4. Practice.
5. Place pieces in order of appearance.
6. Gather children.
7. Place pieces out of sight.
8. Discuss what happened during the activity with children (optional).
9. Store set by keeping pieces flat.
10. Introduce the set with a motivational statement if you wish.

F. What color flannel (or felt) would you use to cover your own board? Why?

G. Finish the following statements.
1. A board is set up slanting back slightly because _____.
2. A folding flannel board with handles is a good idea because _____.
3. If children touch the pieces during a teacher presentation, the teacher should say _____.
4. The main reason teachers like to store set pieces in a flat position is _____.

5. One advantage of a flannel board made from a large Styrofoam sheet is _____.

6. One disadvantage of a flannel board made from a large Styrofoam sheet is _____.

BEGINNING TEACHER ACTIVITIES

The following activities and stories are suggested as a start for the beginning teacher. The flannel board activity set piece patterns that follow are shown at a reduced size. Full-size versions are available at the book companion website at www.cengage.com/education/machado.

THE LION AND THE MOUSE

Author Unknown (a classic story)

Pieces   lion, sleeping   rope
            lion, awake   mouse
            tree   two hunters

(On the board, place the sleeping lion next to the tree. Place the mouse near the lion's back, moving it slowly toward the lion while speaking in a soft voice.)

There once was a little mouse that saw a big lion sleeping by a tree. "Oh, it would be fun to climb on top of the lion and slide down his tail," thought the mouse. So—quietly, he tiptoed close to the lion. When he climbed on the lion's back, the fur felt so soft and warm between his toes that he began running up and down the lion's back.

The lion awoke. He felt a tickle upon his back. He opened one eye and saw the little mouse, which he then caught in his paw. (Move mouse under lion's paw.)

"Let me go—please!" said the mouse.

"I'm sorry I woke you from your nap. Let me go, and I'll never bother you again. Maybe you and I could be friends—friends help each other, you know."

This made the lion laugh. "A little mouse like you, help me? I'm big, I'm strong, and I'm brave!" Then the lion laughed again, and he let the mouse go.

(Take the mouse off the board.)

The mouse ran away, and he didn't see the lion for a long time. But, one day when the mouse was out looking for seeds for dinner, he saw the lion tied to a tree with a rope, and two hunters near him. (Remove sleeping lion. Add awake lion, placing it next to tree, with rope on top. Put the two hunters on the other side of the tree.)

One hunter said, "Well, this rope will hold the lion until we can go get our truck and take him to the zoo." So the hunters walked away.

(Remove the hunters.)

The mouse ran up to the lion as soon as the hunters were out of sight. He said, "Hello, lion."

(Add mouse.)

The lion answered, "Well, I guess it's your turn to laugh at me tied to this tree."

"I'm not going to laugh," said the mouse, as he quickly started to chew on the rope.

(Move mouse close to rope.)

The mouse chewed, and chewed, and chewed. The rope fell apart, and the lion was free.

(Remove rope.)

"You are a good friend," said the lion.

"Hop on my back and hold on. Let's get away from here before those two hunters come back." (Place lion in running position with mouse on lion's back.)

"OK," said the mouse. "I'd like that."

So you see, sometimes little friends can help big friends. The size of a friend isn't really too important.

Cut line

Full-size version of this art can be found on the book companion website at www.cengage.com/education/machado.

THE SEED

Margie Cowsert (while an ECE student)

Pieces
small roots	beaver
green shoot	bird
deer	large trunk
Mr. Man	large leaves
apples (five or more)	large roots
seed	
small trunk	
leaves	

Once upon a time, there was a seed named Abraham. He didn't know what kind of plant he would be, so he asked Mr. Bird. Mr. Bird didn't know but wanted to eat Abraham. Abraham asked him to wait until after he found out what he would be, and the bird agreed to wait.

Abraham grew small roots and green shoots. He asked Mr. Deer if he knew what he would grow up to be. "Do you know what I'll be when I grow up?" Mr. Deer said, "No," but wanted to eat the tender green shoot. Abraham said, "Please wait." So Mr. Deer decided to wait.

Abraham grew a small trunk and leaves. He was glad he was a tree but still didn't know what kind. He asked Mr. Beaver, "Do you know what I'll be when I grow up?" Mr. Beaver didn't know but wanted to eat Abraham's tender bark. He decided to wait also.

Abraham grew big roots, a big trunk, and more leaves, but still didn't know what kind of tree he was. He asked Mr. Man,

Cut as one piece.

Cut as one piece.

Cut as one piece.

Full-size version of this art can be found on the book companion website at www.cengage.com/education/machado.

391

"Do you know what I'll be when I grow up?" Mr. Man didn't know, but he wanted to chop down Abraham to make a house. He decided to wait.

Abraham grew apples. Hooray! He knew that he was an apple tree. He told Mr. Bird he could eat him now. Mr. Bird said Abraham was too big, but that he would like one of the apples. Mr. Deer thought the tree was too big, too, but he did want an apple. Mr. Beaver took any apples that fell to the ground home to his family. Mr. Man loved apples, so he told Abraham Tree that he wouldn't chop him down.

Abraham Apple Tree was so happy to know what he was and that no one was going to eat him or chop him down that he grew lots of apples.

JUST LIKE DADDY

Pieces

little brown bear	green fish (large)
little brown bear's blue vest	green fish (small)
flower	brown mother bear
brown father bear	red boots for little bear
red boots for father bear	blue vest for father bear
yellow coat for father bear	yellow coat for little bear
purple vest for mother bear	

When I got up this morning, I made a big yawn . . .

Just like daddy.

I washed my face, got dressed, and had a big breakfast . . .

Just like daddy.

And then I put on my yellow coat and blue vest and my red boots . . .

Just like daddy.

And we went fishing—Daddy, Mommy, and me.

On the way, I picked a flower and gave it to my mother . . .

Just like daddy.

When we got to the lake, I put a worm on my hook . . .

Just like daddy.

All day we fished, and I caught a big fish . . .

Just like mommy!!!

Flower (cut 1)

Small green fish (cut 1)

Green fish (cut 2)

Yellow coat for father bear (cut 1)

Little bear's blue vest (cut 1)

Little brown bear (cut 1)

Purple vest for mother bear (cut 1)

Full-size version of this art can be found on the book companion website at www.cengage.com/education/machado.

392

Brown mother bear (cut 1)

Brown father bear (cut 1)

Red boots
for father bear
(cut 2)

Red boots
for little bear
(cut 2)

Yellow coat
for little bear
(cut 1)

Blue vest
for father
bear (cut 1)

Full-size version of this art can be found on the book companion website at www.cengage.com/education/machado.

THE TREE IN THE WOODS

Pieces

grass	bird's nest
treetop	bird's egg
tree trunk	bird
tree limb	wing
tree branch	feather

(The flannel board can be used to build the song by placing first the grass and then the treetop, trunk, limb, branch, nest, egg, bird, wing, and feather, as each verse calls for them.)

Now in the woods there was a tree,
The finest tree that you ever did see,

And the green grass grew all around,
around, around,
And the green grass grew all around.

And on that grass there was a trunk,
The finest trunk that you ever did see,
And the trunk was on the tree,
And the tree was in the woods,
And the green grass grew all around,
around, around,
And the green grass grew all around.

And on that trunk there was a limb,
The finest limb that you ever did see,
And the limb was on the trunk,

And the trunk was on the tree,
And the tree was in the woods,
And the green grass grew all around,
    around, around,
And the green grass grew all around.

And on that limb there was a branch,
The finest branch that you ever did
    see,
And the branch was on the limb,
And the limb was on the trunk,
And the trunk was on the tree,
And the tree was in the woods,
And the green grass grew all around,
    around, around,
And the green grass grew all around.

And on that branch there was a nest,
The finest nest that you ever did see,
And the nest was on the branch,
And the branch was on the limb,
And the limb was on the trunk,
And the trunk was on the tree,
And the tree was in the woods,
And the green grass grew all around,
    around, around,
And the green grass grew all around.

And in that nest there was an egg,
The finest egg that you ever did see,
And the egg was in the nest,
And the nest was on the branch,
And the branch was on the limb,
And the limb was on the trunk,
And the trunk was on the tree,
And the tree was in the woods,
And the green grass grew all around,
    around, around,
And the green grass grew all around.

And on that egg there was a bird,
The finest bird that you ever did see,
And the bird was on the egg,
And the egg was in the nest,
And the nest was on the branch,
And the branch was on the limb,
And the limb was on the trunk,
And the trunk was on the tree,
And the tree was in the woods,
And the green grass grew all around,
    around, around,
And the green grass grew all around.

And on that bird there was a wing,
The finest wing that you ever did see,

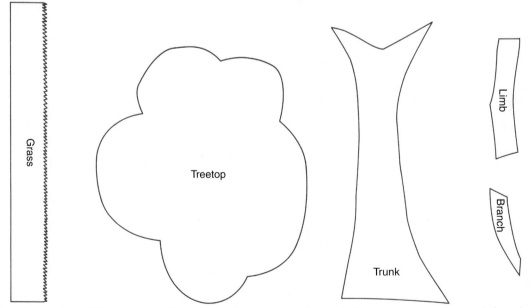

Full-size version of this art can be found on the book companion website at www.cengage.com/education/machado.

394

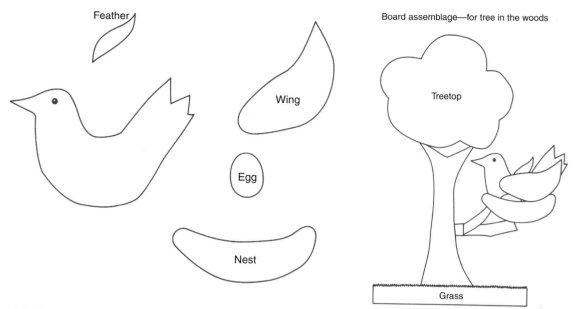

Feather

Wing

Egg

Nest

Board assemblage—for tree in the woods

Treetop

Grass

Full-size version of this art can be found on the book companion website at www.cengage.com/education/ machado.

And the wing was on the bird,
And the bird was on the egg,
And the egg was in the nest,
And the nest was on the branch,
And the branch was on the limb,
And the limb was on the trunk,
And the trunk was on the tree,
And the tree was in the woods,
And the green grass grew all around,
    around, around,
And the green grass grew all around.

And on that wing there was a feather,
The finest feather that you ever did see,
And the feather was on the wing,
And the wing was on the bird,
And the bird was on the egg,
And the egg was in the nest,
And the nest was on the branch,
And the branch was on the limb,
And the limb was on the trunk,
And the trunk was on the tree,
And the tree was in the woods,
And the green grass grew all around,
    around, around,
And the green grass grew all around.

RIDDLE

Pieces   Triangles of felt in red, blue, yellow, green, purple, orange, brown, black, and white

Teacher: Riddle, riddle, ree.

What color do I see?

_____ (child's name) has it on his or her

_____ (shirt, pants, and so forth).
What color can this be? (When the color is identified, the following is said.)

Group: It's _____, _____, _____. (Example: red, red, red)
Mary (instead of Mary substitute name of child who named the color) did say.

Let's see what colors we can find today.

(Teacher puts triangle of same color on flannel board. Child whose name was mentioned is asked whether he or she, or a friend of the child's choice, is going to guess the name of the color. Each child is asked whether he or she wants to guess the color. Activity ends with line of triangles that group names as each triangle is removed.)

ONE, TWO, BUCKLE MY SHOE

Pieces

Numerals 1 through 10   crossed sticks
shoe   straight sticks
door   hen

One, two,
Buckle my shoe;
Three, four,
Knock at the door;
Five, six,
Pick up sticks;
Seven, eight,
Lay them straight;
Nine, ten,
Big fat hen.

Cut line →

0 1 2 3
4 5 6
7 8 9

Full-size version of this art can be found on the book companion website at www.cengage.com/education/machado.

THIS OLD MAN

Pieces
old man	tree
shoe	two clouds (heaven)
door	thumb
sticks	hive
gate	vine
10 bones	hen★
dog	numerals 1 through 10★

★ *Use patterns in previous poem.*

1. This old man, he played one, he played knick-knack on my thumb. With a knick-knack paddy-whack, give a dog a bone.

This old man came rolling home.

2. This old man, he played two, he played knick-knack on my shoe. With a knick-knack paddy-whack, give a dog a bone.

This old man came rolling home.

Full-size version of this art can be found on the book companion website at www.cengage.com/education/machado.

3. This old man, he played three, he played knick-knack on my tree. With a knick-knack paddy-whack, give a dog a bone.

   This old man came rolling home.

4. This old man, he played four, he played knick-knack on my door. With a knick-knack paddy-whack, give a dog a bone.

   This old man came rolling home.

5. This old man, he played five, he played knick-knack on my hive. With a knick-knack paddy-whack, give a dog a bone.

   This old man came rolling home.

6. This old man, he played six, he played knick-knack on my sticks. With a knick-knack paddy-whack, give a dog a bone.

   This old man came rolling home.

7. This old man, he played seven, he played knick-knack up in heaven. With a knick-knack paddy-whack, give a dog a bone.

   This old man came rolling home.

8. This old man, he played eight, he played knick-knack on my gate. With a knick-knack paddy-whack, give a dog a bone.

   This old man came rolling home.

9. This old man, he played nine, he played knick-knack on my vine. With a knick-knack paddy-whack, give a dog a bone.

   This old man came rolling home.

10. This old man, he played ten, he played knick-knack on my hen. With a knick-knack paddy-whack, give a dog a bone.

    This old man came rolling home.

THE AFRAID-OF-STORY

Pieces

mouse	cat
dog	bear
hunter	lion

(Note: Patterns, except cat, can be found in stories in this chapter.)

(Place mouse on board.)

Here is a mouse. Mouse says, "I am the fastest, squeakiest mouse in the forest but I am afraid of cats."

(Add cat. Remove squeaky mouse.)

"I am the cleverest, meowingest cat in the forest but I am afraid of dogs."

(Add dog.)

Cat sneaks away.

(Remove cat.)

"I am the barkingest, bravest dog in the forest but I am afraid of bears."

(Add bear. Remove barking dog.)

"I am the biggest, most ferocious bear in the forest but I am afraid of the hunter."

(Add hunter and remove growling bear.)

"I am the smartest, most fearless hunter in the forest but I am afraid of lions."

(Add lion and remove hunter.)

"I am the fiercest, roaringest lion in the forest but I am afraid of a mouse who runs and squeaks at my feet!"

(Add mouse and remove lion.)

Mouse says "I told you I was the fastest, squeakiest mouse in the forest. Everyone is afraid of something sometimes!"

(One can stop at this point or go through the characters again, stopping at the "but I am afraid of" part in each animal's dialogue for the children to guess. This is also a good story to dramatize.)

Additional flannel board activities are found in the Appendix.

SECTION 5

Speech Growth:

Conversation, Expression,

and Dramatization

CHAPTER **13**

Realizing Speaking Goals

OBJECTIVES

After reading this chapter, you should be able to:

◆ State five goals of planned speech activities.

◆ Describe appropriate teacher behavior in daily conversations with children.

◆ Give three examples of questioning technique.

◆ Explain the role of the teacher in dramatic play.

KEY TERMS

convergent thinking	divergent thinking	expressive jargon
discourse skills	dramatic play	recasting

SWORD PLAY

Two 4-year-old boys were pretending to fence with paper swords. One kept saying "mustard" as he wielded his. After saying it a few more times, the other boy said, "hot dog" in response. They thought this was hysterical. I didn't get it until later, when I realized the first child must have observed someone saying "en garde" while fencing.

QUESTIONS TO PONDER

1. Is this a type of dramatic play?

2. Do you have any other examples of young children copying words they have heard but not understood?

In a well-planned classroom, a child has many opportunities to speak. Oral language is the foundation of literacy learning. Although some activities are planned, others just happen. Classroom discussion is paramount; throw away most or all of your ideas about quiet classrooms and instead aim for a dynamic room where discussion reigns. In this type of atmosphere, true literacy emerges. Help children see the uses of speaking in social interactions in their daily lives and tie speech to print and reading activities when possible. Preschool children do a wonderful job of learning to communicate, and the more they talk, the more their talking improves.

Activities can be divided into three groups: structured, unstructured, and child-initiated. Structured activities are those that the teacher plans and prepares. The teacher may be, for a while, at the center of all action—motivating, presenting ideas, giving demonstrations, eliciting child ideas and comments, and promoting conversation. Unstructured activities, on the other hand, may still be prepared by the teacher, but the children decide the action through self-directed play, and the teacher is cast primarily in the role of cohort, confidant, and interested party (Figure 13–1). The teacher remains conversational and supportive. For optimal child learning, teachers need to appreciate and offer authentic dialogue and real human communication in a reciprocal relationship between learner and teacher rooted in equality, respect, and trust. Educators who are skilled in responsive involvement and responsive conversation make a difference in children's lives. Warm, sensitive, observant, interested listeners who encourage, make suggestions, promote child verbal expression, and are, at times, playful companions of the language arts events are definitely contributing to the quality of children's experiences.

Child-initiated activities are those that follow children's interests and exploration. The teacher may provide materials or activities to further child opportunities. He may act as a resource, someone to share ideas with, someone to discuss discovery, and may also provide help in recording the child's research (Figure 13–2). Teachers take every possible avenue to increase and promote children's expression of ideas.

FIGURE 13–1 Teachers often become "coexplorers" who offer pertinent and language-expanding comments.

FIGURE 13–2 When teachers are close, they can share ideas, discuss happenings, or serve as a resource.

PROGRAM GOALS

Each early childhood center contains a unique group of children and adults. A center has its own geography and its children come from different segments of society, so the goals and priorities of one program may differ from others. There are, however, some common factors among centers. The following goals are acceptable to most programs. They give the teacher a basis for planning speaking activities and daily conversational exchanges. Each child should be helped to attain

◆ confidence in the ability to use speech with others.

◆ enjoyment in speaking experiences in play, conversations, and groups.

◆ acceptance of the idea that another's speech may be different.

◆ a higher level of interest in the meaning of new words.

In addition, each child should be helped to increase his skill in

◆ using speech for ideas, feelings, and needs.

◆ using speech to solve problems.

◆ using speech creatively in play situations.

◆ coordinating speech and body actions.

◆ waiting for a turn to speak.

Teachers realize the importance of children's **discourse skills** that go beyond basic conversation. Discourse skills involve children's use of language in structured ways, like telling a story about a past event, explaining how something works, building a fantasy world with words, explaining classroom rules to a peer, and dictating a "made up" poem.

---

discourse skills — refers to using language in structured ways to go beyond basic conversation, for example, telling a story, explaining a procedure, creating a fantasy, dictating ideas, and elaborating to provide greater understanding.

Thought-provoking and open-ended adult-child conversations support children's discourse efforts.

The overall goal in the development of speech communication in language arts is to increase each child's ability to use the speech he already possesses and to help the child move, when ready, toward the use of Standard English. Program goals can be realized mainly through the planning of daily activities, daily staff-child and child-child interaction, and the use of equipment and materials.

Kindergarten teachers agree that speaking and listening skills have a profound effect on children's success during their first few months at school. Children who know how to express themselves are prepared. Those who listen carefully to others are likely to adjust more readily to changing situations within the classroom.

A wide variety of different experiences can provide many learning opportunities. An activity can follow, review, and add depth to a previous one. One has to consider how much practice time is available. The special interests or needs of each child are considered when planning daily programs. Programs then become more valuable and meaningful.

DAILY CONVERSATIONS

Daily teacher-child conversations become amazingly easy when teachers focus on the "children's agenda." When classrooms seem always to be too hectic to get eye to eye with the child and listen to and pursue the child's interests, the program, environment, and teaching situation need to be evaluated and overhauled, for intimate conversations are severely limited and infrequent. At the other extreme, teachers defeat their purpose when the objective is always to teach or add a new word to the child's vocabulary. The key is to identify the child's interests; words then become meaningful. When the child is engrossed, he will connect the teacher's words with what has fascinated him.

Excellent teachers make their students feel valuable, competent, and worthwhile. The

following are the attitudes and behaviors teachers should cultivate in conversation.

- concern for each child's well-being
- an unwillingness to interrupt a child's conversation to respond to an adult
- a willingness to share the small moments of child accomplishment, sometimes even recognizing a child's achievement in a nonverbal way across a busy classroom
- consideration of children's verbal comments as worthy contributions
- respect for individual opinions
- recognition of each child's potential
- special regard for children as future leaders and discoverers

Teacher actions, questions, or statements that indicate the listener's genuine interest elicit a wealth of oral language (Figure 13–3).

Some of the best activities happen when the teacher notices what the child or group is focusing on and uses the opportunity to expand interest, knowledge, and enjoyment. A rainbow, a delivery truck, or any chance happening can become the central topic of active speaking by the children.

Whether limited or advanced, a child's speech is immediately accepted and welcomed. Teachers carefully guard and protect each child's self-confidence. By waiting patiently and reading nonverbal clues, teachers become understanding listeners.

Every effort should be made to give a logical response, showing the child that the teacher finds value in the communication. Touching, offering a reassuring arm or hand, and giving one's whole attention to the child often seem to relax the child and increase speech production.

Children are more willing to speak when the proper classroom atmosphere is maintained. The following are characteristics of a classroom that is conducive to children's speaking opportunities.

- The tone of the room is warm and relaxed, and children have choices.
- Speaking is voluntary, not mandatory.

FIGURE 13–3 "You want to fill four buckets with sand using the funnel?"

◆ The speaking group is small.

◆ The group listens attentively.

◆ Any speaking attempt is welcomed.

◆ Effort and accomplishments are recognized.

A teacher's willingness to engage in light-hearted dialogue may make the child more open to talking for the fun of it. When the mood is set for discovery, the teacher becomes active in the quest for answers, carefully guiding children through their exploration and expression.

Adults who emphasize the reasons for events and who take a questioning, thoughtful, and systematic approach to problems become model explorers. Thinking out loud while sharing activities is a useful device. "I wonder what would happen if you put the block there?" a teacher might ask. In their speech, young children often deal with the reality of what is happening around them; teachers' speech should also be based on this concept.

In reacting to young children's sometimes awkward, fractured, or incorrect speech, adults intuitively provide useful corrective feedback. The child's "posta put in" would automatically be accepted and corrected with, "Yes, the blocks go on the shelf." Seasoned teachers listen for content and the ideas behind words and matter-of-factly model correct usage so smoothly that the child is not made to feel that his speech usage was in any way deficient. The teacher must know how to make alert, sensitive comments that ensure that the children will continue to see the teacher as a responsive, accepting adult.

Educators and researchers have classified different "functions" of human speech. Some classifications follow. Teachers observing children will notice the young child's increasing use of different speech functions in social situations.

◆ *Instrumental* speech satisfies wants and needs.

"I want to be next."

◆ *Regulatory speech* helps children control others.

"Don't drop the cup because it will break into a zillion pieces."

◆ *Interactional* speech establishes and maintains contact with others.

"M," that's my letter. I'm Monroe." (A child is pointing to an alphabet chart with a friend.)

◆ *Personal function* speech expresses and asserts individuality.

"Let's push it under, and make it stay down." (Child statements made during water play.)

◆ *Heuristic function* speech helps children learn and describe.

"You're the baby, who goes wah, wah, wah."

◆ *Imaginative function* speech creates images and aids pretending.

"Look, I'm flying."

◆ *Representational* speech informs.

"I don't like bananas."

Teachers trying to facilitate children's use of different speech classifications will want to study Figure 13–4. All of these speech functions are present in the average preschool classroom.

What are young children fond of talking about? Themselves and what they are doing! They have their own views and opinions about the world around them. As their social contact increases, they exchange their ideas with other children. When they become older preschoolers, they typically engage in criticism, commands, requests, threats, and questions and answers. As a teacher listens to child-to-child conversations, he can make out both self-interest speech and speech that indicates social-intellectual involvement. Quite a lot of child conversation reflects the child's active, exploring, questioning mind and attempts to try, test, manipulate, control, and discover what speech can do for him. Flights of fantasy and make-believe are also evident.

Certain teacher behaviors and planned programs enhance children's speaking abilities. Are there factors that work counter to the realization of goals? Researchers compared everyday interactions in two child care centers and found one center they describe as lacking language stimulation. They reported that the children spent most of their time in teacher-directed large-group activities and that most of the children's language behavior was receptive, such as listening to and following teachers' directions. Although teachers provided adequate oral language models, they were not active listeners, did not encourage curiosity, and did not spontaneously expand on children's vocabulary or concepts (Hough, Nurss, & Goodman, 1984).

During interactions, children need their conversational partners to provide them with information that relates to the topic of the conversation and is relevant and appropriate to their language level so that they can use it to build upon what they already know. Teachers should try to *avoid* the following behaviors because they discourage healthy speech development.

◆ making inappropriate or irrelevant teacher comments

◆ talking at rather than with children

◆ using a controlling and commanding mode of interaction

◆ repeating oneself often

◆ criticizing child speech

◆ speaking primarily to other classroom adults

These are characteristics of unprofessional practice.

A New York study paired a proficient "talker" with a less proficient preschooler. At a special table, the "talk table," the study authors provided sets of categorized miniature figures and furnishings (Woodward, Haskins, Schaefer, & Smolen, 2004). Rules limited the table to one pair of children for 15 minutes of uninterrupted talk-time play per day. The miniature toys were not to be moved away. Each new set of toys was introduced with vocabulary. Children were urged to "use your words" at the talk table. During the 10-week study, teachers expended efforts to stimulate oral language through interactions and additional literacy activities. Test scores showed statistically significant oral improvement. The authors of the study believe the project clearly indicates that when an assessment suggests that a child has an expressive speech problem, concerned and innovative teachers can do something about it (Woodward et al., 2004).

Personal Speech Expressing Individual Ideas, Feelings, Concerns

Teacher actions include:
1. providing time and opportunity for adult-child and child-adult sharing of personal thoughts and feelings.
2. eye-level listening and impromptu conversations throughout the school day.
3. accepting individual child ideas and feelings and expressing your own.
4. encouraging family visitation, participation, and interaction in classroom activities and affairs.
5. sharing literature that elicits children's personal speech responses.

Speech Helping Children Obtain and Satisfy Wants and Needs

Teacher actions include:
1. listening and responding to children's requests.
2. encouraging children's ability to ask for wants and needs.
3. increasing children's opportunities to help other children by giving verbal directions.
4. explaining in step-by-step fashion the sequence needed to obtain desired results (e.g., how to get a turn with a favorite bike).

Speech That Promotes and Maintains Interaction

Teacher actions include:
1. planning for shared use of materials, areas, or adult help.
2. planning for small group discussion and problem solving.
3. including a mix of child ages and genders in planned activities.
4. celebrating and socializing between children and adults in classrooms.
5. devising activities in which self-worth and diversity are valued.
6. devising activities in which negotiating and compromise are possible.

Speech That Expresses Imaginative Ideas

Teacher actions include:
1. planning for creative individual child and group response.
2. designing activities to promote pretending.
3. prompting child description of creative ideas, actions, and solutions.
4. offering dramatizing, play acting, and role-playing classroom opportunities and providing areas and furnishings.

5. being playful with language and appreciating children's playful language.
6. encouraging children's creative play by providing props and giving teacher attention.
7. using audio or visual taping or group enactment of child creativity to preserve, give status, and promote discussion and provoke additional creativity.

Speech That Enhances Children's Verbal Descriptions and Learning

Teacher actions include:
1. providing child activities to capture child interest and spark curiosity.
2. creating child and group verbal problem-solving opportunities.
3. putting phrases such as the following in daily teacher speech:
   "I wonder what ..."
   "What would happen if ..."
   "Let's see if ..."
   "That's one way, can anyone think of another?"
   "What do we know about ..."
   "Can we try a new way?"
   "What did we see when ..."
4. suggesting real rather than contrived problems to solve.
5. listening closely to child discoveries and prompting children to put ideas into words.
6. noticing child interests. Building interest by following up with further activities.

Speech That Is Representational or Informative

Teacher actions include:
1. keeping record charts with children.
2. planning activities that involve observing carefully and analyzing or drawing conclusions.
3. eliciting additional or more precise information from children.
4. recording memorable classroom events, celebrations, and other happenings.
5. posting child birthdays, individual attributes, milestones, or other facts and data enhancing child self-worth or dignity.
6. graphing class composition factors (e.g., height and weight, food preference). Or presenting simple mapping activities involving school or neighborhood.
7. comparing time-related classroom factors.
8. providing activities that report individual child experiences to the group.

FIGURE 13–4 Suggested teacher strategies to promote child speech in differing classifications of human speech.

Children's Conversational Styles

Early childhood educators need to observe and notice children's conversational styles. Young children vary in their ability to approach others and speak to them and then respond. Conversational styles grow out of children's experiences and conversations with others. Children form their own views of themselves as communicators and "the right" style (Figure 13–5). From your own experience with young children, what types of communication styles have you noticed? Have you encountered children that are eager, shy, self-conscious, self-confident, articulate, silent, questioning, repetitive, loud, advanced, and others? One child may need multiple descriptors, being social yet unclear, or shy but verbal when approached, for example. As one works daily with young children, one makes mental notes (or written ones) to help one decide what possible activities and adult interactions will provide opportunities for speech growth. Beginning teachers need to be aware of teacher tendencies to converse and spend time with children with whom they feel comfortable, perhaps because of that child's particular conversational style, cultural background, ethnic origin, or personality.

Sign Systems

Early childhood educators are aware that young children express themselves in a number of ways. Teachers realize that words are but one of the multiple systems young children use to construct and express meaning. Sign systems, like music, drama, and mathematics, are uniquely different from language yet related. Words often accompany sign systems in both adults' and children's activities. Nonverbal signs, such as gestures, encountered in children's personal experience become associated with particular meanings that may differ widely for individual children.

Teachers meet young children who are more able to express themselves in movement, art, or drama than with words. Actions can sometimes convey more than a child's language ability allows.

Activities that encourage singing, dramatic expression, or use of art media to express what children know and feel expand the "confines" of language, promoting what is called "symbol weaving."

Almost all activities involve communication and expression. It is the teacher's job to see that words are prompted or supplied as a natural part of adult-child interaction so that consequent vocabulary growth is possible. Discussion between teachers and children in all curriculum areas can add and expand meaning to what is jointly experienced. For example, the statement, "You found two cars can fit on the flat bed truck," puts into words the child's discovery. "Joylyn is showing us with her body how she feels about the doll she brought to sharing time" is another example.

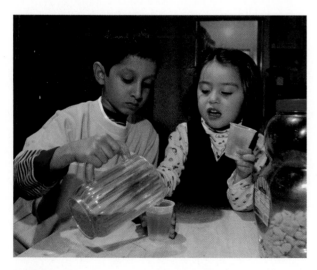

FIGURE 13–5 Anna uses specific terms and mentions small details as she converses with others.

THE AUTHENTIC TEACHER

"Authentic" teachers are quick to issue appreciative comments about a child's persistence at tasks, creative or new elements in child activities, solutions to problems encountered, or other features of children's actions or behaviors. They are good at spotting every child's advances and accomplishments. They also provide honest comments when necessary, and this can be done with specific, detailed words that expand children's understanding. They promote children's ability to put their own feelings into words daily in conflict situations, empowering children in the process.

Of prime importance to most educators is the goal of enhancing each child's growth of self-esteem and feelings of worth and value. Teachers work daily toward this. They attempt to stretch language skills and realize a confident child will converse freely and risk new experiences.

In social conflict situations, teachers channel child problems back to the conflicting parties so that verbal solutions between children are possible (Figure 13–6). They quietly stand near; hoping confrontations can come to satisfactory solutions, and intercede only when child communication breaks down.

It is obvious to teachers that many young children seek validation of their abilities.

FIGURE 13–6 After listening, the teacher will encourage the child to put his distress into words and will suggest that the child return and negotiate a solution.

Children's "Look at me" or "Look what I did" requests can be answered in ways that are both language expanding and self-worth building. "Oh, that's nice" or "Yes, I see" are weak adult statements. A specific comment is more effective: "Your long blocks are standing on their small ends. You built your bridge very carefully" or "To make your cat's tail you had to cut a long thin piece of paper. It looks like a cat's tail because it comes to a small point on the end." These are valuable teacher comments.

INTEGRATING CHILDREN INTO SOCIAL GROUPS

Because adults know children are teachers of other children, they want all children to obtain skills in social interaction. Teachers promote child friendships. The fragile friendships of 2- and 3-year-olds blossom and stabilize at about age 4. The conversation of children in group play is a joy to overhear. A reluctant child is encouraged. Books, puppets, and other language arts media can offer friendship themes and empathy-building models. The story *The Lion and the Mouse* is a good example and usually increases child comments concerning what it means to be a friend. The story ends with ". . . little friends can help big friends. The size of a friend isn't really too important."

SUGGESTED INTERACTION GUIDES

A teacher is a speech model for children. Because preschoolers range in abilities, the following guides for teachers in daily verbal conversations are based on understanding the level of each child. These guidelines help develop speaking ability when dealing with young nonverbal, or slightly verbal, children.

◆ Let the child see your face and mouth clearly, bend your knees, and talk at the child's eye level.

◆ Use simple hand gestures that show meanings.

◆ Watch for nonverbal reactions.

◆ Talk to the nonverbal child slowly, stressing key words such as nouns and verbs.

◆ If you cannot understand a word, repeat it back to the child in a relaxed way.

◆ If a child says "lellow," say, "Yes, the paint is yellow." Articulation will improve with age and good speech modeling.

◆ Answer **expressive jargon** (groups of sounds without recognizable words) or jabbering with suitable statements such as "You're telling me."

◆ Play games in which the child copies sounds or words.

◆ Watch for the child's lead. If he is interested in some activity or object, talk about it in simple sentences.

◆ Make directions simple. Indicate actions as you say the words.

◆ Encourage the child's imitations, whether verbal or nonverbal. Show that the effort is appreciated.

◆ Pause and wait patiently for the child's response.

The following guidelines help children who speak in one-word phrases or simple sentences develop speaking ability.

◆ Enlarge a child's one-word sentences into meaningful simple sentences, for example, "ball" to "The ball bounces."

◆ Use naming words to describe objects and actions: "The red ball is round."

◆ Use conjunctions (*and, but, so, also, or*), possessives (*mine, theirs, ours, Billy's, yours, his, hers*), and negatives (*is not, will not, do not, isn't, don't, won't, am not*).

◆ Help the child talk about his feelings.

◆ Use previously learned words with new words: "The black candy is called licorice." "Your dog is a poodle; this dog is a beagle." "It's a kind of hat called a baseball cap."

◆ Ask simple questions that help the child find out and discover while his interest is high: "Where did you find that round rock?"

◆ Play labeling games with pictures and objects.

◆ Correct speech errors such as "wented" or "goed" by matter-of-factly saying the correct word in a sentence: "Yesterday you went to the store." (Omit any corrective tone of voice.) The child may answer by saying it the same as before, but you have modeled correct usage, and in time it will be copied.

◆ Accept hesitant speech and stuttering in a patient, interested way. When a child is excited or under stress, ideas may not develop into words properly.

◆ Wait patiently while a child tries to speak; silently hold eye contact. The thought may get lost, but if you are a good listener, and if you respond with interest to what is said, the child will try again.

When the child speaks in sentences and comes close to mature speech, the teacher should

◆ include appropriate classifications or categories in sentences to help children form concepts: "Dogs and cats are animals."

◆ ask questions that help the child pinpoint identifying characteristics: "Does it have a tail?"

◆ ask questions that help the child see what is alike and what is different.

◆ after modeling a sentence pattern in conversation, ask a simple question so that the child can imitate the proper form while it is still fresh in his mind: "I think this lemon tastes sour. How does the lemon taste to you?"

◆ help the child keep ideas in order. What happened first? What happened next? What came last?

◆ state instructions clearly, building from one- to two- or three-part directions: "First wash your hands; then you can choose a cracker."

◆ use prepositions in speech. Say them with gestures: "Put the toy on the shelf. Thank

expressive jargon — a term describing a child's first attempts at combining words into narration that results in a mimic of adult speech.

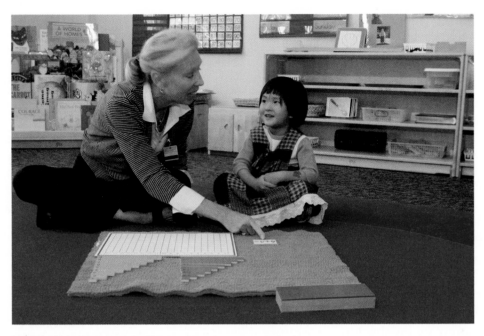

FIGURE 13–7 "Is this how long you want to make it?"

you. The blocks go inside the box." (Use your hand to show position as you speak.)

◆ use adjectives (*big, little, bright, red, soft,* and so forth) and comparatives (*more, less, lighter, heavier, shorter, tallest*): "Tell me about the rubber doll." "Yes, this pink doll is bigger." (Figure 13–7)

◆ ask the child to take simple verbal messages to another staff member: "Tell Mrs. Brown it's time to fix the snack." Alert other staff members to the fact that you are trying to promote verbal memory and self-confidence.

◆ help the child discover cause and effect: "Teacher, I'm afraid of bugs." "Why do bugs make you afraid, Billy?"

◆ remember that what is said in response to the child helps the child in many ways. Really listen. Answer every child if possible. When children talk at the same time, say, "I want to hear each one." "Mary, please say it again." "John, you can tell us next."

◆ give ownership to the ideas children contribute: "Yesterday Nancy told us . . ." "Kate's idea is . . ."

Teachers use a technique in adult-child conversation called **recasting**. This is very similar to expansion and feedback, previously mentioned. Recasting fills in what is missing or gently makes a change in the child's incorrect usage in the adult's answering comment and extends the child's idea. If a child says, "I like apples," for example, the teacher could respond with, "Apples taste good, don't they?" or "I like green ones, don't you?"

When teachers actively listen and observe, questions and teacher responses can better suit individual children. Teachers can grow to understand speech and conceptual errors, miscues, misconceptions, and the ways certain children express themselves with greater depth. With close observation, teachers begin to build a personal and cultural history of

---

recasting — a teaching technique that involves a teacher who supplies children's missing words or gently models correct usage of words or extends the child's idea following the child's verbal statement.

attending children. Some preschool children may have traveled extensively, whereas others have never left their neighborhoods. Both can have rich, full vocabularies but completely different fields of reference. In a conversation about tree blossoms brought into the classroom, the teacher might ask, "Where have you seen trees blossom in your neighborhood?" or "Tell me how the blossoms feel when you rub them gently on your cheek like this" or "What do you see if you look very closely at the blossom in your hand?"

The following teacher verbal interactions are also suggested.

1. When a child achieves success in some communicative setting, the teacher may find ways to extend this to a new and different setting.

2. When children are involved in exploratory activities, the teacher might raise questions such as, "I wonder why this is so?" or "What do you think is happening here?"

3. When children are observed to be troubled with an experience, the teacher can move in and talk about the situation with them and lead them to what they cannot yet do by themselves.

4. Teachers need to trust in children's learning and in their own ability to learn along with their children.★

A number of additional teacher options for extending child conversations can be found in Figure 13–8.

AWARENESS OF INTELLIGENT BEHAVIOR

Over time, a number of researchers have tried to identify effective thinking and intelligent behavior indicators. Would-be teachers observe children and conjecture how young children "come to know" rather than remember or state

★From Goodman, Y. M. (1985). Kidwatching: Observing children in the classroom. In Jaggar, A., & Smith-Burke, M. T. (Eds.), *Observing the Language Learner* (pp. 142–156). Copyright © 1985. Reprinted with permission of Yetta M. Goodman and the International Reading Association.

When a child's attention or focus is upon an object, action, event, animal, person, and so on, try the following:

• *Probe* with comments using your five senses. Discuss visual attributes (color, shiny, round, etc.). Comment on tactile qualities (soft, smooth, etc.). Make sound observations (loud, clang, thud, etc.). Describe smell or taste, if present.

• *Suggest* that the child "describe" using his senses.

• *Provide* data or information that is pertinent.

• *Comment* on significant facts and features, such as function, usefulness, category or class, novelty, origin, timeliness, parts, details, construction, mobility, weight, height, bulk, dimension, movement, and so forth.

• *Compare* it with something similar.

• *Relate* it to present, past, or future.

• *Probe* its relationship to other things.

• *Make guesses* in reference to what has captured the child's attention.

• *Discuss* opinions, impressions, conclusions, and problems that are possible or apparent.

• *Mention* likes and dislikes.

• *Fantasize,* imagine, pretend, or dream out loud.

• *Talk* about humorous, ridiculous, or incongruent features.

To assess your skill:

The child is observing a large ice cube melt in the outside yard. Return to the above and generate extending teacher comments.

FIGURE 13–8 Teacher options and ways to extend child conversations.

what they already know. Most classrooms enroll children whom teachers would call "successful students." By closely observing children, teachers can note behaviors that indicate children's reasoning abilities, insightfulness, strategies, perseverance, creativity, and craftsmanship.

Many indicators are best observed in children's speech behavior. Costa's classic study (1991) outlines intelligent behavior characteristics but also notes that the listing may be incomplete.

1. **Persistence: Persevering when a solution to a problem is not immediately apparent. In preschool some children**

ask abundant questions, others try various and different approaches to reach goals. A child might ask all other teachers in a room if one teacher admits he/she doesn't know the answer to the question. Many children probe the reasons behind happenings and are persistent in getting more and more data to explain happenings.

2. Decreasing impulsivity: A thoughtful pause rather than a quick answer or action may be observed in some preschoolers.

3. Listening to others with understanding and empathy: Some young children hear others' points-of-view and can paraphrase another's ideas. Others may not be able to "overcome ego-centrism" at this age as Piaget observes. Both groups are displaying developmentally appropriate behavior. The first group has achieved a maturity in thinking processes, and is usually slow to ridicule, laugh at, or put down other children's ideas.

4. Flexibility in thinking: No matter what a teacher or parent tells a child on a certain subject, the child may not believe or accept the information. This isn't flexibility in thinking. As children age, however, many will at least consider new possibilities and doubt their previous ideas. Some check out new ideas with others with questions like "Do daddies cook?"

5. Metacognition: Awareness of one's own thinking: Preschoolers may be able to describe the steps they took to achieve some desired outcome, but rarely can they put into words what went on inside their heads or describe their strategies. More often when asked "How did you do that?" they will be silent or say "I just did it." This is a developmentally appropriate answer.

6. Checking for accuracy and precision: The child who shows a printed form

to teacher saying "I made an A" may be simply stating a truth as he sees it. With another child who says "That's not an A. Is it, teacher?" The child is checking for accuracy. In discussions a child may seek a correction. Many teachers have learned this lesson with the child who's a dinosaur buff for the child has learned the distinguishing characteristics of each dinosaur well, and may be better informed than the teacher.

7. Questioning and problem posing: This is a characteristic of many preschoolers who inquire about the "whys" of things and are alert to discrepancies and uncommon phenomena.

8. Drawing on past knowledge and applying it to new situations: At times, teachers have difficulty trying to understand what common element in a present situation the child is connecting to the past. Other connections are readily apparent as when a child reacts negatively to a worker dressed in white.

9. Precision of language and thought: Young children use an increasing number of descriptive words and analogous comments when exposed to adult language that is not vague or imprecise.

10. Using all the senses: Young children readily probe, manipulate, and savor the sensory opportunities presented to them.

11. Ingenuity, originality, insightfulness, creativity: Early childhood professionals treasure child attempts and behaviors in this area, and most teachers can immediately cite examples they've observed.

12. Wonderment, inquisitiveness, curiosity, and enjoyment of problem solving—a sense of efficacy as a thinker: Child attitudes toward problems, thinking games, guessing, and obstacles can enhance or impede their quest for knowledge and solutions. Adults

may model attitudes of "giving up" or "it's too hard" or "I'll never get it right" rather than the preferred "let's find out," "let's see what we can do." Adults can also model enjoyment when in the pursuit of solving some task or dilemma. (p. 203)*

In considering the sixth item in Costa's preceding list, the teacher may consider a child saying, "Sudeh didn't drink her juice," as checking to see if a rule about juice-finishing exists, rather than tattling. The teacher might reply, "At school we can choose to drink as much juice as we want, but everyone should drink all that he pours in his cup."

How can early childhood teachers support children's emerging intellectual abilities? From Costa's list, there are many clues. A teacher begins by having faith in the ability and intelligence of all children and acknowledges that not all children's homes (or all teachers) value intelligent behavior. Intelligent child behavior can be recognized and appreciated.

Children can absorb the idea that often there is more than one solution or answer or way of doing something and that pausing, gathering more data, and "thinking things over" are good strategies. Children can be asked to share their plans and outcomes on chosen activities. Day-to-day happenings and real dilemmas can be talked about and problems solved through actions and discussions where every child's ideas are valued.

The teacher can rig classroom activities to promote children's thinking, problem solving, creative ideas, and imagination. Children can develop the attitude that what they contribute is worthwhile. When teachers listen, paraphrase children's comments, clarify, and try out student ideas, children feel that what they say is meaningful. "Maybe the school's pet bird does eat paper, or maybe it just tears it up. If we watch carefully we can find out, can't we?"

Providing a continually interesting classroom full of exploring opportunities is a must. Classrooms that are rich in firsthand manipula-

tive experiences and are staffed with responsive adults can make this happen. One of the chief causes for failure in formal education is that we begin with language rather than with real and material action. At the preschool level this means that some teachers have a tendency to tell children about reality rather than "providing" reality—real exploring experiences encountered together. Teachers also need to model their own intelligent behaviors and enthusiasm for learning. Nothing works as well as an example.

SETTINGS FOR PREPLANNED SPEAKING ACTIVITIES

Speaking activities occur when children are inside or outside the classroom or when they are on the move. Preplanned activities are more successful when both children and teachers are comfortable and unhurried and when there are no distractions. Peers will be a valuable source of words and meanings.

Close attention should be given to group size and the seating space between children at group times. It is easier to create an atmosphere of inclusion and intimacy in a small discussion group than in a large group, thereby promoting children's willingness to share thoughts. Lighting and heating in the room must also be considered. Soft textures and rugs add warmth and comfort. A half-circle seating arrangement, with the teacher in the center, provides a good view of both the teacher and what is to be seen.

Ease of viewing depends on eye level and seating arrangement. When possible, the objects children are to look at should be at their eye level. Teachers often sit in child-sized chairs while conducting language arts experiences. Screens, dividers, and bookcases can help lessen distractions.

One inventive teacher thought of a way to promote child speech during a family-child "Back to School" night. Children were asked to draw self-portraits. A large mirror was set up beside various drawing supplies and paper. They were asked not to write their names on their self-portraits. Before the meeting, child drawings were posted under signs reading "Can

*From Costa, A. L. (1991). The search for intelligent life. In *Developing minds: A resource book for teaching thinking.* Copyright © 1991 Association for Supervision and Curriculum Development. Used with permission.

you find me?" Signs were done in the home languages of attending children. The activity promoted the children's verbal identification of their artwork and their classmates' drawings and highlighted the children's role as a verbal classroom guide for families.

QUESTIONING SKILLS

A teacher's questions often prompt children to ponder and wonder. Questions checking whether the teacher has understood the child's comment are common. They provide the child feedback concerning the teacher's attention and interest and clarify whether the child's intended message was understood. This gives the child the opportunity to correct the teacher and send further data or explanation or clear up miscommunication. Questions can also help keep conversations afloat and show that the teacher is interested in the child's pursuits.

Questions can help children see details they would otherwise have missed. Sometimes questions help a child form relationships between objects and ideas; they may prompt the child to speak about both feelings and thoughts; they can lead the child to a new interest. Skill in questioning is an important teaching ability. Questions asked by a teacher can often lead children to discovery.

Many experts suggest that teachers need help and specific training in questioning strategies so that they can aid children's ability to see contradictions, move them toward rethinking, and assist concept development. Teachers need to ask questions that are readily understood and require easy responses from the very young child and more challenging, thoughtful responses from language-capable preschoolers. This means modifying questions depending on language levels.

Asking questions may be "the most fragile" of all conversation starters. Teachers can make questions less threatening by asking about a child's activities or interests and by using familiar expressions.

In a situation in a classroom when a window has blown shut and one of the children says, "Someone hit that window, teacher!" a skillful question such as "Is anyone standing near the window?" or "Could anyone reach that window from down on the ground?" or "Can you think of something else that might slam a window shut, something that could push it? Let's look out the window and see if other things are being pushed around," could lead the child to a new conclusion.

The following example illustrates the teacher's role in stimulating the thought process that emerges from play. The teacher, who has created the climate for learning by supplying and arranging the equipment, sees a child playing with cars on ramps that he has constructed with blocks. She knows that if a car is placed on a slope made with blocks, the speed with which it descends and the distance it goes are affected by the slope and length of the ramp. The teacher asks, "Did the blue car go farther than all the others?" or "What might happen if you built your ramp higher?"

The teacher also introduces new words to the child's vocabulary—*slant, ramp, slow, faster, above, below, under, tall, smaller than*—and uses and elicits this vocabulary in conversation.

Teachers need to be sensitive to the anxiety that some children may have. In past experiences, if a child's answers have been overcorrected, or if adults' questions are associated with punishment, teachers' questions can cause children to be silent and tense.

Teachers use "choice" questions at times. This allows them to slip specific, descriptive words into their speech while the child is focused: "Do you want the red paint (pointing) or the blue paint (pointing)?"

Also important in asking questions is the teacher's acceptance of the child's answers. Because each child answers a question based on his own experience, children may give very different answers. The following conversation (observed at the San Jose City College Child Development Center) shows how a teacher handled an unexpected answer. (The conversation had centered on television sets.)

Teacher: "Where could we go to buy a television set?"

Chase: "Macy's."

Chloe: "At a pear store."

Vanda: "The TV store."

Teacher: "Chase says Macy's sells television sets. Chloe thinks we could buy one at a 'pear' store. Vanda thought at a TV store. Maybe we could go to three places to buy one. Chloe, have you seen television sets at the 'pear' store?"

Chloe: "The pear store has lots of 'em."

Teacher: "You've been to a 'pear' store?"

Chloe: "Our TV broke, and we took it to the 'pear' store."

Teacher: "The repair shop fixed my broken television set, too. Yes, sets can be for sale at a repair shop."

The teacher's task is to keep the speech and answers coming, encouraging each child's expression of ideas. Sometimes a question can be answered with a question. When a child says, "What does a rabbit eat?" the teacher might say, "How could we find out?" The teacher knows that a real experience is better than a quick answer.

When using questions, the level of difficulty should be recognized. Early childhood teachers can use carefully asked questions to find the child's level of understanding. Teachers try to help each child succeed in activities while offering a challenge at the same time. Even snack time can be a time to learn new language skills.

Open-ended questions are very useful, and teachers try to increase their ability to ask them. Open-ended questions are defined as questions with many possible answers. Some teachers are so intent on imparting information to children that they forget to assess the ways it may be assimilated. Thus answers to open-ended questions—"Can you tell me about . . . ?" "What do you think about . . . ?"— are often more revealing than answers to questions with a more specific focus. They can be followed by "Tell me more" or "Some people think that . . ." or "What do you think?"

Teachers' questions can be classified into eight main types.

1. *Recall*: Asks the child to remember information, names, words, and so forth. Recall questions are the type most often asked. Many studies report that about 60 percent of teachers' questions require students to recall facts, about 20 percent require students to think, and the remaining 20 percent are procedural. Teachers emphasize fact questions, whereas research indicates an emphasis on higher, cognitive questions would be more effective. The Student Activities section of this chapter asks you to conduct an observational study concerning this point. Could it be that this type of question was modeled constantly in most teachers' own elementary schooling? Example: What color is this ball?

2. **Convergent thinking**: Asks the child to compare or contrast similarities or differences and seek relationships. Example: How are these two toy cars alike?

3. **Divergent thinking**: Asks the child to predict or theorize. Example: If the boy steps on the marble, what might happen?

4. *Evaluation*: Asks the child for a personal opinion or judgment or asks the child to explore feelings. Example: What would be on your plate if you could have your favorite food?

5. *Observation*: Asks the child to watch or describe what he senses. Example: What is happening to the ant on the window sill?

6. *Explanation*: Asks the child to state cause and effect, reasons, and/or descriptions. Example: The clay feels different today. What do you think happened to it?

---

convergent thinking — the process of analyzing and integrating ideas to infer reasonable conclusions or specific solutions from given information.

divergent thinking — the process of elaborating on ideas to generate new ideas or alternative interpretations of given information.

7. *Action*: Asks the child to move his body or perform a physical task. Example: Can you show us how to walk like a duck?

8. *Open-ended*: Many answers are possible. Example: How do children get from their homes to their school in the morning?

Certain types of teacher questions promote children's thinking processes. These include questions seeking child opinion, questions calling for a verbalized child choice, questions promoting a child hypothesis, questions asking for cause-and-effect explanations, and questions seeking child solutions. Teachers can question children's past happenings in light of present happenings to help children form relationships.

Teachers should limit "low-quality" questions that center on isolated bits of knowledge and are designed to test what is learned or remembered. Unfortunately, many adults link the words *teacher* and *test* and doggedly ask continual questions of children, believing this is age-old and appropriate behavior for all "good" teachers. When an adult approaches a young child playing in the sandbox with questions such as "What are you doing?" or "What are you making?" the child may wonder why the adult cannot see for himself or whether he is supposed to be making something. It may be hard for this adult to really focus on the child's activity and make pertinent comments, such as "That's a big mountain of sand you've just made," or to pick up a sand toy cup and say, "Please pour some sand in my cup."

Preschool teachers have many opportunities through questioning to explore children's imaginative responses to books, events, and classroom happenings. Their questions can be child-centered, promoting creative and interpretive child responses. Teachers can improve their ability to stop, listen, and learn from what their charges are saying.

The way questions are phrased may produce short or longer answers. Questions using "what" or "where" usually receive one-word or short-phrase answers. Many questions, such as *Do you? Did you? Can you? Will you? Have you? Would you?* are answered by *yes* or *no*. This type of question fits the level of the very young.

Questions that help a child compare or connect ideas may begin as follows:

> What would happen if ...?
>
> Which one is longer?
>
> How are these two alike?
>
> Why did you say these were different?
>
> What happened next?
>
> If it fell off the table, what would happen to it?
>
> Can you guess which one will be first?
>
> Could this ball fit inside this can?
>
> I wonder why the dog is sniffing?
>
> What do you think is happening?

The following are examples of questions that encourage problem solving or stimulate creative thought.

> If you had a handful of pennies, what would you buy?
>
> Could you tell me what you are going to do when you're as big as your dad?
>
> Can you think of a way to open this coconut?
>
> How could we find out where this ant lives?

These questions can be answered by the more mature speakers. Through close listening and observation, the teacher can form questions that the child will want to answer.

USING A VYGOTSKIAN OR CONSTRUCTIVIST APPROACH

A teacher using a constructivist approach with younger and older children should

◆ make his actions and the children's actions verbally explicit. Label his own actions as he carries them out. Label the child's actions for him as they occur. "Hand me the blue blocks."

◆ model thinking and strategies aloud. As he solves a problem, talk about what he is thinking about. "I could put them together."

◆ when introducing a new concept, be sure to tie it to actions. "When we want to measure something to see how long it is, we put the ruler at the end of the object and read the numbers here."

◆ use thinking while talking to check children's understanding of concepts and strategies. Get children used to talking about what they think and how they solve problems. "You are turning the puzzle piece to see if it fits. If it doesn't fit, what else will you do?"

◆ encourage the use of private speech. This type of self-talk has meaning for the child and should not be discouraged. Coach the child on what he might say to himself as he does something, "The knob turns, and then press the button."

SPEECH IN PLAY AND ROUTINES

Children's play opportunities in early childhood centers are planned for, promoted, and wide ranging. An examination of whether an early childhood center has built conversation and discussion times into its daily schedule can reflect a staff's efforts to encourage child talk and oral expression. A conversational lunch period is an example of a routinely planned "small talk time."

In play, children can symbolize ideas and feelings through gestures and speech and can collaborate with friends. Children reexamine life experiences, adding their imagination and at times manipulating happenings, settings, and people (Figure 13–9).

Play

Play stimulates much child-to-child conversation, and some kinds of play promote talking more than others. Quiet activities such as painting or working puzzles may tend to limit speech while the child is deeply absorbed.

If teachers observe children's play sequences, they will note many child-initiated play situations that involve print, acting, drawing, "reading," and "writing." Props are improvised as dramas unfold. With writing, art, or construction materials handy, children will incorporate these into child-created and child-directed situations.

FIGURE 13–9 Look how intent and careful this child is while she is play ironing.

Teachers plan opportunities for children to play by themselves and with others in small and large groups. Play with another child or a small group almost always requires children to speak. Toddlers may play near each other in a nonverbal, imitative manner using sounds, squeals, and sometimes screams. Interaction with other children promotes the growth of speaking ability.

Studies of children with nonsocial or withdrawn play behavior during preschool found this behavior was a strong predictor of peer rejection, social anxiety, loneliness, depression, and negative self-esteem in later childhood. Extra teacher help and encouragement may be necessary. A child case study by staff, conferencing, and referral to diagnostic experts may be needed if the school is unsuccessful in encouraging a child to engage in more social play behavior.

Early in life, children act out and repeat the words and actions of others. During preschool years, this is called **dramatic play**, and the staff in early childhood centers plan and prepare for it. Dramatic play is believed to have important benefits for children and holds many learning opportunities. It helps children

◆ develop conversational skills and the ability to express ideas in words (Figure 13–10).

◆ understand the feelings, roles, or work of others.

◆ connect actions with words—actions and words go hand-in-hand in dramatic play.

◆ develop vocabulary.

◆ develop creativity—children imagine, act, and make things up as play progresses.

◆ engage in social interaction with other children.

◆ cope with life, sometimes through acting out troubling situations, thus giving an outlet for emotion (for example, almost every doll in an early childhood center gets a spanking periodically when children play house).

◆ assume leadership and group-participant roles.

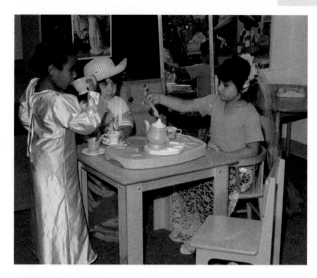

FIGURE 13–10 Tea parties are all-time favorites.

With a rising emphasis on prereading skill development crowding out free play time, some educators may need to justify offering children a curriculum with rich and generous dramatic play time. Hatcher and Petty (2004) suggest that teachers observe and document children's use of cognitive skills during play episodes; they believe that teachers will find plenty of examples of symbolic representation, cognitive flexibility, problem solving, make-believe, divergent thinking, and perspective taking. With close observation, educators can see considerable language growth and learning taking place, including new word use, concept development, linguistic awareness, and language practice. In a research study reported by Marcon (2007), children's later school success appears to have been enhanced by more active, child-initiated early learning experiences, but their progress may have been slowed by overly academic preschool experiences that introduced formalized learning experiences too early for most children's development status.

Pretend play is no easy task, even though it may look to be to the uninitiated observer. It is actually a milestone in development. It requires the ability to transform events and objects

---

dramatic play — acting out experiences or creating drama episodes during play.

symbolically. Pretend play is full of interactive social dialogue and negotiation involving role taking, script knowledge, and improvisation. Considerable vocabulary growth occurs during its duration (Bergen, 2001). For example, when playing house, the child can start out as the grandfather and end up as the baby or the family dog. In each role, the child mixes real and pretend factors simultaneously; acts out thoughts, speech, and actions; and may portray emotions appropriate to the play scenario. Joint planning and problem solving using linguistic skill also have taken place.

In trying to identify children's vocabulary during dramatic play, some educators have cleverly recorded children's dramatic play. From recordings they developed word and comment lists. These were later shared with children during daily recap meetings. One tea party word list included *tea, teapot, cup, spoon, saucer, plate, pour, spill,* and *please*; "No thank you" and "What a beautiful hat!" were on a comment list. This teacher technique is especially helpful for second-language learners when word list words and actions are accompanied by demonstrations.

Much time and effort are devoted to dramatic play in childhood. The child engages in this type of activity often and has the ability to slide easily from the real world into the make-believe world.

Teachers watch dramatic play develop from the simple imitative actions of toddlers and younger preschoolers to the elaborate dramatic play of 4-year-olds, in whom language use blossoms. Teachers support each step along the way by providing the necessary objects and materials that enhance dramatic episodes and by offering assistance (Figure 13–11). Effective teachers must observe and be aware of the adult actions and situations that capture child interest enough to prompt reenactment. One surprised student teacher who dreamed up a shaving activity, complete with mirrors, shaving cream, and bladeless razors, found that the boys rolled up their pants legs and shaved their legs. This brings up two interesting items: first, the wisdom of letting razors, even bladeless ones, become play items, and second, how dramatic play often enlightens teachers. Child safety is always the first criterion used to evaluate whether an activity is appropriate.

Four-year-olds engage vigorously in superhero play. As Indians and cowboys, good guys and bad guys, or monster or ghost enactments captured the imaginations of past generations of

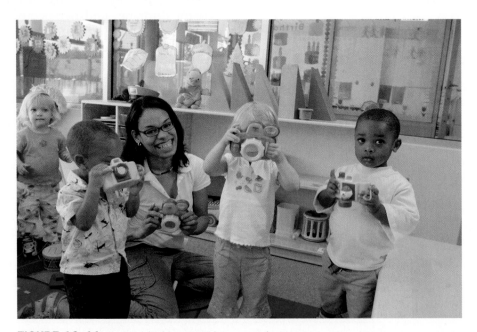

FIGURE 13–11 Pretend photographers need cameras.

American children, new heroes have appeared in television cartoons and movies. Robots and space creatures are common dramatic play themes for 4-year-olds. The children mimic the chosen power figures in actions and words.

Many teachers feel ambivalent when they witness the violence enacted in some of these play episodes, which can require special handling and decisions to intercede to keep children safe. Most teachers set up times for group dialogue about superheroes so that reality and fantasy come under group discussion; such discussions can provide learning opportunities for the entire class or group. Other teachers worry about the perceived lack of child creativity in this type of play because the same theme and action are generally repeated over and over. Some educators believe a positive benefit exists. It may diminish fears associated with scary experiences, powerful people, or fictional media characters. Play may be children's attempt to give themselves extraordinary abilities and strengths.

Rich home and school experiences (going places and doing things) serve as building blocks for dramatic play. One would have a difficult time playing "restaurant" or "wedding" if there had been no previous experience with either. Early childhood centers can provide activities and objects that promote dramatic play, such as

- ◆ field trips.
- ◆ discussions and readings by visitors and guest speakers.
- ◆ books.
- ◆ discussions based on pictures.
- ◆ films, videos, filmstrips, and slides.
- ◆ kits (boxed sets), equipment, and settings for dramatic play.
- ◆ career presentations made by family members or classroom visitors.

In dramatic play, children often use symbols and language to represent objects that are not actually present. An oblong block may become a baby bottle; a pie plate, the kitchen clock; and so on. The enactment of role-appropriate behavior in a make-believe situation is a major step toward literacy. A significant relationship exists between kindergartners' symbolic play and reading achievement. Children with symbolic dramatic play skills seem to have increased ability to comprehend words and understand a variety of syntactic structures.

Dramatic play fosters children's growth in many areas, including verbalization, vocabulary, language comprehension, attention span, imaginativeness, concentration, impulse control, curiosity, problem-solving strategies, cooperation, empathy, group participation, and intellectual development. In play the child is often behaving beyond his age and above his usual everyday behavior.

DRAMATIC PLAY SETTINGS

A playhouse area with a child-size stove, refrigerator, table, and chairs encourages dramatic play. An old boat, a service station pump, and a telephone booth are examples of other pieces of equipment that children enjoy using in their play.

Furniture found at early childhood centers can be moved into room arrangements that suggest a bus, a house, a tunnel, or a store. Large cardboard boxes may become a variety of different props with, or without, word labels. Large paper bags, ropes, blankets, and discarded work clothes or dress-up clothing also stimulate the child to pretend. Items for dramatic play can be obtained from commercial school-supply companies, secondhand stores, flea market sales, garage sales, and other sources.

Dramatic Play Kits

Items that go together and suggest the same type of play can be boxed together, ready for use. A shoe-shine kit, complete with cans of natural shoe polish, a soft cloth, a shoe brush, play money, and a newspaper or a magazine, is very popular. Functional print items can also be added and are a good way to develop print awareness. Children catch on to the activity quickly. Unfortunately, not many may have seen a shoe-shine stand or family member polishing their shoes, so a teacher demonstration of this kit may be necessary.

Community theme prop boxes such as bakery, flower shop, bank, car repair shop, and so forth, are suggested. Children using them make decisions about what community people think and do. Incorporating writing materials natural to the play theme promotes an additional language arts dimension.

Ideas for kits to be used in dramatic play follow.

Post Office. Large index cards, used postcards and letters, stamp pads, stamp blocks, stationery, envelopes, greeting cards, crayons or pencils, stamps (Christmas or wildlife seals), mail boxes (shoe box with slot cut in front and name clearly printed), old shoulder bag purses for mailbags, and men's and women's shirts.

Cleaning Set. Several brooms, mops, sponge mops, dust cloths, dustpans, sponges, shirts with logos, aprons, plastic bottles and spray bottles with water, and paper towels for windows.

Tea Party. Set of cups and saucers, plastic pitchers, napkins, vase, tablecloth, plastic spoons, placemats, place cards, teapot, invitations, small empty food packages such as cereal boxes, and clay or plastic cookies or biscuits.

Hospital and Doctor. Stethoscope, bandages, masking tape, red stickers for play wounds, tongue depressors, play thermometer, medical exam checklist, paper pad and pencil for prescriptions, billing forms for bill, adhesive tape, cotton balls, armband with a red cross on it, bag to carry, paper hospital gowns, white shirt, and photographs of culturally diverse doctors of both sexes.

Teacher. Notebooks, pencils, plastic glasses, chalk, bell, chalkboard, attendance book, photographs of a variety of teachers' desks, chairs, rulers, books, flannel board with sets, book about the first day at school.

Washing the Car. Towels, spray bottles with soapy water, sponges, buckets, cut hose lengths, window squeegees, old plastic rain coats, feather dusters, window cleaner spray bottles with blue-colored water, wax cans, drying line with clothes pins for wet towels, an old car. (A warm, sunny day in an outside grass area works best.)

Supermarket. Cash register, play money, newspaper ads, paper pads and pencils or crayons, hole punch, store name tags, shopping list, paper sacks, empty food cartons, wax fruit, play grocery cart or rolling laundry cart, purse, and wallet.

Hair Salon. Plastic brushes, combs, cotton balls, powder, scarves, colored water in nail polish bottles, old hair dryer (no cord or plug), curlers, water spray bottle, hairpins, book of male and female hairstyles, and mirror.

Service Station. Tire pump, pliers, cans, sponges and bucket, short length of hose and cylinder (for gas pump), hat, plastic charge cards, squirt bottle, paper towels, paper and pencil, and a "Gas for Sale" sign.

Fishing. Hats, bamboo lengths (about 3 feet) with string and magnet at the end, fishing box, a basin, and small metal objects such as paper clips for the fish or cutouts for fish shapes with a paper clip attached to each (to attract the magnet), and bucket.

Gift Wrap. Old wallpaper books, assorted empty boxes or blocks to wrap, used bows, tape, scissors, gift cards, ribbon, crayons, and calendar.

Camping. Old pots and pans, plastic dishes, backpacks, blankets, sleeping bags, foam pads, flashlight, short lengths of logs, red cellophane, large box or tent, food boxes, card table and chairs, old camp stove, canteen, portable radio, pretend child-safe sun tan or protection lotion in plastic bottles, and sunglasses.

Airplane. Chairs in rows, trays, plastic utensils, play food, headphones, little pillows, blankets, tickets, magazines, rolling cart, cups, plastic bottles, napkins, airline attendant clothing, backpack, and snack packages.

More kits can be made for the following:

- TV or computer repair person
- baker
- painter
- picnic
- restaurant
- wedding
- police officer
- construction worker
- mail carrier
- firefighter
- pilot
- circus
- birthday party
- astronaut
- airport
- plumber

The ideas for play kits that have been suggested are based on a few of the many possible themes. Families are good sources of kit items.

Collecting props for favorite stories and putting them in a storage bag or container that has a picture or illustration of the story on its front is another idea. For example, for the story *Stone Soup* (Brown, 1947), the following props could be collected: large pot, large stone, long-handled spoon, assorted vegetables, aprons for cooks, hats for travelers, three-cornered hats for soldiers.

Costumes

Costumes and clothing props let a child step into a character quickly. Strong, sturdy, child-manageable ties and snaps encourage self-help. Elastic waistbands slip on and off with ease. Clothing that is cut down to size (so that it does not drag) can be worn for a longer time. Items that children enjoy are

- hats of all types. (Note: The use of hats, wigs, and headgear may not be possible in some programs where head lice have occurred.)
- shoes, boots, and slippers.
- uniforms (Figure 13–12).

FIGURE 13–12 A hat and uniform can help children step into character.

- accessories, such as ties, scarves, purses, wallets, old jewelry, aprons, badges, and key rings.
- discarded fur jackets, soft fabrics, and fancy fabric clothing.
- wigs.
- work clothes.

A clever idea for a child-made costume is using a large-handled shopping bag. Once the bottom of the bag is cut out, the child can step into it, using the bag handles as shoulder straps. The child can decorate the bag and use it as a play prop.

THE TEACHER'S ROLE IN DRAMATIC PLAY

Dramatic play is child-directed instead of teacher-directed. Play ideas come from the child's imagination and experience.

Teachers can motivate dramatic play before they withdraw to remain in the background. They are watchful but do not hover. Sometimes a new play direction is suggested by a teacher to divert the children away from unsafe or violent play. The flow of play preferably is decided by the children. Teachers' close presence and words can stop or change behavior when the situation becomes unsafe or gets out of hand. If things go smoothly, the ideas, words, and dramatic play actions are those of the children.

Periodic suggestions by the teacher and introduction of material may extend and enrich play. Care is taken not to dominate but rather to be available as a friendly resource.

Play is where reading and writing begin. In dramatic play, children understand its pretend or make-believe nature (although, in certain play situations, a child occasionally may confuse play with reality).

Older preschoolers' dramatic play becomes increasingly mature, involved, complex, and riddled with abstract symbolic representations.

Pioneering attempts to train children who were less able to engage in appropriate pretend play have occurred. Teacher modeling, teacher assuming a play role in reenactments of real-life experiences, and teacher interventions such as suggestions, giving directions, asking questions, and clarifying behavior took place. Study children were encouraged to engage in and sustain sociodramatic play. Teachers let children decide play direction and content. Teachers' actions, it was found, *aided* child elaboration of child-chosen play themes.

Traditionally, teachers have been advised to limit or omit adult interaction and domination of young children's dramatic play. The teacher might be involved by briefly modeling equipment use or making quick statements suggesting children's options—for example, writing a note, selecting menu items, or looking at signs. If children are playing with old cell phones, the teacher might remark, "It says *talk* and *send* on your cell phone buttons," while pointing out the buttons on the phone. Teacher behavior of zooming in and out is believed appropriate. This involves adding to the child's ideas and giving choices for the child to consider without directing or dominating the flow of the child's ideas and play except where child safety is concerned.

When teachers observe dramatic play, lots of language use is occurring, and teachers may be able to provide materials, equipment, or additional play items that facilitate even more language usage. Many times this is done by connecting language in some way to the children's play themes, such as by providing signs, old cell phones, or paper and writing tools so something can be written down, recorded, created, or composed with or without teacher assistance. Teachers try to determine what can be supplied that is naturally connected to the children's play scenarios.

Dramatic Play as an Intellectual Reaction to Book Events

Children's dramatic play and role-playing are ways to synthesize and connect what has been presented in picture books and in their own lives. Any observant teacher knows children's dramatic play mirrors their significant life experiences. The child who first says, "Did you bring home any money?" in a play scenario in which the child playing father enters the play situation has observed or experienced a background event.

What then could be the benefit of playacting a book? Besides the recreating (retelling) of book parts or themes, the experience offers a number of intellectual and literary benefits. Deeper or clearer meaning might be achieved. Early childhood practitioners can conclude that this activity helps children construct knowledge on a number of levels.

Children often retell more detailed and complex stories when they are supplied with simple props, such as small objects or pictures. McGee (2003) suggests using a story clothesline tied between two pieces of furniture with 6 to 10 pictures (created or selected) to depict major story or book events. "Story collars," which represent the clothing story characters might wear, such as a farmer's work shirt collar or a faux fur collar for an animal character, were also suggested.

Props like hats, clothes, and objects and settings connected to the picture book can be created using teacher ingenuity. A teacher can examine a book before presenting it for features that lead to easy enactment; for example, if using *The Three Billy Goats Gruff*, it would be easy to set up a bridge with the materials and equipment found in most preschools.

Most observant teachers find children reliving favorite or captivating picture books with or without their help in groups or as individuals. It is as if in the reliving, the reenactment, the picture book's message becomes "fitted" into what they already know.

When children reenact a picture book with a teacher's help, the teacher may be surprised, because as children reenact they will usually insert objects and events from their own lives into the story context.

The following books lend themselves to child reenactment:

Brown, M. W. (1994). *Big red barn*. New York: Harper.
Eastman, P. (1960/1993). *Are you my mother?* New York: HarperCollins.
Flack, M. (1971). *Ask Mr. Bear*. New York: Young Readers Press.
Marshall, J. (1997). *Goldilocks and the three bears*. New York: Putnam.
Mora, P. (1992). *A birthday basket for Tia*. New York: Macmillan.
Williams, S. (1989). *I went walking*. San Diego: Harcourt, Brace, Jovanovich.

McGee (2003) believes that an intense pressure exists for teachers to justify instructional activities unless they are described as research-based. She notes that research supports "book acting."

Preschoolers and kindergartners who frequently engage in thematic fantasy play (in which children act out stories that have been read aloud to them) have better vocabularies, use more complex language, and have better story comprehension than children who only draw or talk about stories. McGee also notes that children are more likely to enact stories when teachers repeatedly read them. Other techniques mentioned by McGee include:

◆ providing adult supportive assistance and suggestions during enactments to enhance language learning and story comprehension.

◆ promoting interactive sharing of storybooks, where children take on the role of the storyteller, to improve preschoolers' expressive language.

◆ creating activities for kindergartners, to listen to and then retell information contained in stories. Encouraging kindergartners to recall information and use the particular language structures found in written information.

◆ selecting a small group size when retelling to improve children's comprehension.

◆ providing playful replays and dramatization of both stories and informational books.*

According to McGee, these techniques help children

◆ make inferences.

◆ integrate information across the entire text.

◆ use unique literary and content-specific vocabulary.

*From Barone, D. M., & Morrow, L. M. (Eds.). *Literacy and young children*. Copyright © 2003 The Guilford Press. Used with permission.

◆ speak in sentences with more complex grammatical structures.

◆ in group enactments, negotiate, hear others' perspectives, combine perspectives, and integrate more complex dialogue into their own conception of the story.

Daily Routines

Periods designed especially for conversation are included in the program of an early childhood center. A gathering or group time at the start of the day is used to encourage individual recognition and speaking. Snack and lunch periods are set up to promote pleasant conversation while eating. Activities are planned and structured to provide for as much child talk as possible.

Show-and-Tell. One of the most common daily routines is show-and-tell time. It must be noted here that some early childhood educators believe that this routine is outdated and overused and prefer to eliminate it from their daily schedules. In contrast, show-and-tell advocates believe that this activity encourages children to talk about their special interests in front of others. The child can bring something from home or share something made or accomplished at school. Following are some helpful hints for conducting show-and-tell.

◆ Encourage, do not force, children to speak.

◆ If they do not want to talk, they can just show what they brought.

◆ Let the child who is showing something to the group stand or sit near the teacher. A friendly arm around the child's shoulders may help.

◆ Stimulate the other children to ask the child questions: "Mark, you seem to want to ask Gustavo about his blue marble."

◆ Limit the time for overly talkative children by using an egg timer.

◆ Limit the time for the activity so that the children do not become bored.

◆ Thank each child for his participation.

◆ Try something new such as the following:
   a. Display all articles and have the group guess who brought each.
   b. Have children swap (if possible) what they have brought so that they can talk about each other's items.
   c. Bring in a surprise item to share with the children.
   d. Make a caption for each item and display it on a table (for example, "Betty's Green Rock").
   e. Have the child hide the object behind his back while describing it to the others. Then the other children can guess what the object is.
   f. Be sensitive to ethnic and cultural communication styles.

Show-and-tell times can be tedious and stressful, but when well-conducted, they can also be

◆ an activity for closure (ending activities on a satisfying note) and evaluation and for clarification of feelings.

◆ a forum for expressive and receptive language development.

◆ a session for brainstorming, idea catching, and idea expanding.

◆ an opportunity to reflect and engage in group problem solving.

◆ a source for curriculum ideas and materials.

◆ a window into children's thoughts and feelings.

Show-and-tell items are usually kept out of children's reach to prevent the loss of a valued or favorite toy. The teacher can divide the class into groups and name the days on which each group can bring in items or the teacher may prefer to allow the children to share whenever they wish. Show-and-tell helps children develop vocabulary, responsibility, and the ability to speak in front of others. When making these goals known to parents, teachers explain that the children have choices in these sharing times and that items do not have to be brought to school on a daily or regular basis.

Sharing-time objects can be related to a classroom theme, if families are alerted beforehand. Children who brought in objects unrelated to the topic could be given time after topic-centered sharing.

The Daily News or Recap Times. Many centers engage in daily news or recap group time that focuses on important or interesting events of the day. Teachers and children gather to share news, anecdotes, and happenings in both their home and school life. The teacher can initiate this activity with statements such as the following.

> "Keith told me about something new at his house. Would you like to share your news, Keith?"

> "Aliki and Todd built something today that I've never seen before! Please tell us about it Todd. Or would you like me to tell your classmates?"

At group times, the teacher must be aware of group reaction and response. On some days, there may be excited response and conversation; on others, there may be little response, and the activity should be kept brief. To give children an opportunity to talk about problems and their solutions, recap times can be partially devoted to children's verbalizing success or lack of it in proposed courses of action and projects.

◆ "Mosaud was going to try to make a spaceship today. Mosaud, do you want to tell us about it?"

◆ "Megan finished making her book today. Would you like to tell us what happened, Megan?"

Promoting Speech Daily. The following are suggestions that can promote more child speech in daily programs.

◆ Have children give verbal messages or directions to other children often: "Petey, please show Flynn our dustpan and hand broom. Tell him how we empty it." (Then follow through by thanking him.)

◆ Let children describe daily projects.

◆ Relate present ideas and happenings to the children's past when possible: "Shane had a new puppy at his house too. Did your puppy cry at night? What did you do to help it stop? Kathy has a new puppy who cries at night."

◆ Promote child explanations: "Who can tell us what happens after we finish our lunch?"

◆ Promote teacher-child conversations in which the teacher records children's words on artwork, constructions, or any happenings or projects.

◆ Periodically make pin-on badges (for teachers and interested children) like the ones shown in Figure 13–13.

◆ Play "explaining games" by setting up a group of related items on a table and having the children explain how the items can be used. For example, three groups of items might be (1) a mirror, comb, brush, washcloth, soap, and basin of water; (2) shoes, white shoe polish, and new shoelaces; and (3) nuts, a nutcracker, and two bowls. Encourage child volunteers to explain and demonstrate the use of the items by facing the group from the other side of the table. Other possibilities include items to demonstrate peeling an orange, making a sandwich with two spreads, or making a telephone call.

◆ Design and create games that encourage children to speak.

LEADING ACTIVITIES

A child can be chosen to lead others in activities if he is familiar with the routines and activities. The child can alert the others by saying the right words or calling out the names of the children who need items or who are next for a turn at something. One or more children can be at the front of the group, leading songs or finger plays. (Finger plays are discussed in the next chapter.) Often, children can be chosen as speakers to direct routines with words. Also,

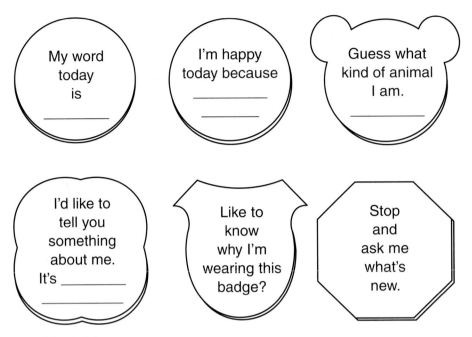

FIGURE 13–13 Pin-on badges.

teachers can promote speaking by asking one child to tell another child something: "Tell Billy when you want him to pass the wastebasket" or "If you're through, ask Georgette whether she wants a turn."

A watchful teacher uses many ways of encouraging the children to speak. The children tend to speak more if their speech is given attention and if speech helps them achieve their ends. It is helpful during group times to point out that the teacher and the other children want to hear what everyone says, and because of this, children should take turns speaking.

SUMMARY

Each early childhood educational program is based on goals. Goals state the attitudes and abilities that a center wishes to develop in children. Planned activities and daily teacher-child conversations help the school reach its goals.

Teachers plan for both group and individual needs. They converse skillfully with children of varying degrees of fluency. There are specific teacher techniques that promote children's expression of ideas.

Questions are asked by both children and teachers. By observing, listening, and interacting, teachers are better able to encourage speaking abilities.

When there is a relaxed atmosphere with interested teachers and many activities, more talking takes place. Playing with others helps vocabulary development and language acquisition in settings where children interact in real and make-believe situations.

The teacher's role in dramatic play is to set the stage but remain in the background so that the children can create their own activities, but teachers may zoom in and out when prudent. Dramatic play settings and kits are made available, and some are boxed and collected by the teacher.

Part of a teacher's work is to encourage children to share their ideas and give children opportunities to lead speaking activities. Teachers ensure that children are talked with rather than talked at. Teachers plan for conversational group times and conduct games and activities that promote verbal comments.

ADDITIONAL RESOURCES

Bloom, P. (2000). *How children learn the meanings of words*. Cambridge, MA: MIT Press.

Boutte, G. S.,Van Scoy, I., & Hendley, S. (1996, November). Multicultural and nonsexist prop boxes. *Young Children, 52*(1), 34–39.

Davidson, J. (1996). *Emerging literacy and dramatic play in early education*. Clifton Park, NY: Thomson Delmar Learning.

Katz, L., & Chard, C. (1998). *Engaging children's minds*. Norwood, NJ: Ablex.

Kieff, J. E., & Casbergue, R. M. (1999). *Playful learning and teaching: Integrating play into preschool and primary programs*. Boston: Allyn and Bacon.

Neuman, S. B., & Roskos, K. (2007). *Nurturing knowledge: Building a foundation for school success by linking early literacy to math, science, art, and social studies*. New York: Scholastic.

Owacki, G. (1999). *Literacy through play*. Westport, CT: Heinemann.

Paley, V. (1984). *Boys and girls: Superheroes in the doll corner*. Chicago: University of Chicago Press.

Vukelich, C., Christie, J., & Enz, B. (2000). *Helping young children learn language and literacy*. Boston: Allyn and Bacon.

Helpful Websites

KidSource Online
http://www.kidsource.com
Discusses areas of intelligence.

National Academies Press
http://www.nap.edu
Provides readings in literacy development.

National Association for the Education of Young Children
http://www.naeyc.org
Includes links to articles and publications.

Book Companion Website

Quotes concerning children's vocabulary development are offered as are additional student activity suggestions. Many focus on the importance of children's opportunities to interact with adults and peers who promote word growth. A question-and-answer section provides information about speaking goals and vocabulary development.

STUDENT ACTIVITIES

1. List five speaking area goals in your own order of priority.

2. Interview a preschool teacher (or teachers). Ask the question, "If you could do only one thing to help young children's speaking ability, what would that be?"

3. Observe a preschool group. What differences do you notice in the children's ability to solve problems with words? Cite specific examples.

4. Observe a preschool classroom. Write down the teacher's questions (word for word). Using the eight question types from this chapter, tell which recorded questions fit which category. Report your findings to the class. Were more recall questions asked?

5. Pair off with another student. Try to find some object (from your pocket or book bag, for example) that might interest a preschool child. Alternate and ask each other two recall, two convergent, two divergent, and two evaluation questions about the objects. Then try asking observation, explanation-seeking, or prediction questions. Which questions were easy to formulate? Which were difficult?

6. Make a list of children in your placement classroom who are the most likely to voice their opinions and ideas, and a second list of children who are least likely to do so. With a peer discuss what you believe has caused the difference and what strategies a teacher might use to promote speaking abilities in both groups of children. Example: Making sure all children in conversations or class discussions are called on to promote their engagement with the topic.

7. With a few classmates, describe a dramatic play-kit idea on a theme that was not included in this chapter. List the items for this kit or theme that you believe would be safe and would stimulate dramatic play. Be sure to include related printed items—for example, seed packets and flower catalogs for a gardening kit. Share with the class, and then judge each kit using the following criteria: safety, creative potential, number of real representative items, kid appeal, connections to theme, literacy value, ease of use, supervision requirement, and teacher demonstrations necessary. Vote on the one play kit created by classmates in this exercise that you believe would be most popular with children. Give the reasons for your vote.

8. Review dramatic play items commercially produced by looking in school-supply catalogs. Report on the cost of three items.

9. Discuss your position concerning show-and-tell time.

10. Pretend you have acquired a very large cardboard packing case, big enough for children to crawl into and stand. In what way would this case enhance dramatic play? In what play situations could the case be used?

11. Read the following observed child behavior. Using Costa's characteristics of intelligent behavior, identify child behaviors that match Costa's listing. With a small group of classmates, write teacher statements that might support and appreciate the child's quest. Do not include possible teacher control or behavior-change-attempt statements.

Damian watched intently as Madison pushed a wheeled popper toy across the floor. Brightly colored wooden balls danced and flew within the toy's transparent dome. Searching for a stuffed animal, Damian selected a green rabbit. With rabbit in hand, he stood in front of Madison saying "What's up, Doc!" while moving the rabbit in jumping motions. Slyly he grabbed the handle of the popper toy. Madison tried to scoot around Damian. Damian held on and Madison howled. As the teacher approached, Damian said, "She won't give me a turn!" Teacher gently removed Damian's hand and said "Let's go find another toy." Damian instead flees to the painting easel. He paints but concentrates on Madison and the toy by peering over the top of the easel. Madison, aware of Damian, sees her friend Bettina, and they proceed to push the popper toy back and forth in front of Damian's easel. Damian makes loud zooming noises with his paintbrush as he strokes vigorously up and down.

Bettina becomes interested and walks around to see Damian's artwork. Madison follows. Damian quickly drops the brush and picks up the popper toy. The girls then paint together at a second easel. The teacher notices Damian has forgotten to take his wet artwork to the drying area, so asks him to do so. With popper toy under his arm, Damian complies and holds the popper between his knees as he pins the wet painting on the drying line. Damian spends about ten minutes pushing the toy and watching colored balls pop upward. His fingers try to pull off the plastic cover to no avail. He slips outside to the yard to an out-of-sight corner. Teacher notices he is seated bent over the toy. She sees Damian pick up a stick and try to wedge off the plastic top using considerable pressure. She approaches and says "Damian, that's an inside toy." Damian shrugs, picks up the toy, and heads for the classroom.

12. Make a dramatic play prop box collection for a child's picture book. On the outside of the storage container put a book illustration or character illustration. Introduce it to a group of preschoolers. Share the results with your classmates.

CHAPTER REVIEW

A. Explain each of the following terms.
  1. structured activities
  2. possessives
  3. negatives
  4. prepositions
  5. comparatives

B. Answer the following questions related to speaking goals.
   1. How can the goals of a program be met?
   2. When children are interested in an object or event, what should the teacher do to help the children learn while they are motivated?

C. Define dramatic play.

D. Answer the following questions.
   1. What is a dramatic play kit?
   2. Name some of the things a teacher does not want to happen during show-and-tell time (for example, one child talking too long).

E. Select the correct answers. Each item may have more than one correct answer.
   1. In daily conversations, the teacher should
      a. answer or respond to nonverbal messages.
      b. pair new word meanings with words the children already know.
      c. listen to children who yell in anger.
      d. patiently accept stuttering and hesitant speech.
   2. If a child says "richlotti-gongo" to you,
      a. repeat it back if you can, hoping the child will show you what he wants to say.
      b. ignore it and wait until you understand the message.
      c. go along with the statement, saying something like, "Really, you don't say."
      d. ask the child to speak more clearly.
   3. In using questions with young children,
      a. suit the question to the children.
      b. always give them the answer.
      c. insist that they answer correctly.
      d. answer some of the children's questions with your own questions, when appropriate.
   4. Planned activities are based on
      a. goals only.
      b. children's current interests only.
      c. goals and children's interests.
      d. knowledge instead of attitudes.

F. Name three ways a teacher can give children confidence in their speaking abilities.

G. From the four question types listed, choose the type that matches questions 1 through 8.
   recall   divergent   convergent   evaluative
   1. What would happen if we left this glass full of ice on the table?
   2. If your shoes and socks are the same color, would you please stand up?
   3. Who can tell me this puppet's name?
   4. If you had a dollar, how would you like to spend it?
   5. What do we need to make a birthday cake?
   6. Why did the basket fall over?
   7. Did the door open by itself?
   8. Who has the smallest cup?

H. Write down teacher questions that could lead a child to a discovery and promote the child's verbal expression of the discovery in the following situations.

1. A bird's nest is found in the yard.

2. The wheel on a bike squeaks.

3. A flashlight is taken apart.

I. Formulate appropriate teacher comments in the following situations (1–3).

1. The child is complaining that easel paint drips and does not stay where he wants it.

2. It is cleanup time, and Sharie (child) says, "Scott and Keith never put anything away!"

3. Carter is talking about the way water is disappearing in the sun.

For 4, 5, and 6, formulate a possible convergent-type teacher question.

4. Megan noticed a bug on the floor.

5. Christa says, "Dana has new shoes!"

6. Ryan brings a toy truck to share at group time.

In 7, 8, and 9, plan evaluation questions that a teacher might use.

7. "I don't like peanut butter," Romana says.

8. "This is my favorite book," Linsay declares.

9. Teacher is introducing a new toy with plastic boats.

J. List Costa's characteristics of intelligent behavior.

K. Write a short paragraph that finishes the following:

The reasons some teachers do not actively plan programs with children leading activities in front of the child group . . .

GAMES PROMOTING SPEECH

Suitcase Game

Teacher: I'm going on a vacation trip. I'm putting suntan oil in my suitcase. What will you put in your suitcase?

Child: A swimming suit.

Child: Candy.

Teacher: (After the group has had an opportunity to contribute.) Let's see how many items we can remember that people wanted to bring on vacation.

Grocery Store Game

Have a bag handy with lots of grocery items. Pull one out yourself and describe it. Have the children take turns pulling out an item and describing it. The teacher can make a shopping list of items named and explain a shopping list's use.

Letter Game

Provide a large bag of letters. Pull one letter out. Talk about a letter you are going to send to a child in the group. "I'm going to give this pretend letter to Frankie and tell him about my new car" or "I want to send this thank-you card to Janelle because she always helps me when I ask for cleanup helpers. Who would like to pull out a letter from this bag and tell us the person they would like to send it to?"

Guess What Is in the Box

Collect small boxes with lids. Put small items inside, such as paper clips, erasers, bottle tops, plastic toys, leaves, flowers, and so forth. Have a child choose a box, guess its contents, open it, and talk about what is in the box.

Describe a Classmate

Choose a child out of the group to stand beside you. Describe or list three of the child's characteristics, for example, red shoes, big smile, and one hand in pocket. Ask who would like to choose another classmate and tell three things about that person.

Guessing Photograph Happenings

Use photographs showing a sequence of actions. Help children express their ideas of what is depicted. Examples: digging in the garden, planting bulbs, a flowering tulip, and mixing pancake batter, frying pancakes, eating pancakes.

The Mystery Bag

An activity children enjoy in small groups is called the mystery bag. The teacher collects a series of common objects. Turning away from the group, the teacher puts one of the objects in another bag. The game starts when a child reaches (without looking inside) into the second bag and describes the object. It is then pulled out of the bag and discussed: "What can we do with it? Has it a name? It's the same color as what else in the room?" The group should be small, because it is hard for a young child to wait for a turn. Examples of objects that could be used include a rock, comb, orange, pancake turner, feather, plastic cup, sponge, hole punch, flower, toy animal, and whistle.

Parts-of-the-Body Guessing Game

I can see you with my _____ (eyes).
I can smell you with my _____ (nose).
I can chew with my _____ (teeth).
I can hear with my _____ (ears).
I can clap with my _____ (hands).
I walk on my _____ (feet).
I put food in my _____ (mouth).
This is not my nose; it's my _____ (point to ears).
This is not my eye; it's my _____ (point to nose).
This is not my mouth; it's my _____ (point to eye).

CHAPTER 14
Group Times

OBJECTIVES

After reading this chapter, you should be able to:

◆ Describe circle and group-time speaking activities.

◆ Perform a finger play with children.

◆ Discuss ways to promote child involvement in simple plays, chants, and circle times.

◆ Plan and lead a group time.

KEY TERMS

chants

circle time

transitional

statements

MR. FUZZ

At a group time, Billy Jay was sharing what had happened to the classroom's visiting teddy over the weekend. Each child in the class has a turn to take Mr. Fuzz home, and Billy Jay had just done so. It was expected that the child taking Mr. Fuzz would then relate some important weekend happenings at Monday morning's circle time. So far, Mr. Fuzz had been hidden by the family dog, accidentally washed in the washing machine, taken up in an airplane, and thrown out of a window on his previous excursions to the children's homes. Billy Jay was excited when he told the group that Mr. Fuzz went to "Three and one." This puzzling statement was soon cleared up when Billy Jay said, "And he likes Jamoca Almond Fudge just like my mom."

QUESTIONS TO PONDER

1. Would it be a good idea to make a book of Mr. Fuzz's adventures for the library corner?

2. Can you think of other literacy activities that also could grow out of the use of Mr. Fuzz?

3. Billy Jay is obviously aware of numbers on signs. Could this lead to an activity for the whole class? If yes, identify one.

The activities in this chapter give children many speaking opportunities. Children involved in the activities have the opportunity to imitate speech, to use creative speech, and to express their own ideas and feelings. However, you should realize that it is difficult to classify activities as listening or speaking activities because they often overlap.

GROUPS

Group time and **circle time** are chances for children to develop understanding about themselves as group members. They enjoy language together by using familiar songs, favorite finger plays, chants, and a wide variety of activities. Children gain self-confidence, feelings of personal worth, and group spirit (Figure 14–1). Group times are often conducted as "sharing times" within programs that are designed for an abundance of child-selected and child-initiated activities.

School administrators and teachers need to clarify their priorities concerning group times. Because it is difficult to conduct intimate conversations and discussions with large groups, many schools prefer working with small groups of children so that conversations can flourish. However, decisions regarding group size may hinge on staffing considerations. Sometimes large groups can be temporarily divided so that there can be "instant replays" of activities for smaller groups.

Strickland and Schickedanz (2004) note that whole group instruction generally occurs once or twice a day and can include read-aloud time, interactive writing, phonological awareness activities, and letter knowledge activities. Interactions during whole group time can encompass (1) explicit instruction in content to which all should be exposed, (2) intentional instruction that builds on stated curriculum goals; and (3) interactions used diagnostically to determine the need for individual and small group follow-up instruction.

FIGURE 14–1 Group time—together time.

circle time — an early childhood term describing a planned gathering of children, usually seated in a half-circle configuration, led by a teacher.

Many educators are debating the value of larger group activities, especially ones that attempt to teach the school's curriculum through large group instruction. Although many programs use large group instruction, educators doubt its developmental appropriateness. Large group times used for news, announcements, morning welcome, a quick class discussion, or closing wrap-up may be part of the established school routine and are common.

When presenting new material during small group sessions, teachers should allow time to receive and react to children's comments and questions. One pitfall in conducting group activities is the tendency for teachers to remain the center of attention, assuming the role of the great dispenser of knowledge. When this occurs, child feedback is ignored.

Some teachers may be unskilled in drawing conversation from children in large group and small group discussions. What is called discussion is the teacher asking questions and calling on children for answers. Then the teacher is apt to rephrase, correct, or evaluate what a child says before asking a new question. If this happens children learn very little about what it means to "talk things over" with a group.

Other questionable teacher skills and behaviors are discussed under the heading "Circle-Time Pitfalls" later in this chapter.

In group settings with 4-year-olds, early childhood teachers become acutely aware of children who are having difficulty paying attention, following directions, getting along, and controlling negative emotions of anger or distress. These children usually will do less well in school. Research on early schooling suggests that the relationships children build with peers and teachers are based on their ability to react in social versus antisocial ways; behaviors can help or hurt academic performance (Raver, 2003). At group times, teachers make every effort to keep children focused and involved in language arts activities.

Language activities add sparkle and liveliness to circle times. The following is a list of words that can be used to describe a successful group experience.

active—Children's participation includes motor and speech involvement.

enthusiastic—The teacher's commitment in making a presentation is communicated by the teacher's facial expressions and manner.

prepared—All necessary materials are at the teacher's fingertips and are used with smooth verbal presentations.

accepting—The teacher is open to children's ideas and feelings and is appreciative of children's contributions.

appropriate—The activity suits the particular group.

clear—The teacher provides purposeful clarification of new concepts.

comfortable—The seating and light source are appropriate.

familiar—The activity includes previously learned and enjoyed material.

novel—New ideas and material are presented.

relaxed—The activity does not pressure or threaten children.

sharing—All children are invited to take turns participating in the activity.

IMPORTANT SKILLS FOR ENTERING KINDERGARTEN

Gamel-McCormick (2000) surveyed 240 kindergarten teachers in Delaware, asking them to rate the importance of a set of 20 skills desirable in entering kindergartners. Two communication-related skills appeared in their top 10 choices: (1) communicates needs and preferences and (2) attends to peer or adult talking. The number one teacher selection was exhibits self-control. Kindergarten teachers were also asked for a hand-written definition of readiness. A summary of their answers follows (Gamel-McCormick, 2000).

◆ Except for physical skills, most teachers included components of all domains in their definitions.

◆ Almost all definitions assessed social and behavioral skills and skills that would allow students to be independent.

◆ A significant minority of teachers included preacademic and academic skills in their definitions.

◆ For most teachers, the definitions focused on children's abilities to interact with peers and adults.

Blair (2003) reports similar results in a nationally represented sample of kindergarten teachers who cited child self-regulation as being essential to school readiness. This included a child's being able to

◆ communicate needs, wants, and thoughts verbally.

◆ sustain attention and be enthusiastic and curious in new activities.

◆ inhibit impulses and follow directions.

◆ take turns and be sensitive to other children's feelings.

What can early childhood educators learn from these studies? Foremost would be that the work undertaken at the preschool level to promote children's self-help, independence, social interaction, cooperation, and group participation skills is highly valued by kindergarten teachers. The child's ability to recognize alphabet letters and write her name was also cited by kindergarten teachers, but these choices followed skills concerned with child self-control and self-help.

The time 4-year-olds spend in small group or circle-time activities during preschool promotes learning group expectations (rules for group behavior), skills in talking, turn taking, listening with focus, and the communication of individual ideas.

GROUPS OF YOUNGER PRESCHOOLERS

Two- and three-year-olds participating in group times are learning social interaction. Their group participation may depend on their feelings of trust and security. After adjustments to seating comfort are made, the teacher welcomes each child by stating or singing their names, or the teacher starts a simple song or finger play. The teacher watches for child focus and involvement. Often, active participation grows slowly as watchers become doers. In well-conducted circle times, children can choose their own level of participation. Teacher flexibility and preplanning, together with the teacher's obvious enthusiasm and delight in each child's presence, breed social acceptance and success. Time will determine whether a teacher decides to expand highly enjoyed circles or cut others short because of children's feedback signals.

Because younger children's classrooms usually are staffed with adults, volunteers, and assisting adults, these adults can sit near or beside children to encourage child participation. An inviting group time may draw in all attending children after it is in progress.

Group time for very young preschoolers can be described as "loose and light" formations or groupings. Children choose to be present and choose their level of involvement. Teachers count on child curiosity and desire to be part of the action. Think of yourself in a new social situation: Wouldn't you watch briefly before entering conversations with strangers and approach those who seem most open and welcoming? And wouldn't you move on if conversations were boring, irrelevant, or obtuse?

PLANNING SMALL GROUP TIME

After considering child capacity to remain involved, a group for either younger or older preschoolers can be planned to occupy a specific time period. What happens and when it happens is roughly outlined. A gathering-together activity can be a song, a finger play, or a recording followed by any number and type of activities. A planned closing and transition ends the experience and moves the group in an orderly fashion onto other classroom pursuits. If group time is of considerable length, then standing and moving activities are interspersed with seated ones.

The seating arrangement needs consideration because it may cause attention to wander. If a large rug is used for circle time and children are asked to sit on the periphery or edge at a distance from the teacher, then intimacy and the ability to see visuals and hear well may be lost. Teachers may need to break up child combinations in seating when children are seated in a "pack." The teacher's physical closeness is part of the "circle-time" experience. In other words, circle time does not necessarily mean children must sit in a circle. A half-circle or arc is a more common seating arrangement.

Group Activities

A group activity is begun by capturing group attention. A signal or daily routine can be used. To make sure all children are focused, a short silence (pause) adds a feeling of anticipation and expectation.

Occasionally varying the signals keeps one signal from becoming old hat. A visual signal, a xylophone ripple, a tap on a musical triangle, an attention-getting record, a puppet announcing a group activity, or reminder stickers placed on children's hands related to the theme of the activity are a few alternatives.

A musical recording can set the mood as children form a group. Singing can serve as a magnet that pulls the group together, and a quiet song is a great means of relaxing and bonding a group. Opening activities that recognize each child help build group spirit. Such recognition is a way of communicating to each child that "You're an important person; we're happy to have you with us." The children can then begin group activities on the right note.

No One Said Leading Groups Would Be Easy

The following is one teacher's internal dialogue while leading a group of children: Are they going to understand this? Should I rephrase this question? How can I get Tony or Sue to participate?

To the outside observer, a skilled teacher leading and interacting with a group may look like a relaxed, interested individual. Under the surface of the teacher's enthusiastic manner, many decisions are being made. Reciprocal interchange is happening; there's internal dialogue going on. The teacher may be watching the clock for time length, watching for both interested and restless behavior, or listening intently for child comments and framing appropriate verbal interaction. With all this going on, many beginning teachers are not able to truly relax.

Circle time often starts with a few children, and others join as they finish chosen pursuits and/or become attracted to circle activities. Early childhood centers differ in philosophy concerning required participation. Staffing may permit other choices.

CIRCLE STARTERS

Many educators suggest using opening and closing circle time with special "hello" and "good-bye" songs. Teachers take the time to sing to each child by name, welcoming them. This singing time quiets the children, allows latecomers to enter the group unobtrusively, acknowledges the importance of each child as he or she is named, and melds the children into a unit ready to listen. Children may be individually touched, and eye contact is maintained.

The following activities are circle-time starters, attention getters, socializers, and wiggle reducers.

Circle Time

I've just come in from outside.

I'm tired as can be.

I'll cross my legs

And fold my hands,
I WILL NOT MOVE.
My head won't move.
My toes are still.
I'll put my hands on my chin,
And when it's quiet, we'll begin!

WHO'S THAT?

(Chant or sing to tune of "Ten Little Indians.")
Who's that _____ in the _____
        (boy, girl, lady, man)   (red, blue, etc.)
_____?
(shirt, pants, shoes, etc.)

(Repeat twice.)
Oh, _____ is _____ name, oh.
(child or adult gives name) (his/her)

(Teacher supplies name when child is hesitant.)

FRIENDSHIP SONG

(Sing or chant the song "The More We Get Together," using hand movements.)
The more we get together, together, together,
(Hug yourself.)
The more we get together, the happier we'll be. (Pull up cheeks in a smile.)
'Cause your friends are my friends, (Point around the circle.)
And my friends are your friends.
The more we get together, the happier we'll be. (Pull up cheeks in a smile.)

A PHONEMIC AWARENESS VERSION

We can find a "t," a "t," a "t"
(Hold up a print "t.")
We can find a "t," if we just look around.
(Hand by side of eye panning room.)
There's your "t," and my "t," (Pointing.)
And my "t," and your "t," (Pointing.)
We can find a "t," if we just look around.
There is tongue (Touch.)
And t-shirt, (Point; substitute attending children's names when possible.)
And table, (Point.)
And teacher, (Point.)

We can find a "t" word, if we just look around.

WIGGLES

I'll wiggle my fingers
And wiggle my toes.
I'll wiggle my arms
And wiggle my nose.
And now that all the wiggle's out,
We'll listen to what circle's about.

CLAPPING START

Turn around and face the wall. Clap, Clap, Clap.
Down upon your knees now fall. Clap, Clap, Clap.
Up again and turn around. Clap, Clap, Clap.
Turn around and then sit down. Clap, Clap, Clap.
Not a sound.

WHERE ARE YOUR _____?

Where are your eyes? Show me eyes that see.
Where are your eyes? Shut them quietly.
Where is your nose? A nose that blows.
Where is your nose? Show me your nose and wiggle it so.
Where is your mouth? Open it wide.
Where is your mouth? With teeth inside.
Smile—Smile—Smile.

CIRCLE ACTIVITIES

A circle group keeps its lively enthusiasm and social enjoyment when well planned. The activities that follow involve both language and coordinated physical movement.

Passing Games

Arrange children in a circle. Have the children pass a small object around the circle. Start the game by having the children pass the object in front of themselves, then behind, then overhead, and then under their legs.

Directions can be changed on command of the teacher, such as "pass it to your left, pass it to your right," and so on. Ask the children for suggestions for other ways to pass the object. Passing a toy microphone can also promote a child's verbal contribution. When a child is done, she passes the microphone to the next child.

TEDDY BEAR CIRCLE PASS

(Have bear in bag behind leader.)
Love somebody, yes, I do.
Love somebody, yes, I do.
Love somebody, yes, I do.
Love somebody, but I won't tell who.
(Shake head sideways.)
Love somebody, yes, I do.
Love somebody, yes, I do.
Love somebody, yes, I do.
Now I'll show (him or her) to you!
Here's a hug—Pass it on.
(Group continues to chant as each child hugs and hands teddy to next child. When teddy returns to leader, last verse is repeated, ending with the following line.)
Now back in the bag; our hugs are through!

Taking Turns and Directing Attention

During circle times, conversations, and other group activities, the following teacher statements are helpful in emphasizing to children the importance of taking turns.

◆ "It's Monica's turn now."

◆ "Barry's turn to talk, and everyone's turn to listen."

◆ "Listen to Bonnie. Bonnie's lips are moving, and ours are resting."

◆ "Just one person talks at a time."

◆ "I am guessing that you really want to say something, Jason, but that you are waiting for your turn."

◆ "Sierra was telling us a story, so it's her turn. What happened next, Sierra?"

◆ "It is time to give Angel a turn to talk, Aki. Angel, do you live in an apartment house?"

◆ "Heiko is answering my question now. Wait and you can answer next, Bradford."

◆ "Raise your hand if you're waiting to tell us about your pet. I see four hands up— September, Ariel, Alexander, and Alwin. You will all have a turn. Alwin, it's your turn now."

◆ "Wait, Collette, Rio hasn't finished his turn."

◆ "My turn to talk, Elias, your turn to listen."

Being a member of a group provides children with two conditions essential for learning: a sense of security and opportunities for social interaction.

Closing Group Activities

Exciting circles and other group activities sometimes need a quiet, settling closing. The following can be used to wind down group activities and prepare excited children for the change to another activity or play.

UP AND DOWN

Up and down,
Up and down,
Clap your hands and turn around.
Up and down,
Up and down,
Clap your hands and sit down.

RAG DOLL

I'm just a limp rag doll.
My arms are limp.
My legs are limp.
My head is limp.
I'm just a limp rag doll.

UP, DOWN, AND REST

Up and down,
Up and down,
Round, round, round,
Up and down.

I stretch, I stretch, I yawn.
I rest and then I start again.
Up and down
(Second time—"I rest, I rest, I rest" is the
  fifth and ending line.)

GOING TO GRANDMA'S HOUSE

Wash the face.
Wash the hands.
Put on a jacket.
Shoes to lace.
Down the stairs
Open the door.
Shut the door.
Jump in the car.
It's not far.
Good-bye.

Transitions

Disbanding a circle or group at an activity's ending calls for a planned approach. If the group is of a larger size, you will need to excuse a few children at a time. When carpet squares are to be picked up and stacked or small chairs returned to tables, a reminder is in order: "When you hear your name, pick up your carpet square and carry it to the stack."

Transitional statements that relate to the just-completed activity work well: "Crawl like Victor the Boa Constrictor to the block center" or "Let the wind blow you slowly to the water table like it blew in the little tree."

TRANSITION POEM

Wiggle both ears.
Touch your nose.
Wiggle your fingers.
Stamp your toes.
Point to your eyes.
Your mouth open wide.
Stick out your tongue.

Put it inside.
Trace your lips.
Go "shh!" Don't speak.
Hands on your neck.
Touch both cheeks.
Shake your hands.
Now let them sleep.
Bend your knees.
Sit on your feet.
Now we finished with this play,
Take your feet and walk away!

GOING TO LINE UP

(To the tune of "The Bear Went over the
  Mountain.")

_____ *is going over to line up.*
(1st child's name)

_____ *is going over to line up.*
(1st child's name)

_____ *is going over to line up.*
(1st child's name)

And _____ *is going next.*
       (2nd child's name)

_____ *went over to line up*
 (1st child's name)

_____ *went over to line up*
 (2nd child's name)

_____ *is going over to line up*
 (3rd child's name)

And _____ *is going next.*
       (4th child's name)

(Last line when all have gone:)
And all are standing tall.

Additional Transitions. A fun way to move children one by one is to recite the rhyme "Jack Be Nimble," substituting the child's name for "Jack": "(Child's name) be nimble, (child's name) be quick, (child's name) jump over the candlestick." (Children clap for the child who jumps or steps over a small plastic candleholder and unlit candle.)

---

transitional statements — teacher statements made to disperse students in small groups or in an orderly fashion.

Another way to disband a group is to make a "tickler" from a 3-foot-long dowel and some yarn. Say to the children, "Close your eyes. When you feel a tickle on your head, it's time to stand and walk carefully through your classmates to the . . ."

Some statements that are helpful in moving a group of children in an orderly fashion are listed here. Many identify language concepts and serve a dual purpose.

- "Everyone with brown shoes stand up. Now it's time to . . ."
- If your favorite sandwich is peanut butter and jelly (ham, cheese, tuna, and so forth) raise your hand. If your hand is up, please tiptoe to the . . ."
- "Richie is the engine on a slow, slow train. Richie, chug chug slowly to the . . ." "Darlene is the coal car on a slow, slow train." (The last child is, naturally, the caboose.)

Multicultural Considerations and Activities

If second-language learners are present, circle times need to include special considerations. Routines that recognize each of the group's children by name will help children feel accepted and included. Activities within circle times that are repeated each day add predictability and promote children's successful participation. Tabors (1997) suggests that the words to songs be introduced without music before singing them. This gives children a better opportunity to catch on and join in. Second-language learners frequently "find their voice" or "go public" for the first time in their new language as they sing, chant, or try physical motions or actions.

The inclusion of multicultural and multiethnic aspects to group activities is not a new idea. Songs and finger plays in the native languages of attending children promote acceptance of diversity. Teachers may need parental help in discovering literary material or for translation. Children usually eagerly learn motions and translated words presented with catchy rhythms. Introduce the name of the language when presenting: "This is a song with Russian words. Gregory's mom taught me how to sing it." As with multicultural and multiethnic picture books, stories, and poetry, these activities are not given extra or special status but are everyday, standard activities—ones that many teachers do not wish to neglect. The problem, at times, is finding them when teacher resources abound with "Anglo-intense" examples.

Circle-Time Pitfalls

Circle times can fall apart for a number of reasons. An examination of the teacher's goals and planning decisions prior to conducting a circle time may clarify what caused child disinterest or lack of enthusiasm. When circles go poorly, the children's behavior may be focused away from the circle's theme and action.

Before examining teacher behaviors, other factors should be reviewed, such as the setting, length, and age-level appropriateness of the activity. Then examine whether the children enjoyed and participated enthusiastically in the activity and how teacher behavior contributed to this. If the activity was not a success, the activity failed the children rather than vice versa.

A teacher whose goals include child conversation and involvement will not monopolize the activity with a constant up-front presentation. Unfortunately, some beginning teachers seem to possess an overwhelming desire to dispense information, eliminating children's conversation and reactions. When this happens, circle times become passive listening times (Figure 14-2).

The size of the circle has also been discussed in this chapter. Teachers attempt large circle times for various reasons. They may be more comfortable with their ability to maintain control when the whole group is involved in the same activity. They may want to be sure everyone in the group learns the same concepts and skills. Unfortunately, these teachers need to understand that large group instruction at the preschool level may cause group disinterest and restlessness by becoming impersonal.

FIGURE 14–2 In successful group times, children offer their comments, ideas, and questions.

Some new teachers have difficulty engaging in spontaneous conversation at circle times, no matter how important or pertinent the child's comments. These teachers are overly reliant on following planned, step-by-step circle time routines that lack back-and-forth flexibility. Unfortunately, one-sided conversations turn off everyone but the speaker.

Waiting a long time for a turn during circle time leads to frustration, which may cause children to tune out. A simple fact that most experienced teachers know is that active, involved children stay focused.

A teacher who constantly asks questions to maintain child attention may defeat her purpose. Some teachers do not understand the difference between asking a question with one right answer (to test a child) and asking questions that encourage thinking, as was mentioned in Chapter 13. Most adults remember from past school experiences how it felt when they missed a question. Unskilled teachers may make children afraid to answer or share their ideas.

Hints for Successful Circle Times

Before you conduct your circle

- review your goals for circle times periodically.
- plan for active child participation and involvement.
- make proposed circle-time duration appropriate to the group's age.
- practice language games and activities so that you can focus on the children.
- think about group size and settings.
- remember that it is better to stop before enthusiasm wanes.
- consider child comfort.
- identify possible room distractions.
- keep rules simple, clear, and at a minimum.

Note that some centers also institute the word *pass* as a circle-time signal that the child does not want to contribute during a discussion. This releases pressure to talk when a child cannot think of a response or chooses not to share her ideas.

During a circle time

◆ focus children at the beginning (Figure 14–3).

◆ state what you expect early, if necessary: "Sit where you can see."

◆ proceed with enthusiasm.

◆ try to enjoy and be unhurried.

◆ think about including activities that promote child decisions, guessing, voting, creativity, expression of personal preferences, problem solving, prediction making, and child questioning.

◆ give children credit for their comments, ideas, and participation.

"Jason's moving his arms and head."

"Shawnita told us what she saw in the mirror."

"Maron thinks our plants need water."

FIGURE 14–3 An active song activity can settle and focus children.

◆ stop the rambling child speaker with "It's time for your friends' turn now, Clyde."

◆ make eye contact with all children.

◆ watch for feedback and act accordingly.

◆ use wind-down activities if the group gets too excited.

◆ use wiggle reducers.

◆ draw quiet children into participation.

◆ reduce waiting times.

◆ watch the length of time allowed for the activity.

◆ think of an orderly transition to the next activity, which may include the children's taking carpet squares to a storage area.

◆ remember that your skill increases with experience.

◆ be aware that sitting still may be a problem for some children.

Most teachers realize that children aren't being rebellious by moving around. They are just moving and they're moving because they need to do it.

Educators will always have children, particularly very young preschoolers or culturally diverse preschoolers, who do not readily choose to participate with speech or actions at group times. The preschool years are a time of rapid language development, and many educators are appropriately concerned with supporting and fostering this language development. Unfortunately, many teachers translate this concern into an insistence that a child speak up individually in group situations. This is not accepted practice.

Aides or volunteers attending a circle time need to be alert to child distractions. Moving closer to or between two children may be helpful, or quietly suggesting an alternative activity to a disinterested child can aid the teacher leader.

Occasionally one child's silliness or mimicking behavior can lead to circle-time disruption as the attention-getting child's behavior challenges the teacher's hold on group focus. Teacher restatement of a circle-time rule may be necessary.

Watching Children's Participation Level. As teachers scan faces and observe child vocalization and movement during circle times, obvious differences in children's ability to focus, stay focused, and participate as fully functioning group members are apparent. Many conditions influence each child's ability to concentrate, actively contribute, and follow group activities—age, health, language deficiencies, weather, distractions, home problems, disabilities, and a multitude of other factors may change child behavior at circle time on any given day. After a teacher has become familiar with her group and leads a few circle times, she mentally categorizes child behaviors. Often at circle time, teachers can tell who is having a bad day. Possible child-attending behavior will vary from not focused to fully engaged, with other behaviors between these two end points. A child may tune in and out, attend but not participate verbally or with body involvement, or attend and participate sporadically.

As teachers monitor children's group behavior, they become increasingly aware of how teacher behaviors and verbalizations affect children's attendance and participation. Ask any practicing teacher about the teacher satisfaction felt at the conclusion of a well-planned and conducted group time during which child interest was held and maintained and something of educational quality or value was accomplished. When teachers feel their child group was eager, responsive, and enjoying the group experience and feel that as the teacher they interacted skillfully, it is a memorable teaching moment.

CHANTS AND CHORUSES

Throughout history, rhythmic **chants** and choruses have been used in group rituals and ceremonies. The individuals in the group gain a group identity as a result of their participation.

Natural enjoyment of rhythmic word patterns can be seen in a child's involvement in group chants. The child and teacher can also playfully take part in call and response during the preschool day. "I made it, I made it," the child says. "I see it, I see it," the teacher answers, picking up the child's rhythm.

This verbal play is common. Sounds in the community and school yard can be brought to the children's attention by teachers who notice them and make comments.

Chants and choruses are mimicked, and sound and word patterns that have regularity and predictability are imitated. Choruses usually involve a back-and-forth conversation (one individual alternating with another) and involve the rise and fall of accented sounds or syllables.

Children need the teacher's examples and directions, such as, "When it's your turn, I'll point to you" or "Let's say it together," before they can perform the patterns on their own. Chants printed on charts with simple illustrations can enhance chanting and chorus times and tie the oral words to written ones.

Chanting promotes successful language experiences regardless of children's background or talent and helps children learn the importance of clear and expressive pronunciation. Teacher charts developed for chanting can be used over and over and are another way for children to discover the relationship of spoken words and print. Many strong-rhythm chants invite clapping, foot stomping, or a wide variety of other physical movements. The chants that follow are some tried-and-true favorites.

THE GRAND OLD DUKE OF YORK

> *The grand old Duke of York*
> *He had forty thousand men.*
> *He marched them up the hill.*
> *He marched them down again.*
> *And when you're up, you're up!*
> *And when you're down, you're down.*

---

chants — rhythmic monotonous utterances.

And when you're half-way-in-between,
You're neither up nor down.

AND IT WAS ME!

I looked in my soup, and who did I see?
Something wonderful . . . and it was me.
Additional verses:
I looked in the mirror, and who did I see?
I looked in the puddle . . .
I looked in a window . . .
I looked in the river . . .
I looked in the pond . . .
I looked at a snapshot . . .
I turned off the television . . .
Ending:
When I'm grown up, I'll still be there.
Right in reflections everywhere.
When I'm grown up, how will it be?
A wonderful world with you and me.

IT'S RAINING, IT'S POURING

It's raining, it's pouring.
The old man is snoring.
He went to bed and he bumped his head
And he couldn't get up in the morning.
Rain, rain go away—come again some
other day.

MISS MARY MACK

Miss Mary Mack, Mack, Mack
All dressed in black, black, black
With silver buttons, buttons, buttons
All down her back, back, back.
She asked her mother, mother, mother
For fifteen cents, cents, cents
To see the elephants, elephants, elephants
Jump the fence, fence, fence.
They jumped so high, high, high
They touched the sky, sky, sky
And never came back, back, back
Till the fourth of July, ly, ly.
July can't walk, walk, walk
July can't talk, talk, talk
July can't eat, eat, eat
With a knife and fork, fork, fork.

She went upstairs, stairs, stairs
To say her prayers, prayers, prayers
She made her bed, bed, bed
She hit her head, head, head
On a piece of corn bread, bread, bread.
Now she's asleep, sleep, sleep
She's snoring deep, deep, deep
No more to play, play, play
Until Friday, day, day
What can I say, say, say
Except hooray, ray, ray!

FILL-IN-THE-BLANK POEM

If I had a dollar,
I'll tell you what I'd do.
I'd spend it all on ice cream,
And I'd give it all to you.
'Cause that's how much I like you! (child's
name)!
(Child's name is said with a deep voice in
vaudeville style.)
'Cause that's how much I like you, (child's
name).
(Substitute other words for ice cream that
children suggest, such as hamburgers,
toys, and so on. Those not wishing to
promote sugar can substitute vegetables
or other items. Examples follow.)
a. *If I had a bike*
   I'll tell you what I'd do
   I'd pedal on the pedals
   And I'd give a ride to you
   'Cause that's how much I like you Tracy
   'Cause that's how much I like you Tracy.
b. *If I had an elephant*
   I'll tell you what I'd do
   I'd put it on a truck
   And take it to the zoo.

Using Accessories

Teachers often use accessories or props to go with chants and choruses used at circle time. The following example, "Little Things," uses accessories. It is a highly enjoyable activity that provokes giggles and "do-it-again" requests.

LITTLE THINGS

> *(to the tune of "Oh My Darling" or chanted)*
> *Little black things, little black things*
> *Crawling up and down my arm.*
> *I am not afraid of them*
> *For they will do no harm.*
> *(Substitute any color for black.)*

Materials. The following colors of yarn are needed.

red	green	black	pink
orange	blue	brown	gray
yellow	purple	white	

Instructions. You will need to make a set of as many colored things as you choose for each child. These can be stored easily in sealed sandwich bags.

Step 1: For each colored thing, cut five yarn pieces, each measuring 8 inches long.

Step 2: Put one yarn piece aside and, keeping the other four together, fold them in half.

Step 3: Using the fifth piece of yarn, tie it around the other four, 1 inch from the folded ends; knot it well, to form a "head" and "legs." Fold the knotted ends down to form more legs.

Give each child a bag of "things." Let the children tell you what color to use. While chanting or singing, have the colored thing crawl up and down arms.

FINGER PLAY

Finger play is a classic preschool group (or individual) activity that parents have probably already introduced to children with "Peek-a-Boo" or "This Little Piggy." Finger plays use words and actions (usually finger motions) together. Early childhood play frequently goes beyond finger movements and often includes whole body actions.

When learning a finger play, the child usually practices and joins in the finger movements before learning the words. Words can be learned and retained by doing the play over and over again.

Finger plays are often done with rhymes. Easy-to-remember rhymes give the children pleasure in listening and a chance to feel good about themselves because (1) they quickly become part of a group having fun and doing the same thing, and (2) they experience a feeling of accomplishment when a rhyme has been learned.

Teachers use finger plays to encourage enjoyment of language, to prepare children for sitting, to keep children active and interested while waiting, and as transitions between activities. Finger plays are also used for special purposes, such as quieting a group or getting toys back on the shelves. They can build vocabulary as well as teach facts and can help a child release pent-up energy.

Teachers should practice a finger play and memorize it beforehand to be sure of a clear and smooth presentation. It should be offered enthusiastically, with the focus on enjoyment. As with other activities, the teacher can say, "Try it with me." The child who just watches will join in when ready. Watching comes first, one or two hand movements next, and then repetitions, using words and actions together. Each child learns at her own rate of speed.

Suggested Finger Plays

Finger plays can be found in many books for early childhood staff members or can be created by the teacher. The following are recommended because of their popularity with both children and teachers.

HICKORY, DICKORY, DOCK

> *Hickory, dickory, dock! (Rest elbow in the palm of your other hand and swing up-raised arm back and forth.)*
> *The mouse ran up the clock; (Creep fingers up the arm to the palm of the other hand.)*
> *The clock struck one. (Clap hands.)*
> *The mouse ran down. (Creep fingers down to elbow.)*
> *Hickory, dickory, dock! (Swing arm as before.)*

OMITTING SOUNDS POEM
(PHONEMIC AWARENESS)

> *This is the "at" I like best. (Make pointed
> hat with hands on head.)*
>
> *I mean my hat. (Make an "oh no" face.)*
>
> *This is an "op," here on my chest. (Hands
> on chest.)*
>
> *No, no, it's my top! (Make face.)*
>
> *This is my "ants." (Touch pants.)*
>
> *Oops, I meant pants. (Make face.)*
>
> *This is my "hoe." (Push out shoe.)*
>
> *No, its my shoe. (Make face.)*
>
> *What's wrong with me today? (Hands on
> head.)*
>
> *Letters left off words that I say. (Point to
> mouth.)*
>
> *I think I better walk out and "lay." (Walk
> fingers up arm.)*
>
> *I did it again, I meant play! (Make face.)*

CHOO! CHOO!

> *Choo-o! Choo-o! Choo! Choo! (Run fingers
> along arm to shoulder slowly.)*
>
> *This little train goes up the track.*
>
> *Choo! Choo! Choo! Choo! (At shoulder, turn
> "train" and head down arm.)*
>
> *But this little train comes quickly back.*
>
> *Choo-choo-choo-choo! Choo-choo-
> choochoo! (Repeat last line.) (Run fin-
> gers down arm quickly.)*
>
> *Whoo-o! Whoo-o! Whoo-o! (Imitate train
> whistle.)*

WHERE IS THUMBKIN?

> *Where is thumbkin, where is thumbkin?
> (Hands behind back.)*
>
> *Here I am, here I am. (One hand out,
> thumb up. Other hand out, thumb up.)*
>
> *How are you today, sir? (First thumb
> bends up and down.)*
>
> *Very well, I thank you. (Second thumb
> bends up and down.)*
>
> *Run away, run away. (First thumb behind
> back; second thumb behind back.)*
>
> *Repeat with:*
>
> *Where is pointer? (Use first finger.)*

> *Where is tall man? (Use middle finger.)*
>
> *Where is ring man? (Use ring finger.)*
>
> *Where is pinkie? (Use little finger.)*
>
> *Where are all the men? (Use whole hand.)*

Newer, less well-known but still popular and
enjoyable finger plays appear in the Activities
section at the end of this chapter.

BODY-ACTION PLAYS

Encourage children to jump in rhythm to the
first chant example while doing what the rhyme
says. Use these for working out pent-up energy.

HEAD, SHOULDERS

> *Head, shoulders, knees, and toes (Stand;
> touch both hands to each part in
> order.)*
>
> *Head, shoulders, knees, and toes.*
>
> *Head, shoulders, knees, and toes. That's the
> way the story goes. (Clap this line.)*
>
> *This is my head, this is not. (Hands on
> head, then feet.)*
>
> *These are my shoulders, these are not.*
>
> *(Hands on shoulders, then knees.)*
>
> *Here are my knees; watch them wiggle,*
>
> *(Wiggle knees.)*
>
> *Touch my armpits and I giggle. (Hands
> under armpits with laugh.)*
>
> *Head shoulders, knees, and toes. (Touch in
> order.)*
>
> *That's the way the story goes. (Clap.)*

BEAT ONE HAMMER

> *My mother told me to tell you*
>
> *To beat one hammer (Pound one fist.)*
>
> *Like you see me do.*
>
> *My mother told me to tell you*
>
> *To beat two hammers (Pound two fists.)*
>
> *Like you see me do.*
>
> *My mother told me to tell you*
>
> *To beat three hammers (Pound two fists;
> stamp one foot.)*
>
> *Like you see me do.*
>
> *My mother told me to tell you*

To beat four hammers (Pound two fists;
*   stamp two feet.)*
Like you see me do.
My mother told me to tell you
To beat five hammers (Add nodding head.)
Like you see me do.
My mother told me to tell you
To beat no hammers (Stop!)
Like you see me do.

SUMMARY

Speaking activities are planned for the young child. Some require simple imitation of words, whereas others call for the child's creative or expressive response.

Finger plays use words and actions together. They are actively enjoyed by children and build feelings of self-worth. Teachers can memorize finger plays and use them daily.

Circle times instill group spirit and social enjoyment of language. Opening activities capture attention. Chants and choruses add rhythmic word play and often involve physical movement. A smooth transition to other activities takes place when teachers are well prepared.

Teachers evaluate circle times comparing outcomes with goals. They monitor child reaction to their behaviors, strategies, and presentation skills. They critique their ability to plan lively, enjoyable, relevant, and language-abundant circle times.

ADDITIONAL RESOURCES

Finger Play Collections

Dowell, R. L. (1987). *Move over Mother Goose.* Pollyanna Productions, Mt. Ranier, MD: Gryphon House Inc.

Ellis, M. J. (1978). *Fingerplay approach to dramatization.* Minneapolis: T. S. Denison.

Finger plays for young children. Scholastic, 2931 East McCarty St., P.O. Box 7502, Jefferson City, MO 65102. (An easel book.)

Glazer, T. (1973). *Eye Winker, Tom Tinker, Chin Chopper: Fifty musical finger plays.* New York: Doubleday.

Kable, G. (1979). *Favorite finger plays.* Minneapolis: T. S. Denison.

Redleaf, R. (1993). *Busy fingers, growing minds: Finger plays, verses and activities for whole language learning.* St. Paul, MN: Redleaf Press.

Rockwell, R., Hoge, D. R., & Searcy, B. (1999). *Linking language and literacy activities throughout the curriculum.* Beltsville, MD: Gryphon House Inc. (Circle-time ideas.)

Wilmes, L., & Wilmes, D. (1981). *Everyday circle times.* Mt. Ranier, MD: Gryphon House Inc. (A collection of ideas for exciting group times.)

Phonemic Awareness Circle-Time Ideas

Jordano, K., & Callella, T. (1998). *Phonemic awareness: Song and rhymes.* Cypress, CA: Creative Teaching Press.

Readings

Carner, K. (Ed.). (1996). *The giant encyclopedia of circle time and group activities for children 3 to 6.* Beltsville, MD: Gryphon House Inc.

Claycomb, P. (1998). *The learning circle: A preschool teacher's guide to circle time.* Beltsville, MD: Gryphon House Inc.

Colgin, M. L. (1982). *One potato, two potato, three potato, four! 165 chants for children.* Beltsville, MD: Gryphon House Inc.

Dowel, R. I. (1995). *Mother Ruth's rhymes: Lyrical finger plays and action verse.* New York: Pollyanna Productions.

Orozco, J. L. (1997). *Diez deditos/ten little fingers and other play rhymes and action songs from Latin America.* New York: Dutton Children's Books.

Helpful Websites

Ask the Preschool Teacher
http://www.askthepreschoolteacher.com
Select Search the Site. Enter "circle time" in Find box and view questions and answers about circle times. A free newsletter is offered.

Child Care Resources, Training and Consultation
http://www.childcarelounge.com
Select Resources for Caregivers; then choose Finger Plays for a collection of finger plays.

Early Head Start National Resource Center
   http://www.ehsnrc.org
      Provides tips concerning group instruction.

Gayle's Preschool Rainbow—Activity Central
   http://www.preschoolrainbow.org
      Click on Rhymes, Songs, and Finger Plays.

Book Companion Website

A new finger play to an old rhyme that can be used at group time is included. Web links and Internet exercises are also available. Resource books promoting additional circle-time teacher activities are listed, along with additional suggested readings.

STUDENT ACTIVITIES

1. With a small group of classmates, practice and present a finger play, chant, chorus, or body-action play. Have each student present the activity until it is learned by the others.
2. Make a list of at least five books that are resources for finger plays.
3. Present a finger play, chant, or chorus to a group of young children.
4. List possible reasons that children become disinterested at circle times.
5. Find a finger play that is seasonal (generally used at only one time a year). Bring a copy to class.
6. Create a finger play, chant, or chorus for young children.
7. Observe a circle time and evaluate it. Share it with the class.
8. Tape-record or videotape a few of your teacher-led discussions at group time. Analyze your listening skills and whether you dominate conversations. Look at your ability to keep group time lively with child participation. If a child-teacher discussion did not hold children's interest, determine the reasons.
9. If you know a song, rhyme, finger play, or movement activity in another language, share it with the class.
10. Create a finger play about making tortillas or using chopsticks. Share with the class.
11. Create finger play motions for one of the following. Share with a small group of peers.

PIZZA

Let's make a pizza big and round
Take tomato sauce and spread it around.
Onions, olives, peppers, and cheese
Add mushrooms, sausage if you please.
Put it in the oven. Careful it's hot!
Bake 'til a warm brown crust you've got.
It's bubbly, spicy, and tastes so nice.
Raise your hand if you'd like a slice.

TAKING OFF

The airplane taxis down the field
And heads into the breeze.
It lifts its wheels above the ground.
It skims above the trees
It rises high and higher
Away up toward the sun.
It's just a speck against the sky and now—
and now—it's gone.

452

CHAPTER REVIEW

A. Finish the following:

1. A transitional statement at the end of group time is necessary because

   _____.

2. History shows that chants and choruses were used for

   _____.

3. A successful circle time for young children can be described by the following terms:

   _____.

B. Why are finger plays so popular with young children?

C. Rearrange and place the following statements in the best order or sequence.

1. Child knows words and actions of a finger play.
2. Teacher knows words and actions of a finger play.
3. Teacher practices finger play.
4. Child participates with actions only.
5. Child watches.
6. Teacher presents finger play to children.
7. Teacher evaluates the results of the finger play.
8. Teacher encourages children to join in actions and words.

D. List five signals or attention getters that a teacher could use at the beginning of a circle time.

E. In what ways should an assistant teacher be helpful when another teacher is leading group language activities?

F. Rate the following teacher statements during planned circles.

G = Good Technique P = Poor Technique

1. "It's my turn to talk."
2. "Stop wiggling, Jimmy."
3. "Everyone's listening; it's time to begin."
4. "When MacKenzie, Tran, and Nan join us, we'll all be together."
5. "The first one standing can be the first one to leave the circle."
6. "We're finished. Let's go."
7. "Speak up, Gisela. It's time to answer."
8. "Thuy is doing our new finger play the 'right' way."
9. "Watch closely, and make your fingers move just like mine."
10. "Everyone listened to what their friends said and took turns talking today."

ADDITIONAL GROUP STARTERS

I LIKE YOU

(Chant or sing.)
I like you.
There's no doubt about it.
I like you.
There's no doubt about it.
I am your good friend.
You like me.
There's no doubt about it.
You like me.
There's no doubt about it.
You are my good friend.
There's my friend (child's name), and my friend
(child's name).
(Continue around circle.)

OH HERE WE ARE TOGETHER

(Chant or sing.)
Oh here we are together, together, together,
Oh here we are together
At (school name) Preschool
There's (child's name) and (child's name), and (names of all children).
Oh here we are together to have a good day.

WE'RE WAITING

(Circle starter.)
We're waiting, we're waiting, we're waiting for (child's name).
(Repeat until group is formed.)
We're here, because we're here, because we're here, because we're here.
And my name is _____, and my name is _____. (Around the circle.)

HELLO

Hello (child's name). Hello, hello, hello.
Shake my hand and around we'll go.
Hello (child's name). Hello, hello, hello.
Shake my hand and around we'll go.

(Teacher starts; children continue around the circle chanting until all are recognized.)

SECRET

I've got something in my pocket
That belongs across my face.
I keep it very close at hand
In a most convenient place.
I know you couldn't guess it
If you guessed a long, long while.
So I'll take it out and put it on
It's a great big friendly SMILE!

TEN FINGERS

I have ten little fingers
And they all belong to me.
I can make them do things.
Would you like to see?
I can shut them up tight
Or open them wide.
I can put them together
Or make them all hide.
I can make them jump high.
I can make them jump low,
I can fold them quietly
And hold them just so.

EVERYBODY DO THIS

Refrain:
Everybody do this, do this, do this.
Everybody do this just like me.
Actions:
Open and close fists
Roll fists around
Touch elbows
Spider fingers
Pat head, rub tummy
Wink
Wave hand good-bye
(Ask children to create others.)

ADDITIONAL CIRCLE ACTIVITIES

ONE AND ONLY

I have two eyes to see all around.
I have two feet to stand on ground.
I have two ears to listen and to hear
Every sound, both far and near.
I have two arms to reach and to fold.
I have two hands to work and to hold.
So many twos it takes to be
The one and only single me.

Reprinted with permission of the publisher Early Years, Inc. From the January 1997 issue of *Teaching K-8* magazine, Norwalk, CT 06854.

IF YOU'RE HAPPY AND YOU KNOW IT

If you're happy and you know it, clap
*   your hands.*
If you're happy and you know it, clap
*   your hands.*
If you're happy and you know it, then
*   your face will surely show it.*
If you're happy and you know it, clap
*   your hands.*
Additional verses:
If you're sad and you know it, wipe
*   your eyes.*
If you're mad and you know it, pound
*   your fist.*
If you're hungry and you know it, rub
*   your stomach.*
If you're silly and you know it, go tee
*   hee.*
If you're cold and you know it, rub
*   your arms.*
If you're hot and you know it, wipe
*   your brow.*
If you're sleepy and you know it, go to
*   sleep . . . snore, snore.*

HANDS ON SHOULDERS

Hands on shoulders, hands on knees.
Hands behind you, if you please.
Touch your shoulders, now your nose.
Now your ear and now your toes.

Hands up high into the air.
Down at your sides then touch
*   your hair.*
Hands up high as before.
Now clap your hands,
One, two, three, four.

BALL ROLLING CIRCLE

The ball will roll across our circle.
Touch toes with your neighbors.
Here comes the ball, Susie. "I roll the
*   ball to Susie."*
(Teacher says: "Susie, roll the ball
*   across the circle and say your*
*   friend's name.")*
"I roll the ball to _____."

THE CARROT SEED WILL GROW

Carrots grow from carrot seeds,
I'll plant this seed and grow one.
I won't be disappointed if my seed
*   doesn't grow.*
What makes seeds grow? I don't know!
So I won't be disappointed if my seed
*   doesn't grow.*
My brother said "Na, na. It won't come
*   up. Na, na. It won't come up.*
Na, na. It won't come up. Your carrot
*   won't come up."*
(Repeat above, ending with the
*   following.)*
Oh, carrots grow from carrot seeds.
I planted one, it grew. I watered it.
*   I pulled the weeds.*
No matter what he said.
Carrots grow from carrot seeds.

ADDITIONAL CHANTS

PANCAKE

Mix a pancake.
Stir a pancake.
Pop it in the pan.
Fry a pancake.
Toss a pancake.
Catch it if you can.

THE BIG CLOCK

Slowly ticks the big clock
Chorus: Tick-tock, tick-tock (Repeat twice.)
But the cuckoo clock ticks double quick
Chorus: Tick-a-tock-a, tick-a-tock-a
Tick-a-tock-a, tick!

LITTLE BROWN RABBIT

Little brown rabbit went hoppity-hop,
All: Hoppity-hop, hoppity-hop!
Into a garden without any stop,
All: Hoppity-hop, hoppity-hop!
He ate for his supper a fresh carrot top,
All: Hoppity-hop, hoppity-hop!
Then home went the rabbit without any stop,
All: Hoppity-hop, hoppity-hop!

WHO ATE THE COOKIES IN THE COOKIE JAR

All: Who ate the cookies in the cookie jar?
All: (Child's or teacher's name) ate the cookies in the cookie jar.
(Teacher points to different child for each verse.)
Named person: Who me?
All: Yes you.
Named person: Couldn't be.
All: Then who?
Named person: (Child's or teacher's name) ate the cookies in the cookie jar.
Newly named person: Who me? (and so forth).

LOCK AND KEY

(A back-and-forth chorus.)
I am a gold lock; I am a gold key.
I am a silver lock; I am a silver key.
I am a house lock; I am a house key.
I am a car lock; I am a car key.
I am a monk lock; I am a monk-key (whoo, whoo, whoo).

ADDITIONAL FINGER PLAYS

THE CAR WASH

The car wash machine, the car wash machine
The strangest thing I've ever seen
We drive the car in dirty and drive it out clean (Pretend to drive car.)
A little light flashes and a door opens wide (Move arms as if opening door wide.)
We go very slowly and drive inside (Driving car motions.)

Water squirts out all over the place (Pretend to squirt water.)
And the brushes seem to be running into my face (Roll hands and move up to face.)
They slide over the car to wash off the dirt (Rub hands.)
I wonder if it's going to hurt. (Cover face.)
It feels like the car is moving away
But the moving brushes make it feel that way!

The car wash machine, the car wash machine
The strangest thing I've ever seen
The car went in dirty and came out clean.

Reproduced by permission. Rhoda Redleaf, *Busy Fingers, Growing Minds.*

FRIENDS AT PLAY

One little child with nothing to do (Hold up one finger.)

Found a friend to play with

And then there were two (Hold up two fingers.)

Two little children, playing happily

Along came another and then there were three (Hold up three fingers.)

Three little children playing grocery store

Along came a customer and then there were four (Hold up four fingers.)

Four little children with cars and trikes to drive

Along came a friend in a wagon, and then there were five. (Hold up all five fingers.)

Reproduced by permission. Rhoda Redleaf, *Busy Fingers, Growing Minds.*

FAMILY OF RABBITS

A family of rabbits lived under a tree, (Close right hand and hide it under left arm.)

A father, a mother, and babies three. (Hold up thumb, then fingers in succession.)

Sometimes the bunnies would sleep all day, (Make fist.)

But when night came, they liked to play. (Wiggle fingers.)

Out of the hole they'd go creep, creep, creep, (Move fingers in creeping motion.)

While the birds in the trees were all asleep. (Rest face on hands, place palms together.)

Then the bunnies would scamper about and run (Wiggle fingers.)

Uphill, downhill! Oh, what fun! (Wiggle fingers vigorously.)

But when the mother said, "It's time to rest," (Hold up index finger.)

Pop! They would hurry (Clap hands after "Pop.")

Right back to their nest! (Hide hand under arm.)

FIREFIGHTERS

Ten little firefighters, sleeping in a row,

Ding, dong goes the bell, down the pole they go.

Jumping on the engine, oh, oh, oh,

Putting out the fire, shhhhhhhhhhhhh-hhhhhhh.

And home again they go

Back to sleep again,

All in a row.

LITTLE HOUSE

I'm going to build a little house (Fingers form a roof.)

With windows big and bright. (Make square with hands.)

With chimney tall and curling smoke (Arm up in the air—waving in spiral.)

Drifting out of sight

In winter, when the snowflakes fall (Hands flutter down.)

Or when I hear a storm (Cup hand to ear.)

I'll go sit in my little house (Stand, then sit down.)

Where I'll be nice and warm. (Hug chest.)

THIS IS THE MOUNTAIN

This is the mountain up so high,
(Form a triangle.)

And this is the moon that sails
through the sky. (Make a circle with
thumbs and index fingers.)

These are the stars that twinkle so
bright. (Make a small circle with
thumb and index, other three fin-
gers moving.)

These are the clouds that pass through
the night. (Make fists.)

This is the window through which I
peep, (Make a square with thumb
and index.)

And here am I, fast asleep.
(Close eyes.)

CLAP YOUR HANDS

Clap your hands high,
Clap your hands low,
Pat your head lightly,
And down you go.
I'll touch my hair, my lips, my eyes,
I'll sit up straight, and then I'll rise.
I'll touch my ears, my nose, my chin,
Then quietly, sit down again.

BUTTERFLY

Roly-poly caterpillar
Into a corner crept.
Spun around himself a blanket
Then for a long time slept.
A long time passed (Whisper.)
Roly-poly caterpillar wakened by and
by.
Found himself with beautiful wings
Changed to a butterfly.

HAMBURGER

A big hamburger bun for you. (Cup
hands together.)

Open it too. (Hands side by side, palms
up.)

What do you see? (Point to palm with
one hand.)

A meat patty? Yes. (Nod head yes.)

Yellow mustard we spread. (Spreading
motion.)

Squeeze catsup that's red. (Pretend to
squeeze bottle.)

Pickle in the middle. (Pretend to place
a pickle.)

Close it tight. (Hands cupped together.)

Yum. Take a bite. (Pretend to bite and
rub tummy.)

Note: Teacher can provide mustard, catsup, and pickles to taste and lead a discussion of who prefers what and where they
like (or do not like) to eat hamburgers.
Some classes have expanded this finger play
into a theme day with many related activities planned, such as a fast food dramatic
play center, hamburger patty–forming center, bun-baking area, sign making, order
counter, chart-preference activity, visit to
a fast food restaurant, money-counting
activity, and so on.

SLEEPY TIME

Open wide your little hands,
Now squeeze them very tight.
Shake them, shake them very loose,
With all your might.
Climb them slowly to the sky.
Drop down like gentle rain.
Go to sleep my little hands,
I'll wake you once again.

A FUNNY ONE

'Round the house
'Round the house (Put fingers around
the face.)

Peep in the window (Open eyes wide.)

Listen at the door (Cup hand behind
ear.)

Knock at the door (Knock on head.)

Lift up the latch (Push up nose.)

And walk in (Stick out tongue and walk fingers in mouth.)

—I caught you! (Bite gently down on fingers.)

Two Little Apples

Two little apples hanging on a tree, (Put hand by eyes.)

Two little apples smiling at me. (Smile.)

I shook that tree as hard as I could. (Shake tree.)

Down came the apples. (Make falling motions.)

Mmmm—they were good. (Rub stomach.)

Peanut Butter And Jelly

First you take the peanuts and you crunch them and you crunch them. (Repeat.)

Peanut butter—jelly! Peanut butter—jelly! Then you take the grapes and you squish them and you squish them. (Repeat.)

Peanut butter—jelly! Peanut butter—jelly! Then you take the bread and you spread it and you spread it. (Repeat.) Peanut butter—jelly! Peanut butter—jelly!

Then you take the sandwich and you eat it and you eat it. (Repeat. Then with your mouth closed hum the refrain as if you had a mouth full of sandwich.)

Peanut butter—jelly! Peanut butter—jelly!

("Peanut butter" is said in the following fashion: "Pea"[medium pitch] "nut"[low pitch] "but"[medium] "ter"[high pitch with hands above head, fingers shaking to side in Vaudeville-type motion]. "Jelly" is said in a low, throaty voice, accompanied by hands to opposite side shaking at knee level.)

Five Little Astronauts

Five little astronauts (Hold up fingers on one hand.)

Ready for outer space.

The first one said, "Let's have a race."

The second one said, "The weather's too rough."

The third one said, "Oh, don't be gruff."

The fourth one said, "I'm ready enough."

The fifth one said, "Let's Blast Off!"

10, 9, 8, 7, 6, 5, 4, 3, 2, 1, (Start with 10 fingers and pull one down with each number.)

BLAST OFF!!! (Clap loudly with "Blast Off!")

ADDITIONAL BODY-ACTION PLAYS

My Little Thumbs

My little thumbs keep moving.

My little thumbs keep moving.

My little thumbs keep moving. Tra-la tra-la tra-la.

My thumbs and fingers keep moving.

My thumbs and fingers keep moving.

My thumbs and fingers keep moving. Tra-la tra-la tra-la.

My thumbs and fingers and hands keep moving.

My thumbs and fingers and hands keep moving.

My thumbs and fingers and hands keep moving. Tra-la tra-la tra-la.

My thumbs and fingers and hands and arms keep moving.

My thumbs and fingers and hands and arms keep moving.

My thumbs and fingers and hands and arms keep moving. And then I stand right up.

My thumbs and fingers and hands and
arms and feet keep moving.

My thumbs and fingers and hands and
arms and feet keep moving.

My thumbs and fingers and hands and
arms and feet keep moving. Tra-la
tra-la tra-la.

My thumbs and fingers and hands
and arms and feet and head keep
moving.

My thumbs and fingers and hands
and arms and feet and head keep
moving.

My thumbs and fingers and hands and
arms and feet and head keep mov-
ing. Tra-la tra-la tra-la.

THE MUSIC'S BEAT

I jump
I hop
I march in place
I twirl around

With style and grace

I wiggle
I squirm
I spin and shake
I move back and forth
Like a human earthquake

I twist
I turn
I kick my feet
I love to move
To the music's beat.

Charley Hoce

Reprinted with permission of the publisher, Early
Years, Inc. From the March 2004 issue of *Teaching
K-8* magazine, Norwalk, CT 06854.

CHAPTER 15

Puppetry and Beginning Drama Experiences

OBJECTIVES

After reading this chapter, you should be able to:

◆ Use puppetry in language arts programming.

◆ Describe young children's puppet play.

◆ List five teaching techniques that offer young children opportunities for simple dramatization.

KEY TERMS

audience
characters
dramas
pantomime

SANTA PUPPET

Blaine, a student teacher, was pleased to be invited to a classroom Christmas party. Blaine's cupcake had a small, inch-and-a-half-high Santa Claus decoration. Other cupcakes had trees, bells, wreathes, and snowmen, but he was served the only one with a Santa. He slipped the small decoration on his little finger and play-fully uttered, "Ho, ho, ho, Santa's here." Every child near was interested and wanted to talk to Santa. Blaine could not believe such a tiny finger puppet could hold their attention. The activity went on until all who wanted to talk to Santa did so. Blaine was amazed at the young children's ability to so quickly accept the fantasy. He then remembered that children don't seem to put together the differences in the various Santa representations they see: the red coat, hat, and beard seem to be enough.

QUESTIONS TO PONDER

1. Was Blaine's activity appropriate? Why or why not?

2. Could you make up a quick, simple poem Santa might say or a simple song Santa might sing that emphasizes the alphabet letter "H"?

3. Can you think of a way that children could create a Santa puppet?

461

Puppets provide countless opportunities for children's speech growth. They match and fulfill many of the preschooler's developmental needs, besides being of high interest. Imagine a lifeless puppet lying on a table. Suddenly, a child slips his hand into the puppet and it awakens to a life and personality of its own. Magic happens and the world of make-believe begins. Children love to pretend and puppetry allows them to create their own magic.

When used by a child, puppets can be

◆ moved and controlled by the child (Figure 15–1).

◆ a challenge because of the need to coordinate speech and movement.

◆ talked to as an accepting companion.

◆ used individually and in group play.

◆ used to create and fantasize.

◆ used to explore another's personality.

◆ used as a way to release pent-up emotions.

◆ used to relive and imitate experiences.

◆ seen as an adult-like activity.

◆ used to entertain others.

◆ constructed by children.

Many of these uses build and develop children's confidence in their own speaking ability. There are many ways the teacher can use puppetry in language development activities. When used by a teacher, puppets can

◆ motivate.

◆ gain and hold attention.

◆ provide variety in the presentation of ideas and words.

◆ provide a model to imitate.

◆ tell stories.

◆ promote child creativity and pretending.

◆ provide a play opportunity that encourages speech and motor-skill coordination.

◆ introduce new information.

◆ promote positive attitudes toward speaking and dramatic activities.

◆ build audience skills.

◆ provide construction activities.

◆ help children express themselves.

◆ build vocabularies.

◆ make activities entertaining and enjoyable.

◆ provide a wide range of individual personalities through puppets.

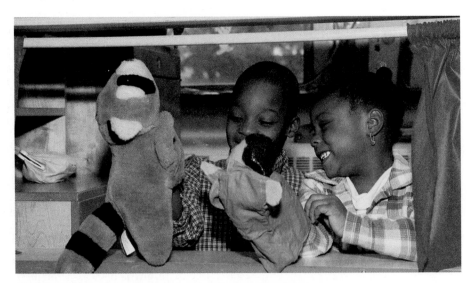

FIGURE 15–1 Controlling puppet actions can be great fun.

What can puppets offer both children and their teachers? For the child, the introduction of puppets can create a fresh and creative learning environment. Young children can usually accept the puppet as a nonthreatening, sympathetic friend with whom they can share their thoughts and feelings without fear of ridicule, rejection, or reprimand. This friend is privy to the child's inner world and able also to communicate with the outer world as an intermediary. It is perhaps here that the teacher finds in puppetry its most valuable asset for contributing to the process of education. A skillful teacher can take advantage of special moments of puppet-inspired communication to tune in to the child's thinking and to open up new avenues for learning.

AUDIENCE SKILLS

Audience skills are quickly learned, and teachers encourage them through discussion and modeling. Clapping after performances is recommended. Listening and being a quiet audience is verbally appreciated. Teachers and staff need to decide whether a child in the audience can leave during a performance. Most schools adopt this plan of action, and the child is expected to choose a quiet play activity that does not disturb others.

STIMULATING CHILDREN'S USE OF PUPPETS

Teachers can expand children's experiences with puppets in the following ways.

- Present puppet plays and skits.
- Find community resources for puppet presentations: puppeteer groups, children's theater groups, high school and elementary classes, and skilled individuals.

- Introduce each puppet periodically and provide new ones when possible.
- Display and store puppets invitingly.
- Provide props and puppet theaters.
- Keep puppets in good repair.

A puppet carried in a teacher's pocket can be useful in a variety of teaching situations, as mentioned previously. Children imitate the teacher's use of puppets, and this leads to creative play.

TEACHER PUPPETRY

Children sit, excited and enthralled, at simple skits and dialogues performed by the teacher. Continually amazed by young children's rapt attention and obvious pleasure, most teachers find puppetry a valuable teaching skill (Figure 15–2).

Prerecording puppet dialogue (or attaching puppet speeches inside the puppet stage) helps beginning teacher puppeteers. With practice, performance skills increase and puppet coordination can then become the main teacher task.

Many books are available that give valuable suggestions for increasing teacher puppetry skill, including tips on developing a puppet voice and personality. Some advise becoming skilled at giving puppets a voice that contrasts to your own and looking at the puppet to see what characteristics its physical features suggest. A deep commanding voice, for example, may be appropriate for a large mouth while sleepy eyes may connote a slow, tired voice. Become fully involved with the character and experiment freely. A puppet's personality can evolve over time, but a name should come to mind fairly quickly. It is sometimes easier to pattern a puppet's personality and character after a real person than to fashion an imaginary one.

---

audience — the respondents to drama presentation; a group of listeners or spectators.

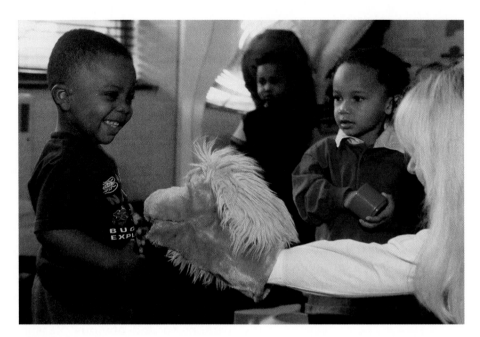

FIGURE 15–2 A teacher delights this child with impromptu puppet interaction.

Naturally, puppet **characters** in plays or from printed sources already have built-in personalities, but a teacher's daily puppets have no such script and challenge teacher creativity.

Planning and performing simple puppet plays requires time and effort. The plays are selected for suitability and then practiced until the scene-by-scene sequence is firmly in mind. Good preparation helps ensure a smooth performance and adds to children's enjoyment.

Several helpful tips on puppetry follow.

◆ A dark net peep-hole enables performers to watch audience reactions and helps dialogue pacing.

◆ Puppets with strong, identifiable personality traits who stay in character are well received. Another way to enhance a puppet's personality is to give it an idiosyncrasy that sets it apart.

◆ Plan your puppet's personality in advance and stick to it. For example, Happy Mabel has the following characteristics: she is always laughing; says "Hot Potatoes!" often; likes to talk about her cat, Christobel; lives on a farm; is an optimist; speaks in a high-pitched voice; lives alone; and likes young visitors.

◆ Use your favorite puppet in at least one activity weekly.

PUPPET ACTIVITIES

Child participation with puppets can be increased when planned puppet activities are performed. The following are a few of the many possible puppet play activities.

◆ Invite children to use puppets (with arms) and act out that a puppet is sleepy, hungry, dancing, crying, laughing, whispering, saying "hello" to a friend, climbing a ladder, waving good-bye, and shaking hands. (A large mirror helps children build skill.)

characters — persons (or puppets) represented in or acting in a story or drama.

◆ Ask two volunteers to use puppets and act out a situation in which a mother and child are waking up in the morning. The teacher creates both speaking parts, then prompts two children to continue on their own. Other situations include a telephone conversation, a child requesting money from a parent to buy an ice cream cone, and a puppet inviting another to a party.

◆ Urge children to answer the teacher's puppet. For example:

Teacher: "Hi! My name is Mr. Singing Sam. I can sing any song you ask me to sing. Just ask me!"

or

Teacher: "I'm the cook. What shall we have for dinner?"

or

Teacher: "My name is Randy Rabbit. Who are you? Where am I?"

◆ Record simple puppet directions (such as the following) and have a large mirror available so that the children can see their actions.

1. Make your puppet touch his nose.
2. Have your puppet clap.
3. Kiss your hand, puppet.
4. Rub your eyes, puppet.
5. Reach for the stars, puppet.
6. Hold your stomach.
7. Scratch your ear.
8. Bow low.
9. Hop.

◆ Record simple puppet **dramas**. After a teacher demonstration, make them available to children on a free-choice basis.

◆ Let children speak for a puppet that has not learned to talk.

◆ Give one special puppet the role of the teacher's helper. This puppet gives

directions, rings the clean-up or snack-time bell, and introduces new children.

◆ Invent a singing puppet that sings new songs or sings to pieces of music karaoke style.

◆ Have puppets say character lines in a simple drama.

◆ Have a puppet read a picture book.

◆ Make a set of alphabet letter stick puppets that sing the alphabet song. (It is best to line these up beforehand in an upright position on a foam block.)

Storage and Theaters

Store puppets in an inviting way, face up, begging for handling; shoe racks, wall pockets, or upright pegs within the child's reach are suggested. An adjacent puppet theater tempts children's use. Old television cabinets (with insides removed and open backs) make durable theaters that the children can climb into. Other theaters can be constructed by the teacher using large packing crates that can be painted and decorated by the children. For additional ideas, see Figure 15-3.

As soon as a child physically picks up a puppet, he wants to make it talk and move. He gives it a voice and it comes to life. In the puppet corner children will experiment without inhibition using different vocal sounds and movements. No other form of expression, except creative dramatics, offers such a broad range of opportunities for verbal experimentation.

In most early childhood centers, rules are set for using puppets. The puppets should stay in certain designated areas and should be handled with care.

Visiting Puppet Idea

Many centers create a "visiting puppet." This puppet is sent to children's homes in a tote bag containing a pen and pad for a family to record the child's account of what the puppet did during its visit. During group time, when the puppet returns to school, the teacher reads

---

dramas — plays; stories in dramatic form, typically emphasizing conflict in and among key characters.

Fiberboard Theatre
Use hinges on sides so it can be folded.

Puppet Screen
For shadow puppets. Make by stapling old sheet to picture frame.

Light

Spring-pressure adjustable window curtain rod.

Doorway
Tape sheet across bottom half.

Refrigerator Box
Cut one side all the way down. Cut a window stage about 24″ wide. Add curtains and paint.

Hat Box
Tie around neck. Place hand through bottom to manipulate puppet.

Table Theatre
Use a table turned on side. Children work puppets from behind.

Window
On a warm day children go outside, some stay to work puppets from open windows.

Blanket
Hang a blanket from two chairs. Easy and quick.

FIGURE 15-3 Ideas for puppet theaters

the family's comments and invites the visited children and/or other children to elaborate on the puppet's adventures.

Puppet Plays

Familiar and favorite stories make good puppet dramas. Many contain simple, repetitive lines that most of the children know from memory. Children will often stray from familiar dialogues in stories, however, adding their own lines, actions, or settings. Older preschoolers speak through puppets easily; younger children may be more interested in manipulating alone or simple imitating (Figure 15–4). Wooden spoons with cutout felt details can be created for use in *The Three Billy Goats Gruff* reenactments.

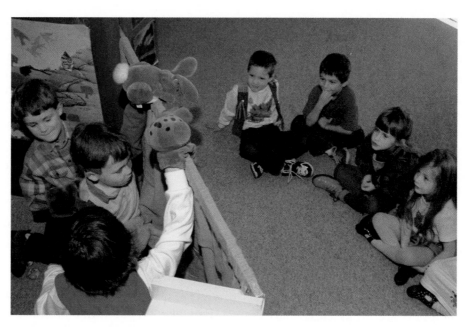

FIGURE 15–4 These puppeteers have a rapt audience.

When children enlarge or change dialogue or a character's personality, their individuality directs and creates. Schools can wind up with many versions and interpretations of familiar favorites.

Other Puppetry Tips

◆ Some children are fearful of puppets. They may even think that a puppet has died when they see the puppet limp on the shelf. With reassurance and additional exposure to teacher puppet use, fear subsides.

◆ The act of becoming the puppet's persona (such as an alligator or wolf, for example) may be frightening to 3-year-olds (Figure 15–5).

◆ Aggressive puppet play of the "Punch and Judy" type should be avoided. Having puppets punch and hit is common behavior in traditional Punch and Judy shows, and consequently is not presented to young children in school settings. Any modeling of aggressive and violent behavior in puppetry is inappropriate, for it is quickly imitated by some children. Unfortunately, because of violence in society,

FIGURE 15–5 Children can feel comfortable or uncomfortable with puppet play at any age.

young children may attempt to use puppets roughly.

◆ The following are a few other points to keep in mind concerning puppets.

◆ Most public libraries offer puppet shows periodically.

◆ Parents and volunteers can help construct sturdy classroom puppets.

◆ Commercial school-supply companies offer well-made, durable puppets and theaters for group use.

◆ Elementary or high school drama classes may provide puppet shows.

PUPPET CONSTRUCTION

Puppets can be divided into two general categories—those worked with the hands and fingers and those that dangle on strings. Hand puppets are popular in the preschool because they are so versatile and practical. Teacher-made, child-made, and commercially manufactured hand puppets are an essential part of most centers. Actually, almost any object of the right size given eyes can become a puppet! Bleach bottle puppets are common.

Moving arms and pliable faces on puppets increase the possibilities for characterization and action. Rubber, plastic, and papier-mâché puppet heads are durable. Cloth faces often permit more expressive facial expressions.

Teacher Puppet Presentations

Many simple stories can be shared with children through teacher puppetry. The following story is an example of a tale that lends itself to a puppet presentation. Teachers can create their own stories that appeal to the interests of the children with whom they work.

THE PANCAKE

Narrator: Once upon a time, an old woman made a pancake. When it was nice and golden brown, it hopped out of the frying pan and began rolling down the road, saying:

Pancake: Whee! I'm free! Nobody will ever eat me! What a nice day! I'll just roll along till—hey! I wonder what that funny looking round thing is by the river!

Narrator: He didn't know it, but it was a bridge.

Pancake: I'll bet I can roll over that thing. Watch this! I'll just get a head start back here—(backs up) one . . . two . . . three! (As the pancake starts over the bridge, frog comes up and grabs it.)

Pancake: Let me go! Let me go!

Frog: I want to eat you! I love pancakes! (Pancake pulls away and rolls out of sight.)

Frog: Oh, dear . . . it got away . . . (Frog down. Bridge down. Pancake rolls in.)

Pancake: That was a close one! I hope I do not meet any other—(Off stage is heard the sound of barking . . .)

Pancake: What's that sound? I do not think I like it . . . (Dog in, tries to grab pancake.)

Dog: I want a bite! I love pancakes! (Pancake cries "No! No!" and rolls off.)

Dog: It got away. Well, better luck next time . . . (Dog out, pancake rolls in.)

Pancake: Goodness! Everybody seems to love pancakes, but I do not want to be loved that way! (Off stage is heard the sound of "meow!")

Pancake: Meow? What kind of animal makes that sound? (Cat in, tries to grab pancake, pancake escapes as before.)

Cat: Meow? Meow, no breakfast now! (Cat out, pancake rolls in panting.)

Pancake: This is dreadful! Everybody I meet wants to eat me! (Bird flies in.)

Bird: A pancake! Delicious! I'll just peck a few pieces out of it! (Bird starts to peck at pancake, which rolls away crying, "No! No!" Bird follows, and then returns alone.)

Bird: It's too hot to chase it. Besides, it can roll faster than I can fly. (Bird out. Put bridge up again.)

Narrator: And all day long the pancake rolled until it finally found itself back at the same bridge. (The pancake rolls in.)

Pancake: (Wearily) Oh, dear . . . here I am again, back at the same bridge . . . I must have been rolling around in circles. And I'm too tired to roll another inch. I must rest. I'll just lie down here next to this round thing over the river . . .

(Pancake lies down flat, or leans against the bridge, if possible.)

(Now puppeteer has two free hands to put on frog and dog. But before they come in, we hear their voices.)

Frog's
Voice: (half-whisper) It's mine!

Dog's
Voice: (half-whisper) No, it's mine. I saw it first!

Frog's
Voice: (same) You did not! I saw it first!

Dog's
Voice: (same) Who cares—I'm going to eat it! (Dog and Frog enter and grab the pancake between them.)

Pancake: Let me go! Let me go! (Frog and dog tussle, drop pancake out of sight, look after it.)

Frog: Oh no! You dropped it in the water!

Dog: Not me! You're the one who dropped it!

Narrator: And as the pancake disappeared beneath the water, they heard it say, (far away voice) "Nobody will ever catch me . . ." and nobody ever did.

Teachers find that play situations containing a puppet, animal, or other character that is less knowledgeable and mature than the children themselves promote a feeling of bigness in children. The children are then in the position of taking care of and educating another, which often produces considerable child speech and self-esteem. A well-known commercial language

development kit cleverly contains a puppet that has no eyes. Children are urged to help this puppet by describing objects and events.

SIMPLE DRAMA

Children often playact familiar events and home situations. This allows them to both try out and work out elements of past experiences that they remember for one reason or another. Their playacting can be an exact imitation or something created by their active imaginations.

Much of children's imaginative play (pretend play) reenacts life situations and leads to creative embellishment (Figure 15–6). It happens all the time in preschool. Children often need only a jumping-off place provided by a room setting, real or toy telephone, story, or teacher suggestion. Picture what might happen if a teacher says

"Here comes the parade, let's join it and march."

"A kitten is lost in the play yard, what can we do? Where can we look?"

"The bus just stopped at the gate. Let's go places. Where will we go first? First we need to step up inside and pay our money."

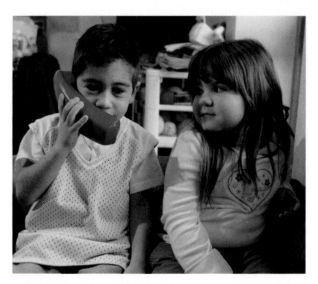

FIGURE 15–6 In today's world, almost everyone has a telephone.

"The astronauts' rocket ship crashed on the moon. Our rocket ship is here. Let's get on and rescue them."

"Let's pretend we're hummingbirds searching for sweet nectar in all the brightly colored flowers."

"My goodness, teddy bear has fallen out of the bed. His leg is hurt. What can we do?"

The teacher's watchfulness and skillfulness will be necessary. Unfortunately, exposure to television violence may seep into play, or play may lead to unwise, unsafe actions, depending on one's particular play group. The teacher may need to redirect or stop children's actions. More commonly, however, the astronauts will be rescued and returned to earth, the kitten will be found, and the bus ride will lead to adventures without difficulties.

In creative drama, the teacher's role is to be a fellow participant that follows children's creative lead. The benefits of creative drama experiences are multiple—social, intellectual, linguistic, and sometimes therapeutic. Creative language use and increased self-esteem are natural outcomes.

Four-year-olds, because of their ability to conceptualize and fantasize, are prime candidates for beginning exposure to this literary form. They pick up both acting skill and audience skill quickly. Three-year-olds enjoy drama presentations and are good audiences. They profit from exposure but can have a difficult time with the acting role. Imitative, pretend play and **pantomime** suit their developmental level. Pantomime becomes the foundation on which 4-year-olds build their acting skills for created and scripted parts.

Young preschoolers will need teacher prompting and suggestions for acting out. Teachers can ask children how someone might feel or act under certain circumstances. They can also ask children to think about what takes place in their homes, at school, at various times of the day, or in other life settings and situations to determine possible acting scenarios. Positive, appreciative teacher and peer comments concerning convincing or appropriate acting behavior provide additional pointers.

In both drama and pantomime, children can act out all the joy, anger, fear, and surprise of their favorite characters. This gives children the opportunity to become someone else for a few minutes and to release their frustration and energy in an acceptable way.

After young children become familiar with stories, they thoroughly enjoy reenacting or dramatizing the stories. By using both physical motions and verbal comments, children bring the words and actions of the stories to life. Because most stories deal with a character with a problem, decision, or challenge, part of the draw of drama for young children is their interest in figuring out how the characters are going to resolve their dilemmas.

Playacting Tips

Children will act out parts from favorite stories as well as scenes from real life. The teacher sets the stage, keeping some points in mind.

- The children must be familiar with the story to know what happens first, next, and last.
- Activities in which the children pretend to perform certain actions, to be certain animals, or to copy the actions of another help prepare them for simple drama.
- Video-recorded plays and films are good motivators.
- A first step is to act without words or while listening to a good story or record.
- The teacher can be the narrator, while the children are the actors.
- Children should be encouraged to volunteer for parts.
- Props and settings can be simple. Ask, "What can be used for a bridge?" or a

---

pantomime — creative communication done with nonverbal physical actions.

Chapter 15 • Puppetry and Beginning Drama Experiences

similar question so that children can use their creativity.

- Any of the children's imaginative acts should be accepted, whether or not they are a part of the original story, unless they endanger others.
- Individual and group dramatizations should be appreciated and encouraged.
- Every child who wishes a turn playing the parts should be accommodated.
- No-touching guidelines are necessary when vigorous acts are part of dramas.
- With large groups, the teacher can limit acting roles to a manageable number to prevent chaos.
- In child-authored dramas, the teacher may need to clarify the child's intent in story sequences.
- Reenacting stories with different children playing parts is usually done with popular stories.
- Include multicultural stories when possible.

Some classic stories that can be used for playacting (drama) include:

- *Goldilocks and the Three Bears*
- *The Three Little Pigs*
- *The Little Red Hen*
- *The Gingerbread Boy*
- *Little Red Ridinghood*
- *Little Miss Muffet*

Fast-action and simple story lines are best for the young child. Playacting presents many opportunities for children to develop

- self-expression.
- use of correct speech.
- coordination of actions and words.
- creative thinking.
- self-confidence.
- listening skills.
- social interaction.

As mentioned in Chapter 10, children's own dictated stories are excellent vehicles for dramatization. In child-authored stories, the most popular procedure is for the child-author to choose the role he would like to play, and then which classmates will play the rest. Teachers read previously dictated stories before and as children act the roles.

Problem-Solving Drama

Early childhood practitioners may want to try problem-solving dramas with older preschoolers. Imaginary problem-solving situations are suggested by the teacher and are then enacted creatively by children working toward a solution. Children are not given words to say, but character parts are assigned. Sample problems might include the following:

- A child's shoes are missing, and it is time to go to a party. Characters include the mother, grandmother, dog, cat, brother, and sister.
- While at the zoo on a preschool field trip, the class learns that a giraffe is loose. The teacher asks a group of children to guess where a giraffe might hide. Characters include a zookeeper, police officer, four children, and their preschool teacher.

Teachers trying this type of creative drama may need to slip in and out of the dramatization, serving as a confidant, collaborator, and helpful but not dominating coach.

Drama from Picture Books

A seasoned teacher tells a funny story about children's love of dramatization. Because picture books are often enacted at her center, a child who readily identifies with a particular book character often speaks up, saying, "I want to be the rabbit," long before the reading session is finished.

In enacting stories from books or storytelling sources, the teacher may have to read the book or tell the story many times so that it is digested and becomes familiar to the children. A discussion of the story can promote children's expression of opinions about enjoyed parts, the feelings of characters, and what might be similar in their own lives. The teacher can then ask, "Who's good at crying and can go 'Boo-hoo'?" or "Who can act mad and stomp around the floor?" Most child groups have one or more children ready to volunteer. The teacher can play one of the parts.

The following is a step-by-step teacher guide for child enactment of a book.

- Start by keeping dramatization simple. Forget props or rehearsing. Props can be added later after subsequent readings or when highly enjoyed enactments are identified.
- Read the book (or child's dictated book or story).
- Announce that you will reread the book and that children can pretend to be book characters by acting out what happens in the story.
- Select roles from volunteers by asking questions such as, "Who can bark like a big red dog?"
- Then ask the selected children to stand together in front of the group to the side of the teacher or in any classroom space that lends itself to drama production.
- Reread the story more slowly than before.
- Feel free to interrupt the text and give clues to actors, such as, "Beady Bear was surprised. How might his face look?"
- Promote audience skills, such as clapping, and cast skills, such as holding hands and taking bows.
- Time permitting, if child attentiveness hasn't waned, go through a second enactment giving all children a chance to act or change characters.
- Think about asking another group or class in as an audience occasionally.

Many action- and dialogue-packed picture books, such as the following, lend themselves to child reenactment.

Carle, E. (1996). *The grouchy ladybug*. New York: HarperCollins.
Gág, W. (1999). *The funny thing*. New York: Smithmark.
Galdone, P. (1975). *The gingerbread boy*. New York: Seabury Press.
Hogrogian, N. (1971). *One fine day*. New York: Macmillan.
Hutchins, P. (1972). *Rosie's walk*. New York: Simon & Schuster.
Keats, E. J. (1998). *Peter's chair*. New York: Viking.
Krauss, R. (1974). *The carrot seed*. New York: Scholastic.
Mayer, M. (1983). *Me too!* New York: Golden Press.
Rylant, C. (1987). *Birthday presents*. New York: Orchard Books.

A number of well-known children's songs and popular poems set to music can also be enacted, including:

Aliki. (1996). *Go tell Aunt Rhody*. New York: Aladdin Paperbacks.
Cauley, L. B. (1992). *Clap your hands*. New York: Putnam.
Oxenbury, H. (1999). *Clap hands*. New York: Simon & Schuster.
Oxenbury, H. (1999). *Say goodnight*. New York: Simon & Schuster.

DRAMATIZING FAIRY TALES AND FOLKTALES

A number of educators urge teachers to dramatize classic fairy tales and folktales.

For 2½- and 3-year-olds:

The Three Little Pigs
The Three Billy Goats Gruff
Goldilocks and the Three Bears

For 4-year-olds:

Cinderella
Jack and the Beanstalk
The Wolf and the Seven Little Kids
The Shoemaker and the Elves

Some teachers are reluctant to offer children many of these classic tales because of their inherent violence, but some educators try to persuade them to do so. Their argument for using these books is based in their belief that in order to solve life's problems one must not only take risks, one must confront the worst that might happen. Children, like the rest of us, ruminate and worry about these worst things. Fairy tales confront them. This is the chief reason many adults have trouble with fairy tales. They think they can protect children from the hard realities of life. Children think about death, separation, and divorce. None of us wants to think about these painful possibilities, yet we must. Teaching staffs decide whether fairy and folk tales are appropriate for their group of children.

Nonfiction books can also be dramatized. Content such as bears hibernating in their dens or dinosaurs moving through swamps, for example, might lend itself to dramatization. When acting, children appear to be thoroughly absorbed and enjoying themselves. At play they may retain more of the information presented than during the book's reading. Nonfiction books should not be overlooked by early childhood teachers when looking for dramatization possibilities.

Progressive Skill

Dramatizing a familiar story involves a number of language skills—listening, auditory and visual memory of actions and characters' speech lines, and remembered sequence of events—as well as audience skills. Simple pantomime or imitation requires less maturity. Activities that use actions alone are good as a first step toward building children's playacting skills. Children have imitated others' actions since infancy, and as always, the joy of being able to do what they see others do brings a feeling of self-confidence. The children's individuality is preserved if differences in ways of acting out a familiar story are valued in preschool settings.

Pantomime

Among the all-time favorites for pantomime is the following.

THE BEAR HUNT

> *We're going on a bear hunt*
> *We're going where?*
> *We're going on a bear hunt.*
> *OK, let's go! I'm not afraid!*
> *Look over there!*
> *What do you see?*
> *A big deep river.*
> *Can't go around it.*
> *Can't go under it.*
> *Have to swim across it.*
> *OK, let's go. I'm not afraid!*
> *What's this tall stuff?*
> *What do you see?*
> *Tall, tall grass.*
> *Can't go around it.*
> *Can't go under it.*
> *Got to go through it.*
> *OK, let's go. I'm not afraid!*
> *Hey, look ahead.*
> *What do you see?*
> *A rickety old bridge.*
> *Can't go around it.*
> *Can't go under it.*
> *Got to go across it.*
> *OK, let's go. I'm not afraid!*
> *Now what's this ahead.*
> *It's a tall, tall tree.*
> *Can't go under it.*
> *Can't go over it.*
> *Have to climb it.*
> *OK, let's go. I'm not afraid!*
> *Do you see what I see?*
> *What a giant mountain!*
> *Can't go around it.*
> *Can't go under it.*
> *Got to climb over it.*
> *OK, let's go. I'm not afraid!*
> *Oh, look at that dark cave.*
> *Let's go inside.*
> *It sure is dark in here.*
> *I think I feel something.*
> *I think it's a nose.*
> *And two furry ears.*
> *HELP! It's a bear!!!!!!!!!!!!!!*
> *Let's get out of here . . . I'm afraid.*

(Pretend to climb back over the mountain and down the tree, run across the bridge, swish through the tall grass, swim the river, open the door, run in, slam the door, and collapse in a heap.)

> *Whew . . . Home at last . . . I was afraid!*

CREATIVE DRAMA PROGRAMS

Starting a language program that includes creative drama requires planning. Props and play materials must be supplied for children to explore. When children see simple plays and pantomimes performed by teachers, other children, and adult groups, they are provided with a model and a stimulus. Some drama activity ideas for the older preschool child include

- pantomiming action words and phrases: tiptoe, crawl, riding a horse, and using a rolling pin.
- pantomiming words that describe a physical state: cold, hot, and sleepy.
- pantomiming feeling words: happy, sad, hurt, holding a favorite teddy bear lovingly, feeling surprise.
- acting out imaginary life situations: such as opening a door with a key, climbing in and out of a car, helping to set the table.
- acting familiar character parts in well-known stories: "She covered her mouth so the clown couldn't see her laugh." "The rabbit dug a big hole and buried the carrot." "He tiptoed to the window, raised the shade, and opened it."
- saying familiar lines from known stories: "And he huffed and he puffed, and he blew the house down."
- playing a character in a short story or song that involves both spoken lines and actions.
- pantomiming actions of a character in a short, familiar story that the teacher reads (or from a teacher-recorded story tape). There are a vast number of commercially recorded stories available at school-supply stores.
- making story sequence cards for a favorite book.

The following pantomimes for young children are good initial exercises.

- Drink a glass of water. "Oh! It turned into hot soup and burned your mouth!"
- Pick a flower. Smell it.
- Eat a bowl of spaghetti.
- Row a boat.
- Bounce a ball.
- Pour your milk from the carton to a glass. Drink it.
- Play the piano, trumpet, drums, or guitar.
- Shoo away a fly.
- Chew a piece of bubble gum and blow a bubble. It gets bigger, bigger, and bigger. Suddenly it breaks.
- Blow up a small paper bag, and then pop it.
- "You and your grandmother are in a supermarket. Suddenly, you cannot find her and you feel scared. You look up and down all the aisles trying to find her. There she is. You see her."

COSTUMES, PROPS, AND STAGE

Imagination and inexpensive, easy-to-make costumes are a great performing incentive. Accessories such as aprons, shirts, canes, and gloves can be used in a variety of play and drama situations, and hats are popular when head lice problems do not exist. A "stage" area can be a semipermanent part of the classrooms. Comfortable audience seating and viewing should be considered.

Cutout art board (or cardboard) heads and figures held by the child quickly aid his ability to step into character (Figure 15–7). (Make sure that the board is lightweight and the hand holes are comfortable.) Older children may be able to draw their own patterns, or patterns for figures can be found in children's books and can be enlarged with the use of an opaque projector. These props allow children to put their faces into the spaces cut out of the characters' faces and are useful in child dramatization. However, some teachers feel that these props are physically awkward and prefer, instead, simple costumes.

SUMMARY

Using puppetry for language development is a widely accepted practice in preschools. Many puppet types are available to choose from. The

FIGURE 15–7 Story character boards.

ability to coordinate puppet actions and words takes practice and maturity. Teachers find that the more children watch puppets being used, the more they will use them. Puppets that are stored attractively and upright near puppet theaters encourage children's exploration.

There is a wide range of uses for puppets as instructional devices. Puppets are interesting and capture attention as an enjoyable play activity.

Drama is another step on the road to literacy. Simple child dramatizations of favorite stories begin during preschool years. Language programs provide many playacting opportunities. Props, playacting, and pantomime activities motivate this expressive art. Skills are acquired through increased experiences with drama. Planning by the teacher aids children's acquisition of dramatization abilities.

ADDITIONAL RESOURCES

Sources for Puppet and Drama Visuals

Career dress-ups. Dexter Educational Toys, P.O. Box 630861, Aventura, FL 33163.

Door puppet playhouse. Fabric Farms, 3590 Riverside Drive, Columbus, OH 43221.

Dress-ups for dramatic play. DRESS-UPS, 652 Glenbrook Road, Stamford, CT 06906.

Felt puppets. Pat's Puppets, 121 W. Simmons, Anaheim, CA 92802.

Puppet patterns. Plaid Enterprises Inc., P.O. Box 7600, Norcross, GA 30091.

Books for Creative Dramatization

Burton, B. (1973). *Buzz, buzz, buzz.* New York: Macmillan.

DePaola, T. (1975). *Strega Nona.* New York: Scholastic.

Domanska, J. (1969). *The turnip.* New York: Macmillan.

Ets, M. H. (1955). *Play with me.* New York: The Viking Press.

Ets, M. H. (1963). *Gilberto and the wind.* New York: The Viking Press.

Flack, M. (1952). *Ask Mr. Bear.* New York: Macmillan.

Green, N. B. (1975). *The hole in the dike.* New York: Harper and Row.

Hutchins, P. (1969). *The surprise party.* New York: Macmillan.

Hutchins, P. (1972). *Goodnight owl.* New York: Macmillan.

Hutchins, P. (1986). *The doorbell rang.* New York: Greenwillow Books.

Keats, E. J. (1962). *The snowy day.* New York: The Viking Press.

Keats, E. J. (1966). *Jennie's hat.* New York: Harper and Row.

Lionni, L. (1969). *Alexander and the wind-up mouse.* New York: Pantheon.

Mayer, M. (1968). *There's a nightmare in my closet.* New York: The Dial Press.

McGovern, A. (1976). *Too much noise.* New York: Scholastic.

Miller, E. (1964). *Mouskin's golden house.* Englewood Cliffs, NJ: Prentice Hall.

Murphy, J. (1980). *Peace at last.* New York: The Dial Press.

Slobodkina, E. (1947). *Caps for sale.* New York: William R. Scott Inc.

Young, M. (1964). *Miss Susy.* New York: Parents' Magazine Press.

Readings

Breyer, M. A., & Seho, R. (1999). *A guide for using the master puppeteer in the classroom.* Westminister, CA: Teacher Created Materials.

Crepeau, I. M., & Richards, M. A. (2006). *A show of hands: Using puppets with young children.* St. Paul, MN: Redleaf Press.

Fox, M. (1987). *Teaching drama to young children.* Portsmouth, NH: Heinemann.

MacLennan, J. (1988). *Simple puppets you can make.* New York: Sterling.

McCaslin, N. (1996). *Creative drama in the classroom.* White Plains, NY: Longman.

Wagner, B. (Ed.). (1998). *Educational drama and language arts: What research shows.* Portsmouth, NH: Heinemann.

Helpful Websites

Axtell Expressions
http://www.axtell.com
Discusses puppet manipulation.

Drama Kids International
http://www.dramakids.com
Provides information about an American company that offers worldwide franchises for children's drama programs.

Folkmanis Puppets and Children's Books
http://www.kidsbooksandpuppets.com
A commercial site that sells puppets and puppet-book combinations.

National Academies Press
http://www.nap.edu
Summarizes publications concerned with early literacy.

Pioneer Drama Service, Inc.
http://www.pioneerdrama.com
A resource for inexpensive scripts. Search catalog for folktales or fairy tales that are appropriate for young children.

Book Companion Website

Have you attempted to use a puppet to read a picture book? The book companion website suggests you do so and then critique the experience for your training group. Paper-plate puppets are also described. Phoneme puppets have been used in some classrooms; read about them. The website includes many puppet sources to investigate, and quiz questions.

STUDENT ACTIVITIES

1. Make a puppet described in this chapter, or make one of your own choosing.
2. Present a simple puppet play with a few classmates.
3. Collect 10 easy-to-make costume ideas that promote creative drama. Share your ideas with the class.
4. Record a puppet drama and enact the drama with the help of classmates.
5. Construct a puppet theater.
6. Invite a local puppeteer group to share ideas with the class.
7. Bring one simple puppet play script or drama script to class.
8. Create a short puppet play.
9. Find commercial resources for ethnic puppets. Share names of companies and the prices for puppets.
10. Create a puppet from a household item such as a cup or a tube. Share with the class.
11. List community resources that might help young children in your community become more familiar with drama.
12. What fiction or nonfiction books dealing with the African-American experience or the Vietnamese-American experience might be appropriate for a preschool dramatization activity? List and discuss with a group of three to four classmates. Report your findings to the class.

CHAPTER REVIEW

A. Write a short paragraph describing the reasons puppets are a part of preschool language arts programs.

B. Rate the following teachers using the following scale.

A	B	C
Definitely promotes puppet interest and use.	Unable to determine or cannot decide.	Turns children off.

1. Mrs. G. (teacher) pulled a small puppet from her smock pocket. Reaching behind Mark, age 3, she talked through the puppet. "Mark Allen Graham? Rupert sees what you're doing, and he doesn't like children who break crayons." Mark returns the crayon to the container.

2. Miss R. (teacher) is introducing a small group of children to an activity involving a poem on a chart. "Well, there's Petey, Sam, Scott, Adam, Renee, and Jonathan," Miss R. begins. The puppet in her hand moves and claps, and the puppet's voice is low pitched and deep. "I came to talk to you about rabbits. Does anyone know what rabbits look like? I live in a pocket, you know. I've heard about rabbits, but I've never seen one."

3. Mr. O. (teacher) has a large packing carton in the middle of the classroom. Two children notice the carton and ask, "What's that for?" Mr. O. tells the two children that he noticed the school puppets do not have a puppet theater. "How could we make one from this box?" he asks the children. "You need a window," one child says. "Yes, that's true. I'll draw one. Stand here, please. I'll need the window the right height." The conversation and the project have drawn a larger group of children.

4. Mr. T. (teacher) has noticed a puppet lying on the ground in the playground. He picks it up, examines it, and puts it in his pocket. During circle time, he says, "Orvil (puppet's name) was on the ground in the yard today. Raise your hand if you know where he should be put after we play with him. Olivia, I see your hand. Would you please put Orvil in the place in the classroom that's just for him? Thank you, Olivia. What could happen to Orvil, our puppet, if we left him on the floor or ground?" "He'd get stepped on," Thad offers. "That could happen, Thad," said Mr. T. "Can anyone else think of what might happen to Orvil on the ground outside?" Mr. T. continues. "The ants would crawl on him," Jessica comments.

5. Ms. Y. (teacher) announces to a group of children, "It's talking time. Everyone is going to talk to Bonzo (the puppet dog) and tell him their names." She reaches behind her and pulls Bonzo from a bag. "Willy, come up and take Bonzo," Ms. Y. says. "Now, Cleo, you come up here, too. Willy, have Bonzo say, 'Woof, woof, I'm Bonzo.'" Willy fiddles with the puppet and still has not slipped it onto his hand. "We need a barking Bonzo. Who would like to come up, put Bonzo on his hand, and bark?" Ms. Y. asks.

6. Miss W. (assistant teacher) has created an alphabet puppet set. In storytelling and other activities, these puppets brag about how many words start with their letter names.

Share your rating with the training class.

C. Select the best answer for each statement.
1. Because puppets are so appealing, teachers
   a. motivate, model, and plan child activities to enhance the children's experiences.
   b. rarely use puppets in a conversational way, because it interrupts children's play.
   c. feel the large expense involved in supplying them is well worth it.
   d. find child language develops best without teacher modeling.

2. Puppets in preschool centers are used
   a. only by children.
   b. most often to present teacher-planned lessons.
   c. by both teachers and children.
   d. only when children ask for them.

3. Creative playacting (dramatization) is probably more appropriate
   a. for younger preschoolers, aged 2 to 3 years.
   b. for older preschoolers.
   c. when children are chosen for familiar characters' parts rather than selected from those children who volunteer for parts.
   d. when teachers help children stick to story particulars rather than promoting new lines or actions.

4. Identifying with a familiar story character through puppet use or playacting may give the child
   a. skills useful in getting along with others.
   b. greater insight into others' viewpoints.
   c. speaking skill.
   d. a chance to use creative imagination.
   e. all of the above.

5. If one is looking for a puppet with an expressive and active movement ability, one should use a
   a. plastic-headed puppet.
   b. papier-mâché puppet head with arms.
   c. cloth-headed puppet with arms.
   d. stick puppet.
   e. all of the above are equally active and expressive.

6. Punch and Judy types of child's play with puppets are
   a. to be expected and need teacher attention.
   b. a rare occurrence.
   c. best when teacher's performance sticks to the script.
   d. expected and should be ignored.
   e. a good puppetry modeling experience.

TEACHER-CONSTRUCTED AND CHILD-MADE PUPPETS

PAPIER-MÂCHÉ PUPPET HEADS

Materials

Styrofoam egg or ball (a little smaller than the size you want for the completed head), soft enough to have a holder inserted into it

neck tube (made from cardboard—about 1.5 inches wide and 5 inches long, rolled into a circle and taped closed, or plastic hair roller)

bottle (to put the head on while it is being created and to hold it during drying)

instant papier-mâché (from a craft store)

paints (poster-paint variety)

spray-gloss coat (optional)

white glue

(Use instant papier-mâché in well-ventilated teacher work areas.)

Construction Procedure

1. Mix instant papier-mâché with water (a little at a time) until it is like clay—moist, but not too wet or dry.

2. Place Styrofoam egg on neck tube (or roller) securely. Then place egg (or ball) on bottle so that it is steady.

3. Put papier-mâché all over head and half way down neck tube. Coating should be about a half-inch thick.

4. Begin making the facial features, starting with the cheeks, eyebrows, and chin. Then add eyes, nose, mouth, and ears.

5. When you are satisfied with the head, allow it to dry for at least 24 hours in a well-ventilated place.

6. When the head is dry, paint the face with poster paint. When that is dry, coat it with spray gloss finish to seal paint (optional).

7. Glue is useful for adding yarn hair, if desired.

SOCK PUPPETS

Materials

old sock
pink felt
sewing machine

Construction Procedure (Figure 15-8)

1. Use a wool sock or other thick sock. Turn it inside out and spread it out with the heel on top.

2. Cut around the edge of the toe (about 3 inches on each side).

3. Fold the mouth material (pink felt) inside the open part of the sock and draw the shape. Cut the mouth piece out and sew into position.

4. Turn the sock right side out and sew on the features.

FIGURE 15–8 Sock puppet construction.

480

EASY PUPPET

Obtain a stuffed animal. Try yard sales or outgrown shops. Cut a slit in the back of the animal large enough to insert a hand and remove the stuffing from the upper half. Use stiff cardboard or paper folded and cut for the animal's mouth. A sock or soft glove can be sewn to the slit opening to prevent stuffing escape. Note: Choose a stuffed animal with a cloth instead of molded face.

PAPER-BAG PUPPETS

Materials

> paper bags
> scissors
> crayons or marking pens
> paste
> yarn or paper scraps
> paint (if desired)

Construction Procedure

1. Making paper-bag puppets is quick and easy. Give each child a small paper sack. (No. 6 size works well.)

2. Show the children how the mouth works and let them color or paste features on the sack (Figure 15–9a).

3. You may wish to have the children paste a circle on for the face. Paste it on the flap part of the bag and then cut the circle on the flap portion so the mouth can move again.

4. Children may want to add special features to their paper-bag puppets, for example, eyes, tail, or ears (see Figure 15–9b). Another puppet face pattern is shown in Figure 15–9c.

STICK PUPPETS

A stick puppet is a picture or object attached to a stick (Figure 15–10). It moves when the puppeteer moves the puppet up and down or from side to side, holding the stick.

Materials

> paper
> glue
> scissors
> crayons
> craft sticks (or tongue depressors or
>   cardboard strips)

Construction Procedure

1. Characters and scenery can be drawn by children or can be preoutlined. Depending on the age of the children,

(a)   (b)   (c)

FIGURE 15–9 Paper-bag puppets.

FIGURE 15–10 Stick puppets.

the characters and scenery can then be colored or both colored and cut out.

2. Older children may want to create their own figures.

3. Stick puppets with verse pasted or written on their backs can introduce a poem. Stick puppets are easily made by tracing book characters or coloring-book figures, cutting them out, adding a stiff backing, and attaching a tongue depressor.

POP-UPS

Materials

heavy paper
glue
yarn
stick (tongue depressor or thinner sticks)
scissors

plastic
Styrofoam or paper cup
felt pens

Construction Procedure

1. Cut circle smaller than cup radius. Decorate face.

2. Slit the cup bottom in the center to allow sticks to move up and down.

3. Glue the face to the stick. Glue on yarn hair.

4. Slip puppet in the cup with stick through cup bottom so that the puppet disappears and can pop up.

SHADOW PUPPETS

Shadow puppets are easy to construct. Simple shapes made of stiff paper allow the audience to see the puppet's mass.

Materials

stiff paper
scissors
doweling sticks (hardware store)
tape
fabric
staple gun or thumb tacks
large picture frame (thrift store)

Construction Procedure

1. Cut puppet.

2. Attach rods using heavy tape (adhesive or electrical).

3. Stretch fabric over frame using a staple gun.

Hints

When purchasing fabric, take a flashlight to make sure light shines through it.

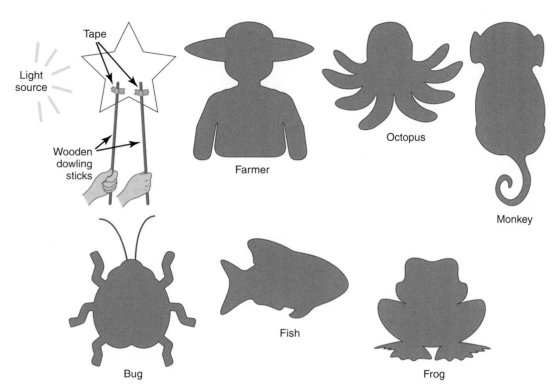

Light source

Tape

Wooden dowling sticks

Farmer

Octopus

Monkey

Bug

Fish

Frog

FIGURE 15–11 Shadow puppets.

Fabric, such as an old sheet, can be stretched and secured across a doorway.

Make sure a strong light source is available. It should be strong enough to shine on the back of the puppet when it is held up to the screen (Figure 15–11).

BOX PUPPET

Materials

one small (individual size) box with both ends intact
one piece of white construction paper, 6-by-9 inches
crayons or poster paints and brush
scissors
sharp knife
glue

Construction Procedure

1. Refer to Figure 15–12. Cut box in half as in view 1, with one wide side uncut. Fold over as in view 2.

2. On construction paper, draw the face of a person or an animal. Color or paint features and cut out the face.

3. Add yarn for hair, a few broom straws for whiskers, and so on, if desired.

4. Cut face along the line of the mouth and glue to box, as in view 4, so that lips come together as in view 5.

JUMPING JACK

Materials

stiff paper or oak tag brads
string
hole punch

FIGURE 15–12 Box puppet.

dowel
glue
curtain pull (optional)

Construction Procedure

1. Design and cut pattern, making arms and legs long enough to secure behind figure. Cut two body pieces (Figure 15–13).

2. Glue figure to dowel by inserting between front and back.

3. Brads act as joints. Hole-punch and add arms, legs, and string.

FINGER PUPPETS

Materials

fabric or cardboard
scissors
sewing machine
pattern
elastic ribbon

Construction Procedure

Cut and sew pieces. Insert stuffing after attaching elastic ring. Stiff paper or cardboard can also be used to make a puppet front (Figure 15–14).

FIGURE 15–13
Jumping jack.

Elastic band for finger

Band for finger

Cardboard

Tabs to press together to make finger ring

FIGURE 15–14 Finger puppets.

DECORATED PAPER-BAG PUPPETS

Materials

   5-by-8-inch paper bag
   string
   crayons or paint
   newspapers or cotton
   paste
   crepe paper or cloth for dress
   scissors

Construction Procedure

Draw a face on the upper part of bag; color. Stuff with cotton or newspaper. Put neck cylinder into head and tie string around neck. (Neck cylinder is made by rolling a piece of tag board and taping together. The roll should fit around the first finger.)

If the puppet needs hair, paste on. Add other distinguishing characteristics. Cut hole in paper or cloth and stick neck cylinder through the hole. Paste, sew, or otherwise fasten. Add hands or paws cut from tag board.

Movement

Place forefinger in neck tube to create movement.

STUFFED CLOTH PUPPET

Materials

   cloth (for head and dress)
   scissors
   needle and thread
   tag board for hands and feet
   material for hair (cotton, yarn, and so forth)

Construction Procedure

Draw head pattern and cut around it on a fold of cloth (white, tan, or pink). Sew around front and back, turn inside out, and stuff with cotton or rags. Insert neck tube and tie. Paint on face. Cut body (Figure 15–15) and sew to neck tube. Add hands and feet.

STUFFED PAPER PUPPET

Construction Procedure

Have the child draw himself or any character he chooses on a piece of butcher paper. Then trace and cut second figure for the

FOLD

Place this pattern on the fold of a piece of material, pin to it, then cut out piece. Cut another—you need a front and back. With right sides together, sew making 1/4" seams on sides. Turn right side out and press. Fold top of neck inside 1/4" and place around neck tube and glue.

Puppet hand—cut 2 for each hand and sew or glue together. Glue or sew to sleeve.

FIGURE 15–15 Basic puppet body.

Full-size version of this art can be found on the Online Companion™ at http://www.earlychilded.delmar.com

back. Staple edges together and stuff with crumpled tissue paper or other stuffing. Attach stick to hold it up, if desired.

ADDITIONAL PUPPET IDEAS

- ◆ plastic-bottle-head puppet
- ◆ Dust-mop-head puppet
- ◆ favorite-television-character puppet
- ◆ garden-glove puppets (different faces can be snapped on or attached with Velcro) (Figure 15–16)
- ◆ suspended-toy-from-stick puppets (add beads to feet to give them sound effects.)

DRAMA OUTLINE—ITSY BITSY SPIDER

Materials

black yarn spider with metal washer sewn on back or sewn on the "spider's" stomach
rainwater spout
flashlight
yellow cellophane circle big enough to cover flashlight's end
rubber band
watering can
bucket (optional)
water (optional)

FIGURE 15–16 Garden-glove puppets.

Preparation

1. Make spider from black yarn. Sew on washer. Make extra "dry" spider if using real water for this activity.

2. Buy water spout tubing from hardware store or construct from two milk cartons.

3. Cover flashlight front with yellow cellophane using rubber band. (This will represent the sun.)

4. Fill watering can. Place bucket if using real water.

Procedure

1. Present lyrics with hand motions or use sequence cards to refresh children.

2. Ask for child volunteers to act as spider, spout, rain, or sun. Give props.

3. Place volunteers in order of appearance.

4. Sing lyrics, hesitating to demonstrate parts: moving spider up spout to top, making rain, dropping spider down spout, shining sun, and crawling spider up the spout again.

5. Go through "Itsy, Bitsy Spider" with total group, cueing volunteers with hand motions.

6. Repeat with other volunteers if group is still interested. (Using imaginary water is best, but some teachers conduct this activity outside or in water play areas.)

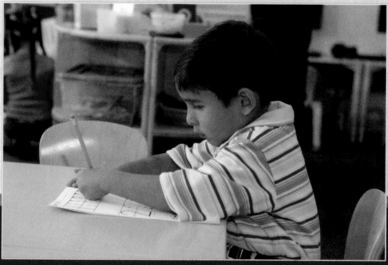

SECTION 6

Writing:

Print Awareness

and Use

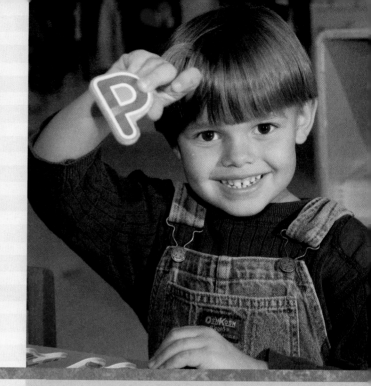

CHAPTER 16
Print—Early Knowledge and Emerging Interest

OBJECTIVES

After reading this chapter, you should be able to:

♦ Discuss children's development of small-muscle control in the hands.

♦ Outline the probable sequence of events occurring before a child prints her first recognizable alphabet letter.

♦ Describe printscript alphabets.

♦ Print both the lowercase and uppercase printscript alphabet.

♦ Describe classroom equipment and settings that promote printscript development.

♦ Plan a print-awareness activity.

KEY TERMS

alphabetic principle	orthographic	sight reading
interactive writing	awareness	writing
invented spelling	print awareness	

UPS

Cheney and Ong, 4-year-olds, are busy stuffing toy animals into boxes provided by their teacher, Mr. Sanchez. They ask for tape, and their teacher supplies strips of masking tape. He watches them struggle to carry the box outside and then pretend to knock on the door. Mr. Sanchez goes to the door. "Well hello. Is this for me?" he says. Cheney pretends to look at his hand and says, "Is this Cherrywood Preschool?" "Yes," the teacher answers. "Are you the deliverymen?" "No, we're from U-P-S," Ong says.

QUESTIONS TO PONDER

1. What does this vignette tell you about Ong and Cheney?

2. Could the teacher turn this dramatic play into some kind of additional print-awareness learning?

3. What type of teacher-supplied materials could have added depth to the boys' play and print knowledge?

Preschool teachers ask themselves two pertinent questions concerning print and teaching children to write in printscript: (1) is it appropriate to offer lessons (activities) that teach print letter recognition and formation at this age? And (2) how is instruction in printscript undertaken? Resolving these questions is made easier by this chapter's discussion.

Current ideas about the child's development of **writing** (printing) skill have undergone a major change. Preschool children are seen as writers. Older ideas promoted the idea that teaching children to print and read should not be undertaken until children are in kindergarten or first grade. It was believed that at that stage children are mature enough or possess the readiness skills that would make these tasks much easier. Writing and reading skills were thought to be different from listening and speaking skills. Speech was accomplished without direct or formal teaching over a long period, beginning in infancy. Educators have revised their thoughts.

The concept of early literacy suggests that the foundations of literacy develop from a child's early experiences with print before the onset of formal reading instruction. Educators take children's writing seriously, and they listen for their intended message and support writing development.

Symbol making is the essence of what it means to be human. Young children often talk about what they have done, constructed, and drawn, and they "read" meaning into their creations, a meaning they wish to communicate to others. Through talk with others, children invest their marks with meaning. Giving attention to children's work prompts children to translate their work's meaning to the interested adults. It is believed that this type of speech in children paves the way for their eventual use of written forms.

At some point, children gain the insight that print is categorically different from other kinds of visual patterns in their environment, and eventually they learn that print symbolizes language and can be produced by anyone. Children also begin to realize that print holds information. Educators urge teachers to help children see that print holds ideas, observations, stories, and plans.

A review of current research with preschoolers would agree that (1) adult-child shared book reading that stimulates verbal interaction can enhance language (especially vocabulary) development and knowledge about concepts of print, and (2) activities that direct young children's attention to the sound structure within spoken words and to the relationships between print and speech can facilitate learning to read with greater ease.

Preschool children already know something about the world of print from their environment. Most children form primitive hypotheses about letters, words, and messages, both printed and handwritten. West, Denton, and Germino-Hausken (2000), studying kindergartners, found that 37 percent of children entering kindergarten have a basic familiarity with print. It is a widely held view that learning to read and write will be easier for the child who has had rich preschool literacy experiences than for the child who has had little or limited literacy opportunities.

Much of young children's writing is a kind of exploratory play, common in the developmental beginnings of all symbolic media. **Print awareness** and beginning printing skill and reading awareness and beginning reading skills are now viewed as developing at younger ages, simultaneously with children's growing understandings of a number of other symbol systems. Print awareness describes the child's sensitivity to the presence and use of print in the world around her. When supported by an educative environment, young children compose connected written discourse using emergent forms long before they hold conventional ideas about writing. Children's scribbling, drawing-used-as-writing, nonphonetic strings of letters, and invented spellings

---

writing — the ability to use print to communicate with others.
print awareness — in early literacy, the child's growing recognition of the conventions and characteristics of a written language. It includes recognition of directionality in reading (left to right and top to bottom), that print forms words corresponding to speech, and that spaces separate words and other features.

are now accepted and honored as reflecting underlying understandings about writing.

The clues have been there for some time. Early childhood educators have always had children that asked questions and displayed early attempts and interest in printing. Preschool children can respond to and learn about visual features of print, know some letters, write some words, make up pretend writings such as letters to people, and dictate stories they want written before they have begun to consider how the words they say may be coded into print, and in particular how the sounds of speech are coded in print. Through informal daily literacy events and adult-child interactions (such as making useful signs), children learn the many purposes and the power of print in their lives and in those of adults. Adults expect children to talk before they read but may not have noticed that children are interested in writing before they can read.

Alphabet letters appear in 4-year-olds' drawings. Young children go through the motions of reading books, and some have a keen interest in numbers and measurement. This supports the idea that children are attempting to make sense out of what they encounter and are expanding their understandings of symbol systems on a number of fronts (Figure 16–1).

Children do not leap from illiteracy to an understanding that our writing system is alphabetic. They may have hypothesized many conclusions, and they may have tried writing with a variety of their own inventions after puzzling over the relationship between print and speech.

Professional practice promotes teachers' supporting, welcoming, and recognizing children's efforts and accepting children's correct and incorrect conclusions about printing, just as they accepted and supported incorrect or incomplete speech and welcomed it. Earlier practice may have led some teachers to either ignore or defer supportive guidance in printing, the rationale being that this instruction would come later in the child's schooling. Teachers are encouraged to have faith in children's ability to discover and develop their own writing theories and symbol systems, as they did when they taught themselves to speak. This takes place in a print-rich environment with responsive adults. Some educators worry about providing too many literacy-focused activities, materials, and furnishings in classrooms, fearing that they may displace other toys and other curricula. This may turn children's play into literacy work.

Teachers must be willing to introduce, demonstrate, and discuss print's relationship and use

FIGURE 16–1 Teachers promote interest by showing interest in children's printing attempts.

in daily activities to pique child interest. Optimal developmental opportunities can be missed in the very best equipped and print-prolific classroom environments. An environment conducive to a child's development of print awareness is a place where print is important and where interactions with print are a source of social and intellectual pleasure for individual children and the people who surround them. Preschoolers who observe and interact within a print-rich environment with sensitive and responsive teachers may discover that

- print is different from other kinds of visual marks and patterns.
- print appears on all kinds of surfaces and objects (Figure 16–2).
- print is almost everywhere.
- adults read picture books aloud but also read silently at times.
- print symbolizes oral language.
- print holds information.
- lots of different people and children know how to print and know what print says.

Through being read to frequently, preschoolers may know

- where one starts reading on a page.
- that reading moves from left to right.
- that at the end of a line, the reader returns to the left margin.
- that pages in a book are in a sequence usually starting with page 1.
- that there is a difference between letter, word, and sentence.
- that there are spaces between words.
- that there are marks, called punctuation marks, that have different names and meanings.
- that there are uppercase (big) and lowercase (little) letters.

Preschoolers will discover a number of other print-related concepts. For example, they also may become aware that written language functions to label, communicate, remind, request, record, and create.

A child will not learn the name of the letter *B*, the sound of the letter *B*, or how to print it, simply by being with adults, or by being with an adult who likes to read. Children learn these critical concepts because adults take the time and effort to teach them in an exciting, engaging, and understanding manner. Figure 16–3 is an example of a teaching assistant's approach.

Writing awareness and beginning writing attempts make more sense to children who have

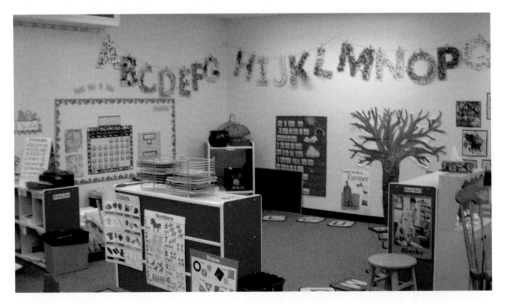

FIGURE 16–2 Print is at eye level and saturates this classroom area.

GRADUATE TEACHING ASSISTANT'S APPROACH

Child 1:	(3-year-old): I'm writing a letter to my daddy. How do you write "Daddy"?
Teacher:	Well, let's think about that. /d/, /d/, /d/. What letter do you think we might use to write /d/?
Child 2*:	[5-year-old]: D!
Teacher:	Yes. We do use D, but let's let Ana (fictitious) think about it. She's the one who is writing the word. If she needs help, I'll tell you and then you can tell me what your idea is.
Child 2:	OK.
Child 1*:	I can't make a D.
Child 2:	I can. I will show you. (*Gets up from his chair and puts his arm down next to the child's paper, indicating that he is ready to demonstrate.*)
Teacher:	Well, actually, wait just a minute. I'll grab the chart. (*Reaches toward an alphabet letter chart that is hanging from a book on the side of the paper display shelf in the writing center.*)
Child 2:	But I know how. I can show her.
Teacher:	I know that you know how, but Ana might like to know how you learned it, and she might like to know that this chart can show us how, so we'll just take a quick look at it, and, Allen (fictitious), get another piece of paper, honey. Let's not do our demonstration on Ana's paper. She'll write her own *D* after we show her how.
Child 2:	(*Draws a straight, vertical line, very deliberately on his paper.*)
Child 1:	(*Watches Child 2 with eyes wide and bright.*)
Teacher:	Ok, that's just great. Now, Ana, you make that part of the D on your paper. Where was it you thought you wanted to write "Daddy"?
Child 1:	(*Points to the middle of her paper.*)
Teacher:	Ok, you want it down here in the middle. OK, start a little over here (*gesturing to the left side of the paper, across from where the child had pointed*) so that you will have enough room for all of the letters we'll need to write "Daddy."
Child 1:	(*Moves to the spot indicated by the teacher's finger and draws a pretty good straight, vertical line.*) Now what?
Teacher:	Well, now, there's a curved line that comes out like this (*uses index finger to trace curved line in the D on the chart*), and then it goes back in to touch the line down here. Allen is going to show you how to do that on the *D* he is making on his paper.
Child 2:	(*Draws the curved line very carefully to complete the* D.)
Teacher:	OK, now you can add that curved line to finish your *D.* Start right up here at the top of the vertical line you have already drawn, and then move your marker out this way and then gradually down to touch the line down here (*uses finger to trace the path*).
Child 1:	(*Draws curved line.*) Now what?
Teacher:	Well, let's see. D /ae/, /ae/, Daddy. That's a really hard sound to know how to write.
Child 2:	No it isn't. My name starts with that sound.
Teacher:	That's right, it does, and you know what's really funny? Ana's name also starts with that sound, and the sound in her name is spelled with the same letter as the sound in your name. What a coincidence! (*Said as if she had just noticed this herself and thought that it was a remarkable discovery.*)
Child 2:	A!
Child 1:	A?

FIGURE 16–3 A teaching assistant helps a child print the word *Daddy*. *Child 1 = Ana; child 2 = Allen. (From Barone, D. M., & Morrow, L. M. [Eds.] [2003]. *Literacy and young children* [pp. 136–137]. Copyright © 2003. The Guilford Press. Used with permission.) *(continued)*

GRADUATE TEACHING ASSISTANT'S APPROACH–cont'd

Teacher:	Yes, *A*. Just as in (*says both names, one after the other, isolating the first vowel phoneme in each name before saying the rest of it.*)
Child 1:	I know how to write A! (*Proceeds to do it.*) Now, what is next?
Teacher:	Da /d/, /d/ . . .
Child 1:	D?
Teacher:	Yes, there are two of them.
Child 1:	I already did one.
Teacher:	Well, I mean there are two more in the middle.
Child 1:	(*Writes the two D's.*)
Teacher:	(*Offers verbal guidance to support recall of lines needed and their direction.*)
Child 1:	OK. Now what?
Teacher:	Daddy, Dadd /i/.
Child 1:	E! (*Child begins to position her marker to begin making an E.*)
Teacher:	Well, the sound is /i/, but we write it with the letter Y. Let me show you one on the chart. (*Same process as was used before is used to instruct Child 1 on making Y and then to help Child 1 to make one of her own.*) OK, that says "Daddy." (*Underlines it with her finger.*) Did you want to write something else?
Child 1:	No, I'm finished.

FIGURE 16–3 (*continued*)

experienced an integrated language arts instructional approach. The areas of speaking, listening, reading, and writing are interrelated. The child's ability to see how these areas fit together is commonly mentioned in school goals. Adults in classrooms communicate with others daily—both orally and in written form. Written communication offers daily opportunities for teachers to point out print's usefulness. Print's necessity can be discussed and shared.

Increased focus on children's early reading success in the United States has provided additional impetus for researching early writing and reading relationships. An increasing number of experts believe children establish early ideas about printing (writing) that serve as a basis for early printing and reading attempts. Some children can print a word (or many words) the first day they enter kindergarten, and a good number of children come to school believing that they can write. Their first attempts to print concentrate on messages rather than perfection. Generations of children have been asked to learn the letters of the alphabet,

sound and symbol correspondences, and a vocabulary of sight words before they learned to write or read. If the same were true of learning to speak, children would be asked to wait until all letter sounds were perfected at age 7 or 8 before attempting to speak. Early on children begin to understand that reading is getting meaning from print and they become increasingly aware of the different functions and uses of written language.

Based on the notion that the child constructs from within, piecing together from life experiences the rules of oral language, educators believe that if children are given time and supportive assistance, they can crack the writing and reading code by noticing regularities and incongruence, thus creating their own unique rules. Children would progress at their own speeds, doing what is important to them and doing what they see others do. Without formal instruction, they experiment with and explore the various facets of the writing process. They decorate letters and invent their own symbols—sometimes reverting to their own inventions even after they are well into distinguishing and reproducing different, recognizable alphabet letters. Some children expect others to know what they have written, regardless of their coding system.

Natural curiosity leads children to form ideas about print and its use in their lives. It used to be assumed that children know little or nothing about written language before they receive formal instruction. However, evidence indicates that children have extensive knowledge of some aspects of written language.

A few children may have developed both phonological awareness and phonemic awareness. Researchers report that roughly 15 percent of 3- and 4-year-old children can identify words that begin with a particular phoneme and about 25 percent can reliably identify rhyming words. Tests designed to measure print awareness have been found to predict future reading achievement. Children who live in an alphabetical, literate environment begin to hypothesize that there are relationships between oral and written language.

The concept of writing readiness began with some important figures from the past that influenced the directions that early childhood education has taken. It became popular to talk about writing readiness as being that time when an average group of children acquired the capacity, skills, and knowledge to permit the group to accomplish the task. Figure 16–4 compares traditional, readiness, and "natural" instructional approaches. It would be difficult to find an early childhood center that does not use some elements of each of the three approaches in the instructional program.

TRADITIONAL APPROACH

- providing play materials and free time
- supplying art materials, paper, writing tools, alphabet toys and games, chalkboard
- reading picture books
- planning program that excludes instruction in naming or forming alphabet letters
- providing incidental and spontaneous teaching about print

READINESS APPROACH

- providing writing materials and models
- planning program with introduction to tracing, naming alphabet letters, and naming shapes
- reading picture books
- providing a language arts classroom center
- channeling interested children into print and alphabet activities by offering supportive assistance

NATURAL APPROACH

- providing writing and reading materials and models
- planning program that emphasizes print in daily life
- promoting dramatic play themes that involve print, such as grocery store, restaurant, newspaper carrier, print shop, and office
- creating a writing center for the classroom
- supplying alphabet toys and models
- answering questions and supporting children's efforts
- making connections between reading and writing and speaking
- reading picture books

FIGURE 16–4 Comparisons of instructional approaches in printing.

STARTING FROM A DIFFERENT PLACE

At about 16 to 20 months, some toddlers become interested in scribbling. One sees them grasp a drawing or marking tool in their fist and use it in sweeping, whole-arm motions to make marks. Motions can be vigorous, rhythmic, scrubbing, and repetitive and may include sharp stabs at the paper, which tears because of the pressure applied. Adults can wisely provide sturdy, large pieces of paper taped down onto a surface that can take the punishment. Large flattened brown grocery bags work well.

Scribbling involves decision making. It coincides with young children's emerging sense of autonomy. Children make decisions about line, color, and the placement of marks on the paper. They also use and gain control over the tools of their home and classroom—crayons, markers, pencils, paper and so on—if it is regarded as a valued activity.

Teachers need to consider all enrolled children ready to learn and progress in language and literacy, with each child possessing a different past experience. Past opportunity may have dramatically molded the individual child's literacy behaviors and language competency. Teachers hope to expand language competencies that exist and introduce children to new activities and opportunities.

Much of young children's writing is exploratory. When children show interest and share in discussions about written marks, they begin to understand print's meaning and functional use.

Through personally motivated and personally directed trial and error—a necessary condition of their literacy development—children try out various aspects of the writing process. They sometimes interact and collaborate with peers who are more literate (Figure 16–5). Competent others provide help and eventually children function without supportive assistance.

Should One Systematically Teach Writing Tool Grip?

Although somewhat controversial, some early childhood programs are instituting implicit instruction for 3- and 4-year-olds on how to grip a writing tool. These programs purposefully provide broken crayons (ones of a short length that glide well) and promote young children's use of a finger gripping motion rather than whole hand grasping. Children are shown what these programs believe to be the most efficient and comfortable finger gripping position. It is believed that this type of grip allows the best control of the writing tool and aids eventual speed in writing (printing). Children who have already found their own unique grip are shown a second way that they can choose to adopt. Program plans include enjoyable activities that promote small motor control with a finger pinching action, such as picking up small objects. Instructions for the "right" tool grip are as follows: hold the writing tool between a bent thumb and a first finger (index) pointed at the tool's marking tip, with the tool resting on the middle finger; the ring and little finger should be bent inward toward the palm.

Some educators are less enthusiastic about this instructional approach for many reasons, including research that points out that about half of all 3-year-olds have already mastered the grip. Other educators feel that child motivation and interest is paramount before grip instruction takes place.

Advocates counter by describing a writing fundamentals curriculum that is without

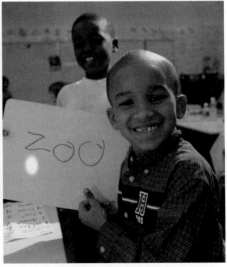

FIGURE 16–5 Teachers promote both individual and collaborative printing activities.

pressure, game-like, and uses songs with clever rhythms to introduce concepts and terms. Each early childhood program will decide how or if grip instruction or writing fundamentals instruction will be included in its program. Parents frequently demonstrate their own writing grip to their children, and educators usually initiate instruction with a child who exhibits awkwardness or frustration. A right-handed teacher may find that demonstrating a writing grip is difficult with a left-handed child because the paper is slanted in a different direction than for right-handed children. Teachers routinely tape or secure writing paper to tables or large surfaces so the paper won't slip away from early writers or they may show how holding the paper with the other hand solves the problem.

RESEARCH IN WRITING DEVELOPMENT

In *Literacy Before Schooling* (1982), researchers Ferreiro and Teberosky revolutionized educators' thinking about young children's development of print knowledge and writing. Subsequent research in children's self-constructed knowledge of alphabet forms and printing has followed, using anthropological, psychological, and other investigative approaches. Ferreiro and Teberosky identified three developmentally ordered levels.

First Level

In this level, children

- search for criteria to distinguish between drawing and writing. Example: "What's this?" referring to their artwork.
- realize that straight and curved lines and dots are present but organized differently in print. Example: Rows and rows of curved figures, lines, and/or dots in art.
- reach the conclusion that print forms are arbitrary and ordered in a linear fashion.
- accept the letter shapes in their environment rather than inventing new ones.

Example: Rows of one letter appear in linear fashion in art.

- recognize from literacy-rich environments written marks as "substitute objects" during their third year. Example: "What does this say, teacher?" or "This says 'Mary.'"

Second Level

In this level, children

- look for objective differences in printed strings.
- do not realize that there is a relationship between sound patterns and print.

Third Level

In this level, children

- accept that a given string of letters represents their name and look for a rational explanation of this phenomenon.
- may create a syllabic hypothesis.
- may print letter forms as syllables heard in a word. Example: I C (I see).
- may develop knowledge about particular syllables and what letters might represent such a syllable.
- may look for similar letters to write similar pieces of sound.
- begin to understand that printing uses alphabet letters that represent sounds; consequently, to understand print, one must know the sound patterns of words.

What conclusions of this landmark research may affect language arts program planning and early educators' interaction techniques? Certainly, teachers will note attending children's active attempts to understand print. They will realize that each child constructs her own ideas and revises these understandings as more print is noticed and experienced. The seemingly strange questions children ask or off-the-wall answers some children give in classroom discussions about print may now be seen as reflecting their inner thoughts at crucial points in their print development. As teachers view children's artwork, they will see more readily early print forms, and they will continue their attempts to provide literacy-rich, print-rich classroom environments.

Some preschoolers demonstrate that they know the names and shapes of alphabet letters. They may also know letters form words and represent sounds. They might have grasped the idea that spoken words can be written and then read. They may be able to express daily uses of written words. Why would a young child write or pretend to write? It is not an easy motor task. Is it simple imitation or is it done for adult reaction? Do children do so because there is an inner drive to know or become competent? Research has yet to answer these questions. Teachers conjecture reasons with each young child they meet who has beginning printing skills. The reasons why children pretend to write are not the most important thing; what matters more are teacher reactions and their commitment to providing additional opportunities to nourish and expand what already exists.

YOUNG CHILDREN'S PROGRESS

Baker and Schiffer (2007) suggest that learning to write begins as children gain familiarity with the alphabet, learn about writing instruments, and recognize simple words in everyday places, such as *STOP* on the familiar red street sign. At some point, children learn that written marks have meaning. Just as they sought the names of things, they now seek the names of these marks and, later, the meanings of marks. Because each child is an individual, this may or may not happen during the preschool years. One child may try to make letters or numbers. Another child may have little interest in or knowledge of written forms. Many children are somewhere between these two examples.

Preschool children may recognize environmental print words before they know the name of any alphabet letters. This is termed **sight reading**, and some preschool children may recognize most of the children's names in their group. Quite a few researchers believe a period of time exists when a young child conceives of a certain alphabet letter as representing a person or object (for example, all "B" words remind the child of her own name). At that point, the child may say, "'B', that's my name." A child may not understand that the alphabet is a complete set of letters representing speech sounds used in writing, but rather, she may have a partial and beginning view of the **alphabetic principle**. Figure 16–6 displays possible child understandings concerning the alphabetic principle.

Writing (printscript) is complex. Many subcomponents of the process need to be understood. Development may occur at different rates, with spurts and lags in different knowledge areas. Besides the visual learning of letter features and forms, the ability to manually form shapes, and knowing that writing involves a message, a writer must listen to the sounds of her inner speech and find matching letters representing those sounds. Because letter follows letter in printing, the

---

THE ALPHABETIC PRINCIPLE

The child may:

- understand that letters have different shapes.
- identify some letters by name.
- notice some words start with the same letter.
- realize letters make sounds.
- match some sounds to letters correctly.
- possess a sight word vocabulary—usually her own and peer's names.
- realize alphabet letters are a special category of print.

FIGURE 16–6 The alphabetic principle.

---

sight reading — the ability to immediately recognize a word as a whole without sounding it out.
alphabetic principle — the awareness that spoken language can be analyzed as strings of separate words and that words, in turn, as sequences of syllables and phonemes within syllables.

child needs to make continuous intellectual choices and decisions.

Many events happen between the ages of 3 and 5. Children begin to vary their marks and move from imitation to creation. They produce a mixture of real letters, mock letters, and innovative symbols. A few written messages are readable. These actions signal several new behaviors and child discoveries. These follow.

- ◆ They are attending to the fine features of writing, noting shapes and specific letters.
- ◆ They are developing an early concept of sign—the realization that symbols stand for something.
- ◆ They are recognizing that there is variation in written language.

Children refine and enlarge these concepts by experimenting with writing. They draw, trace, copy, and even invent marks and letter forms of their own.

Print awareness is usually developed in the following sequence:

1. The child notices adults making marks with writing tools.
2. The child notices print in books and on signs. When this time comes, a child is increasingly aware of all the print in the world around her—street signs, food labels, newspaper headlines, printing on cartons, books, billboards, everything. He may try to read everything. Already having a good foundation in translating spoken words to print, she may move on and try printing. If help is provided when she asks for it, she progresses. It can be a very exciting time for her.
3. The child realizes that certain distinguishable marks make her name.
4. The child learns the names of some of the marks—usually the first letter of her name. While building a sizable store of words recognized on sight, children will begin to make finer and finer distinctions about print by using more and more visual cues. They begin to pay attention to individual letters, particularly the first ones in words.

The child's imitation of written forms usually develops in the following sequence:

1. The child's scribbles are more like print than artwork or pure exploration (Figure 16–7).
2. Linear scribbles are generally horizontal with possible repeated forms. Children's knowledge of linear directionality may have been displayed in play in which they lined up alphabet blocks, cut out letters and pasted them in a row, or put magnetic board letters in left-to-right rows (Figure 16–8).

FIGURE 16–7 Scribbles are sometimes print-like.

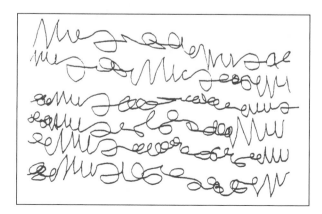

FIGURE 16–8 Linear scribbles.

3. Individual shapes are created, usually closed shapes displaying purposeful lines (Figure 16–9).

4. Letter-like forms are created.

5. Recognizable alphabet letters are printed and may be mirror images or turned on sides, upside down, or in upright position (Figure 16–10).

6. Words or groupings of alphabet letters with spaces between are formed.

7. **Invented spelling** appears; this may include pictured items along with alphabet letters (Figure 16–11).

8. Correctly spelled words with spaces separating words are produced.

FIGURE 16–10 Recognizable alphabet letters.

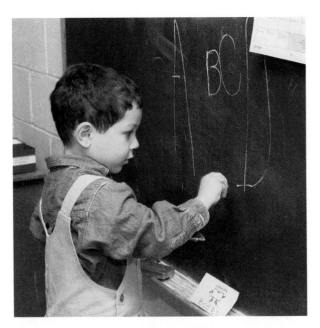

FIGURE 16–9 This boy has just made a closed-shape letter with purposeful lines.

FIGURE 16–11 Child read as "Blast off rocket to the moon."

invented spelling — the result of an attempt to spell a word whose spelling is not already known, based on a writer's knowledge of the spelling system and how it works.

INVENTED SPELLING (DEVELOPMENTAL SPELLING)

Invented spelling is something children do naturally. It is a temporary phenomenon that is later replaced with conventional spelling. Teachers, until the mid to late 1980s, gave young children the idea that until they learned to read, they needed to write only those words they had memorized or copied. Research has changed educational philosophy and methods. It suggests that children's literacy emerges during a span of several years. As young children slowly begin to understand what letters mean and how to string them together, some children will invent spelling. Often, the beginning consonant sound of a particular word is printed. A whole sequence might shortly appear and consist of single-letter words.

The invented-spelling stage casts teachers in the role of detectives trying to ascertain meanings that the child may perceive as obvious. In their early attempts to write, preschool children invent a system of spelling that follows logical and predictable rules before they learn the conventional forms.

Vowels are commonly omitted in invented spellings. Words appear that may look like a foreign language—*dg* for dog, and *jragin* for dragon.

Identifiable stages in invented spelling are followed by some children and are given here for teacher reference.

1. Spelling awareness—alphabet letters represent words. Example: C (see), U (you).
2. Primitive spelling with no relationship between spelling and words—numbers and letters are differentiated. Example: tsOlf..DO.
3. Prephonetic spelling—initial and final consonants may become correct. Example: KT (cat), CD (candy), RT (write), WF (with).
4. Phonetic spelling—almost a perfect match between the symbols and sounds. Some vowels are used. Some sight words may be correctly spelled. Example: SUM (some), LIK (like), MI (my), ME (me).
5. Correct spelling.

Invented spelling serves as an important stage in the process of deciphering the sound-symbol system of written language. It is believed that at this point, phonics becomes important to children. Early on, the child selects letters in her inventive spelling that have some relationship to how the word is pronounced. Large items such as "elephants" may be written in huge letters and with more letters than small objects, because the child is operating under the misconception that bigger necessitates more letters. A perfectly logical conclusion! The names of letters may represent words (*u* for you) or parts of words. Young writers' invented spelling uses personal logic rather than or in conjunction with standard spelling, and the child's strategy of using a name of a letter has a frustrating side. There are only 26 alphabet letters but almost twice that many phonemes, or sound units. What do children do when they encounter a sound for which there is no ready letter-name match? They use a system of spelling logic based primarily on what they hear but also influenced by subconscious knowledge of the general rules of language usage and of how sounds are formed in the mouth when spoken.

What should an early childhood educator do when confronted with invented spelling in a child's work? Faith that children who are given help will evolve toward conventional spelling is needed. Invented spelling gives young writers early power over words. Professional writers do not worry about correct spelling on their first drafts and neither do inventive spellers.

Many primary teachers write out the standard spelling for words below a child's invented spelling. By doing so, teachers honor the original but provide further information so children can compare their spelling inventions with regular standard spellings. Inventive spellers who realize their spelling differs from text in books and the world around them may experience frustration and confusion. Teachers at this juncture may introduce phoneme spelling by "sounding out" words that they print.

Some educators recommend putting a small teacher translation on papers containing invented spelling. They record the child's intended message (or a translation of what the child has tried to write) using small letters on a remote corner of the page or on its back. This can be a satisfying arrangement if the child has no objection to the practice. It also gives the teacher the opportunity to observe and hear the child decode her message in her own words.

In this way a family examining "sent-home papers" can possibly understand the thought processes the child used to write the message and understand the child's great accomplishment. A parent-teacher discussion is usually necessary for parents to realize that beginning attempts are not immediately corrected.

Teachers need to use these techniques carefully with older preschoolers, being mindful of the child's inventiveness and pride in her work. Many preschoolers object to teachers adding any marks on their papers.

When a child asks the teacher to write a specific word, the teacher has a chance to help the child with letter sounds (rather than letter names), saying *d-o-g* as she writes it. Time permitting, the teacher can add, "It starts with the alphabet letter d, like Dan, D-a-n."

GOALS OF INSTRUCTION

Providing experiences that match a child's interests and abilities is the goal of many early childhood centers. Most schools plan activities for those children who ask questions or seem ready and then proceed if the children are still interested. Others work with children on an individual basis. Yet others believe in providing a print-rich environment where the child will progress naturally with supportive adults who also model an interest in print and point out uses of print in daily activities. Teachers should plan activities involving authentic writing (printing), that is, writing done for the "real world" rather than for contrived school purposes. An authentic written message often involves a child's need or desire. It is possible to combine these approaches. A teacher might

say, "Let's say the word you are trying to print very slowly, and stretch it out so we can hear its sounds."

As with other language abilities, goals include stimulating further interest and exploration. This should be done in such a way that the child is not confused by instruction that is too advanced or boring.

As stated previously, an important goal concerning print awareness is relating writing to other language arts areas. It is almost impossible to not do so. Teachers are encouraged to consciously mention connections so that children will understand how writing fits in the whole of communicating. Figure 16–12 is a listing of both print and book awareness understandings that early childhood educators endeavor to promote before a child begins kindergarten.

Another important teacher goal would be having the ability to print every lowercase and uppercase alphabet letter in excellent form, so as to offer children the best model possible.

PRINT AND BOOK AWARENESS GOALS

The child understands that:

- reading obtains information from books.
- writing communicates thoughts and ideas.
- print can carry messages.
- letters are different from numerals.
- book illustrations carry meaning.
- print can be read.
- books have authors who create books and their titles.
- print is read from left to right and top to bottom.
- alphabet letters in print can form words.
- alphabet letters have names.
- words are separated by spaces.
- spoken words can be written down.
- print has everyday functional uses (for example, shopping lists, messages, recipes, signs).
- one can follow print with one's eyes as it is read aloud.

FIGURE 16–12 Print and book awareness goals.

COORDINATION

Children's muscle control follows a timetable of its own. Control of a particular muscle depends on many factors—diet, exercise, inherited ability, and motivation, to name a few. A baby can control her neck and arms long before her legs. A child's muscle control grows in a head-to-toe fashion. Muscles closer to the center of the body can be controlled long before those of the hands and fingers. Large-muscle control comes before small-muscle control (Figure 16–13). Think of a toddler walking; the toddler's legs seem to swing from the hips. Just as each child starts walking and develops muscle control at different ages, so too does each child develop fine motor control, which influences her ability to control a writing tool.

Precise writing is extremely difficult for some 3- and 4-year-olds, who typically grasp writing tools in their fists and guide them with movements started at the shoulder, elbow, or wrist. With the pivot and the writing tool point so far apart, children can't help but write large. Preschoolers' spatial skills are limited, and it can be difficult for them to construct and combine lines. Four-year-olds with more advanced fine motor skills can hold a pencil in a well-controlled finger and thumb grasp (Figure 16–14).

COGNITIVE DEVELOPMENT

Realization that written symbols exist is a first step in writing. The discovery that written language is simply spoken language, ideas, or communication is another step. Mental growth, which allows a child to see similarities and differences in written symbols, comes before the ability to write. The child recognizes that a written mark is a shape made by the placement of lines.

Seven prerequisite skill areas for handwriting follow.

- small-muscle development and coordination
- eye-hand coordination
- ability to hold writing tools properly
- ability to form basic strokes (circles and straight lines)
- letter perception

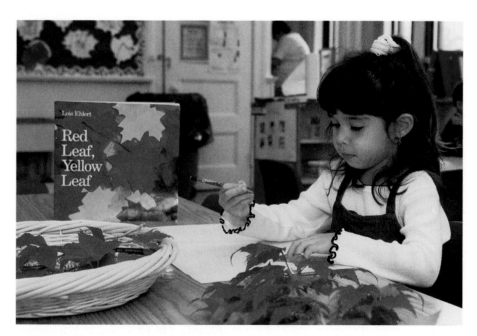

FIGURE 16–13 The small-muscle control Ria is using to trace a leaf will be needed when she begins to print.

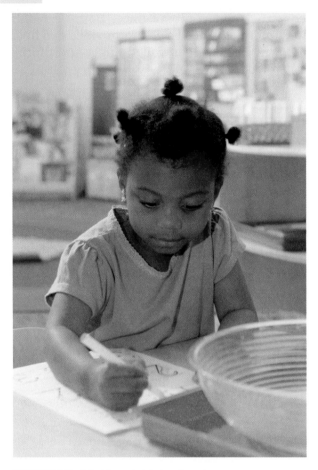

FIGURE 16–14 This child displays her own unique finger-and-thumb grasp.

◆ orientation to printed language, which includes a desire to write and communicate, including the child's enjoyment of writing her own name

◆ left-to-right understanding

A number of listed skills deal with the child's cognitive development. Through past experiences, including child's play, ideas about print and writing have been formed.

PLAY AND WRITING

Print, signs, and writing imaginary messages often become part of a dramatic play sequence. During play, children may pretend to read and write words, poems, stories, and songs, and they may actually make a series of marks on paper. Play encourages children to act as if they are already competent in and able to control the activity under consideration. Through pretend play, they may feel that they are already readers and writers; at least a beginning move toward eventual literacy takes place. Children observe families using reading and writing in their daily lives. These activities are given status. Early childhood teachers can build on children's early attitudes by modeling, demonstrating, and providing dramatic play opportunities involving print, which promote collaborative peer printing.

DRAWING EXPERIENCE

A young child scribbles if given paper and a marking tool. As the child grows, the scribbles are controlled into lines that she places where desired (Figure 16–15). Gradually, the child begins to draw circles, then a face, later a full figure, and so on. Children draw their own symbols representing what they see around them. Educators urge teachers to examine one child's drawings over a few weeks' time; they may discover that the child is working on a basic plan. Perhaps a child makes the same pattern or schema again and again. It may seem as if the child has learned a plan of action for producing the pattern or schema. This gives the child enough control over pencil and paper

FIGURE 16–15 Children start writing by scribbling and, when older, drawing symbols of the world around them.

to play with variations, which often leads to new discoveries. The length of time it takes this process to develop differs with each child.

A profound connection exists between experience and ability in drawing and interest in and ability to write (Figure 16–16). Drawings and paintings not only communicate children's thinking (when they reach the level of drawing that is representative of the environment) but also often display early attempts to create symbols. Some of these symbols may be recognized by adults, but others seem to be unique and represent the world in the child's own way. Children often want to talk about their work and create stories to accompany graphics.

Because alphabet letters are more abstract than representative drawing, most educators suggest that drawing precedes writing. One research study identified a characteristic that was common to almost all children in the study who read early and continued to hold their lead in reading achievement: the children were described by their parents as "pencil-and-paper kids," whose starting point of curiosity about written language was an interest in scribbling and drawing.

FIGURE 16–16 Nontoxic felt-tip pens (markers) are standard preschool materials.

WRITING AND EXPOSURE TO BOOKS

Probably the most common experience that promotes a child's interest in print is hearing and seeing picture books read over and over. Through repeated exposure, the child comes to expect the text to be near or on the same page as the object depicted. Two- and three-year-olds think that pictures in a book tell the story; as they gain more experience, they notice that the reader reads the print, not the pictures. Memorized story lines lead to children's questions about print on book pages. Once a word is recognized in print, copying that word onto another piece of paper or manipulating magnetic alphabet letters to form the word is a natural outgrowth. This activity usually leads to parent attention and approval and further attempts. Scribblers, doodlers, drawers, and pencil-and-paper kids are all labels researchers have used to describe children who have an early interest in writing, and much of what they do has been promoted by seeing print in their favorite books.

Stages of print recognition are believed to exist, starting with a stage in which the text and the picture are not differentiated. Then children begin to expect that the text is a label for the picture. In a third stage, the text is expected to provide cues with which to confirm predictions based on the picture. Some important concepts that young children gradually understand concerning print are

- the print, not the pictures in a book, tells the story.
- there are alphabet letters.
- words are clusters of letters.
- there are first letters and last letters in words.
- alphabet letters exist in uppercase and lowercase.
- spaces in printing are there for a reason.
- punctuation makes words have meaning.

Children may notice the left-to-right and top-to-bottom direction of printing and also the left-page-first directional feature.

It is important to promote the idea that there are different purposes for print and text, and that it appears in different forms depending on its purpose. Road signs have large block print and may be colorful and reflective to alert pedestrians and drivers both day and night. This fact is an example of both purpose and form.

There are other examples in classrooms, such as hot and cold written on water handles. Lists of print words, newspapers, dictionaries, and poetry usually look different from picture book text, whose purpose usually is to tell a story.

The acquisition of skills in writing and reading and the development of the attitude that books are enjoyable involve more than academic or technical learning. These skills flourish with a warm physical and emotional base with shared enjoyment and intimacy. Most experts believe that considerable support exists for the notion that oral language provides a base for learning to write. The importance of emotionally satisfying adult-child interactions in all areas of language arts cannot be overestimated.

Alphabet Books

Children's books in print before the twentieth century were mostly informational and moralistic. Alphabet books suited the then prevailing public view that a good children's book should promote learning. Presently, library collections for young children include a variety of alphabet books. Although many are in print and some are classic favorites, new titles continually appear. It is said that almost every author of young children's literature yearns to develop a unique alphabet book. The following are some recommended titles:

Bunting, E. (2002). *Girls A to Z.* Honesdale, PA: Boyd Mills Press. (A girl-can-be-anything theme.)

Fleming, D. (2002). *Alphabet under construction.* New York: Henry Holt and Company. (Suits toddlers and preschoolers, with colorful and playful illustrations.)

Kirk, D. (2002). *Miss Spider's A B C.* New York: Scholastic. (Preparing for a birthday party.)

Lester, A. (1998). *Alice and Aldo.* Boston: Houghton Mifflin. (Alphabet letters A to Z introduced through Alice's chronological daily activities [like breakfast in bed].)

Paul, A. (1999). *Everything to spend the night from A to Z.* New York: DK Publishing. (The overnight bag brought for an overnight stay with Grandpa yields A to Z objects.)

When children are asking for alphabet letter names, and when alphabet letters are appearing in their art or writing, alphabet books can become favorites. Teachers notice that a first interest in alphabet letters often appears when the child sees her printed name and then notices similar letters in friends' names.

Ideas for ways to build alphabet books into further classroom activities follow.

◆ Paint on a giant alphabet letter shape.

◆ Hide an alphabet letter in a large drawing and have children search for it.

◆ Make a class alphabet book by outlining large alphabet letters on pages and encouraging interested individual children to decorate a letter.

◆ Create a "Who looked at this book today?" chart. Add children's names to the chart if they browsed the book.

PLANNING A PROGRAM FOR PRINT AWARENESS AND PRINTING SKILL

Program planning is often done on an individual basis, but standards have been initiated and used as a basis for program planning in an increasing number of child development centers (Figure 16–17). If group instruction is planned, it deals with general background information concerning print use during the school day and how it relates to children's lives, including print use in the home and community.

A great deal of spontaneous and incidental teaching takes place. Teachers capitalize on children's questions concerning mail, packages, signs, and labels. In most preschool settings, print is a natural part of living, and it has many interesting features that children can discover and notice when teachers focus attention on print.

STANDARDS

- understands that print is used for different functions
- understands that speech can be written down
- understands that print carries a message
- understands that illustrations carry meaning but cannot be read
- understands that books have titles and authors
- understands concept of word—letters are grouped to form words, and words are separated by spaces
- understands concepts of directionality—front-to-back, left-to-right, and top-to-bottom movement on a page
- understands that letters function differently than numbers

LEARNING EXPERIENCES

- observes varied uses of print for various purposes (e.g., shopping lists, recipes and other simple directions, and letters and messages) and participates in their use
- observes adults writing as they say the words aloud
- participates in composing process by offering ideas and language for others to write down
- attends to print during Big Book activities
- refers to books by their titles; is beginning to understand that a book represents a person's ideas and that this person is the author
- engages in opportunities to draw and "write" independently
- observes and follows along as adults track print from left to right while reading aloud; browses through books from front to back
- participates in opportunities to write own name

FIGURE 16–17 Typical standards and learning experiences: concepts of print. From Strickland, D. S., & Schickendanz, J. A. (2006). *Learning about print in preschool: Working with letters, words, and beginning links with phonemic awareness.* Newark, DE: International Reading Association.

Most teachers realize that children will explore graphic symbols on their own, often inventing as they go and constructing and revising understandings as they proceed. A supportive classroom environment allows children to design their own route to further knowledge about print. It is critical for children to have a literacy-rich, risk-free environment that includes time to invent, to play, and to experiment with written language for meaningful purposes in an authentic context while interacting with knowledgeable others. Such experiences allow children to work through questions and perplexities, and to build conceptualizations and understandings in ways meaningful to them. As children compare their inventions with the written language around them,

particularly their names, they deepen their understandings of the complexities of our written language system.

A discussion is necessary here concerning the practice of asking the child to form alphabet letters and practice letter forms. The dangers in planning an individual or group experience of this nature are multiple. One has to consider whether a child has the physical and mental capacity to be successful and whether the child has an interest in doing the exercise or is simply trying to please adults.

The logical progression in learning about letters is to first learn letter names and then learn letter shapes. The child then has a solid mnemonic peg on which to hang the concept of "letter" as the concept is learned. Activities such as singing the alphabet song, reading alphabet books, and playing with alphabet magnets or puzzles help preschoolers learn letters. The uppercase letters are larger and research suggests that they are the easiest forms for preschoolers to reproduce.

Parents often offer only uppercase letters when asked by their child to print. Before learning to read, a child will need to know both forms. Preschools often present "big" and "little" together in the school's visual environment. It is the uppercase letters that most children recognize when they enter kindergarten. Preschool and kindergarten teachers also print children's names with an uppercase first letter followed by lowercase letters in printscript.

Teachers encourage children to print ("write") their own names on their artwork when they believe children have an interest in printing. Any child attempt is recognized and given attention. These teachers may also say, "May I write your name on the back? With two names, one on the front and one on the back, we will find your work quickly when it's time to leave school." Teachers print names on the upper left corner of the children's work because that is the spot reading starts on any given page written in English.

Early writing instruction is not a new idea. Maria Montessori (1967a) (a well-known educator and designer of teaching materials) and numerous other teachers have offered instruction in writing (or printing) to preschoolers. Montessori encouraged the child's tracing of letter forms using the first two fingers of the hand as a prewriting exercise. She observed that this type of light touching seemed to help youngsters when writing tools were later given to them. Montessori (1967a) designed special alphabet letter cutouts as one of a number of prewriting aids. These cutouts were thought to help exercise and develop small muscles and create sight-touch sensations, fixing the forms in memory.

In seventeenth- and eighteenth-century England, a gingerbread method of teaching alphabet letters was developed. As a child correctly named a letter-shaped cookie or a word formed by cookies, she was allowed to eat it (or them).

This is offered here to point out past educators' practices rather than to recommend.

This text recommends print activity planning that concentrates on awareness of print and its uses in everyday life plus helpful teacher interaction and encouragement given to children who show more than a passing interest. When a child asks for information concerning print or asks to be shown how to print, she is displaying interest and following her own curriculum.

How to Make the ABCs Developmentally Appropriate

When a print-rich classroom environment includes books, charts, labels, printed children's names, and other functional daily use of print in the classroom's daily activities, children are bound to see alphabet letters as a natural part of their world and develop curiosity about them.

Teachers examine activities and take advantage of teachable moments. Educators realize alphabet knowledge prompts phonemic awareness. Teachers promote children's fluency in naming alphabet letters. Fluency can be defined as speed and accuracy. Children fluent in alphabet letter names can recognize and correctly name alphabet letters without hesitation, thereby indicating that letter names have been well learned.

Introduction of alphabet books is probably the most common and professionally acceptable vehicle for teaching letter names; the alphabet song is a close second. Alphabet activities can be enjoyable and game-like or can be a natural outgrowth of daily schedules and happenings.

Following are samples of alphabet-related activities.

Name of the Day. One child's name is chosen and discussed at circle time. The first alphabet letter in the child's name is named and searched for in room displays.

Alphabet Letter Sorting Game. A teacher-made box with slots under alphabet letters is provided, along with a deck of teacher-made alphabet cards. A child (or children) decide what card is slotted, and then the box is lifted and the cards retrieved for the next child. The box can be a large cardboard box upended with letters on the box and adjacent cut slots. This game needs a simple introduction and demonstration.

Alphabet Chart Game. The teacher posts large alphabet letters on large paper around the room. Child volunteers choose how to get to one letter from the starting place to touch the letter and then how to get to the next. (Every child gets a turn.) The teacher may have to start by saying, "Let's tiptoe to the letter C" or "Who can think of a way to get to 'M'"?

Designing Game Activities. When designing games, remember that in developmentally appropriate games

- everyone gets a turn.
- clear directions (rules) are introduced.
- everyone wins.
- competition is inappropriate.
- cooperation is promoted.
- praise or prizes are omitted.
- musical games are enjoyed.
- movement games are wiggle reducers if they end on a cooling-down note.
- every child who wants to play is included.
- game parts or visuals are sturdy.
- frustrating game elements should not be included.

Remember also that these games are meant to promote listening skills and problem solving. It is recommended that alphabet letters be introduced. Most early childhood program staffs specifically designate exactly which letter form they will offer first and affirm alphabet letters named by children in either uppercase or lowercase. Teaching the sounds of alphabet letters is an instructional decision based on children's age, interest, and ability. Schools decide if it is developmentally appropriate and whether it is done only on a one-to-one basis.

A phonetic alphabet pronunciation guide is included in the Appendix. Teachers offering letter sounds should know this guide well.

ENVIRONMENT AND MATERIALS

Children's access to drawing tools—magic markers, chalk, pencils, crayons, brushes—is important so that children can make their own marks. It is suggested that teachers create a place where children can comfortably use these tools.

The following early childhood materials help the child use and gain control of small arm and finger muscles in preparation for writing.

- puzzles
- pegboards
- small blocks
- construction toys
- scissors
- eyedroppers

Most early childhood centers plan activities in which the child puts together, arranges, or manipulates small pieces. These are sometimes called tabletop activities and are available for play throughout the day. A teacher can encourage the use of tabletop activities by having the pieces arranged invitingly on tables or resting on adjacent shelves.

The following are examples of materials common in print-immersion classrooms.

- labels—pictures or photographs accompanied by corresponding words
- charts and lists—charts that convey directions, serve as learning resources (pictures and names of children in alphabetical order), organize the class (attendance roster or class calendar), show written language as a reminder (children's sign-up lists)
- materials and activities—various materials, including alphabet toys, puzzles, stamps, magnetic letters, and games, along with clever teacher-made materials (Figure 16–18) or commercial furnishings, such as blocks, stuffed alphabet-shaped pillows, alphabet rugs, and wall hangings
- books and other resources—a variety of books and magazines, poetry, newspapers, computer software, picture dictionaries, riddle and novelty books, and other printed material

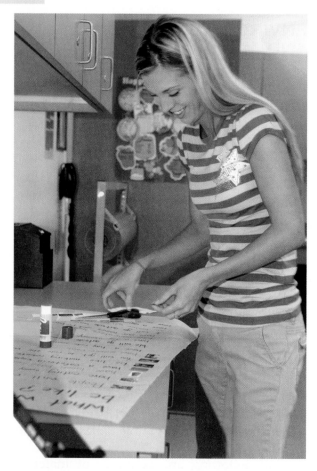

FIGURE 16–18 Making charts that alert children to print's usefulness is a common teacher task.

Early childhood centers create rooms that are full of symbols, letters, and numbers in clear view of the child. Room print should reflect teacher and child interests. Many toys have circles, squares, triangles, alphabet letters, and other common shapes. Recommended symbol size for preschool playroom display is at least 2 to 2½ inches in height or larger.

Labeling

Labeling activities revolve around the purpose and function of labels and signs in daily life. One educator created handheld signs for use during daily scheduled activities such as clean-up, line-up, circle time, listening time, and washing hands. Each sign had printed words and a visual clue, such as a wastebasket for clean-up, an ear for listening time, and so on.

In a classroom, many needs usually exist. A "Park bikes here" sign alerts bike riders to the proper storage area and may prevent yard accidents and be useful for a child looking for an available bike.

A labeling activity initiated by a teacher to introduce the need for road signs and environmental signs can lead to an activity in which children decide the appropriate wording.

Common classroom labeling includes the following.

◆ artwork

◆ name tags

◆ lockers and storage areas (Figure 16–19)

◆ belongings

◆ common objects in the room, such as scissors, paper, crayons, fishbowl, chair, water, door, window, sink

◆ school areas, such as block, library or reading center, playhouse, art center, science center

◆ place cards for snacks

Display Areas

Display areas often include the following.

◆ magazine pictures with captions

◆ current interest displays, for example, "Rocks we found on our walk"

◆ bulletin boards and wall displays with words

◆ wall alphabet guides (Aa Bb . . .)

◆ charts

◆ child's work with explanations, such as "Josh's block tower" or "Penny's clay pancakes"

◆ folding table accordion display (Figure 16–20)

◆ signs for child activities, such as "store," "hospital," "wet paint," and "Tickets for Sale Here"

Message-Sending Aids

Classroom mailboxes, suggestion boxes, and message boards are motivational and useful. Writing short notes to children piques an

FIGURE 16–19 Large printscript letters are used to label boxes.

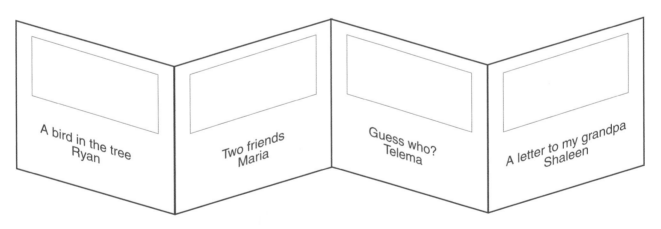

FIGURE 16–20 Folding table accordion.

interest about what is said. Large-sized stick-on notes are great for this purpose and can be attached to mirrors, plates, toys, and so on.

Teacher-Made Materials, Games, and Toys

The following teacher-made materials will help children with letter and word recognition skills.

◆ brightly colored alphabet letters from felt, cardboard, sandpaper, leather, plastic
◆ games with letters, numbers, or symbols
◆ alphabet cards
◆ games with names and words
◆ greeting cards
◆ hats or badges with words

Writing Centers

Writing centers are planned, teacher-stocked areas where printing is promoted. A writing center can be a separate area of a room, or it can exist within a language arts center. Child comfort and proper lighting are essential, along with minimized distractions. Often, dividers or screens are used to reduce outside noise and activity. Supplies and storage areas are provided at children's fingertips so that children can help themselves. Teacher displays or bulletin board areas that motivate printing can be close by. If water-based marking pens are provided, pens with distinct bright colors are preferred.

Through dialogue and exploration at a writing table or center, children are able to construct new ideas concerning print and meaning in a supportive mini-social setting.

There should be a variety of paper and writing tools. Printing stamps and printing ink blocks, a hole punch, and brads are desirable. Old forms, catalogs, calendars, and computer paper may be inviting. Scratch paper (one side already used) or lined paper and crayons placed side-by-side invite use. Most local businesses or offices throw away enough scratch paper to supply a preschool center.

Colored or white chalk has an appeal of its own and can be used on paper, chalkboards, or cement. For variety, use brightly colored oil pastels or soft-lead pencils on paper. Most schools install a child-high chalkboard; table chalkboards are made quickly by using chalkboard paint obtained at hardware or paint stores and scrap wood pieces. Easels, unused wall areas, and backs of furniture can be made into chalkboards.

Primary print typewriters and computers capture interest. Shape books with blank pages and words to copy and trace appeal to some children, as do large rub-on letters or alphabet letter stickers (these can be made by teachers from press-on labels). Magnetic boards and magnetized letter sets are commonly mentioned as the favorite toy of children interested in alphabet letters and forming words.

Letters, words, and displays are placed for viewing on bulletin boards at children's eye level. Displays in writing centers often motivate and promote print. McNair (2007) suggests that young children are particularly fascinated by their own names. A name list or name cards can be used throughout the classroom.

FIRST SCHOOL ALPHABETS

Parents may have taught their children to print with all capitals. Early childhood centers help introduce the interested child to the letter forms that are used in the first grades of elementary school.

In kindergarten or first grade, printing is done in printscript, sometimes called manuscript printing (Figure 16–21), or in a form called D'Nealian print (Figure 16–22). Centers should obtain guides from a local elementary school, because letter forms can vary from community to community.

Teachers need to be familiar with printscript (or any other form used locally). It is easier for a child to learn the right way than to be retrained later. All printing seen by young children in a preschool usually will be either printscript, using both uppercase and lowercase letters, or D'Nealian style. Names, bulletin boards, and labels made by teachers should model correct forms. Printscript letters are formed with straight lines, circles, and parts of circles. In Figure 16–21, the small arrows and numerals show the direction to follow in forming the letters as well as the sequence of the lines.

The D'Nealian form, developed by teacher-principal Donald Neal Thurber and introduced in 1978, has grown in acceptance. Its popularity stems in part from its slant and continuous stroke features, which provide an easy transition to slant and stroke used in cursive writing introduced to children after second grade. Thurber (1988) notes that it takes 58 strokes to print the circle-stick alphabet but it takes only 31 strokes to print the same in D'Nealian print. Further

FIGURE 16–21 Printscript alphabet.

$\bar{a}\, d\, k\, H\, R\, U$

$a\, d\, k\, H\, R\, U$

$2\, 4\, 7\, 9\, 10$

FIGURE 16–22 Samples of D'Nealian print and numerals.

start making number symbols before showing an interest in alphabet letters. Numeral forms (Figure 16–23) are also available from elementary schools. The numeral forms in one geographical area may also be slightly different from those of another town, city, or state.

BEGINNING ATTEMPTS

In beginning attempts to write, children commonly grasp writing tools tightly and press down hard enough to tear the paper. With time and the mastery of small muscles, children's tense, unschooled muscles relax and forms and shapes start to resemble alphabet forms and recognizable shapes. Deep concentration and effort are observed. All attempts are recognized and appreciated by early childhood teachers as signs of the children's growing interest and ability.

Figure 16–24 arranges alphabet letters in manuscript print from the easiest for children to manage and form to the most difficult. **Orthographic awareness** is the ability to notice and use critical features of the graphic symbols in written language. Children learn what makes a letter unique and that these features are often very finely drawn. The visual difference between the alphabet letters *n* and *m*, or

information about this alphabet and teaching suggestions can be obtained from Thurber's publisher, Scott Foresman.

Numbers in printed form are called numerals. Children may have used toys with numerals, such as block sets. Young children will probably hold up fingers to indicate their ages or to tell you they can count. They may

orthographic awareness — the ability to notice and use critical features of graphic symbols in written language.

FIGURE 16–23 Printscript numerals.

1. I	14. V	27. Z	40. Y
2. o	15. c	28. t	41. d
3. L	16. x	29. B	42. R
4. O	17. T	30. Q	43. G
5. H	18. h	31. s	44. a
6. D	19. w	32. n	45. u
7. i	20. J	33. z	46. k
8. v	21. f	34. r	47. m
9. l	22. C	35. e	48. j
10. X	23. N	36. b	49. y
11. E	24. A	37. S	50. p
12. P	25. W	38. M	51. g
13. F	26. K	39. U	52. q

FIGURE 16–24 Listing of letters from easiest to form to most difficult.

n and *h*, are subtle, but many preschoolers have no difficulty. Educators realize that each child's knowledge is a very personal matter, with children finding their own ways of weaving understanding around a letter to help them remember it and reproduce it.

PLANNED ACTIVITIES—BASIC UNDERSTANDINGS

Most planned activities in this language arts area, and most unplanned child-adult exchanges during the school day, involve basic understandings. Rules exist in this graphic art as they do in speech. Children form ideas about these rules.

Print concerns the use of graphic symbols that represent sounds and sound combinations. Symbols combine and form words and sentences in a prescribed grammatical order.

Alphabet letters are spaced and are in uppercase and lowercase form. They are written and read from left to right across a page. Margins exist at beginnings and ends of lines, and lines go from the top to bottom of pages. Punctuation marks end sentences, and indentations separate paragraphs. It is amazing how many rules of printing interested children discover on their own and with teacher help before they enter kindergarten.

DAILY INTERACTIONS AND TECHNIQUES

The techniques listed in this section are purposeful actions and verbalizations used by teachers in printscript instruction. The teacher uses a natural conversational style rather than a formal teaching tone.

Putting the children's names on their work is the most common daily use of printscript. The teacher asks the children whether they want their names on their work. Many young children feel their creations are their very own and may not want a name added. When a paper is lost because it has no name on it, children see the advantage of printing a name on belongings.

All names are printed in the upper left corner of the paper, if possible, or on the back if the child requests. This is done to train the children to look at this spot as a preparation for reading and writing. Children's comments about their work can be jotted down at the bottom or on the back of their papers.

The teacher can be prepared to do this by having a dark crayon or felt-tip pen in a handy place or pocket. Dictation is written without major teacher editing or suggestions concerning the way it is said. The teacher can tell the child that the teacher will be writing down the child's ideas and then follow the child's word order as closely as possible. Some teachers prefer to print the statement, "Chou dictated these words to Mrs. Brownell on May 2, 2008," before or after the child's message. Most teachers would print the child's "mouses went in hole" as "mice went in the hole," which is minor editing. All child-dictated printing should be in printscript, using both uppercase and lowercase letters and proper punctuation.

When a child asks a teacher to print, the teacher stands behind the child and works over the child's shoulder (when possible). This allows the child to see the letters being formed in the correct position. If the teacher faces the child while printing, the child sees the letters upside down. Some teachers say the letter names as they print them.

Letters or names written for the child should be large enough for the child to distinguish the different forms—more than 1 inch high. This may seem large to an adult (Figure 16–25).

Some schools encourage teachers to print examples on lined paper if a child says, "Make an *a*" or "Write my name." Others suggest that teachers blend letter sounds as they print words. Many centers expect teachers to respond to the child's request through conversation and by searching for letters on alphabet charts. This encourages the child to make her own copy before the teacher automatically prints it.

Teacher techniques often depend on the circumstances of a particular situation and knowledge of the individual child. One technique common to all centers is supportive assistance and voiced appreciation of children's efforts. Teachers can rejoice with a young child over approximations of intent in writing, just as we do with a toddler who makes an imprecise attempt to say a new word.

Children may show their printing attempts to the teacher or point out the names of letters they know. A positive statement to the child is appropriate: "Yes, that is an *a*" or "I can see an *a*, *t*, and *p*" (the teacher points to each) or "Marie, you did print the letters *a* and *t*."

With these comments, the teacher encourages and recognizes the child's efforts. Often, the child may have the wrong name or form for a letter. The teacher can react by saying, "It looks like an alphabet letter. Let's go look at our wall alphabet and see which one" or may simply say, "Look. You made a *w*."

Encourage, welcome, and keep interest in print alive by providing attention. Children have many years ahead to perfect their skill; the most important thing at this early stage is that they are interested in the forms and are supplied with correct models and encouragement.

One technique is to have children who ask for letter forms trace over correct letter models or symbols. This can be done with crayons, felt-tip pens, or other writing tools. To explain the meaning of the word *trace*, the teacher gives the child a demonstration.

When reading charts or books to children, a teacher may move her hand across the page beneath words. This is done to emphasize the left-to-right direction in reading and writing and separations between words. Introducing authors' names periodically helps children realize that they also can create stories, and what they create can be written.

Maryellen Donald

FIGURE 16–25 Letters should be large enough for the child to see easily.

ENVIRONMENTAL PRINT IN DAILY LIFE

A teacher of young children makes connections between print and daily classroom happenings. This is not difficult, but it does require teacher recognition and purposeful action. Print can be noticed starting with children's names and print on clothing, shoes, food, toys, and almost every object in the classroom, including light switches and faucet handles. Print is part of classroom life.

Children need to learn what print can do for them in satisfying personal needs. This makes print real. Children become aware of print by using it for real and meaningful purposes when they dictate and write stories, make signs for the block area, read names on a job chart, write messages, look for EXIT signs, follow recipes, have conversations and discussions, or listen to stories. Children may need teacher assistance in recognizing the usefulness of written messages. Many instances of sending or reading print messages are possible during a school day. For example, because print often protects one's safety, there are many opportunities to discuss and point out words that serve this function.

Dramatic play themes that involve print and printing labels for dramatic play props are shown in Figure 16–26.

Teachers look for functional activities such as

◆ making necessary lists of children's names with children. Example: Teacher creates a waiting list.

◆ making holiday or special occasion cards.

◆ making group murals and labeling parts at a later date. Example: Teacher uses color words or children's ideas (Jane says, "This looks like a cat.").

◆ writing what-we-found-out activities. This can be done with many discovery experiences. Example: What floats, and what does not?

◆ classifying experiences. Example: "Shoes Are Different"—Teacher elicits from the group the kinds of shoes children see others wearing. It might be brown shoes, sandals, shoes with laces, and so on. Once these are listed across the top of the chart paper children can choose under which heading their name should go.

◆ sharing the lunch or snack menu by discussing printed words on a chart or chalkboard.

◆ making classroom news announcements on a large sheet of paper posted at children's eye level. Examples follow: Enrico moved to a new apartment. Mrs. Quan is on a trip to Chicago.

Creating a large classroom journal will allow the teacher a daily or weekly opportunity to model writing a class-dictated sentence. The teacher can also talk aloud about her writing while using a large sheet of paper. The first step would be a joint discussion concerning what is to be written. The teacher can then "think aloud" as she writes, leveling her comments to the children's ability.

When working on the journal, the teacher may simply say, "We planted seeds," and emphasize the number of words in the sentence by making three spaced lines. Or the teacher may say, "We will start by looking at the left side of the paper because the first word on a page is printed on the top left side of the page. We will put the first word of our sentence here." This can be repeated on other "journal days" before the teacher decides to think aloud about the names of the first letter in each word. No matter the journaling activity, the children will be watching their teacher form letters, use capital letters, form words, leave spaces between words, and end messages with a period. Depending on the class and its ability, the teacher may not think aloud about the sounds of the letters, but as journaling progresses she may choose to do so depending on the philosophy of the program.

(Teachers using journaling must know how each alphabet letter is to be formed. Go back to Figure 16–21 and notice the small numbered arrows.)

Daily journal sheets can be bound with large metal rings to make a class big book. Child art is often attached to the blank area under the sentence on each page. Large sheets are used so large teacher print is easily observed by a group of children. See the Activities section at the end of this chapter for more ideas related to classroom journaling.

PLAY THEMES

Classroom Post Office

Suggested play items:

stamps (many come with magazine advertisements), old letters, envelopes, boxes to wrap for mailing, scale, canceling stamp, tape, string, play money, mailbag, mailbox with slots, alphabet strips, writing table, felt-tip pens, counter, postal-employee shirts, posters from post office, stamp-collector sheets, wet sponge, teacher-made chart that lists children by street address and zip codes, box with all children's names on printed individual strips, mailboxes for each child

Taco Stand

Suggested play items:

counter for customers, posted charts with prices and taco choices, play money, order pads, labeled baskets with colored paper taco items (including cheese, meat, lettuce, salsa, sour cream, avocado, shredded chicken, and onions), customer tables, trays, bell to ring for service, folded cards with numbers, receipt book for ordered tacos, plastic glasses and pitchers, cash register, napkins, tablecloth, plastic flowers in plastic vase, cook's jacket, waiter/waitress aprons, busperson suit and cleaning supplies, taped ethnic music, plastic utensils, soft pencils or felt-tip pens, line with clothespins to hang orders, paper plates

A hamburger stand or pizza parlor are other possibilities.

Grocery Shopping

Suggested items:

shopping-list paper, bookcase, pencils or felt-tip pens, chart with cut magazine pictures or labels from canned goods or vegetables labeled in print by teacher for children to copy if they desire, empty food cartons and cans, plastic food, shopping cart, purse and wallet, play money, brown bags, cash register on box, dress-up clothes for customers and store clerks

Letter-Writing Classroom Center
(for writing to relatives and friends)

PRINT-AWARENESS ACTIVITIES

Classroom Newspaper

Make a class newspaper. Print children's dictated news or creative language after sharing a local paper with them. Child drawings on ditto master can be duplicated. Add teacher and parent news, poems, captions, drawings, and so forth. Some children may wish to print their own messages. These may range from scribble to recognizable forms and words.

T-Shirt Autograph Day

Each parent is asked to bring an old T-shirt (any size) to school for T-shirt autograph day. Permanent felt markers are used by children under teacher supervision. (Washable markers can also be used, but teachers must iron or put T-shirts in a clothes dryer for 5 minutes on a hot setting.) T-shirt forms are necessary and can be made of cardboard. Material must be stretched over a form so marks can be added easily. It is a good idea to have children wear plastic paint aprons to protect clothing from permanent markers. Children are free to autograph shirts in any manner they please. A display of T-shirts with writing usually prompts some children to add letters to their own shirts. Most teachers own or can borrow T-shirts with writing.

FIGURE 16–26 Dramatic play themes and activities that promote print awareness and use.

WRITING TABLE OR AREA

Many classrooms include a writing table or area for children's daily free-choice exploration. Stocked with different paper types, a variety of writing instruments, alphabet letter stencils, letter stamps, and letter model displays, this type of setup makes daily access available and inviting. However, just providing a writing center is not enough. Teachers need to be in it daily, as motivators and resources. Some writing areas have considerable use. In other classrooms, teachers spend little or no time there (Smith, 2001). Whether a writing center appeals to children, grabs children's attention, and is child-functional depends on the ingenuity of teachers.

Respecting "I'll Do It My Way!"

Recognizing that children need time as well as opportunity, teachers notice that individual children involve themselves in classroom literacy events based on their maturity and interest. When a child senses a reason and develops a personal interest in writing or reading, she acts on her own timetable. There seems to exist in the child at this point a desire to do something her own way; the child wants to retain ownership of early literacy behaviors. The child who examines a classroom alphabet chart and then copies letter forms may choose to share her marks with other children and avoid the teacher. Another child the same age may prefer to consult the teacher. Other children may ask, "What's this say?" or "What's this called?" In all situations, teachers aim to preserve and promote each child's idea of competency as a writer or reader.

LEFT-HANDED CHILDREN

Left-handedness or right-handedness occurs as the child's nervous system matures. Preschool teachers notice hand preferences when children use writing tools. Some children seem to switch between hands as though hand preference has not been established. Most left-handers use their right hands more often than right-handers use their left hands. Writing surfaces in preschools should accommodate all children, and both right-handed and left-handed scissors should be available.

Teachers should accept hand preference without attempting to change or even point out a natural choice. Seating left-handed children at the ends of tables (when possible) during activities or making sure left-handers are not crowded against right-handers is a prudent course of action.

LINED PAPER

Some children acquire the necessary motor control and can use lined, printed paper (Figure 16–27), so some programs provide it.

Lines can easily be drawn on a chalkboard by the teacher. This provides a large working surface and an opportunity for children to make large-size letters.

CHART IDEAS

Printscript can be added to playrooms by posting charts that have been made by the teacher. Charts can be designed to encourage the child's active involvement. Pockets, parts that move, or pieces that can be added or removed add extra interest. Charts made on heavy chart

FIGURE 16–27 Example of a 5-year-old kindergartener's printing accompanying art.

The Picnic

We had lunch
in the park.
We sat
on the grass.

FIGURE 16–28 Experience chart.

board or cardboard last longer. Clear contact paper can be used to seal the surface. Chart ideas include:

◆ experience charts (Figure 16–28).
◆ color or number charts.
◆ large clock with movable hands.
◆ chart showing the four seasons.
◆ picture story sequence charts.
◆ calendars.
◆ room task charts ("helpers chart").
◆ texture charts (for children to feel).
◆ poetry charts (Figure 16–29).
◆ recipe charts using step-by-step illustrations.
◆ classification or matching-concepts charts.
◆ birthday charts.
◆ height and weight charts.
◆ alphabet charts.
◆ rebus charts (Figure 16–30).

Many teachers make "key word" charts. Key words can be words inspired by a picture-book title, character, and so forth; words solicited from children; or words taken from some classroom event or happening. The chosen word is printed by the teacher at the top of a chart. The teacher then asks a small group, "When I say

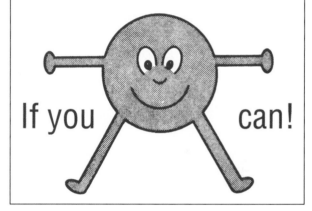

Mix a pancake
Stir a pancake
Pop it in a pan,
Fry the pancake,
Toss the pancake,
Catch it

If you   can!

FIGURE 16–29 Poetry chart.

this word, what do you think of?" or "Salt and pepper go together. We see them in shakers sitting on the kitchen table. What goes with [key word]?" or "Tree is the word at the top of our chart. What can we say about the trees in our play yard?" or some such leading question. Children's offered answers are put below the key word on the chart. This activity suits some older 4-year-olds, especially those asking, "What does this say?" while pointing to text.

Charts of songs or rhymes in the native languages of attending children have been used successfully in many classrooms. Parent volunteer translators are often pleased to help put new or favorite classics into their native tongue.

like (eye) on my

like very red.

like with lots of noise.

like to play with and

like (rocks) and (balls) and

like lots of funny (hats)

like and and

like (walking on fallen logs)

like riding on my (bike)

like sleeping in the (night)

What do U like?

FIGURE 16–30 Rebus chart.

It is easy to see that placing pictures alongside print makes the task of choosing easier. Simple pictures are drawn by the teacher. This works well. The best charts relate to classroom themes or happenings.

When making a chart, first draw sketches of the way words and pictures could be arranged. With a yardstick, lightly draw on guidelines with a pencil or use a chart liner (see Activities section). Then, add printscript words with a felt-tip pen or dark crayon. Magazines, old elementary school workbooks, old children's books, and photographs are good sources for pictures on charts. Brads or paper fasteners can be used for movable parts. Book pockets or heavy envelopes provide a storage place for items to be added later to the chart.

Experience Charts: A Chart Story Activity

The purpose of experience charts is to have children recognize that spoken words can be put in written form. Most centers keep large chart-making paper and felt tip markers or thick black crayons in stock for chart making.

After an interesting activity, such as a field trip, visit by a special speaker, party, celebration, or cooking experience, the teacher can suggest that a story be written about the experience. A large sheet of paper or chart sheet is hung within the children's view, and the children dictate what happened. The teacher prints on the sheet, helping children sort out what happened first, next, and last. Figure 16–32 and Figure 16–33 show examples of other word and picture charts.

Chart Stands

Homemade chart stands can be made by teachers. Commercial chart holders, chart stands, chart rings, and wing clamps are sold at school-supply stores. Teachers using charts daily will attest to preferring commercially manufactured chart stands because of their mobility and stability.

"*Uno, Dos, Tres Inditos*," a Spanish version of "Ten Little Indians," has been frequently enjoyed and learned quickly.

A technique adopted in many schools involves using a color-code system when recording individual child contributions to a group-dictated chart. This enables a child to return to the chart and find her comments.

Think of all the charts that can include a child's choice, vote, or decision! These charts are limitless. A child can indicate her individual selection under the diverse headings by making a mark, printing her name, using a rubber stamp and ink pad, or moving her printed name to a basket or pasting it onto the chart as shown in Figure 16–31.

FIGURE 16–31 Examples of charts. *Note: Teacher writes child's answer, reads it aloud, and later displays a complete animal drawing to discuss. Example: "Tia says a dog."

Letter Patterns

Commercially made letter patterns or teacher-made sets are useful devices that can be traced for teacher use in game making or for wall displays. Made of sturdy card stock or oak tag paper, they can be quickly and easily traced. See the Activities section for letter pattern samples.

Chart Books

A number of books called chart books, big books, or easel books are in print. These giant books are poster size and easily capture children's attention. The print stands out and cannot be missed. Creative teachers have produced their own versions with the help of overhead projectors that enlarge smaller artwork. Chart paper or poster board is used.

GENERATING STORY SENTENCES

Story sentence activities are similar to chart activities. A child, or a small group of children, becomes an author. After a classroom activity or experience, the teacher encourages generating a story (a written sentence). The activity is child-centered thereafter, with the teacher printing what the child or group suggests. The teacher can use a hand-wide space between words to emphasize the end of one word and spacing between words, and may talk about letters or letter sounds found at the beginning or end of children's names. It is not unusual for all children in a group of 4-year-olds to recognize all the names of other students in their class. Ideas and contributions from individual

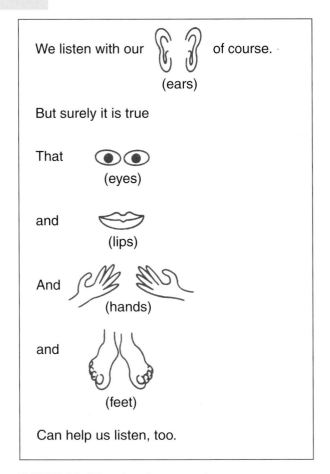

We listen with our 👂👂 of course.
(ears)

But surely it is true

That 👀
(eyes)

and 👄
(lips)

And 🖐🖐
(hands)

and 🦶🦶
(feet)

Can help us listen, too.

FIGURE 16–32 Rebus listening chart.

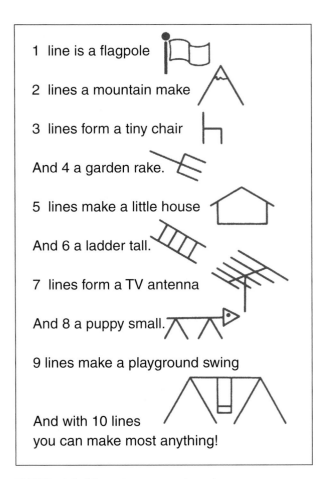

1 line is a flagpole

2 lines a mountain make

3 lines form a tiny chair

And 4 a garden rake.

5 lines make a little house

And 6 a ladder tall.

7 lines form a TV antenna

And 8 a puppy small.

9 lines make a playground swing

And with 10 lines
you can make most anything!

FIGURE 16–33 A chart using line drawings.

children are accepted, appreciated, and recognized by the teacher, and generated sentences are read and reread with the group. Long strips of chart paper or rolled paper can be used. Story sentences are posted at children's eye level.

See the Activities section of this chapter and the book's companion website for additional teacher-created printscript activity ideas.

Interactive and Scaffolded Writing

Interactive, or shared, **writing** times take place in many kindergartens and first-grade classrooms. They are described here to acquaint preschool practitioners with what lies ahead and what might be adapted, modified, or individualized for the few individual children who read (not memorize) simple text in picture books and write messages during their preschool years.

This kindergarten strategy is receiving an increased amount of use and attention from educators. Educators define interactive writing as an instructional context in which a teacher shares a pen—literally and figuratively—with a group of children as they collaboratively compose and construct a written message. Children participate in every element of the writing process—deciding on a topic, thinking about the general scope and form of the writing,

interactive writing — (1) an instructional strategy popular in American kindergartens; (2) a process involving a teacher who verbally stretches each word so that the child (children) can distinguish sounds and letters. This is also known as shared writing.

determining the specific text to write, and writing it word by word, letter by letter. Rereading, revising, and proofreading take place during and after the experience and usually lead to a child's (or children's) reading words, phrases, sentences, and the whole of what has been written.

Using the interactive writing process, a teacher focuses attention on letter sounds, names, forms, left-to-right and top-to-bottom progression, spaces between words, capitalization, punctuation, and spelling. Researchers believe interactive writing is an instructional strategy that works well for children of all linguistic backgrounds.

Looking at a skilled kindergarten or first-grade child composing and constructing a message, one finds the child must think about and keep in mind the message, choose a first word, decide where to place it on the paper, consider what alphabet letter she knows makes the wanted sound, remember how the letter is formed, manually form it, decide if there are other sounds and other letters needed, know when the word ends, and know a space is needed before the next word. Immediately, an early childhood educator can see foundational understandings concerning writing must have been well learned.

Teachers who work individually with a child might define scaffolded writing as a process that involves supportive teacher assistance.

Assistance by the teacher enables a child to do what she can't do by herself, but may be able to do if parts of the writing task are gradually handed over to the child. Bennett-Armistead, Duke, & Moses (2005) suggest that scaffolded writing consists of the following steps:

- Ask the child the message he would like to write. He may say something like "I played with my friend Matt yesterday."
- Repeat this message to the child.
- Draw one line for each word using a highlighter or ball point pen. Have the child write one "word" per line at the level that is most comfortable for the child.
- Read and reread the message together as necessary, as he writes, to help him

remember the whole message. For instance, he may get as far as "I played" and not remember what came after "played." At this point, you can remind him that he played with his friend Matt yesterday.

Bennett-Armistead and colleagues note that the teacher helps children sound out words and focus on letters during the above steps.

PARENT COMMUNICATION

A conversation with or note to the parents of a child who has asked about or started printing can include the following.

- The teacher has noticed the child's interest in printing alphabet letters, numerals, and/or words.
- The teacher is including a printscript and numeral guide for parents who wish to show their children the letter forms at home.
- The early childhood center encourages printing attempts but does not try to teach printscript to every child. Many children are not interested, and others would find it too difficult at their present developmental level.
- A parent can help by having paper and writing tools for the child at home and by noticing and giving attention to the child when she comes to the parent with written letters.
- Children who start printing early often write letters and numerals in their paintings. The printing may be backward, upside down, or sideways; this is to be expected. (Many parents worry unnecessarily when this is noticed.)

Parents also may need an explanation concerning child-dictated papers or child printing, which teachers accept rather than edit or correct.

Centers plan parent meetings for joint discussion of the appropriateness of printing instruction during preschool years. If the center's position is clear, staff members will be able to give articulate answers concerning the center's programming. Most parents are responsive when teachers explain to them that early child dictation is written with only minor editing, respecting early attempts. As children become more skilled, more teacher corrective help is offered. The assurance teachers give parents that they will provide both basic experiences and opportunities on an individual basis most often satisfies the parents' need to know that the school cares about each child's progress.

SUMMARY

The alphabet and printed words are part of preschool life. A center's goals rarely include teaching all attending children to print, but instead attempt to offer a print-rich environment. For the great majority of preschool children attending child centers, sit-down practice of letter forms is developmentally inappropriate. Some preschool children, on the other hand, will attempt repeatedly to form alphabet letters and practice writing them on their own or with the teacher's supportive guidance. However, many children will show beginning interest in the uses of print and print in books.

Numerals are also interesting to young children. These symbols appear daily at school, at home, and in the neighborhood.

The ability to print depends on the child's

◆ muscle control.

◆ skill in recognizing symbols.

◆ ability to note the placement of lines in a symbol.

Printscript is used in preschool, kindergarten, and first grade. Letters are formed with lines and circles in uppercase and lowercase symbols.

Children are ready for printing at different ages. They learn alphabet letters at different rates. Printscript is used for display and other activities at early childhood centers.

Equipment and settings for giving children an opportunity to explore printing are available in a childhood center. Materials are arranged within reach. Printing seen on wall displays and charts helps motivate interest.

Printscript is used in a variety of ways. The most common is in planned activities and labeling artwork. A name or sentence should start in the upper left corner and move toward the right.

New teachers practice printscript forms so that good print models are supplied. It is also important to encourage children and to recognize their efforts, even if they cannot make correct forms.

Parents should be alerted to children's printing attempts and to the center's policy and practices concerning this language arts skill.

ADDITIONAL RESOURCES

Readings

Bloom, C. A. (1997). *Playing with print: Fostering emergent literacy.* Glenview, IL: Good Year Books.

Collins, J. L. (1998). *Strategies for struggling writers.* New York: Guilford.

Dufflemeyer, F. A. (2002). Alphabet activities on the Internet. *The Reading Teacher, 55,* 631–635.

Johnson, P. (1997). *Pictures and words together: Children illustrating and writing their own books.* Portsmouth, NH: Heinemann.

Prior, J., & Gerard, M. R. (2004). *Environmental print in the classroom.* Newark, DE: International Reading Association.

Schickedanz, J. A., & Casbergue, R.E. (2005). *Writing in preschool: Learning to orchestrate meaning and marks.* Newark, DE: International Reading Association.

Strickland, D. S., & Schickedanz, J. A. (2004). *Learning about print in preschool.* Newark, DE: International Reading Association.

Thurber, D. N., & Jordan, D. R. (1987). *D'Nealian handwriting.* Teacher's Edition. Glenview, IL: Scott Foresman and Company.

Children's Books with Writing Themes

Ahlberg, J., & Ahlberg, A. (1986). *The jolly postman.* Waltham, MA: Little, Brown & Co. (Letter writing.)

Barton, B. (2001). *My car.* New York: Greenwillow. (Discusses road signs and other functional print.)

de Groat, D. (1996). *Roses are pink, your feet really stink.* New York: HarperCollins. (Writing or dictating Valentine rhymes.)

de Paola, T. (1978). *Pancakes for breakfast.* New York: Harcourt Brace Jovanovich. (Recipes.)

Numeroff, L. (1991). *If you give a moose a muffin.* New York: HarperCollins. (Recipes.)

Williams, M. (2003). *Don't let the pigeon drive the bus.* New York: Hyperion Books for Children. (Text connects spoken word to print.)

Alphabet Books

Catalanotto, P. (2002). *Matthew A. B. C.* New York: Atheneum. (A child's adventures.)

Cleary, B. (1998). *The hullabaloo A-B-C.* Boston: Morrow Junior Books. (Alphabet experiences through farm noises explored by three children.)

Isadora, R. (1999). *ABC pop!* New York: Viking Press. (A clever introduction of alphabet letters.)

Lester, A. (1998). *Alice and Aldo.* Boston: Houghton Mifflin. (Alphabet letters A to Z introduced through Alice's chronological daily activities, such as breakfast in bed.)

Marzollo, J. (2000). *I spy little letters.* New York: Scholastic. (Finding letter shapes.)

Paul, A. (1999). *Everything to spend the night from A to Z.* New York: DK Publishing. (The overnight bag brought for an overnight stay with Grandpa yields A to Z objects.)

Satin, A. S. (2004). *Mrs. McTats and her house full of cats.* New York: Simon & Schuster. (Alphabet cats.)

Helpful Websites

America Writes for Kids
http://usawrites4kids.drury.edu
Encourages child writers.

KidSource Online
http://www.kidsource.com
Provides tips on helping children with writing.

National Association for the Education of Young Children
http://www.naeyc.org
Select the Read NAEYC Position Statements link.

SIL International
http://www.sil.org
Use key words "invented spelling topics" in the site's Search feature.

Book Companion Website

Putting together a "birthday" gift book is an activity idea that combines children's art and children's dictated messages. This and other print-awareness activities are included on the book companion website. In the internet exercises, students are asked to brainstorm and create activities that promote children's concepts about the printed text in picture books. Further readings are provided.

STUDENT ACTIVITIES

1. Observe a morning program for 4-year-olds. Cite as many examples as possible of adults' use of written communication.

2. Expand the following statement: Practicing alphabet letter formation when a teacher requests it could result in the child's . . .

3. Without turning back to review the printed alphabet guide given in this chapter, print the alphabet in both uppercase and lowercase letters in printscript. Obtain a printscript alphabet from the nearest public school. With a red crayon or pen, circle letters that differ (even slightly) from your attempted alphabet. Print all letters you circled on the remaining lines using proper form.

4. Observe a preschool program. Notice and list all printscript forms found in the classroom that are within the children's view. Report the findings to classmates.

5. Secure some examples of young children's attempts to make letters and numerals in their drawings. What do you notice about the symbols? Are the lines large, small, slanted, or straight? Are capitals or small letters used? What else do you notice?

6. Take tracing paper to a classroom of 4-year-olds. Trace examples of child printing (writing) and bring to your next class period. (Talk to your instructor first concerning making school visits and appointments.)

7. Use the following checklist to observe a 4- or 5-year-old child. Interview the child's teacher for items you were unable to determine. (Note: Make sure the teacher knows that this is not a test but an instrument to make you aware of children's emerging abilities.)

Checklist of Print Interest and Understandings

Rate each item as follows. **Y:** Most of the time:
                                               S: Sometimes
                                             H: Has not attempted as yet
                                             U: Unable to determine

The child
_____ sits through a book reading and enjoys it.
_____ asks for a book's rereading.
_____ "reads" to another parts or lines of a book from memory.
_____ shows an interest in alphabet letters.
_____ shows an interest in books or environmental print.
_____ reads children's name tags or signs.
_____ puts alphabet letters in artwork.

_____ knows when words are skipped in favorite books.

_____ plays with marking tools.

_____ shares written letters or words with others.

_____ points to print in the work of others.

_____ wants name on work.

_____ wants to write own name on work.

_____ knows that print says something.

_____ produces a row of symbols.

_____ attempts to copy symbols, letters, or words.

_____ reads symbols she has written.

_____ invents spellings.

_____ discusses a use of print.

_____ knows print can be read.

_____ wants her talk written down.

_____ recognizes individual alphabet letters.

_____ recognizes words that start with the same letter.

_____ can read some environmental signs.

_____ follows along in chart activities.

_____ looks at books while alone.

_____ has an active interest in something else that then gives a low priority to literary activities.

_____ is best described by which of the following statements?

   a. has yet to develop an interest in print

   b. is developing a possible interest

   c. has about the same degree of interest as others her age

   d. has a fairly strong interest

   e. has a continual interest that has led to experimentation and printing attempts

   f. is very interested in some other area that takes up her time and energy

   g. prints almost daily and has invented spellings or spells many words correctly

8. Watch the children's use of crayons or other writing tools. Take notes. Make observations about the following.
   a. time spent with marking tools
   b. manner used (for example, how do the children hold the crayons?)
   c. whether they have good control of both paper and marking tool

9. Role-play with peers the following scenario.

   Arianna's dad meets her preschool teacher in the hallway and says, "How come you don't correct Arianna's papers? Look at these I'm taking home today. Don't you have time to print _car_ right? How is she going to learn?"

10. Make chart paper or tag board patterns for the full uppercase and lowercase alphabet. School-supply stores and practicing teachers are good resources for letter models.

CHAPTER REVIEW

A. Select the correct answer. Most questions have more than one answer.

1. Child care programs
   a. teach all children to print.
   b. try to teach correct printscript form.
   c. all teach the same printscript form.
   d. help children with printing attempts.

2. Small-muscle control
   a. comes after large-muscle control.
   b. depends on many factors.
   c. is difficult for some preschoolers.
   d. is the only thing involved in learning to print.

3. If drawings have upside-down alphabet letters, teachers should
   a. immediately begin printing lessons.
   b. know that the child may be interested in activities with printed forms.
   c. quickly tell the child that the letters are upside down.
   d. worry about the child's ability to form the letters perfectly.

4. A child's readiness to print may depend on her
   a. ability to gather information from her senses.
   b. knowledge that letters are formed by placing lines.
   c. home and family.
   d. feelings for the teacher.

B. Answer the following questions.

1. What are some possible reasons that children ages 2 to 5 years may start to print?

2. What should teachers consider about the printscript form they use?

3. Muscle control is only part of learning to write. What other factors affect readiness for written communication?

4. When a child says, "Is this M?" how should one reply?

5. If a child says a *b* is an *f*, what might a teacher say?

C. Describe a print-rich classroom.

D. Answer the following questions.

1. If a child goes to a teacher to show letters she has drawn, how should the teacher react?

2. If two children are arguing over the name of a letter, how should the teacher handle the situation?

3. List three ways a teacher can use printscript during the school day.

E. Referring to Figure 16–34, list all of the things the teacher might have done to encourage the children's attempts.

F. Select the correct answers. All have more than one answer.

1. When a child's first name is to be printed on her work, it should be
   a. in the center on top.
   b. in the upper right corner.

FIGURE 16–34

c. in the upper left corner.
d. done with an uppercase first letter and then lowercase letters.

2. The size of the printscript used with young children
   a. does not really matter.
   b. should be large enough to see, at least 1 inch.
   c. can be of any size.
   d. should be at least 2 inches high.

3. The teacher who does not know how to form printscript letters can
   a. practice.
   b. use an individual style.
   c. get a copy from an elementary school.
   d. write instead.

G. A note to the parents of a child who is interested in learning to print should include what kind of information? List four items that should be included.

OTHER CHART IDEAS AND PRINT AWARENESS ACTIVITIES

NAME-A-PART CHART

Enlarge a figure of a face, animal, house, car, bird, bike, or any familiar object that has parts or features children can name. (Draw freehand or use an overhead projector to enlarge a small drawing.) After introducing the chart, discuss and have the children identify what is pictured or a part of what is pictured. Make a printscript label or strip following children's suggestions.

Children can glue strips or labels on the chart. Glue sticks work well, or children can apply glue to the back of the label or strip. Children sometimes creatively think up silly names, and that is part of the fun. At other times, they may discuss seriously what they believe are the correct labeling words. In a variation of this activity, the teacher draws an outline and parts are drawn as they are named by children.

CHART LINER INSTRUCTIONS

See Figure 16–35. Use Figure 16–36 for letter shapes if necessary.

INSTRUCTIONS TO MAKE A CHART LINER

Cut a piece of Masonite® 12" by 36". Make 7 sawcuts 1½" apart, beginning and ending 1½" from either end. Then glue or nail 1½" square pieces of wood 12" long to each end.

Note: A teacher-made chart liner is a useful device that helps teachers make evenly spaced guidelines on charts that use lines of print. By placing the chart liner over chart paper, quick guidelines are accomplished by inserting a sharp pencil in sawcut slots.

FIGURE 16–35 Making a chart liner.

ABCDEF

GHIJKL

MNOPQ

RSTUV

WXYZ

FIGURE 16–36 Letter patterns. Note: Letters will need to be enlarged for display in the classroom. *(continued)*

abcdef
ghijkl
mnopq
rstuv
wxyz

FIGURE 16–36 *(continued)*

534

PRINTSCRIPT ACTIVITIES

The following activities are based on (1) a particular group of enrolled children, (2) an individual child's interest, or (3) a classroom's project or study theme. Some suit younger preschoolers; others were enjoyed by older preschoolers who had developed considerable interest in print and print form. Activities suggested represent a variety of skill levels and do not appear in a simple-to-complex order.

A Word-a-Day Activity. Printing and defining just one word a day is a useful strategy for building vocabulary and promoting word recognition. Best if the word is drawn from the children at a group time, but teachers can add a word that might be encountered in the theme of study or for another purpose. A special display spot for word-of-the-day is recommended, and children can be asked when they might speak the word or how they might tell a short story using the word. Lots of activity possibilities exist.

Clay-On Patterns. These patterns can be used to enhance small, manipulative-muscle use and tracing skills.

Materials needed include clay and 9 × 12 inch contact-covered cardboard sheets with patterns (Figure 16–37). The activity involves children making clay cylinders to form the patterns. The teacher demonstrates how to roll clay in cylinders and place them on patterns where clay can dry and later be painted.

Commercial Names and Trademarks. Some children delight in reading their favorite brand names. Many trademarks and product logos have appeared on television, in magazines, in fast-food restaurants, or on products seen in the home. It is surprising how familiar children are with this type of print.

Materials:
scissors
cardboard
contact paper (optional)

Use commercial print cut from ads or packaging of home products. Mount on stiff paper or cardboard. Get as close to the color and original letter type as possible. Collect pictures of the product, toy, food, drink, cereal, and so on, the print represents. Mount on cardboard or stiff paper. Cover with clear contact paper.

Activity: The child pairs print with picture. The child may want to "read" print labels to adult or another child.

Connecting Dots. The dot patterns for this activity can be made quickly by the teacher on paper or chalkboard and used as a free-play choice. The purpose of this activity is to enhance small-muscle use and children's skills in forming and recognizing symbols.

Materials: paper, writing tools (or chalkboard and chalk)

Activity: Children connect dots to form symbols (Figure 16–38).

FIGURE 16–37 Patterns.

FIGURE 16–38 Connecting-dots activity.

Sorting Symbols. This activity enhances small-muscle use and children's skills discriminating symbol differences.

Materials:
paper
writing tool
scissors
paste

Activity: After the teacher cuts the symbols in squares from sheets, the children are asked to mix them all together and then find the ones that are the same to paste onto another sheet of paper.

Variation: The teacher can make a cardboard set of symbols that can be sorted by children as a table game (Figure 16–39).

Alphabet Song Slowly. The rhyming song is an easy and fun way for children to recognize letter names. Sing it slowly, exposing each letter as it is named.

Materials include a complete teacher-made printscript alphabet line (Figure 16–40).

ALPHABET SONG

ABCDEFG
HIJKLMNOP
QRS and TUV
WX and Y and Z.
Now I've said my ABCs,
Tell me what you think of me.

FIGURE 16–39 Symbol card for sorting game.

Activity: Children sing the song while one child or the teacher touches the corresponding letter on the alphabet line. The teacher can ask the group to sing slowly or quickly, in a whisper or a loud voice, or in a high or low voice.

Gift Wrap. Children are given the opportunity to creatively wrap gifts while learning the usefulness of print.

Materials:
empty boxes
wrapping paper
scissors
decorative stickers
thin-line markers
list that includes the names of all in the class (including teachers)
stamps
masking tape
card strips or paper strips preprinted with "To" and "From"
small inexpensive gift items or clay child-made objects

Activity: Children wrap the gifts in boxes with wrapping paper and dictate messages or try to write names on paper or card strips.

Secret Words. This activity promotes visual discrimination and children's recognition of symbols.

Materials:
white crayon
white paper
water color brushes
water colors

Activity: The teacher uses white crayon to write a symbol or word on white paper.

FIGURE 16–40 Printscript alphabet line (partial sample).

536

The crayon should be thickly applied. The teacher demonstrates how the symbol appears when water color is painted over the whole paper. The children can guess the shape names.

Sticker Pictures. The children are shown the relationship between objects and words.

Materials:
stickers
paper strips
felt markers

Activity: The teacher has each child choose a sticker for her paper strip. The child names the sticker, and if the child desires, the teacher writes the name of the sticker on back of the strip. The children can then decorate the sticker strips.

Label Fun. The children recognize the print word forms for classroom objects.

Materials:
press-on labels (large size)
felt marker

Activity: Each child is given 5 to 10 labels and told to choose items on the child's body or in the room on which she will stick word labels. Children are told to stick labels on something that has not been labeled by another. Teacher prints child's dictated word(s).

Alphabet Walk. This is another group activity to promote children's recognition of alphabet letters.

Materials:
large newsprint
art paper
felt marker or dark crayon
masking tape

Activity: The teacher makes giant letters on art paper, one letter per sheet. The children are told that the teacher is going to place giant letters around the room. Have two children choose one friend each to walk to the letter A, which the teacher points out to them. The teacher selects another child to think of a way, besides walking, that the four children can move to the second letter. The teacher can give suggestions like crawling, hopping, tip-toeing, walking like an elephant, and so forth. Children clap for the first four, and another four are selected and directed to walk to another letter.

Find Your Shoe. This group activity shows the usefulness of print.

Materials:
press-on labels
marking pen

Activity: The children are asked to take off their shoes and put them in front of them. The teacher asks what will happen to the shoes if everyone puts the shoes in one pile and the teacher mixes up the pile. The teacher introduces the idea that shoes would be easier to find if the children's names were added to each shoe by putting a press-on label on the inner sole. Labels preprinted with the child's name are given to each child. The child puts the labels on her shoes. The shoes go in a pile, which the teacher mixes. Each child describes her shoes to a friend and asks the friend to find the shoes. Two or three friends look in the pile for the shoes at a time.

Alphabet Macaroni Prints. This activity promotes shape discrimination and small-muscle activity.

Materials:
alphabet soup macaroni (sand, seeds, rice, sand or salt can also be used)
glue and brushes
paper
felt-tip pen

Activity: Each child traces her name or a shape by painting over lines with thinned white glue. The macaroni is then spooned over the glue. When the glue is dry, shake the loose macaroni into a container. The result will be raised, textured letters (Figure 16–41). The teacher should demonstrate this process.

ABC "Paste-On" Group Wall Poster. Small-muscle use and symbol recognition are enhanced.

Materials:
alphabet letters or words cut or torn from magazines or newspapers
large-size poster paper or chart paper

Activity: A montage effect is created by having children paste letters where they choose on a piece of paper. During a period of 1 week, the children can return to the work and paste on more letters. At a group time, children are asked to point to three letters or words (or phrases) that they wish the teacher to read.

Alphabet Eaters. Large-muscle use and visual discrimination are enhanced.

Materials:
cards with printscript
alphabet letters (small enough to be slipped into animal's mouth)
sturdy boxes on which animal heads and alphabet strips are glued (holes are cut in the opposite sides of boxes so that children can reach in for cards)

Activity: A child selects a card and "feeds" it to the animal that has a similar alphabet letter on the strip under its mouth (Figure 16–42).

Footprint Alphabet Walk. This activity promotes large-muscle use and symbol recognition.

Materials:
large cardboard (or cloth) on which 26 footprints have been traced
cardboard footprint cutouts each with a printscript alphabet letter (three sets

FIGURE 16–41 Alphabet macaroni pictures.

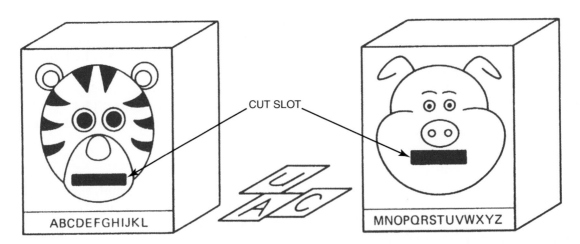

FIGURE 16–42 Alphabet "eaters" and cards.

can be made—lowercase, uppercase, and numerals, if desired), covered with clear contact paper or made from plastic-like material.

Activity: Children place cutout footprints over footprint of the correct letter (Figure 16–43).

Tracers. Tracers can be used over and over again. Waxy crayons or felt markers wipe off with a soft cloth. They can be used to help children recognize and discriminate among symbols and enhance small-muscle coordination.

Materials:
acetate or clear vinyl sheets
cardboard
scissors
strapping or masking tape
paper
felt-tip pen or marker

Construction Procedure: Attach acetate to cardboard, leaving one side open to form a pocket. Make letter or word guide sheets. Simple pictures can also be used (Figure 16–44).

Activity: A child or the teacher selects a sheet and slips it into the tracer pocket. A wax crayon or marker is used by the child to trace the guide sheet. A soft cloth erases the crayon or marker.

Rebus Recipe Cards. Picture cues to "read" with words and numerals help children complete a cooking task. Teacher-made recipe cards or small charts are created before the activity takes place.

Materials:
recipe ingredients
measuring cups, spoons, etc.
plastic bowl, spoon and other necessary utensils
heated surface, refrigerator, microwave or conventional oven, if necessary
teacher-prepared recipe cards

FIGURE 16–43 Footprint alphabet walk.

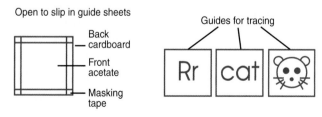

FIGURE 16–44 Tracers.

Activity: With the teacher's help, children complete a cooking task. Suggestions: cup cakes, gelatin with bananas, sandwiches, and salads.

DRAWING ACTIVITIES

Words on Drawings. In this labeling activity, children select words that can be added to their drawings.

Materials:
felt-tip pen or crayons

Activity: The teacher asks each child individually whether words can be added to her painting, drawing, or illustration. Make sure the child realizes that the teacher is going to write on the drawing. It is a good idea to show the child what has been done to another child's picture beforehand. Most children will want words added, but some will not. It is best to limit this activity to the children who are making symbols of faces, figures, houses, and so forth, in their work. Younger children might not be able to decide what to have written on their work when asked, "Would you like me to put a word name on something you've drawn in your picture?"

Rebus Stories. Teachers can use drawings or photographs to encourage child participation during storytelling time. At a crucial point in the story, the teacher pauses and holds up a picture, and the children guess the next word in the story. Teachers can name the picture and resume the story if the children have not guessed the word. Any guess that is a close approximation is accepted; for example, "It is a truck, Josh, a fire truck." The rebus story in Figure 16–45 is an example of teacher authorship. Many additional teacher-created rebus stories are possible.

PRESCHOOL AND KINDERGARTEN ACTIVITIES USING CHILDREN'S NAMES

- Use a morning child sign-in sheet. Give choice of placing sticker by name or printing name.
- Sing name games at circle time.
- Mara's name starts with M, starts with M, starts with M, (repeat), and she is sitting next to Elizabeth. (To the tune of "Mary Had a Little Lamb.")
- Make name tags with raised letters: Use white glue. Soak thick yarn in glue and place over letters, or pour sand over the painted-on glue letters while it is still wet. "Can you feel the letters in your name? Here's an *A*; it comes first," and so on.
- Find and circle the children's names on a chart or chalkboard.
- Paint oversized cutout letters of the children's names.
- Use an ink stamp set of alphabet letters to stamp children's names.
- Find and match name cards.
- Have children find their place at a table that has name place mats.
- Play the name bag game. The cutout letters of the children's names are put in a bag. The children decide the order in which to paste them. Preparation includes making cutout letters for each child and putting them in individual brown bags.
- Shake materials on letters. Children use a glue stick or liquid white glue to trace letter shapes and then sprinkle on hole-punch confetti circles or another similar fine-grained material.
- Have children place colored letter cutouts on wax paper. The teacher covers with a sheet of wax paper the same size and irons with a warm iron. They are displayed on windows.

540

DUCK AND BEAR TAKE A TRIP

This is and this is his friend .

 cried one day and said, "Let's take a vacation!" had not

learned to fly. "I get tired walking," said . "Let's ask

wise old how we can take a trip when a won't walk

and a can't fly." Wise old said, "That's not a problem.

Both of you can ride your to the airport. Buy a ticket

FIGURE 16–45 This rebus story, created by a teacher, uses computer-generated graphics. *(continued)*

and watch the . On an

can sit down and doesn't have to know how to fly.

When the lands, rent a .

In a   can sit and can sit too."

"Thank you, wise old ." "You're very welcome, ."

"Now take along a so you can write me a postcard," said .

FIGURE 16–45 *(continued)*

- Make name necklaces. Use hole-punched colored discs.
- Make a name hat and paste on cutout letters.
- Make pancake letters at snack time.
- Teacher prepares and bakes while children watch.
- Create a teacher-made personalized name book. Polarized photos are added. Child dictates captions.
- Hold up individual name strips for children to identify and perform a task such as standing up, choosing a partner or leaving the circle when dismissed, and so on.
- Line up printed letter cars and let them roll down a block incline. Children choose letters to roll.
- Have children find their names somewhere in the room. Teacher has hidden names beforehand.
- Hang the children's names on a clothesline one letter at a time. Make letter cards with T-shirt shapes.
- Make name puzzles for each child. Use a middle-sized flapped envelope. Print child's name on the envelope with a wide black marking pen, making the letters at least 1½ inches high. On a strip of cardboard or oak tag paper print the name again but use a different colored felt or marking pen for each letter. Cut the strip into

interesting puzzle pieces and insert into the envelope. This puzzle is best when demonstrated with a puzzle using the teacher's name.
- Lick and stick names. Use gummed paper cutout alphabet letters.
- Play stick-it note name activities. Print children's names on stick-it notes. Children stick their notes on something they choose to do or play with.
- Make giant generic gingerbread figures out of flattened large brown bags. Children decorate and name their figures. They are added to a large wall display.
- Count letters in name.
- Think of a word that rhymes with a child's name.
- Ring a bell for each letter of name.
- Draw alphabet letters in the air.
- Clap syllables in names.
- Cut apart your name and paste it back together.
- Find alphabet letters that are a full circle or have a full circle.
- Find alphabet letters that are made with straight lines only and then find letters made with both circles or half circles, and straight lines.
- Create a name word wall with names starting with a similar letter in groups.

SECTION 7

Reading:

A Language Art

CHAPTER 17

Reading and Preschoolers

OBJECTIVES

After reading this chapter, you should be able to:

- Describe reading skills.
- List three methods used to teach reading.
- Discuss the early childhood teacher's role in reading.

KEY TERMS

phonetic
instruction

reading
method

transitional
kindergarten

MACKENZIE'S ABILITY

During group time, Mackenzie's teacher makes a discussion chart that reflects what the children in her class of 3-year-olds "love to eat" at breakfast. Later, she notices the following poorly formed letters in Mackenzie's painting: BBRY PNKS.

QUESTIONS TO PONDER

1. What does the teacher know about Mackenzie's literacy development?

2. Is this precocious behavior or just precious behavior?

3. What course of action should Mackenzie's teacher pursue?

4. Could it be assumed that Mackenzie may be reading a few words?

At one time, it was thought that there was a magic age when all children became ready for "sit-down" reading instruction. Now it is believed that early childhood teachers at every level must be considered teachers of reading, even if they do not offer formal reading instruction. Research and theory suggest that teachers of young children need to be actively engaged in providing experiences that will build children's language and eventually lead children to become readers. These experiences are deemed appropriate if they match the individual child's level of language development and promote new competence in oral and written language. When children learn to read, they use what they know about oral language to comprehend written language.

A wide range of age-appropriate activities involving understanding oral language, awareness of print, intimate experiences with picture books, dramatization, listening, musical activities, and diverse kinds of language arts activities discussed in this text promote early literacy and prepare children for the discovery of reading. Neuman and Roskos (2007) remind educators of the importance of preschool children's quest for knowledge and discovery in all content areas that is the true foundation for reading success. A strong literacy (language arts) curriculum is thought to be tremendously valuable but in itself not enough.

> Reading achievement in the earliest years may look like it's just about letters and sounds—but it's not. Successful reading, as will become abundantly clear by grades 3 and 4, consists of knowing a relatively small store of unconscious procedural skills, accompanied by a massive and slowly built-up store of conscious content knowledge. It is knowledge and the disposition to want to learn more that encourages children to question, discover, evaluate, and invent new ideas and that enables them to become successful readers. (p. 8)

Some children who are in early childhood centers and kindergartens can read. Some have picked up the skill on their own; others have spent time with an older brother or sister,

parents, or others. Although reading is considered the fourth language art, this chapter does not intend to suggest reading instruction for groups of young children or even encourage formal instruction for the 1 to 5 percent of children who can read words during preschool years.

It is clear from research that the process of learning to read is a lengthy one that begins very early in life. A lot of teacher effort during preschool years involves setting up young children to learn to read with ease. Many experts have discussed children's disposition to read. This disposition can be defined as a desire; a positive attitude toward the act of reading; or a feeling that reading is worthwhile, enjoyable, and fun (Figure 17–1). It includes the knowledge that one can find helpful or important information if one can read.

There is now empirical evidence that differences in pre-literacy experiences are associated with varied levels of reading achievement during the early years of elementary school. Children who begin school with few experiences in and less knowledge about literacy are unable to acquire the prerequisites quickly enough to keep up with formal reading instruction in the first grade.

Preschoolers who are given training in phonological awareness evince significant acceleration in their later acquisition of reading. Pre-readers' letter knowledge was found to be the single best predictor of first-year reading achievement, with the ability to discriminate phonemes ranking a close second. Strickland (2003) believes that a child's ability to write his own name is also a predictive characteristic. Children who will probably need additional support for early language and literacy development should receive it as early as possible. Preschool practitioners should be alert for signs that children are having difficulties.

Children Who May Need Special Help

Research has identified children who are likely to begin school less prepared. Their characteristics include:

◆ living in a low-income family or a poor neighborhood.

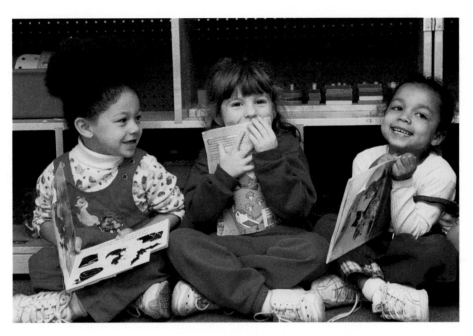

FIGURE 17–1 Enjoying their books? Oh yes!

◆ having limited English proficiency.

◆ being slated to attend an elementary school where reading achievement is chronically low.

◆ speaking a dialect of English that differs substantially from one used in schools.

◆ having specific cognitive deficiencies, hearing impairments, and early language impairments.

◆ having parents who have a history of reading problems.

Preschool educators are increasingly involved in individual state efforts to increase children's present and future ability to learn to read with ease. They have been identified as instrumental and important contributors to their elementary school educators' efforts to increase child success.

Early childhood educators are looking closely at what their individual language arts curricula contain and how to provide supportive assistance for those individual children and individual families they assume to be at risk.

Research-derived indicators for potential problems include:

◆ in infancy or during the preschool period, significant delays in expressive language, receptive vocabulary, or intellectual capacity (IQ).

◆ at kindergarten or elementary school entry, delays in a combination of abilities, including the following.
letter identification
understanding of the functions of print
verbal memory for stories and sentences
phonological awareness
lexical skills such as naming vocabulary
receptive language skills in the areas of
  syntax and morphology
expressive language
overall language development

Prior experiences necessary for young children to acquire reading skill follow.

◆ Children have had experiences in early childhood that fostered motivation and provided exposure to literacy in use.

◆ Children get information about the nature of print through opportunities to learn letters and to recognize the internal structure of spoken words.

◆ Children get explanations about the contrasting nature of spoken and written language.

Optimal environments in preschool and kindergarten require teachers who are well prepared and highly knowledgeable and who receive ongoing administrative support. Forms of support can include in-service training, financial aid, tutoring or mentoring, administrative participation and communication, and other assistance.

READING

The language arts approach and whole-language approach to reading consider reading as one part of the communication process. The language arts are interrelated instead of separate, isolated skills. The teacher is responsible for showing the relationship between the various areas of language arts. In other words, the goal is to help children understand that communication is a whole process in which speaking, listening, using written symbols, and reading those symbols are closely connected (Figure 17–2).

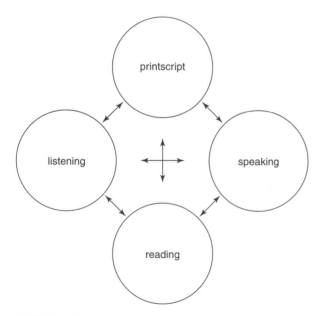

FIGURE 17–2 The four language arts are interrelated and interdependent. Note: Some educators accept a fifth language art—viewing and visual representation.

In the past, the logical connection between listening, speaking, using written words, and reading was overlooked. The subjects were often taught as separate skills, and the natural connection between each area was not clear to children. In the language arts, whole-language, or natural approach, the connection (the way these areas fit together) is emphasized.

The preschool teacher realizes that certain skills and abilities appear in children before other skills do, and also appear concurrently. One researcher studied the literacy development of a group of 4- and 5-year-old children exposed to prenatal maternal drug use (Figure 17–3). She believes that the children's literacy development was appropriate and similar to unexposed 4- and 5-year-old children.

Early learning experiences in listening and speaking serve as a foundation for further language and communication. Children's beginning ideas about print, writing, and reading form concurrently, and children may display understanding and skill in all of these areas.

Activities with young children can move easily from listening, speaking, seeing, or using printscript to beginning reading attempts: from passive to active participation. Many preschool youngsters are able to read most of the names of the children in their group after being exposed to the daily use of name tags.

Past and Current Thinking Concerning Early Reading Instruction

The National Reading Panel Report (2000) and the Elementary Education Act, which includes the No Child Left Behind Act passed in 2002, deal with ways to improve early literacy instruction and prepare young preschool children for school success. Morrow and Asbury (2003) describe what was suggested.

> The report suggests that instruction in early literacy needs to be organized and systematic. It also identifies areas on which to concentrate during instruction. The elements identified are (1) phonemic awareness, (2) phonics, (3) comprehension, (4) vocabulary, and (5) fluency.

NAME	BOOK CONCEPTS	READING	ORTHOGRAPHIC KNOWLEDGE	CONCEPT/ WORD
Jose	tight scribble	aware of book organization	retells/oral and book connected	not aware of letters	no/focus on illustration
Jamal	beginning letter/ unable to make letters	aware of book organization	only listens to stories when storytelling strategy used	not aware of letters	no/focus on illustration
Anna	yes	aware of book organization	retells/oral and book connected	aware of letters in name	pointing synchronized to rhythm not to words
Mark	yes	aware of book organization	retells/oral and book connected	aware of letters in name	aware of words/ not able to track
Billy	yes	aware of book organization	retells/oral and book connected memorizes predictable text	initial consonants semiphonemic	rudimentary
Jennifer	yes	aware of book organization	retells/oral and book connected	initial consonants semiphonemic	rudimentary
"Getting the Idea of Reading and Writing"				
Mario	yes	aware of book organization	retells/prefers book language	initial consonants semiphonemic	track/not pointing to words
Donette	yes	aware of book organization not aware of word	retells/prefers book language	initial consonants semiphonemic	track/not pointing to words
Melisha	initial letter then circles	beginning/end top/bottom sequence of pages	retells/oral and book language	initial consonants semiphonemic	track/not pointing to words
Melina	yes	aware of book organization	retells/oral and book language predictable	initial consonants semiphonemic	rudimentary
"Beginning Readers and Writers"				
Ray	yes	aware of book organization	fluent nonpredictable text/word X word	letter-name	full
Curtis	yes	aware of book organization	fluent nonpredictable text/word X word	letter-name	full
Josh	yes	aware of book organization	fluent nonpredictable text/word X word	letter-name	full

FIGURE 17–3 Four-year-olds' literacy summary. "Getting the Idea of Reading and Writing." (From Barone, D. [1994, Oct.]. The importance of classroom context: Literacy development of children prenatally exposed to crack cocaine—year two. *Research in the Teaching of English, 28*[3], 286–312. Copyright © 1994 by the National Council of Teachers of English. Reprinted and used with permission.)

The report also highlights the importance of qualified teachers in developing successful readers. (p. 51)*

Early childhood educators are still taking these research-based suggestions to heart and are concerned about the approximately 30 to 40 percent of children who do not have an easy time learning to read in elementary school. They have increased recognition that young children, especially disadvantaged ones, often need concentrated instructional support. These children should learn important skills and strategies that they would have difficulty discovering on their own. Teachers are doing more assessment and documentation to help them identify children's individual needs and progress. Their efforts include attention to guidelines for developmentally appropriate practice and standards. They are planning a full and well-balanced early childhood language arts curriculum.

Why is phonemic awareness mentioned so frequently in early childhood literacy readings and in centers' program goals? Because at the beginning of kindergarten it is one of the two best predictors of how well children will learn to read during their first 2 years of school (Ehri & Nunes, 2006). It involves how children learn to read and write words and the unique structure of the English writing system. Ehri and Nunes (2006) point out that to remember how to decode new words, beginners must know how to blend phonemes; and to remember how to read individual words, beginners must be able to segment words into phonemes that match up to graphemes and phonemes and store them in memory.

Professional literature urges preschool teachers to use an integrated approach to language arts. Concerns over national literacy and children's reading success have promoted study and discussion. Many state legislatures have passed new child literacy laws reacting to the enactment of the Federal Reading Excellence Act (1998). Most experts recommend a literature-based program for both elementary school and preschool. Ideal classrooms are

described as "language rich" or "literacy developing." Key ideas presently stress instruction offered in meaningful contexts with children developing strategies to achieve skills they view as useful to them.

Many researchers agree that early school experiences play a crucial role in the child's future literacy development. They believe that teachers should explore effective ways to facilitate language learning by involving children in authentic language uses.

Early childhood professionals want to make sure that their programs of activities offer the best in children's literature, not watered-down versions of classics (Figure 17–4). There is thought to be both older and contemporary literature and language-related activities that have depth, meaning, and linguistic charm. Meaning and comprehension are aided by discussion and familiarity and can be guided by sensitive teachers who also monitor the appropriateness of what is offered.

Pressure for Formal Reading Instruction in Preschools

Some families, for one reason or another, may hold the mistaken idea that their child will have an educational advantage if he receives formal reading instruction in preschool. This idea is often expressed during initial enrollment interviews. Fortunately, early childhood educators can explain that foundational literacy experiences and activities are a standard part of a quality preschool curriculum and that individual growth activities are planned for each child based on his developing capabilities. Durkin's research in the 1960s received considerable publicity, and subsequent studies by many others cite instances of young children reading before kindergarten. Some parents and educators are intrigued by this idea, and still promote formal, sit-down instruction with 3- and 4-year-olds today. Cullinan (1977) attempted to stem this practice and explained the error of this plan of action. Current educators often cite her position today. Some of Cullinan's ideas follow.

. . . a major fallacy in basing programs on early reading studies is that children

*From Morrow, L. M., & Asbury, E. (2003). Current practices in early childhood literacy development. In Morrow, L. M., et al. (Eds.). *Best practices in literacy instructions*, pp. 43–63. Copyright © 2003 Guilford Press.

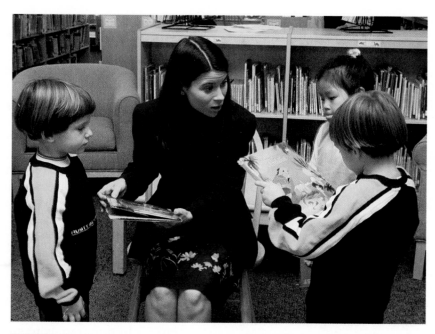

FIGURE 17–4 Quality children's literature is offered by professional early childhood educators.

who learned to read early did not do so from exposure to formal reading instruction. Findings show that children who learned to read early were the ones who were read to, who showed interest in paper and pencil activities, and who were interested in visual distinctions in signs and labels. Their families valued reading as an activity.

Someone answered their questions. Children learned messages encoded in writing can be decoded, or read, and that letters represented sounds used in speaking. (p. 10)

In other words, typically children who learned to read while quite young did so by discovering decoding in responsive, literacy-enriched family situations. Most early childhood experts and educators fear that concentrating on early reading-skill instruction may reduce time for play and take away symbolic enrichment time. Play provides the interaction of imagery, imitation, and language, which builds a foundation necessary for learning to read. Chenfeld (2007) worries: "We have permitted developmentally

inappropriate practices to become realities, squeezing the joy from children's early days in 'real school'". (p. 20)

The pressure preschool staffs may feel to begin formal reading instruction grates against the belief system that values the importance of play. Educators react to the tragedy of finding a number of children in a few preschools with worksheets to complete before they can play. Researchers have yet to find that early reading instruction is advantageous or better than later instruction. In fact, starting formal academics too early may do more harm than good. Some educators point out that formal reading instruction in Denmark, where illiteracy rates are very low, is delayed until age 7. Studies show that children who are pushed to read early may not be such avid readers when they're older—which is when it matters—while their classmates who started slower may read often and spontaneously.

Standards, Benchmarks, and Behaviors

A research-based document that helps preschool curriculum planners identify their standards for pre-kindergarten reading and writing curriculum is available. Based on work sponsored wholly, or in part, by the Office of Educational Research and Improvement (OERI), a publication titled *A Framework for Early Literacy Instruction: Aligning Standards to Developmental Accomplishments and Student Behaviors: Pre-K through Kindergarten* (Bodrova et al., 2000) is available. A standard is defined in the publication as a general statement that represents information, skills, or both that a child (student) should understand or be able to do by the end of his or her pre-K school experience. A benchmark is defined as a sub-component of a standard.

The authors state that their publication was not intended as an assessment checklist and that curriculum should not be "dumbed-down" versions of higher-grade benchmarks. Supporting knowledge listings in reading and writing standards will be of particular interest to early childhood educators and provide clarity as to the purposes of their planned activities and daily interactions. Preschool teachers will be better able to recognize emerging preschool behaviors after studying the document in total.

This document is available from McREL (Mid-continent Research for Education and Learning), 2550 S. Parker Rd., Suite 500, Aurora, CO 80014. In examining supporting knowledge sections of the publication, early childhood educators may be able to more effectively examine their language arts curriculum, their teaching behaviors, and their daily interactions.

Most states have developed state reading standards for public school instruction that are available from local school districts and state departments of education.

Standards for Reading Teacher Preparation

Standards for Reading Professionals (2003), developed by the professional standards and ethics committee of the International Reading Association (IRA), is a reference used by community colleges, college and university faculties, and state departments of education. It is designed to guide the development of elementary school teacher preparation programs and the evaluation of teacher candidates and their training programs through the use of identified candidate performance-based assessment. The standards recognize five categories of professionals: the paraprofessional (2-year degree with specific course work), the classroom teacher, the reading specialist/literacy coach, the teacher educator, and the administrator.

Newly graduated reading professionals must demonstrate they can meet the needs of all students and that they possess the following capabilities or attitudes:

1. Candidates have knowledge of the foundations of reading and writing processes and instruction.
2. Candidates use a wide range of instructional practices, approaches, methods, and curriculum materials to support reading and writing.
3. Candidates use a variety of assessment tools and practices to plan and evaluate effective reading instruction.
4. Candidates create a literate environment that fosters reading and writing by integrating foundational knowledge, use of instructional practice, approaches and methods, curriculum materials, and the appropriate use of assessments.
5. Candidates view professional development as a career-long effort and responsibility.

TEACHER AWARENESS OF CHILD INTEREST AND UNDERSTANDING

Each child will probably hold a totally different view concerning reading (Figure 17–5). Possible understandings a preschooler may have include:

◆ pictures and text have different functions.
◆ print contains the story.
◆ the words the reader says come from the pictures.
◆ stories tend to have some predictable segments and features.

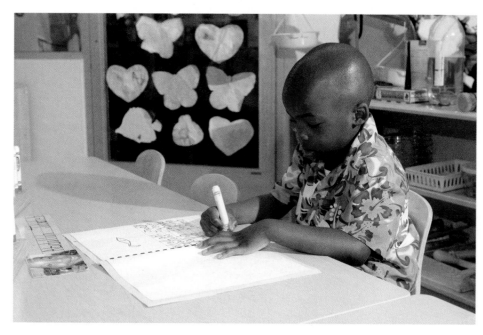

FIGURE 17–5 An interest in printing can lead to an interest in reading.

◆ it is possible to write messages.

◆ there are words, and written words are made up of letters.

◆ letters are arranged from left to right.

◆ letters appear in linear fashion to represent the sequence of sounds in spoken words.

◆ spaces delineate word boundaries.

◆ letters come in capitals, in small print, and even in script, but they all have the same significance.

◆ some marks are used to show beginnings and ends of text.

The ability to read is present if the child understands and acts appropriately when he sees a printed word. In other words, the child must be able to understand the concept that (1) all "things" have a name, (2) the name of the thing can be a written word, (3) the two are interchangeable, and (4) the "word symbols" can be read.

Most teachers have had children "read" to them from a favorite, memorized storybook. Generally, a word from the book will not be recognized out of context and read by the child when seen elsewhere. However, this behavior—imitative reading—can be an indication of early literacy development.

A child may develop the ability to recognize words because of an interest in printing letters. Another child may pick up the sounds of alphabet letters by listening and finding words that start with the same letter. Books and stories can also lead children into early interest and recognition of words. Some children have the ability to distinguish one word from another by sight and can easily remember words. Other children do not develop this ability until a later age.

Early readers are children who have a desire to read. They also have had interactions with others who have answered their questions and stimulated their interest. A few children will read between the ages of 4 and 5, but many will not have the capability or interest to read until a later age. About one to three preschoolers out of a hundred can read simple books. A teacher should be aware of each child's capabilities. Educators remind teachers that reading pictures is beginning reading (Figure 17–6). In daily observations and verbal conversations, a child's responses give valuable clues. The wrong answers are as important as the right ones.

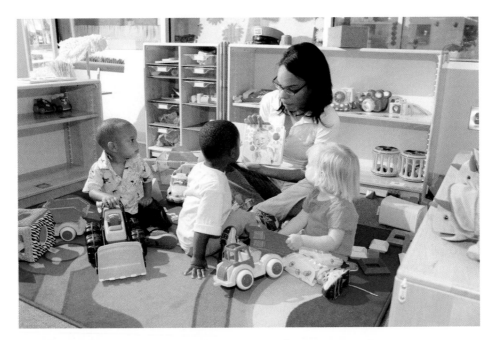

FIGURE 17–6 Reading pictures (illustrations) is beginning reading.

Attempts to identify young children's emerging ideas about the act of reading have been undertaken. Children were asked what they knew about reading at age 3, and the study continued through ages 5 or 6. The following developmental sequence seemed apparent to the researchers.

Young children

1. see reading as one aspect of social interaction. Children comment, look at illustrations, and observe page turning.

2. notice that readers eyes are on the book's pages, and if asked to read the book themselves will turn pages (front to back), and may read labeled objects or actions aloud. Some may talk to themselves, asking rhetorical questions, or speak memorized lines or words.

3. may show they realized a story has a meaningful sequence of actions or events that is reflected in the illustrations. Some children "read" from the pictures. Other children may mimic an adult's oral reading style.

4. may realize each book tells a unique story, and believe the reader has memorized it word for word.

5. grasp the idea that print tells the story and provides clues to the reader. The sounding out of simple words may begin.

6. use different and varied strategies to interpret the print.

Kindergarten teachers facing a wide range of enrolled children's language arts abilities often attempt to assess children's progress in letter identification, phonemic awareness (sound-symbol relationships), sight words, concepts of words, and printing skill. In a typical kindergarten class, children's literacy skills and functioning may span a 5-year range; that is, some may possess skills typical of 3-year-olds and others, those of 8-year-olds. Informal testing is common. Some common informal testing probes and questions follow.

1. Cards with an uppercase and lowercase printscript alphabet are displayed one by one.
   "What alphabet letter do you see?"
   "Can you tell me the sound it makes?"
   "Do you know a word that starts with this letter?"

2. The child is given paper and pencil.
"Please write alphabet letters you know."
"Tell me about the letters you've written."

3. The child is asked to write known words.
"Write all the words you know."
"Can you write your name?"

4. The child is presented a list of common sight words.
"Do you know any of these words?"

5. The child is asked to describe/tell about his favorite book.

Individualized activities can become an easier task when assessment data have been gathered.

Cambourne (1988) has also identified "reading-like" child behaviors, which follow.

1. recreating text from memory, turning pages randomly

2. recreating a text from pictures only (Each picture represents a complete text—no continuity of story line.)

3. same as 1 and 2, with a continuous story line that may or may not match the text in the book

4. recreating text from memory, running eyes and/or finger over text but not one-to-one matching of print with meaning

5. just turning pages, frontward and backward, but obviously engaging with pictures

6. Sitting next to someone else engaged in behaviors 1 through 5 and sometimes collaborating with or intervening in others' reading-like behavior

Child Knowledge of Alphabet Letters

In comparing two children—one who knows the alphabet and reads a few words and one who crudely writes his own name and makes up barely understandable stories—one may conclude that the first child is bright. However, creativity and logic are important in literacy development, and the second child may be outdistancing the first by progressing at his own speed. Literacy at any age is more than merely naming letters or words. A child's fluency and ease at recognizing letters is also deemed important. The speed and accuracy of letter naming is an index of the thoroughness or confidence with which the letters' identities have been learned. Children's effortlessness may indicate an ability to see letters as "wholes" and then see words as patterns of letters.

Other educators suggest that it is other knowledge that is learned along with the ability to name letters that is crucial. More often than not, alphabet letter names are first encountered in the alphabet song (to the tune of "Twinkle, Twinkle Little Star") or in alphabet books at ages 2, 3, and 4. Children usually memorize the oral names of a few alphabet letters. Children then develop a sense that different letter shapes have different names, and it is an easy jump to children understanding that their names are different in print than their friends' names. "That's my letter," a child may say when encountering a letter in the environment that is similar to or the same shape as the first letter of his first name.

Teachers and parents need to understand that young children have 2 to 4 years to master the letter shapes before entering kindergarten. Instruction in letter recognition usually is begun during preschool years. The goal is to ensure that letter shapes are highly familiar and recognizable to the children before they are faced with the task of learning the letters' sounds or, more generally, of learning to read words. The sounds that letters make are commonly introduced after the names of the letters are well learned, but some programs choose to introduce the letter name and sound together. Still other programs follow the recommendation of McGuiness (1997) and call letters by their sounds.

Understanding the alphabetic principle involves the knowledge that there is a systematic relationship between letters and sounds. A child's grasp of the alphabetic principle may be the single most important step toward acquiring the code that eases early reading. Many prereaders figure this out without adult help. Letter-to-sound correspondence teaching has currently and historically been the subject of countless arguments and disputes among reading instruction professionals. Many teachers believe that knowing the names of letters helps some children remember sounds.

Increasingly, early childhood educators are finding or creating new ways to include more focus on alphabet letters by capitalizing on opportunities to point out print and its uses in classroom life, by saturating their classrooms with print, and by reading quality picture books with ABC themes. It is not beneficial to force print instruction; rather, teachers should draw it into conversations and design an environment where print is hard to miss.

Head Start programs are using the Head Start Outcomes Framework to guide their program goals (U.S. Department of Health and Human Services, 2003). They are working on preschool children's ability to identify at least 10 alphabet letters, their knowledge of sound-letter associations, their ability to pay attention to separate and repeating sounds, their ability to form lines and circles, and their attempts to form alphabet letters. These teachers are also busy relating the uses and functions of print to young children's lives.

Word Recognition

The typical 4-year-old relies on idiosyncratic cues to identify words, rather than intuitively making use of letter sounds. For example, when name tags are used with different types of stickers accompanying different children's names, the sticker is usually read (recognized) rather than the print.

A CLOSER LOOK AT EARLY READERS

Researchers studying both gifted children and early readers notice that parents overwhelmingly report that they have read to their children from birth on or from the time the children learned to sit up. Research shows that early readers who learned to read without systematic instruction had one common experience, despite their different backgrounds: they were all introduced to books between the ages of 3 and 5. Home activities mentioned by the parents of early readers are shown in Figure 17–7. Frequently, parents also spend time with their young child using the computer or other kinds of electronic media—both educational program and entertainment varieties, and someone reads books aloud on a regular basis. Many reading experts believe that children who achieve at an outstanding level have families that did not impose their learning priorities upon their very young but instead followed the child's lead, emphasizing play and a rich, stimulating environment rather than formal instruction. Studies of the early reader indicate that the child was usually exposed to a variety of reading material and enjoyed watching educational television, spending close to equal time in both pursuits. An interest in print characterizes

TYPE OF ACTIVITY	FREQUENCY OF REPORT
daily readings with pointing at words	6/6
showing words in magazines	2/6
teaching names of letters	6/6
teaching sight vocabulary	5/6
making rhymes with words	5/6
playing letter games	6/6
helping learn sounds of letters	6/6
helping put words together	6/6
playing spelling games	6/6
playing add-a-letter games	1/6
listening to child read aloud	5/6
having child read after parent	1/6
doing alternative reading	2/6
working on sounding out words	2/6
providing books on an appropriate level	3/6

FIGURE 17–7 Six parents' reading activities with their children. (From Anbar, A. [1986, March]. Reading acquisition of preschool children without systematic instruction. *Early Childhood Research Quarterly, 1*[1], 69–83. Copyright © 1986 Elsevier. Used with permission.)

precocious readers, and their parents are described as responsive—noticing child interests and providing help when asked. Many child-centered family activities were part of the early reader's family lifestyle. These children seemed fascinated and obsessed with the alphabet, and parents reported that they answered questions, read to the child, and engaged in play activities with letters and words but had not set out with a systematic plan to teach reading. One study of early readers identified possible stages in these children's learning process (Figure 17–8).

If we could examine parent-child storybook readings closely, simply reading aloud does not describe most parent actions accurately. Pointing out book features, relating book happenings to shared family experiences, defining words, engaging in turn-taking dialogue, prompting children's identification and naming of illustrations, listening to children's memorized "readings," and engaging in other parental interactions are all part of the experience (Figure 17–9). Educators use the same techniques.

Adults support efforts to ease children's difficulty in learning to read. These efforts can include

◆ finding good books in which the pictures closely match the words.

◆ prompting, "Will you point to the words as you read them?"

◆ letting children ponder the problem that what they are saying does not match the number of words they are pointing to in the print and hoping children self-correct themselves.

◆ saying, "Great self-correcting," when it happens.

◆ watching for confusion and modeling the strategies readers use when they encounter problems. For example, pausing to see whether the child backs up and rereads on his own or saying, "Try it again, that's what I usually do."

The goal is for the black marks on the page to give the child enough feedback that the child can adjust his approximation. This marks a huge step in the process of learning to read.

Other effective strategies that early readers use to help themselves include

◆ orienting themselves to a book as a whole.

◆ studying the pictures to heighten their sense of what the words say.

◆ guessing at what the print probably says.

◆ checking to confirm or disprove their guesses.

◆ pointing to words.

For early readers, many experienced teachers recommend books with repetitive, patterned text and books with a jazzy, rhythmic phrase on every page that may change just a word or two as text moves ahead. Teachers watch out for and avoid books that consist of meaningless, silly ditties. Looking for logical books that are both interesting and tailored to a child's life and past experience is the

Stage I	a preliminary period of gaining awareness and general knowledge of books and print (starting any time during the first year)
Stage II	learning to identify and name the letters and acquiring beginning sight vocabulary (starting around 12–18 months)
Stage III	learning the sounds of the letters (starting around 20–24 months)
Stage IV	putting together words (starting around 24–32 months)
Stage V	active reading from familiar books (starting around 20–30 months)
Stage VI	sounding out short, unfamiliar words (starting around 32–34 months)
Stage VII	reading easy, unfamiliar books (around 36 months)
Stage VIII	reading for enjoyment of content (around 48 months)

FIGURE 17–8 Stages in the learning process of early readers. (From Anbar, A. [1986, March]. Reading acquisition of preschool children without systematic instruction. *Early Childhood Research Quarterly, 1*[1], 69–83. Copyright © 1986 Elsevier. Used with permission.)

FIGURE 17–9 Teachers, like parents, often point out and discuss features in books.

prudent course of action. A list of suggested books follows.

Barton, B. (1984). *Building a house*. New York: Puffin

Boelts, M. (2007). *Those shoes*. Cambridge, MA: Candlewick.

Christelow, E. (1989). *Five little monkeys jumping on the bed*. New York: Clarion Books.

Gravett, E. (2007). *Orange pear apple bear*. New York: Simon & Schuster.

Hutchins, P. (1968). *Rosie's walk*. New York: Macmillan.

Krauss, R. (1974). *The carrot seed*. New York: Scholastic Book Services.

What should happen when a child expects to learn to read the first day of school or kindergarten? Many kindergarten teachers suggest a teacher should "make it happen." The child should go home after the first day able to read a simple sentence such as "My name is _____." This enhances the child's perceptions that he can read. A big portion of the battle to improve children's self-esteem occurs and allows the child to believe in himself.

SHARED READING

Many pre-kindergartens, kindergartens, and lower elementary school classes conduct group reading activities called shared readings. Often, 14-by-17-inch or larger books, called Big Books, or teacher-made charts are introduced, discussed, and read. On a first reading, the book's cover and illustrations are examined. Predictions about the story or other content take place. Text is large, and colorful illustrations are directly connected to the text. Words are repeated frequently. After a first reading, children may be prompted to share something they noticed in the book. While reading, the teacher puts one hand under each word and moves from top to bottom and left to right. Children may be asked to guess words or predict story outcomes.

Shared reading promotes both letter and sound recognition, especially after repeated readings. In the course of shared reading, children query what a particular word says, notice that some words rhyme, and notice words with

Chapter 17 • Reading and Preschoolers   **561**

the same sound or letter. The teacher encourages discussion and children's touching or pointing to book features. Pleasant attitudes toward the experience are built through accepting and appreciating each child's comments and ideas. It is easy to see that this exercise will result in children's efforts to point out letters, words, or rhymes that they know. Both fiction and nonfiction titles are used.

VOCABULARY AND EARLY READERS

A child's vocabulary is strongly related to his comprehension and ease of learning to read. Reading comprehension involves applying letter-sound correspondence to a printed word and matching it to a known word in the reader's oral vocabulary. Oral vocabulary is a key in making the transition from oral to written forms. Many studies agree that reading ability and vocabulary size are related (National Reading Panel, 2000).

In trying to measure children's vocabulary, one finds that different vocabularies exist. Receptive vocabulary is seen in toddlers, who follow requests such as "get Grandpa's brown shoes" before they can say the words. Productive vocabulary is used when we speak or write to another. Oral vocabulary refers to words that are recognized in speaking or listening. For example, the toddler may bring Grandpa's black shoes because color words are not part of his oral vocabulary. Reading vocabulary refers to words that are used or recognized in print. Many young children can be described as having a reading vocabulary when they correctly recognize street signs and commercial fast-food symbols. Sight vocabulary is a subset of reading vocabulary. A sight word is immediately recognized as a whole and does not require word analysis for identification. Early childhood teachers rarely know the size of preschoolers' sight vocabularies unless they do assessments. When they do, they find some preschoolers have amazingly large ones.

Early childhood educators consciously promote and prompt vocabulary development.

They relish and model an interest in words, their definitions, and dictionary use. New words enter children's vocabularies daily in a developmental environment. Teachers explain new words and relate them to children's experience by giving examples. Sight vocabulary words are composed of alphabet letters that can be named and sounded out, so-called teaching moment naturals. Kindergarten classrooms (and some preschools) have word charts, word lists, word walls, words used for labeling, and words in displays. Preschools have abundant alphabet letters and words used in functional ways.

Considerable study suggests that a small vocabulary is one major determinant of poor reading comprehension for Latino children and others who lag in readiness in the first grades of elementary school. Every effort in early childhood centers is made to aid children's oral vocabulary and work toward depth of understanding through firsthand experience, exposure to books, classroom discussion, play with peers, and the scheduling of frequent daily literacy events.

Some preschools develop a "Words I Know" file box for children who wish to have one. It can be taken home occasionally. Words are dictated by children then printed by the teacher. An oblong box with strips of sturdy paper works well. Printing with a wide-tip black marker is recommended. Strips can be used for tracing and other activities, when appropriate. Some preschoolers have sizable sight word vocabularies, as was mentioned. Sylvia Ashton-Warner (1963) believed, as do many other early childhood educators, that first words have intense meaning for a child. Ashton-Warner's conviction gave rise to her articulation of what she called the organic reading method, which used key vocabulary for teaching reading and writing.

OBJECTIVES

Differences exist in the objectives of instruction between (1) educators who believe in readiness activities and (2) educators who advocate natural self-discovery of reading skills.

The first group hopes to facilitate learning and enjoyment of reading. The second group foresees the child's experimentation—creating ideas about reading, based on his notions of the use of writing and reading, and attempting to crack the code with supportive assistance. Both groups favor a print-rich classroom, and objectives in many programs are based on a consideration of a blending of the two positions. Both groups also agree that experiences with classic and quality literature and dramatic activity help children's early literacy.

Programs that choose to include reading readiness among their instructional goals and objectives plan activities that promote the following skills and attitudes.

- recognizing incongruities—the ability to see the inappropriateness of a situation or statement, such as "The mouse swallowed the elephant"
- recognizing context clues—realizing that pictures on the same page give visual clues to the words
- acquiring the ability to listen
- building vocabulary through firsthand experiences
  recognizing likenesses and differences
  identifying through sight and sound
  rhyming
  increasing memory span
  recalling sequence and content
  following directions
- increasing speech output
  developing attitudes of each child's ability and worth
  increasing imaginative and creative speech
- building critical thinking and problem solving with language
  identifying through clues
  classifying, sorting, and organizing
  developing concepts and recognizing relationships
  anticipating outcomes
  seeing cause-and-effect relationships
- developing self-confidence—attitudes of competence

- increasing interest and motivation through enjoyment of and success in language activities
- developing left and right awareness
- developing positive attitudes toward books and skills in book use
  turning pages
  storing and handling books with care

Phonemic awareness, the awareness that words are composed of sounds, is important in facilitating learning to read. What can early childhood educators do to encourage phonemic awareness? Reading experts suggest literature that focuses on some kind of play with the sounds of language to help children "naturally" develop awareness. Books including alliteration, rhyme, repetition, and sound substitution fit this category.

Educators seriously consider each child's attitude development concerning reading times and reading in general. In both their actions and words, teachers convey their attitudes. If actions and words value reading and express enthusiasm (and joy) for finding out what enjoyment or information is possible in a book, young children also tend to adopt an "Oh boy, a book" orientation. They may then accept the idea that reading books can be a pleasurable pursuit—a treat, a door to adventure, fantasy, fun!

SEQUENCE OF READING BEHAVIOR

In the absence of adult intervention that emphasizes another sequence, children generally seem to develop reading and writing abilities as follows:

1. The child develops an awareness of the functions and value of the reading and writing processes before becoming interested in acquiring specific knowledge and skills.
2. The child is likely to give greater attention to words and letters that have some personal significance, such as his name or the names of family, pets, and so forth.

3. The child develops both reading and writing skills simultaneously as complementary aspects of the same communication processes, rather than as separate sets of learning.

4. The child develops an awareness of words as separate entities (as evidenced when he dictates words slowly so that the teacher can keep pace in writing them down) before showing awareness or interest in how specific letters represent sounds.

5. The child becomes familiar with the appearance of many of the letters by visually examining them, playing games with them, and so forth, before trying to master their names, the sounds they represent, or their formation.

6. The child becomes aware of the sound similarities between high-interest words (such as significant names) and makes many comparisons between their component parts before showing any persistence in deciphering unfamiliar words by blending together the sounds of individual letters.

As stated earlier, the teacher will probably encounter a few preschool children who have already learned how to read simple words and simple books, but there may be others reading at much higher levels. Some children, usually older 4-year-olds, seem quite interested in alphabet letters, words, and writing. Teachers know the center's goals for each child.

It is important for teachers to be able to help the child's existing reading abilities and actively plan for future reading skill. Figure 17–10 lists accomplishments during kindergarten.

The Transition to Kindergarten

A relatively new entity, the **transitional kindergarten**, exists in some communities. It may have a curriculum designed to support each child's early skill or address at-risk status through special summer intervention classes and/or increased parental and community participation in the child's learning. Its goal is to offer children a transitional period to enhance their effectiveness as prereaders. The goals of most transitional programs involve both child self-regulation and social interaction. Playing appropriately with others, collaborating, planning play directions, sharing, taking turns, approaching peers to play, and knowing some of the other children's names are social interaction skills. Self-regulation includes watching peers to find out what is expected, imitating behaviors, following classroom routines and rules, changing behavior when necessary, waiting, standing in line, and taking care of personal items. To perform some of these tasks the child needs to accept the teacher as an authority figure.

The communication goals that a transitional program might target are similar to those targeted in preschool, such as responding to teacher questions; offering ideas in group discussions; expressing needs, fears, and feelings; following simple "school-talk" directions; remembering items and actions previously seen or heard; and knowing how to appropriately ask for adult help. In a transitional program, children are expected to listen when it is time to listen, sit when it is time to sit, and finish assigned tasks. The child's ability to make a transition from a parent at arrival and back to parent's authority at departure is another program goal.

READING METHODS

Research studies conducted to try to pinpoint the one best **reading method** for teaching children to read have concluded that there is no proven best method. A position statement

---

transitional kindergarten — a relatively new feature of some elementary school districts that offers supportive literacy activities and classroom access (usually during the summer before the child is to enroll in kindergarten).
reading method — any of several relatively specific procedures or steps for teaching one or more aspects of reading, each procedure embodying explicitly or implicitly some theory of how children learn and of the relationship between written and spoken language.

KINDERGARTEN ACCOMPLISHMENTS

- knows the parts of a book and their functions
- begins to track print when listening to familiar text being read or when rereading own writing
- "reads" familiar texts emergently (i.e., not necessarily verbatim from the print alone)
- recognizes and can name all uppercase and lowercase letters
- understands that the sequence of letters in a written word represents the sequence of sounds (phonemes) in a spoken word (alphabetic principle)
- learns many, although not all, one-to-one letter sound correspondences
- recognizes some words by sight, including a few very common ones (a, the, I, my, you, is, are)
- uses new vocabulary and grammatical constructions in own speech
- makes appropriate switches from oral to written language situations
- notices when simple sentences fail to make sense
- connects information and events in texts to life and life to text experiences
- retells, reenacts, or dramatizes stories or parts of stories
- listens attentively to books teacher reads to class
- can name some book titles and authors
- demonstrates familiarity with a number of types or genres of text (e.g., storybooks, expository texts, poems, newspapers, and everyday print such as signs, notices, labels)
- correctly answers questions about stories read aloud
- makes predictions based on illustrations or portions of stories
- demonstrates understanding that spoken words consist of sequences of phonemes
- given spoken sets like "dan, dan, den," can identify the first two as being the same and third as different
- given spoken sets like "dak, pat, zen," can identify the first two as sharing a same sound
- given spoken segments, can merge them into a meaningful target word
- given a spoken word, can produce another word that rhymes with it
- independently writes many uppercase and lowercase letters
- uses phonemic awareness and letter knowledge to spell independently (invented or created spelling)
- writes (unconventionally) to express own meaning
- builds a repertoire of some conventionally spelled words
- shows awareness of distinction between "kid writing" and conventional orthography
- writes own name (first and last) and the first names of some friends or classmates
- can write most letters and some words when they are dictated

FIGURE 17–10 Kindergarten accomplishments in reading. (Reprinted with permission from Snow, C., Burns, S., & Griffin, P. [Eds.]. [1998]. *Preventing reading difficulties in young children.* Washington, DC: National Academy Press. Copyright 1998 by the National Academy of Sciences. Courtesy of the National Academies Press, Washington, DC.)

developed by the International Reading Association (1999) reads:

> There is no single method or single combination of methods that can successfully teach all children to read. Therefore, teachers must have a strong knowledge of multiple methods for teaching reading and a strong knowledge of the children in their care so they can create the appropriate balance of methods needed for the children they teach. (p. 1–2)

The important factors seem to be the teacher's (1) enthusiasm for the method or technique used and (2) understanding of the method used. The ideal situation for a child learning to read is a one-to-one child/teacher ratio, with the reading activity suited to the child's individual capacity, learning style, and individual interests. This is difficult to fulfill in an early childhood learning center because of the number of children per group and the many other duties required of a teacher. Other limitations can include the teacher's amount of training, knowledge of a variety of methods to teach reading, and ability to plan interesting and appropriate activities within a print-rich classroom.

What preschool teachers need to understand is that advocates of many differing methods used to teach reading agree that a rich, strong base in quality children's literature and well-developed oral language and listening skill aid success in whatever reading method is eventually used. Most educators, including Farstrup (2006), acknowledge that even with repeated reform efforts and the existence of data that demonstrates the overall success of public schools, many students, especially minority and poor children, fail to succeed in learning to read. Reading instruction integrates attention to the alphabetic principle with attention to the construction of meaning and opportunities to develop fluency. Integration means that opportunities to learn these two aspects of skilled reading should be going on at the same time, in the context of the same activities, and that the choice of instructional activities should be part of an overall, coherent approach to supporting literacy development, not a haphazard selection from unrelated, varied activities.

How best to teach beginning reading may be the most politicized topic in the field of education. Shanahan (2006) notes that arguments about whole language, phonics, and the best way to teach children to read have been epidemic.

The Natural Approach

Popular approaches to reading include what has been termed "natural" reading. The basic premise of this method centers on the idea that a child can learn to read as he learned to talk, that is, with adult attention and help with early skills. Advocates feel that children learn to read in a literate society the same way they learned to talk, walk, draw, and sing: by seeing and hearing reading modeled skillfully and by noticing and understanding that this is an interesting and useful thing to do.

In the natural approach, an interest in print (words) leads to invented spelling and reading. "Organic" and natural reading systems propose that children learn to read by authoring from their own experiences, and by being exposed to great classic literature as well as child-authored literature.

Educators associated with natural reading include Ashton-Warner (1963), Johnson (1987), and Fields (1987). The well-known work of Allen (1969) has led to a method called the language-experience approach and can be thought of as a popular early form of the natural method. Stauffer (1970) points out the specific features of the language-experience approach that he believes make it especially appropriate for young children.

- a base in children's language development and firsthand experiencing
- stress on children's interests, experiences, and cognitive and social development
- respect for children's need for activity and involvement
- requirement for meaningful learning experiences
- integration of school and public library resources with classroom reading materials
- encouragement of children's creative writing as a meaningful approach to using and practicing reading and writing skills

Johnson (1987), influenced by the work of Sylvia Ashton-Warner, recommends starting 5-year-olds reading through a procedure that elicits children's images. The images are then connected to printed captions. Individual important images merge as meaningful words to be shared with others through sight reading. Slowly, visual discrimination, capitalization, sentence sense, phonetics, and punctuation are accomplished at each child's particular pace.

Sylvia Ashton-Warner's method of teaching reading inspired a whole generation of teachers during the 1960s. Thompson (2000) believes that Ashton-Warner gives today's teachers an early model for teaching multicultural children to read. Thompson describes Ashton-Warner's techniques.

> What she called her "scheme" for working in the New Zealand bicultural context may be, in some very basic ways, universally adaptable to intercultural or transcultural education for the new millennium. Organic teaching requires the teacher to listen to the pupils, to truly hear them and encourage what is important to them, and to use that as the working material for teaching and learning. This concept, Ashton-Warner asserts, embodies the kind of attitude necessary for building trans-cultural bridges for sharing understanding of cultures, ultimately a possible direction leading to peace in our shrinking global village. (p. 155)

The author recommends, as most teacher-training programs recommend, the early childhood educator's reading of Ashton-Warner's book *Teacher* (1963), for it is as pertinent today as it was more than 45 years ago.

To many people, the terms natural and organic methods and language-experience and language arts approaches are synonymous and describe the same or similar methods of reading instruction. Robisson (1983) recommends the language-experience approach to young children's teachers because this method is a natural way to build on children's expressive and cognitive activities and because it is flexible and adaptable. She suggests that new teachers collect a large repertoire of activities from the many writers who have contributed to the development of this method. Allen and Allen's *Language Experience Activities* (1982) is a valuable resource. Because no one reading method is superior, teachers should be able to use features of phonic, linguistic, or sight-word recognition that seem useful at any given time

(Robisson, 1983). In other words, combine methods.

The language arts approach to reading instruction introduces children to written words through their own interest in play, through their enjoyment of speaking, and by listening to language. Often, children's first experience with written words comes from their own speech and actions. A sign that says "John's Block Tower" or "Free Kittens" may be the child's first exposure to reading. The emphasis is on the fact that words are part of daily living.

Educators' attitudes toward reading instruction have been influenced by various factors: current research, some American children's struggle to read, poor national reading performance (National Assessment of Educational Progress, 1995), and children's lack of school success because of their reading ability. Natural and organic approaches have lost favor. They are thought to be incomplete—good as far as they go, but not as systematic or explicit as they might be.

The Whole-Language Movement

Enthusiasm for a reading philosophy and approach called "whole language" is apparent in some elementary schools.

Whole-language advocates believe in offering children meaningful and functional literature in full literary texts rather than through worksheets or dittoed handouts. The approach emphasizes the interrelated nature of the language arts. It believes that learning in any one area of language arts helps learning in others.

The whole-language approach is similar to what is termed the "natural-language" approach in early childhood books, journals, and professional teacher-training literature. The whole-language approach is a philosophy that suggests that children learn language skill by following the natural learning behavior that governs the way they learn to talk, and that writing, listening, reading, and speaking activities grow from a child's experiences and interests (Figure 17–11). The teacher directs natural curiosity into activities that develop skills.

FIGURE 17–11 Because Evan has displayed an interest in a special topic, the teacher provides a related book.

All sorts of literature (instead of basal readers) are used in whole-language classrooms, including posters, comics, classic literature, quality books, magazines, and newspapers, to mention a few. Poetry, songs, chants, and simple drama activities are among the language activities offered. The whole-language teacher presents opportunities for learning and development by relating activities to a single theme. Spontaneous conversational exchanges are typical and seen as enhancing and extending learning. Teachers using this approach draw attention to connections between speaking, writing, and reading by saying things like, "I heard you say *boat*. This is how you write that. Now let's read it." There are usually no ability-grouped reading circles, and classrooms are described as busy, active, and full of talk.

Goodman (1986) has listed basic beliefs that most early childhood educators attempting whole-language instruction believe are crucial.

◆ Whole-language learning builds around whole learners learning whole language in whole situations.

◆ Whole-language learning assumes respect for language, for the learner, and for the teacher.

◆ The focus is on meaning, not on language itself, in authentic speech and literacy events.

◆ Learners are encouraged to take risks and invited to use language, in all its varieties, for their own purposes.

◆ In a whole-language classroom, all the varied functions of oral and written language are appropriate and encouraged. (p. 99)

Critics point out that there are no formulas for planning, developing, organizing, and managing whole-language curriculum and that consequently, whole-language teachers with similar philosophies may differ in what curriculum they present. Other criticism usually centers on the teacher's ability to assess each child's reading progress and the lack of instruction in phonics.

Walmsley and Adams (1993) speak about the challenge apparent in translating whole-language theory into practice.

> Letting go some or all of the traditional teacher's control of the classroom's activities and behaviors does not come easily to teachers, even if they subscribe to a child-centered philosophy. And the consequences of liberating oneself from traditional practice are often not easy to accept. Many of the teachers are finding it hard to adjust to a changed classroom environment, even though few of them have serious doubts about the instructional philosophy they have newly embraced. (p. 17)

Walmsley and Adams (1993) predict that the whole-language movement will survive but not dominate American public education. This has proved to be true. Exclusion of phonics instruction by some whole-language teachers and lower reading achievement test scores in some whole-language classrooms have caused additional concern. In 1987 California adopted a reading program focused on teaching children to read simply by exposing them to literature. Reading achievement scores fell, and California fourth-graders tied for last place among states in the 1994 National Assessment of Educational Progress's reading report card.

Many educators today believe that whole language has become a full-fledged, although still evolving, theory of learning and teaching. It exemplifies a constructionist view of learning, believing concepts and complex processes are constructs of the human brain; therefore, research suggests that the greater the intellectual and emotional involvement in learning, the more effectively the brain learns, uses, and retains what is learned.

Resources for early childhood teachers wishing to know more about reading instruction are found in the Additional Resources section at the end of this chapter.

Literature-Based Reading Programs

A literature-based reading curriculum has been adopted or recommended in many states. Au (2006) describes literature-based instruction as involving a continuum of strategies to be applied as children move up through the grades in elementary school: shared reading, guided reading, guided discussion, and literature discussion groups (also known as literature circles or book clubs). In addition, two strategies are used and considered important across the grade levels: teacher read-alouds and sustained silent reading.

Teachers using this approach to reading instruction usually fall into three groups (or types) depending on how "literature-based" is defined and carried out in their classrooms. The three types may vary somewhat with each teacher.

1. Literature-based readers. Basal reading programs that use literature content texts are adopted. In about 80 percent of these texts, the stories are faithful to the original writing. Books are based on selections of stories, not whole books. Teachers' guides and workbooks suggest fragmented kinds of word study and fill-in-the-blank exercises.

2. Basalization of literature. A literature-based reading program uses real books to study but treats them as basal readers.

3. Comprehensive literature program. Literature permeates the curriculum. Teachers read aloud to children; they give children a choice of real books for their own reading; they make use of the fine informational books that we have today to use literature in every area of the curriculum; and they encourage children's response to books through discussion, drama, art, and writing. Their primary goal is to produce children who not only know how to read but also become readers.

Educators are examining New Zealand's literature-based reading approach because New Zealand is recognized as the most literate country in the world. New Zealand's instructional approach is similar to whole-language theory put into practice. The instructional model was instituted after educational research pointed to the success of literature-based models. An influx of culturally diverse children who were not adequately progressing in reading prompted New Zealand's use of newer instructional methodology.

The Decoding, or Phonetic, Reading Approach

Decoding, using a phonetic approach to reading instruction, is based on teaching children the 44 language sounds (phonemes), which are 26 alphabet letters and combinations (graphemes). This approach assumes that, to read, children first must be able to "decode"; that is, they must be able to pronounce the letter sequences they see on a page based on what they know about the link between spelling and sound. An underlying skill is phonemic awareness, the understanding that words, even simple ones like *cat*, are composed of individual sounds called phonemes, which make a difference in meaning. Only one phoneme makes the difference between rope and soap.

Although phonetic approaches differ widely, most users believe that when children know which sounds are represented by which letters or letter combinations, they can "attack" an unknown word and decode it. Some schools using this approach begin decoding sessions when all sounds have been learned; others expose children to select sounds and offer easily decoded words early. A few phonetic approach systems require teachers to use letter sounds exclusively and later introduce the individual letter names, such as *a, b, c,* and so forth.

Five "word-attack" (or decoding) skills are helpful in the complicated process of learning to read.

1. picture clues—using an adjacent picture (visual) to guess at a word near it (usually on the same page)
2. configuration clues—knowing a word because you remember its outline
3. context clues—guessing an unknown word by known words that surround it
4. phonetic clues—knowing the sound a symbol represents
5. structural clues—seeing similar parts of words and knowing what these symbols say and mean

Phonics may be most useful when a reader already has some general notion of what a word should be. A child trying to guess a word he does not know at the end of a sentence read by an adult, such as "the cup fell on the f____," might guess "fire." Such a guess would be phonetically reasonable, but a child relying on meaning would guess "floor."

Cunningham (2003), who attempted to identify the best way to teach phonics, cites the findings of the National Reading Panel:

> **The National Reading Panel (2000) reviewed the experimental research on teaching phonics and determined that explicit and systematic phonics is superior to non-systematic or no phonics, but that there is no significant difference in effectiveness among the kinds of systematic phonics instruction. They also found no significant difference in effectiveness among tutoring, small-group, or whole-class phonics instruction. (p. 74)**

Advocates of **phonetic instruction** are often critical and vocal about the exclusive use of any one reading approach that neglects phonics. Most teachers recognize that some children can learn to read with little or no phonetic instruction. They also note that many children may have difficulty without it.

See additional readings on phonetic instruction in the Additional Resources section at this chapter's end.

Look-and-Say Method

Many of the children who do read during preschool years have learned words through a "look-and-say" (whole-word) approach. That is, when they see the written letters of their name or a familiar word, they can identify the name or word. They have recognized and memorized that group of symbols. It is believed that children who learn words in this fashion have memorized the shape or configuration of the word. They often confuse words that have similar outlines, such as "Jane" for "June" or "saw" for "sew." They may not know the alphabet names of the letters or the sounds of each letter. This approach was prevalent in public school reading instruction in the twentieth century, but it is rarely used today. Children who are good at noticing slight differences and who have good memories seem to progress and become successful readers.

Other Approaches to Reading Instruction

Many elementary school districts emphasize that their approach to reading instruction is a combined or balanced approach. This approach offers a rich diet of quality literature and literary experiences plus a sound foundation of phonics. Cowen (2005) defines a balance reading approach as follows:

> A *balanced reading approach* is research-based, assessment-based, comprehensive, integrated and dynamic, in that it

---

phonetic instruction — instruction in phonics is instruction that stresses sound-symbol relationships. It is a strategy used in beginning reading instruction.

empowers teachers and specialists to respond to the individual assessed literacy needs of children as they relate to their appropriate instructional and developmental levels of decoding, vocabulary, reading comprehension, motivation, and socio-cultural acquisition, with the purpose of learning to read meaning, understanding, and joy. (p. 10)

Morrow and Asbury (2003) recommend and describe a comprehensive approach as follows:

A comprehensive approach that acknowledges the importance of both form (phonetic awareness, phonics mechanics, etc.), and function (comprehension, purpose, meaning) of the literacy processes, and recognizes that learning occurs most effectively in a whole-part-whole context. This type of instruction is characterized by meaningful literacy activities that provide children with both the skills and the desire to achieve proficient and lifelong literacy learning. There are multiple experiences with word study activities; guided, shared, silent, collaborative, independent, and content-connected reading and writing; and oral reading to build fluency. The reading and writing take place in whole-class, small-group, one-on-one, teacher directed, and social center settings in which children can practice what they have learned. Materials used include instructional texts, manipulative objects, and meaningful children's literature. The instruction is spontaneous, authentic, and not only involves students in problem solving, but it is also direct, explicit, and systematic. (p. 45)

Cassidy and Cassidy (2004) conducted a survey of 25 literacy leaders from prominent literacy organizations. They found that scientific evidence-based reading research and instructional approaches are the hottest topics in literacy learning. Other survey topics of very decided interest were reading comprehension, direct/explicit instruction, English as a second language learners, fluency, high-stakes assessment, literacy coaches/reading coaches, phonemic awareness, phonics, and political/policy influences on literacy.

Reading Instruction in Public Elementary Schools

An individual teacher's method of reading instruction is heavily influenced by many factors, including teacher experience regarding what works, politics, economics, and the popular wisdom of the day.

Cunningham and Creamer (2003) have reviewed what has happened since 2000. These authors note that reading instruction up to the present has experienced a "pendulum swing"—from whole language and silent reading in the middle to late 1990s to intensive phonics and oral reading today.

Other eras are identified as follows:

◆ phonics era (1956–1964)
◆ language, literature, and discovery-learning era (1965–1974)
◆ individualized specific skills instruction era (1975–1986)
◆ language, literature, and discovery-learning era (1987–1995)
◆ phonics and oral reading era (1996–)

In a review of current reading instruction research, one finds the terms *balanced, eclectic, research-based, accountable, phonetic awareness, phonics instruction, fluency, comprehension,* and *alphabetics.* The field of reading instruction seems to lack consensus concerning what constitutes the best practices for the teaching of reading.

Educators that understand different eras, trends, and schools of thought can make a real contribution to children's literacy learning and reading success. Teachers can influence most schools and construct their own version of best practices in reading instruction, particularly if they get results.

Standards, assessment, and accountability are current factors in public school classrooms. The No Child Left Behind Act (NCLB) is driving change. School boards and school districts are promoting reading instruction based on standards. Teachers and teacher groups realize their instructional methods and strategies must match and fit within identified language arts parameters. Testing will take place, and the results will be published. Every effort is being made to make parents and early childhood educators aware of the foundations of literacy, particularly the language skills and abilities necessary for successful participation in kindergarten. These include phonological and phonemic awareness, an understanding of the alphabetic principle, alphabet letter recognition, social and group skills, concepts about print, an adequate vocabulary, oral language, listening ability, early reading, writing and invented spelling development, and visual-perceptual skills.

It must be noted here that although many advocates and educators are pleased with the NCLB Act, other teachers and administrators are critical of the requirements imposed by the NCLB legislation and are hopeful that a new president and/or Congress will change the law or in some way improve it.

THE READING RECOVERY PROGRAM

Reading Recovery (RR), a well-known beginning reading intervention program, was designed for first-graders experiencing difficulty learning to read. The program provided one-on-one tutoring by teachers who received extensive training in beginning reading theory and practical application. Marie Clay (1993), a New Zealand educator, is credited as being the "architect" of the program.

Teacher-tutors' daily routine with identified children included the rereading of familiar books, working with alphabet letters, writing a sentence, and learning a new book (Invernizzi, 2003). Tutored lessons lasted 30 minutes and continued for 12 to 20 weeks, or until the child reached the level of the classroom's middle-level reading group.

RR evaluation studies conducted by Shanahan and Barr (1995) found that

. . . children who received Reading Recovery instruction make sizable gains in reading achievement during the first grade year [comparing] favorably with those of higher achieving first graders who received only classroom instruction, along with compensatory support. (p. 11)

Other researchers suggest that earlier intervention aimed at preventing problems would yield more powerful benefits than later attempts of remediation. In other words, intervention should occur before problems are apparent.

RR, a model used by many other later tutoring programs, has its critics. These criticisms mention RR's use of an incidental, student-centered approach to phonics and vocabulary development and its expense.

A controversy exists concerning the stability of RR student gains. Some evaluators believe gains diminished substantially during the students' third and fourth school years.

THE ROLE OF STORY TIMES AND BOOK-READING EXPERIENCES

Many teachers who are faced with the responsibility of teaching reading believe that the ease in learning to read is directly related to the amount of time a child has been read to by parents, teachers, and others. Think of the difference in exposure hours between a child who has been read to nightly and one who has not.

Books have a language of their own; conversation is quite different. Books are not just written oral conversation but include descriptions, primarily full sentences, rhythm, dialogue, and much more. Listen to adults as they read books to young children; they adopt special voices and mannerisms and communicate much differently from everyday speech. Through repeated experience, children learn that illustrations usually reflect what a book is saying; this knowledge helps them make educated guesses of both meanings and printed words adjacent to pictures.

Storybook sessions are reading sessions and can greatly affect the child's future with books. If teachers wish to evaluate how well they are doing in making books important to children in their programs, the following set of questions will help.

1. During free-choice periods, how many children go to the library corner and look at books by themselves (Figure 17–12)?

2. How many requests to read during the day do adults get from children?

3. How many children listen attentively during story time?

4. How many books have been borrowed by parents during the week?

5. Which books have become special favorites, as shown by signs of extra wear?

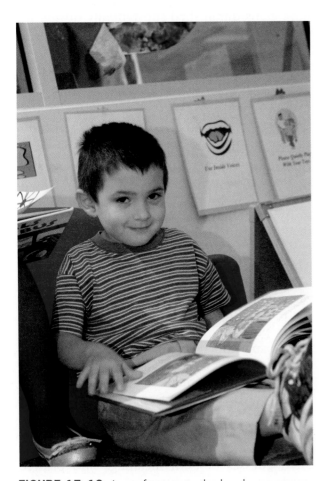

FIGURE 17–12 Aram frequents the book area more than most others in his class.

PARENTS' ROLE IN READING

Parents often want to find ways to help their children succeed in school. Because the ability to read is an important factor in early schooling, parents may seek the advice of the teacher.

Many programs keep parents informed of the school's agenda and goals and the children's progress. An early childhood center's staff realizes that parents and teachers working together can reinforce what children learn at home and at school.

The following are suggestions for parents who want to help their children's language and reading-skill development. Many are similar to suggestions for teachers in early childhood centers.

◆ Show an interest in what children have to say. Respond to children, giving clear, descriptive, full statements.

◆ Arrange for children to have playmates and to meet and talk to people of all ages.

◆ Make children feel secure. Encourage and accept their opinions and feelings.

◆ Develop a pleasant voice and offer the best model of speech possible.

◆ Encourage children to listen and to explore by feeling, smelling, seeing, and tasting, when possible.

◆ Enjoy new experiences. Talk about them as they happen. Each community has interesting places to visit with young children—parks, stores, museums, zoos, buses, and trains are only a few suggestions.

◆ Read to children and tell them stories; stop when they lose interest. Try to develop children's enjoyment of books and knowledge of how to care for them. Provide a quiet place for children to enjoy books on their own.

◆ Make an alphabet book with your preschooler.

◆ Listen to what children are trying to say rather than how they are saying it.

◆ Have confidence in children's abilities. Patience and encouragement help language skills grow.

◆ If parents have questions about their children's language skills, they should consult the children's teachers.

SUMMARY

The fourth area of the language arts is reading. Early childhood centers do not offer formal reading instruction because it is developmentally inappropriate. A few preschoolers do have actual reading skill. Most preschoolers, however, are only beginning to form ideas about reading. Early childhood educators offer systematic and explicit instruction in literacy skills. They work to prepare and promote children's ability to learn to read with ease when formal reading instruction begins.

The goal of the teacher is to blend the language arts skills—listening, speaking, reading, printscript, and viewing—into successful experiences. Because the skills are so closely connected, one activity can flow into another activity in a logical fashion. This gives young children a clearer picture of communication.

Experiences in classic and contemporary quality literature and other language arts activities provide a background for reading. Abilities, attitudes, skills, and understanding grow at an individual rate. There are many methods of teaching language arts; each center decides which course of action or activities are best suited for attending children. Children exposed to a rich offering of language opportunities that includes paying attention to the understanding of written and oral materials are judged to have the best chance of becoming competent and lifelong readers.

This chapter reviewed a number of reading methods and approaches used to teach reading, and it cited current practice and the factors influencing it. The child's crucial development of positive attitudes concerning reading, books, and their own communicating competencies was emphasized.

Parents and teachers work together to give children the opportunity to gain reading skill and to keep children's interest alive and personally rewarding.

ADDITIONAL RESOURCES

Readings

Anderson, N. A. (2007). *What should I read aloud? A guide to the 200 best-selling picture books.* Newark, DE: International Reading Association.

Ashton-Warner, S. (1963). *Teacher.* New York: Simon & Schuster.

Calkins, L. M. (2000). *The art of teaching reading.* New York: Longman.

Clay, M. M. (1997). *The early detection of reading difficulties.* Portsmouth, NH: Heinemann.

Morrow, L. M. (2005). *Literacy development in the early years: Helping children read and write.* Boston: Allyn and Bacon.

Pianta, R., & La Paro, K. (2003). Improving early school success. *Educational Leadership, 60,* 24–29.

Venn, C., Jahn, M., & Shreve, R. (2002). *All ready reading and writing preschool guidebook.* Casper, WY: All Ready LLC.

Readings on Phonetic Instruction

Cowen, J. E. (Ed.). (2003). *A balanced approach to beginning reading instruction: A synthesis of six major U. S. research studies.* Newark, DE: International Reading Association.

Cunningham, P. M. (2000). *Phonics they use: Words for reading and writing.* New York: Addison-Wesley/Longman.

National Reading Panel. (2000). *Teaching children to read: An evidence-based assessment of the scientific research literature on reading and its implications for reading instructions.* Washington, DC: National Institute of Child Health and Human Development.

Yopp, H. K., & Yopp, R. H. (2000). Supporting phonemic awareness development in the classroom. *The Reading Teacher, 54,* 130–143.

Helpful Websites

High/Scope Educational Research Foundation
http://www.highscope.org
Explains how children learn to read in High/Scope programs.

International Reading Association (IRA)
http://www.reading.org
Provides additional standards information and readings. Search for IRA's position statement, "What Is Evidence-Based Reading?"

Jumpstart
http://www.jstart.org
Provides information about Jumpstart, a national early education organization that matches children from low-income backgrounds with adults who focus on literacy.

National Center for Learning Disabilities
http://www.GetReadytoRead.org
Features screening tools, literacy activities, checklists, and games.

National Council of Teachers of English
http://www.ncte.org
Search for position papers titled *On Reading, Learning to Read,* and *Effective Reading Instruction.*

National Reading Panel
http://www.nationalreadingpanel.org
Presents research report conclusions and findings by a panel of notable researchers in 2000.

Starfall
http://www.starfall.com
This free educational website focuses on learning to read.

Book Companion Website

On the book companion website, you will find a checklist for children's social and developmental behaviors. These behaviors have been associated with school readiness and learning to read. This is not a screening instrument but rather an inventory of the possible behaviors that indicate a successful beginning kindergarten experience. Also included is a questionnaire a teacher might use for self-evaluation of teaching and planning behaviors; it helps pinpoint areas for future development of skills. Suggested web activities are numerous. Preschool alliteration activities can be fun and challenging. The book companion website provides a list of activity ideas.

STUDENT ACTIVITIES

1. Invite a kindergarten teacher and a first-grade teacher to discuss their experiences and knowledge about young children and reading.
2. Observe a kindergarten class. List and describe any activities that increase a child's interest in reading or actual reading instruction.
3. Make a chart of printscript words (common words such as *dog* and *cat* and highly advertised words such as those naming commercial beverages or cereals; include children's names). Test these words with a group of 4-year-olds in a game-like way. Describe the children's response to your game.
4. Observe an older 4-year-old. Using Figure 17–13, attempt to rate the child's behavior. Interview the child's teacher, putting the teacher's ratings in another color ink. Discuss the outcome of this exercise with others in your training group.

Rating Scale

  1 = often
  2 = frequently
  3 = sometimes
  4 = infrequently
  5 = rarely
  6 = unable to determine

1. requests adult to read a picture book
2. asks about story time
3. shares a book with a friend
4. spends time in classroom library area
5. has a favorite book
6. likes to leaf through picture books
7. joins story times eagerly
8. hurries to story time
9. pretends to read
10. says remembered words while book browsing
11. spends time choosing a book to browse
12. shares pages in books that have captured his attention
13. memorizes repeated words or phrases in books with others
14. looks focused or displays delight in book's happenings

15. wants to take books home
16. displays knowledge of a book taken home
17. talks about his home book collection
18. talks about visits to a community library
19. laughs at humorous portions of picture books
20. asks about illustrations at times
21. treats books with care
22. enjoys books on certain topics of interest to him
23. discusses book characters
24. loses self in a book and blocks out room happenings
25. can describe a book's story line (in part)
26. asks questions about book's happenings at times

Additional Comments:

_____

_____

_____

_____

FIGURE 17–13 Checklist of reading attitudes and behaviors.

5. In a small group, discuss what you would do and what your limitations would be if you were working with a group of young children and found that two of them were reading a few words.

6. Stage a debate. Divide the class into two groups: one presenting the disadvantages of teaching young children to read before first grade and the other presenting the advantages. Do some library research. Have each group discuss its position separately. Then, debaters from each team meet to substantiate their arguments by citing experts or written sources. Each team gets one point for substantiations used during the actual debate.

7. Have volunteers role-play the following situation.

   A parent states to a teacher: "I know you believe in teaching Jonathan (her child) about alphabet letters, and all the other parents are teaching them to their children. Jonathan is just unable to learn his letters. The other children will seem bright to their kindergarten teacher, while Jonathan will seem slow. What should I do to help him?"

8. Read the following excerpt and write your reaction in preparation for a class discussion.

   Children begin reading signs and other environmental print (Jell-O and cereal boxes, McDonald's milk cartons, soup cans, tooth paste tubes) on their own when they find it useful or interesting to do so. Take any 3- or 4-year-old to the grocery store, and you will quickly see what they are capable of reading.

9. State your position concerning the need to offer selected activities and experiences before kindergarten to children who may be at risk for having difficulties learning to read.

CHAPTER REVIEW

A. Discuss the following situations briefly.

   1. A child asks you to listen while he reads a favorite book to you.

   2. You have noticed a young child who is able to read all of the printscript in the playroom.

   3. A parent notices his child is reading a few words and asks advice as to what to do.

B. How can a teacher include the four language arts in activities?

C. Explain what is meant by each of the following terms—reading readiness, reading method, phonics, configuration, and incongruities.

D. Select the phrase that best completes each of the following sentences.
1. At the age of 4 and 5,
   a. many children learn to read.
   b. a few children learn to read.
   c. children should be given reading instruction.
   d. most children will be ready to read.
2. The language arts are
   a. reading, printscript, and listening.
   b. speaking, reading, and listening.
   c. listening, speaking, writing (print), and reading.
   d. reading readiness, listening, speaking, and alphabet knowledge.
3. Children may begin reading because they
   a. have an interest in alphabet letters.
   b. have an interest in books.
   c. want to see what they say written down.
   d. have an interest in speaking, listening, or writing (printscript).
   e. all of the above
4. Reading-like behavior
   a. includes a variety of skills, motives, and attitudes.
   b. can be defined as having an interest in reading.
   c. means at a certain age a child will perfect all the skills needed to read.
   d. means that reading should be taught to most preschoolers.
5. Parents and early childhood teachers work together so that
   a. parents will teach their children to read at home.
   b. teachers can teach reading during preschool years.
   c. what children learn at home and school can be reinforced by both parents and teachers.
   d. children's experiences at home and school will be the same.

E. Describe which of the reading instructional methods reviewed in this chapter seems more logical to you and why. Mention the distinguishing features of the method you choose, and contrast or compare it to another reading method.

F. What factors tend to predict child ease in learning to read?

SECTION 8

Settings Promoting Literacy:

At School and Home

CHAPTER 18

Developing a Literacy Environment

OBJECTIVES

After reading this chapter, you should be able to:

◆ Explain the need for materials in language-development activities.

◆ Assist teachers in the care, storage, and replacement of materials.

◆ Describe early childhood language games.

KEY TERMS

audiovisual
  equipment

language center
listening center

software

"CAN I HAVE ANOTHER TURN?"

Four-year-old Emma found computer use to be the high point of her day, and as her computer involvement grew her other interests narrowed. Her preschool teacher noticed she had lost interest in art projects, was socially less involved, spent less and less time with other children, and often tried to negotiate more time on the school's computer. Her teacher observed that Emma seemed distracted and restless, and she felt that Emma's gross-motor skills might be lagging. She also believed that Emma had shortened her attention span for everything else offered in class.

Emma's family noted that she immediately rushed to their home computer after school and had lost interest playing with neighborhood friends. Most of them stopped dropping by to ask her to play. Emma's interest in toys also seemed diminished.

QUESTIONS TO PONDER

1. Is it possible that a 4-year-old could develop addictive behavior?

2. Emma's parents sought professional advice but they also wanted Emma to continue to develop computer skill. What plan of action do you think might have been recommended to the parents?

3. What teacher plan of action would you suggest?

This text has emphasized the need to provide children with a variety of interesting classroom materials, objects, and furnishings. Such materials are important in keeping programs alive, fascinating, and challenging.

Classroom materials and objects promote language skills in many ways.

- They provide the reality behind words and ideas.
- They provide the child with opportunities for sensory exploration. This increases children's knowledge of relationships and ability to identify the things around them.
- Materials capture attention, motivate play, and build communication skills.
- Familiar and favorite materials can be enjoyed over and over, with the child deciding how much time to devote to them.
- Many materials isolate one language and perceptual skill, allowing it to be practiced and accomplished.

In language arts centers, related instructional materials are located in one convenient area. Stocking, supervision, and maintenance of materials, furnishings, and equipment are easily accomplished. The classroom can be a place to grow, expand, test ideas, and predict outcomes of questions. A prepared environment provides successful experiences for all children in a climate in which ideas and creative learning flourish.

A limited body of knowledge exists regarding how the physical features and equipment of a literacy-based classroom enhance learning. A preliminary study examining the impact of literacy-enriched play areas (ones with meaningful print) found that preschool children who played in such areas spontaneously used almost twice as much print in their play. Consequently, teachers are urged to experiment and creatively design language arts centers and other play centers and monitor the effect of the room and its furnishings on children's language arts skills.

SUGGESTIONS FOR PRINT-RICH ENVIRONMENTS

The following ideas for print-rich classrooms are from Du and Stoub (2004). Note that labels can be symbols, pictures, photos, or stickers.

- Label all area signs with pictures and words.
- Label all shelving units and containers.
- Label everything in the classroom as you find connections to current curriculum—doors, windows, tables, lights, and so on.
- Post a picture of the children's daily routine.
- Create a message board or daily newsletter where teachers can relate messages to children and vice versa.
- Create a place where children can sign in and out daily.
- Create a question for the day in print and discuss it.
- Use name cards that children select and put in slot pockets, if an area holds only a certain number of children.
- Make classroom games that include print and symbols.
- Have a helper chart.
- Have a pocket attendance chart.
- Design graphs with children's names.
- In housekeeping areas include cookbooks, phone books, recipe books, menus, and newspapers.
- Make lists with children concerning the functional use of print.*

THE LANGUAGE ARTS CENTER

Full of communication-motivating activities, every inch of floor and wall space of a language arts center is used. Small areas are enlarged by building upward with lofts or bunks to solve floor-space problems in crowded centers (Figure

*From Du, L., & Stoub, S. (2004). Options pre-K literary curriculum, session guide, February 21, 2004.

FIGURE 18–1 Solving space problems.

18–1). Adding areas that children can climb into is another useful space-opening device.

A **language center** has three main functions: (1) it provides looking and listening activities for children, (2) it gives children an area for hands-on experiences with communication-developing materials, and (3) it provides a place to store materials. The ideal area has comfortable, soft furnishings with ample work space, proper lighting, and screening to block out other areas of active classrooms. Teachers make centers cozy and inviting with pillows, a covered crib mattress, or a bean bag chair or two. The area can become a place of refuge for the child who needs to get away from the bustle of the group and a nice place for the teacher to spend some time with children individually.

Language arts centers should be quiet places that are separated from the more vigorous activities of the average playroom. Suggested furnishings are listed by category.

General-Use Materials
    one or more child-size tables and a few
      chairs

shelving dividers or screens
soft-cushioned rocker, easy chair, or couch
soft pillows
crawl-into hideaways, lined with carpet or
    fabric (Figure 18–2)
individual work space or study spots
audiovisuals and electrical outlets
book racks that display book covers
chalkboard
storage cabinets
flannel board
pocket chart
children's file box (Figure 18–3)
bookcase (Figure 18–4)
bulletin board
carpet, rug, or soft floor covering
chart stand or wall-mounted wing clamps
wastebasket

Writing and Prewriting Materials
    paper (scratch, lined, newsprint, and typ-
      ing paper in a variety of sizes)

FIGURE 18–2 A crawl-into listening area for quiet language activities furnished with headsets.

language center — a classroom area specifically set aside and equipped for language arts–related activities and child use.

table

file or index cards

paper storage shelf

writing tools (crayons, nontoxic washable felt markers, and soft pencils in handy contact-covered containers)

primary-school typewriter

small, sturdy typewriter table or desk

word boxes

picture dictionary

wall-displayed alphabet guides

cutouts of colorful alphabet letters

tabletop chalkboards with chalk

blank book skeletons

scissors

tape

erasers

alphabet letter stamps and ink pads

tracing envelopes, patterns, wipe-off cloth

chart paper

magnet board with alphabet letters

hole punch

yarn

write-on, wipe-off boards

stick-on notes

notepads

pencil sharpener

envelopes baskets, desk trays, and flat boxes

stationery

brass paper fasteners

set of printscript strips with attending children's and staff's names

FIGURE 18–3 Children's work file box.

FIGURE 18–4 Bookcases can be used as room area boundaries.

stickers

glue sticks

stencils

Reading and Prereading Materials

books (including child-made examples)

book and audiovisual combinations (read-a-longs)

cutouts of favorite story characters

rebus story charts

an alphabetized chart of enrolled children's names

Speech Materials

puppets and puppet theaters

flannel board sets

language games

Audiovisual Equipment

overhead projector

record, tape, or CD/DVD player; headsets; and jacks

story records

language master, recording cards

picture files

television screen and VCR

computer and printer

video camera

digital camera

Adults usually supervise use of **audiovisual equipment** in a language center, and a number of the simpler machines can be operated by children after a brief training period. Tape recorders, CD/DVD players, electronic media, and headsets require careful introduction by the teacher.

The Teacher's Role in Language Centers

Teachers are congenial, interested companions for the children: sharing books; helping children with projects; recording children's dictation; playing and demonstrating language games; making words, word lists, signs, or charts (Figure 18–5 and Figure 18-6); and helping children use the center's equipment.

FIGURE 18–5 Stickers, words, or children's work may be added to charts.

audiovisual equipment — any mechanical or nonmechanical item useful in offering sight or hearing experience.

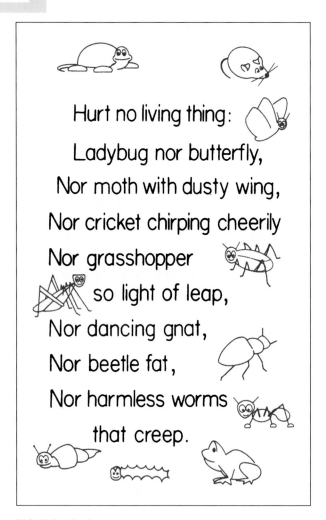

Hurt no living thing:

Ladybug nor butterfly,

Nor moth with dusty wing,

Nor cricket chirping cheerily

Nor grasshopper

so light of leap,

Nor dancing gnat,

Nor beetle fat,

Nor harmless worms

that creep.

FIGURE 18–6 Language center chart.

Teachers slip in and out as needed and monitor equipment use. Vigorous or noisy play is diverted to other room areas or outside yard areas. Children who have been given clear introductions to a language center's materials and clear statements concerning expectations in use of the center's furnishings may need little help. It may be necessary, however, to set rules for the number of children who can use a language center at a given time.

The teacher explains new materials that are to become part of the center's collection. Many materials are demonstrated before they are made available to the children.

Posting children's work on the center bulletin board and planning chalkboard activities and printing messages that may catch the children's attention motivate interest in and use of the center. Plants and occasional fresh flowers in vases add a pleasant touch. To help children use equipment, materials, and machines on their own, teachers have become inventive, using step-by-step picture charts posted above or near materials. Color-coded dots make buttons or dials stand out. Some centers control machine use by giving training sessions in which children obtain "licenses." Children without licenses need to have adult companions.

Another task the teacher may want to undertake is making read-along recordings to accompany favorite books. The popularity of read-alongs cannot be denied, nor can the educational benefits. Children who use read-alongs are learning word recognition as well as some of the more advanced reading skills. For fun and pleasure, the lure of read-alongs makes them another gateway into the world of books. Teachers should consider the following when making recordings:

A narrator's pacing is important. It cannot be too fast, or the child trying to follow along will be lost. If it is too slow, the child will become bored. The inflection and tone of the voice are also vital. The narrator cannot be condescending or patronizing; neither should there be an attempt to "act out" the story and run the risk of making the story secondary to the performance.

Besides these factors, a teacher needs to estimate audience attention span and use a pleasant page-turning signal. With story recordings, either on tape or CD (with or without a story visual), the child may be a passive listener or can be an active, responsive participant. Some commercial manufacturers and teachers have cleverly designed interactive features, but these, though enjoyable and educational, cannot match what is possible with a "live" book reading and are a second-best activity.

HOUSEKEEPING AND BLOCK AREAS

Educators emphasize the importance of housekeeping and block areas, both of which encourage large amounts of social interaction and the use of more mature, complex language. High levels of dramatic play interaction are also encouraged in theme (unit) centers. Teachers design spacious, well-defined, well-stocked (theme-related) partitioned room areas for block play and dramatic play.

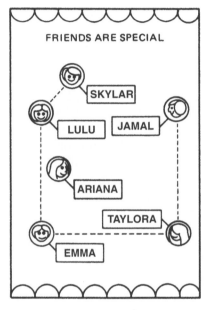

FIGURE 18–7 Bulletin board ideas.

FIGURE 18–8 Plastic lid chalkboard activities.

DISPLAYS AND BULLETIN BOARDS

Interesting eye-level wall and bulletin board displays capture the children's attention and promote discussion. Displaying children's work (with children's permission), names, and themes based on their interests increases their feelings of accomplishment and their sense of pride in their classroom. Displays that involve active child participation are suggested. Many can be designed to change daily or weekly.

Printscript is used on bulletin boards with objects, pictures, or patterns. Book pockets, picture hooks, ¼-inch elastic attached to clothespins, and sticky bulletin board strips allow pieces to be added and removed.

Figure 18–7 shows one bulletin board idea. The child selects a spot to paste her picture (photo) and name. A colored line is drawn between the photo and name. Later, colored lines can be drawn, connecting friends' pictures.

CHALKBOARD ACTIVITIES

One of the most underutilized instructional items in early childhood centers can be the chalkboard. The following chalkboard activities are suggested to help children's language development.

Tracing templates and colored chalk. Using a sharp tool, cut large plastic coffee can lids into a variety of patterns (Figure 18–8). Suspend the patterns on cord or elastic with clothespins over the chalkboard.

Pattern games. Draw Figure 18–9 on the chalkboard. Ask the children what shape comes next in the pattern. Then draw Figure 18–10 and see whether the children can make a line path from the dog to the doghouse.

FIGURE 18–9 What comes next in the pattern?

FIGURE 18–10 A left-to-right skill builder.

AUDIOVISUAL EQUIPMENT

Budgets often determine the availability of audiovisual materials in an early childhood center. Care of equipment and awareness of operating procedures are important. Special fund-raising projects, rental agreements, borrowing arrangements, or donations have secured audiovisuals for some programs. The machine's instruction manual should be studied for the proper care and maintenance necessary for efficient use.

The following audiovisual equipment enriches a center's language arts program activities.

◆ *Camera* (including Polaroid and video cameras). A camera can be used to provide images and photos that are useful in speaking activities, displays, and games.

◆ *Projector and Screens.* Common home, school, field trip, and community scenes can be discussed, written about (experience stories), or used for storytelling.

◆ *Lite-bord™.* This is a special display board that uses nontoxic erasable crayons for making colorful drawings and words that glow.

◆ *Video Cameras.* Children enjoy being recorded while displaying and explaining their creations. It has multiple uses.

◆ *Overhead Projectors, Screens, and Transparencies.* Stories with silhouettes or numerous transparency activities can be designed.

Small patterns and alphabet letters can be enlarged and copied by teachers for a variety of uses. McDonald and Simons (1989) suggest drawing or placing images on the screen while storytelling or reading poetry (for example, using a "Humpty Dumpty" picture sequence while reciting the rhyme). Meier (2004) recommends supplying children with overhead projector sheets, or other kinds of plastic sheets, so that they can project their images and words onto a large screen. Some, but not all, picture books work well with this instructional technique. If text and illustration appear on the same page, this type of sharing is recommended. Teachers may have limited access to equipment used to make transparencies, but if available, the author strongly recommends this type of alternative storybook reading. Illustrations can be enlarged and enjoyed. Text appears giant-sized.

◆ *Opaque Projector.* Pages of picture books can be projected on wall areas to offer a new way to read books. Guessing games are also possible. Characters from picture books can become life-size companions.

Listening Center Equipment

The following equipment is useful for the center's **listening center**.

---

listening center — a classroom area designed to accommodate children's listening experiences.

◆ *Headsets and Jack Box.* Accommodating up to eight children at one time adapt to cassette, CD, and record players. Volume control is set on the jack box.

◆ *CD Players.* Most centers have this piece of equipment. Commercial suppliers of story CDs are plentiful.

◆ *Digital Camera.* Classroom photographs can be displayed on the computer, and prints can be made for display. Photo printers are available from many manufacturers.

◆ *Digital Camcorder.* Classroom action photography can be displayed on television sets and computers, or prints can be made.

◆ *Pocket Wall Charts with Stands.* This handy teacher's aid displays alphabet letters, words, sentences, shapes, pictures, colors, names, and so on. It is easy to use. Teachers prefer see-through pocket styles. These can be teacher-made.

◆ *Big Book Storage Rack.* See-through individual hanging bags can be used for big books and oversized materials; this visual solves the problem of storing large items.

◆ *Write and Wipe Boards and Easels.* Colored markers glide on and wipe off quickly. They are useful for teacher activities or child use. They are made in free-standing or tabletop styles, and some are magnetic, so plastic alphabet letters and numerals with magnets will stick.

◆ *Computer.* Besides computer use with software programs and use as a word processor, the computer has become a versatile piece of equipment.

◆ *Tape Recorders.* This is still a popular audiovisual aid that is used in early childhood centers. The tape recorder opens up many activity ideas. Suggestions for language development activities with tape recorders follow.
Record children's comments about their artwork or project. "Tell me about . . ." is a good starter. Put the tape and artwork together in the language center so that it is available for the children's use.

Let the children record their comments about a group of plastic cars, human figures, animals, and so on, after they arrange them as they wish.
Have children discuss photographs or magazine pictures.
Record a child's comments about a piece of fruit that she has selected from a basket of mixed fruit.
Record a "reporter's" account of a recent field trip.
Gather a group of common items, such as a mirror, comb, brush, and toothbrush. Let the child describe how these items are used.
Record a child's description of peeling an orange or making a sandwich with common spreads and fillings.
Record a child's comments about her block structures. Take a Polaroid photo and make both tape and photo available in the listening and looking area.

◆ *Television Sets and VCRs.* These can be purchased as separate units or as combined machines. Children's classic literature is available. Local video rental stores and public libraries stock a variety of titles. Active discussion of what is viewed is recommended.

◆ *Discussion or Study Prints.* A collection of large posters, photographs, mounted magazine pictures, and life-size book characters can be used in activities. Visuals can increase child verbalization and serve as creative "jumping off" spots.

The Use of Picture Files

Picture files consisting of collections of drawings and photographs are made available to children in classroom language centers. Teachers find that they are invaluable motivators for many language-related child activities. Magazine photos and photos showing classroom scenes or attending children are popular with children. Images can be rotated and used to supplement a present course of study.

It is a good idea to start with enlarged photographs of each child and staff (affix to a firm backing). Resources for pictures include coloring books, shape books, inexpensive children's books, calendars, catalogs, trade journals, travel folders, and toy advertisements.

Suggested activities include:

◆ writing captions.

◆ storytelling from a series of pictures.

◆ giving names to animal pictures.

◆ finding hidden objects.

◆ categorizing pictures.

◆ finding objects that have alphabet letters printed on them.

◆ putting illustrations in a sequence and telling a story.

◆ matching pictures with related objects.

◆ finding alphabet letters in signs.

◆ identifying logos or outdoor signs from familiar fast-food restaurants or other local businesses.

◆ singing or creating a song to go with a picture.

◆ rhyming with pictures.

◆ finding things of the same shape, color, and category.

◆ classifying pictures by season.

◆ making a sound to fit a picture.

◆ writing a letter to someone shown in a picture.

◆ finding an object in the classroom that looks like something in a picture.

◆ choosing a favorite from a picture collection of food or other objects.

◆ labeling everything in a picture.

◆ finding things that start with the same alphabet letter sound.

◆ making an alphabet book as a group project or promoting each child's creation of an individual alphabet book.

It is easy to see that there are many possibilities. Teacher ingenuity creates others. Teachers often protect pictures with clear contact paper or lamination. Classrooms may have a teacher's set and a children's set. Smart teacher substitutes pack them along for "filler" or "spur of the moment" activities.

Technology and Literacy Learning

What do early childhood educators believe concerning the use of technology? Most will agree that machines, whether computers or other audiovisuals, can teach, support, assist, motivate, and be used for the practice and application of literacy skills. Technology cannot "be the teacher of literacy," but it can be a useful tool in assessing and tracking children's literacy skill development.

More academic research is necessary to help educators and families understand how both school and home electronic media affect the informal learning of young children. Some manufacturers and associations, such as Microsoft and the national PTA (Parent-Teachers Association), are urging parents to use "PACT" to determine what types of media are appropriate for young children.

> The "P" stands for parental involvement. The "A" is for determining what a child can access on line. "C" is for selecting content deemed appropriate for little ones. And "T" stands for time, as in how long children can play a game console, TV or computer (*USA Today*, 2008).

New products are building in features that encourage children's group play (e.g., Nintendo Wii) and other features such as co-viewing. A new website, WhatTheyPlay.com, helps families examine ratings of children's program titles. IBM and Zula USA are developing "educational virtual worlds" that attempt to teach 4-year-olds about math and science. PBS has created online neighborhoods for preschoolers (Snider, 2008). The site allows 3- to 6-year-olds to play and learn with the help of characters such as Curious George and the Berenstain Bears. Homes and schools will decide whether subscription fees and program content is suitable.

PLANNING LANGUAGE CENTERS AND COMPUTER CENTERS

Once rooms or areas are designated as language centers, staff members classify materials into "looking and listening" or "working with" categories (Figure 18–11). Display, storage, working space, and looking and listening areas are determined. Activities that require concentration are screened off when possible. Many different arrangements of materials and equipment within a language arts center are possible. Most centers rearrange furnishings until the most functional arrangement is found. For sample arrangements with different functions, refer to Figure 18–12.

Many children like to escape noise with a favorite book or puppet. Most centers provide

FIGURE 18–11 Writing tools are always found in classroom language centers.

these quiet retreats within a language arts center. School staffs have found creative ways of providing private space. Old footed bathtubs with soft pillows, packing crates and barrels, pillow-lined closets with doors removed, tepees, tents, and screened-off couches and armchairs have been found workable in some classroom language arts areas.

With the fears mentioned earlier in this text concerning the overuse of television and videos, some educators see computer programs as offering a "cartoon world" rather than the real experiences and human interactions upon which real knowledge and literacy depends. Early childhood educators realize that computer skills and knowledge may be necessary in elementary school grades; however, they may be unsure about the best time to introduce them to young children.

Slowly but steadily computer centers are becoming standard in 3- and 4-year-olds' preschool classrooms. Staffing, expense, and time for teacher preview of programs are important considerations. Many educators agree that computer centers are compatible with developmentally appropriate practice. Computers can offer problem solving, creative experiences, and literacy opportunities. Benefits cited by many early childhood advocates of child computer use include the following.

◆ Child cooperation and turn taking are promoted.

◆ The need for adult supervision is minimal once "rule use" is accepted and initial child training on mechanics has taken place.

◆ Children can work at their own speed.

◆ Opportunities for child collaboration, mentoring, negotiation, and joint solutions to problems are provided.

◆ Use builds children's self-confidence and also builds children's feelings of independence.

Additional benefits children may experience when computers become part of classroom life that are related to language arts skills and development include children's

◆ verbal interactions with a peer partner or others (Figure 18–13).

FIGURE 18–12 Language arts center.

FIGURE 18–13 One peer can often instruct another.

◆ experiences with alphabet letters, print, and words.

◆ ability to see uses of print, which include recording, informing, sending, and receiving messages.

◆ opportunity to create literary works that then can be recorded.

◆ experience in making greeting cards.

◆ exposure to rhyme.

◆ opportunity to match letters, patterns, rhymes, and words with pictorial representations.

◆ exposure to visual and interactive storybooks.

Teachers with computers in their classrooms will agree that it is appropriate to step in when children are frustrated or lack necessary user skills. They tend to offer minimal help if they believe that the child can work out a problem on her own, thereby allowing the child to experience mastery and the resulting feeling of accomplishment. Most teachers periodically join children at the computer to ask questions or make comments that encourage the expansion of skill.

Some educators are concerned about the fact that some elementary school children and adolescents have displayed obsessive and addictive behaviors, and have indulged in computer video game overuse. These "gamers" have less social contact with peers and less interest in reading, which affects their school performance. Research undertaken at the early childhood level on this subject is scarce.

Centers develop simple computer area rules that are appropriate to their classroom, children, and equipment. Rules usually involve clean hands, number of children allowed at one time, how to ask for help, taking turns, time allowed per turn, use of earphones, and what training is required before use.

Research seems to suggest that 3- and 4-year-old children who use computer programs that support and reinforce the major objectives of their curricula have significantly greater developmental gains when compared with children who have not had computer experiences in similar classrooms. Among the gain areas researched were nonverbal skills, verbal skills, problem solving, and conceptual skills (Figure 18–14).

Interestingly, computer program use has been found to improve the speech skills of children with dyslexia and other language-based learning disabilities. Researchers noted that language comprehension improved to normal, near-normal, or above normal in children who had been 2 to 3 years behind peers in speech skills. The findings are especially encouraging for children who have difficulty learning to talk (developmental dysphasia) or who have subsequent reading problems (developmental dyslexia).

For preschool classrooms, educators recommend an initial training period, turn taking, cooperative learning in small groups, peer tutoring, hands-on experience, waiting lists, and a sufficient number of adults who make an "adult time" investment. **Software** variety should also be offered.

Software Selection

Developmentally appropriate integration begins with selecting hardware and software that will complement goals. The following is

---

software — a wide range of commercial programs developed for computer users' convenience, education, entertainment, and so on.

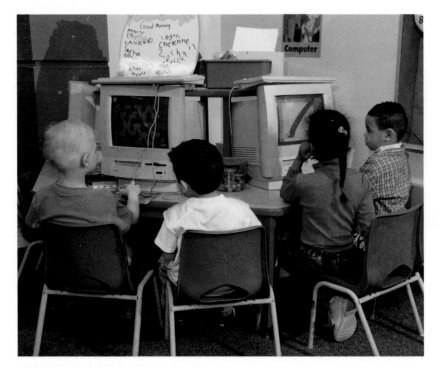

FIGURE 18–14 Problem-solving programs can be experienced by one child or with one peer.

a list of software characteristics to check and consider.

◆ does not include violence

◆ provides positive verbal and visual cues and responses (feedback)

◆ allows the child to control pace and action

◆ allows the option of practicing a skill or moving on

◆ supports working alone or with others

When teachers provide open-ended software that encourages creativity, rather than drill-and-practice software, this is developmentally appropriate. Open-ended programs encourage children to explore and to extend their thinking. They spark children's interest as well as social and cognitive development.

Other software features teachers need to examine include content, age appropriateness, pacing, child choices available, meaningful graphics and sound, clear directions for yet-to-read children, approaches to learning, and appropriate cost. The integrity and craftsmanship

in a software program determines its effectiveness and quality. Four critical steps to maximize children's learning through computer use follow.

1. selecting developmental software

2. selecting developmental websites

3. integrating these resources into the curriculum

4. selecting computers to support these learning experiences

Websites may offer many rich educational opportunities and provide opportunities that appear to enhance problem solving, critical thinking skills, decision making, language skills, knowledge, research skills, the ability to integrate information, social skills, and self-esteem.

The following magazine is a good resource for information about software selection: *Children's Technology Revue*, 120 Main Street, Flemington, NJ 08822; http://www.childrens-software.com. (This publication reviews software programs, evaluating each program in six

Sign-up sheet · Earphones · Alphabet letter chart · Study carrel · Clock · Earphones · Computer · Timer · Study carrel · Printer · Storage

Child chair · Computer · Mouse · Timer · Mouse · Adult chair

FIGURE 18–15 Computer center.

areas using a 1 to 5 rating scale; reviews include a description of the program and a list of features and teaching goals.)

Computer Location

The ideal classroom location for computers is a visible location where monitors can be seen throughout the classroom. This setting enables supervision and quick assistance (Figure 18–15). A computer center or activity area in a preschool or kindergarten classroom usually operates well with two or three computers and one or two printers.

SUMMARY

When there is a language arts center within an early childhood playroom, language development materials are arranged in one central room location. Children follow their own interests, according to their preferences.

A language center's material can include a wide range of teacher-made and commercially purchased items. Activities in listening, speaking, writing, and reading (or combinations of these) are side-by-side, promoting the child's ability to see relationships among them.

Audiovisual materials and equipment are useful language center devices. Costs sometimes limit their availability. Training in the use and care of audiovisual machines is necessary for efficient operation. Computer use in young children's classrooms continues to expand, and teacher screening of software programs is important.

ADDITIONAL RESOURCES

Readings

Anderson, G. T. (2000, March). Computers in a developmentally appropriate curriculum. *Young Children*, 55(2), 90–93.

Children's Technology Revue (monthly magazine), Scholastic Active Learning Associates, 120 Main St., Flemington, NJ 08822.

Elkind, D. (1996, July). Young children and technology: A cautionary note. *Young Children*, 51(6), 28–34.

Haugland, S., & Wright, J. (1997). *Young children and technology: A world of discovery*. Boston: Allyn and Bacon.

Ingraham, P. (1997). *Caring and managing learning centers: A thematic approach*. Peterborough, NH: Crystal Springs.

Kritchevsky, S., & Prescott, E. (1996). *Planning environments for young children: Physical space*. Washington, DC: National Association for the Education of Young Children.

Wood, J. M. (2004). *Literacy online: New tools for struggling readers and writers.* Portsmouth, NH: Heinemann.

Helpful Websites

Computing With Kids
http://www.computingwithkids.com
Offers a free weekly newsletter.

Playworld Systems
http://www.playdesigns.com
Reviews commercial equipment and furniture.

KidSource Online
http://www.kidsource.com
Provides access to articles on computers in the early childhood curriculum.

NAEYC Technology & Young Children
http://www.techandyoungchildren.org
A special interest and discussion forum.

Sesame Workshop
http://www.sesameworkshop.org
Provides information and activities to download.

Book Companion Website

The digital camera is a possible tool to be added to the teacher's collection. The book companion website describes how some pre-K teachers are using these cameras. Take a short quiz on chapter contents. A reference list will acquaint the reader with readings concerning computers and young children, classroom work spaces, and language arts bulletin boards.

STUDENT ACTIVITIES

1. Observe an early childhood program. Describe the use and storage of language development materials.
2. Listen to three commercial story recordings. Judge and compare the quality of the recordings.
3. Invite an audiovisual company's sales representative to the class to demonstrate the company's product. (Seek instructor approval first.)
4. Develop a price list for five pieces of audiovisual equipment found in this chapter.
5. Interview two early childhood teachers on their use of audiovisuals in their language arts curriculum. Report the findings to the group.
6. Plan and conduct an activity for a group of preschoolers using a tape recorder.
7. Investigate three children's computer (software) programs. Report your findings.
8. Observe preschoolers interacting with a computer in an early childhood classroom. Take written notes during a 15-minute observation period. Share notes with a group of peers. Develop a list of classroom rules for child computer use.
9. Make an "L" poster chart by cutting out pictures of "L" words (or use another alphabet letter). Introduce it to a group of older 4-year-olds. Think about how you will connect the chart to children's interests and lives while creating the chart. Print the items recognized in a list or on the chart and underline the beginning letter. Report your experiences.

CHAPTER REVIEW

A. List the advantages of an early childhood language arts center. What are the disadvantages?
B. List the teacher's duties in a well-functioning classroom language arts center (for example, supervision).
C. Describe or draw a picture of an imaginary language arts center that has a crawl-into bunk or loft area. It should be a place where a child could be alone to enjoy a book.
D. List seven useful machines mentioned in this chapter for classroom language arts centers.
E. Describe a well-designed classroom computer center.

CHAPTER 19

The Parent-Center Partnership

OBJECTIVES

After reading this chapter, you should be able to:

◆ Describe the parent-teacher partnership that affects language arts programs.

◆ Compare strategies used to enhance family-school communication.

◆ Identify ways in which parents can strengthen a child's language growth.

KEY TERMS

family literacy   outreach
  programs   socioeconomic

THE POWER OF PERSISTENCE

At pick-up time, when Martin's mother arrived, Mei Lin, Martin's teacher, observed a behavior she had not previously seen in Martin. Martin immediately started what Mei Lin would describe as vocal badgering. His verbal assault included a steady stream of, "But you promised . . . , I want one . . . , You said so . . . , I didn't have one yesterday . . . , I want it . . . , You told me I could . . . , I'm ready . . . , Let's go." His voice got louder and louder and didn't stop when his mother attempted to talk to Mei Lin. It continued as Martin and his mother exited to the porch. Mei Lin then heard Martin's mother say, "All right. We'll go to McDonalds!"

QUESTIONS TO PONDER

1. What is happening here?

2. Should Mei Lin discuss the situation with Martin's mother? Why or why not?

3. Does this have anything to do with language development?

4. Is there anything positive about Martin's way with words?

FAMILIES AND CHILD LITERACY

Although families and teachers are partners in a child's education, parents are always the child's foremost teachers and models, and the home is the child's first and most influential school (Figure 19–1). Many parents are eager consumers of information about what is best for their offspring. Six in ten parents read books about parenting or early childhood development before their children were born, and about 32 percent took classes for new parents.

Families are usually informed of the school's language and literacy curriculum during enrollment interviews. Most families want to find out how teachers interact with their children on a daily basis to realize their instructional goals. Many educators believe that some parents have a great need to be told what to do in terms of their children's education and are vulnerable as a result. It is suggested that anxious parents need reassurance and can be encouraged to trust their instincts.

Early childhood teachers can enhance their ability to work with the families of children in their classrooms. They should not make assumptions about a family's parenting practices. Within any cultural group—be it ethnic, racial, **socioeconomic**, or religious—individuals and families vary in their beliefs and adherence to the social conventions of their community.

Significant changes in family structure have occurred. More than 25 percent of all children and about 57 percent of African-American children are living with an unmarried parent. Whatever family type exists, the family should be viewed by educators as having knowledge on a wide range of topics that might be accessed by schools and educators. Family members are experts concerning how the home supports their child's emerging literacy. Questions teachers ask during initial and later interviews can gather valuable information concerning family literacy goals, home conversations with children, home literacy settings and materials including books and other publications, and their children's particular preferences and developing interests. Information gathered can influence the classroom library book selection as well as individual and group instructional planning.

Early childhood teachers and centers examine a wide range of strategies to enhance their relationships with families. Researchers urge educators to consider a family-by-family approach. When reaching out to families, teachers are likely to find that intra-group differences may be as great as inter-group differences. Efforts could include hiring bicultural and bilingual staff to increase a program's ability to communicate and create trust.

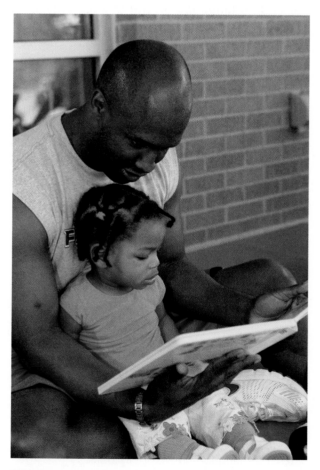

FIGURE 19–1 The child's foremost teachers and educators are the child's parents and family.

socioeconomic — relating to or involving a combination of social and economic factors.

Child literacy at home and school is influenced by three important factors: (1) setting, (2) models, and (3) planned and unplanned events. The setting involves what the home or school provides or makes available, including furnishings, space, materials and supplies, toys, books, and so forth. Family "connectedness" is crucial. Interactions with parents, siblings, grandparents, and other relatives enrich children's lives. Sharing hobbies, trips, chores, mealtimes, community and neighborhood happenings, conversations, and stories are all language-development opportunities. Access to additional settings outside the home is also considered. Time allowed or spent in community settings can increase or decrease literacy.

Preschools planning to maintain the continued literacy development of attending children must face the fact that a home's low socioeconomic status often affects their children's literacy growth. Au (2006) notes that poverty appears to be the factor most highly associated with poor reading achievement in elementary school. Middle-class families usually offer their children the advantage of more home book reading, more library visits, and more print-related experiences. Families with low educational aspirations for their children and low motivation, which sometimes results from poverty, stress, fatigue, and other unfortunate living conditions, are the families who most need sensitive professional **outreach** from their children's teacher and school.

Family economics may determine the opportunities and materials that are available, but family ingenuity and know-how may overcome a lack of monetary resources. Most things that parents can do to encourage reading and writing involve time, attention, and sensitivity rather than money. All families can be instrumental in fostering literacy if they spend time doing so. The usefulness of speaking, writing, and reading can be emphasized in any home. Children's literature may be borrowed from public libraries and other sources in almost all communities.

Although preschools are not as programmed as elementary schools and much of the learning in preschools goes hand-in-hand with firsthand exploration, families still have a big edge over group programs in offering intimate, individualized adult-child learning opportunities. Family interactions during activities involve both the quality and quantity of communication (Figure 19–2). The supportive assistance given at home, the atmosphere of the home, parent-child conversations, and joint ventures can greatly affect the child's literacy development.

Successful parents listen to what children say and respond to them. They interpret the child's language attempts and reply with related action accompanied by words and sentences. Learning is greater where children are supported by caring adults who share their world with them and enter into the children's worlds of play and talk, tuning in to their feelings and experiences. The essential element is the intimacy between child and adult who share a common environment; this fosters the understanding of meanings and child curiosity.

FIGURE 19–2 Some parents consult their child's teacher for language-developing ideas.

Children who find their efforts and attempts at language received and valued develop the confidence to continue. Children's learning flourishes when they are allowed some degree of control over their own actions and when they interact with adults who are receptive, less concerned with the correctness of child speech, and more likely to respond in ways that stretch thinking.

Early childhood centers design their own unique parent involvement programs. With increased federal and state emphasis on early childhood educators' working jointly with parents and families, educators working in publicly funded programs will need to clarify their goals and analyze their efforts. Most educators would agree any parental involvement must start with the development of a trusting relationship (Figure 19–3).

Developing Trust

Developing trust grows from parental feelings of being respected, accepted, and valued for their individual and cultural diversity, and it also grows when staff members are sensitive to family economics. Educators need to be aware of what parents' desire for their children. All of this starts the day parents walk through the school's door. What is on the walls and how they are welcomed and treated by staff are important. This calls for a consideration of parents' comfort and requires staff preparation and planning.

Identifying Supportive Assistance

Identifying exactly what a center can offer in supportive assistance is a necessary task. A school's list can be long or short depending

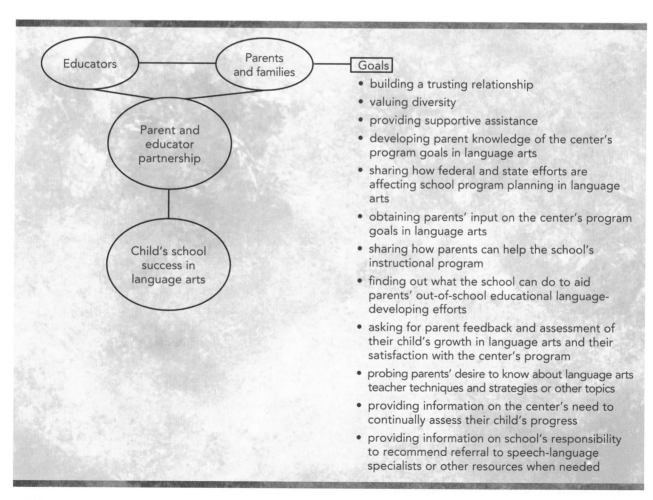

FIGURE 19–3 Parent involvement goals.

on the financial and human resources available. Some schools have generous budgets; others do not. Some have committed and dedicated staff members who realize working with and through parents and families is a priority. Most educators are familiar with data and research showing that a family's socioeconomic status, cultural and linguistic group membership, parenting style, and home literacy experiences correlate with the knowledge and skills that children bring to school. They realize that excellent instructional help will be necessary to prepare some children for kindergarten.

Early Childhood Language Arts Program Planning

It is a staff's task to explain how a center's program addresses "the whole child" and, in this case, especially language arts instruction. In some states, early childhood programs will need to follow curricular standards and requirements specified in licensing and/or federal or state guidelines or standards. Individual states have established standards and practices to ensure program quality after their state legislators became aware of research concerning young children's brain capacity and growth. The No Child Left Behind Act provided additional focus on early reading and the skills developed during preschool years. Many programs, including Head Start, continue to update program standards in language arts. Other groups have developed or are currently developing guidelines and benchmarks, including the U.S. Department of Education, the International Reading Association, NAEYC, the National Reading Panel, the Administration for Children and Families, and the National Goals Panel. Every effort to develop research-based recommendations is undertaken. Goldenberg (2002) lists what he terms the "emerging consensus" of current instructional practices (preschool through third grade) in beginning literacy:

1. **Literate environments in which print is used for diverse and interesting** purposes, including opportunities for student choice and ample time for looking at books and reading or "pretend reading."

2. **Direct, explicit, systematic instruction in specific skills (e.g., phonological awareness, letter names/sounds, decoding, and comprehension strategies), with sufficient practice in successful use of skills in order to promote transfer and automaticity.**

3. **Discussions and conversations about materials children read or that are read to them.**

4. **Focus on word-recognition skills and strategies (direct instruction, but also use of techniques such as word walls and making words).**

5. **Strategically sequenced instruction and curriculum materials to maintain optimal challenge (instructional or independent, as appropriate).**

6. **Organizational and classroom management strategies to maximize academic engagement and appropriate use of materials.**

7. **An explicit focus on language (including vocabulary development).**

8. **Valid and frequent assessments, using multiple measures as needed and appropriate, to allow teachers to gauge developing skills and target instruction appropriately.**

9. **A home-school connection component that links the school's efforts with children's home experiences and enlists parents in supporting their children's academic development. (p. 282)**

Some of this curriculum may be difficult to explain to parents without using specific examples over an extended period. Schools and centers that are privately funded may not use the "consensus" goals listed and instead may use other goals as the basis for their language arts instruction.

Obtaining Family Input

Schools have developed vehicles to ensure that parental input is part of a school's operational plan. These include parent (classroom) mailboxes, parent advisory committees, and parent councils. Parent questionnaires, surveys, and checklists often probe parents' ideas. Other efforts to reach out and communicate include e-mail, parent reading groups, planning workshops, and on-the-fly daily contacts.

PARENT GUIDELINES FOR LITERACY AND LANGUAGE DEVELOPMENT

The techniques or actions recommended to help children's language and literacy development apply to both teachers and parents. Parents have different and more varied opportunities to use these techniques. The following guidelines have been gathered from various sources dealing primarily with parent-child relations, and some have been mentioned previously in this text.

How Parents Can Promote Overall Literacy Skills

- Spend some time with your child every day. At school, the teacher has many children to attend to and may not give a child individual attention.

- Have your child match buttons, beans, blocks, or toys by colors, shapes, sizes; this kind of categorizing is an important thinking skill.

- Sort groceries by categories (canned goods, vegetables, fruits, and so on).

- Keep in mind that your child's early experiences with print, writing tools, alphabet letters, and books can be puzzling. When your child asks questions, he should readily be given assistance and answers, while he is focused.

- Slip quickly in and out of your child's play, encouraging child discovery. This type of on-the-move teaching is natural and different from sit-down structured teaching, to which your child tunes out as interest wanes.

- Offer what is just a little beyond what your child already knows in a supportive, enthusiastic, discovery setting. Interactions should be shared and enjoyable.

- Turning conversations into commands aimed at teaching language arts turns your child away.

- Arrange things so that your child has many opportunities to see operations from beginning to end. For example, make butter from whipping cream or applesauce from picked apples. Your child may not be aware of the origins of the things adults take for granted.

- Encourage each success or honest effort with a smile of approval or loving words.

- Be available as a resource person. When your child asks questions that you cannot answer, do not hesitate to seek help from others or books.

- Help your child feel secure and successful. Your interactions can build feelings of self-worth—if your child's ideas and opinions are valued—or feelings of worthlessness—if his ideas and opinions are negated or ignored.

- Realize that young children's self-control is developing and is necessary in group activities. In preschool and kindergarten, behavioral expectations create the climate for learning. Parenting means setting behavioral standards. Disciplined work habits promote school success.

How Parents Can Stimulate Speaking Abilities

- Talk to children lovingly, taking care to speak naturally and clearly. Listen when children want to tell you something; do not nag or interrupt children when they are speaking (but do make an effort to correct speech errors casually, that is, without drawing attention to the error).

◆ Read stories, poems, jingles, and riddles to children.

◆ Encourage play with puppets, bendable family dolls, dress-up clothes, play stores, doctor kits, and play telephones, letting the children act out various events and practice the language patterns we use in our daily lives.

◆ Encourage children to tell you stories.

◆ Increase your attempts to build vocabulary by including new and descriptive words in your vocabulary.

◆ Give attention; listen for intent rather than correctness. Show children that what they say is important. Communicate with children at their eye level, when possible. Expand and tactfully extend children's comments; talk on the children's chosen subjects.

◆ Use your best speech model—Standard English, if it comes naturally. If you speak a language other than English, provide a good model of that language.

◆ If one is a member of a cultural or ethnic group, examining attitude concerning adult-child verbal interactions is prudent. Meager quantity of home conversations can limit a young child's vocabulary development.

◆ Become a skilled questioner by asking questions that promote thinking, predicting, and a number of possible answers based on the children's viewpoints.

◆ Encourage children to talk about whatever they are making, but do not keep asking them, "What is it?"

◆ Talk frequently, give objects names, describe the things you do, speak distinctly and be specific, use full sentences; encourage children to ask questions, and include children in mealtime conversations.

The following are 11 suggestions from Mavorgenes (1990).

◆ Talk about what children are interested in and patiently answer their questions.

◆ Encourage children to develop their interests and talk about them.

◆ Do things together and talk about them: trips to stores, the zoo, museums, movies, concerts, and worship services; television; library visits; sports; and hobbies.

◆ Allow children to take the lead and direct the talk.

◆ Listen to your children so that you learn about them and show that you are interested in them.

◆ Provide young children with a play telephone and teach them how to use it.

◆ Ask children to describe objects they see.

◆ Talk with children to describe objects they see in a picture. Then hide the picture and see how many objects they can recall.

◆ Sing to and with children.

◆ Make games of spontaneous rhyming.

◆ Make up chants to do chores by.★

How Parents Can Build Print Awareness and Skill

◆ Provide literature and a language-rich setting in the home.

◆ Write down the things children tell you about their pictures. Make books of each child's work and photographs, and talk about the books.

◆ Read family letters and mail to children, along with circulars, junk mail, restaurant menus, wrappers and packaging, signs, labels, building identifications, catalogs, brand names, and calendars.

◆ Provide scrap paper and writing tools, and reserve an area in the home as a writing center for children's use (Figure 19–4).

◆ Make or buy alphabet letter toys or word books.

◆ Ask teachers for copies of the alphabet your children will use in kindergarten.

◆ Encourage scribbling and doodling.

◆ Write messages to children or make signs for their play, such as "Mark's boat."

★From Mavorgenes, N. A. (1990, May). Helping parents help their children become literate. *Young Children, 45*(4):4–9. Copyright © 1990 National Association for the Education of Young Children. Reprinted with permission.

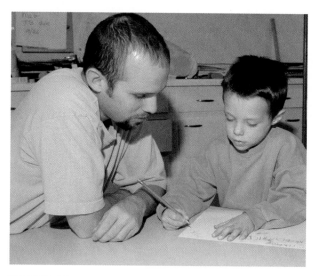

FIGURE 19–4 Some homes provide home "writing" areas and parents who show an interest in children's writing attempts.

- Talk about what you are writing and its use to you.
- Read signs when driving or walking, especially safety signs.
- Point out print on home equipment and products.
- Encourage interest in paper-and-crayon activities by showing children their names in print. Give attention to their attempts to copy their names or write them from memory.
- For pretend play, provide bank forms, memo pads, doctors' prescription pads, school forms, store order pads, and ordering pads used in restaurants. This kind of play stretches children's imaginations and broadens their experiences.
- Help children in writing letters to grandparents, sick friends, book authors, or famous people.
- Put little notes in children's lunch boxes or backpacks. These can be picture notes or simple messages like "Hi, I love you."
- Make "books" for children's writing and drawing. Fold several sheets of paper together or staple sheets together.
- Model writing for children; write private notes, grocery lists, and recipes with children. These things show how useful writing is.

- Praise children's attempts to invent their own spelling; these show that they are learning the relationship between print and speech. "Correct" spelling will follow later.
- Do not criticize neatness, spelling, or grammar; it is important that children learn that writing is communication and fun.
- Write down shared experiences or often-told family stories; the written stories can support early readers by helping them anticipate a sequence of events or by helping children figure out words of personal importance emphasized in the story.

How Experiences Outside of the Home Can Promote Literacy

- Take trips to interesting places: bowling alley, shoe-repair shop, bakery, zoo, farm, airport, different kinds of stores. Also consider train and bus trips. When the family returns, make drawings related to the trip. Discuss and relive your experiences and adventures and promote expression of child idea and remembrances in recordings or other media. Recreate the trip in creative dramatics. Effective trips can be quite simple but need careful planning. Visit community events such as 4-H fairs, craft shows, antique-auto shows, new-car shows, and farm-equipment displays.
- Having children accompany family members to the store, bank, post office, zoo, or park can turn the trip into an educational excursion. A home has many advantages that a school cannot duplicate.

How Parents Can Promote Listening Skills

- Try teaching children to listen to and identify sounds, such as the whine of car tires, bird calls, insect noises, and sounds of different kinds of doors closing in the house. Recordings, television, and storybooks also stimulate interest in listening.
- Be a good listener—pause before answering, and wait patiently for children to formulate answers or speech.

How Parents Can Promote an Interest in Reading

Some families create an environment that supports reading by making sure it is impossible to avoid books. They always bring a backpack full of books along on car rides, and keep books in the pockets on the back of car seats. These families understand that young children can make tremendous progress as readers while "just pretending." This happens when a child pretends to read books, reads illustrations, or flips pages as he tells his own story or imitates the actions or voices of those who have read to him.

Parents with positive attitudes about reading will usually find that their children are motivated, spend more time at reading, and expend more effort in learning to read. Put simply, parents who value reading have children with a greater interest in reading skills.

Reading is dependent on facility with oral language. Children who talk easily, handle words skillfully, ask questions, and look for answers usually become good readers. Families have more opportunities for one-on-one time with children compared with teachers who have groups of children to help. Skilled adults reading picture books stop when a child has lost concentration. They try to obtain enthralling books. They restrain themselves and do not go overboard in their attempts to educate children. Instead they have fun, enjoy humor, and encourage questions. Literacy-promoting families read to children every day. Figure 19–5 displays the amount of time children are reading or being read to and the time children spent engaging in other activities, as reported in a survey by the Kaiser Family Foundation (2003).

Many families consult librarians for help. See Figure 19–6 for a list of books with an element of predictability. Finding predictable picture books that include repetitive features enhances the child's feelings of being part of the telling. Competency increases when the child knows what comes next after a few readings. An appealing book selected by a parent can be read with enthusiasm and animation. Children enjoy active participation when chanting lines, pointing to illustrations, and speaking in characters' voices. Families can give reading status and importance;

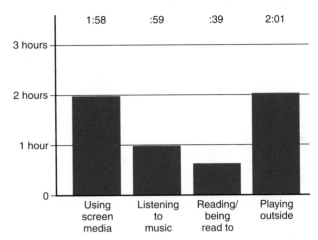

Amount of time children 0–6 spend each day, on average

Note: Average is among all children, across all days of the week, including those who don't do certain activities yet at all.

FIGURE 19–5 *Zero to six: Electronic Media in the Lives of Infants, Toddlers, and Preschoolers*, (#3378), The Henry J. Kaiser Family Foundation, Fall 2003. Copyright © 2003. (This information was reprinted with permission of the Henry J. Kaiser Family Foundation. The Kaiser Family Foundation, based in Menlo Park, California, is a nonprofit, independent national health care philanthropy and is not associated with Kaiser Permanente or Kaiser Industries.)

they can read recipes and directions with their children to show print's purpose (Figure 19–7).

A child's age will determine, in part, what he will find interesting in a book. The preschooler is interested in rhyming words, repetitions, characters the child's own age, bright colors, and fun things to feel. The more a child is exposed to pleasurable reading activities, the greater will be his interest in reading. Families can provide books for browsing and a special place to keep the collection.

Children will become readers only if their emotions are engaged and their imaginations are stretched and stirred by what they find on the printed page. The truly literate are not those who know how to read, but those who read fluently, responsively, critically, and because they want to.

It is wise to select from among the best books for even the youngest children. The best books are well-designed with uncluttered pages, interesting text, and colorful pictures that stimulate young imaginations.

AUTHOR	TITLE	PUBLISHER
Arno, E.	The Gingerbread Man	Crowell
Bang, M.	Ten, Nine, Eight	Greenwillow
Baum, A., & Baum, J.	One Bright Monday Morning	Random House
Berenstain, S., & Berenstain, J.	Bears in the Night	Random House
Bonne, R., & Mill, A.	I Know an Old Lady Who Swallowed a Fly	Holiday House
Brown, M. W.	Goodnight Moon	Harper Festival
Charlip, R.	What Good Luck! What Bad Luck!	Scholastic
Charlip, R., & Supree, B.	Mother Mother I Feel Sick Send for the Doctor Quick Quick Quick	Tricycle Press
Flack, M.	Ask Mr. Bear	Simon & Schuster
Galdone, P.	The Three Billy Goats Gruff	Seabury
Graham, J.	I Love You, Mouse	Harcourt Brace
Hoban, T.	Just Look	Greenwillow
Hogrogian, N.	One Fine Day	Macmillan
Hutchins, P.	The Surprise Party	Simon & Schuster
	Rosie's Walk	Simon & Schuster
Isadora, R.	Max	Simon & Schuster
Langstaff, J.	Oh, A-Hunting We Will Go	Simon & Schuster
Martin, B., Jr.	Brown Bear, Brown Bear, What Do You See?	Holt
Mayer, M.	What Do You Do with a Kangaroo?	Macmillan
Sendak, M.	Chicken Soup with Rice	HarperCollins
Shaw, C. B.	It Looked Like Spilt Milk	HarperCollins
Slobodkina, E.	Caps for Sale	HarperCollins
Spier, P.	The Fox Went out on a Chilly Night	Doubleday
Stevenson, J.	"Could Be Worse!"	Morrow, William & Co.
Stover, J.	If Everybody Did	McKay
Thomas, P.	"Stand Back," Said the Elephant, "I'm Going to Sneeze"	HarperCollins
Viorst, J.	Alexander and the Terrible, Horrible, No Good, Very Bad Day	Simon & Schuster
Zolotow, C.	If It Weren't for You	HarperCollins

FIGURE 19–6 Predictable books.

Parents often think that children learn about reading in school. The truth of the matter is that many children already know a lot about reading when they enter kindergarten, because parents have been teaching their children about reading since they were born. Methods that parents use to teach differ and some parents may not realize that experience with print gives a broad and meaningful introduction to reading. Reading really cannot be learned very well if it is first taught only with lessons on isolated letters and sounds. If reading is to make sense to children, they must see how it is used in life. The following is some additional reading-related advice for parents.

◆ When children select books, show a genuine interest; do not criticize children's selection.

AUTHOR	TITLE	PUBLISHER
Brown, M.	*Stone Soup*	Simon & Schuster
Carle, E.	*The Very Hungry Caterpillar*	Putnam
de Paola, T.	*Pancakes for Breakfast*	Harcourt Brace Jovanovich
de Regniers, B. S.	*May I Bring a Friend?*	Simon & Schuster
Galdone, P.	*The Gingerbread Boy*	Houghton Mifflin
	The Little Red Hen	Houghton Mifflin
Hoban, R.	*Bread and Jam for Frances*	HarperCollins
Marshall, J.	*Yummers*	Houghton Mifflin
Mayer, M.	*Frog Goes to Dinner*	Dial
McCloskey, R.	*One Morning in Maine*	Viking
	Blueberries for Sal	Penguin Putnam
Patz, N.	*Pumpernickel Tickle and Mean Green Cheese*	Baltimore Sun
Sendak, M.	*Chicken Soup with Rice*	HarperCollins
Seuss, Dr.	*Green Eggs and Ham*	Random House

FIGURE 19–7 Books that encourage reading recipes and home cooking experiences.

◆ When children ask for the pronunciation of words, tell them; do not analyze the words or sound them out.

◆ Discuss authors and illustrations at times.

◆ Enjoy humor or fun in books. Relate book happenings to the child's real-life experiences.

◆ Subscribe to children's magazines or borrow copies from libraries.

◆ Ask warm-up questions to set the stage and help children anticipate what will happen.

◆ Point as you read. For very young children, point to things in pictures as you talk about them. Pointing helps focus attention, thus lengthening the time children will sit still for a story. It also develops visual literacy—the idea that pictures have meaning.

◆ Try asking what the child expects the book to be about from looking at the cover.

◆ Look for ways to involve the child during readings.

◆ Stop and let the child supply words.

◆ Talk about words (unusual ones) the child may not understand.

Parents can benefit from knowing they have a greater chance to instill a love of books than teachers do because of their intimate knowledge of their child's life experiences. Parents are able to connect book story features not only to past happenings experienced together but also to the unique characteristics of their child's personality, interests, desires, and abilities. They have an emotional bond that can connect book-reading times to "pleasantness." They can start book reading during infancy and toddlerhood and make parent-child book time a special "together" time. Parents can ask questions, point to objects in illustrations and hesitate to promote guessing, and prompt their child to see details and cause-and-effect relationships. All of these things will increase the child's literacy and vocabulary. Parents can become active listeners who add information a little above what the child knows. When they accept their child's comments and ideas, parents reinforce the child's efforts and desire to share his ideas. Storybook illustrations can also be "read" and discussed in detail. Parents can find books along their child's particular line of interest and select ones that challenge by presenting more complex ideas or information.

Encouraging parents to read in their native language is an important consideration. Schools enrolling other-than-English-speaking children include foreign language picture books in their classroom collection and often stock additional copies that parents can borrow. Local library staffers may be able to provide others.

Parents and other family members play important roles in promoting early literacy. Those who wish to rate themselves using Figure 19–8 may discover that they are already promoting child language and literacy in a number of ways.

Parent Storytelling

The magic of parental storytelling not only improves child listening but also broadens child interests and opens new worlds of discovery. Following are tips from professional storytellers.

1. Select a story that will interest both you and the children. Your enthusiasm for a story is important in helping the children enjoy the story too.

2. Practice the story several times before you share it with the children. Learn all you can about the characters, settings, and events within the story.

3. Decide how to animate the story. Practice some hand gestures, facial expressions, or body movements that will spice up the story for the children.

4. Practice different accents, voice inflections (angry, sad, joyous), and loud and soft speech patterns to help make characters come alive and to add drama to your presentation.

5. Create some simple puppets from common household objects such as wooden

---

Use the following ratings: O = often, S = sometimes, I = infrequently, D = does not apply

Family attempts to:

_____ 1. initiate family discussions at mealtimes.

_____ 2. give full attention to child's comments.

_____ 3. add descriptive or new words in conversation.

_____ 4. take child to library.

_____ 5. take time at post office to discuss letters and postage.

_____ 6. discuss children's books.

_____ 7. read to child daily.

_____ 8. point out print around the house.

_____ 9. accept child's opinions.

_____ 10. use dictionary with child.

_____ 11. talk on the child's chosen subject.

_____ 12. ask questions that promote child's descriptions or predictions.

_____ 13. listen patiently.

_____ 14. discuss television programs.

_____ 15. plan community outings.

_____ 16. invite interesting people to home and promote interactions with child.

_____ 17. correct child's speech casually with little attention to errors.

_____ 18. encourage child hobbies.

_____ 19. answer questions readily.

_____ 20. discuss care and storage of books.

_____ 21. play word games or rhyme words playfully.

_____ 22. talk about how print is used in daily life.

_____ 23. find books on subjects of interest to child.

_____ 24. consult with child's teacher.

_____ 25. give attention and notice accomplishments.

_____ 26. take dictation from child.

_____ 27. try not to interrupt child's speech frequently.

_____ 28. initiate family reading times and family discussions of classics.

_____ 29. establish a book center in the home.

_____ 30. create child writing or art center in the home.

_____ 31. give books as gifts.

_____ 32. provide different writing tools and scrap paper.

_____ 33. provide alphabet toys in the home.

FIGURE 19–8 Family self-rating.

picnic spoons, paper plates, or lunch bags. Draw individual character features on each item and use them during your story.

6. Promote your storytelling time. Make an announcement about an upcoming story or design a simple "advertisement" for a story and post it in advance.

7. Design a simple prop for the children to use during the telling of a story: a paper boat for a sea story, a magnifying glass or camera for a mystery story, or a paper flower for a springtime story.

8. Have the children suggest new props, gestures, or voice qualities that would be appropriate for retelling of the story at a later date.

9. After telling a story, talk about it with the children. Ask them to tell you the most enjoyable or memorable parts.

Being a good storyteller takes a little practice, but the time invested can make a world of difference in helping children appreciate good literature.

Games with Rules

A lot of family language interaction takes place in family game playing. Games have rules and encourage child self-regulation, focused attention, and memory. Outdoor games have an added physical component. To play by the rules, children must regulate their behavior and regulate the rule-abiding behavior of others. Acquiring self-regulation, a skill appropriate and desired in further schooling, is a major accomplishment during early childhood. Many researchers point out that the emotional, social, and behavior competence of young children (such as higher levels of self-control and lower levels of acting out) predicts children's academic performance in their first grades of school, over and above their cognitive skills and family backgrounds.

Home Reading and Writing Centers

Home reading centers are a lot like school reading areas. A comfortable, warm, private, well-lighted place free of distraction works best. Adjacent shelving and a chair for parent comfort is important to book-sharing times. Window seats and room dividers make cozy corners. Parents can get creative in selecting and furnishing reading centers.

Family book collections encourage children's positive attitudes concerning books as personal possessions and give books status. Home-made books often become children's favorite volumes. Families model appropriate storage and care in home reading centers. A special area with writing supplies, an alphabet chart, table, and chair should be suggested to parents.

Parents interested in purchasing books can be alerted to the opportunity to buy books through school-sponsored book clubs, local library book sales, used-book stores, thrift shops, and yard sales. Pointers should be shared concerning selecting quality books.

Library Services

Parents are sometimes unaware of children's library services. Children's librarians, as mentioned before, are great sources of information and often offer children a wide-ranging program of literary events and activities. They are good at finding books that match a particular child's interest. Teachers who are in touch with a preschool child's emerging interests can alert parents.

Building home book collections can be a real problem for some parents. Economics and library availability may thwart parent desires. Some parents living in the inner city in unsafe neighborhoods may leave their homes only to get food and to take children to school.

Home Visits

In trying to understand attending children, especially "silent ones" or culturally diverse ones, a home visit may help to plan for children's individual needs. Most early childhood centers with strong home-school partnerships schedule yearly visits to each family.

Parents Who Speak Languages Other Than English

Early childhood centers have become increasingly sensitive to other-than-English-speaking families who are often eager to promote their child's literacy. Many children with limited English proficiency also have in common that their parents are poorly educated, that their family income is low, that they reside in communities in which many families are similarly struggling, and that they attend schools with student bodies that are predominantly minority and low achieving. Gamble, Ramakumar, and Diaz (2007) suggest that educators may be able to enhance co-parenting solidarity, if differing parenting styles and perhaps child-rearing disagreements exist in a Hispanic family. This is accomplished by promoting the idea that family members can be supportive of each other and work out their differences through communication, negotiation, coordination, and respect for a different perspective. The center staff members would also be respectful and sensitive in home-school interactions and communications.

Family literacy programs attempt to break the cycle of intergenerational illiteracy by providing services to both parent and child. Programs vary from community to community as each program tries to meet the needs of participants. Participants are often parents who lack basic literacy skills and may need to acquire positive self-concepts to encourage their children's school success. Family literacy programs and adult literacy programs can be located through county Offices of Education or state agencies.

Directors and administrators can receive information and a multitude of resources concerning exemplary family literacy programs from the following two agencies:

National Center for Family Literacy
325 W. Main St., Suite 300
Louisville, KY 40202-4237

Division of Adult Education and Literacy
 Clearinghouse
U.S. Department of Education
400 Maryland Ave. S.W.
Washington, DC 20202-7240

Early childhood centers can often locate family literacy programs and identify resources by contacting the Director of Adult Education in their state. A growing number of communities are instituting publicly funded family literacy programs. Many of these programs are designed to provide

◆ child care.

◆ transportation.

◆ introduction to literacy-building home activities.

◆ access to community services.

◆ involvement in children's school activities.

◆ bilingual support and promotion of pride in language and culture.

◆ increased parental self-esteem.

Many parent education projects working with immigrant parents reject the idea that the best way to help parents is to hold group parenting classes. They instead attempt to increase parents' confidence in their teaching abilities by other means. They encourage parent picture-book readings and after-book discussions in the child's native language. They provide books, book bags with suggested activities, or recorded books or may use other strategies.

African-American School Success

Murphy (2003) conducted case studies on four high-achieving elementary school children of African-American heritage. She states:

> These children's academic success is no accident. All four benefited from the continuous, active involvement of their parents in guiding and influencing their school success. (p. 17)

---

family literacy programs — community programs attempting to provide literacy-building opportunities and experiences for families. Services are available for both adults and children.

Murphy describes five factors that "maintained and sustained" these African-American families:

◆ a high-achievement orientation
◆ strong kinship bonds
◆ strong work orientation
◆ adaptability of family roles
◆ a religious orientation

Murphy also cites additional contributing family characteristics. These include:

◆ the family's beliefs and values.
◆ the quality interactive behavior of parents.
◆ parents' placing an extraordinarily high value on education.
◆ their maintaining a social environment in which learning flourished.

Early childhood educators working with diverse groups of children will find this study interesting, for it alerts teachers to the strength, resolve, and commitment to education that exists in many American families.

One of the four children that Murphy studied, a 10-year-old, was asked why he has done so well in school. He cited

"great teachers, parents who cared about my school work, friends who helped me with my school work, and a great staff"; and about his parents, he said, "They helped me learn about the world and my environment"; and he added, "I'm special because God made me special. He sent me to this earth to have fun, get an education, and go to college." (p. 21)*

What child wouldn't do well with a similar attitude toward school, teachers, parents, and himself as a "learner"?

Parent Education Projects— Working Together

Minnesota initiated parent training programs during the late 1970s, and Missouri is credited as the first state in the United States to

mandate that all school districts provide parent education and support services. The Parents as Teachers (PAT) project was initiated in 1981 with 350 families. It has been replicated under different names in more than 50 sites nationwide. Starting at a child's birth, the project helps parents understand their child's individual development and promotes early literacy. Personalized home visits, group meetings, ongoing monitoring, periodic screening, and referral and guidance services have effectively worked toward the project's goal of having children reach age 3 without undetected developmental delay or handicapping conditions. Among the literacy-building activities considered "particularly powerful" in the PAT methodology is in-home parent storybook reading. Read-aloud activities seemed to influence family social-interaction as well as child literacy. Further information about the project is available by contacting Parents as Teachers National Center, 2228 Ball Drive, St. Louis, MO 63146.

The fact that many young families today may be less prepared to care for children than were their predecessors has not escaped educators. Nor has it escaped our national government. A government program called "Good Start, Grow Smart," is an early childhood initiative that helps state and local governments strengthen early learning for young children. The initiative focuses on young children's literacy and cognitive, social, and emotional development. During the 1990s, 25 percent of the nation's children who did not have any risk factors in their lives—such as poverty, parents with limited education, single-parent homes, or lack of English-language experience—entered kindergarten bereft of the necessary oral language or early literacy skills critical for learning. Because of this alarming percentage of unprepared preschoolers, as well as other factors, U.S. school systems, reading educators, school administrators, and community leaders have increased efforts to support additional family literacy programs. Most programs are designed to promote family storybook reading (Paratore, 2006).

In an effort to reduce the stark contrast some young children and their family members

*From Murphy, J. C. (2003, Nov.). Case studies in African-American school success and parenting behaviors. *Young Children*, 58(6):85, 89. Copyright © 2003 NAEYC. Used with permission.

experience between home and school, family literacy programs and early childhood programs currently are attempting to become aware of each enrolled child's family literacy proficiency, their culture-specific literacy practices, and family literacy knowledge. This type of collaboration and connection between home and school, it is felt, will promote better planning for school instruction and increase the school's ability to relate school activities to children's daily lives. Promoting home literacy events and activities, particularly storybook reading, is still an important goal, but collaborating and understanding what families know, what they do, and how they do it, has been given increased emphasis and attention.

Paratore (2007) describes Project Flame (Family Literacy Aprendiendo, Mejorando, Educcando) as follows:

> Although Project Flame is clearly based on teaching parents how to support their children in the acquisition of school-based literacy behaviors (including sessions on creating home library centers, book sharing, library visits, teaching the ABC's, and helping with homework), parents' personal perspectives and cultural knowledge provide an essential foundation for literacy conversation. This collaborative learning provides opportunities for participants to share the "multiple literacies"' of their home lives. (p. 59)

THE FEDERAL EVEN START FAMILY LITERACY PROGRAM

Even Start, a federally funded program (1989–1997), consisted of a variety of family literacy projects that integrated low-income children's early childhood education classes with parent education and family supportive services. Family participation criteria included (1) family eligibility for adult basic education (ABE), (2) a child younger than 8 years of age, and (3) residence in a geographical area receiving funds for Even Start services.

The Even Start program was modeled after a 1980s Kentucky program that involved parents with low-literacy skills and their 3- to 4-year-old children. Even Start was based on the following assumptions:

◆ Intervention is more effective when focused on the family rather than just on the parent or just on the child.

◆ A planned, structured classroom time involving parent and child in literacy skill development might also promote parent-child relationships when staff guidance was present.

◆ Families need supportive services and help in accessing them.

The goals of Even Start were to intervene and offer a developmentally appropriate, meaningful, and useful child curriculum that promoted school readiness and children's language and literacy skills. It also aimed to increase parents' involvement in their child's schooling by decreasing parental barriers, such as fear of school, transportation problems, and low self-esteem. It attempted to provide a stable, capable staff that could integrate all services.

Federal legislation required an evaluation of Even Start at both local and national levels. These evaluations took place from 1989 to 1997. Results showed that adults gained literacy skills similar to those of adults in the control group, but more Even Start adults earned a GED (general education diploma). Even Start children learned school readiness skills significantly faster than children in the control group, but those in the control group caught up after receiving school services.

Many current educators accept the assumptions espoused by Even Start, and programs and projects have adopted similar ones, believing they have value and merit. Although criticisms based largely on the findings from the U. S. Department of Education's national evaluation in 2003 of Even Start's effectiveness have resulted in drastic funding cuts, there are existing state programs. To find out about state programs and the National Even Start Association, consult www.evenstart.com.

TELEVISION VIEWING AND YOUNG CHILDREN'S LANGUAGE DEVELOPMENT

Parents often ask teachers about the value of television and videos and about their child's viewing habits. A national survey of more than 1,000 parents conducted by the Henry J. Kaiser Foundation (Antonucci, 2003) suggests that parents have divided opinions concerning whether television viewing "mostly helps" (43 percent) or "mostly hurts" (27 percent) children's learning. The foundation's survey also notes that in homes where television is on for the longest periods, children were less likely to be able to read. A review of research generally supports the idea that children's television viewing casts children as "watchers" rather than active participants in language exchanges with others. The effect of viewing on particular children differs. After children become readers, studies show that reading development is adversely affected when viewing is excessive. A newer (2006) report by the Kaiser Health Foundation found that 8 in 10 of the nation's 1- to 6-year-olds watched TV and/or played video games about 2 hours on a typical day (Neergaard, 2006). This estimated figure had not changed significantly since the Kaiser foundation's first report in 2003. Approximately 19 percent of children under age 2 have TVs in their bedroom even though the American Academy of Pediatrics recommends that *no* TV or other multimedia use should happen for children younger than the age of 2—a time of the brain's most rapid development (Broughton, 2006).

Television programs for children older than age 2 that stress educational or informative material do not seem to have harmful potential. Again, the amount of viewing time is critical. Because research offers so many conflicting views, teachers cannot give definitive answers to parents. Educators can express their concern that heavy television and video viewing rob a child of a literacy-rich home environment, one that is necessary for the child's optimal growth. Real firsthand experiences, exposure to books, and conversations with interested and responsive family members stack the odds in the favor of early literacy and cannot be replaced by television or videos.

What is excessive viewing? Research suggests that more than 10 hours of viewing weekly is excessive. Young Americans, on average, now spend more hours in front of the set than at any other activity except sleeping.

An increasing number of alarmed educators and researchers warn that excessive, unsupervised television and video viewing by young children promotes negative effects, including

◆ aggressive and violent behavior.

◆ decreased imagination, cooperation, and success in relationships.

◆ vulnerability to stimulus addiction, resulting in the child needing overstimulation to feel satisfied.

◆ immunity to vicarious emotional stresses, resulting in the inability to produce socially acceptable emotional responses.

◆ poor reading comprehension and inability to persevere to an outcome.

◆ listening problems.

◆ pronunciation difficulty.

◆ inability to make mental pictures (visual imagery).

◆ inability to remember or decipher meaning from what is viewed or heard because of the passive aspect of television viewing.

◆ hindered development of metalinguistic awareness (e.g., understanding that letters make up words, written words are linked together into meaningful sentences, a word is made from printed marks, one reads from left to right in English, and the meaning of terms such as *author*, *title*, *illustration*, etc.).★

◆ decreased verbal interactions with family.

◆ decreased opportunities to experience life and exercise verbal problem solving.

Very few research studies have attempted to reduce preschoolers' television watching. Dennison, Russo, Burdick, and Jenkins (2004) were successful in doing so. Their 2-year study with 16 early childhood centers was funded in part

★From Jane M. Healy, Ph.D., *Endangered Minds.*

by the National Institutes of Health. Intervention sessions emphasized reading and alternatives to television viewing. They also stressed the importance of families eating meals together. Children in the study group were rewarded with stickers for choosing television alternatives. A children's book, *The Berenstain Bears and Too Much TV*, featuring an anti-television theme, was introduced to children in the study. Results indicated that children in the study session reduced television watching time by 3.1 hours per week. For a full description of the intervention program, consult the February 2004 issue of *Archives of Pediatrics & Adolescent Medicine*.

Some studies suggest that children, even those who have been taught critical analysis skills, do not generate critical thinking during television commercials. Children and adults think differently, using different parts of their brain. In other words, they tend to believe the images they see!

Educators are beginning to understand that children's excessive television viewing, electronic gaming, and other media use, combined with societal attitudes concerning reading and intellectual pursuits, are our nation's greatest threat to literacy and the development of our children's thinking abilities.

What can parents do? They can place firm limits, participate in children's television viewing, discuss program content, turn off the set, and give substitute care providers clear instructions concerning screen time.

Other Electronic Media

Video and other types of media games may be a topic of interest for some parents and families. Because video games are interactive in nature, causing players to imitate violence and not merely to watch it in the process of play, their potential for altering brain structures and function is even more significant than repeated film or television viewing. It is a very good idea to review the media material available to one's child. Cartoon graphics that look like they suit young children are often misleading. More than 2,000 research studies link media violence to children's violent behavior. It is plain that most of the media advertised for children is expensive and has extremely little educational value. It cannot hold a candle to real life experience!

HOME-SCHOOL COMMUNICATION

Schools differ widely in both the amount of written home-school communication and the amount of time spent talking or meeting with parents. Teachers are struggling, particularly in urban, coastal, and border states, to learn about family practices, beliefs, and educational needs and desires. They wish to find common ground and acknowledge parents' cultural values while also sharing their programs' philosophies and teaching techniques. That can be a challenging goal to achieve, particularly in areas with a diverse population. In places such as California's Silicon Valley, it is common to find children from as many as 10 to 29 different ethnic or culturally diverse groups in one elementary classroom.

Most preschool teachers desire more time and more conversations and additional written communication with parents. This suits some parents who seem to be seeking supportive assistance in child-rearing. Each parent group and center is unique, and consequently, tremendous differences exist in the degree to which preschool centers and families work together. Most centers try to provide some type of family assistance. Families who receive help and support feel more open to contribute to the school's activities.

Family-school contacts usually take place in at least four ways:

1. daily conversations
2. written communications
3. planned family meetings, workshops, and social events
4. individual conferences

At the beginning of the child's school year, a telephone call welcoming the family establishes communication. Weekly newsletters and personal notes from teachers maintain links thereafter.

Communication on the Fly

Teachers have a good chance to share children's interests and favorite school activities when parents arrive to take their children home from the center; teachers can discuss with parents such things as books, play objects, and child-created or constructed work. Children spend time with and talk about what excites them; the observant teacher can be aware of attending children's developing interests. Families are usually curious about what their children have shared about their homes and out-of-school activities.

Bulletin Boards

Many schools use "family" bulletin boards as a communicative device. Schools receive more announcements of literary happenings in their communities than do parents. Language-developing local events and activities can be advertised so parents can view them when picking up or dropping off their children. Short magazine and newspaper articles of interest can be posted at eye-catching levels.

Planned Meetings and Conferences

Planned meetings include individual and group gatherings (Figure 19–9). Conferences let families know what plans the school has in place to address their children's individual interests and growth, and whether their plans are working. When children have interests in alphabet letters, dramatizing, special-topic books, or other pursuits, families and teachers can discuss related school and home activities.

Method and Material Review Meetings

A meeting can be planned to take a closer look at the early childhood center's planned language program, materials, and language arts center. Families then get a firsthand look and an opportunity to explore what is at hand. Teachers often conduct sample activities and demonstrate material and equipment use. Families are able to ask questions about their children's use of or interest in a center's planned opportunities.

Family and Teacher Study Meetings

Some possible themes of study meetings might include (1) the effects of television viewing on children's language development, (2) bilingualism, or (3) free and inexpensive toys that promote language or involve multiple and wide-ranging other subjects. The center's staff, parents, outside experts, or films can present ideas to be studied and discussed. This type of meeting helps inform all present. Differing views clarify everyone's thinking.

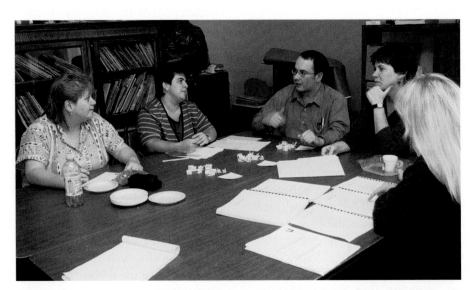

FIGURE 19–9 Parents' wishes and concerns are often aired in parent-staff meetings.

It is a good idea to analyze what is really important to communicate to parents concerning children's language arts development. The following items are the author's high-priority topics. Many parents show concern over their children's articulation and vocabulary, particularly children's speech errors. Parents may be worried when they notice that a child's language, which at 3 was apparently error-free and highly grammatical, becomes full of errors a year later. They need to know that this indicates progress. At each successive stage a child masters a limited range of simple speech structures. When more complicated structures are attempted due to his more complicated thinking, his hypotheses are tested by whether he is understood or not. It is helpful to assure parents that the school's staff monitors fluency and to share typical child speech characteristics. Such discussions often relax parents and dispel their fears. Hints concerning simple modeling of correct forms are well received by most parents.

Sharing information on school interaction techniques used to increase children's speech by listening, following children's leads, and expanding interest in daily conversation is also very important. Families need to realize how influential they are in modeling an interest in and positive attitudes toward reading, writing, and speaking. Their ability to listen closely to ideas rather than judging correctness of grammar or ideas should be discussed. Alexander (2004) notes that research has found that before a child reaches age 14, parents are twice as important as school is for a child's learning. Educators urge adults to engage in intellectually challenging conversations, offer new and increasingly descriptive words, and extend conversations with unpressured questioning. Another topic to discuss with parents is the warm, unpressured social environments that promote conversations about pleasurable happenings, such as reading picture books and sharing stories. Discussing quality books and "advertising" books to children can perhaps combat electronic media dominance in the home. Analyzing books, pictures, text, and their messages is a great idea. The child's home access to creative materials, such as drawing and marking tools, is important.

Parents have many questions about early reading and writing of alphabet letters. Both reading and writing acquisition is aided by a widely enriching home and preschool curriculum that preserves children's feelings of competence by offering that which is slightly above their level and related closely to their present interests.

Last on this list may be the most important topic teachers can discuss with parents. A lot of language development is possible when parents and other adults share activities they love—the ones they can speak about enthusiastically in detailed specific terms; the ones that are vital to them and for which they have a passionate interest. Examples are easy to find and role-play for a parent and family groups: the dad who does carpentry, the grandma who grows garden vegetables, the aunt who dances the flamenco, the mom who makes noodles from scratch, the brother who plays the flute, the sister who collects butterflies, and the uncle who restores motorcycles. So many times parents and families do not see themselves as resources and do not understand the power of shared experiences with their young child. Parents and family members supply the daily experiences that give words meaning and depth, as do teachers, but they are more instrumental because of the amount of time spent with the child and their access to the world of children's lives out of school.

Fathers and Language Development

More than 25 percent of children do not live with their fathers (Child Care Bureau, 2004). For young children, good fathering contributes to the development of emotional security, curiosity, and math and verbal skills, a national study concludes. Many preschools are rethinking their parent involvement and planning to include fathers and children's male relatives to a greater degree. Some schools require "father classroom time," and family meetings are designed to cleverly interest and increase male attendance.

Fathers play an important role in their children's school achievement, and the earlier they become involved with their children's learning and socialization, the better. Educational research suggests that a father's ability to support his child's learning can affect the child's engagement with books.

Explaining Phonemic Awareness to Parents

Many parents are well read, but a definition of phonetic awareness and why it has become important is a good idea. Main points to transmit to parents follow.

- Current research suggests that phonemic awareness is an essential skill in learning to read.
- Preschoolers become aware and play with sounds, rhymes, and silly words frequently.
- Speech is composed of small units called phonemes (sounds).
- Each phoneme represents a particular sound. (In *cat*, there are three different phonemes: c-a-t.)

What can parents do to help make their child aware of the phonemic structure of language?

- Clap to music.
- Clap to syllables.
- Sing repetitive and rhyming songs.
- Say words slowly and stretch sounds out in a game-like way at times.
- Play games with rhyming words.
- Blend sounds together in games.
- Say "When I say 'c-a-r' slowly, what word do you hear?"
- Find things that start with "T," and so on.
- Seek computer games that play with word sounds.
- Make up stories with word sounds.
- Have plenty of alphabet books, games, and toys available.
- Know that a child's learning an alphabet letter's name precedes introducing its sound.
- Look for teachable moments rather than planned sit-down instruction.

School Lending Libraries. Increasingly, early childhood centers are aware of the benefits of maintaining a school lending library. Although extra time and effort are involved in this provision to parents, centers are sensitive to the plight of parents who are economically distressed and pressed for time. Lending libraries should give families book-reading tips. Books in the first language of enrolled children are included in a center's book collection.

Rules and procedures for checkout and return are prepared in print for families. Staff time, center budget, and staff availability are key factors in deciding whether a family lending library is a viable activity.

Working with Hard-to-Reach Parents

Centers incorporate family dinners and provide child care to increase parental attendance at home-school meetings. Every effort is made to make the center staff and facility as nonintimidating as possible and to convince every family that they can contribute to child literacy.

Chang (2001) describes family literacy night meetings to engage families, grandparents, and family friends as a way to more effectively share ideas and activities. Night sessions helped families apply research-based classroom interventions, strategies, and activities at home. Called "The Scaffold for Family Literacy Development," family literacy night's six major guidelines follow.

1. Always work with and help your child produce something that conveys what and how much he really knows. This involves working jointly to produce something that will clarify and reflect the child's learning.

2. Always help your child develop language used at home and in school by modeling, talking, or working together. Always give your child opportunities to use new words in different ways. This informs families of the importance of talking and listening to their child while restating, probing, or praising the child's ideas,

opinions, or judgments related to specific topics in a calm and encouraging manner. Families were urged to use multiple paths to encourage learning and the discovery of similarities and differences in words or phases.

3. Always help your child relate what he has learned in school to daily life. Families were encouraged to use related events to strengthen vocabulary comprehension.

4. Always help your child think or ask questions using on- and under-the-surface questions. Always help your child see how ideas or concepts are related. Always give positive feedback.

5. Always talk with your child about school or lifelong learning. Always listen to your child when discussing how he can think about learning and what he can plan or do for it.

6. Always value your child's abilities in multiple ways. Always help your child learn through multiple paths that he would like to try. This enhances families' abilities to verbalize how their child may develop a healthy and productive sense of self-respect and confidence.*

Although Chang's described family literacy evening meetings for parents and families were used at the elementary school level, they also suit preschool-level families.

Washington Elementary School and Preschool (Santa Ana, California) devotes the first 20 minutes of every school day to classroom reading. They call it "Book Choice Time." Family members, volunteers, and older brothers and sisters attending the same elementary school enjoy good literature together, often in their home language. More than 600 family members participate on any given day.

---

*From Chang, J. (2001, April). Scaffold for school–home collaboration: Enhancing reading and language development." Research brief #9, p. 13. Center for Research on Education, Diversity, and Excellence.

DAILY CONTACTS

Greeting both parents and children as they arrive starts a warm, comfortable atmosphere; encourages talking; and sets the tone for conversation. Short, personal comments build parent-school partnership feelings and help children enter the school discussing the morning's happenings. Children are offered choices of possible activities through statements such as, "We've put red play dough on the table by the door for you" or "The matching game you told me you liked yesterday is waiting for you on the shelf near the bird cage."

Family mailboxes can hold daily teacher messages. Important milestones, such as the child's first interest in or attempt at printing alphabet letters or his name or his first created stories, should be shared. A short note from the teacher about a child's special events is appreciated by most families. A note about special daily happenings such as, "I think Toni would like to tell you about the worm she found in the garden" or "Saul has been asking many questions about airplanes," keeps families aware of their children's expanding interests.

WRITTEN COMMUNICATION

Often, centers prepare informal letters or newsletters that describe school happenings or daily themes. Figures 19–10 and 19–11 are two examples of this type of teacher-family communication.

A written communication may concern the following.

◆ local library addresses or a description of services or programs, such as story hours or puppet shows
◆ local children's theater or drama productions
◆ children's book stores
◆ film presentations of interest to the young child
◆ special community events
◆ adult programs, workshops, meetings, and so forth, that include topics concerned

---

SMALL, SMALLER, SMALLEST

Dear Parents,

We are studying the size of things and will have many discussions this week comparing two or more objects or people. In similar discussions at home, emphasize the endings of size words (-er, -est).

Following are some activities you may wish to try in which size can be discussed. Note the words *big, bigger,* and *biggest* or *tall, taller, tallest,* or others could also be appropriately used.

1. Sort bottle caps, canned food cans, spoons, or crackers.
2. Discuss your pet's size in relation to a neighbor's pet.
3. Take a large piece of paper and cut into square pieces. Discuss small, smaller, smallest.
4. Look for round rocks or pebbles and compare sizes. Ask the child to line them up from small to smallest.
5. Play games involving finding objects smaller than your shoe, finger, a coin, and so on, or smaller than a ball but larger than a marble.

You will find many opportunities to compare size in your neighborhood or on walks, or in the course of daily living.

Sincerely,

Your partner in your child's education
Your child's preschool teacher

FIGURE 19–10 Sample of informal letter to parents to strengthen school learning. Note: Adding child drawings might create additional interest.

with the development of children's language arts

◆ requests for donated materials useful in language arts games or activities

Monthly Newsletters

If a school is trying to help families expand their children's experiences, newsletters can suggest family outings and excursions to local community events and low-cost and free entertainment. Dates, times, costs, telephone numbers, and simple maps can be included.

Completed newsletters can be handed out to adults at pick-up or drop-off time. It is suggested that newsletters be upbeat, with humor, quotes, and anecdotes scattered throughout the pages.

FAMILY RESOURCES

Centers sometimes provide informational articles, magazines, and books that may be borrowed for short periods or available at the school's office. Photocopied magazine articles in manila folders that have been advertised on the school's family bulletin board are a good resource for busy families.

Family information about children's books and reading can be obtained from

American Library Association, 50 E. Huron St., Chicago, IL 60611.
Children's Book Council Inc., 12 West 37th St., 2nd Floor, New York, NY 10018-7480.
Cullinan, B. E. (1992). *Read to me: Raising kids who love to read.* New York: Scholastic.

A free public library card can be the smartest card in a family's wallet because the more their children read the better they do in school. Libraries offer a wide variety of services that promote child (and adult) literacy. Many public libraries offer the following: help locating material for children's homework assignments and/or research, books, magazines, periodicals, microfiche, newspapers, videos, movie rentals, CDs, DVDs, CD-ROMs, Internet access, laser printers, copy machines, photographs, audio books, and entertainment media. Libraries frequently sponsor and create children's programs and cultural events, bulletin boards posting

Dear Family,

This week we have talked about many means of transportation—of how we use animals and machines to take us from one place to another.

We built things, painted things, and learned songs and heard stories about different vehicles such as bikes, cars, trucks, buses, boats, trains, airplanes, horses and wagons, etc., and we even took a bus ride.

Here are some suggested home activities to reinforce school learning.

• Talk about places you go together in your car.

• Save large cardboard boxes—line them up, and pretend they are railroad cars.

• Save old magazines. Let your child find "vehicles that move things from place to place." The child may want to find, cut, and paste pictures.

• Take a walk, and find all the moving vehicles you can.

• Sing a train song, "I've Been Working on the Railroad," or any other.

• Plan a ride on or in a vehicle that is new to the child.

As you enjoy life together, you may want to point out and talk about transportation.

Sincerely,

P.S. Here's a rebus poem to share.

 Sam wanted to go to the zoo.

The family wanted to go there too.

The was out of gas.

And the [bus image] didn't go past

their [house image] , so what could they do?

How could they get to the zoo?

FIGURE 19–11 A partnership letter.

local happenings that promote learning opportunities, and they hold periodic used-book sales where inexpensive books and other literacy-promoting items can be obtained.

PARENTS AS PROGRAM VOLUNTEERS

The role of families, relatives, neighbors, and community volunteers has changed. Early childhood educators realize that home and school literacy learning are intimately intertwined. Family and community volunteers and resources are seen as vital parts of language arts instruction

(Figure 19–12). The teacher's goal is to involve and invite resource people to participate in a relationship that urges them to become active participants in children's language learning and literacy. Families can help teachers plan relevant curriculum topics. Most parent groups include willing volunteers who donate their time, talents, skills, and abilities or share hobby collections with the children. The following are some of the ways families can contribute.

◆ Celebrate "book week."

◆ Explain occupations. Encourage parents to be guest speakers, discussing their occupations. Ask them to bring in items used in

FIGURE 19–12 This parent volunteer adds cultural songs with vigorous movements.

FIGURE 19–13 Blake and Ethan's dad volunteers as a computer consultant so he comes to the center with his sons one morning a week.

their occupations and to wear the clothing associated with their jobs.

◆ Demonstrate special skills. From yoga to weaving, parents' simple demonstrations interest children.

◆ Provide cooking demonstrations. Cooking demonstrations can add words to children's vocabularies.

◆ Organize field trips. Families can offer to volunteer their time or provide suggestions.

◆ Organize fund-raisers.

Many parents often work in businesses where useful language arts materials are discarded, such as scrap paper, cardboard, and so forth. The parent is usually more than willing to obtain these previously discarded materials, especially if they are unable to volunteer their time to the center.

Many family volunteers enjoy making language-developing games and visuals. Art,

photography, sewing, and carpentry talents lend themselves to creating and constructing many classroom materials. Repairing a school's books, flannel board sets, and puppet collections can be an ongoing task. Even the busiest families seem to find time to share their expertise as visiting guest speakers. Through the joint efforts of home and school, centers are able to provide a wider range of language-developing experiences for attending children (Figure 19–13).

SUMMARY

Schools differ in both the amount and types of interactions between families and the center. School personnel need to clarify priorities that they wish to communicate to parents concerning children's language development. By

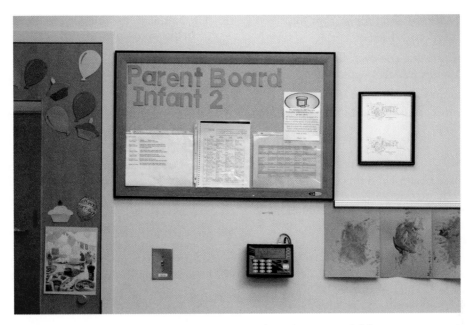

FIGURE 19–14 Family message boards are found in most child centers.

teachers and families working together, children's learning experiences can be reinforced and expanded. A first step involves gaining family's trust.

Contact with families takes place in a variety of ways, both planned and unplanned, including daily conversations, written communications, meetings, and scheduled conferences (Figure 19–14). Centers are interested in promoting the reading of quality books in the home and alerting parents to community opportunities. Volunteers can aid goal realization in the language arts by sharing their talents, hobbies, labor, time, and energy. Together, home and school work toward children's language growth and competence.

ADDITIONAL RESOURCES

Readings

Berenstain, S., & Berenstain, J. (1984). *The Berenstain bears and too much TV.* New York: Random House. (A child's book that deals with television issues).

Henderson, A. T., Mapp, K. L., Johnson, V. & Davies, D. (2007). *Beyond the bake sale: The essential guide to family-school partnerships.* New York: The New Press.

International Reading Association. (2002). *Beginning literacy and your child.* Newark, DE: Author.

Jones, E., & Cooper, R. M. (2006). *Playing to get smart.* New York: Teachers College Press.

Lipson, E. R. (2000). *Parent's guide to the best books for children.* New York: Three Rivers Press.

Schon, I. (2002, July). Pars los ninos . . . Picture books in Spanish for young children. *Young Children, 57*(4), 92–85.

Thernstrom, A., & Thernstrom, S. (2003). *No excuses: Closing the racial gap in learning.* New York: Simon & Schuster.

Wells, R. (2005). *My shining star: Raising a child who's ready to learn.* New York: Scholastic Press.

International Reading Association Brochures

The following brochures are free with a self-addressed, stamped envelope. Send requests to 800 Barksdale Rd., P.O. Box 8239, Newark, DE 19714-8139. Brochures are also available in Spanish.

Explore the Playground of Books: Tips for Parents of Beginning Readers

Get Ready to Read!: Tips for Parents of Young Children

Library Safari: Tips for Parents of Young Readers and Explorers

Making the Most of Television: Tips for Parents of Young Viewers

See the World on the Internet: Tips for Parents of Young Readers—and "Surfers"

Summer Reading Adventure!: Tips for Parents of Young Readers

Helpful Websites

Centers for Disease Control and Prevention (CDC)
http://www.cdc.gov/actearly
Offers descriptions of young children's developmental milestones and early warning signs of developmental problems.

ECRP—Early Childhood Research & Practice
http://www.ecrp.uiuc.edu
Provides links to readings that describe how new teachers can develop relationships with parents.

HIPPY USA (Home Instruction for Parents of Preschool Youngsters)
http://www.hippyusa.org
Provides information about this parent involvement program that promotes 3- to 5-year-old children's school success.

National Child Care Information Center
http://nccic.org
A clearinghouse for information of interest to families and educators. Spanish-language resources are available.

The National Institute for Literacy
http://www.nifl.gov
Provides information about this federal organization that supports state, regional, and national literacy services.

Parents as Teachers
http://www.parentsasteachers.org
Describes a well-respected parent education program serving families.

U.S. Department of Education—Especially for Parents
http://www.ed.gov
Serves educators as well as parents. Select Parents link.

U.S. Department of Education, Office of Communications and Outreach
http://www.nochildleftbehind.gov
Select Publications link and request the free 62-page booklet *Helping Your Child Become a Reader: With Activities for Children from Infancy Through Age 6.*

Book Companion Website

Lots of web activities provide information on family literacy resources. Internet exercises delve into the issue of parents' and kindergarten teachers' opinions (based on a U.S. Department of Education survey) concerning children's school readiness skills. Take a short quiz that probes your ability to assist families.

STUDENT ACTIVITIES

1. Photocopy the following list of scenarios, and cut the sections into cards. Rate each card before joining a group of classmates to discuss ratings.

Rating Scale:

1	2	3
teacher used good judgment	uncertain about teacher's behavior	teacher used poor judgment

A field trip is in progress. Mrs. Winkler, a parent, is acting as a volunteer supervisor. A teacher over-hears Mrs. Winkler tell her group to be quiet and listen to her explanation of what is happening at the shoe factory. The teacher tactfully suggests to Mrs. Winkler that the children may wish to ask questions.	During a study meeting, two parents are having a heated discussion concerning television's value. A teacher offers her views. Her views happen to support one side of the argument.
Mr. Sousa is a violinist. He is also Tami's father. Tami's teacher sends a special note to Mr. Sousa, inviting him to share his talents with the class. The note mentions that he will be allowed to play the violin for a 5-minute period.	Mr. Thomas, a teacher, knows about a book sale at a local children's book store. He includes the item in the school's newsletter to parents.
Sending written messages to parents is not personal, Ms. Garcia (a teacher) feels. She telephones parents in the evening with news of milestones their children have accomplished in the school's language arts program.	Parent bulletin board posting is part of Miss Alexian's duties. She feels that parents rarely read posted materials. At a staff meeting, she asks others for helpful ideas for displays that would grab parents' attention.
Mr. Washington, a teacher, greets the children by waving from across the room or saying, "Hi, Mark. I'm glad you're here."	"Oh, that's not the right way to ask a child about his artwork," Mrs. Yesmin, a teacher, says to Patsy's father.
"You're her teacher. Why ask me what she does at home? It's what goes on at school I'm interested in!" says Mrs. McVey, Pam's mother. "Knowing how Pam spends her time at home helps me plan school activities," explains Mrs. Lerner, Pam's teacher.	"Do you read to your child?" Miss Hernandez asks Mike's mother. "Of course, didn't you think I did?" the child's mother answers.
"There's an article on the parent bulletin board about children's use of slang words that you might want to look over, Mrs. Chung," says Mr. Benjamin (a teacher) to one of the parents.	During a parent-teacher meeting, Mrs. Texciera says, "Jill's work is always so messy." Miss Flint, the teacher, answers, "With time, it will improve. She's working with small puzzles and painting. This will give her more practice and control."
"Oh, don't worry about Jon watching television, Mr. Dunne," says Jon's teacher.	"There isn't one good video for preschoolers, Mr. Perez!"

625

2. With a group of classmates, list ideas for parents to obtain inexpensive quality books for home libraries and book corners.

3. Plan a parent newsletter for a local preschool center with helpful information concerning children's language development.

4. Invite a school's director to discuss parent involvement in a school's language arts goals.

5. Identify three books that might help parents understand children's language development or that might provide home activity ideas. Cite the title, author, and copyright date.

6. If you were to design a literacy packet for parents to use over the summer before their child starts kindergarten, what would it include and why?

7. Interview a few parents of preschoolers. Ask, "What three communication skills do you believe are important for your child's success in elementary school (which he will attend after preschool)?"

8. Visit a public library in a multilingual, culturally and racially diverse community to search for other-than-English picture books. Were other literacy-promoting resources available to parents who do not read English? Report back to your training group.

9. Construct an example of a homemade book that you could use for a parent meeting discussion. Think about book features that might delight children. Use photos or illustrations that might stimulate child interest and conversation. Share with the class.

10. Discuss the things you observe concerning the lives of single parents you know that you think might have escaped the notice of their child's teachers. Especially mention factors that may affect children's language arts development.

11. Arreola (2003) believes that many Latino parents are intimidated and are reluctant to visit their child's school:

    Our culture believes that it is their territory, you don't get in their territory— if you do, you're not respecting them. (p. 4a)

    How could you encourage these parents to visit school?

CHAPTER REVIEW

A. In a short paragraph, describe family involvement in an early childhood center's language arts program.

B. List the teacher's duties and responsibilities in school-home communications.

C. What is the meaning of the following statement? "Early childhood centers reinforce home literacy just as homes can reinforce the center's literacy activities." Be specific.

D. Describe the kinds of problems schools may face when they plan family-teacher study meetings on enhancing young children's ease in learning to read.

APPENDIX

SUGGESTED MUSIC (CHAPTERS 2 AND 8)

The following are available from Educational Activities, 516-223-4666; Kimbo Educational, 732-229-4949; and Lakeshore Learning Materials, 800-778-4456.

Tonja Evetts Weimer

Fingerplays and Action Chants
 Vol. 1—Animals
 Vol. 2—Family and Friends
Pittsburgh, PA: Pearce-Evetts Productions

Kathy Poelker

Look at My World

Amazing Musical Moments!

Wheeling, IL: Look At Me Productions

Raffi

Singable Songs for the Very Young

More Singable Songs

Corner Grocery Store

Baby Beluga

Rise and Shine

Raffi's Christmas Album

One Light, One Sun

Ontario, Canada: Troubadour Records

Hap Palmer

Sea Gulls (1978)

Walter the Waltzing Worm

Freeport, NY: Educational Activities

One Little Sound

Classic Nursery Rhymes

Getting to Know Myself

Carson, CA: Lakeshore Learning Materials

Greg and Steve

We All Live Together, Vols. 1–5

On the Move with Greg and Steve

Holidays and Special Days

Los Angeles, CA: Youngheart Records

Greg & Steve's Fun & Games

Carson, CA: Lakeshore Learning Materials

L. Campbell Towel

 "Spotlight," Cat Paws: Music for Playing

Milwaukee, WI: Hal Leonard Publishing

Tom Glazer

Tom Glazer's Treasury of Songs for Children

Garden City, NY: Doubleday

J. Warren

Piggyback Songs for Infants and Toddlers

Everett, WA: Totline Press

J. Weissman

The I Love Children's Song Book

Overland Park, KS: Miss Jackie Music Co.

Fred Koch

Did You Feed My Cow?

Lake Bluff, IL: Red Rover Records

Ella Jenkins

Early Childhood Songs

You'll Sing a Song and I'll Sing a Song

Carson, CA: Lakeshore Learning Materials

Multicultural Music

Children of the World

Carson, CA: Lakeshore Learning Materials

DEVELOPMENTALLY APPROPRIATE PRACTICE (CHAPTER 6)

Language and Communication Development— Widely Held Expectations

For 3-year-olds:

- shows a steady increase in vocabulary, ranging from 2,000 to 4,000 words;

- tends to overgeneralize meaning and make up words to fit needs

- uses simple sentences of at least three or four words to express needs

- may have difficulty taking turns in conversation; changes topics quickly

- pronounces words with difficulty; often mistakes one word for another

- likes simple finger plays and rhymes and learns words to songs that have much repetition

- adapts speech and style of nonverbal communication to listeners in culturally accepted ways but still needs to be reminded of context

- asks many *who, what, where,* and *why* questions but shows confusion in responding to some questions (especially *why, how,* and *when*)

- uses language to organize thought, linking two ideas by sentence combining; overuses such words as *but, because,* and *when*; rarely makes appropriate use of such temporal words as *before, until,* or *after*

- can tell a simple story but must redo the sequence to put an idea into the order of events; often forgets the point of a story and is more likely to focus on favorite parts

For 4-year-olds:

- expands vocabulary from 4,000 to 6,000 words; shows more attention to abstract uses

- usually speaks in five- to six-word sentences

- likes to sing simple songs; knows many rhymes and finger plays

- will talk in front of the group with some reticence; likes to tell others about family and experiences

- uses verbal commands to claim many things; begins teasing others

- expresses emotions through facial gestures and reads others for body cues; copies behaviors (such as hand gestures) of older children or adults

- can control volume of voice for periods of time if reminded; begins to read context for social cues

- uses more advanced sentence structures, such as relative clauses and tag questions ("She's nice, isn't she?") and experiments with new constructions, creating some comprehension difficulties for the listener

- tries to communicate more than his or her vocabulary allows; borrows and extends words to create meaning

- learns new vocabulary quickly if related to own experience ("We walk our dog on a belt. Oh yeah, it's a leash—we walk our dog on a leash")

- can retell a four- or five-step directive or the sequence in a story

For 5-year-olds:

- employs a vocabulary of 5,000 to 8,000 words, with frequent plays on words; pronounces words with little difficulty, except for particular sounds, such as *l* and *th*

- uses fuller, more complex sentences ("His turn is over, and it's my turn now")

- takes turns in conversation, interrupts others less frequently; listens to another speaker if information is new and of interest; shows vestiges of egocentrism in speech, for instance, in assuming listener will understand what is meant (saying "He told me to do it" without any referents for the pronouns)

◆ shares experiences verbally; knows the words to many songs

◆ likes to act out others' roles, shows off in front of new people or becomes unpredictably very shy

◆ remembers lines of simple poems and repeats full sentences and expressions from others, including television shows and commercials

◆ shows skill at using conventional modes of communication complete with pitch and inflection

◆ uses nonverbal gestures, such as certain facial expressions in teasing peers

◆ can tell and retell stories with practice; enjoys repeating stories, poems, and songs; enjoys acting out plays or stories

◆ shows growing speech fluency in expressing ideas

Excerpt from Bredekamp, S., & Copple, C. (Eds.). (1997). *Developmentally appropriate practice in early childhood programs.* Washington, DC: NAEYC.

PROFESSIONAL STANDARDS (CHAPTER 6)

Language and literacy. Early language and literacy form the basis for much later learning, and well-prepared early childhood teaching candidates possess extensive, research-based knowledge and skill in the area, regardless of the age group or setting in which they intend to practice.

Listening, speaking, reading, and writing are integrated elements. Verbal and nonverbal communication in its diverse forms, combined with competence as a reader and writer, are essential for children's later development. Even as infants and toddlers, children are building the foundations for literacy through early experiences.

Teaching candidates—including those who are not currently teaching linguistically diverse young children—also demonstrate knowledge of second-language acquisition and of bilingualism. They know the home language environments of the children they teach and the possible effects on children when their classroom environment does not reflect the home language. Candidates know the sociopolitical contexts of major language groups and how those may affect children's motivation to learn English. Candidates understand the benefits of bilingualism and the special needs of young English language learners (ELLs), building on the home language systems that children already have developed and assisting them to add a second language to their repertoire. For young English language learners who are learning to read, candidates use, adapt, and assess research-based literacy activities and teaching methods that build on prior knowledge and support successful transitions for those learners.

Candidates are able to articulate priorities for high-quality, meaningful language and literacy experiences in early childhood, across a developmental continuum. Across the years from infancy through third grade, those experiences should help children to, for example:

- explore their environments and develop the conceptual, experiential, and language foundations for learning to read and write
- develop their ability to converse at length and in depth on a topic in various settings (one-on-one with adults and peers, in small groups, etc.)
- develop vocabulary that reflects their growing knowledge of the world around them
- use language, reading, and writing to strengthen their own cultural identity, as well as to participate in the shared identity of the school environment
- associate reading and writing with pleasure and enjoyment, as well as with skill development
- use a range of strategies to derive meaning from stories and texts
- use language, reading, and writing for various purposes
- use a variety of print and nonprint resources
- develop basic concepts of print and understanding of sounds, letters, and letter-sound relationships

*From Hyson, M. L. (Ed.). NAEYC Initial Licensure Standards in Preparing Early Childhood Professionals: NAEYC's Standards for Programs. Copyright © 2005 NAEYC. Reprinted with permission from the National Association for the Education of Young Children.

ASSESSMENT TOOLS (CHAPTER 6)

Bricker, D., Capt, B., Johnson, J., Pretti-Frontezak, K., Slentz, K., Straka, E., & Weddel, M. (2002). *Assessment, evaluation, and programming system for infants and children (AEPS)*. Baltimore, MD: Brookes Publishing Co.

Clay, M. (1996). *Observational survey of early literacy achievement*. Portsmouth, NH: Heinemann.

Early Language and Literacy Classroom Observation Toolkit (ELLCO). Baltimore, MD: Brookes Publishing Co.

PALS PreK: *Phonological Awareness Literacy Screening for Preschool*. (2002). Publisher: University of Virginia Press (http://pals.virginia.edu/default.asp).

Peabody Picture Vocabulary Test (3rd. Ed.). (1997). Publisher: American Guidance Service; ages: 2½ and up.

Preschool Language Scale (4th Ed.). (1992). Publisher: Psychological Corporation; ages: birth to 7.

Preschool Outcomes Checklist. Venn, E. C., & Jahn, M. C. (2004). *Teaching and learning in the preschool: Using individually appropriate practices in early childhood*. Newark, DE: International Reading Association (May be copied for classroom use.)

Reading Skills Competency Tests—Readiness Level. Publisher: The Writing Company (http://www.writingco.com).

Test of Early Language Development (1999). Publisher: PRO-ED (http://www.proedinc.com); ages: 2 to 7.

Test of Early Reading Ability (2001). Publisher: PRO-ED (http://www.proedinc.com); ages: 3 to 10.

Test of Oral Language Development. Publisher: PRO-ED (http://www.proedinc.com).

Test of Phonological Awareness. Publisher: PRO-ED (http://www.proedinc.com); level: kindergarten

Woodcock-Johnson Educational Battery. Publisher: Riverside Publishing (www.riverpub.com); ages: 2 and up.

Woodcock-Johnson Reading Mastery. Publisher: American Guidance Services/Pearson AGS Globe (www.agsnet.com; select "assessment," "early childhood," "language screening."); level: K–12.

ADDITIONAL STORY (CHAPTER 10)

THE CROOKED-MOUTH FAMILY

There are many versions of this action story. This one, however, appeals to young children and never fails to bring laughter and requests to have it repeated. Before the teacher begins the story, she can quietly light a candle—preferably a dripless one.

Once there was a family called The Crooked-Mouth Family.

The father had a mouth like this.

(Twist mouth to the right.)

The mother had a mouth like this.

(Twist mouth to the left.)

The Big Brother had a mouth like this.

(Bring lower lip over upper lip.)

The Big Sister had a mouth like this.

(Bring upper lip over lower lip.)

But the Baby Sister had a pretty mouth just like yours.

(Smile naturally.) (Repeat mouth positions as each character speaks.)

One night they forgot to blow the candle out when they went upstairs to bed. The father said, "I'd better go downstairs and blow that candle out."

(With mouth still twisted to the right, blow at the flame being careful not to blow it out.)

"What's the matter with this candle? It won't go out."

(Repeat blowing several times.)

"I guess I'd better call Mother. Mother!

Please come down and blow the candle out."

Mother said, "Why can't you blow the candle out? Anybody can blow a candle out. You just go like this."

(She blows at the flame, mouth still twisted to the left.)

"I can't blow it out either. We'd better call Big Brother."

(Change to father's mouth.)

"Brother! Please come down and blow the candle out."

Big Brother said, "That's easy. All you have to do is blow hard."

(With lower lip over upper, hold the candle low and blow.)

Father said, "See. You can't blow it out either. We'll have to call Big Sister.

Sister! Please come down and blow the candle out!"

Big Sister said, "I can blow it out. Watch me."

(With upper lip over lower, candle held high, blow several times.)

Father said, "That's a funny candle. I told you I couldn't blow it out." Mother said, "I couldn't blow it out, either." Big Brother said, "Neither could I." Big Sister said, "I tried and tried, and I couldn't blow it out."

Father said, "I guess we'll have to call Baby

Sister. Baby! Please come down and blow the candle out."

Baby Sister came downstairs, rubbing her eyes because she had been asleep. She asked, "What's the matter?" Father said, "I can't blow the candle out." Mother said, "I can't blow it out either." Big Brother said, "Neither can I." Big Sister said, "I can't either." Baby Sister said, "Anybody can blow a candle out. That's easy." And she did.

Author Unknown

FLANNEL BOARD ACTIVITY SETS (CHAPTER 12)

THE HARE AND THE TORTOISE

Pieces: rabbit dog   rabbit running   rabbit sleeping   finish-line   flag

One day the rabbit was talking to some of the other animals. "I am the fastest runner in the forest," he said. "I can beat anyone! Do you want to race?" "Not I," said the dog.

"Not I," said the hen.

"I will race with you," said the turtle.

"That's a good joke," said the rabbit. "I could dance around you all the way and still win."

"Still bragging about how fast you are," answered the turtle. "Come on, let's race. Do you see that flag over there? That will be the finish line. Hen, would you stand by the flag so that you can tell who wins the race?"

"Dog, will you say the starting words—get on your mark, get ready, get set, go!"

"Stand there," said the dog. "Get on your mark, get ready, get set, go!"

The rabbit ran very fast. He looked over his shoulder and saw how slowly the turtle was running on his short little legs. Just then he saw a shady spot under a tree. He thought to himself—that turtle is so slow I have time to rest here under this tree. So he sat down on the cool grass, and before he knew it, he was fast asleep.

While he slept, the turtle was running. (Clump, Clump—Clump, Clump) He was not running very fast, but he kept on running. (Clump, Clump—Clump, Clump) Pretty soon the turtle came to the tree where the rabbit was sleeping. He went past and kept on running. (Clump, Clump—Clump, Clump) The turtle was almost to the finish line. The hen saw the turtle coming and said, "Turtle, keep on running. You've almost won the race." When the hen spoke, the rabbit awoke. He looked down by the finish line and saw the turtle was almost there. As fast as he could, the rabbit started running again. Just then he heard the hen say, "The turtle is the winner!"

"But I'm the fastest," said the rabbit.

"Not this time," said the hen. "Sometimes slow and steady wins the race."

Put on turtle, dog, hen, and rabbit at left edge of board.

Add finish-line flag on right edge of board. Move hen by flag.

Put on running rabbit. Remove standing rabbit.

Add sleeping rabbit while removing running rabbit.

Change sleeping rabbit to running rabbit.

Full-size version of this art can be found on the book companion website at www.cengage.com/education/machado.

The Big, Big Turnip

(Traditional)

Pieces: farmer   turnip   daughter   mouse
         farmer's wife   large piece of ground   dog

A farmer once planted a turnip seed. And it grew, and it grew, and it grew. The farmer saw it was time to pull the turnip out of the ground. So he took hold of it and began to pull.	Place farmer on board. Cover turnip so that only top is showing with ground piece, and place on board.
He pulled, and he pulled, and he pulled, and he pulled. But the turnip wouldn't come up. So the farmer called to his wife who was getting dinner.	
Fe, fi, fo, fum.	
I pulled the turnip,	
But it wouldn't come up.	
And the wife came running, and she took hold of the farmer, and they pulled, and they pulled, and they pulled, and they pulled. But the turnip wouldn't come up.	Move farmer next to turnip with hands on turnip top. Place wife behind farmer.
So the wife called to the daughter who was feeding the chickens nearby.	
Fe, fi, fo, fum.	
We pulled the turnip,	
But it wouldn't come up.	
And the daughter came running. The daughter took hold of the wife. The wife took hold of the farmer.	Place daughter behind farmer's wife.
The farmer took hold of the turnip. And they pulled, and they pulled, and they pulled, and they pulled. But the turnip wouldn't come up. So the daughter called to the dog who was chewing a bone.	
Fe, fi, fo, fum.	
We pulled the turnip,	
But it wouldn't come up.	
And the dog came running. The dog took hold of the daughter. The daughter took hold of the wife. The wife took hold of the farmer. And the farmer took hold of the turnip. And they pulled, and they pulled, and they pulled. But the turnip wouldn't come up.	Place dog behind daughter.
The dog called to the cat that was chasing her tail. Fe, fi, fo, fum.	
We pulled the turnip,	
But it wouldn't come up.	

And the cat came running. The cat took hold of the dog. The dog took hold of the daughter. The daughter took hold of the wife. The wife took hold of the farmer. The farmer took hold of the turnip.

And they pulled, and they pulled, and they pulled.

But the turnip wouldn't come up.

So the cat called the mouse that was nibbling spinach nearby.

Fe, fi, fo, fum.

We pulled the turnip,

But it wouldn't come up.

And the mouse came running.

"That little mouse can't help," said the dog. "He's too little." "Phooey," squeaked the mouse. "I could pull that turnip up myself, but since you have all been pulling, I'll let you help too."

So the mouse took hold of the cat. The cat took hold of the dog. The dog took hold of the daughter.

The daughter took hold of the wife. The wife took hold of the farmer. The farmer took hold of the turnip. And they pulled, and they pulled, and they pulled. And up came the turnip.

And the mouse squeaked, "I told you so!"

Place cat behind dog.

Place mouse behind cat.

Remove ground.

Full-size version of this art can be found on the book companion website at www.cengage.com/education/machado.

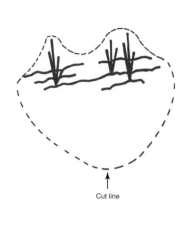

Full-size version of this art can be found on the book companion website at www.cengage.com/education/machado.

THE LITTLE RED HEN

Pieces: fire   sticks rooster   mouse   little red hen pot
               two large rocks   sack fox   table

It was morning. In the cottage where the little red hen and the rooster and the mouse lived, little red hen was happily setting the table for breakfast. "Who will get some sticks for the fire?" said little red hen. "I won't," grumbled the rooster.	Place cottage, table, and hen on board. Add rooster. Add mouse.
"I won't," squeaked the mouse.	
"Then I'll do it myself," said the little red hen, and off she went to gather them.	Remove hen.
When she returned with the sticks and had started the fire, she asked, "Who will get water from the spring to fill the pot?"	Replace with hen and sticks. Place fire over sticks.
"I won't," grumbled the rooster.	
"I won't," squeaked the mouse.	
"Then I'll do it myself," she said and ran off to fill the pot. "Who will cook the breakfast?" said the hen. "I won't," grumbled the rooster.	Place pot over fire.
"I won't," squeaked the mouse.	
"Then I'll do it myself," said the hen, and she did. When breakfast was ready, the hen, the mouse, and the rooster ate together but the rooster spilled the milk, and the mouse scattered crumbs on the floor.	Remove hen. Return hen. Move hen, mouse, and rooster near table.
"Who will clear the table?" said the hen.	
"I won't," grumbled the rooster.	
"I won't," squeaked the mouse.	

"Then I'll do it myself," said the hen. So she cleared everything and swept the floor.

The lazy rooster and mouse by this time had moved closer to the fire and had fallen fast asleep.

Move rooster and mouse near the fire.

"Knock, knock, knock," the noise at the door awakened them.

"Who's that?" said the rooster. "Oh it might be the mail carrier with a letter for me," so the mouse went to the door and opened it without looking out the window first to see who was there. It was a fox. "Help," said the mouse, but the fast old fox, quick as a wink, caught not only the mouse, but also the rooster and the little red hen. Quickly he popped them all into his sack and headed off toward home, thinking about the fine dinner he was bringing to his family.

Place fox and sack on board. Hide rooster, mouse, and hen behind sack.
Remove cottage.

The bag was heavy, and home was a long way, so the fox decided to put it down and rest.

Put fox in horizontal position.

"Snore, Snore, Snore," went the fox.

Little red hen said to the rooster and mouse, "Now we have a chance to escape. I have a pair of scissors and a needle and thread in my apron pocket. I've cut a hole in the bag. Hurry and jump out, find a rock, the biggest one you can carry, and bring it back quickly. "Snore, Snore, Snore," went the fox.

Soon the mouse and the rooster returned with large rocks. They pushed them into the sack, and the hen sewed the hole up. Off they ran to their home. They closed the door and locked it, and they bolted the windows. They were safe now. The fox didn't know he'd been fooled until he got home and opened his sack.

Remove hen, rooster, and mouse from sack. Add rocks.
Move rocks behind sack.

Remove fox and sack with rocks.

The mouse and the rooster were so happy to be home that they didn't grumble and fight anymore; they even helped to cook the dinner with smiles on their faces.

Place cottage, hen, rooster, and mouse beside it on board.

Full-size version of this art can be found on the book companion website at www.cengage.com/education/machado.

Full-size version of this art can be found on the book companion website at www.cengage.com/education/machado.

HUSH, LITTLE BABY

(Flannel-board song)

Pieces:	mother	ring	bull	sleeping baby	looking glass	dog
	crying baby	billy goat	horse	mocking bird	cart	

Courtesy of *Adventures in Felt* © Copyright 1972.

Hush, little baby, don't say a word; Mama's going to buy you a mockingbird.	Place mother and crying baby on her lap.
If that mockingbird won't sing, Mama's going to buy you a diamond ring.	Add ring.
If that diamond ring turns to brass, Mama's going to buy you a looking glass.	Add looking glass.
If that looking glass gets broke, Mama's going to buy you a billy goat.	Add billy goat.
If that billy goat won't pull, Mama's going to buy you a cart and bull.	Add cart and bull.

If that cart and bull turn over, Mama's going to buy you a dog named Rover.

Add dog.

If that dog named Rover won't bark, Mama's going to buy you a horse and cart.

Add horse and move cart from bull.

If that horse and cart break down, YOU WILL be the sweetest little baby in town.

Lullaby, baby sweet of mine, you'll be asleep by half past nine.

Replace crying baby with sleeping baby.

Cut line

Full-size version of this art can be found on the book companion website at www.cengage.com/education/machado.

ALPHABET PRONUNCIATION GUIDE (CHAPTERS 16 AND 17)

Symbols	*Sounds as in the Words*	*Symbols*	*Sounds as in the Words*
a	fat, apple, asks (short *a*)	m	him, me, custom
$\bar{a}$	ate, name (long *a*)	n	sun, not, even
b	rib, big	o	ox, on, not (short *o*)
c	cereal (soft *e*)	$\bar{o}$	go, open, home (long *o*)
c	traffic, cat, certain (hard *e*)	p	sip, pat
d	lid, end, feed	r	ran, rip, very
e	end, wet, pen (short *e*)	s	kiss, so, last, sugar
$\bar{e}$	me, Elaine, eat (long *e*)	t	hit, top
f	if, leaf, full	u	up, rug, custom (short *u*)
g	grape (hard *g*)	$\bar{u}$	useful, unite (long *u*)
g	rag, go, gem (soft *g*)	v	give, have, very
h	hat, how, high	w	we, win, watch
I	it, individual, pin (short *i*)	x	box
I	piece, niece	y	yea, you
$\bar{i}$	ice, while (long *i*)	$\bar{y}$	my, cry
j	jump, jeep	z	zoo, fuzz
k	lick, kiss, milk		
l	will, late, little		

Vowel Digraph Sounds

ai . . . snail
ay . . . say
ea . . . lead
ea . . . tea
ee . . . sheep
ei . . . receive
ie . . . believe

ey . . . key
ey . . . they
oa . . . float
oe . . . hoe
ow . . . grow
ou . . . though

Vowel Diphthongs

oi . . . toil
ou . . . though
oy . . . soy
ue . . . sue
ew . . . new

Consonant Digraph Examples

ch as in chess
gh as in ghost
ph as in phonic
sh as in shoe
th as in thank

GLOSSARY

A

accent — prominence or emphasis given to a word or syllable through one or more of the following factors: loudness, change of pitch, or longer duration.

accommodation — the process by which new experiences or events change existing ideas or thought patterns.

activity plans — written, detailed, step-by-step teaching plans, often including an evaluation section.

acuity — how well or clearly one uses senses; the degree of perceptual sharpness.

affective sphere — the affectionate feelings (or lack of them) shaped through experience with others.

alliteration — the repetition of the initial sounds in neighboring words or stressed syllables, for example, "The foam flowed free and fizzy."

alphabetic principle — the awareness that spoken language can be analyzed as strings of separate words, and words, in turn, as sequences of syllables and phonemes within syllables.

articulation — the adjustments and movements of the muscles of the mouth and jaw involved in producing clear oral communication.

assessment — a broad repertoire of behaviors involved in noticing, documenting, recording, and interpreting children's behaviors and performances. Testing is a subset of assessment behaviors in which performances are controlled and elicited in standardized conditions.

assimilation — the process that allows new experiences to merge with previously stored mental structures.

assonance — the repetition in words of identical or similar vowel sounds followed by different consonant sounds.

attachment — a two-way process formed through mutual gratification of needs and reciprocal communication influenced by the infant's growing cognitive abilities. It is sometimes referred to as bonding or a "love affair" relationship.

audience — the respondents to drama presentation; a group of listeners or spectators.

audiovisual equipment — any mechanical or nonmechanical item useful in offering sight or hearing experience.

auditory — relating to or experienced through hearing.

auditory processing — the full range of mental activity involved in reacting to auditory stimuli, especially speech sounds, and in considering their meanings in relation to past experience and their future use.

B

babbling — an early language stage in sound production in which an infant engages in vocal play with vowel and consonant sounds, including some sounds not found in his or her language environment.

behaviorism — the theoretical viewpoint, espoused by theorists such as B. F. Skinner, that behavior is shaped by environmental forces, specifically in response to reward and punishment.

bilingual — refers to an individual with a language background other than English who has developed proficiency in the primary language and a degree of proficiency in English.

Black English — a language usually spoken in some economically depressed African-American homes. A dialect of non-Standard English that has its own rules and patterns, it is also called African-American English.

C

chants — rhythmic, monotonous utterances.

characterization — the way an author presents a character by describing character verbalizations, actions, or thinking, or by indicating what other characters say, think, or do about the character.

characters — persons (or puppets) represented in or acting in a story or drama.

child-initiated curricula — a basic tenet underlying this type of curriculum is the belief that *true* growth occurs when children are free to develop intrinsic interests naturally.

circle time — an early childhood term describing a planned gathering of children usually seated in a half-circle configuration led by a teacher.

classify — the act of systematically grouping things according to identifiable common characteristics, for example, size.

closure — a conversation technique that prompts children to verbally guess and complete or fill in a teachers' sentence. The teacher pauses or hesitates, which prompts the child to finish a teacher verbalization.

cluttering — rapid, incomplete speech that is often jerky, slurred, spoken in bursts, and difficult to understand; nervous speech.

cognition — the process that creates mental images, concepts, and operations.

communication — the giving (sending) and receiving of information, signals, or messages.

concept — a commonly recognized element (or elements) that identifies groups or classes; usually has a given name.

conceptual tempo — a term associated with Jerome Kagan's theory of different individual pacing in the perceptual exploration of objects.

consonant — (1) speech sound made by partial or complete closure of the vocal tract, which obstructs air flow. (2) An alphabet letter used to represent any of these sounds.

constructivist theory — a theory such as that of Jean Piaget, based on the belief that children construct knowledge for themselves rather than having it conveyed to them by some external source.

continuant — a consonant or vowel that may be continued or prolonged without alteration during one emission of breath.

convergent thinking — the process of analyzing and integrating ideas to infer reasonable conclusions or specific solutions from given information.

cooing — an early stage during the prelinguistic period in which vowel sounds are repeated, particularly the *u-u-u* sound.

couplets — stanzas of two rhyming lines.

cues — prompts or hints that aid recognition, such as a parent pointing to and/or saying "teddy bear" when sharing a picture book illustration. This is done because the infant is familiar with his own teddy bear.

cultural literacy — literacy that reflects a culture's knowledge of significant ideas, events, values, and the essence of that culture's identity.

culture — all the activities and achievements of a society that individuals within that society pass from one generation to the next.

curriculum — an overall plan for the content of instruction to be offered in a program.

curriculum models — refers to a conceptual framework and organizational structure for decision making about educational priorities, administrative policies, instructional methods, and evaluation criteria.

D

deafness — hearing is so impaired that the individual is unable to process auditory linguistic information, with or without amplification.

dialect — a variety of spoken language unique to a geographical area or social group. Variations in dialect may include phonological or sound variations, syntactical variations, and lexical or vocabulary variations.

dialogue — a conversation between two or more persons or between a person and something else.

diction — clarity of speech; enunciation.

discourse skills — refers to using language in structured ways to go beyond basic conversation, for example, telling a story, explaining a procedure, creating a fantasy, dictating ideas, and elaborating to provide greater understanding.

divergent thinking — the process of elaborating on ideas to generate new ideas or alternative interpretations of given information.

dramas — plays; stories in dramatic form, typically emphasizing conflict in and among key characters.

dramatic play — acting out experiences or creating drama episodes during play.

dual coding — the belief that infants' experiences and emotions influence cognition.

E

early literacy — speaking, listening, print awareness and writing behaviors, reading of alphabet letters and words, and other skills that evolve and change over time, culminating in conventional literacy.

Ebonics — a nonstandard form of English, a dialect often called Black English that is characterized by not conjugating the verb "to be" and by dropping some final consonants from words.

echolalia — a characteristic of the babbling period. The child repeats (echoes) the same sounds over and over.

equilibrium — a balance attained with consistent care and satisfaction of needs that leads to a sense of security and lessens anxiety.

expansion — a teaching technique that includes the adult's (teacher's) modeling of words or grammar, filling in missing words for children's utterances, or suggesting ideas for child exploration.

explanatory talk — a type of conversation characterized by a speaker's attempt to create connections between objects, events, concepts, or conclusions to promote understanding in the listener.

expressive jargon — a term describing a child's first attempts at combining words into narration that results in a mimic of adult speech.

expressive (productive) vocabulary — the vocabulary a person uses in speaking and writing.

extension — a teaching strategy in which an adult expands the child's information by adding new, additional, related information or meaning.

F

fable — a short tale in prose or verse that teaches a moral, usually with talking animals or inanimate objects as main characters.

fairy tales — folk stories about real-life problems, usually with imaginary characters and magical events.

family literacy programs — community programs attempting to provide literacy-building opportunities and experiences for families. Services are available for both adults and children.

fiction — imaginative narrative in any form of presentation that is designed to entertain, as distinguished from that which is designed primarily to explain, argue, or merely describe.

figurative language — language enriched by word images and figures of speech.

G

gaze coupling — infant-mother extended eye contact.

genre — a category used to classify literary works, usually by form, technique, or content.

grammar — the rules of a specific language that include both written and spoken utterances and describe how that specific language works and the forms of speech that conform to the rules that well-schooled speakers and writers observe in any given language.

H

hearing — the facility or sense by which sound is perceived.

hearing disorders — characterized by an inability to hear sounds clearly. Loss may range from hearing speech sounds faintly or in a distorted way, to profound deafness.

holophrases — the expression of a whole idea in a single word. They are characteristic of the child's language from about 12 to 18 months.

I

impulsive — quick to answer or react to either a simple or complex situation or problem.

inflections — the grammatical "markers" such as plurals; also can involve a change in pitch or loudness of the voice.

inner speech — mentioned in Vygotsky's theory as private speech that becomes internalized and is useful for organizing ideas.

interactionists — those who adhere to the theory that language develops through a combination of inborn factors and environmental influences.

interactive writing — (1) an instructional strategy popular in American kindergartens; (2) a process involving a teacher who verbally stretches each word so that the children can distinguish sounds and letters. It is also known as shared writing.

invented spelling — the result of an attempt to spell a word whose spelling is not already known, based on a writer's knowledge of the spelling system and how it works.

J

joint attention — child's awareness that he or she must gain and hold another's focus during communicational exchanges to get his or her message understood.

L

language — the systematic, conventional use of sounds, signs, or written symbols in human society for communication and self-expression. It conveys meaning that is mutually understood.

language center — a classroom area specifically set aside and equipped for language arts–related activities and child use.

listening — a mental process that includes attending, hearing, discriminating, understanding, and remembering.

listening center — a classroom area designed to accommodate children's listening experiences.

listening comprehension level — the highest grade level of material that can be comprehended well when it is read aloud to a child.

literacy — involves complex cognitive interactions between readers and their texts and between background knowledge and new information. It involves both skill and knowledge and varies by task and setting. Different types of literacy are described—prose, document, quantitative, academic, workplace, and functional.

M

mental image — a "perceptual representation" or mental picture of a perceptual experience, remembered or imagined.

metalinguistic awareness — a conscious awareness on the part of a language user of language as an object in itself.

metalinguistic skills — the ability to think about language as a separate entity.

metaphors — figures of speech in which a comparison is implied by analogy but is not stated.

moderation level — an individual preferred state of arousal between bored and excited when learning and pleasure peak.

modifiers — words that give a special characteristic to a noun (for example, a *large* ball).

monologue — literally "speaking alone."

morpheme — the smallest unit in a language that by itself has a recognizable meaning.

morphology — the study of the units of meaning in a language.

multiple literacies – refers to the many diverse ways families promote children's literacy through cultural and other home and life experiences that may be similar or different from school instruction.

N

narrative — in general, a story, actual or fictional, expressed orally or in writing.

nativists — those who adhere to the theory that children are born with biological dispositions for learning that unfold or mature in a natural way.

neurolinguistics — a branch of linguistics that studies the structure and function of the brain in relation to language acquisition, learning, and use.

nonfiction — prose that explains, argues, or describes; usually factual.

nursery rhymes — folk sayings with rhyming words for very young children.

nurturist — one who adheres to the theory that the minds of children are blank or unformed and need educational input or direct instruction to develop and "output" knowledge and appropriate behavior.

O

onsets — any consonants before a vowel in a syllable.

orthographic awareness — the ability to notice and use critical features of graphic symbols in written language.

otitis media — inflammation and/or infection of the middle ear.

outreach — an early childhood program's attempt to provide supportive assistance to attending children's families to promote their children's success in school and developmental growth.

overextension — in the early acquisition of words and their meanings, the application of a word to include other objects that share common features, such as "water" being used to describe any liquid.

over-regularization — the tendency on the part of children to make their language regular, such as using past tenses like -*ed* on verb endings.

P

pantomime — creative communication done with nonverbal physical actions.

parentese — a high-pitched, rhythmic, singsong, crooning style of speech. It is also known as "motherese" or baby talk.

participation stories — stories with some feature children can enact through physical movements, verbal expression, or both.

perception — mental awareness of objects and other data gathered through the five senses.

personification — a metaphorical figure of speech in which animals, ideas, things, etc., are represented as having human qualities.

phonation — exhaled air passing through the larynx's vibrating folds and producing "voice."

phoneme — one of the smallest units of speech that distinguishes one utterance from another.

phonemic awareness — the insight that every spoken word can be conceived as a sequence of phonemes.

phonetic instruction — instruction in phonics is instruction that stresses sound-symbol relationships. It is used especially in beginning reading instruction.

phonetics — pertaining to representing the sounds of speech with a set of distinct symbols, each denoting a single sound.

phonological awareness — the whole spectrum from primitive awareness of speech sounds and rhythms to rhyme awareness and sound similarities; at the highest level, awareness of syllables or phonemes.

phonology — the sound system of a language and how it is represented with an alphabetic code.

plot — the structure of the action of a story.

poems — metrical forms of composition in which word images are selected and expressed to create powerful, often beautiful impressions in the listener and/or enjoyable rhythmic responses in young children.

pragmatics — the study of how language is used effectively in a social context; varying speech patterns depending on social circumstances and the context of situations.

print awareness — in early literacy, children's growing recognition of the conventions and characteristics of a written language. It includes recognition of directionality (left to right and top to bottom), that print forms words corresponding to speech, and that spaces separate words and other features.

prosodic speech — the child's use of voice modulation and word stress to give special emphasis and meaning.

psychosocial theory — the branch of psychology founded by Erik Erikson; development is described in terms of eight stages that span childhood and adulthood.

R

reading method — any of several relatively specific procedures or steps for teaching one or more aspects of reading, each procedure embodying explicitly or implicitly some theory of how children learn and of the relationship between written and spoken language.

realism — presents experiences without embellishment to convey life as it appears in a natural world limited by the senses and reason.

recasting — a teaching technique that involves a teacher who supplies children's missing words or gently models correct usage of words or extends the child's ideas following the child's verbal statement.

receptive (comprehensive) vocabulary — the comprehension vocabulary used by a person in listening (and silent reading).

reflective — taking time to weigh aspects or alternatives in a given situation.

regularization — a child's speech behavior that indicates the formation and internalization of a language rule (regularity).

resonation — amplification of laryngeal sounds using cavities of the mouth, nose, sinuses, and pharynx.

responsive mothers — mothers who are alert and timely in responding to and giving attention to infants' needs and communications.

rhythm — uniform or patterned recurrence of a beat, accent, or melody in speech.

rimes — the vowel and any consonants after it in a syllable.

S

scaffolding — a teaching technique helpful in promoting languages, understanding, and child solutions. It includes teacher-responsive conversation, open-ended questioning, and facilitation of children's initiatives. It is a process that starts with supportive adult assistance that enables the child to do what he is unable to do by himself. Child learning usually proceeds gradually, and less and less adult assistance is necessary.

selective (elective) mutism — a behavior that describes child silence or lack of speech in select surroundings and/or with certain individuals.

semantics — the study of meanings associated with words and the acquisition of vocabulary.

semiotics — observant of signs or symbols. The study of how groups come to share meaning.

sensory-motor development — the control and use of sense organs and the body's muscle structure.

sight reading — the ability to immediately recognize a word as whole without sounding it out.

signing — a body positioning, sound, action, or gesture or combination of these undertaken by an infant that represents an effort to communicate a need, desire, or message.

similes — comparisons of two things that are unlike, usually using the words *like* or *as*. Example: "Love is like a red, red rose."

social connectedness — a term associated with the following human characteristics: is stable and secure, develops close relationships with others, has supportive family and friends, and is deemed a worthy individual by others. Often seen by others as able to transcend stress and possess an individual identity.

social constructivist theory — such as Vygotsky's emphasis on the importance of language and socially shared cognition, scaffolding exchanges, and the child's private speech.

socioeconomic — relating to or involving a combination of social and economic factors.

software — a wide range of commercial programs developed for computer users' convenience, education, entertainment, and so on.

spatial-temporal reasoning — the mental arrangement of ideas and/or images in a graphic pattern indicating their relationships over time.

speech and language disorders — communication disorders that affect the way people talk and understand; range from simple sound substitutions to not being able to use speech and language at all.

Standard English — substantially uniform formal and informal speech and writing of educated people that is widely recognized as acceptable wherever English is spoken and understood.

story — an imaginative tale with a plot, characters, and setting.

story map — a timeline showing an ordered sequence of events.

subculture — an ethnic, regional, economic, or social group exhibiting characteristic patterns of behavior sufficient to distinguish it from others within an embracing culture or society.

symbols — things that stand for or suggest (such as pictures, models, word symbols, and so forth).

synapses — gap-like structures over which the axon of one neuron beams a signal to the dendrites of another, forming a connection in the human brain. It involves memory and learning.

syntax — the arrangement of words as elements in a sentence to show their relationship.

T

telegraphic speech — a characteristic of young children's sentences in which everything but the crucial word(s) is omitted, as if for a telegram.

transitional kindergarten — a relatively new feature of some elementary school districts that offers supportive literacy activities and classroom access (usually during the summer before the child is to enroll in kindergarten).

transitional statements — teacher statements made to disperse students in small groups or in an orderly fashion.

V

verses — lines of a poem or poetry without imaginative or conceptual power.

visual literacy — the ability to interpret and communicate with respect to visual symbols in media other than print.

visualization — the process, or result, of mentally picturing objects or events that are normally experienced directly.

vowel — a voiced speech sound made without stoppage or friction of air flow as it passes through the vocal tract.

W

webbing — a visual or graphic method of mapping or planning a possible course of study.

whole-language approach — a philosophy and reading-instruction approach integrating oral and written language. Advocates believe that when children are given literature-abundant and print-rich environments, they will follow their natural curiosity and learn to read as they learned to speak. A thematic focus is used. Teachers seize opportunities to connect and integrate related language arts areas.

writing — the ability to use print to communicate with others.

REFERENCES

Acredolo, L., & Goodwyn, S. (1985). Symbolic gesturing in language development. *Human Development*, *28*, 53–58.

Acredolo, L. & Goodwyn, S. (2000). *Baby minds: Brain-building games your baby will love to play.* New York: Bantam Books.

Adams, M. J. (1990). *Beginning to read: Thinking and learning about print.* Cambridge, MA: The MIT Press.

Ainsworth, M. D. S., & Bell, S. M. (1972). Mother-infant interaction and development of competence. *ERIC Digest*, ED-065-180.

Alexander, L. (2004, Summer). Putting parents in charge. *Education next*, *4*(3), 39–44.

Allen, R. V. (1969). *Language experiences in early childhood.* Chicago: Encyclopedia Britannica.

Allen, R. V., & Allen, C. (1982). *Language experience activities.* Boston: Houghton Mifflin.

American Speech-Language-Hearing Association. (2001, 2004). *How does your child hear and talk?* [Brochure]. Rockville, MD: American Speech-Language-Hearing Association.

Antonucci, M. (2003, October 29). Gaga over TV. *San Jose Mercury News*, pp. 1A, 5A.

Arreola, A. (2003, October 17). Quote in Slonaker, L., Learning a lesson about school visits: Parent-teacher meetings key for kids, experts say. *San Jose Mercury News*, pp. 4A, 12A.

Ashton-Warner, S. (1963). *Teacher.* New York: Simon & Schuster.

Atienza, H. (2004, June 27). Kindergarten: As a parent, you knew the day would come eventually. *The Idaho Statesman*, p. L2.

Au, K. (1993). *Literacy instruction in multicultural setting.* Orlando, FL: Harcourt Brace.

Au, K. H. (2006). Multicultural factors and the effective instruction of students of diverse backgrounds. In A. E. Farstrup & S. J. Samuels (Eds.), *What research has to say about reading instruction* (pp. 392–413). Newark, DE: International Reading Association.

Baker, I., & Schiffer, M. B. (2007, May). The reading chair. *Young Children*, *62*(3), 44–49.

Barnett, W. S., Yarosz, D. J., Thomas, J., Jung, K., & Blanco, D. (2007). Two-way and monolingual English immersion in preschool education: An experimental comparison. *Early Childhood Research Quarterly*, *22*(3), 277–293.

Barone, D. M. (2003). Caution: apply with care. In D. M. Barone & L. M. Morrow (Eds.), *Literacy and young children: Research-based practice* (pp. 291–308). New York: The Guilford Press.

Barrett, J. (2003, November 10). Tune in or tune out? *Newsweek*, 71.

Bennett-Armistead, V. S., Duke, N. K., & Moses, A. M. (2005). *Literacy and the youngest learner: Best practices for educators of children from birth to 5.* New York: Scholastic.

Bergen, D. (2001, November). Pretend play and young children's development. *ERIC Digest*, EDO-PS-01-10.

Bergren, D., Reid, R. & Torelli, L. (2001). *Educating and caring for very young children.* New York: Teachers College Press.

Biber, B., Shapiro, E. & Wickens, D. (1977). *Promoting cognitive growth: A developmental-interaction point of view.* Washington, DC: National Association for the Education of Young Children.

Blair, C. (2003, July). Self-regulation and school readiness. *ERIC Digest*, EDO-PS-03-7.

Bodrova, E., & Leong, D. (1996). *Tools of the mind.* Englewood Cliffs, NJ: Prentice Hall.

Bodrova, E., Leong, D. J., Paynter, D., & Semenov, D. (2000). *A framework for early literacy instruction: Aligning standards to developmental accomplishments and student behaviors: Pre-K through kindergarten.* Aurora, CO: Mid-continent Research for Education and Learning.

Booth, D. (1999). Language delights and word play. In I. Fountas & G. S. Pinnell (Eds.), *Voices on word matters: Learning about phonics and spelling in the literacy classroom* (pp. 121–137). Portsmouth, NH: Heinemann.

Bornstein, M. (December 1991–January 1992). In S. Goodman (Ed.), Presumed innocent, *Modern Maturity, 34*(6), 24–28.

Boser, U. (2006, October). Say what? *Smithsonian, (37),* 7, 84.

Brady, S., Fowler, A., Stone, B., & Winbury, S. (1994). Training phonological awareness: A study with inner-city kindergarten children. *Annals of Dyslexia, 44,* 27–59.

Bredekamp, S., & Copple, C. (1997). *Developmentally appropriate practice in early childhood programs* (Rev. ed.). Washington, DC: National Association for the Education of Young Children.

Broughton, D. (2006, Thursday May 25). Quoted in Neergaard, L., Parents turn small fry on to the screen. *Idaho Statesman,* p. 18M.

Burmark, L. (2002). *Visual literacy: Learn to see, see to learn.* Alexandria, VA: Association for Supervision and Curriculum Development.

Cambourne, B. (1988). *The whole story: Natural learning and the acquisition of literacy in the classroom.* New York: Ashton Scholastic.

Campbell, F. A., & Ramey, C. T. (1994). Effects of early intervention on intellectual and academic achievement: A follow-up study of children from low-income families. *Child Development, 65,* 684–689.

Cassidy, J., & Cassidy, D. (2004, December/2005, January).What's hot, what's not for 2005. *Reading Today, 22*(3), 1, 8.

Center for Research on Education, Diversity & Excellence. (2001, Summer). Some program alternatives for English language learners, *Practitioners Brief #3.* Santa Cruz, CA: University of California

Chang, J. (2001, April). Scaffold for school-home collaboration: Enhancing reading and language development. *Research Brief #9.* Santa Cruz, CA: Center for Research on Education, Diversity, & Excellence, University of California.

Chenfeld, M. B. (2007, August/September). Handcuffed in the garden of thorns. *Reading Today, 25*(1), 20.

Child Care Bulletin (2007, Winter/Spring). Introduction to quality rating systems. (32) 2. Washington, DC: U.S. Department of Health and Human Services, Administration for Children and Families, Child Care Bureau.

Child Care Bureau. (2004, May). *Promoting responsible fatherhood through child care.* Washington, DC: U.S. Department of Health and Human Services, Administration on Children, Youth and Families.

Chomsky, C. (1971, August/September).Write now, read later. *Childhood Education, 47*(2), 42–47.

Chomsky, N. (1968). *Language and mind.* New York: Harcourt, Brace, and World.

Christakis, D. A., & Zimmerman, F. J. (2007). Violent television viewing during preschool is associated with antisocial behavior during school age. *Pediatrics, 120,* 993–999. Retrieved Jan. 23, 2008, from http://pediatrics.aapublication.org/egi/gca?aii ch=&SEARCHED=1&FULLTEXT=toddle.

Chukovsky, K. (1963). *From two to five.* Berkeley, CA: University of California.

Ciccarelli, S. K. (2006, April 11). Quoted in J. Phillips, Straight talk on baby talk: It's OK for awhile—or is it? *San Jose Mercury News,* p. 3E.

Clark, A. (2007, May). A hundred ways of listening: Gathering children's perspectives of their early childhood environment. *Young Children, 62*(3), 76–84.

Clay, M. (1966). *Emergent reading behaviors.* Unpublished doctoral thesis, University of Auckland Library.

Clay, M. (1987). *The early detection of reading difficulties.* Hong Kong: Heinemann.

Clay, M. (1991). *Becoming literate: The construction of inner control.* Portsmouth, NH: Heinemann Educational Books.

Clay, M. (1993). *An observational survey of early literacy achievement.* Auckland, New Zealand: Heinemann.

Coles, G. (2004, January). Danger in the classroom: 'Brain glitch' research and learning to read. *Phi Delta Kappan,* pp. 344–351.

Collins, R., & Ribeiro, R. (2004). Toward an early care and education agenda for Hispanic children. *Early Childhood Research & Practice, 6*(2), 161–192.

Cooper, P. (1993). *When stories come to school.* New York: Teachers & Writers Collaborative.

Costa, A. L. (1991). The search for intelligent life. In *Developing minds: A resource book for teaching thinking.* Alexandria, VA: Association for Supervision and Curriculum Development.

Covey, S. R. (1989). *The seven habits of highly effective people.* New York: Simon & Schuster.

Cowen, J. E. (2005). *A balanced approach to beginning reading instruction.* Newark, DE: International Reading Association.

Cowley, G. (1997, Spring/Summer). Off to a good start [Special Edition]. *Newsweek,* pp. 27–34.

Cowley, G. (2000, Fall/Winter). For the love of language [Special Edition]. *Newsweek,* pp. 12–15.

Cox, V. E. L. (1927). The literature curriculum. In L. Lamme (Ed.), *Learning to love literature* (pp. 1–12). Urbana, IL: National Council of Teachers of English.

Crawford, A. N. (2005). Communicative approaches to second-language acquisition: The bridge to second-language literacy. In G. G. Garcia (Ed.), *English learners: Reaching the highest level of English literacy* (pp. 152–181). Newark, DE: International Reading Association.

Cullinan, B. E. (1977). Books in the life of the young child. In B. E. Cullinan & C.W. Carmichael (Eds.), *Literature and young children* (pp. 1–16). Urbana, IL: National Council of Teachers of English.

Cullinan, B. E. (1992, October).Whole language and children's literature. *Language Arts*, 69(6), 426–430.

Cunningham, J. W., & Creamer, K. H. (2003). Achieving best practices in literacy instruction. In L. M. Morrow, L. B. Gambrell, & M. Pressley (Eds.), *Best practices in literacy instruction* (pp. 333–346). New York: The Guilford Press.

Delacre, L. (1988). *Nathan's fishing trip.* New York: Scholastic.

Delpit, L. (1995). *Other people's children: Cultural conflict in the classroom.* New York: The New Press.

DeMarie, D. (2001, Spring). A trip to the zoo: Children's words and photographs. *Early Childhood Research and Practice*, 3(1), 27–49.

Dennison, B. A., Russo, T. J., Burdick, P. A., & Jenkins, P. L. (2004, February). An intervention to reduce television viewing by preschool children. *The Archives of Pediatrics and Adolescent Medicine*, 158, 170–176.

Descartes, R. (1978). *Descartes: His moral philosophy and psychology.* New York: University Press.

Dewey, J. (1916). *Democracy and education.* New York: Free Press.

Dickinson, D. K. (2001). Putting the pieces together. In D. K. Dickinson & P. Tabors (Eds.), *Beginning literacy with language* (pp. 257–287). Baltimore: Brookes.

Dietrich, C., Swingley, D., & Werker, J. T. (2007, October 8). Native language governs interpretation of salient speech sound differences at 18 months. *PNAS*, 104(41), 16027–16031. (Proceedings of the National Academy of Sciences of the United States of America.)

Donegan, P. (2002). Normal vowel development. In M. J. Ball & F. E. Gibbon (Eds.), *Vowel disorders* (pp. 1–35). Woburn, MA: Butterworth-Heinemann.

Dondi, M., Messinger, D., Colle, M., Tabasso, A., Simion, F., Barba, B., & Fogel, A. (2007). A new perspective on neonatal smiling: Differences between the judgments of expert coders and naïve observers. *Infancy*, 12(3) 235–255.

Dori, J. (2007, July). Think aloud! Increase your teaching power. *Young Children*, 62(4) 101–105.

Du, L., & Stoub, S. (2004, Bebruary 21). *Options pre-K literacy curriculum.* Session guide. California Association for the Eucation of Young Children, Annual Conference. San Diego, CA.

Duke, N. K. (2007, May). Let's look in a book. *Young Children*, 62(3), 12–16.

Dworak, M., Schierl, T., Bruns, T., & Struder, H. K. (2007, November). Impact of singular excessive computer game and television exposure on sleep patterns and memory performance of school-aged children. *Pediatrics*, 120(5), 978–985.

Edwards, C., Gandini, L., & Forman, G. (Eds.). (1998). The hundred languages of children: The Reggio Emilia approach—Advanced recollections. Greenwich, CT: Ablex Publishers.

Ehri, L. C., & Nunes, S. R. (2006). The role of phonemic awareness in learning to read. In A. E. Farstrup & S. J. Samuels (Eds.), *What research has to say about reading instruction* (pp. 110–139). Newark, DE: International Reading Association.

Eiserman, W. D., Shisler, L., Foust, T., Buhrmann, J., Winston, R., & White, K. R. (2007). Screening for hearing loss in early childhood programs. *Early Childhood Research Quarterly*, 22(1), 105–117.

Elleman, B. (1995). Handling stereotypes. *Book Links*, 4(5), 4.

Erikson, E. (1950). *Childhood and society.* New York: W.W. Norton.

Ezell, H. K., & Justice, I. M. (2000). Increasing the print focus of shared reading through observational learning. *American Journal of Speech-Language Pathology*, 9, 36–47.

Falk, D. (2004, July). Quote in Wong, K., Baby talk beginnings: Infant pacification may have led to the origins of language. *Scientific American*, 291(1), 30–32.

Farstrup, A. E. (2006). There is more to effective reading instruction than research. In A. E. Farstrup & S. J. Samuels (Eds.), *What research has to say about reading instruction* (pp. 1–7). Newark, DE: International Reading Association.

Farstrup, A. E. (2007, February/March). Five years of NCLB: Where do we go from here? *Reading Today*, 24(4), 20.

Ferreiro, E., & Teberosky, A. (1982). *Literacy before schooling.* Exeter, NH: Heinemann.

Fields, M. (1987). *NAEYC developmentally appropriate guidelines and beginning reading instruction.* Presentation made at the annual conference of the National Association for the Education of Young Children, Chicago.

Freeman, M. (2007, February/March). A wild restraint: Reading education and *The Cat in the Hat*. *Reading Today*, 24(4), 21.

Froebel, F. (1974). *The education of man.* Clifton, NJ: Augustus M. Kelly.

Gainsley, S. (2003, Summer). Write it down. *High/Scope Resource, 22*(2), 26–27.

Gallas, K. (2003). *Imagination and literacy: A teacher's search for the heart of learning.* New York: Teachers College Press.

Gamble, W. C., Ramakumar, S., & Diaz, A. (2007). Maternal and paternal similarities and differences in parenting: An examination of Mexican-American parents of young children. *Early Childhood Research Quarterly, 22*, 72–88.

Gamel-McCormick, M. (2000, November). Exploring teachers' expectations for children entering kindergarten and procedures for sharing information between pre-K and K programs. Conference presentation at the annual conference of the National Association for the Education of Young Children, Atlanta.

Gandini, L. (1997). Examples of practice. In J. Hendrick (Ed.), *First steps toward teaching the Reggio way* (136–158). Upper Saddle River, NJ: Prentice Hall.

Gardner, H. (1993). *Multiple Intelligences.* New York: Basic Books.

Gardner, H. (1999). *Disciplined mind: What all students should understand.* New York: Simon & Schuster.

Gardner, H. (2000). *Intelligence reframed: Multiple intelligences for the 21st century.* New York: Basic Books.

Gartrell, D. (2007, November). Guidance matters. *Young Children, 62*(6), 72–73.

Gerber, E. B., Whitebook, M., & Weinstein, R. S. (2007). At the heart of child care: Predictors of teacher sensitivity in center based care. *Early Childhood Research Quarterly, 22*, 327–346.

Gesell, A. (1940). *The first five years of life.* New York: Harper & Brothers.

Glazer, J. J. (1986). *Literature for young children.* Columbus, OH: Charles E. Merrill.

Goldenberg, C. (2002). Making schools work for low-income families in the 21st century. In S. Neuman & D. Dickinson (Eds.), *Handbook of early literacy research* (pp. 211–241). New York: The Guilford Press.

Goodman, K. S. (1986). *What's whole in whole language.* Portsmouth, NH: Heinemann Educational Publishers.

Gonzalez-Mena, J. (2006). *Diversity in early care and education: Honoring differences.* New York: McGraw-Hill.

Gonzalez-Mena, J. (2007, September). What to do for a fussy baby: A problem-solving approach. *Young Children, 62*(5), 20–24.

Gopnik, A. (1999, December 25). Quoted in K. Corcoran, Babies blossom without gimmicks, psychologist says. *San Jose Mercury News,* pp. 1A, 28A.

Gopnik, A., Meltzoff, A., & Kuhl, P. (1999). *The scientist in the crib: Minds, brains, and how children learn.* New York: William Morrow and Company.

Gordon E. (1986, August). Listen to the Music! *American Baby, 48*(8), 46, 67–69.

Gould, B. (2002). Stress and the developing brain. *Head Start Bulletin, 73*, 16–18.

Gowen, J.W. (1995, March). The early development of symbolic play. *Young Children, 50*(3), 75–84.

Greenberg, P. (1998, November). Thinking about goals for grownups and young children while we teach writing, reading, and spelling (and a few thoughts about the 'J' word). Part 3. *Young Children, 53*(6), 31–42.

Greenspan, S. I. (1997). *The growth of the mind and the endangered origins of intelligence.* Reading, MA: Addison-Wesley.

Greenspan, S. I. (1999). *Building healthy minds: The six experiences that create intelligence and emotional growth in babies and young children.* Cambridge, MA: Perseus Books.

Harris, T., & Hodges, R. (Eds.). (1995). *The literacy dictionary: The vocabulary of reading and writing.* Newark, DE: International Reading Association.

Harris, V. J. (1993). *From the margin to the center of the curricula: Multicultural children's literature.* In B. Spodek & O. Saracho (Eds.), *Language and literacy in early childhood education* (Vol. 4, pp. 123–140). New York: Teachers College Press.

Harrison, M., Roush, J., & Wallace, J. (2002). Trends in age of identification and intervention in young children with hearing loss. *Ear and Hearing, 24*, 89–95.

Hartley, E. A. (1991). Through Navaho eyes: Examining differences in giftedness. *Journal of American Indian Education, 31*(1), 53–64.

Hatcher, B., & Petty, K. (2004, November). Visible thought in dramatic play. *Young Children, 59*(6), 79–82.

Hendrick, J. (Ed.). (1997). *First steps toward teaching the Reggio way.* Upper Saddle River, NJ: Prentice Hall.

Hess, R. D., & Shipman, V. C. (1966). Early experience and the socialization of cognitive modes in children. *Child Development, 28*(4), 221–257.

Honig, A. S. (1999, March). The amazing brain. *Scholastic Early Childhood Today, 13*(6), 17–22.

Honig, A. S. (2007, September). Play: Ten power boost for children's early learning. *Young Children, 62*(5), 72–78.

Hostetler, M. (2000, January).We help our children create books. *Young Children, 55*(1), 28–32.

Hough, R. A., Nurss, J. R., & Goodson, M. S. (1984). Children in day care: An observational study. *Child Study Journal, 14.1,* 33–41.

Hunter, T. (2003, May). What about Mr. Baker? *Young Children, 58*(3), 77.

The Idaho Statesman. (1999, June 9). Poor daycare hurts kids' language, math skills, study says. *The Idaho Statesman,* p. 4A.

Interlandi, J. (2007, August 20). Turn it off, baby. *Newsweek* (CL) 8/9, 14.

International Reading Association (1998). *Phonemic awareness and the teaching of reading: A position statement from the Board of Directors of the International Reading Association.* Newark, DE: Author. (Brochure).

International Reading Association. (1999). *Using multiple methods of beginning reading instruction: A position statement of the International Reading Association.* Newark, DE: Author. (Brochure).

International Reading Association. (2003). *Standards for reading professionals.* Newark, DE: Author.

International Reading Association & The National Association for the Education of Young Children. (1999). *Learning to read and write: Developmentally appropriate practices for young children.* Washington, DC: National Association for the Education of Young Children.

International Visual Literacy Association. (2004). Retrieved July 23, 2004, from http://www.ivla.com.

Invernizzi, M. A. (2003). The complex world of one-on-one tutoring. In S. B. Neuman & D. K. Dickinson (Eds.), *Handbook of early literacy research* (pp. 459–470). New York: The Guilford Press.

James, J. Y., & Kormanski, L. M. (1999, May). Positive intergenerational picture books for young children. *Young Children, 54*(3), 37–43.

Johnson, C. Quoted in P. Wingert & M. Brant (2005, August 18). Reading your babies. *Newsweek,* 32–38, 39.

Johnson, K. (1987) *Doing words.* Boston, MA: Houghton Mifflin.

Justice, L. M., & Lankford, C. (2002). Preschool children's visual attention to print during storybook reading: Pilot findings. *Communication Disorders Quarterly, 24*(1), 11–21.

Justice, L. M., & Pence, K. L. (2006). *Scaffolding with storybooks: A guide for enhancing young children's language and literacy achievement.* Newark, DE: International Reading Association.

Kagan, J. (1971). *Change and community.* New York: John Wiley & Sons.

Kaiser Family Foundation Family Survey. (2003, 2006). Menlo Park, CA: Kaiser Family Foundation. Retrieved October 26, 2004, from http://www.kff.org and retrieved December 4, 2006, from http://www.kff.org.

Kalmar, K. (2008, January). Let's give children something to talk about: Oral language and preschool literacy. *Young Children, 63*(1), 88–92.

Kantrowitz, B. (1997, Spring/Summer). Off to a good start [Special Edition]. *Newsweek,* pp. 5–8.

Kantrowitz, B. (2000, Fall/Winter). 21st century babies. [Special Edition]. *Newsweek,* pp. 4–7.

Karchmer, R. A., Mallette, M. H., & Leu, D. J. Jr. (2003). Early literacy in a digital age: Moving from singular book literacy to the multiple literacies of networked information and communication technologies. In D. M. Barone & L. M. Morrow (Eds.), *Literacy and young children: Research-based practices* (pp. 175–194). New York: Guilford.

Katz, L., & Chard, S. (1989). *Engaging children's minds: The project approach.* Norwood, NJ: Ablex.

Katz, L., & Schery, T. K. (2006, January). Including children with hearing loss in early childhood programs. *Young Children, 61*(1), 86–95.

Kendall, J. S., & Marzano. R. J. (2004). *Content knowledge: A compendium of standards and benchmarks for K-12 education.* Aurora, CO: Mid-continent Research for Education and Learning. Online database: http://www.Mcrel.org/standards-benchmarks.

Kibby, M. (2005). Thinking aloud and reading comprehension. University at Buffalo, Center for Literacy and Reading Instruction. Retrieved January 7, 2006, from www.readingcenter.buffalo.edu/center/think.htm.

Koralek, D. (2007, May). Incorporating books throughout the curriculum. *Young Children, 62*(3), 10–11.

Kotulak, R. (1996). *Inside the brain: Revolutionary discoveries of how the mind works.* Kansas City, MO: Andrews and McMeel.

Kucan, L. (2007, November). Insights from teachers who analyzed transcripts of their own classroom discussions. *The Reading Teacher, 6*(13), 228–236.

Kupetz, B. N., & Green, E. J. (1997, January). Sharing books with infants and toddlers: Facing the challenges. *Young Children, 52*(2), 22–27.

Lair, J. (1985). *I ain't much baby but I'm all I've got.* New York: Fawcett.

Lally, J. R. (1997). Curriculum and lesson planning: A responsive approach. Unpublished manuscript. Sausalito, CA: West Ed.

Lloyd-Jones, L. (2002). Relationship as curriculum. *Head Start Bulletin, 73,* 10–12.

Love, J. M. (2003). Instrumentation for state readiness assessment: Issues in measuring children's early development. *Assessing the State Assessments: Special Report.* Greensboro, NC: The Regional Laboratory at SERVE.

Lynch-Brown, C., & Tomlinson, C. (1998). Children's literature past and present: Is there a future? *Peabody Journal of Education, 73*(3), 228–252.

MacDonald, M. R. (1996). Quoted in Mooney, B., & Holt, D. *The storyteller's guide.* Little Rock, AR: August House Publishers.

Machado, J. (2008, April 18). Recorded observation notes. Busy Bee Children's Center. Santa Clara, CA.

Machado, J., & Botnarescue, H. (2008). *Student teaching: Early childhood practicum guide.* Clifton Park, NY: Thomson Delmar Learning.

Marcon, R. A. Quoted in S. J. Oliver & E. Klugman (2007, January/February). Building a play research agenda: What do we know about play? *Exchange, 173,* 14–18.

Mavrogenes, N. A. (1990, May). Helping parents help their children become literate. *Young Children, 45*(4), 4–9.

McDonald, D. T., & Simon, G. M. (1989). *Musical growth and development.* New York: Schirmer Books.

McGee, L. M. (2003). Book acting: Storytelling and drama in the early childhood classroom. In D. M. Barone & L. M. Morrow (Eds.), *Literacy and young children: Research-based practices* (pp. 157–172). New York: The Guilford Press.

McGuiness, D. (1997). *Why our children can't read and what we can do about it: A scientific revolution in reading.* New York: Free Press.

McMullen, M. B. (1998, May). Thinking before doing. *Young Children, 53*(3), 65–70.

McMullen, M., & Dixon, S. (2006). Building on common ground: Unifying practices of infant toddler specialists through a mindful relationship-based approach. *Young Children, 61*(4), 46–52.

McNair, J. C. (2007, September). Using children's names to enhance early literacy development. *Young Children, 62*(5), 84–89.

Meier, D. R. (2004). *The young child's memory for words.* New York: Teacher's College Press.

Mody, M., Schwartz, R., Gravel, J., & Ruben, R. (1999, October). Speech perception and verbal memory in children with and without histories of otitis media. *Journal of Speech, Language, and Hearing Research, 42*(5), 1069–1077.

Montessori, M. (1967a). *The absorbent mind.* New York: Holt, Rinehart, and Winston.

Montessori, M. (1967b). *The discovery of the child.* New York: Holt, Rinehart, and Winston.

Morphett, M. V., & Washburne, C. (1931). When should children begin to read? *Elementary School Journal, 31,* 496–508.

Morrow, L. M., & Asbury, E. (2003). Current practices in early childhood literacy development.

In L. M. Morrow, L. M., Tracey, D. H., Woo, D. G., & Pressley, M. (1999). Characteristics of exemplary first grade literacy instruction. *Reading Teacher, 52,* 462–476.

Munir, K., & Rose, S. C. (2008, January 21). How to solve three puzzles. *Newsweek,* 64–66.

Murphy, J. C. (2003, November). Case studies in African American school success and parenting behaviors. *Young Children, 58*(6), 85–89.

Nash, J. M. (1997, February 3). Fertile minds. *Time, 149*(5), 48–56.

National Assessment of Educational Progress. (1995). The NAEP reading: A first look—Findings from the National Assessment of Educational Progress. Washington, DC: U.S. Government Printing Office.

National Association for the Education of Young Children. (1996, January). Position statement: Responding to linguistic and cultural diversity—Recommendations for effective early childhood education. *Young Children, 51*(2), 4–12.

National Association for the Education of Young Children, and the International Reading Association. (1998, July). Learning to read and write: Developmentally appropriate practice for young children. A position statement. *Young Children, 53*(4), 30–46.

National Association for the Education of Young Children and the National Association of Early Childhood Specialists in State Departments of Education. (2003, November). *Early childhood curriculum, assessment, and program evaluation.* Position statement summary. Paper presented at National Association for the Education of Young Children Annual Conference. Chicago: Authors.

National Association for the Education of Young Children. (2005a, July). National Association for the Education of Young Children governing board approves new NAEYC early childhood program standards and accreditation performance criteria. *Young Children, 60*(4), 50–54.

National Association for the Education of Young Children. (2005b). Standards and Accreditation Performance Criteria for Early Childhood Programs. Washington, DC. Author.

National Association for Hearing and Speech Action (NAHSA). (1985). *Recognizing communication disorders.* Rockville, MD: NAHSA.

National Association for Hearing and Speech Action (NAHSA). (2000). *What do you hear?* Rockville, MD: NAHSA.

National Black Child Development Institute. (2006). *Love to Read.* Retrieved September 13, 2006, from http://www.nbedi.org/programs/LTR/research.asp.

National Education Association. (2005). *Children's favorite books.* Retrieved March 16, 2005, from www.nea.org/readacross/resourses/kidsbooks.html.

National Reading Panel. (2000). *Teaching children to read: An evidence-based assessment of the scientific research literature on reading and its implications for reading instruction* (NIH Publication No. 00-4769). Washington, DC: National Institute of Child Health and Human Development.

National Reading Panel Report. (2000). *Teaching children to read.* Washington, DC: National Institute of Child Health and Human Development.

National Research Council. (1998). *Preventing reading difficulties in young children.* Washington, DC: National Academy Press.

National Research Council. (2000). *How people learn: Brain, mind, experience and school.* Washington, DC: National Academy Press.

Neergaard, L. (2004, June 8). New guidelines call for vision screening for preschoolers. *The Idaho Statesman,* p. 1.

Neergaard, L. (2006, Thursday, May 26). Parents turn small fry on to the small screen. *Idaho Statesman,* p. 18.

Nelson, K., & Shaw, L. (2002). Developing a socially shared symbolic system. In E. Amsel & J. Byrnes (Eds.), *Language, literacy and cognitive development: The development and consequences of symbolic communication* (pp. 27–57). Mahwah, NJ: Erlbaum.

Neuman, S. B., & Roskos, K. (2007). *Nurturing knowledge: Building a foundation for school success by linking early literacy to math, science, art, and social studies.* New York: Scholastic Inc.

New, R. S. (2002). Early literacy and developmentally appropriate practice: Rethinking the paradigm. In S. Neuman & D. Dickenson (Eds.), *Handbook of early literacy research* (pp. 254–262). New York: Guilford.

Nicopoulou, A., Scales, B., & Weintraub, J. (1994). Gender differences and symbolic imagination in stories of four-year-olds. In A. H. Dyson & C. Genishi (Eds.), *The need for story* (pp. 102–123). New York: National Council of Teachers of English.

Ohl, J. (2002, Fall). Linking child care and early literacy: Building the foundation for success. *Child Care Bulletin,* 27, 1–4.

Okagaki, L., & Diamond, K. (2000, May). Responding to cultural and linguistic differences in the beliefs and practices of families with young children. *Young Children,* 55(3), 47–55.

O'Leary, C., Newton, J., Lundz, B., Hall, M., O'Connell, K., Raby, C., & Czarnecka, M. (2002, June 1–4). Visual Communication Group Summary. ACM SIGGRAPH Workshop. Snowbird, UT.

Padron, Y. N., Waxman, H. C., & Rivera, H. H. (2002, August). Educating Hispanic students: Effective instructional practices. *Practitioners Brief #5.* Santa Cruz, CA: Center for Research on Education, Diversity and Excellence, University of California.

Paley, V. (1990). *The boy who would be a helicopter: The uses of storytelling in the classroom.* Cambridge, MA: Harvard University Press.

Paley, V. (1994). Princess Annabella and the black girls. In A. H. Dyson & C. Genishi (Eds.), *The need for story: Cultural diversity in classroom and community* (pp. 145–154). Urbana, IL: National Council of Teachers of English.

Pan, B. A., & Gleason, J. B. (1997). Semantic development: Learning the meanings of words. In J. Gleason (Ed.), *The development of language* (4th ed., pp. 311–331). Boston: Allyn and Bacon.

Papadaki-D'Onofrio, E. (2003, September/October). Bilingualism/multilingualism and language acquisition theories. *Child Care Information Exchange,* 153, 46–50.

Paratore, J. (2006). Home and school together! Helping beginning readers succeed. In A. E. Farstrup & S. J. Samuels (Eds.), *What research has to say about reading instruction* (pp. 48–68). Newark, DE: International Reading Association.

Piaget, J. (1952). *The language and thought of the child.* London: Routledge and Kegan Paul.

Piaget, J. (1970). *Science of education and the psychology of the child.* New York: Orion.

Poole, C. (1999, March). You've got to hand it to me! *Scholastic Early Childhood Today,* 13(6), 34–39.

Quindlen, A. (2001, February 12). Building blocks for every kid. *Newsweek,* 68.

Raines, S., & Isbell, R. (1994). *Stories: Children's literature in early education.* Clifton Park, NY: Thomson Delmar Learning.

Rauscher, F. H. (2003, September). Can music instruction affect children's cognitive development? *ERIC Digest,* EDO-PS-03-12.

Raver, C., & Knitzer, J. (2002). *Ready to enter: What research tells policymakers about strategies to promote social and emotional school readiness among three- and four-year-old children.* New York: National Center for Children in Poverty.

Raver, C. C. (2003, July).Young children's emotional development and school readiness. *ERIC Digest,* EDO-PS-03-8.

Raymond, J. (2000, Fall/Winter). Kids, start your engines [Special Edition]. *Newsweek,* 8–11.

Reading Today. (2004, December/2005, January). New report: States are narrowing achievement gaps and raising achievement, but not fast enough. *Reading Today, 22*(3), 4.

Renzulli, J. (1986, October). Interview quote in Alvino, J. Guiding your gifted child. *American Baby, 48*(10), 54, 57–58.

Rimm-Kaufman, S. E., Pianta, R. C., & Cox, M. J. (2000). Teachers' judgments of problems in the transition to kindergarten. *Early Childhood Research Quarterly, 15*(2), 147–166.

Robisson, H. F. (1983). *Exploring teaching in early childhood education.* Boston: Allyn and Bacon.

Rones, N. (2004, August). Listen to this. *Parents,* pp. 167–168.

Rousseau, J. J. (1947). L'Emile ou l'education. In O. E. Tellows & N. R. Tarrey (Eds.), *The age of enlightenment.* New York: F. S. Croft.

Rusk, R., & Scotland, J. (1979). *Doctrines of the great educators.* New York: St. Martin's Press.

Sachs, J. (1997). Communication development in infancy. In J. Gleason (Ed.), *The development of language* (4th ed., pp. 261–282). Boston: Allyn and Bacon.

Schickedanz, J. A. (1982). The acquisition of written language in young children. In B. Spodek (Ed.), *Handbook of research in early childhood education.* New York: The Free Press.

Schickedanz, J. A. (1986). *More than the ABCs: The early stages of reading and writing.* Washington, DC: National Association for the Education of Young Children.

Schickedanz, J. A. (1989, August/September). What about preschoolers and academics? *Reading Today, 7*(1), 24.

Schickedanz, J. A. (1999). Written language use within the context of young children's symbolic play. *Early Childhood Research Quarterly, 4,* 225–244.

Schickendanz, J. A. (2003). Engaging preschoolers in code learning. In D. M. Barone & L. M. Morrow (Eds.), *Literacy and young children: Research-based practices* (pp. 121–139). New York: The Guilford Press.

Shanahan, T. (2004, November 12). Laying the groundwork for literacy: The National Early Literacy Panel synthesis for research on early literacy education. Conference presentation. National Association for the Education of Young Children Annual Conference. Anaheim, CA.

Shanahan, T. (2006). What reading research says: The promises and limitations of applying research to reading education. In A. E. Farstrup & S. J. Samuels (Eds.), *What research has to say about reading instruction* (pp. 8–24). Newark, DE: International Reading Association.

Shanahan, T., & Barr, R. (1995). Reading Recovery: An independent evaluation of the effects of early instructional intervention for at-risk learners. *Reading Research Quarterly, 30,* 58–69.

Shore, R. (1997). *Rethinking the brain.* New York: Families and Work Institute.

Singhal, J. (1999, March). Tuning in to the musical brain. *Bay Area Parent, 16,* 21–23.

Slobin, D. I. (1971). *Psycholinguistics.* Glenview, IL: Scott Foresman.

Smilansky, S. (1968). *The effects of sociodramatic play on disadvantaged preschool children.* New York: Wiley.

Smith, M. W. (2001). Children's experiences in preschool. In D. Dickinson & P. Tabors (Eds.), *Beginning literacy with language* (pp. 149–174). Baltimore: Brookes.

Smith, T., Kleiner, A., Parsad, B., & Farris, E. (2003). *Prekindergarten in U.S. Public schools: 2000-2001 (NCES 2003-019),* 1021–1059. Washington, DC: Department of Education, National Center for Educational Statistics.

Snow, C., Burns, S., & Griffin, P. (Eds.). (1998). *Preventing reading difficulties in young children.* Washington, DC: National Academy Press.

Snider, M. (2008, Tuesday January 15). The digital download. *USA Today,* p. 7D.

Soto, L. D. (1991, January). Understanding bilingual/bicultural young children. *Young Children, 40*(2), 30–36.

Spivak, L. (2000, Fall/Winter). In G. Cowley (Ed.), For the love of language [Special Edition]. *Newsweek,* pp. 12–15.

Stark, D. R., Chazen-Cohen, R., & Jerald, J. (2002). The infant mental health forum. *Head Start Bulletin, 73,* 46–47, 53.

Stauffer, R. C. (1970). *The language experience approach to the teaching of reading.* New York: Harper and Row.

Stieglitz, M. G. (2008). The visual differential: An experimental study of the relation of varied experiences with visuals to shape discrimination. Unpublished doctoral dissertation, University of Wisconsin.

Stoel-Gammon, C. (1997). Phonological development. In J. Gleason (Ed.), *The development of language* (4th ed., pp. 138–201). Boston: Allyn and Bacon.

Stott, F. (2003, November/December). Making standards meaningful: Aligning preschool standards with those established for K-12 can be an important step toward offering equality in early educational experiences. *Early Childhood Today, 18*(3), 19–20.

Strickland, D. S. (2003, November). Exemplary practice in organizing skill development in the early literacy classroom. National Association for the Education of Young Children Annual Conference. Chicago.

Strickland, D. S., Shanahan, T., & Escamalia, K. (2004, November 12). Laying the groundwork for literacy: The National Early Literacy Panel synthesis of research on early literacy education. National Association for the Education of Young Children Annual Conference. Anaheim, CA.

Strickland, D. S., & Schickedanz, J. A. (2004). *Learning about print in preschool: Working with letters, words, and beginning links with phonemic awareness.* Newark, DE: International Reading Association.

Strickland, D. S., & Riley-Ayers, S. (2006, April). Early literacy: Policy and practice in the preschool years. *Preschool Policy Brief 10,* 1–10. New Brunswick, NJ: National Institute for Early Education Research.

Tabors, P. O. (1997). *One child, two languages: A guide for preschool educators of children learning English as a second language.* Baltimore, MD: Paul H. Brookes.

Tabors, P. O., Paez, M. M., & Lopez, L. M. (2003). Dual language abilities of bilingual four-year-olds: Initial findings from the early childhood study of language and literacy development of Spanish-speaking children. *NABE Journal of Research and Practice, 1,* 70–91.

Taylor, R. (2002, March). Helping language grow. *Instructor, III*(6), 25–26.

Teachout, C., & Bright, A. (2007, July). Reading the pictures: A missing piece of the literacy puzzle. *Young Children, 62*(4), 106–107.

Thompson, N. S. (2000, January). Sylvia Ashton-Warner: Reclaiming personal meaning in literacy teaching. *English Journal, 89*(3), 90–96.

Thurber, D. (1988). *Teaching handwriting.* Glenview, IL: Scott Foresman.

Trautman, L. S. (2003, November/December). If your child stutters. *Parent & Child, 11*(3), 64–67.

Trelease, J. Quoted in Neuman, S. B., & Roskos, K. (2007). *Nurturing knowledge: Building a foundation for school success by linking early literacy to math, science, art, and social studies.* (Forward). New York: Scholastic Inc.

Trousdale, A. M. (1990). Interactive storytelling: Scaffolding children's early narratives. *Language Arts, 69*(2), 164–173.

USA Today. (Thursday, January 10, 2008). Tech show tackles what's appropriate (or not) for kids, p. 4B.

U.S. Department of Education. (1991). *Help your child become a good reader.* Washington, DC: Author.

U.S. Department of Education. (1998). *Federal Reading Excellence Act.* Washington, DC: U.S. Government Printing Office.

U.S. Department of Education. (2002). *The No Child Left Behind Act.* Washington, DC: Author.

Retrieved June 17, 2003, from http://www.edgov/nclb/overview.

U.S. Department of Health and Human Services, Administration for Children and Families. (2003). *The Head Start leaders guide to positive child outcomes.* Washington, DC: Author.

U.S. Department of Health and Human Services Fatherhood Initiative. (2001). Retrieved June 6, 2002, from http://hhs.fatherhood.hhs.gov/index.shtml.

U.S. Department of Health and Human Services. (2003). *The Head Start path to positive child outcomes.* [The Head Start Child Outcomes Framework]. Retrieved May 21, 2004, from http://www.hsnrc.org/CDI/outcontent.cfm.

Venezky, R. (1970). *The structure of English orthography.* The Hague, Netherlands: Mouton.

Venezky, R. (1999). *The American way of spelling.* New York: Guilford.

Volk, D., & Long, S. (2005, November). Challenging myths of the deficit perspective: Honoring children's literacy resources. *Young Children, 60*(6), 12–19.

Vygotsky, L. S. (1976). *Mind and society: The development of higher psychological process.* Cambridge, MA: Harvard University Press.

Vygotsky, L. S. (1978). *Mind and society. The development of higher psychological process.* Cambridge, MA: Harvard University Press.

Vygotsky, L. S. (1980). *Mind in society.* Cambridge, MA: Harvard University Press.

Vygotsky, L. S. (1986). *Thought and language.* Cambridge, MA: MIT Press.

Walley. A. C., Metsala, J. L., & Garlock, V. M. (2003). Spoken vocabulary growth: Its role in the development of phoneme awareness and early reading ability. *Reading and Writing: An Interdisciplinary Journal, 16,* 5–20.

Walmsley, S., & Adams, E. L. (1993, April). Realities of "whole language." *Language Arts, 70*(4), 272–280.

Walpole, S., & McKenna, M. (2004). *The literacy coach's handbook: A guide to research-based practice.* New York: The Guilford Press.

Wardle, F. (2003, September/October). Language immersion programs for young children. *Child Care Information Exchange, 153,* 54–57.

Wasik, B. A. (2006, November). Building vocabulary one word at a time. *Young Children, 61*(6), 70–78.

Weissbourd, R. (1996). *The vulnerable child.* Reading, MA: Addison-Wesley.

Weitzman, E. (1992). *Learning language and loving it.* Toronto: A Hanen Centre Publication.

Wells, G. (1981). *Learning through interaction: The study of language development.* Cambridge, MA: Cambridge University Press.

West, J., Denton, K., & Germino-Hausken, E. (2000). *America's kindergartners*. Washington, DC: National Center for Educational Statistics.

White, B. L. (1987). *The first three years of life*. Englewood Cliffs, NJ: Prentice Hall.

Williams, K. C. (1997, September). What do you wonder? *Young Children, 52*(6), 78–81.

Williams, A. E. (2008, January). Exploring the natural world with infants and toddlers in an urban setting. *Young Children, 63*(1), 22–25.

Wingert, P., & Brant, M. (2005, August 18). Reading your baby's mind. *Newsweek*, p. 32–38, 39.

Winsler, A., Manfra, L., & Diaz, R. M. (2007). "Should I let them talk?" Private speech and task performance among preschool children with and without behavior problems. *Early Childhood Research Quarterly, 22*, 215–231.

Wolf, J. (2000, March). Sharing songs with children. *Young Children, 55*(2), 19–31.

Woodward, C., Haskins, G., Schaefer, G., & Smolen, L. (2004, July). Let's talk: A different approach to oral language development. *Young Children, 59*(4), 92–95.

Zambo, D., & Hansen, L. (2007) Love, language, and emergent literacy. *Young Children, 62*(3), 32–37.

Zimmerman, F. J., & Christakis, A. (2007, November). Associations between content types of early media exposure and subsequent attentional problems. *Pediatrics, 120*(5), 986–992.